Contents

ACKNOWLEDGEMENTS

The authors wish to express their thanks to those members of staff in the Plymouth Business School who have offered encouragement, discussed many of our ideas and given us pointers to examples in their various specialist fields where business and professional ethics play a role.

Thanks are also due to Dr D. A. T. Thomas of the Open University, for help on the section on Ethics and International Business and to Business in the Community Information Officer, Reena Chuda, for her generous supply of BITC literature.

Setting the scene 1

Why business ethics?
The history of business ethics

WHY BUSINESS ETHICS?

This is intended as a 'bumper book' on business ethics. Not only have we attempted to cover a wide range of issues which are typically encountered in the world of business; but we have also used a variety of materials, spanning original essays on key topics, readings from definitive writers, case studies and discussion topics. It is our hope that this book will be useful to students, teachers and researchers alike. Not least, we hope that it will help those who have graduated beyond the student stage, and that it will be of value to men and women who are already in the world of business and who are almost certainly facing some of the moral dilemmas which are dealt with in this book.

The field of business ethics is an area of growth, both in educational circles and in the world of business. Most recent work on the subject has been carried out in the USA which means that most of the issues have a distinctively American character. Because American legal, political and economic systems are different from those in Europe, and more specifically the UK, ethical dilemmas in business are inevitably different. Both of the present writers are British, which gives this book a slant which we hope will help to redress the imbalance which currently exists in the field. However, having said this, the reader will find that we have included a significant amount of American material. We cannot ignore the works of writers like Milton Friedman, whose seminal writings raise key issues in business ethics which affect the USA and Europe alike.

Having declared this particular slant, we have continued to look over our shoulders at the United States, where the field has been pioneered, and also cast our nets into the rest of the world. Business values and business ethics have an international dimension which it would be foolish to ignore. Perhaps the most difficult ethical dilemmas to resolve are those which result from conflicts of values that are an inevitable consequence of the culture clashes which result from international business.

This book is therefore quite an ambitious one. No doubt there will be those who feel that we have done less than justice to certain areas or to certain countries and cultures. But one has to make a start and it is our hope that we will encourage our readers to pursue in greater depth some of the areas we have identified. With this in mind, we have endeavoured to provide pointers to further reading in each area.

There are no doubt several reasons which account for the rise of interest in the field of business ethics. Through the media the public are becoming increasingly aware of some of the scandals in the business world and some of the disasters which appear to result from too little regard to morality. *The Herald of Free Enterprise*, the *Piper Alpha* disaster and the BCCI scandal, to name but a few, raise questions in the public mind about the ethics of business.

The scandals which linger in the public mind give rise to the conviction that maxims such as 'business is business' or principles like *'caveat emptor'* (let the buyer beware) fall far short of what the public have a right to expect. Businesses are therefore increasingly coming under pressure to define their standards and often to express these formally in written codes of practice.

The accelerating interest in business ethics, we believe, has been further increased by recent trends towards Total Quality Management (TQM). Total Quality does not necessarily have to mean high quality – a common misunderstanding of the concept. What it does mean is that the management of a business organization is called upon to define in advance what kind of quality is acceptable within the firm and particularly to ensure that appropriate systems are in operation which ensure that this pre-determined standard of quality exists. This includes the knowledge of who is responsible for each stage of the necessary operations, what materials and equipment are needed and at what places and times, to ensure that overall quality is maintained.

TQM has a two-fold consequence for business ethics. First, the necessity of defining the level of quality which is to be maintained forces the management at least to consider the question of what is acceptable to the consumer at the end of the process. Do consumers want a product that is built to last, or will they settle for the 'cheap and cheerful' (or even 'cheap and nasty') second best because it costs less? Raising the question of the final quality of goods and services means that the consumer's interests cannot be ignored; the principle of *caveat emptor* will no longer suffice as a principle on which one's business should operate.

Second, the fact that management is required to define procedures and codify them meticulously is an appropriate cue for the introduction of codes of practice. What ought management to expect of employees at various points in a production process, and indeed what may employees expect the management to do at various levels?

The precise codification of procedures has a number of roles. It assigns duties which, at least, impart a moral concept. It crystallizes an organization's ideas on what is acceptable and what is not, and even a decision that a second-rate product is acceptable is in itself a value judgment, entailing ethical decisions (such as the decision to produce and sell goods and services of inferior quality).

THE HISTORY OF BUSINESS ETHICS

Although there has been a marked increase in interest in business ethics in recent times, the subject has in fact quite a long pedigree. The Roman Catholic Church, particularly in the Medieval period, defined very carefully pieces of canon law which prescribed clearly what was legitimate behaviour in certain fields in the business world. 'Canon', incidentally, means a standard or measure; hence canon law is the ideal standard by which one measures one's behaviour. For example (and we shall return to this later in chapter 6) there were doctrines relating to just wages and just prices. A doctor must not increase the price of medicine to a dying patient, thus taking advantage of his or her serious predicament; an employer must not pay a worker less than a living wage. Indeed, in the Judaeo-Christian tradition an interest in business ethics is apparent long before the scholastic theologians came on the scene. The Law of Moses prevented reapers from harvesting all their crops: they were obliged to leave some at the edges of the field for the poor to have the benefit. Servants were entitled to their sabbath rest day, just like their masters. There was to be an amnesty period every fifty years in which all debts were cancelled (personal or business) – the Year of the Jubilees, as it was called.

Other religious traditions have been equally concerned in their history with prescribing ways in which business affairs are to be conducted. Islam insists that monies are not lent with the purpose of attracting unearned interest (or usury); any loan must share risk and possible profit with the borrower. Although the Buddha is not normally associated in the popular mind with worldly affairs such as business transactions, three of the points in the Eightfold Path (the fundamental teaching about the way to nirvana) are perfect speech, perfect action, and perfect livelihood. In other words, one may not earn one's living by deception, by misappropriation of goods or monies, or by working in employment which involves the taking of life (human or animal) or trading in intoxicants or drugs (other than those which are for medical use).

The reason for the relatively recent eclipse of business ethics is a matter for conjecture. One explanation, which the present writers endorse, is that it is connected with the Protestant Reformation which paralleled the rise of modern capitalism. This had a two-fold effect on business activity. First, the Protestant Reformation, by calling into question the doctrine of papal infallibility, jettisoned the whole system of Roman Catholic canon law. The Church was no longer to be the intermediary between humanity and God, and salvation was no longer to be obtained by works (which included not only religious rites such as receiving the sacrament, but also honest and just dealings with one's fellow men and women), but by unearned divine grace. (Grace means unmerited favour or undeserved benefit.) The emphasis on grace and faith rather than works rather left the Protestant Churches, which represented the majority of people in Great Britain and other European countries such as Germany, and (in due course) the USA, in somewhat of a moral vacuum. The Protestant Churches were not prone to giving official pronouncements about the nature of morality or how one should conduct one's affairs in public, thus leaving moral decisions to the individual conscience.

Secondly, allied to this moral vacuum, the rise of capitalism came to enhance the standards of living of many employers and workers. True, there is much criticism of the conditions of life for the poverty-stricken factory workers of the Victorian era who had to leave the land and live in over-crowded housing in towns, but it is arguable that they would actually have been worse off if they had remained working on the land. In the absence of any system of church law to regulate one's conduct, it is human nature for the seller of goods, services or labour to want to exact as high a price as possible and for the buyer to want to pay as little as possible. Students of business will of course be familiar with the account of how it is possible for business transactions to occur when the aims of buyer and seller seem incompatible in this way. The classical economists such as Adam Smith devised the theory of the price mechanism to explain how the two forces of supply and demand worked together to determine the market rate for the buying and selling of goods and labour. What is worth noting is that Adam Smith's 'invisible hand' of the price mechanism explains how market forces **do** operate; it does not give any ethical guidance on how, morally, they **should** operate. (We shall return to Adam Smith in the readings in Chapter 2.)

It is perhaps this emphasis on the almost relentless operation of market forces which has led to public scepticism about business ethics. Indeed a former professor of one of the authors expressed surprise at our project, declaring that there was no such thing as business ethics. Business ethics, he declared, was a contradiction in terms. It may therefore be appropriate to say something which reassures the sceptic that business ethics is indeed a proper and legitimate field of study.

Whether the situation in the business world is quite as bleak as this professor believed is open to debate. As we have acknowledged, there have been some very serious instances of unethical behaviour in the business world. But of course it is the scandalous cases which attract public attention, and if a firm behaves well towards its employees and the public, this is scarcely newsworthy. The economist J. K. Galbraith has argued, in fact, that the present way in which many large companies are structured provides little incentive for salespeople to give the customer a bad deal. Unlike the privately owned corner shop, where it could possibly be to the financial disadvantage of the owner (at least in the short term) to replace defective goods, workers in the chain-store or the multi-national company earn a wage which is pre-determined and which does not depend on their maximizing profits by denying customers their rights. Their managers are in a similar position, and indeed manager and shop floor are at quite a far remove from the shareholders, who are – the evidence shows – content with an adequate financial return for their investment. Indeed, who is able to tell whether a firm's management has maximized its profits anyway? When a firm's Annual Report shows a healthy profit it does not follow that, with better management, profits could not have been even higher, when a firm incurs heavy losses, this may have been the best that could have been achieved in the circumstances.

However, for the sake of argument, let us assume the worst. Let us suppose that the business world is a jungle, where dog eats dog, and where fraud, deception and subterfuge reign supreme, and it is a matter of the survival of the fittest. Would this mean that there is no role for business ethics?

On the contrary. Even if one asks rhetorically, 'Who can find a virtuous woman?',[1] this does not mean that one cannot define what a virtuous woman (or man, for that matter) would be like. Even if at present there were little evidence of ethical business people, we can still try to define what it would be like if those in the business world were to act ethically. Unless it was actually impossible for business people to implement standards of ethical conduct, there would be everything to be gained by directing their attention to the study of business ethics.

Having said this, it should be made clear that the function of business

---

[1] *Proverbs 31.10.*

ethics is not a missionary task. Many a layperson and many a college fresher have assumed that our task in teaching business ethics is 'telling people to be more ethical'. This is a misconception of the function of business ethics as an academic discipline and it is important to explain why.

Matters of business ethics are controversial. Some readers may believe in 'reverse discrimination' while others may oppose it; some may feel that it is justifiable to 'blow the whistle' on firms who are recalcitrant about improving standards of behaviour, while others may hold that company loyalty takes precedence over any public benefit; some may believe that company directors do not deserve their apparently astronomical salaries, while others may take the view that reducing their earnings would make little difference to the average shop floor worker.

The good teacher of business ethics (and the good writer) has to leave students, business people and other readers to make up their own minds. After all, men and women in the business world have to live with the consequences of their decisions, and what a reader may feel comfortable with may be different from that of the authors. The value of business ethics as a field of study lies in being able to identify the salient issues in controversies surrounding business ethics and to understand the main arguments in favour of the various stances which it is possible to take. Thus the reader is at least in a position to make an informed and considered decision on ethical matters, which is an advance on the state of affairs where often our moral stance is simply a matter of 'gut feeling'. (This point will be expanded in chapter 2.)

Because the area of business ethics is controversial, we have endeavoured to give a fair hearing to various competing viewpoints on the areas covered. At times it will be obvious what we, the authors, think, while at other times we shall simply identify the issues and rehearse the relevant arguments on each side. The readings have been chosen, not necessarily to reflect our own standpoints on the matters under discussion, but to provide readers with a balanced diet which takes into account the variety of opinions which have been expressed in the relevant fields. Where our own colours have shown it is not our intention to make the reader submit to our own viewpoint, but rather to demonstrate how a case can be made out in favour of one's preferred position. Readers who find they do not share our opinions are positively encouraged to do likewise in favour of the competing point of view.

We have referred to the causes within the business world for the revival of interest in business ethics. Although business ethics may have been eclipsed for a century or two, ethics as a wider discipline has by no means been neglected, and throughout the history of western thought has been regarded as a well accredited branch of philosophy. Students who undertake to study ethics as a branch of philosophy have often been surprised – and sometimes disillusioned – to find that much of the time spent on the discipline is about analyzing words and concepts, rather than tackling more substantive issues of personal and social morality. 'What do we **mean** by "right"?' or 'What do we **mean** by "justice"?' are more probable questions dealt with in the philosophy ethics class than, 'Should we enjoy high standards of living when two thirds of the world is in poverty?' or 'Can industrial espionage ever be justified?'

Some of the material in the present book will, of necessity, be analytical. We shall consider questions like, 'What do we mean by "right" and "wrong"?', 'What is justice?', 'What do we understand by "equality"?' and even 'What do we mean by "ethics"?'. We have done this, partly because these questions are deeply embedded in the Anglo-Saxon philosophical tradition in which the present authors have been educated, but also – more importantly – because linguistic analysis provides us with the 'tools of the trade', so to speak. Unless we have first decided what we mean by 'justice', we are in no position to determine whether wages or prices are just; if we are unclear as to what we mean by 'equality', we cannot decide whether or not a policy of 'affirmative action' contributes to the equality of the sexes (and we need to determine what we are to understand by 'equality of the sexes' too).

Unfortunately, many modern philosophers, until very recently, have done little or nothing else than analyze words. The philosopher Wittgenstein stated that 'All philosophy is a critique of language,'[2] and many philosophers have followed Wittgenstein, claiming that philosophy is 'about words', not about the world. We cannot here enter into the debate in which those linguistic philosophers maintained their position and what its merits and demerits are. Suffice it to say that their critics have increasingly come to accuse the Wittgensteinians of playing an esoteric parlour game which – to use Wittgenstein's own words – 'leaves everything as it is';[3] it may be an interesting game in its own right, its critics maintain, but it is a pointless activity unless it really does make a difference in the way we live our lives.

It is our belief that the analytic tools which have been developed

[2] Ludwig Wittgenstein, *Tractatus Logico-Philosophicus* (London: Routledge & Kegan Paul, 1922, 1961) 4.0031.
[3] Ludwig Wittgenstein, *Philosophical Investigations* (Oxford: Blackwell, 1963) 1:124.

within the tradition of linguistic philosophy can and should be used in the sphere of business ethics. Regrettably a significant amount of American material which passes for business ethics has been written by well-intentioned business people who, unfortunately, lack the analytical skills which would enable them to be clear as to what precisely key concepts such as fairness, justice, truth and the like might mean. The opposite danger, of course, is that philosophers in the Anglo-Saxon tradition can become so absorbed in analyzing concepts that they never get around to saying anything which impinges on the real world of business. As trained philosophers who have worked for many years within a business school, the present authors hope that they can combine the best of both worlds – but of course we must leave the reader to decide whether we have truly succeeded in this aim.

In attempting to combine the two ingredients of analysis on the one hand and the practicalities of real life business situations on the other, readers will find that some material is highly abstract and analytical while other material is very firmly anchored in the kinds of decisions which have to be made in business. The chapter on Ethical Theory (chapter 3) may be found particularly difficult by readers who are unfamiliar with the philosophical background which has generated these often turgid debates about the nature of morality and what is the underlying basis of ethics. We have done our utmost to present readers with the gist of these debates, and hope that, if the going gets tough, readers will persevere none the less. Unless we can decide what lies at the basis of our ethical decision making, we cannot proceed to make well-founded moral decisions.

In other places we have used the analytical tools of modern philosophy to break fresh ground in defining concepts. As far as we are aware, no writers on business ethics have attempted, as we have done, to give a detailed conceptual analysis of the question, 'What is capitalism?' (This is surprising, in view of the fact that the nature of capitalism lies at the heart of so many issues in this field.) In chapter 10, similar analysis is given to the concept of 'greenness' – a key word which is frequently bandied about in European and US business, but which in fact does not have a single obvious and clear meaning. It is simply not possible to consider the extent to which businesses have obligations to be 'green' or 'greener' unless we have a very clear idea of what precisely this means (and it evidently means different things to different business managers and consumers).

Other issues are more 'down-to-earth'. Readers from a business background will no doubt relate very readily to issues such as corporate responsibility, the right to work, the position of women in industry, the ethics of advertising and the possible limits to economic growth.

We hope that this book will appeal to those in the business world and to philosophers alike. If it encourages business men and women to be somewhat more reflective, and philosophers to come down a little from their ivory towers, then we will have amply succeeded in our task.

Business ethics: its scope and purpose $\boxed{2}$

What is business ethics?
How is it done?
How is it possible?
Why do it?
Does it work?

Introducing the readings

Moral issues in business   Richard T. De George
The ethical side of enterprise   Verne E. Henderson
The wealth of nations   Adam Smith
Why 'good' managers make bad ethical choices   Saul W. Gellerman

Case study
Ethically active business: the work of business in the community

Discussion topics

WHAT IS BUSINESS ETHICS?

Confronted with an unfamiliar subject, many people insist on starting with a definition. How, they ask, can we know what is being talked about unless first we are told what it is. How shall we define business ethics? A simple definition is easy enough. The term is, after all, just a combination of two very familiar words, namely 'business' and 'ethics'. Unsurprisingly then, what the term refers to is simply ethics as it applies to business. Just as we can talk of medical ethics as concerned with the morality of medical practices and policies, or political ethics as concerned with the morality of political affairs, so also can we talk of something called 'business ethics' as being peculiarly concerned with moral issues in business.

This is hardly very enlightening, not only because in this case the answer was obvious, but because all any definition can do is offer an alternative form of words. It helps us know what the term refers to of course; but unless this is something very simple, we can hardly be said to 'know' that thing merely because we have understood a few words of definition. With a complex subject, a definition is only as good as the long and complicated account which it encapsulates. With the complex subject that is business ethics, we arrive at such an account by looking at the problems which raise moral issues in business, and by critically examining the various proposals for solving them. This entire book is just such an account. At the end of it readers should have a broad idea of what business ethics is. Acquiring that idea is not the point of the exercise though. It is at best a by-product. What really matters is acquiring an appreciation of the nature of the issues and, even more importantly, how they might be resolved. This is because business ethics, like ethics in general, is centrally concerned with conduct. Ethical questions are essentially questions about whether we ought or ought not to perform certain kinds of actions; about whether those actions are good or bad, right or wrong, virtuous or vicious, worthy of praise or blame, reward or punishment, and so on. Consequently, with business ethics as with any other branch of ethical enquiry, the point of the exercise is to resolve questions of conduct. It has, then, an essentially practical purpose. We inquire not simply in order to be informed, but to inform our actions; to provide those actions with a better and sounder basis than they might otherwise have.

Does this mean that business ethics is a matter of producing moral codes? Is it a series of guides to morally good business practices, replete with lists of do's and don'ts? It can be. But if it were only that then it would be a branch of what is known as 'normative' or, alternatively, 'prescriptive' ethics. (We shall use the latter term.) It would be ethics understood as a matter of laying down 'norms' of behaviour, of 'prescribing' conduct – a matter, that is, of issuing instructions regarding what should and should not be done; with business ethics concerning itself with those instructions that have particular reference to the world of business.

Laying down the law with regard to what should and should not be done is, as we have acknowledged, very much what ethics is about. But it is not what it is all about, or even primarily about – at least not if 'ethics' is understood in its traditional philosophical sense of a disciplined enquiry into morality. (Broadly speaking, 'ethics' is the inquiry, 'morality' is what is inquired into.)

What does such a conception of ethics require? Does it mean a scholarly detachment from moral commitment, as talk of 'disciplined enquiry' seems to imply? Is ethics, as a discipline, concerned merely to observe what it is that people say and do regarding moral matters without any attempt to pass judgement?

If so, it would be subsumed under what can be called 'descriptive ethics'. Here, in contradistinction to prescriptive ethics, the concern is merely to describe what goes on regarding moral matters. We seek to discover, by observation, surveys, interviews, tests, and the like, what it is that people do, say or believe about what is good and bad, right and wrong, and so on. The concern is not to assess the moral correctness or incorrectness of what is discovered, nor is it to come up with amendments or alternatives. It is merely to give a descriptive account of actual moral behaviour and attitudes; with the behaviour and attitudes of business people as the special concern of business ethics.

Again, there is more to ethics than this. It is not that accounts of what people actually do, say and think about morality are set aside. Still less is it that no pronouncements on what is right and wrong are to be made. But what is missing from both a purely descriptive or purely prescriptive approach is that vital critical element which is at the heart of ethics as a disciplined inquiry. We have to subject the behaviour and attitudes exhibited, and the rules and principles propounded, to a rigorous critical examination to see if we can determine why they are, morally speaking, right or wrong. It is this which is attempted here and in books on business ethics generally, and is, in terms of a disciplined enquiry, what is traditionally understood by the word ethics, whether it is applied to business or any other area of life.

HOW IS IT DONE?

This is all very well, but how is it to be done? How will we arrive at these conclusions about moral rights and wrongs in business?

It is not entirely facetious to answer, 'With difficulty!' Business ethics is hardly going to concern itself with issues for which there are straightforward and obvious solutions. It is not much help, for example, to be told that theft and fraud are morally wrong. We already know that. It is barely conceivable that anyone would wish to defend activities such as stealing the design of a new product and selling it to a competitor, or keeping two sets of accounts, one for oneself and the other for the Inland Revenue. It is the more complex and contentious issues that are going to be of the greatest concern in the study of business ethics: issues like corporate responsibility, environmental protection, worker participation, and so on.

Yet we are still left with the question of just how these admittedly difficult issues are to be tackled. By what method do we decide on answers to questions of moral right and wrong in business? There is no special or unique process to do this. It is nothing more or less than is involved in any disciplined enquiry into complex problems, whether in business or anywhere else. We consider the problem and come up with possible solutions which we then subject to three broadly different kinds of test.

- Firstly, and most obviously, there is the test of agreement with the evidence as we understand it. Does the evidence support or deny the explanation we have put forward? If, for example, we are arguing for the benefits of greater worker participation in the running of companies, what is the evidence that employees actually want such involvement?
- Secondly, there is the test of internal coherence. Are all the parts of the explanation in agreement with each other or is it self-contradictory in some way? Does it say things which are somehow in opposition and so cannot be, or are unlikely to be, equally true at the same time? We cannot, for example, accept that workers are exclusively interested

in maximizing wages and argue for the importance to them of an enhanced self-esteem that would come from participation in decision making.

- Thirdly, we can subject our conclusions to the test of its compatibility with our more general system of belief. Does it fit in with what we generally take to be true in this area or does it somehow contradict our assumptions, or at least rest uncomfortably with them? How well, for example, does the claim that workers are exclusively interested in maximizing wages fit in with what we generally accept about human motivation?

In widening the issue out to consider compatibility with our more general assumptions, we invariably become involved in theoretical issues. The debate about worker participation will, as we have just seen, sooner or later involve theories of human motivation.

What are theories? Very roughly, they are overarching, large scale explanations in terms of which other and smaller explanations are both generated and evaluated. A theory of human motivation which gave pride of place to the desire for economic rewards would, for example, both lead to and endorse the claim that workers are exclusively interested in maximizing wages. Conversely, a theory giving priority to a need for social relationships would be difficult to reconcile with such a claim.

Theories are no less a feature of ethical enquiry than of any other, and have just the same generating and evaluating role. If, for example, we base our argument for worker participation on the claim that workers have a moral right to have a say in the running of the companies for which they work, then this will certainly raise theoretical questions about the nature of moral rights – questions about what they are and why (or whether) they should include workers having their particular say.

·Though theories have this overarching role, they are not themselves immune to evaluation of course. They are subject to much the same tests of agreement with evidence, internal coherence, and compatibility with other beliefs as any other, but more particular, kind of explanation. The only real difference is that the testing is done at a larger and more abstract scale when theories are at stake. It is one thing, for example, to discuss the question of workers' rights to participation, but quite another to discuss moral rights in general.

Summing up then, we can say that we attempt to solve ethical problems in much the same way as we would any other complex and contentious question. There is the same range of tests available and the

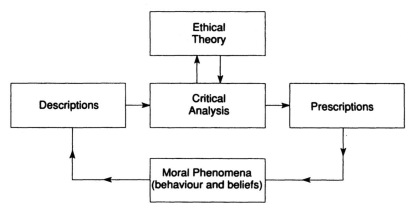

Figure 2.1 Ethical enquiry.

same kind of critical relationship to theory. (This is why this book contains a chapter on ethical theory.)

Diagrammatically, the situation with regard to ethical enquiry can be put this way. (see Figure 2.1.) Here, what we have labelled 'critical analysis' is at the centre of a dynamic system where it both uses and assesses ethical theory (hence the two way relation) to examine existing moral behaviour and beliefs in order to arrive at critically evaluated moral prescriptions which aim to replace, endorse, modify, or add to existing ideas of morality and thereby alter or reinforce existing moral practices in some way. Business ethics then is simply that particular sub-division of this activity which deals with conduct in business affairs as opposed to any other particular kind or to conduct in general.

HOW IS IT POSSIBLE?

This is all very well, a sceptic might say, but are not ethical problems just too complex, too contentious, for this pretty picture to apply? Is it not the case that we just do not have definitive answers to these problems? Hence, there can be no 'critical analysis' of ethical issues in business or anywhere else. All we can have is a very uncritical prescriptive or descriptive ethics. Ethics as an enquiry to provide us with answers to moral problems, it might be said, is just not possible.

Clearly, this objection cannot mean that arriving at answers to ethical problems is impossible. This book, for one, will be full of them. The key word is 'definitive'. There are plenty of answers, it would have to be admitted, the trouble, the sceptic would have to say, is that none of them are definitely correct. They are all uncertain; we can never be sure we have the right answer.

That much can be admitted. As well as being complex, ethical problems are, as we noted, contentious. We have not just different, but opposing answers, based very often on strongly contrasting theoretical perspectives.

Much the same is true of many other kinds of enquiry of course. It is not unknown even in the natural sciences of physics, biology, chemistry, and the like. It is a commonplace, perhaps even the norm, in social sciences such as psychology, sociology, and economics, and it is as true of the study of business as of any other study of social phenomenon. There are many different and sometimes conflicting theories, for example, of worker motivation, marketing, and even the function of management itself. In fact, if definitive answers are demanded for difficult questions, then it is doubtful if we get anywhere near this in any but the hardest of hard sciences – and no one would count management science or the study of business in general as being in that category.

This does not mean we give up these enquiries into business or any other social phenomenon. What we very sensibly do is settle for something less than certainty. We recognize the scope for genuine differences and so are prepared to entertain a wider range of possible solutions than would be normal in more exact forms of enquiry.

For an introductory text book dealing with one of these uncertain enquiries, this means setting out, as fairly as is possible, the various contending positions and inviting the reader to choose between them. Instead of the comfort of a single definitive answer which can be relayed to the reader simply, we have the challenging and often confusing situation of a variety of possible answers. This is so in much of the social sciences, in many of the more theoretical areas of business studies, and is very much the situation here.

However, though a text book such as this is forced, in fairness to the reader, to be neutral between various contending answers, this does not mean that therefore there is nothing to choose between them; that the choice is an entirely arbitrary one, subject only to whim or fancy. If this were so then any old answer would do. We could decide how to act in business by tossing a coin or by looking at our horoscope – or we could simply decide that following our own personal whims at the time was the right thing to do.

Even in the most uncertain of enquiries it is obvious that not any old answer will in fact do. Not any answer could equally well agree with the evidence, be equally coherent, or be equally compatible with our other beliefs as any other. Some (such as the ones mentioned above) could be wildly implausible. Others, though plausible enough, could run into difficulties of varying degrees of severity. Even though they never approach certainty, some answers can still be more evidential, more coherent, more generally compatible than others. This has to be so in even the most contentious areas of social science and of the study of business – including the study of business ethics.

All right, it might be retorted, but is there not greater uncertainty in ethical matters? Are we not much less able to arrive at a better answer in ethics than in these other, admittedly uncertain, enquiries? This may be so, but how much less certain is it? Just saying ethical enquiry is particularly problematical still leaves it possible for us to decide between competing answers to moral problems on an objective basis. We can keep on trying, even though success is likely to be particularly hard to achieve.

The attempt to arrive at conclusions on matters of business ethics would be doomed to failure if it were shown that any objective justification in ethics was impossible. If this were the case, then anything goes in ethics, and no answer is intrinsically better than any other. This is a very large claim indeed. Can it be defended, and, if so, how? To uphold such a view, it would need to be demonstrated that the whole of morality lay outside the realm of objective justification. This would amount to a full blown theory of the nature of morality itself – albeit that the whole of morality was, in a sense, to be dismissed.

Theories about the nature of morality are called 'meta-ethical' theories. A meta-ethical theory is a large scale theory which attempts to answer questions **about** ethics rather than questions **in** ethics. The distinction can be explained more readily by considering examples of these respective types of question. 'Is it sometimes right to break confidentiality?' is a question **in** ethics, whereas, 'Are moral judgments simply expressions of our personal emotion?' is a question **about** ethics. Meta-ethics, then, attempts to explain the nature of morality as a whole and not just some particular area such as the nature of moral rights or whatever.

The theory that ethical statements cannot be objectively justified is a meta-ethical theory. We certainly need to look at a meta-ethical theory which denies the very possibility of ever really knowing moral right from wrong, but we can do so adequately only in the context of an examination of equally grand though opposing meta-ethical theories. A fuller presentation of this question must therefore wait for the chapter on ethical theories (chapter 3).

In the meantime, however, consider the consequences of such a denial of ultimate objective justification for the ethical. Would it follow that ethical enquiry must be abandoned? We do not think so. What would have to go is any 'evidential test' for moral conclusions: there could no longer be an appeal to evidence as an ultimate test of ethical correctness. But this would still leave us with the test of internal coherence: some answers to ethical problems could still fit together better than others and it is still necessary to avoid having one part of an answer inconsistent with another. Also, and perhaps more importantly, there is still the test of compatibility with our general system of belief.

This last test is particularly important because very prominent among our moral beliefs is adherence to the correctness of some set of moral rules. As a matter of fact, a great number of people in all societies, perhaps the great majority, **do** believe they know right from wrong. More significantly still, all but a tiny pathological minority accept they **should** adhere to rules of right and wrong. They may not always adhere to these rules in practice; they may even have just those intellectual doubts about knowing right from wrong that we have touched upon. Nonetheless, they accept they ought to adhere. And for the most part, they do. Moreover, there is for the most part agreement about what those rules should be; at least for the most fundamental and important of them. Consequently, and unsurprisingly, society will be structured around those rules. Transgression of them will meet sanctions of various kind: disapproval, ostracism, even legal penalties.

The upshot of this is, notwithstanding whether or not these ethical rules can be objectively justified, they will inevitably form a living part of the structure of any and every society. Decision making will have to accommodate them, and this will be as true of business decision making as of any other. Those responsible for the conduct of business will have little option, therefore, but to fit their activities around this inescapable social fact. They will simply have to reconcile our business conduct with ethical expectations or run the risk of social disapproval, ostracism, or worse. Barclays Bank's very reluctant withdrawal from South Africa, because of a boycott by UK student unions, illustrates the kind of price they might pay (a bank which does not attract students does not later have high income graduate customers), while the jailings of prominent business men following the Guinness affair demonstrates another.

Moreover, moral rules are not simply one of many kinds of social rules. There are many different kinds of social rules but the moral kind is peculiarly privileged among them. They constitute the basis upon which the correctness of the others are evaluated. Rules of etiquette, for example, can be rigidly adhered to; but not at the cost of immorality. No one, for example, would adhere to the niceties of polite conversation when warning of a life or death emergency. Even legal rules are subordinated to the moral. The (perceived) immorality of a law can be such that it is only morally proper to disobey it. The recently repealed apartheid laws in South Africa are a prime example of laws too morally discreditable to be respected.

As with acceptance of any kind of social rule, operating within a moral framework is not simply a question of blindly following instructions. It will always involve some kind questioning and enquiry even when it puts question of ultimate justification aside. There are at least three reasons for this:

- The first is that even the best ordered set of moral rules is inevitably going to involve some clashes. How, for example, are we to reconcile the moral rule that we should obey the law with the apparent immorality of certain laws?
- A second reason is the problem of applying the rules to particular cases. No rule can possibly specify every circumstance it might apply to. It is one thing, for example, to have a moral rule against cheating, quite another to decide in any particular case what constitutes cheating. Why, for instance, is insider dealing taken to be a form of cheating, and what in any instance constitutes insider dealing?
- The third reason why morality is never simple rule following is that even though there is a wide measure of moral agreement in society about what rules are to hold, the agreement is never total. Some rules are controversial; others will be revised, repealed or replaced. Is there, for example, a right by workers to participate in the running of companies? If so, what of the supposition that managers have 'a right to manage' or primary duty to shareholders to maximize the value of their holdings?

All the above examples illustrate the possibility of moral debate without necessarily raising the meta-ethical issue of whether anything ultimately justifies competing claims. That issue certainly could arise were the questioning to be pushed far enough in a theoretical direction. But it need not be. A high level of debate can be conducted simply within the framework of a generally shared set of moral beliefs. The compatibility of any particular moral position with that system can by itself provide the basis for rational debate. Indeed, the great majority of moral debates are conducted at just this level.

We can conclude then that, even without recourse to ultimate justification, ethical enquiry remains not only possible but, in terms of social functioning, absolutely inescapable. We simply cannot function in society without operating within and reasoning about moral rules, and this (as we shall see in chapter 3), is a good reason for regarding them as ultimately justifiable.

WHY DO IT?

Granted then that ethical inquiry is all too possible, why engage in it? Why, in particular, engage in inquiring into the ethics of business activity?

One very good reason has already been given. It is inescapable. Societies are, we have seen, structured around moral rules in a peculiarly fundamental way. Businesses have to operate in a social structure which in some ways is as much ethical as it is legal, political, economic, or anything else. Business decisions can therefore be as much constrained by the ethical environment as by the legal, political, economic, or whatever. Some things are better to do than others given the demands of the legal, political, or economic environments; and likewise some things are better than others to do given the demands of the ethical environment within which a business must also operate.

Another reason to be concerned with the ethics of business activity is that as an activity business is overwhelmingly important. Most of the working population depend on it for their livelihoods. The rest are at least dependent on it as consumers. As a force in society it can certainly stand comparison with religion, politics, or anything else. Some would argue it has long been the dominant force in western societies at least, with governments of various hues only distinguished by the varying degrees of enthusiasm with which they bend to the economic power exerted by business. Certainly it is a growing power. With world-wide privatizations of what were state-owned assets, business methods and business attitudes are moving into more and more areas of economic activity in more and more countries. Multi-national corporations grow ever bigger. Their turnovers dwarf the entire gross national product of many small and even medium sized countries (Shell's is bigger than

Morocco's, ICI's is bigger than Jordan's.) Business generally is becoming ever more global in character with a world-wide market in money, services, and products which is beyond the power of even the largest of individual national governments to control. Never, in short, has there been more need for attention to the ethics of business.

A third reason is much more parochial. It is peculiar to the people at whom this and other books on business ethics are chiefly aimed. They are the people who exercise, or will exercise, power in businesses; that is, managers and those studying to be managers. For them a concern with the ethics of business is part of a now well established and seemingly inevitable process of professionalization.

In this managers are no more than part of a general social trend. Many groups from librarians to school teachers, engineers to accountants, have attempted in varying ways and with varying degrees of success to follow lawyers and doctors in professionalizing their occupations. The motivation is almost certainly a desire for that high social esteem which professional status brings. The justification for this is broadly based on two considerations: the first is a claim that the job involves a high degree of intellectual difficulty; the second is a claim that it involves a high degree of responsibility.

This first factor justifies that great distinguishing mark of the professional; a period of formal education and training, replete with examination and certification. The second justifies that other great mark of the professional; a concern with ethics, usually replete with codes of conduct and enforcement procedures.

With managers, the intellectual difficulty factor is rooted in the complexity, and sometimes scale, of business operations. Managers plan, organize, command, control, lead, and so on. These are complex tasks. If the organization is large enough and the manager senior enough, it is complexity compounded by scale. Increasingly, but by no means universally, this complexity and possible scale is seen to warrant formal educational requirements for managers.

As for the responsibility factor, this virtually holds by definition. In planning, organizing, commanding, and so on, managers take on responsibilities. This is not just for technical matters: for manufacturing processes, bureaucratic procedures, financial budgets, and the like. There are responsibilities towards people. Managers must safeguard investors' money, protect the environment, keep consumers from harm, take care of the health and safety of employees, and the like. When the organization is very large and the manager very senior, these are responsibilities on a vast scale; with financial ruin, ecological disaster, human suffering, and even death, following on from mistakes, misdeeds, or mishaps. Think of Barlowe Clowes, Polly Peck, the Bank of Credit and Commerce International, of Bhopal, *Exxon Valdez*, *Piper Alpha* and so on. Here size has brought notoriety. However, for those involved, the activities of senior managers in small organizations can be no less dire – no less a question of ruin, disaster, suffering or even death. All managers, even the most junior, are all the time making decisions which affect some people's lives to some degree. And because of the complexity of organizational structures, even the most junior of managers will sometimes make decisions which have far reaching consequences. They might antagonize an important customer, upset a key group of workers, or fail to follow a vital safety procedure. All in all then, we can conclude that in terms of responsibility, managers have as much reason to have a concern with ethics as any lawyer, doctor, or other professional.

A fourth reason for inquiring into the ethics of business activity may be surprising. It is self-interest. By this we do not mean the self-interest of the groups at the receiving end of business activities: the employees, customers, trading partners, or society at large. It is easy enough to see their interest in businesses being aware of their ethical responsibilities; for these responsibilities are owed to them. They are the ones who could be cheated, exploited, or defrauded, if businesses pay no heed to moral matters. The claim we want to make is the altogether more problematic one that it can be in the interest of businesses themselves to inquire into the ethics of business activity. More specifically, because of course 'businesses' can't inquire, we want to claim that managers can serve the interests of the businesses if they inquire into the ethics of business activity. Moreover, it is 'self-interest' understood by the normal business criteria of survival, growth, and profitability which is meant and not some notion of virtue as its own reward. There are three ways in which ethical inquiry can serve that interest: firstly, in terms of relations with consumers and the public at large; secondly, in terms of relations with employees; and thirdly, in terms of relations between businesses.

Relations with consumers and the public

With regard to the first way, we only have to note that there is, as was pointed out above, a penalty in terms of social disapproval facing any company which transgresses generally accepted moral rules. Such transgressions could threaten the prosperity or even survival of a company just as much as misjudging the political or economic climate, or running foul of the law. Moreover, the ethical environment is no more a discrete system than are the others. They all overlap and interact with each other: economic factors influence politics, political action effects changes in law, laws restrict and permit particular economic activities, and so on. Ethical factors can very obviously figure in such interactions. Because of the peculiarly fundamental character of moral rules, they can even be the initiating factor in the process. For example, moral disapproval of certain economic activities can lead to political pressure for legal controls, resulting in laws against such matters as insider dealing, pollution, or unsafe working practices.

Here the role of the moral environment is restrictive, as we would expect it to be. It places limitations on business activity. But this need not always be so. Like any other social environment, the ethical can be a source of business opportunity. For example, since the 1970s there has been a 'mushrooming' of 'ethical investment funds' aimed at what market research tells us is an 'ethical investor' who wants to avoid putting money into armaments manufacture, tobacco, gambling, and the like. Recently, the Co-operative Bank in the UK has launched a 'customer charter' guaranteeing, amongst other things, not to release information about the credit-worthiness of its customers to other financial institutions without the express permission of the customer involved. This breaks what has become a normal banking practice of releasing such information without the customer even being aware of it. The stand the Co-operative Bank has taken against this morally dubious activity has evoked, it says, 'hostility' from its competitors, praise from the press, and will, it presumably hopes, be an inducement to existing and potential customers to bank with them. Finally, there is the by now classic case of Body Shop where a whole marketing strategy has been built around an image of moral rectitude: no polluting, no testing on animals, no projecting of an unattainable ideal of feminine beauty, and so on.

Whether as opportunities to be exploited or, as is more usual, as limitations to work within, there is no doubt that businesses have a very sound prudential reason for being concerned with ethical matters. It is quite simply in their interest. Moral disapproval of company activities can convert into political pressures, legal controls and even consumer boycotts; at the very least, it does the company image harm. Moral approval on the other hand, not only avoids political pressures and legal controls; it can even lead to consumer support; and it does the company image untold good. For example, and in sharp contrast to other major producers of cosmetics and toiletries, Body Shop spends no money at all on advertising. It does not need to. Instead, it has the free publicity provided by frequent media exposure. This tends to centre around the personality of the firm's co-founder, Anita Roddick. But interest in that personality and in the company at large is inextricably bound with that high moral profile which she so successfully promotes and projects. The Body Shop exemplifies the kind of actively benevolent image which probably most companies would like to have. Certainly no company would like to have a malevolent image; public relations departments and public relations consultants exist largely to make sure they do not. A now common form of public relations activity is for companies to engage in the sponsorship of sporting and artistic events, and the funding of community projects – anything from athletics, to opera, to employment schemes for inner city youth. The beneficiaries are carefully chosen for lending a particular association to the company name. Acknowledgement of the company's 'generous assistance' is made in some suitably discreet fashion. The objective is not so much to make the company known as to make it known as a health conscious, cultured, and above all caring organization. Multi-nationals in particular spend millions on 'corporate advertising' which has nothing to do with selling the company's products and everything to do with making the public feel good about the company and its activities. Assurance that the environment is safe in their hands is a particular favourite here. When, for instance, the beautifully modulated voice in a TV commercial asks us, 'Why all the pretty pictures of flamingos?', it is so that we can be told what a good job the British Oxygen Company is doing in cleaning up the environment. Why, one might ask, does such a largely anonymous industrial concern want to be known to the public at large except in order to be loved by them?

Relations with employees

That the moral approval of consumers and society generally is in the interest of businesses can hardly be disputed. There is room for more contention with the second of the three ways in which ethical concern can serve that interest; when that concern is directed inwards, towards the company's own employees. Here a claim for self-interest is very much dependent on a particular approach to the management of people. Very roughly, it is an approach which assumes that if an organization shows care and consideration towards its employees then they will work so much more effectively for it. They will respond with a loyalty and a commitment to the organization which will translate into increases in productivity and quality that will more than pay for any increased financial cost of being caring and considerate.

This is the belief which lies behind that tradition of enlightened, if sometimes paternalistic, management which looks to good working conditions and company health and welfare schemes to keep workers happy and productive. It is a tradition with a very long pedigree. Examples can be found in most countries. In Great Britain it can be traced back to reforms instituted by Robert Owen at the New Lanark cotton mills at the start of the nineteenth century. A later example is Titus Salt with his building of the model industrial community of 'Saltaire' around the middle of that century. The Quaker founders of the Cadbury and Rowntree chocolate making firms are also notable examples of this approach. Marks and Spencer would probably be the most cited modern instance. At an international level, one could point to the policy of protecting jobs and attempting to provide lifetime employment which is practised by companies such as IBM, Hewlett-Packard, and major Japanese corporations in general, as proof that 'looking after' employees pays productive dividends.

Relations between businesses

With the third and final way which moral concern serves the self-interest of business – that of relations between businesses – there is a very simple yet rather profound and, we think, indisputable point to be made. It is that businesses just could not function in an environment devoid of ethical constraint. If fraud, theft or deception were the norm rather than the exception in business dealings, then those dealings would eventually become impossible to sustain. They would be too uncertain, too fraught with danger, to be worth engaging in for most people. As Plato noted many centuries ago, there must be a measure of trust, even amongst thieves.[1] For business to be carried on successfully there has to a reasonable expectation that most people will behave reasonably honourably most of the time. So in this third way also, a concern with the ethical on the part of those running businesses will serve the interest of those businesses.

[1] Plato, *The Republic*, Book One.

Ethics and self-interest

Put all three ways together and it amounts to substantial convergence between morally correct behaviour and commercial success. To study business ethics is to try to identify what is morally correct behaviour for business. It is, therefore, to study something which can make a substantial contribution to the commercial self-interest of businesses.

As a reason for studying business ethics this is anything but novel. It is the reason given by a former head of the US Securities and Exchange Commission, Mr James Shad, when in 1987 he gave $20 million to a $30 million ethics programme at the Harvard Business School. What he reputedly said then, and he has certainly repeated similar sentiments since,[2] was that: 'ethics pays . . . It's smart to be ethical.' More generally, we find this same justification for business ethics in the oft-repeated contention that 'good ethics is good business'.

This slogan has obvious attractions for business people. It seems to offer what might be called an 'instrumental' view of business ethics, the idea that it is there simply as an instrument of business efficiency. Like cost accounting, marketing research, or any other tool of modern management, ethical investigation is, on this view, merely something to further the commercial aims of business.

For this to be true without qualification, it has to be that there can never be any conflict between the moral and the commercial; that 'good ethics' is always, and unreservedly, 'good business'. This is obviously not so. Take the case of low wages paid to Third World plantation workers by British tea companies. ('Low' in this instance means that at best they only permit a subsistence standard of living.) To make the assumption that 'good ethics is always good business' and generously increase the workers' wages could well be disastrous in commercial terms. Any company which did this would suffer a cost disadvantage relative to any rival company which did not. Its products would therefore be at a price disadvantage relative to those of these rival firms, and this could lead to falling sales and so falling profits.

No unqualified version of the instrumental view is going to be remotely plausible. There is obviously a limit to the degree to which morality and commercial self-interest can converge. This is no more than could be expected. There are obviously limits to the degree to which morality and any kind of self-interest can converge. In one way self-interest is integral to morality; in another, wholly antithetical.

The integral way amounts to no more than the rather obvious but very

[2] *'Business Matters'*, BBC2, 11 July 1991.

profound fact that we all have a vested interest in the maintenance of morality. This holds in both a negative and a positive sense. In the negative sense it is because it is in our interest not to be the victims of wrongdoing: to be wronged is to be harmed. In the positive sense it is because it is in our interest to have moral obligations fulfilled towards us, such as obligations to fulfil commitments, to afford assistance, repay debts of various kinds. Morality is all about prohibiting wrongdoing, on the negative side, and compelling obligations to be fulfilled on the positive side. Therefore, morality serves our interests in both respects.

That self-interest is also antithetical to morality stems from an equally obvious but profound fact; it is that the self-interest which morality serves is universal in character. It is both reciprocal and collective. We are all protected from being wronged by others because we are all prohibited from wronging others. We are all entitled to have moral obligations towards us fulfilled by others because we are all compelled to fulfil our obligations to others. The satisfaction of our individual interests does not extend to being allowed to do wrong or set aside obligations when it suits us. Morality serves the interests of individuals only up to the point that it is broadly compatible with the interests of everyone else. The social role of morality, in fact, is to reconcile individual with collective self-interest; in short, to serve the common good. This is why though it serves self-interest, morality is also the most threatened by it, for nothing is more antithetical to the common good than the unrestrained self-interest of individuals.

In business, as anywhere else, it is this requirement of universality which sets limits on the extent to which morality and self-interest can coincide. In the case of the tea companies, for instance, what makes the commercial self-interest in low wages wrong is that it at the expense of a reciprocal and collective self-interest. It violates limits set by the common good.

It is because commercial self-interest, like any other kind of self-interest, can so easily extend beyond the common good that 'good business' does not necessarily follow 'good ethics' and an unqualified version of the instrumental view of business ethics is so untenable. But we are still left with the possibility of a qualified version. It can be argued that 'good ethics is good business' in the sense that while it is not always true, it is true generally, on balance, or in the long run. There is acceptance that being ethical imposes limits and even extra costs on businesses. They cannot pursue profit regardless of harm to the common good; and things such as environmental protection, welfare provision for workers, community programmes and the like, cost money. But on balance, it is argued, the benefits and opportunities outweigh the costs and limitations. As a general business strategy 'ethics pays'. Companies which strive to be ethical will, on balance and all other things being equal, have a competitive advantage over those which do not. So as business ethics is an aid to companies being ethical, it is also, on balance, an aid to companies being commercially successful, So arguably, in this qualified, broadly true sense, the instrumental view of business ethics holds good.

Whether ethically orientated firms actually are commercially more successful than those that are not is a very vexed question indeed. The evidence is mixed. Most findings seem positive to some degree, a few are netural, a few are negative. This shows a balance in favour of the 'ethics pays' thesis and not much evidence that being ethical will actually damage a company's wealth.[3] What it is not, though, is conclusive proof that the thesis 'ethics pays' is true. In the absence of such proof, probably the best that can be done is to point again to the benefits in terms of consumer and public esteem, employee loyalty, and the trust of other businesses which accrue to ethically concerned companies. These are assets of obvious commercial worth which no business would want to lose and most would strive to acquire.

They are assets which would be denied the actively unethical firm, the company which will do anything at all, no matter how unethical, for financial gain. In the long run, all it will acquire is disdain, disloyalty and distrust. Provided it could keep out of the courts, it could still no doubt survive and prosper. Other factors, such as a commanding market position, scarcity value, unemployment, and political influence, could all offset the liabilities acquired as a consequence of immorality. But liabilities they would remain and the company is so much the poorer in having them and not the contrasting assets which being actively ethical would bring.[4]

What of the firm which we might describe as the 'ethically passive'? (This could well be your average business.) Either from conscience or caution it is not prepared to do just anything in the pursuit of financial

[3] K. E. Aupperle *et al.*, 'An empirical Examination of the Relationship Between Corporate Social Responsibility and Profitiability'; *Academy of Management Journal*, 1985, vol. 28, no. 2, pp. 446–63. Their survey of past studies comes up with a majority of positive findings, but their own investigations point to a neutral correlation.

[4] The idea that being actively ethical is connected with risk avoidance is supported by J. B. McGuire *et al.*, 'Corporate Social Responsibility and Firm Financial Performance', *Academy of Management Journal*, 1988, vol. 31, no. 4, pp. 854–72.

gain. It conforms to whatever minimum standards the law and public opinion are prepared to tolerate, but beyond that it does nothing. It does not actively seek to promote the common good in any way. It seeks only, up to the maximum limits tolerated, to promote its own financial self-interest. 'Minimum morals, maximum mammon' could sum up its creed. Inevitably, it does some good. For a start, it is avoiding the grosser forms of corporate immorality, and like any business, even the most actively unethical, it will be providing products, services, jobs and (possibly unlike the unethical firm) paying taxes. Such public benefaction, if that is what it is, will be incidental to its exclusively financial objectives; an unavoidable by-product of making money in a minimally moral fashion. What then of such a business? Without any trouble and expense, will not at least a portion of the commercial advantages which accrue to the 'ethically active' business accrue to it also?

We think not. If we look again at those advantages we see that they follow from being thought deserving of moral credit. The ethically active business has earned the esteem of consumers and public, the loyalty of employees, the trust of other business, as credit for doing good. But to earn such credit it is not enough just to do good. The intention must be to do good. If, as it is with the ethically passive business, the good it does through producing, employing, and paying taxes is incidental to an exclusively financial objective, then no credit is deserved. This is merely serving one's own self-interest, and there is nothing morally credit worthy in that. It is not immoral provided the collective interest is not harmed. But in the fact that it is not directed at serving that common good, it is not moral either.

It might be said that at least there is an intention on the part of the morally passive business to refrain from the grosser forms of corporate immorality. But this is no more than can be expected and so, very properly, earns little or no credit. In contrast, credit is heaped on the ethically active business precisely because it does more than can be expected. For what this demonstrates is a commitment to the common good. It is only if such a commitment can be demonstrated that beneficial deeds earn moral credit for those who perform them.

All this raises interesting questions about motives of course. Are the people directing the ethically active business doing it just to have the ensuing advantages without a thought for the common good? Or are their motives totally altruistic, wanting nothing but the common good? Are they perhaps a mixture of altruism and self-interest, mindful of the advantages but also sincerely desiring to benefit society?

If the wholly self-interested motive applies, then there is certainly a problem about how much moral credit, if any, is deserved. Here too, good is being done merely incidentally by people who are setting out only to serve their own interests. Worse, there is scope for insincerity, even deception; there is the setting of moral objectives without a real moral intent. Fortunately though, moral credit does not demand the other extreme of total altruism. Being moral is one thing, being saintly is something extra. Morality is, as we saw, a mixture of self-interest and altruism; it is self-interest within the limits of the common good. So, provided it is desired to advance the collective interest along with the personal and that the latter has priority in the event of a clash, then moral credit is perfectly well deserved. In point of fact, the people directing the morally active business are unlikely to be either totally self-interested or totally altruistic; they are unlikely to be either total villains or saints. Their motives are almost certainly mixed. But provided they are mixed in the way prescribed, with consideration and priority given to the collective interest, the business is perfectly entitled to reap those rewards of esteem, loyalty and trust.

Ethics and the bottom line

In being entitled to these rewards, the ethically active business does enjoy competitive advantages denied even to the ethically passive business, let alone the actively unethical one. But even accepting the qualified instrumental view that on balance such advantages outweigh the costs and limitations of being ethical, the fact that sometimes they will not entails that on occasions being ethical must mean giving ethical objectives priority over commercial ones. The optimistic response to this is to think in terms of small losses and gains within particular firms. Sometimes being ethical will cost more than it brings in, but the business can absorb these costs and in the long run the policy of being ethical pays off. No doubt under normal circumstances this is how it happens; but normal circumstances presuppose extraordinary ones. Sometimes the cost of being ethical will be far from minor; it might even threaten the very survival of the business. Take the vital foreign order scenario; does the company take an order from a tyrannical regime? Many western companies supplied weapons and weapons making plant to Iraq before the Gulf War of 1991, for example. Does the company bribe the corrupt official to win that vital foreign order? The American Lockheed Corporation did this in Japan, for example. Situations can and do arise in business, as in life generally, where to take the moral line is to pay a heavy price. Talk of an 'on balance' gain from being ethical can overlook the fact that the balance is also across the whole spread of businesses and not just within a particular business. Overall most businesses might gain, but this still leaves the possibility that particular businesses might lose, and lose heavily.

Given this sobering thought, it could seem to many business people that being ethical can be taken too far. The attraction of the instrumental theory, even in its more plausible qualified form, is that it seems to offer an apparently painless absorption of business ethics into business practice. If 'good ethics' is always 'good business' then there is no question of any conflict between ethical and commercial aims. On the contrary, the ethical is always an aid to achieving the commercial. Even if 'good ethics' is only, generally speaking, 'good business', this still might seem to promise only harmony and benefit in the long run. Now it stands revealed that even though there might be gains overall, there could be losses – and crucial losses at that. At this point many business people could indeed decide that maybe business ethics is not such a good idea after all, for what it now seems to be doing is threatening another idea to which (for good and not so good reasons) many business people are very attached; the idea that in business profit maximization must be the ultimate guiding objective, the 'bottom line'.

The not-so-good reason for being attached to this idea is, to put it bluntly, machismo. It has connotations of toughness, hard-headedness, even ruthlessness, which are very attractive to some people – particularly males. A vivid illustration of this was when the Abbey National was converted from a not-for-profit building society to a for-profit bank. This meant that what were 'surpluses on income' would now count as 'profit'. Asked about this, the then chairman, Campbell Adamson, said in support of the change that as far as he was concerned 'surpluses were for choirboys'. (He was making a pun between 'surpluses' and 'surplices'.)

On this particular score we think we can, as far as it is warranted, offer some comfort. Ethical objectives in business are a far from soft option. The fact they must interconnect with commercial ones makes them complex; the fact they can collide with the commercial makes them uncomfortable; and they are, as we have seen, no less vital to the prosperity and even survival of the company than any other kind of objective which business people are called upon to determine and realize. All this is dramatically demonstrated in the phenomenon of 'crisis management'. Why there is a crisis is invariably because management is faced with a combination of moral and commercial demands. In 1990, for example, the French company Perrier was faced with just such a dilemma with the discovery of a relatively minor degree of contamination of its bottled water. The Perrier management had then to make delicate and difficult decisions involving financial, marketing, medical, and moral considerations. (Perrier eventually removed millions of bottles from circulation and so restored public confidence in the product.)

The good reason why business people are attached to the idea of profit as the bottom line is the obviously crucial role which profit does play in business. Profit is generally why businesses are set up in the first place and they will not normally survive without it. Added to this, the drive for profit is an undeniable inducement to efficiency in business.

All this is true; but if (as we presume it does) 'bottom line' means the ultimate guiding principle which takes precedence over everything else then it is simply false. None but a small minority of businesses, and then not all the time, do or possibly could operate on this principle. What they generally do, and generally must do, is to contain their drive for profit within broad legal and moral limits.[5] If all businesses attempted to take the drive for profit beyond legal limits then most business people would be in jail – and there is only limited scope for entrepreneurial activity there. If they all attempted grossly to exceed moral limits for the sake of profit then not only would public and political opinion stop them, but the conduct of business itself would become impossible. As we have seen, there has to be an expectation that most businesses will behave reasonably morally most of the time for commercial relations between businesses to be possible, otherwise these relations are just too uncertain to be worth the risk.

Does this mean the legal is the bottom line in business? After all, no one goes to jail for breaking rules that are merely moral. Despite this notable fact, it is moral rules which have precedence as social rules. As we have also seen, the legitimacy of the legal is judged in terms of the moral. If a law is deemed immoral then there are grounds for altering or repealing it, or even disobeying it. Basic though legal rules are to society, it is the moral which are the most fundamental kind of social rules. Nor is it the case that the moral are totally without the sanctions of state-administered punishment: they are to some extent replicated in law; particularly the more basic kind – rules against murder, fraud, theft,

---

[5] It can be disputed whether even within broad legal and moral limits profit maximization is the overriding aim of businesses. See Peter Drucker, *The Practice of Management* (London: Pan, 1968).

and the like. But even when they are 'merely moral', without legal enforcement and with perhaps only the (considerable) sanction of public opinion as support, in virtue of being moral they still have that logical priority over other social rules. Just as a profitable activity can be ruled out on grounds of illegality, so an activity which is both profitable and legal can be ruled out on the grounds that it is immoral.

The moral is therefore the 'bottom line' in business just as it is anywhere else in social life. This means that there has to be a fifth, last and overriding reason for studying business ethics. It is to help businesses get it right morally; to discover the moral limits within which businesses have to operate, and how they might better further the common good along with their morally legitimate business aims.

In adding this reason we recognize that ethically active business is attempting to operate according to the most fundamental of social rules. It is attempting to align itself with the common good; the collective self-interest of society. Without that organizing principle, not just business activity, but social life in general, would be impossible. There would just be competing self-interest without hope of reconciliation. So what the ethically active business is doing is organizing itself and its relations with the wider society in harmony with the guiding principle of social life, the very basis of social cooperation. That is why it is likely to be rewarded with esteem, loyalty, trust, and so on.

Conclusion

Finally, where does the addition of this fifth reason leave the (qualified) instrumental view of ethics? Not totally abandoned; there are still good grounds for thinking that being ethically active is generally sound business sense. What must be abandoned is the notion that this can alone stand as a reason for studying the ethics of business. Rather, self-interest must take its place alongside inescapability, importance, professionalism and above all, the objective of moral correctness, as a reason for engaging in this study.

DOES IT WORK?

Given that moral correctness is the overriding reason for studying business ethics, the inevitable question is: Will it work? Will studying business ethics make business people – and hence businesses as institutions – more ethical?

If what is being demanded is some necessary connection between study and practice, then the answer is no. All the knowledge in the world cannot guarantee to make a person more ethical. The ancient Greek philosopher Socrates thought it did.[6] He believed that wrongdoing was a kind of ignorance; if we knew what was right we could only do what was right. Alas, this is not so; people can very well know what is right and still, through weakness or wilful disregard, do what is wrong. Business ethics cannot alter this fact of life. What it can perhaps do is to help people become more ethical, and it may do this in two ways.

Firstly, it can make it more difficult for people to behave immorally. Ignorance may not be the sole cause of wrongdoing but it can be a contributory factor. If one is given exposure to ethical issues and ways of resolving them, then it is that much more difficult not to be aware of what is at stake or retreat behind the excuse it is beyond one's competence.

This is the thinking behind the increasingly popular practice of issuing company codes of ethical practice; no one can claim they did not know. It is also, incidentally, the thinking of an American judge who sentenced Chicago exchange dealers to take an ethics course at a law school after they were found guilty of illegal trading practices. Their comment was that it was a bit ironic being taught ethics by lawyers. But that was a comment on lawyers, not ethics courses.

The second way in which studying business ethics might help business people become more ethical is nothing more than the assumption made in any academic study of any area of business. It is that the ability to tackle the problems of business can be enhanced by formal, rigorous study. In the case of business ethics, this means that the ability to tackle the ethical problems of business is enhanced. That study can lead to excellence in practice is not guaranteed; but neither is it in accounting, marketing, personnel, or anything else. With any study, it is up to individuals how well, or even whether, they translate learning into practice.

---

[6] Plato, *loc cit.*.

INTRODUCING THE READINGS

The first reading is a broad survey of the whole field of business ethics by Richard T. De George. It starts by considering the issue of objectivity in morals, moves on to the 'macro-moral' problem of morally evaluating entire societies and economic systems (principally capitalism) and concludes with a six-fold classification of the kinds of 'micro-moral' problems that arise **within** a given social and economic framework. (A similar division features in this book with chapter 3 dealing with objectivity, chapter 4 with the macro-moral, and subsequent chapters with specific micro-moral issues.)

The second reading, by Verne E. Henderson, is explicitly 'micro-moral'. It seeks to show how ethical considerations fit into business decision making in general. It makes the point that businesses must operate within an environment that is as much moral as legal. Stress is placed on tackling the particular 'situation' rather than operating with a fixed set of principles, and the assumption is made that ethics is essentially about promoting 'human welfare'. (As we shall see in chapter 3, both claims are questionable.)

This same identification of the moral with the common good is made in the third reading. It is the classic defence of self-interested individualism by the Scottish philosopher and economist, Adam Smith (1723–1790). In it he propounds his famous 'invisible hand' argument. This says that provided there is competition to satisfy customer wants, then the common good is best served by the pursuit of individual self interest. That way, human welfare will be maximized even though it is no part of the intention of the self-interested individuals that it should be. Smith adds, however, a warning that business people will do anything to avoid the competition necessary to ensure this happy harmony between individual interest and the common good – a point we shall return to in chapter 4.

The final reading by Saul W. Gellerman is very much an example of 'applied business ethics'. In it he analyses three notable cases of business misconduct in order to isolate the factors which lead competent managers to go morally wrong. Having isolated them, he concludes with recommendations on how to avoid their occurrence.

Moral issues in business

RICHARD T. DE GEORGE

The position that ethics has nothing to do with business has a long history. But it is a position that takes too narrow a view of both ethics and business. Ethics is concerned with the goods worth seeking in life and with the rules that ought to govern human behavior and social interaction. Business is not just a matter of economic exchange, of money, commodities, and profits; it involves human interactions, is basic to human society, and is intertwined with the political, social, legal, and cultural life of society.

There is an obvious connection between business and ethics. A businessman whose employees rob him blind could no more survive than a businessman who through lying and fraud sold only products that did not work. Such examples, however, do not settle any real issue between business and ethics. For if lying, fraud, or theft lead to the failure of a business, then a businessman might condemn and eschew them not because they are immoral but because they are bad business practices. Actions that are contrary to moral norms may in some, perhaps even in many, instances be bad for business. But we can distinguish acting in a certain way because it is moral from so acting because it is economically profitable. The distinction is between an action done from duty (i.e., because the action is morally correct) and an action which happens to coincide with one's moral duty, done from some other motive. The claim that morality is inapplicable in business affirms that one's calculation should be based on business, not moral, considerations. Where both coincide, so much the better; where they diverge, so much the worse for morality.

It would be nice to be able to show that moral action is always best for business. But this seems not to be true, especially in the short run. Lying, fraud, deception, and theft sometimes lead to greater profits than their opposites. Hence, moral judgments sometimes differ from business judgments. Businesses need not be run from moral motives. But the actions of businesses affect individuals, society, and the common good. If moral actions are ultimately in the common good, then running businesses in accord with moral norms is in the common good. To the extent that profit maximization conflicts with moral norms, it leads to actions which are not in the common good. In such cases, if the common good is to be protected, and if businessmen do not on their own act in accordance with moral norms, they should be forced to do so. Either public pressure or legal measures should be brought to bear to make the immoral practices unprofitable. If the penalties for not acting morally are sufficiently severe and if the enforcement of norms is sufficiently diligent, then conforming to moral norms will in the long run be in the business interests of business as well as in the general interests of society.

Discussions of morality and business, if the above points are conceded, often lead to three different kinds of questions. First, whose morality is to be imposed on business? Secondly, can economic systems be morally evaluated, and how is morality to serve as a guide between different economic systems and different societies with varying moral norms? Thirdly, which specific practices within a given system are in the public's good?

I

The first question is in several ways a specious one, though seriously and frequently raised. It assumes that there are many different moralities, perhaps that each person has his own, that each is equally valid, and that there is no way to choose among them. When fleshed out as a theory, the position has come to be known as moral relativism. As a philosophical position, it has been refuted at some length,[1] and I think cogently. For present purposes, however, we need look only at the argument based on the fact of cultural diversity and on the fact of moral pluralism within our own contemporary American society. Do either of these facts provide adequate grounds for arguing that there is no morality we can collectively and appropriately apply in the moral evaluation of business practices? I think not, for three reasons.

First, despite the differences in many customs and moral practices from society to society and age to age, there is and has been basic agreement on a large number of central issues. The most basic agreement, though completely formal, is that good should be done and evil avoided. Substantively, there are moral requirements that the members of any society must follow if it is to survive. These include, among others, respect for the lives of its members; respect for the truth (without which it would be impossible to communicate and carry on social life); and respect for cooperation and helpfulness. Each society, for instance, holds that it is immoral for any ordinary member without good reason to kill other members of that society. A society may not have any compunction about killing members of other societies. But unless a society holds that killing its own members without sufficient reason is wrong, the society could not long endure.

Secondly, even in those cases in which the members of a society are allowably killed – e.g., executions, infanticide, euthanasia – the society usually has a network of beliefs which justifies the practice. Beliefs differ, however, and some people believe what is false. A false belief may lead to a different practice than a true belief, but mistaken beliefs do not validly ground a practice. The fact of differing practices, therefore, does not by itself support the claim that there is no way to decide between them. Sometimes there is. In those cases in which moral practices are based on false beliefs, bad reasoning, inconsistent premises, and so on, we have a means of sorting out practices and choosing or rejecting one rather than another. Progress in morality and changes in moral practices, in fact, frequently follow upon the growth of knowledge and changes in belief. The basic similarity of human beings, for instance, is now sufficiently clear and established that we can rightly say it is morally improper to exclude women, or blacks, or men, or any sub-group from the moral community. Criteria of sex, race, nationality, and so on are not morally relevant criteria. This was true even before it was recognized. Unless it was true, it is difficult to understand how it could have come to be recognized.

Thirdly, many differences in moral practices from culture to culture can be shown to be the result of differing circumstances, not of differing moral principles. Morris Ginsberg argues this persuasively and at length.[2]

Thus, the fact that different parts of the world have somewhat different moral practices shows neither that they are all equally valid nor that any one of them is necessarily invalid or immoral.

What about moral pluralism within our own society? Does it justify the claim that all moral judgments are equally good or valid, sound or proper? No, it does not. Reasoning analogous to that used above with respect to differences between cultures applies here as well. For differences are data to be explained, not premises from which moral relativism can be validly deduced.

In American society, despite the rather large amount of disagreement on some issues – e.g., abortion, birth control, capital punishment – there is an enormous amount of agreement. This is true of any viable society; for without such agreement the fabric of society would disintegrate. Not only is there general agreement that murder, theft, lying, fraud, and so on are immoral, but the public reaction both to the events connected with what has become known as 'Watergate' and the public reaction to bribes by corporations is evidence of a large degree of agreement on moral issues such as these. That peoples in some other parts of the world did not understand American public reaction in these cases might indicate that they are cynical about morality, that they do not expect national leaders or businessmen to behave morally, or that they hold different moral values. But their reactions are beside the present point.

In those realms where there is real difference of moral opinion in our country, moreover, there is some consensus about how to deal with that difference. Thus, there is general agreement that morally different opinions are to be tolerated and actions not legally controlled if their results fall exclusively or almost exclusively on the consenting, informed adults who participate in the actions. Fornication and adultery are two cases in point. Other actions, though perhaps not considered immoral, may harm persons other than the participants. Here, there is general agreement that the use of laws to prevent such harm is appropriate. Whether a particular law gets passed, however, depends on the support which can be generated for it through debate, argument, and other means (e.g., lobbying). The recent history of abortion laws is an example of how differing moral judgments are handled where there is disagreement about whether the rights of innocent persons are being infringed.[3]

The pertinent conclusion for our purposes is that the morality which is to be applied to business in our society is the morality which is generally held by the members of our society; that this covers a large area on which there is agreement;

and that, on those topics on which there is disagreement, there should be informed debate about the nature of the activity in question, the circumstances, and the moral principles which differing groups think are applicable. Progress is made this way in other areas, and it is the only way that progress can be made in this area as well. Whether slavery is immoral is not just a matter of opinion; whether discrimination is immoral is not just a matter of opinion; whether bribery is immoral is not just a matter of opinion. These are all matters on which a consensus has been reached (at least in our country, though also in a great many other parts of the world as well), and reached for good and substantial reasons. That these and other moral judgments cannot or should not be applied to the realm of business is simply not true.

The morality held by the American people is expressed in their moral beliefs, institutions, and laws. In areas where there is no specific legislation, the norms implied in legislation should be applied. In disputed areas, the moral judgments which can be best defended and articulated should hold sway. Yet, three points should be made. First, morality is broader than legality. Not everything that is immoral can or should be made illegal. Public reaction, however, is not expressed only in law. Informed public opinion can affect business, and improper business activities should be protested in the market as well as in the ballot box or in the legislature.

Secondly, members of the business community are also members of society. Both should and usually do have a sense of what is immoral, of what they would perceive to be immoral in the business activities of others, and of what the public would perceive as immoral in their own business activities. Just as individuals do not exist in a vacuum but in a society, so businesses do not exist in a vacuum but in a society. As part of that society, they, as individuals, have responsibilities to the society as well as to themselves. Ignoring unethical practices where engaged in by others so that they will be ignored when engaged in by oneself leads to the undermining of confidence in business by the public and will eventually lead to legislation or the wider public enforcement of moral norms.

Thirdly, the view that business practices should be restricted not by moral considerations but only by legal considerations fails to recognize two points. First, one of the bases for making practices illegal is that they are immoral. Second, if immoral practices are not policed by an industry but are engaged in until made illegal, the resulting legislation is frequently excessively restrictive, over-determined, and more costly than uncoerced compliance with moral norms. Thus, industry-wide self-regulation is frequently preferable to legislation. Self-imposed codes of ethics, if honestly drawn up and followed industry-wide (because policed by the industry) – providing they are not self-serving or a means of controlling that legitimate competition which benefits society – can both protect the public interest and keep the conditions of competition within an industry fair.

Our discussion thus far has not addressed itself to borderline cases, and has not suggested that it is always clear exactly what is moral and what is not. It has argued in various ways, however, that despite these uncertainties there is a large area of agreement about the morality of business practices and that the claim of ignorance about what is moral, based on moral pluralism either cross-culturally or within our own society, is largely spurious.

II

Following the economic model, the second group of questions arising from the connection between morality and business can be called macro-moral. These questions involve the moral evaluation of entire economic systems or the moral evaluation of countries and peoples vis-à-vis one another in the economic realm. Issues of the second type arise, for instance, from the fact that there are at the present time some rich countries, some poor countries, and some countries in between. Wealth may come from natural resources or from industrial development. There are some persons who question the right of any people or of any nation to control the resources of a given territory when these resources are needed by others, as well as the right of a manufacturing country, for instance, to exploit the natural resources of another country. An example of the first type would be whether oil-rich countries are morally justified in collectively raising the price of oil to any level they like, regardless of the effect on the oil-using nations – both the relatively well-to-do ones and the poor ones. Is this a moral question at all, or only an economic one? If human welfare is affected by these actions, as it obviously is, then there does seem to be a moral dimension. But exactly how moral suasion can be brought to bear among nations and peoples is far less clear than how it can be brought to bear in a given society. From a moral point of view, the problem is exacerbated by the fact that we are not dealing with individuals but with countries and peoples; how responsibility is to be assigned is consequently less clear than when dealing with individual cases.

The matter of economic exploitation poses a similar problem. Suppose that a manufacturing country did at some time in the past exploit the raw materials of a colony or of an underdeveloped country. Does the former country now owe reparations to the latter? If so, who precisely owes what, if the exploitation is no longer practiced and those who practiced it are now dead? How exploitation is to be defined and how one is to decide whether it was in fact or is in fact practiced remain problematic. But exploitation aside, whether one country which enjoys a high standard of living has any responsibility to help another country which has a low standard of living or whose people are unable to subsist on what they have is a large moral problem, the dimensions of which have yet to be adequately described.

I shall not attempt to solve these problems. Rather, I shall briefly turn to a second type of macro-moral problem, viz., whether economic systems can be morally evaluated.

Hardly anyone would deny that we all have a *prima facie* moral obligation not to engage in immoral practices. So if a given economic system is built on an immoral practice or practices, we have a *prima facie* moral obligation not to engage in the system. But showing that any economic system – which is always bound up with the legal, political, and social system of a society – is both inherently immoral and practicably replaceable is frequently no easy feat.

We can rest secure in the moral judgment that slavery is always *prima facie* morally wrong and to be avoided. We can be less sure that because they were built on slavery, ancient Greece or Rome or Egypt were immoral societies. For we may have some doubts about whether, in those cases, there were any viable better alternatives. I am not arguing that there were not; I am simply affirming that not every *prima facie* immoral practice must be avoided, since some such practices may be the least bad of the available alternatives. Nor should the judgment that slavery is immoral be confused with the judgment that everyone in a slave-holding society is acting in a subjectively immoral way. For they may not realize that the practice they are engaged in is immoral. Yet despite these caveats, we can be sure that slavery is an immoral economic – as well as social and political – system for present-day Americans to adopt.

Granted, therefore, that economic systems can be morally evaluated, we can legitimately ask: is the capitalistic system inherently immoral? Though it is not clear that Marx himself raised moral objections to capitalism, Marxists certainly have, and some of them have come to a negative conclusion. How valid is this assessment?

Four arguments have been used to show the inherent immorality of the capitalist system. One holds that capitalism is built on the exploitation, and so in a sense on the cheating or robbing, of either its own workers – the proletariat – or those of less developed countries. A second and related argument says that capitalism involves a kind of slavery – wage slavery – which is as immoral as physical slavery. A third claims that capitalism yields alienation and similar ills and is therefore immoral. The fourth claims that though capitalism may not have been immoral when it was necessary to develop the productive resources which alone could raise the standard of living of mankind and make a better life possible, it is now restrictive, hampers further development, could and so should be replaced by a preferable – from a human and so moral point of view – alternative. The last claim is not that capitalism is necessarily immoral but that it is immoral to choose it over some better available alternative.

We can examine each claim in turn.

The claim that capitalism is built on the exploitation of workers is sometimes attributed to Karl Marx. Marx's interpretation of the labor theory of value holds that the only way an entrepreneur can make a profit is by paying his workers less than they produce. He does not claim this is immoral. For they are paid what their replacement value is, and so in that sense they are paid what they are worth. But the entrepreneur profits by the discrepancy between what the workers produce and what he pays them, and, if successful, he, not they, gets rich.

The view that maintains that the appropriation of surplus value by the entrepreneur is stealing and so inherently immoral, however, must hold that all value belongs by right to the person who produces it. There are a number of good reasons why this view should not be held. First of all, it does not take sufficient account of how machines multiply the value produced by human labor. An individual worker who has to gather his own raw materials, fashion his own tools, and make whatever he produces individually should get the value of what he produces. With industrialization, however, the labor power of a worker is multiplied by the machines he uses. If a worker today using machines can make ten times as many shoes as he could make without machinery, does it follow that he should be paid ten times as much? It would seem not. For in the first place, as Marx saw, someone has to pay for the machines. More importantly, it took the creative genius of someone – not the particular worker who uses the machines – to invent the machine. It also took the initiative of the entrepreneur who risked his capital and the invested capital of the stockholders who put up the money for the enterprise. So although the worker is able to produce a great deal of value in a short amount of time due to the multiplication made possible by machines, all the credit should not go to him, nor therefore should all the value of what he produces. On this first interpretation, if all of the owner's profit is stolen from the workers, he gets nothing for initiative, risk, inventiveness, and so on.

A second interpretation maintains that the owner's profit is not entirely theft but is so when excessive. With the rise of labor unions, workers banded together to force management to share some of the profits that an enterprise realizes, to improve working conditions, to shorten working hours and days, and to get legislation passed that favors or protects them in various ways. If the difference between what the owners and managers of an industry get and what the lowest paid worker gets is too great, this may be unfair for some reason. A system of taxation or some other form of redistribution may well be in order. But this is compatible with private ownership of industries and admits that a certain portion of surplus value may legitimately go to the owners of industry.

Nor for similar reasons can the case be made out that capitalism or some variety of it has been able to continue because it has shifted its exploitation from its own workers to underdeveloped countries and it is those workers who are being exploited. The argument concerning individual workers in the country in question parallels the above analysis. If it is claimed that the country as a whole is exploited by the richer country, then the technique of exploitation must be characterized otherwise. If this was the case in the relation between mother countries and their colonies, then it does not seem to have been the case *because* of capitalism. Industrial countries today still import raw materials from other countries which are sometimes less developed. This fact by itself does not equal exploitation. Moreover, the raw materials can be sold to countries run more or less on the capitalistic model or to countries run on the socialistic model. The price at which the materials is sold does not depend on the economic system of the buyer country. Hence, the case cannot be sustained that the capitalistic countries depend on exploitation unless the socialistic countries are to be blamed likewise. The evil, in that case, would not be an evil of capitalism, but an evil of well-to-do or industrial as opposed to poor and non-industrial countries. This kind of charge would then become the kind we looked at above; but it would not be the kind of claim we are presently examining, viz., that capitalism as a system is inherently immoral. The claim that exploitation is necessarily ingredient in capitalism and that it is inherently immoral, therefore, does not hold up well under analysis.

The second attack – namely, that capitalism involves wage slavery and that wage slavery is almost as bad as absolute physical slavery – is also defective. The view might be plausible if it could be shown that capitalism pushes workers down to a lower and lower level of life; that they have no bargaining power and are dependent for their subsistence on selling themselves to the owners of the means of production; that they work under inhuman conditions; that they are forced by the system to work at whatever job is available; and that not only heads of households but all members of a household, small children included, are forced to work under inhuman conditions. This is the situation Marx so poignantly describes in *Capital*. Had his analysis that the plight of the workers would get worse and worse until they had nothing to lose but their chains been true, then it could well be argued that the workers had a moral right to seize the instruments of production and change the system. For the system would not allow them to develop their human potentiality, would deprive them of human dignity, and would rend society dangerously apart. If that is the result of capitalism, then it should be morally condemned. Everyone in the society would be alienated, set one against another, lose his sense of human dignity, and be alienated not only in labor but also in society, in politics, and so on. But once again, that situation does not seem to be a necessary ingredient of what has come to be called capitalism. If there ever was such a situation as that described (it never got quite that bad, and so Marx's revolution never took place in the capitalist countries of the West), then it could be branded immoral, just as slavery is branded immoral. But that situation does not prevail today, and we cannot therefore validly make the claim that the economic system of the so-called capitalist countries is inherently immoral because it involves workers in such dehumanizing, slave-like conditions.

The third claim is that private ownership of the means of production results in the alienation of man from the product of his labor, from the labor process, from himself and other men. There is something wrong with a society that values goods more than people, that dehumanizes people in the labor process, and that fragments human beings into competitors, preventing them from social cooperation and mutual respect. And if it could be shown that these were the results of private ownership of the means of production, we would all have to agree that any system built on such ownership is inherently immoral. The link between such conditions and their source, however, is not a conceptual one but an empirical one. And it seems clear that in those societies in which the private ownership of the means of production has been done away with, there is no perceptible decline in alienation, in the desire for goods, in the dehumanization that is tolerated in factories, and so on. And in societies which continue to have private ownership of the means of production, we find growing numbers less interested in goods than their parents; we find a stronger defense of human rights than elsewhere; we find a consciousness that certain types of work can be dehumanizing and stultifying and attempts to change such conditions; and we find not only competition but also cooperation and a willingness to work together.

How we deal with alienation and dehumanization are real problems which we must face. But that they are the result of private ownership of the means of production and will disappear with the disappearance of such ownership seems clearly not to be true.

The fourth charge has the most plausibility. The claim is that capitalism was not (and so is not) inherently immoral. It was historically necessary to develop the industrialization without which mankind could not produce the wealth and the goods necessary for it to increase its standard of living and of dignity. But the capitalist system now serves as a brake, precluding the distribution of the wealth it produces for the benefit of all mankind; it fosters conspicuous consumption; it continues alienation when it would be possible to eliminate or at least substantially reduce it; it protects the vested interests of the rich at the expense of the still poor; it stands in the way of change. It therefore prevents the development of a better, fairer, juster, more moral, humanly preferable society. The charge is not that it is inherently unjust but that it is morally wrong because it inhibits a system which is morally preferable.

Several claims are bound up in this charge, and it is well to separate them out. The first is that there is a better system which would be non-capitalist, or at least non-capitalist in the sense that capitalism exists in some countries today. What the more moral alternative would be and how to achieve it, however, are crucial questions. The Marxist position is that the more moral system would be communism, which would have as its first essential ingredient the abolition of private ownership of the means of production. But what is to take its place? The model of the Soviet Union suggests that state capitalism takes its place. Are the workers better off in the Soviet Union than in the United States? No. Do they enjoy a higher standard of living? No. Do they have more control over their work and working conditions? No. Do they have a less repressive government as a result of their non-capitalistic economic conditions? No. They have, in some respects, more security. But that they have more freedom for self-development and self-expression can at least be argued. Alienation has not disappeared with the abolition of private ownership of the means of production. So if the Soviet model is what is to replace the capitalist model, not only from a human point of view but even from an economic point of view, the case has not been made that capitalism as practiced in the United States is preventing Americans from enjoying the better life available to them if they switch to the Soviet model. The planned economy of the state-owned system has not shown itself superior to the individual initiative still possible in less planned and at least partially privately owned systems.

The Soviet model, of course, is not the only possible alternative, though it is one frequently suggested by Marxist critics. A system of non-Soviet socialism is another alternative; a mixed system is a third possibility; and there are others. But among these, we should consider each on its own merits, first to see if it is in some ways superior. We have no clear model that has developed historically, no particular society which we can turn to as the moral model to emulate.

Secondly, if we did have a model, we would still have the question of how to arrive at it in fact. Seizure of the means of production in the United States, for instance, seems both unlikely and implausible. For what would the workers do once they seized control? Workers, through their retirement plans, presently control large portions of the stock of major industries. What they want is what every stockholder wants – they want their stock to go up. They are not demanding that the companies be run differently. The counter might be that they must be taught to want the companies to be run differently. If there is good reason for such a claim, then they should be taught. But exactly what that way is, is still not clear. A workers' revolution is not in the offing; and a led revolution runs all the dangers of ending up with a totalitarian government at the helm.

The American system is clearly not without fault; it has immoral aspects, it includes immoral practices, it does not achieve distributive or social justice, it is not without corruption, it contains unjustifiable inequalities of wealth, treatment, and so on. As these are slowly or more vigorously corrected, we may develop a kind of society that no longer deserves the name of capitalism. But the arguments we have looked at do not show that the system as a whole deserves moral censure, nor do they present us with a better viable alternative. We have no moral panacea to apply; we have no utopia waiting to be grasped or formed. But we do have possibilities for improvement which will make our society, and so our system, more moral. Piece-meal change, however, from a moral point of view, brings us away from what I have termed the macro-moral questions of evaluating worldwide problems of justice and the morality of systems, to a consideration of micro-moral problems – e.g., the morality of particular practices, states of affairs, and so on within a given system.

III

Micro-moral problems are not less important than macro-moral problems and do not deal necessarily with small issues, but they take as their frame of reference the existing situation and seek to make judgments within the system rather than about the system.

Since I cannot in the space of a short essay even begin to enumerate the vast array of micro-moral problems, much less solve them, I shall simply categorize a few of them.

The problems of morality in business, taken within a given framework or economic system, can be divided broadly and somewhat arbitrarily into six kinds.

The first of these concerns the determination of the justice of distribution of resources. It involves questions of the right to property, questions of ownership and use, questions of just wages, return on capital investment, appropriate reward for risk and skill and inventiveness, as well as questions of providing for the members of a society so that they do not fall below a certain level of welfare or respect. All these questions demand for their solution prior agreement on what in general constitutes justice for the society, as well as how justice is to be weighed when it comes into conflict with welfare, liberty, and other values which are socially important. The development of a theory of justice, not only an ideal theory but also a theory by which we can determine present-day injustices and the proper remedies for past injustices, is required. We do not have an adequate comprehensive theory as yet. Many competing claims are made even in the name of distributive justice: allocation according to equality, need, effort, achievement, contribution, ability, and so on. These must be weighed and balanced as best we can with each other and with commutative and other kinds of justice.

Even with a definite notion of what is just, a second set of questions arises in trying to apply any given concept of justice of particular cases. Since no two cases are exactly alike, it is often difficult to know exactly how to apply the principles. Easy cases can be handled. The more difficult ones pose moral problems which can be resolved only by discussion, debate, and ultimately by making some decision on the basis of the best information and insight available.

A third group of moral problems arises from a conflict among different values, especially when there seems to be no good alternative. Justice, security, liberty, productivity, efficiency, and other values frequently conflict, with no optimal solution available. Here the determination and choice of the least bad alternative is the best one can do.

The fourth kind of moral problem comes from the development of moral insights and the task of applying them to previously accepted practices. For a long while in the United States, for instance, segregation was generally accepted, at least in some parts of the country. Though now seen as immoral, and though it is now recognized that it was immoral when practiced in the past, it took a long while and a whole program of reeducation to get people to see this. Discrimination and sexism are other cases of this kind. How many other practices do we engage in without the consciousness of their immorality? Some claim that our treatment of animals, especially in slaughterhouses, is immoral. Only in the fairly recent past have we come to consider the industrial pollution of the environment to any serious degree immoral, and have we acted to make some instances of it illegal. It is not always clear who is morally responsible. If the pollution of the air by automobiles is injurious to the health of all of us, do we have a moral obligation to drive less or not at all, or to force manufacturers to build cars with antipollution devices? Are the manufacturers morally culpable if they produce automobiles which do not have such devices?

The fifth general kind of moral problem arises from new activities, products, and techniques. The problems raised by scientific advances are in some ways new problems. We now have the capability of wiping out the human race, of despoiling the environment in a way that will make it unfit for future generations, of using up unrenewable resources, of manipulating genes, and so on. Each of these problems has aspects that affect business: whether industries should engage in the production of certain materials and whether workers should work in such industries.

Lastly, and perhaps most prosaically, are the questions of the application of ordinary accepted moral values and prohibitions in the conduct of business and industry. It is generally accepted that lying is wrong; that stealing is wrong; that harming another is wrong; that giving and taking bribes is wrong; and so on. Each of these leads to specific cases in business as well as in other branches of life. If lying in advertising can make more money for a company, should a company do so? What exactly constitutes lying in advertising? How near to lying can one come? How much exaggeration for emphasis is allowed? How much must one disclose about the bad parts of one's products? Is telling half the truth lying? Whether these questions are asked about a corporation or about members within a corporation – either of management or of workers – they are not new questions; nor do they raise really new problems. The obligation to be moral applies to all aspects of our lives, and our business activities are not exempted. This does not mean that morality is always observed. And where it is not self-imposed, there is the need for its being imposed from the outside with appropriate sanctions to preserve the common good.

The case of bribery to foreign government officials in the recent past is interesting. The argument advanced in defense of the practice was that in dealing with certain foreign officials, since bribery was a way of life for them, a business could not successfully compete unless it paid bribes; if it did not, other companies from one's own nation or from other nations would pay them and win the contracts.

When the practice was disclosed publicly, it raised a small furor in the United States. It led to the dismissal of a number of officers of corporations. Some claimed that it would place American businesses at a disadvantage. The results, however, are noteworthy. Gulf Oil was involved in such practices, and several members of the Board were forced to resign. Since then, the corporation has been following a strict set of self-imposed rules with regard to bribes. Despite this, it has been able to compete successfully. And in some countries in which bribes were previously the way of life, officials have come under pressure themselves and have been forced to reform the practice. Public disclosure of immoral practices in this instance served to help reform the practices not only of American companies but of companies and governments in other parts of the world as well.

IV

Moral philosophers do not have all the answers to all moral problems and dilemmas. Some moral philosophers are skilled at moral reasoning; some know the ways by which moral claims can be defended or presented better than those untrained. But they do not have any monopoly on knowledge or moral values. They cannot and should not be expected to solve moral riddles. But they can be expected to clarify moral alternatives, articulate moral values, and pass on techniques of moral reasoning.

If my claim is correct – that the morality which should be applied to questions of business ethics is the socially accepted morality, as open to correction and development – then disputed questions should be discussed openly and publicly. The public debate should be articulate, informed, intelligible, clear, and should proceed in a rational manner if a rational conclusion is to be reached. It should be free of demagoguery, or at least, people must learn how to distinguish the demagoguery from the reasoned argument. People can and should be trained to think clearly on moral issues, just as in other areas. The moral philosopher can attempt to develop a theory of morals which accounts for and coheres with our consistent moral intuitions, and there are disputes about which theory does this best. But most theories agree in large part on which actions are moral and which are immoral. We cannot wait until all the theoretical issues are all solved before we undertake practical moral problems. Moral education helps all the members of a society take part in the debate about the common good, about the values to be realized and sacrificed, about the balance to be struck between justice and welfare and liberty, and so on. It also helps each member of society to be more conscious of his own responsibility to act morally; it motivates him not to engage in immoral practices either on or off the job; and it makes him sensitive to the possible immoral practices that can be found in the business world as well as in any other sector of life.

Many facets of our system have not yet caught up with our social needs, and the people as a whole, as well as the managers of business, have not yet faced up to the social responsibilities – much less devised techniques for handling them – of business. It is inherently easier to decide how to produce a product at the best price than to worry also about the social impact of that decision. But the wags who wink at immorality in business, arguing that ethics and business are two separate spheres and never the twain shall meet, are short-sighted and look only as far as the last line of their financial statements. Society is larger than that; business is part of society; and ethics has as much a place in business as in any other part of social life. When all members of society realize that fact and act accordingly, society will be that much better off.

NOTES

1. See, for instance, W. T. Stace, *The Concept of Morals*, N.Y.: The Macmillan Company, 1937; Paul Taylor, *Principles of Ethics*, Encino and Belmont, Calif.: Dickenson Publishing Co., Inc., 1975; Brand Blanshard, *Reason and Goodness*, London: George Allen & Unwin Ltd., 1961. A useful collection of essays on the topic is John Ladd (ed.), *Ethical Relativism*, Belmont, Calif.: Wadsworth Publishing Co., Inc., 1973.
2. See his *Essays in Sociology and Social Philosophy*, vol. I: *On the Diversity of Morals*, London: William Heinemann, Ltd., 1956.
3. For further development of this point, see my article, 'Legal Enforcement, Moral Pluralism and Abortion,' *Philosophy and Law: Proceedings of the American Catholic Philosophical Association*, XLIX (1975), pp. 171–180.

The ethical side of enterprise

VERNE E. HENDERSON

'What! Another article on business ethics? What are they trying to ram down my throat this time?' This is a common reaction by businesspeople to what is becoming the latest fad. Peter Drucker recently called it that and stated flatly that there is no such thing as 'business ethics.'[1] However, there is an ethical side to enterprise, and Drucker's article convinces me that it is not well understood. In *Death in the Afternoon*, Ernest Hemingway wrote that 'What is moral is what you feel good after and what is immoral is what you feel bad after.' Ethics is different; it is what you do hoping that others will feel good after.

My experience indicates that business management is particularly wary and sometimes even incensed when ethical issues are raised by spokespeople from the religious community. R. H. Tawney noted the prevalence of that attitude more than half a century ago: 'Trade is one thing, religion is another.'[2] Yet my conversations with businesspeople reveal their frustrations and concerns: 'How can we talk about ethics without raising fanatical religious or denominational flags?' 'Can't we find a fresh approach, some new words, or something so that we can talk about a subject we all secretly know is very important?'

As a spokesman from the religious community, I affirm the need to remove religious brand names and denominational labels. Moreover, I believe that this new age of ever-advancing technology will require significant ethical innovation. The word 'ethics' should generate a new set of feelings and perceptions.

Ethics in the broadest sense provides the basic conditions of acceptance for any activity. The ethics of a game or sport both implies its purpose and specifies rules of fair play. Business schools, for example, have traditionally focused on what we might call the business side of enterprise (finance, accounting, economics, marketing, forecasting), explaining the rules and imparting winning tactics. The human and the legal sides of enterprise have assumed increasing importance as the rules and tactics have become complex and the unresolved disputes numerous. Out of weariness and frustration, we ask a basic question: Should we play this game at all? Of course, we have to play. Business, after all, is a survival activity, isn't it . . . putting food on the table? So instead we ask: Can't we play the business game differently? The ethical side of enterprise emerges as this questioning of corporate activity grows in breadth and depth. At the macro level, one may question the legitimacy of both the corporation and capitalism as a viable economic system.[3] This article focuses on the micro level, addressing the specific decisions of enterprise on a variety of issues.

Reading taken from *Sloan Management Review*, 23, pp. 37–47. Copyright © 1982 Sloan Management Review Association.

THE NEED TO DEFINE ETHICS

As a senior corporate executive recently described the major problems his firm faces in contemplating joint ventures abroad, it became clear to me that his primary concerns were ethical ones. For instance, how do you establish trust and share risk? How do you deal with two governments that have significant cultural differences? What motivates top management to undertake such complex efforts? These joint ventures are new cultural configurations in the marketplace and, as such, they will cause us to question old values and to establish new ones. The role of the ethicist is to aid the manager in negotiating the uncharted depths of this new environment. But first, the term 'ethics' must be defined.

A Static Definition

Ethics is commonly defined as a set of principles prescribing a behavior code that explains what is good and right or bad and wrong; it may even outline moral duty and obligations generally. However, given the dynamic environment in which business must operate today, this conventional definition is far too static to be useful. It presumes a consensus about ethical principles that does not exist in this pluralistic age. The absence of such a consensus can be attributed to numerous changes that have occurred over time in the business environment, including the growth of conflicting interest groups, shifts in basic cultural values, the death of the Puritan ethic, and the increasing use of legal criteria in ethical decision making.

Multiple Clients Edgar Schein cites the increasing number of clients and interests the manager must satisfy: the stockholders, the customer, the community and/or government, the enterprise itself, subordinate employees, peers and colleagues, a superior, and perhaps the standards of a profession.[4] Since these clients may possess different and sometimes conflicting expectations, their ethical assessments of a management decision are also likely to differ. With so many clients and ethical expectations, it is never easy to know what is right or which client to heed. The multiple clients (or constituencies) factor requires a careful balancing of priorities and a situational approach to ethical issues.

Shifting Values George Lodge argues that a new American ideology has emerged as a result of five major shifts in basic values within the American culture:[5]

1. From rugged individualism to 'communitarianism';
2. From property rights to membership rights;
3. From competitive markets as the means to determine consumer needs to broader societal determination of community needs;
4. From limited government planning to explanded and extensive government planning;
5. From scientific specialization to a holistic utilization of knowledge.

These shifts in values can give rise to two types of ethical dilemmas. First, an industry can be divided in its loyalties to both old and new ideologies (i.e., to a free market versus a controlled market). Second, society at large may be divided in its loyalties to the needs of an industry versus the needs of the environment. These are tough choices: open markets or managed markets; industry or the environment. Such shifting values increase individuals' and firms' uncertainty regarding ethical issues. Moreover, this uncertainty is not likely to be resolved by simply choosing one ideology over another or one constituency over another.

Death of the Puritan Ethic According to Daniel Bell, the 'Puritan temper' or 'Protestant ethic,' which allegedly inspired the spirit of capitalism, is dying.[6] In the past this ethic promoted hard work, thrift, saving, moderation, and equality of opportunity or means. However, commercial success has spawned contradictory values that emphasize leisure, spending, debt accumulation, hedonism, and equality of condition or ends. The major consequence of this change is the erosion of a unifying social ethic. The fact that these two ethical systems exist simultaneously motivates and justifies a schizophrenic life-style where one is encouraged to be 'straight' at work but a 'swinger' on weekends. It is hardly surprising that managers often concede that their most vexing ethical dilemmas involve personnel.

Identical developments are evident at the corporate level. John K. Galbraith perceives a dichotomy within the production system; he labels one part a planning system and the other a marketing system.[7] The inordinate power of the planning system of large corporations gives them a monopoly over consumer needs; they even determine which needs will be served. If this is true, it means that large corporations have also deserted the Puritan ethic, that their only ethic is survival and self-perpetuation, and that their primary constituency consists of themselves.

The death of the Puritan ethic as the dominant ethical force in society has left us visionless. The individual and the corporation, confronting contradictions which foster uncertainty, turn inward and respond to the one constituency over which they have some sense of certainty and control – themselves. Achievement horizons are shortened: individuals expect rapid promotion, and corporations focus exclusively on quarterly progress.

Lawyers as Priests We used to be able to look to religion for ethical guidance; the priest would bless and legitimize our enterprise. That is no longer the case. In fact, the entry of brand-name religion into the marketplace seems to divide loyalties further and inhibit ethical discussion. This vacuum has been filled by the legal profession.

Lawyers maintain that they only interpret the law and that they do not make it (at least not until they are elected to legislative office). But, as both practitioners and legislators, lawyers increasingly serve our culture as the priest once did. The law determines what is right and implicitly blesses it. In effect, the equation seems to be: if it's legal, it's ethical.

Yet this equation has its limitations. Christopher Stone argues that neither the 'invisible' hand of the market nor a court of law is capable of delineating and enforcing the principles and behavior needed to solve society's problems, although both can play a positive role.[8] In his description of the history of corporations and the law, Stone documents numerous cases in which regulation of business by law has been ineffective. In addition, such regulation is rarely cost-effective, and it usually produces unanticipated and/or unacceptable consequences. Thus, while our growing dependence on the law as a substitute for ethics may be understandable, it is not necessarily desirable.

A Dynamic Definition

In these rapidly changing times, both the underlying purpose and the rules of the business game have become increasingly unclear. One consequence of these changes is that ethics can no longer be viewed as a static code or a set of principles that is understood and agreed upon by all. Charles Powers and David Vogel address this problem by providing a simple but dynamic working definition: 'In essence ethics is concerned with clarifying what constitutes human welfare and the kind of conduct necessary to promote it.'[9]

The first part of this definition implies both a constellation of values and a process of discussion or debate. While some values will be widely shared, individuals and groups will sometimes differ on 'what constitutes human welfare.' The Powers and Vogel definition is particularly suitable to the U.S., where no 'ultimate authority' issues quick, precise answers. Rather, the process of clarification is an ongoing response to changing values, emerging technological or economic developments, and shifting political forces. For example, government's increasing role as an income transfer agent in recent years signifies a change in the definition of human welfare. The fact that some portion of the national income is distributed on the basis of need rather than merit affirms a particular perception of economic justice. Lester Thurow notes a correlation between environmentalism and income distribution, suggesting that environmentalism is one of the newest consumer wants for those whose basic needs already have been satisfied.[10] This represents a further refinement of the definition of human welfare.

The second part of the Powers and Vogel definition focuses on behavior. Once we have conceptualized or reached some consensus about what constitutes human welfare, the debate then focuses on the kind of conduct necessary to promote that concept of human welfare. For instance, having determined that some national income should be distributed on the basis of need rather thn merit, we can use income tax legislation to establish a new code of conduct: taking from some and giving to others. In this way a new ethic is established. Most of the regulation of business that began in the last century can be viewed from this same perspective – a higher state of human welfare was clarified and complementary conduct was subsequently mandated.

New political and economic forces are continually reshaping our perception of the highest state of human welfare and altering our conduct accordingly. At the corporate level, deciding what is good and right or bad and wrong in such a dynamic environment is necessarily 'situational.' Therefore, instead of relying on a set of fixed ethical principles, we must now develop an ethical process. In order to do this, this article will next outline a conceptual ethical framework and then present an algorithm designed to deal with ethical questions on a situational basis.

A CONCEPTUAL FRAMEWORK

Business executives regularly wrestle with the new factors of the business environment: multiple clients and goals, shifting values and cultural contradictions, and increasing dependence on legal staffs. Although the profit-priented corporation will naturally focus *primarily* on economic goals, decisions that focus *exclusively* on profit maximization are being challenged. Typically, all of these decisions are fashioned with care in the guarded privacy of corporate offices and boardrooms. This is due in part to the nature of the competitive business game; undoubtedly, some secrecy is also occasioned by less noble motive. Once a product or service reaches the market, these decisions face exposure to public scrutiny.

The process has become even more complex in our turbulent environment. Focusing on legal considerations, let us assume that the vast majority of businesspeople intend to function within the boundaries of the law. Unfortunately, the legal status of an increasing number of manufacturing or marketing decisions is unclear when they are initially conceived and put into operation. Public scrutiny of these decisions (by Congress, a federal or state agency, or perhaps some other client) often raises questions of legality. In cases where some law or legal precedent exists, a clear determination of status can be achieved (although this may take years).

Over time many products and services have fallen from presumed legality into illegality, including cyclamates, DDT, firecrackers, recombinant DNA, and payments to foreign officials and governments. Thus, not only must products and services face final acceptance or rejection by the consumer, but their legal status may change as new information becomes available.

According to our dynamic definition of ethics, ethical issues emerge when our perception of what constitutes human welfare receives or requires clarification. More specifically, ethical issues arise when laws or legal precedents are either unclear or at variance with shifting cultural values. The proliferation of multinational and transnational corporations has provided numerous examples of this process. Positioned between two or more legal/ethical systems, these firms face scrutiny by publics that may differ radically on significant issues: the use and distribution of material resources, the source and exercise of authority, perceptions of time, measurement of productivity, and the use of competition as a motivating force. These differences alter ethical objectives and their complementary customs and legal sanctions.

Many multinationals have been affected by the existence of the Foreign Corrupt

Practices Act of 1977. Under this law, of course, it is illegal for U.S. firms to make payments to foreign officials or governments. Yet, some would argue that the Act itself is unethical insofar as it restricts international trade and thereby diminishes both human welfare and our national interest. When the Act was proposed, the Securities and Exchange Commission took the position that secret payments deprived current and prospective stockholders of potentially relevant information about company operations. The Internal Revenue Service questioned the deduction of such payments as business expenses. In effect, the Act was passed to satisfy a constituency that includes an unknown percentage of domestic and foreign consumers, unidentified current and prospective stockholders, and an agency of the federal government (which presumably acts on behalf of taxpayers). But are there consumers, stockholders, and taxpayers who would take a different ethical stance? Probably. None of the available choices satisfies the total constituency; this is characteristic of ethical dilemmas.

The issue of foreign payments illustrates how ethical questions develop from corporate decisions that are privately conceived and executed in advance of public scrutiny and without clear legal or ethical precedent. Aside from blatant corruption and dishonesty, the above process describing the emergence of ethical issues accounts for much of the consternation and confusion about business ethics today. It is the failure to understand and anticipate this process that creates the vast majority of ethical dilemmas.

The conceptual framework described above is summarized in Figure 1. The inner circle of this figure represents corporate decisions before they are revealed to the public. Once these decisions are manifested (middle circle), they may become the subject of considerable public debate. The result of this debate is the codification

Figure 1 A conceptual framework.

process (outer circle), in which society determines the legal and ethical status of each decision.

One question continually confronts business executives as they privately ponder alternatives: What happens when our decisions become public? This question can be particularly difficult to answer, since the legal and ethical status of a decision may change over time. Decision makers need to answer the question: into which quadrant of Figure 2 will an issue with ethical implications fall?

Consider the business executive who aspires to function in Quadrant I. When his or her decisions become manifest and codified, they will prove to be both ethical and legal. In the past this was a reasonable expectation for most decision makers. While it is dangerous to make assumptions about the intentions of businesspeople today, it seems that more of their decisions now fall into Quadrants II, III, and IV.

In Quadrant II (ethical and illegal), we find a host of controversial issues that divide the country because their ethical and legal statuses conflict: selling marijuana, 'whistle blowing,' windfall profits, and payments to foreign officials. While many individuals will attempt to resolve such conflicts by focusing on an issue's legal status, the ethical questions surrounding an issue also should be examined. According to

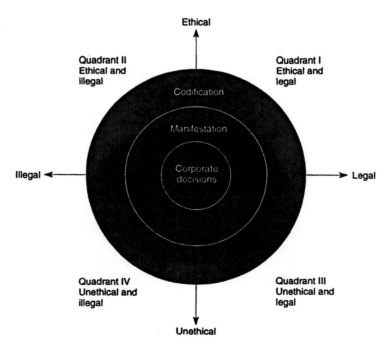

Figure 2 Classifying decisions using the conceptual framework.

our conceptual framework, the ethical perceptions concerning an issue must be addressed before its legal status can be changed. This is a time-consuming task that business has been unwilling or unable to assume on a large scale.

Quadrant III contains another series of controversial subjects – those which are legal but unethical. For example, while the marketing of infant feeding formulas to developing countries is legal, a recent vote at the United Nations called it unethical. (The U.S. abstained from voting.) The following examples are legal as well, but some have questioned their ethical underpinnings: the manufacture of pesticides, the use of laetrile in cancer treatment, plant relocation based on labor cost differentials, and interlocking directorships. As in Quadrant II, it is tempting to focus corporate attention on the legal status of these issues, rather than on their ethical foundation.

In Quadrant IV (unethical and illegal), we find a wide variety of actions that have been censured, including discrimination against minorities and women, occupational hazards, disposal of chemical waste, and political slush funds. In these areas, the laws are clear and ethical support is sufficiently strong to silence open dissent.

While some issues clearly belong in one quadrant or another, there are many others whose status is unclear. How then do we decide which quadrant an issue belongs in? This is determined not only by *which* action is being examined, but also by *how* that action is undertaken. One interesting example is 'whistle blowing.' To the extent that some forms of whistle blowing are ethical but in clear violation of company rules or expectations, they may be placed in Quadrant II. However, where such behavior jeopardizes trade secrets or national security, we might want to place it in Quadrants III or IV. The fact that whistle blowing may be placed in any of these quadrants underscores the turbulence in our legal and ethical environments.

The conceptual framework presented here depicts a dynamic environment filled with legal and ethical uncertainty. Since decision making in such an environment must frequently be based on situational factors, an algorithm is needed that will allow us to judge each ethical issue on its own merits.

A SITUATIONAL ETHIC ALGORITHM

According to Joseph Fletcher, the basic tenet underlying situation ethics is that circumstances alter cases.[11] This theory maintains that honesty is not always the best policy – it depends on the situation. In Fletcher's judgment, complex, significant ethical decisions are made based on the situation at a given moment in time, and, therefore, no two judgments will ever be the same. As the consequences of business decisions become more complex and unpredictable, the situation ethic becomes a necessity. There is a danger, however, that disastrous outcomes will be rationalized too easily as 'we did the best we could.' Since a situation ethic is without ready-made answers, it is important to develop a rigorous, rational process for examining ethical issues. Such homework should precede the implementation of a decision and serve as the ethical equivalent of a cost-benefit analysis.

Fletcher identifies four factors that can serve as check points in sorting out the ethical dimensions of a given situation.[12] These factors, translated into the business context, are goals, methods, motives, and consequences. Analyzing situations from these four perspectives constitutes an ethical algorithm which can increase our sense of certainty about decisions and ultimately provide a defendable decision-making *process*. Users of the algorithm plug in their own values as they examine goals, methods, motives, and consequences. Careful consideration of these four factors before selecting a course of action is likely to yield a variety of significant insights.

Goals

The goal structure of an organization should be examined from the perspectives of goal multiplicity, constituency priority, and goal compatibility.

Goal Multiplicity While profit maximization (subject to certain constraints) is an implicit goal of most business corporations, many firms simultaneously pursue other goals as well. Moreover, an organization's goal structure is often complicated by the imposition of constraints from outside sources. For example, a firm that relocates to another part of the country in order to maximize profits must consider the reactions of public officials and employees. A company that does business in South Africa must weigh the effect of its actions on the 'ethical investor' who is opposed to apartheid. In some cases constraints such as these can eventually function as goals themselves. To the extent that these new goals can be measured, they will figure prominently in the minds of stockholders, employees, the government, and various segments of the population at large. Decision makers must be clear about this multiplicity of goals from the outset, particularly if constraints are incorporated into the goal structure.

Sometimes, however, constraints are not included in the goal structure. Some corporations, for example, treat affirmative action strictly as a constraint. It never becomes part of the goal structure, at least not in a formal sense. Minimum compliance with affirmative action guidelines may be perceived as an acceptable policy, but not as a corporate objective. Such a policy may be difficult to defend publicly, but it illustrates the importance of goal clarity and the handling of constraints.

Constituency Priority Multiple goals can be identified as serving only corporate purposes, a specific national interest, or a minority constituency. Ranking these constituencies in terms of priorities enriches the definition of the goal structure. In most corporations, top priority is usually assigned to the enterprise itself and/or the stockholders to varying degrees. Secondary and lower priorities are given, for example, to a national interest (affirmative action) and a minority constituency (employee satisfaction), respectively. The ranking exercise itself can be illuminating, spotlighting inconsistencies and potential conflicts within the goal structure. In particular, inconsistencies are likely to appear in matching up constituent priority with goal priority. Clarity and management consensus are the operational objectives in this exercise.

Business is not always happy with morality that is legislated by others. Adopting a hierarchy of multiple goals (including those previously perceived as constraints) builds a stronger, broader ethical foundation for enterprise.

Goal Compatibility After a firm has identified and ranked its multiple goals, the goals should be checked for compatibility. Because the ethical side of enterprise is intangible and unpredictable, an organization will frequently find that its goals conflict with one another. For example, one company that was doing business in South Africa publicly adopted the dual goals of modest profit and effective opposition to apartheid.[13] While profit was easy to measure, 'effective opposition to apartheid' proved to be a much more nebulous goal. Different groups applying different standards argued that the firm should use significantly different methods to achieve these goals. One suggestion was for the firm to withdraw from South Africa, thereby sacrificing the profit goal entirely. When it finally became clear that the two goals were incompatible, the company was forced to choose between them.

Methods

Before selecting appropriate methods to achieve its goals, a firm must carefully consider the acceptability of various methods to constituents. In addition, the organization should decide whether these methods are intended to maximize goals or merely to satisfy them; whether the methods are essential, incidental, or extraneous to the goals themselves.

Constituent Acceptability Where ethical issues emerge, the firm must consider the acceptability of various methods to its constituents. Today a corporation has more constituencies than ever before. Over time these groups have voiced a greater number of expectations and concerns, which have resulted in much new legislation. Consequently, manufacturing methods must meet new standards of product and employee safety and environmental protection. Increased SEC and IRS regulation governs investment and marketing activities in foreign countries. The passage of ERISA has regulated the vesting of employee pension benefits. As such changes in regulation and legislation continue, business can help shape them by carefully evaluating the acceptability of its methods to multiple constituencies.

Methods That Satisfy or Maximize Goals Should the decision maker select methods that satisfy a goal or methods that maximize achievement? How safe is safe? Should a firm simply satisfy affirmative action requirements, or should it make a maximum effort to increase the employment of minorities and women? The fact that corporations have not really confronted and answered these questions has created ethical confusion. For example, such confusion has arisen in the debate over what constitutes excess or windfall profits. What is a fair or ethically acceptable return on investment? Over what period of time? The situation ethic algorithm suggests that businesspeople must confront such questions as part of the decision-making process.

Essential, Incidental, or Extraneous It has been suggested that the decentralization of management at General Electric under Ralph Cordiner in the 1950s was a major contributor to the pricing conspiracy which ensued.[14] However, the real goals behind GE's decision to decentralize remain shrouded in controversy. Was decentralization absolutely *essential* to goal achievement? Was it *incidental?* Did management believe that it would probably have a positive impact and was worth trying at little risk? Or was it really *extraneous* to the goal itself and more a whim or personal predilection of top management? Such questions are always relevant as a firm attempts to select the most effective methods for achieving its goals.

Formal contractual arrangements and informal commitments to employees may be areas offering a number of significant choices for the future. These include such issues as the vesting of pensions, flextime, educational opportunities and on-the-job training, salary bonuses for production workers, and lifetime work contracts. In each case, business can evaluate whether such changes are essential, incidental, or extraneous to success.

Motives

It is often difficult to distinguish between motives and methods. Simply stated, corporations do not have motives. Rather, individuals have motives which find their way into corporate life through goal and method selection. In some instances, it is readily apparent that the motives of a strong or influential executive are the driving force behind a corporation's goals and methods. What drives a manager or executive to take certain actions? An instinct for survival, an innate competitive urge, a desire for power? Although employees' motives are often difficult to discern, they are the lifeblood of any institution, determining its character, climate, and degree of success. The more influential an employee, the more his or her motives will affect the firm's goals and methods. While we can only infer from an individual's behavior what his or her motives are, there are nevertheless some useful check points in this third step of the ethical algorithm.

Hidden or Known Do others know what your motives are? As decisions with ethical implications are revealed to the public, the underlying motives of business executives tend to emerge as well. The revelation of these motives often determines the ethical or legal labeling that follows.

Motives of corporate decision makers are often suspect simply because they are somewhat hidden. The invisibility of corporate leaders makes it easy for them to be labeled 'greedy' or 'power hungry.' If there is any substance to such accusations or if decision makers remain silent regarding their motives, the worthy goals or methods of corporate enterprise can be drowned in a sea of outraged voices. The situation ethic does not stipulate that all motives should be revealed at all times. Rather, it argues that executives should know what their motives are and when it is essential to make them public.

Shared or Selfish In *The Gamesman*, Michael Maccoby identifies four distinct executive types, each distinguished in large measure by his motives: the Craftsman, the Companyman, the Jungle Fighter, and the Gamesman.[15] The Craftsman is absorbed in his creative process; the Companyman bases his identity on that of the firm. The Jungle Fighter is a power seeker; the Gamesman thrives on competitive activities that allow him to mark himself as a winner. In addition to underscoring the critical role that motives play, Maccoby implies that leaders driven by narrow personal or selfish motives are less likely to achieve corporate success, especially over the long term. Executives who question whether their motives are purely selfish or widely shared are moving in the direction of consensus management. Again the situation ethic does not argue that consensus is always desirable or possible, only that it is an important check point in the ethical algorithm.

Value Orientation Commitments to certain basic values and/or religious beliefs tend to enter corporate life through the motives of key business leaders. It is becoming increasingly important for executives to be able to articulate these values and beliefs in the context of their work life. The value shifts noted by Lodge appear to have received only indirect, inconsistent attention from the business community.[16] It is not clear why business has been silent in this arena. However, it is clear that this silence has had negative effects on the ethical soundness of enterprise. In the future the success of capitalistic enterprise will be largely determined by what business leaders' motives are and by how effectively they can articulate them.

Consequences

In the final step of the ethical algorithm, the firm reviews its goals, methods, and motives and considers the potential consequences of its actions. Each of the multiple goals and methods is matched with one or more consequences. Decision makers must ask: What are the consequences of using a particular method or reaching a specific goal? These potential outcomes can be grouped into several categories.

Time Frames Most firms will find it instructive to project the consequences of their policies over several different time periods. Of course, the appropriate time frames will vary with each firm's products and goals.

Constituency Impact Possible consequences must be considered from the perspective of each of the firm's constituencies. This is especially important if ethical and legal precedents are unclear or if new technology is to be introduced.

Exogenous Effects Firms must also anticipate the probable consequences of the efforts of others. In some companies such a notion is standard marketing practice. These exogenous effects are likely to grow in importance with advancing technology, increasing interdependence, global markets, and shifting values and political climates.

CONCLUSION

Sensitivity to the ethical side of enterprise means searching arduously for decisions and actions that warrant and receive the affirmation of an expanding multifarious constituency. The conceptual framework presented here is one attempt to perceive this constituency in all of its complexity. The ethical algorithm is one means of working with this constituency, rather than against it. The singular importance of enterprise to our daily lives and our collective future demands our careful attention and finest efforts.

NOTES

1. See P. E. Drucker, 'Ethical Chic,' *Forbes*, 14 September 1981, pp. 160–173.
2. See R. H. Tawney, *Religion and the Rise of Capitalism* (New York: Harcourt & Brace, 1926).
3. See P. Berger, 'New Attack on the Legitimacy of Business,' *Harvard Business Review*, September–October 1981.
4. See E. H. Schein, 'The Problem of Moral Education for the Business Manager' (Paper prepared for the Seventeenth Conference on Science, Philosophy, and Religion, August 1966).
5. See G. C. Lodge, *The New American Ideology* (New York: Alfred A. Knopf, 1979).
6. See D. Bell, *The Cultural Contradictions of Capitalism* (New York: Basic Books, 1976).
7. See J. K. Galbraith, *Economics and the Public Purpose* (Boston: Houghton Mifflin, 1978).
8. See C. D. Stone, *Where the Law Ends: The Social Context of Corporate Behavior* (New York: Harper Torchbooks, 1975).
9. See C. Powers and D. Vogel, *Ethics in the Education of Business Managers* (Hastingson-Hudson: Institute of Society, Ethics and the Life Sciences, The Hastings Institute, 1980).
10. See L. Thurow, *The Zero-Sum Society* (New York: Basic Books, 1980).
11. See J. Fletcher, *Situation Ethics: The New Morality* (Philadelphia: The Westminster Press, 1966). Dr. Fletcher is former Professor of Ethics at the Episcopal Divinity School, Cambridge, MA).
12. Ibid.
13. See D. T. Verma, 'Polaroid in South Africa (A),' #9-372-624 (Boston: Intercollegiate Case Clearing House, 1971).
14. See R. A. Smith, 'The Incredible Electrical Conspiracy,' *Fortune*, April 1961.
15. See M. Maccoby, *The Gamesman* (New York: Bantam Books, 1976).
16. See Lodge (1979).

The wealth of nations

ADAM SMITH

Extract I

This division of labour, from which so many advantages are derived, is not originally the effect of any human wisdom, which foresees and intends that general opulence to which it gives occasion. It is the necessary, though very slow and gradual consequence of a certain propensity in human nature which has in view no such extensive utility; the propensity to truck, barter, and exchange one thing for another.

Whether this propensity be one of those original principles in human nature of which no further account can be given or whether, as seems more probable, it be the necessary consequence of the faculties of reason and speech, it belongs not to our present subject to inquire. It is common to all men, and to be found in no other race of animals, which seem to know neither this nor any other species of contracts. Two greyhounds, in running down the same hare, have sometimes the appearance of acting in some sort of concert. Each turns her towards his companion, or endeavours to intercept her when his companion turns her towards himself. This, however, is not the effect of any contract, but of the accidental concurrence of their passions in the same object at that particular time. Nobody ever saw a dog make a fair and deliberate exchange of one bone for another with another dog. Nobody ever saw one animal by its gestures and natural cries signify to another, this is mine, that yours; I am willing to give this for that. When an animal wants to obtain something either of a man or of another animal, it has no other means of persuasion but to gain the favour of those whose service it requires. A puppy fawns upon its dam, and a spaniel endeavours by a thousand attractions to engage the attention of its master who is at dinner, when it wants to be fed by him. Man sometimes uses the same arts with his brethren, and when he has no other means of engaging them to act according to his inclinations, endeavours by every servile and fawning attention to obtain their good will. He has not time, however, to do this upon every occasion. In civilised society he stands at all times in need of the cooperation and assistance of great multitudes, while his whole life is scarce sufficient to gain the friendship of a few persons. In almost every other race of animals each individual, when it is grown up to maturity, is entirely independent, and in its natural state has occasion for the assistance of no other living creature. But man has almost constant occasion for the help of his brethren, and it is in vain for him to expect it from their benevolence only. He will be more likely to prevail if he can interest their self-love in his favour, and show them that it is for their own advantage to do for him what he requires of them. Whoever offers to another a bargain of any kind, proposes to do this. Give me that

Extracts taken from *The Wealth of Nations*. Book I, ch. III; Book IV, ch. II and Book I, ch. X (respectively). Originally published in 1776.

which I want, and you shall have this which you want, is the meaning of every such offer; and it is in this manner that we obtain from one another the far greater part of those good offices which we stand in need of. It is not from the benevolence of the butcher, the brewer, or the baker that we expect our dinner, but from their regard to their own interest. We address ourselves, not to their humanity but to their self-love, and never talk to them of our own necessities but of their advantages. Nobody but a beggar chooses to depend chiefly upon the benevolence of his fellow-citizens. Even a beggar does not depend upon it entirely. The charity of well-disposed people, indeed, supplies him with the whole fund of his subsistence. But though this principle ultimately provides him with all the necessaries of life which he has occasion for, it neither does nor can provide him with them as he has occasion for them. The greater part of his occasional wants are supplied in the same manner as those of other people, by treaty, by barter, and by purchase. With the money which one man gives him he purchases food. The old clothes which another bestows upon him he exchanges for other old clothes which suit him better, or for lodging, or for food, or for money, with which he can buy either food, clothes, or lodging, as he has occasion.

Extract II

Every individual is continually exerting himself to find out the most advantageous employment for whatever capital he can command. It is his own advantage, indeed, and not that of the society, which he has in view. But the study of his own advantage naturally, or rather necessarily, leads him to prefer that employment which is most advantageous to the society.

First, every individual endeavours to employ his capital as near home as he can, and consequently as much as he can in the support of domestic industry; provided always that he can thereby obtain the ordinary, or not a great deal less than the ordinary profits of stock.

Thus, upon equal or nearly equal profits, every wholesale merchant naturally prefers the home trade to the foreign trade of consumption, and the foreign trade of consumption to the carrying trade. In the home trade his capital is never so long out of his sight as it frequently is in the foreign trade of consumption. He can know better the character and situation of the persons whom he trusts, and if he should happen to be deceived, he knows better the laws of the country from which he must seek redress. In the carrying trade, the capital of the merchant is, as it were, divided between two foreign countries, and no part of it is ever necessarily brought home, or placed under his own immediate view and command. The capital which an Amsterdam merchant employs in carrying corn from Konnigsberg to Lisbon, and fruit and wine from Lisbon to Konnigsberg, must generally be the one-half of it at Konnigsberg and the other half at Lisbon. No part of it need ever come to Amsterdam. The natural residence of such a merchant should either be at Konnigsberg or Lisbon, and it can only be some very particular circumstances which can make him prefer the residence of Amsterdam. The uneasiness, however, which he feels at being separated so far from his capital generally determines him to bring part both of the Konnigsberg goods which he destines for the market of Lisbon, and of the Lisbon goods which he destines for that of Konnigsberg, to Amsterdam: and though this necessarily subjects him to a double charge of loading and unloading, as well as to the payment of some duties and customs, yet for the sake of having some part of his capital always under his own view and command, he willingly submits to this extraordinary charge; and it is in this manner that every country which has any considerable share of the carrying trade becomes always the emporium, or general market, for the goods of all the different countries whose trade it carries on. The merchant, in order to save a second loading and unloading, endeavours always to sell in the home market as much of the goods of all those different countries as he can, and thus, so far as he can, to convert his carrying trade into a foreign trade of consumption. A merchant, in the same manner, who is engaged in the foreign trade of consumption, when he collects goods for foreign markets, will always be glad, upon equal or nearly equal profits, to sell as great a part of them at home as he can. He saves himself the risk and trouble of exportation, when, so far as he can, he thus converts his foreign trade of consumption into a home trade. Home is in this manner the centre, if I may say so, round which the capitals of the inhabitants of every country are continually circulating, and towards which they are always tending, though by particular causes they may sometimes be driven off and repelled from it towards more distant employments. But a capital employed in the home trade, it has already been shown, necessarily puts into motion a greater quantity of domestic industry, and gives revenue and employment to a greater number of the inhabitants of the country, than an equal capital employed in the foreign trade of consumption: and one employed in the foreign trade of consumption has the same advantage over an equal capital employed in the carrying trade. Upon equal, or only nearly equal profits, therefore, every individual naturally inclines to employ his capital in the manner in which it is likely to afford the greatest support to domestic industry, and to give revenue and employment to the greatest number of people of his own country.

Secondly, every individual who employs his capital in the support of domestic industry, necessarily endeavours so to direct that industry that its produce may be of the greatest possible value.

The produce of industry is what it adds to the subject or materials upon which it is employed. In proportion as the value of this produce is great or small, so will likewise be the profits of the employer. But it is only for the sake of profit that any man employs a capital in the support of industry; and he will always, therefore, endeavour to employ it in the support of that industry of which the produce is likely to be of the greatest value, or to exchange for the greatest quantity either of money or of other goods.

But the annual revenue of every society is always precisely equal to the exchangeable value of the whole annual produce of its industry, or rather is precisely the same thing with that exchangeable value. As every individual, therefore, endeavours as much as he can both to employ his capital in the support of domestic industry, and so to direct that industry that its produce may be of the greatest value; every individual necessarily labours to render the annual revenue of the society as great as he can. He generally, indeed, neither intends to promote the public interest, nor knows how much he is promoting it. By preferring the support of domestic to that of foreign industry, he intends only his own security; and by directing that industry in such a manner as its produce may be of the greatest value, he intends only his own gain, and he is in this, as in many other cases, led by an invisible hand to promote an end which was no part of his intention. Nor is it always the worse for the society that it was no part of it. By pursuing his own interest he frequently promotes that of the society more effectually than when he really intends to promote it. I have never known much good done by those who affected to trade for the public good. It is an affectation, indeed, not very common among merchants, and very few words need be employed in dissuading them from it.

Smith includes the following famous warning to his account:

Extract III

People of the same trade seldom meet together, even for merriment and diversion, but the conversation ends in a conspiracy against the public, or in some contrivance to raise prices. It is impossible indeed to prevent such meetings, by any law which either could be executed, or would be consistent with liberty and justice. But though the law cannot hinder people of the same trade from sometimes assembling together, it ought to do nothing to facilitate such assemblies, much less to render them necessary.

Why 'good' managers make bad ethical choices

SAUL W. GELLERMAN

How could top-level executives at the Manville Corporation have suppressed evidence for decades that proved that asbestos inhalation was killing their own employees?

What could have driven the managers of Continental Illinois Bank to pursue a

Reading taken from *Harvard Business Review*, July–August 1986. Copyright © 1986 *Harvard Business Review*.

course of action that threatened to bankrupt the institution, ruined its reputation, and cost thousands of innocent employees and investors their jobs and their savings?

Why did managers at E. F. Hutton find themselves pleading guilty to 2000 counts of mail and wire fraud, accepting a fine of $2 million, and putting up an $8 million fund for restitution to the 400 banks that the company had systematically bilked?

How can we explain the misbehavior that took place in these organizations – or in any of the others, public and private, that litter our newspapers' front pages: workers at a defense contractor who accused their superiors of falsifying time cards; alleged bribes and kickbacks that honeycombed New York City government; a company that knowingly marketed an unsafe birth control device; the decision-making process that led to the space shuttle Challenger tragedy.

The stories are always slightly different; but they have a lot in common since they're full of the oldest questions in the world, questions of human behavior and human judgment applied in ordinary day-to-day situations. Reading them we have to ask how usually honest, intelligent, compassionate human beings could act in ways that are callous, dishonest, and wrongheaded.

In my view, the explanations go back to four rationalizations that people have relied on through the ages to justify questionable conduct: believing that the activity is not 'really' illegal or immoral; that it is in the individual's or the corporation's best interest; that it will never be found out; or that because it helps the company the company will condone it. By looking at these rationalizations in light of these cases, we can develop some practical rules to more effectively control managers' actions that lead to trouble – control, but not eliminate. For the hard truth is that corporate misconduct, like the lowly cockroach, is a plague that we can suppress but never exterminate.

Three cases

Amitai Etzioni, professor of sociology at George Washington University, recently concluded that in the last ten years, roughly two-thirds of America's 500 largest corporations have been involved, in varying degrees, in some form of illegal behavior. By taking a look at three corporate cases, we may be able to identify the roots of the kind of misconduct that not only ruins some people's lives, destroys institutions, and gives business as a whole a bad name but that also inflicts real and lasting harm on a large number of innocent people. The three cases that follow should be familiar. I present them here as examples of the types of problems that confront managers in all kinds of businesses daily.

Manville Corporation

A few years ago, Manville (then Johns Manville) was solid enough to be included among the giants of American business. Today Manville is in the process of turning over 80% of its equity to a trust representing people who have sued or plan to sue it for liability in connection with one of its principal former products, asbestos. For all practical purposes, the entire company was brought down by questions of corporate ethics.

More than 40 years ago, information began to reach Johns Manville's medical department – and through it, the company's top executives – implicating asbestos inhalation as a cause of asbestosis, a debilitating lung disease, as well as lung cancer and mesothelioma, an invariably fatal lung disease. Manville's managers suppressed the research. Moreover, as a matter of policy, they apparently decided to conceal the information from affected employees. The company's medical staff collaborated in the cover-up, for reasons we can only guess at.

Money may have been one motive. In one particularly chilling piece of testimony, a lawyer recalled how 40 years earlier he had confronted Manville's corporate counsel about the company's policy of concealing chest X-ray results from employees. The lawyer had asked, 'Do you mean to tell me you would let them work until they dropped dead?' The reply was, 'Yes, we save a lot of money that way.'

Based on such testimony, a California court found that Manville had hidden the asbestos danger from its employees rather than looking for safer ways to handle it. It was less expensive to pay workers' compensation claims than to develop safer working conditions. A New Jersey court was even blunter: it found that Manville had made a conscious, cold-blooded business decision to take no protective or remedial action, in flagrant disregard of the rights of others.

How can we explain this behavior? Were more than 40 years' worth of Manville executives all immoral?

Such an answer defies common sense. The truth, I think, is less glamorous – and also less satisfying to those who like to explain evil as the actions of a few misbergotten souls. The people involved were probably ordinary men and women for the most part, not very different from you and me. They found themselves in a dilemma, and they solved it in a way that seemed to be the least troublesome, deciding not to disclose information that could hurt their product. The consequences of what they chose to do – both to thousands of innocent people and, ultimately, to the corporation – probably never occurred to them.

The Manville case illustrates the fine line between acceptable and unacceptable managerial behavior. Executives are expected to strike a difficult balance – to pursue their companies' best interests but not overstep the bounds of what outsiders will tolerate.

Even the best managers can find themselves in a bind, not knowing how far is too far. In retrospect, they can usually easily tell where they should have drawn the line, but no one manages in retrospect. We can only live and act today and hope that whoever looks back on what we did will judge that we struck the proper balance. In a few years, many of us may be found delinquent for decisions we are making now about tobacco, clean air, the use of chemicals, or some other seemingly benign substance. The managers at Manville may have believed that they were acting in the company's best interests, or that what they were doing would never be found out, or even that it wasn't really wrong. In the end, these were only rationalizations for conduct that brought the company down.

Continental Illinois Bank

Until recently the ninth largest bank in the United States, Continental Illinois had to be saved from insolvency because of bad judgment by management. The government bailed it out, but at a price. In effect it has been socialized: about 80% of its equity now belongs to the Federal Deposit Insurance Corporation. Continental seems to have been brought down by managers who misunderstood its real interests. To their own peril, executives focused on a single-minded pursuit of corporate ends and forgot about the means to the ends.

In 1976, Continental's chairman declared that within five years the magnitude of its lending would match that of any other bank. The goal was attainable; in fact, for a time, Continental reached it. But it dictated a shift in strategy away from conservative corporate financing and toward aggressive pursuit of borrowers. So Continental, with lots of lendable funds, sent its loan officers into the field to buy loans that had originally been made by smaller banks that had less money.

The practice in itself was not necessarily unsound. But some of the smaller banks had done more than just lend money – they had swallowed hook, line, and sinker the extravagant, implausible dreams of poorly capitalized oil producers in Oklahoma, and they had begun to bet enormous sums on those dreams. Eventually, a cool billion dollars' worth of those dreams found their way into Continental's portfolio, and a cool billion dollars of depositors' money flowed out to pay for them. When the price of oil fell, a lot of dry holes and idle drilling equipment were all that was left to show for most of the money.

Continental's officers had become so entranced by their lending efforts' spectacular results that they hadn't looked deeply into how they had been achieved. Huge sums of money were lent at fat rates of interest. If the borrowers had been able to repay the loans, Continental might have become the eighth or even the seventh largest bank in the country. But that was a very big 'if.' Somehow there was a failure of control and judgment at Continental – probably because the officers who were buying those shaky loans were getting support and praise from their superiors. Or at least they were not hearing enough tough questions about them.

At one point, for example, Continental's internal auditors stumbled across the fact that an officer who had purchased $800 million in oil and gas loans from the Penn Square Bank in Oklahoma City had also borrowed $565 000 for himself from Penn Square. Continental's top management investigated and eventually issued a reprimand. The mild rebuke reflected the officer's hard work and the fact that the portfolio he had obtained would have yielded an average return of nearly 20% had it ever performed as planned. In fact, virtually all of the $800 million had to be written off. Management chose to interpret the incident charitably; federal prosecutors later alleged a kickback.

On at least two other occasions, Continental's own control mechanisms flashed signals that something was seriously wrong with the oil and gas portfolio. A vice president warned in a memo that the documentation needed to verify the soundness of many of the purchased loans had simply never arrived. Later, a junior loan officer, putting his job on the line, went over the heads of three superiors to tell a top executive about the missing documentation. Management chose not to investigate. After all, Continental was doing exactly what its chairman had said it would do: it was on its way to becoming the leading commercial lender in the United States. Oil and gas loans were an important factor in that achievement. Stopping to wait for paperwork to catch up would only slow down reaching the goal.

Eventually, however, the word got out about the instability of the bank's portfolio, which led to a massive run on its deposits. No other bank was willing to come to the rescue, for fear of being swamped by Continental's huge liabilities. To avoid going under, Continental in effect became a ward of the federal government. The losers were the bank's shareholders, some officers who lost their jobs, at least one who was indicted, and some 2000 employees (about 15% of the total) who were let go, as the bank scaled down to fit its diminished assets.

Once again, it is easy for us to sit in judgment after the fact and say that Continental's loan officers and their superiors were doing exactly what bankers shouldn't do: they were gambling with their depositors' money. But on another level, this story is more difficult to analyze – and more generally a part of everyday business. Certainly part of Continental's problem was neglect of standard controls. But another dimension involved ambitious corporate goals. Pushed by lofty goals, managers could not see clearly their real interests. They focused on ends, overlooked the ethical questions associated with their choice of means – and ultimately hurt themselves.

E. F. Hutton

The nation's second largest independent broker, E. F. Hutton & Company, recently pleaded guilty to 2000 counts of mail and wire fraud. It had systematically milked 400 of its banks by drawing against uncollected funds or in some cases against nonexistent sums, which it then covered after having enjoyed interest-free use of the money. So far, Hutton has agreed to pay a fine of $2 million as well as the government's investigation costs of $750 000. It has set up an $8 million reserve for restitution to the banks – which may not be enough. Several officers have lost their jobs, and some indictments may yet follow.

But worst of all, Hutton has tarnished its reputation, never a wise thing to do – certainly not when your business is offering to handle other people's money. Months after Hutton agreed to appoint new directors – as a way to give outsiders a solid majority on the board – the company couldn't find people to accept the seats, in part because of the bad publicity.

Apparently Hutton's branch managers had been encouraged to pay close attention to cash management. At some point, it dawned on someone that using other people's money was even more profitable than using your own. In each case, Hutton's overdrafts involved no large sums. But cumulatively, the savings on interest that would otherwise have been owed to the banks was very large. Because Hutton always made covering deposits, and because most banks did not object, Hutton assured its managers that what they were doing was sharp – and not shady. They presumably thought they were pushing legality to its limit without going over the line. The branch managers were simply taking full advantage of what the law and the bankers' tolerance permitted. On several occasions, the managers who played this game most astutely were even congratulated for their skill.

Hutton probably will not suffer a fate as drastic as Manville's or Continental Illinois's. Indeed, with astute damage control, it can probably emerge from this particular embarrassment with only a few bad memories. But this case has real value because it is typical of much corporate misconduct. Most improprieties don't cut a corporation off at the knees the way Manville's and Continental Illinois's did. In fact, most such actions are never revealed at all – or at least that's how people figure things will work out. And in many cases, a willingness to gamble thus is probably enhanced by the rationalization – true or not – that everyone else is doing something just as bad or would if they could; that those who wouldn't go for their share are idealistic fools.

Four rationalizations

Why do managers do things that ultimately inflict great harm on their companies, themselves, and people on whose patronage or tolerance their organizations depend? These three cases, as well as the current crop of examples in each day's paper, supply ample evidence of the motivations and instincts that underlie corporate misconduct. Although the particulars may vary – from the gruesome dishonesty surrounding asbestos handling to the mundanity of illegal money management – the motivating beliefs are pretty much the same. We may examine them in the context of the corporation, but we know that these feelings are basic throughout society; we find them wherever we go because we take them with us.

When we look more closely at these cases, we can delineate four commonly held rationalizations that can lead to misconduct:

A belief that the activity is within reasonable ethical and legal limits – that that it is not 'really' illegal or immoral.

A belief that the activity is in the individual's or the corporation's best interests – that the individual would somehow be expected to undertake the activity.

A belief that the activity is 'safe' because it will never be found out or publicized; the classic crime-and-punishment issue of discovery.

A belief that because the activity helps the company the company will condone it and even protect the person who engages in it.

The idea that an action is not really wrong is an old issue. How far is too far? Exactly where is the line between smart and too smart? Between sharp and shady? Between profit maximization and illegal conduct? The issue is complex: it involves an interplay between top management's goals and middle managers' efforts to interpret those aims.

Put enough people in an ambiguous, ill-defined situation, and some will conclude that whatever hasn't been labeled specifically wrong must be OK – especially if they are rewarded for certain acts. Deliberate overdrafts, for example, were not proscribed at Hutton. Since the company had not spelled out their illegality, it could later plead guilty for itself while shielding its employees from prosecution.

Top executives seldom ask their subordinates to do things that both of them know are against the law or imprudent. But company leaders sometimes leave things unsaid or give the impression that there are things they don't want to know about. In other words, they can seem, whether deliberately or otherwise, to be distancing themselves from their subordinates' tactical decisions in order to keep their own hands clean if things go awry. Often they lure ambitious lower level managers by implying that rich rewards await those who can produce certain results – and that the methods for achieving them will not be examined too closely. Continental's simple wrist-slapping of the officer who was caught in a flagrant conflict of interest sent a clear message to other managers about what top management really thought was important.

How can managers avoid crossing a line that is seldom precise? Unfortunately, most know that they have overstepped it only when they have gone too far. They have no reliable guidelines about what will be overlooked or tolerated or what will be condemned or attacked. When managers must operate in murky borderlands, their most reliable guideline is an old principle: when in doubt, don't.

That may seem like a timid way to run a business. One could argue that if it actually took hold among the middle managers who run most companies, it might take the enterprise out of free enterprise. But there is a different between taking a worthwhile economic risk and risking an illegal act to make more money.

The difference between becoming a success and becoming a statistic lies in knowledge – including self-knowledge – not daring. Contrary to popular mythology, managers are not paid to take risks; they are paid to know which risks are worth taking. Also, maximizing profits is a company's second priority, not its first. The first is ensuring its survival.

All managers risk giving too much because of what their companies demand from them. But the same superiors who keep pressing you to do more, or to do it better, or faster, or less expensively, will turn on you should you cross that fuzzy line between right and wrong. They will blame you for exceeding instructions or for ignoring their warnings. The smartest managers already know that the best answer to the question, 'How far is too far?' is don't try to find out.

Turning to the second reason why people take risks that get their companies into trouble, believing that unethical conduct is in a person's or corporation's best interests nearly always results from a parochial view of what those interests are. For example, Alpha Industries, a Massachusetts manufacturer of microwave equipment, paid $57 000 to a Raytheon manager, ostensibly for a marketing report. Air force investigators charged that the report was a ruse to cover a bribe: Alpha wanted subcontracts that the Raytheon manager supervised. But those contracts ultimately cost Alpha a lot more than they paid for the report. After the company was indicted for bribery, its contracts were suspended and its profits promptly vanished. Alpha wasn't unique in this transgression: in 1984, the Pentagon suspended 453 other companies for violating procurement regulations.

Ambitious managers look for ways to attract favorable attention, something to distinguish them from other people. So they try to outperform their peers. Some may see that it is not difficult to look remarkably good in the short run by avoiding things that pay off only in the long run. For example, you can skimp on maintenance or training or customer service, and you can get away with it – for a while.

The sad truth is that many managers have been promoted on the basis of 'great' results obtained in just those ways, leaving unfortunate successors to inherit the inevitable whirlwind. Since this is not necessarily a just world, the problems that such people create are not always traced back to them. Companies cannot afford to be hoodwinked in this way. They must be concerned with more than just results. They have to look very hard at how results are obtained.

Evidently, in Hutton's case there were such reviews, but management chose to interpret favorably what government investigators later interpreted unfavorably. This brings up another dilemma: management quite naturally hopes that any of its borderline actions will be overlooked or at least interpreted charitably if noticed. Companies must accept human nature for what it is and protect themselves with watchdogs to sniff out possible misdeeds.

An independent auditing agency that reports to outside directors can play such a role. It can provide a less comfortable, but more convincing, review of how management's successes are achieved. The discomfort can be considered inexpensive insurance and serve to remind all employees that the real interests of the company are served by honest conduct in the first place.

The third reason why a risk is taken, believing that one can probably get away with it, is perhaps the most difficult to deal with because it's often true. A great deal of proscribed behavior escapes detection.

We know that conscience alone does not deter everyone. For example, First National Bank of Boston pleaded guilty to laundering satchels of $20 bills worth $1.3 billion. Thousands of satchels must have passed through the bank's doors without incident before the scheme was detected. That kind of heavy, unnoticed traffic breeds complacency.

How can we deter wrongdoing that is unlikely to be detected? Make it more likely to be detected. Had today's 'discovery' process – in which plaintiff's attorneys can comb through a company's records to look for incriminating evidence – been in use when Manville concealed the evidence on asbestosis, there probably would have been no cover-up. Mindful of the likelihood of detection, Manville would have chosen a different course and could very well be thriving today without the protection of the bankruptcy courts.

The most effective deterrent is not to increase the severity of punishment for those caught but to heighten the perceived probability of being caught in the first place. for example, police have found that parking an empty patrol car at locations where motorists often exceed the speed limit reduces the frequency of speeding. Neighborhood 'crime watch' signs that people display decrease burglaries.

Simply increasing the frequency of audits and spot checks is a deterrent, especially when combined with three other simple techniques: scheduling audits irregularly, making at least half of them unannounced, and setting up some checkups soon after others. But frequent spot checks cost more than big sticks, a fact that raises the question of which approach is more cost-effective.

A common managerial error is to assume that because frequent audits uncover little behavior that is out of line, less frequent, and therefore less costly, auditing is sufficient. But this condition overlooks the important deterrent effect of frequent checking. The point is to prevent misconduct, not just to catch it.

A trespass detected should not be dealt with discreetly. Managers should announce the misconduct and how the individuals involved were punished. Since the main deterrent to illegal or unethical behavior is the perceived probability of detection, managers should make an example of people who are detected.

Let's look at the fourth reason why corporate misconduct tends to occur, a belief that the company will condone actions that are taken in its interest and will even protect the managers responsible. The question we have to deal with here is, How do we keep company loyalty from going berserk?

That seems to be what happened at Manville. A small group of executives and a succession of corporate medical directors kept the facts about the lethal qualities of asbestos from becoming public knowledge for decades, and they managed to live with that knowledge. And at Manville, the company – or really, the company's senior management – did condone their decision and protect those employees.

Something similar seems to have happened at General Electric. When one of its missile projects ran up costs greater than the air force had agreed to pay, middle managers surreptitiously shifted those costs to projects that were still operating under budget. In this case, the loyalty that ran amok was primarily to the division: managers want their units' results to look good. But GE, with one of the finest reputations in U.S. industry, was splattered with scandal and paid a fine of $1.04 million.

One of the most troubling aspects of the GE case is the company's admission that those involved were thoroughly familiar with the company's ethical standards before the incident took place. This suggests that the practice of declaring codes of ethics and teaching them to managers is not enough to deter unethical conduct. Something stronger is needed.

Top management has a responsibility to exert a moral force within the company. Senior executives are responsible for drawing the line between loyalty to the company and action against the laws and values of the society in which the company must operate. Further, because that line can be obscured in the heat of the moment, the line has to be drawn well short of where reasonable men and women could begin to suspect that their rights had been violated. The company has to react long before a prosecutor, for instance, would have a strong enough case to seek an indictment.

Executives have a right to expect loyalty from employees against competitors and detractors, but not loyalty against the law, or against common morality, or against society itself. Managers must warn employees that a disservice to customers, and especially to innocent bystanders, cannot be a service to the company. Finally, and most important of all, managers must stress that excuses of company loyalty will not be accepted for acts that place its good name in jeopardy. To put it bluntly, superiors must make it clear that employees who harm other people allegedly for the company's benefit will be fired.

The most extreme examples of corporate misconduct were due, in hindsight, to managerial failures. A good way to avoid management oversights is to subject the control mechanisms themselves to periodic surprise audits, perhaps as a function of the board of directors. The point is to make sure that internal audits and controls are functioning as planned. It's a case of inspecting the inspectors and taking the necessary steps to keep the controls working efficiently. Harold Geneen, former head of ITT, has suggested that the board should have an independent staff, something analogous to the Government Accounting Office, which reports to the legislative rather than the executive branch. In the end, it is up to top management to send a clear and pragmatic message to all employees that good ethics is still the foundation of good business.

CASE STUDY

Ethically active businesses: the work of business in the community

Business in the Community (BITC) is an organization dedicated to getting businesses involved in tackling the social and economic problems of the communities in which they operate. From a founding membership of 30 firms in 1982, BITC has grown to around 500 member firms by 1992. They include many of the largest and best-known companies operating in Great Britain. In the words of the *Financial Times*, the list of their representatives reads like 'a who's who of British Industry and Commerce'.

BITC is concerned with an extremely wide range of issues which it divides into four main areas. These are education, the environment, economic development and enterprise, and promoting the business case for community involvement. They all overlap in practice, but the last mentioned is perhaps the most pervasive. This is because the role of BITC is essentially that of a co-ordinating body rather than an agency acting on behalf of businesses. For example, it administers the Per Cent Club through which companies commit themselves to spending at least 0.5% of pre-tax UK profits (or 1% of dividends) on community-based projects, but it is the individual companies themselves which decide on and carry out the projects.

The key word in perhaps all BITC's activities is 'partnership'. For example, under the 'education' heading, BITC seeks to have the needs of business met by educational institutions in return for making the expertise and resources of business available to those institutions. Under the 'environment' heading, BITC not only attempts to promote environmental awareness in businesses but seeks also to get them to co-operate with each other and with local communities and government bodies in tackling problems. Under the 'economic development and enterprise' heading, the partnerships include those of businesses and business people with local authorities and voluntary organizations in promoting the re-generation of economically depressed areas. In addition, there is within this category the very close partnership of BITC itself with Local Enterprise Agencies. (These were established to assist new and growing business and setting them up was the original focus of BITC's work.)

The idea of partnership permeates even the organizational structure of BITC. Though very much business-led, its governing bodies are not exclusively composed of company executives. They include trade union leaders, as well as representatives of local authorities, government departments, and voluntary organizations.

In keeping with this consensual approach, BITC strives to be non-partisan. It expressly declares political non-alignment and is careful to present itself as such in its publications. It cannot though, entirely escape controversy. There is the fundamental question of whether or not business should leave social problems to governments (a question to be explored in chapter 5). In its exploratory publication 'Directions for the Nineties', BITC shows itself sensitive to the charge that it might be acting in the place of governments when it declares that 'asking business to do more does not mean that Government should do less.' However, it almost immediately goes on to recommend that governments 'adopt a social franchise approach' inviting existing public–private partnerships to tender for programmes instead of creating new organizations which increase duplication and dissipation of resources – a recommendation which, rightly or wrongly, many might see as an open invitation for governments to do less.

When it comes to justifying community involvement by businesses, BITC seems to have difficulty reconciling an altruistic 'philanthropic' approach with a self-interested one. For the most part it emphasises the latter; perhaps recognizing that discomfort with the moral which, this chapter has suggested, is prevalent in business circles.

The self-interest is seen as operating in ways that, again, correspond with suggestions made in this chapter. It is, on BITC's schema, to do with 'building reputations', 'building people' and 'building markets'. The first is concerned with that enhanced public image which comes with acting in an ethically active way. The second is concerned with helping in the recruitment and retention of staff as well as the improvement in management skills which hopefully comes from staff involvement in community projects. The third concerns that broad and admittedly long term interest which companies have in expanding markets for their products through the economic regeneration of local communities. On the evidence of BITC's impressive membership list, there would seem to be many prominent business people who would at least go some way in supporting the arguments of this chapter on the relationship between ethics and self-interest in business.

Sources: BITC publications, including annual corporate reviews (with acknowledgement to BITC Information Officer, Reena Chuda, for her generous supply of these items).

DISCUSSION TOPICS

1. Find out whether the organization in which you are working or studying has a code of practice. Has its appearance made any difference to the behaviour of those who work there? Are there changes you would like to see?

If your organization does not have a code of practice, consider what main points you would like to see included in it. (If the organization is an educational establishment, consider the possibility of having codes of practice for students as well as staff.) Give reasons for the points you have included.

2. Is good business ethics good business? Consider the arguments for and against. Identify examples where good business ethics has been particularly profitable or unprofitable.

Ethical theory | 3

Cognitivism and non-cognitivism
Religious morality
Consequentialism versus non-consequentialism
Utilitarianism: an ethic of welfare
Kantianism: an ethic of duty
Natural law: an ethic of rights
Applying ethical theories

Introducing the readings

Is business bluffing ethical?   Albert Carr
Does it pay to bluff in business?   Norman E. Bowie
Rule utilitarianism, equality and justice   John C. Harsanyi
Virtues and business ethics   Joseph R. DesJardins

Case study
Assessing the ethics of business: the new consumer survey

Discussion topics

In the previous chapter we looked at the role of values in business and considered how business ethics was becoming part of the professional-ization of business. But what exactly **are** ethical judgments, and how do we justify them?

At first appearance this may seem a needless difficulty. After all, is it not obvious what is happening when we make ethical decisions? Do we not do so almost every day of our lives?

It is one thing to engage in an activity, but often quite another to state what exactly is going on when we do it. For example, someone may have a tremendous gift for selling goods to people, but may not necessarily be aware, until he or she is taught, exactly what is going on when a successful strategy is put into operation. In a similar way, we can make moral judgments, but find some difficulty in explaining exactly what is taking place when we do so.

In the case of ethical judgments, the situation is perhaps more difficult. If I state that a product is – say – red, we have little difficulty in understanding and explaining what is meant. Red is a colour, and is a physical property which can be seen with the eyes. Ethical judgments seem to be different. If we describe something as good or bad, right or wrong, we do not seem to be talking about a property we can see, touch, hear or experience in any obvious way with our senses. So what are we doing when we make an ethical judgment? Are we making a statement about the physical world in which we live, which can be true or false, or are we doing something different? Are there moral truths which can be known like empirical statements about the world, such as 'The product I am selling is red'?

COGNITIVISM AND NON-COGNITIVISM

The first and most profound division in ethical theory is between the claim that it is possible to know moral right from wrong and the denial of that claim. Because this is claim and counter-claim about what we can and cannot know, the position which declares we can know is called 'cognitivism' and the contrary position 'non-cognitivism'.

According to cognitivism, there are objective moral truths which can be known, just as we can know other truths about the world. Statements of moral belief, on this view, can be true or false, just as our statement that something is a certain colour can be true or false. According to the non-cognitivist, by contrast, 'objective' assessment of moral belief is not possible. It is all 'subjective'. There is no truth or falsity to be discovered. There is only belief, attitude, emotional reaction, and the like. As Hamlet puts it, 'There is nothing either good or bad but thinking makes it so'.

When non-cognitivism claims that there are only attitudes, its proponents do not usually mean that moral judgments are simply expressions of one's feelings. Advocates of non-cognitivism acknowledge the essentially social nature of morality by invariably arguing that these are group attitudes. They are cultural preferences; attitudes of races, religions, societies, sub-groups, or whatever. The scope can vary, but they remain merely preferences without any supporting basis in reality. There is nothing to make one set of preferences any more true or false than another. There can be no appeal to anything outside the fact of group norms to validate moral belief. Moral right and wrong is whatever particular cultural groups say it is. It is culturally relative; a view usually referred as 'moral relativism'.

What lends plausibility to moral relativism is the fact of moral diversity. Different cultural groups do have different moral practices. All globe-trotting business people know this. Their in-flight reading tells them; books with titles like 'Tips for travellers', government pamphlets with titles like 'Advice for visitors to . . .'. They give warnings about types of action considered acceptable in one's own culture, but liable to cause offence when exported to a different part of the globe. They state that 'here' bribes are condemned as immoral, while 'there' they are accepted as normal; that while 'here' drinking alcohol is perfectly acceptable, 'there' it is forbidden by law; 'there' women wear short skirts, 'here' their dress must be modest, covering the body from the neck to a maximum of twenty centimetres above the ankle.

True enough; but how much of this is a difference in morals? Is there really a culture which thinks that bribery is morally all right, for example? We have to separate practice from principle. Consider a country in which there are pitifully low wages for public officials. They can only support themselves and their families by accepting bribes, and only by paying them bribes will the public get things done. It has become normal practice, but no one likes it and no one thinks it is morally right. The public would rather not pay and the officials would rather have a living wage. Circumstances have thrown principles and practice out of joint. So perhaps morals there are not so different from here; only the circumstances? Where also is the difference in moral principle between allowing and prohibiting alcohol consumption? Is it not rather a difference in calculations of the social cost of the practice? No society thinks drunkenness, alcoholism or the attendant bad behaviour and illness are good things. They all would rather be without them. But one culture thinks a total ban on consumption is neither a publicly acceptable nor practicable solution to the problem. (The USA tried it and the result was Al Capone.) Another thinks it is. They have had the ban for a long time, people have broadly accepted it, and what is the worth of a little artificially induced merriment against the benefits of keeping drunkenness and alcoholism at bay? Differing estimations of likely social consequences could also lie behind the differing views on how women should dress. Those societies insisting on neck to ankle coverage might, in part at least, do so in the belief that any further exposure would cause men to sexually abuse women. No society wants to encourage such abuse. There could well be disagreement as to likely causes and to appropriate measures for removing them; questions about whether men really are this unrestrained, and whether it would be more effective to restrict men's behaviour rather than women's dress. If this is the nature of the disagreement, it is not a difference in morals.

Another situation in which a cultural difference need not amount to a moral difference is in those areas in which the word 'culture' is applied in the restricted, but very usual sense of being connected with differences in aesthetic sensibility, manners, fashions, customs and the like. Admittedly, the moral and the merely cultural are not always easily separable, and societies do have a tendency to conflate them – particularly where the cultural is about what is 'clean' and 'unclean'. This could be the case then with rules about the permissible length of women's dress. They could be based on ideas of etiquette, aesthetics or sartorial tradition, which are no less passionately held for being merely cultural rather than moral?

The lesson of all these examples is that we cannot read off diversity in underlying moral principle from diversity in practices. We must first sift through differences in social circumstance, strategy, causual belief, and cultural preference. When we do, we could well find that what looks like a difference in morals is nothing of the kind. However, at the end of the day we could of course still be faced with a genuine moral difference. Even after allowing for all the complications, we could very well find that behind different ideas on appropriate dress for women are fundamentally opposing views on sexual equality. But even given such genuine and fundamental moral diversity, this is no proof of the correctness of moral relativism. In morals, as in anything else, the fact people believe different things to be true does not, of itself, prove there is no truth to be found. The truth could be there but none have yet arrived at it; or perhaps some have got at the truth and others have not. The fact of moral diversity can therefore simply mean that either no culture has yet arrived at the truth on certain moral matters, or else that some have arrived at it and others have not.

In other words, some cultures have got it morally right and others have got it wrong. The latter can be a rather uncomfortable possibility for liberal minded people. A motive behind moral relativism has undoubtedly been a wholly laudable desire for cultural and racial tolerance. If the opposing moral beliefs of different cultural groups are all equally unfounded, then none are superior or inferior to any other. None are true and others false. In particular, for this is the great historical exemplar, western moral values have no claim to superiority over non-western ones. There are no poor benighted heathens for western imperialists and western Christian missionaries to rescue from moral depravity. The claim of a 'civilizing mission' which was often used to justify western imperialism is without moral foundation because (at least according to the non-cognitivist) all morality is without foundation in either fact or reason.

This all looks suspiciously like trying to have one's cake and eat it. There is an implicit appeal to the moral virtue of tolerance while denying, as the moral relativist must, any objective justification for such an appeal. But if morality is relative then nothing stops any particular group opting for intolerance. If we are free to choose whatever set of moral standards we like, we are free to be as intolerant as we like. Moral relativism does not entail tolerance.

That is a loss of a supposed advantage to the theory but not a mortal blow. However, this issue of toleration poses an altogether deeper and more serious dilemma for a consistent moral relativism; one which any form of non-cognitivism in ethics must face. It is that there are then no objective grounds for opposing any activity no matter how morally repellent it might seem. Having denied any objective basis to morality, there is then nothing to make it either true or false that an action is right or wrong. There are therefore no objective reasons for either supporting or opposing any particular activity on moral grounds. All culturally sanctioned practices are on an equal footing. Thinking that racism, sexism, corruption, exploitation and genocide are bad things is no more or less justifiable than thinking they are good things. Both are simply matters of cultural consensus. For societies opposing these things to take action against societies supporting them is merely to exercise preference for one set of attitudes over another. The opposing societies can perfectly well indulge in their opposition for there is nothing to make them wrong in this; but equally, there is nothing to make them right either.

Faced with the consequence that societies are free to pick and choose whether or not to engage in something like genocide, it might well seem to many that moral relativism, along with non-cognitivism in general, is really not a very plausible position to adopt. Can we really believe that no action of any kind no matter what it involves in the way of human suffering is 'objectively' right or wrong? Do we really have no rational reason for preferring respect for human life to total disregard, kindness to cruelty, honesty to dishonesty? Have whole systems of morality really only evolved to organize subjective preferences? It hardly seems credible. If it does not we must start considering what objectivity in ethics might be based on. The merits of various cognitivist theories must be examined.

RELIGIOUS MORALITY

One obvious source of morality might be thought to lie in religion. After all, if God exists, who better than God himself to decide what is right and what is wrong? If God is omniscient, then surely he must be the infallible authority on matters of ethics (as indeed everything else). Accordingly many people throughout the ages, including some modern business men and women, have built their ethics upon religion. Thus, for the evangelical Christian, the ethical rule book is the Bible; for the Muslim it is the Qur'an; for the Jew it is the Torah (the first five books of the Christian's Old Testament) interpreted by the Talmud.[1]

The theory that actions are right solely because God commands them is sometimes known as the 'Divine Command' theory. As a theory it is hugely popular and temptingly simple, but also radically incoherent.

This is not simply the obvious problems of proving that God exists and demonstrating that we know his will. The deeper problem is that

---

[1] The Talmud is a legal compilation of encyclopaedic proportions, compiled around 500 BCE, and is acknowledged to be the authoritative Jewish legal work, second only to the Torah itself.

even supposing God is the final arbiter on ethical matters, how does he himself decide what it right and wrong? If God can make an action either right or wrong just by deciding that this should be so, then God turns out to be no more than a dictator whose will is arbitrary, and humankind is subject to his whims which have no good underlying reasons. On the other hand, if God has **reasons** for commanding one thing rather than another, then it is these reasons held, independently of what God decides or tells humanity. If God commands humans not to steal on the grounds that this causes human suffering, then it is human welfare that forms the basis of morality – the fact that God commands it is incidental.

Some religious believers may add that God, being ruler of the universe, not only has the power to make laws on behalf of humanity, but is able to back them up by sanctions. According to classical Christian and Islamic teaching, God will reward the righteous with the joys of heaven, and consign the wicked to the torments of hell. Thus, it may be argued that what makes actions right and wrong is the fact (if it is a fact) of divine reward and retribution. This though, clearly gets things the wrong way round. It is never the fact of reward or punishment that makes actions right or wrong, rather it is *because* actions are right or wrong that they should be rewarded or punished. Thus, we still require reasons independent of God's will to explain why an action is right or wrong.

The argument so far assumes that being religious is to be equated with believing in God. This is not necessarily the case; Buddhists and Jains, for example, are religious, yet a creator God does not feature in their scheme of things, and with their religions comes very clearly defined codes of ethics. Although morality can exist without religion, religion will not usually exist without morality. Few, if any, religions do not have moral codes.

So what, if anything, does a religion add to a moral code? One respect in which a religious morality might extend beyond a secular morality is that religion typically holds that there are dimensions of reality beyond the purely physical world. The Christian does not merely seek for the secular well-being of humanity, but for the 'kingdom of heaven' (however that is to be understood); the Jew may seek for the messianic age of peace, justice and harmony.

Believers in a religious morality will often claim that the actions they are prescribed will help to bring about that supernatural goal. There is a belief among some Jews that if all Jews were to observe two successive sabbaths impeccably the Messiah would come immediately. Within a religion it is possible to hold that there are special obligations which will enable the distinctively religious goal to be brought about.

There is therefore much at stake for the follower of a religion, which is why the freedom to practise the religion of one's choice is generally regarded as a fundamental human right. Those involved in international business are therefore ill advised to ride rough shod over the religious convictions of their trade partners, who may well believe that their entire eternity could be at stake. Here readers may recall the scene in Shakespeare's *Hamlet*, where Hamlet, in his deliberations on whether to kill the king in order to avenge his father's murder, entertains the idea of waiting until the king has committed some grave misdeed, so that he will be punished for all eternity.

A religion can also enable its followers to experience a sense of belonging to a tradition or a community. The root meaning of the word 'religion' is the Latin word *religio*, which means, 'I bind'. Religion binds people together; thus the Jew can feel an identity with fellow Jews by knowing that they keep the same dietary rules, observe the sabbath and come together for the festivals of Passover, Weeks and Booths. The Muslim's undertaking of the hajj (pilgrimage to Mecca) and the Christian's coming together for the sacrament are all ways in which these respective communities are bound together in a brotherhood (a word frequently used in the context of Islam) or a fellowship (a word often employed by the Christian). Belonging to a community entails having distinctive characteristics, and one way of ensuring that a community is distinctive is by imposing special obligations upon its members.

A religion can also provide its followers with a distinctive **means** of achieving a desired end. For example, many religions deplore extremes of wealth and poverty and aim for an age where there will be compassion and justice. (This need not entail absolute equality – a notion explicitly rejected by most religions, in fact). The Jews in ancient times prescribed several ways in which inequalities of wealth could be levelled down; one way of doing this was the institution of the 'Jubilee Year' which occurred every fiftieth year in ancient times, and in which all debts were automatically cancelled. Contemporary Islam prescribes that a certain proportion of one's wealth should be given as alms for the poor (*zakat*), and that unearned interest may not be gained from moneys lent. The Roman Catholic Church, through the centuries, has propagated the doctrines of the just wage and the just price. The Jain religion makes the interesting recommendation that people in the business world should decide, in advance of achieving their fortune, what standard of wealth they hope to achieve; then, if such fortune is surpassed, the surplus should be given away to worthy causes. Of course it would be possible to practise these ideals without belonging to a religion at all. But, as we all know, individual resolutions (such as those made at New Year or during a period such as Lent) are much easier to break than obligations which are assumed by a whole community.

Religions, too, can also have the function of imposing special forms of discipline on their followers. In theory at least, supporters of a religion strive for perfection, and few believers regard the present physical world and its values as affording a perfect state of affairs. Accordingly, many believers will perform activities which are in effect attempts to detach themselves from the physical world. One of the reasons why certain Christians fast during Lent and Muslims fast during the month of Ramadan is to demonstrate their ability not to depend on the physical world – or at least to depend on it to a lesser degree than those ordinary mortals who eat a normal diet.

These activities take on a specifically religious dimension on account of the fact that believers perform these activities *en masse*, as part of a community. The Christian Sunday, the Jewish sabbath or a religious retreat are not simply means of ensuring that followers take sufficient rest from their work, important though that is. The fixing of a definite day or a pre-determined period enables the religion to 'bind together' its followers into a definite community which shares such activities. (Incidentally, there are now secular organizations which offer retreats for business people – contemporary secular materialism at least sometimes draws on the legacy of a religious society.)

Finally, religions provide their followers with myths or stories, which serve as a source of inspiration and illustration for a moral life. The Parable of the good Samaritan encourages Christians to love their neighbour; the story of Job assists Jews, Christians and Muslims to exercise patience and loyalty in the face of adversity. The stories of the previous lives of the Buddha (the *Jatakas*) help Buddhists to understand the lengths to which compassion can go, and how good can triumph over evil. Most people think in concrete rather than abstract terms, and religions can provide examples as well as theories.

To sum up, then, the writers hold that it is perfectly possible to have morality without religion, and that religious morality ultimately draws on reasons which are independent of religion. However, one can talk about 'religious moralities' in the sense that each particular religion has its distinctive moral code, which followers pursue in the context of that religious tradition.

CONSEQUENTIALISM VERSUS NON-CONSEQUENTIALISM

The great divide in cognitivist thinking is between theories which assess moral right and wrong in terms of the consequences of actions and those which do not. Those which do are 'consequentialist' theories; those which do not are 'non-consequentialist'.

Deep though the division is, this is a distinction which must be treated with some caution. It is doubtful if non-consequentialist theories, even the most extreme, can or do totally ignore consequences in assessing right and wrong. On the whole, consequentialist theories are the more exclusive. With them it is generally true that only consequences count. Yet even so, concessions are possible and modifications which take other factors into the reckoning have been proposed. The division into consequentialist and non-consequentialist theories is therefore a broad one. In some cases and to some extent, it can be distinguished by where the emphasis is put rather than by a total concentration on consequences or, less probably, their total exclusion. That said, even the difference in emphasis is marked and profound.

With consequentialist theories we look to the results of actions to determine the truth or falsity of moral judgements about them. If what follows from an action is, on balance, of benefit then it is a 'good' action and so we are 'right' to do it; conversely, if the outcome is, on balance, harmful then the action is 'bad' and we are 'wrong' to do it. For consequentialism, the test of whether an action is right or wrong is whether it is good or bad in the sense of resulting in benefit or harm. Right or wrong is a question of good or bad; and good or bad a question of benefit or harm.

For non-consequentialism, there is no immediate appeal to beneficial or harmful consequences to determine good or bad. Nor do good and bad directly determine right and wrong. Rather, it is the other way about; it is right and wrong that determines good and bad. We start from some conception of what it is for an action to be right or wrong, and that determines for us whether or not an action is good or bad. Calculations as to the likely consequences of the action need play no part in that conception. It can be solely in virtue of being an activity of a certain kind that the action is right or wrong, and therefore good or bad.

A Divine Command theory offers an illustration of the difference between consequentialism and non-consequentialism. If religious believers were to obey God's commands in order to attain a desirable state after death, or because they believed that obedience was rewarded by material success (a view held by some Protestant Christians and also, historically, by Jews, who associated covenant keeping with the coming of the promised messianic age), then such motives presuppose a consequentialist view of ethics. If, however, the believer obeys God's commands, not for any expected reward, but for the sole reason that God has commanded them, then he or she presupposes a strictly non-consequentialist account of morality. It is not what follows from our actions which then makes them right or wrong but only the fact of their conformity or non-conformity to God's commands. It is solely in virtue of being activities of such a conforming or non-conforming kind that actions are right or wrong, and therefore good or bad.

The non-religious theories which we shall go on to examine embody the contrast between consequentialism and non-consequentialism in more complicated ways. Given such complexity, it is easy to assume that all we have here is a high-flown theoretical difference. This would be a mistake. What the theoretical difference of opinion highlights and elaborates is a contrast which is a widespread and fundamental feature of the way people in general approach ethical problems. Faced with an ethical problem, the habitual approach of some people is to weigh up the costs and benefits. They ask 'Where's the good in that?, or 'Where's the harm in it?'. In so doing they adopt, whether they know it or not, a consequentialist approach to ethics. In contrast, other people tend to disregard such calculations. For them the issue is one of 'simple right or wrong'; something is either right or wrong and that is the end of the matter.

Take, for example, different management approaches to the problem of 'shrinkage' – the loss of stock which occurs through employees illicitly taking or consuming the company's products. A determinedly non-consequentialist approach would be to take the line that this is stealing pure and simple and as such demands the culprits to be caught and punished regardless of consequences. A consequentialist approach would want to weigh up the pros and cons of imposing sanctions. Is the loss of stock worth the cost of increased surveillance and supervision of staff? Is it worth the resentment these actions would cause? What also if the culprits are caught? Are they to be dismissed regardless of their personal circumstances as the non-consequentialist might insist? Or are factors such as the effect of their dismissal on their families to be taken into account? Although these are very practical issues, the question they pose of how the ethical dilemmas should be resolved is a matter of theoretical concern.

This difference in the underlying theoretical approach is not to be confused with having a different moral code in the sense of a competing list of moral rights and wrongs. It is to have competing explanations of **why** actions are right or wrong. This can justify different stances on particular moral issues and so lead to different listings of rights and wrongs; but it need not. Both a consequentialist and a non-consequentialist are likely, for example, to agree that stealing by employees is wrong. Where they would differ is in their understanding of why it is wrong. For the consequentialist it is, broadly speaking, because of the socially disruptive effects of the practice. For the non-consequentialist it is because there is something intrinsically wrong in the act of taking someone else's property.

Taken item by item, a consequentialist and non-consequentialist listing of rights and wrongs will probably not differ very much. This does not mean this is mostly a purely theoretical dispute with little bearing on substantive moral issues. There will be some disagreement on substantive moral issues and they are, unsurprisingly, likely to concern just those issues which divide society the most. The classic example is abortion. Here consequentialist arguments about the social effects of unwanted pregnancies tend to be utilized by the pro-choice lobby, while non-consequentialist arguments about the unborn child's right to life tend to be used by the pro-life lobby.

The division between consequentialists and non-consequentialists is also likely to manifest itself in their respective responses to moral issues; they have a radically different conception of the nature of the problem and therefore radically different approaches to its solution. On the issue of shrinkage, for example, we saw that an uncompromisingly non-consequentialist response is that wrongdoing should meet its just deserts whatever the cost, while for the consequentialist the question of what to do depends on a careful calculation of costs. Adherence to principle is the basis of the non-consequentialist approach, pragmatic flexibility that of the consequentialist. Whereas with the non-consequentialist there could normally be only one response in any circumstance, with the consequentialist the response will certainly vary with the circumstances. In the case of shrinkage, sometimes the decision could be to do nothing whatsoever; sometimes it could be to take even harsher action than the non-consequentialist would regard as proper. It all depends on what would produce the best result.

UTILITARIANISM: AN ETHIC OF WELFARE

The best known consequentialist theory of ethics is called 'utilitarianism'. The name derives from the use of the word utility to denote the capacity in actions to have good results. This choice of word proclaims the consequentialist nature of the theory. Utility means usefulness – underlying the point that it is the usefulness of actions which determines their moral character rather than anything in the nature of the action itself. Actions are not good or bad in themselves, but only in what they are good or bad **for**. This is their utility or, when the result is bad, their disutility. In utilitarian terms, the more good which results from an action the more utility it has; the worse the result, the more disutility. (Although, strictly speaking, good and bad are the results while utility and disutility are the capacities for those results, they amount to the same thing in practice and can, for convenience, be treated as synonymous.)

Though utilitarianism in one form or another goes back to the earliest thinking on ethical matters, the classic formulation is owed to the British philosopher and social reformer, Jeremy Bentham (1748–1832). The formulation he offered was characteristically bold and unequivocal. Utility is one thing and one thing only, he said, it is happiness. Disutility is unhappiness. Actions are right to the extent they maximize happiness or at least minimize unhappiness, wrong to the extent they maximize unhappiness or minimize happiness.

Faced with a choice between two actions, one which will result in happiness and the other in unhappiness, we should choose the one producing happiness. Given a choice between two actions which will both produce happiness, we should select the one producing the most happiness. Given that both will produce unhappiness, we must choose the one producing the least unhappiness – the lesser of the two evils. Where the same amount of happiness or unhappiness will result, either option may be chosen, and where neither happiness nor unhappiness will follow our actions, we are morally free to do whatever we like.

Why identify utility with happiness? Because, Bentham said, it is the only thing desirable as an end in itself. All other things are only desirable as a means to the end of happiness. All the other things we seek – fame, fortune, sanctity, serenity, knowledge, power, love, friendship, or whatever – are of value only in so far as they are conducive to happiness. They are good only in so far as they lead to that single ultimate good. Happiness is therefore the only thing good in itself. Conversely, unhappiness is the only thing bad in itself, the only ultimate evil.

An obvious objection is to ask how happiness can be measured. Bentham hoped for a precise, scientific measure. In this he was clearly being unrealistic. What is perfectly possible, though, is a set of crude but effective calculations. They are made all the time; they are even put to exactly that moral use which utilitarianism supposes. We make consequentialist assessments of the rightness or wrongness of actions, and this invariably involves some sort of rough and ready calculation of the impact on human happiness of the actions. There is, moreover, proof of the general effectiveness of such calculations in the fact that they also often feature in our often very successful attempts to predict and control behaviour. In our everyday dealings with people we usually know perfectly well what will please or displease them and, in order to control and predict their behaviour, act accordingly. We are even able to make effective estimates of the differing degrees of happiness or unhappiness that actions are likely to produce. It is likely that the harder the blow the more unhappiness, the more generous the gift the more happiness, and so on. It is not always known with certainty of course. Sometimes we can have no idea of the effect on happiness of actions. Sometimes we get it wrong. But we can make reasonable estimates most of the time, and get them reasonably correct enough of the time to have a practicable guide to conduct in the idea of utility as happiness.

There is even the possibility of admitting an element of quantification into these estimates provided we settle for what is admittedly a very indirect approach. It is found in economics. In economics, consumption of goods and services is said to satisfy wants. The greater the proportion of our income we are prepared to devote to purchasing one set of items rather than another, the greater the relative satisfaction obtained. We are presumed to seek only to maximize that satisfaction. Calculations and predictions of economic behaviour are made on that basis. In so far as economics endeavours to explain why we are assumed to behave in that way, it appeals to a conception of human beings as, at least in the economic sphere, essentially pleasure seeking. We are presumed to seek to maximize satisfaction because of the happiness it brings. This has obvious parallels with utilitarianism. It is even the case, as anyone who has studied economics will know, that the terminology is shared. The capacity in goods and services to provide satisfaction is spoken of as their utility. The greater the capacity of any particular set of goods or services to satisfy our wants, the more utility it has for us. This conceptual and terminological overlap is no accident. Economics and utilitarian ethical theory have a long historical connection. The economic concept of utility gradually separated itself from any direct relationship with moral good and became the measure of relative consumer preference that it is today; but even with this momentous break, economics and utilitarianism are still not entirely separate. There remains that same underlying conception of human beings as pleasure seeking. There are still also traces of the old moral sense of utility in attempts by economists to calculate the relative welfare that societies as a whole will derive from alternative patterns of expenditure. Conversely, modern utilitarian theory attempts to use measurements of welfare in the economic sense to solve moral problems; often in rather complicated mathematical ways.

In so far as economics goes along with the Benthamite notion that happiness plays a peculiarly fundamental role in human conduct, it shares in a commitment to a doctrine known as 'hedonism' (from the Greek for 'pleasure'). This is a theoretical perspective which has taken various forms in its long and continuing history, but can be broadly divided into two sorts of claims. The first centres around the idea of happiness as the ultimate goal of human behaviour. This is called 'psychological hedonism' and is, as we have seen, explicit and unrestricted in Bentham but merely implicit and restricted (to economic behaviour) in economics. The second sort of claim is called 'ethical hedonism' and centres around the idea that moral good is identical with happiness – something from which the science of economics has very properly come to distance itself, but is the very basis of Benthamite utilitarianism.

Though Bentham's general commitment to both these ideas is undoubted, precisely what he subscribed to is difficult to assess. He is certainly a psychological hedonist in the sense that he accepted that happiness was the guiding aim of human behaviour. He was also certainly an ethical hedonist in the sense that he accepted that happiness was the ultimate measure of moral right and wrong. However, the position he adopts must be carefully distinguished from two others which also go under the same headings. He is probably not a psychological hedonist in the sense that he thinks our behaviour can only be directed towards our own happiness, that it is a psychological fact about human beings that they are only capable of performing acts directed at achieving their own happiness. He is certainly not an ethical hedonist in the sense that he believes that only our own happiness counts in determining right and wrong, that we ought to do whatever maximizes our own happiness.

Had Bentham accepted such purely individualistic interpretations of psychological and ethical hedonism, his would be the kind of hedonism known as 'egoism' (from the Greek for 'I'). He is very clear, however, that the good which we must seek is the common good. It is the total sum of human happiness which must be maximized and not simply our own individual happiness. We must follow what he called the 'Greatest Happiness Principle' and aim for the greatest happiness of the greatest number. In this our own happiness should have no priority. It should simply be part of the sum. If our own happiness can only be enhanced by diminishing the total sum of happiness, then it must be sacrificed for the greater happiness.

Bentham's ethical hedonism is therefore explicitly and diametrically opposed to egoism. This means that, at least by implication, he rejects an egoistical interpretation of psychological hedonism also, for in requiring us to sometimes sacrifice our own happiness for the greater happiness, Bentham must allow that sometimes we are capable of acting in a non-egoistical fashion – that is, of not just seeking our own happiness. Otherwise we would not be capable of following the Greatest Happiness Principle and there would be no point in proposing it as a guide to conduct.

That Bentham should oppose ethical egoism is unsurprising. Any unqualified identification of morality with self-interest will perhaps inevitably run foul of the requirement, noted earlier, that the pursuit of self-interest be compatible with the common good (see Chapter 2). In making the common good the arbiter of right and wrong, Bentham avoids that problem. What he does though, is make it the sole arbiter: only the common good counts. Only optimizing the total sum of human happiness counts in distinguishing right from wrong. This is a position that brings its own peculiar problems, for then some morally dubious practices would seem not only to be allowed, but positively required.

Take a situation in which the happiness of society as a whole is maximized by the creation of an underclass. There is a section of the population, say 20%, which, through no fault of its own, suffers from low wages, high unemployment, limited access to educational and welfare provision, and has little or no political influence. They are unhappy with their lot but cannot do much about it. The other 80% of the population gain from having this underclass. They reap the benefits of having cheap labour (particularly in the service sector) and a pool of disposable labour to take up the slack in times of economic recession. They also enjoy a somewhat larger share of educational resources, of welfare provision, and of political influence than their numbers and needs might be supposed to entitle them. They are very happy with their lot. When the total sum of happiness is added up it is found that this is the arrangement which maximizes happiness given the total resources available. An alternative arrangement could make the 20% minority a lot happier but this would not be enough to offset a marginal decrease in the happiness of the 80% majority. (We invite readers to think of societies which might come close to this scenario.)

Modifications of the greatest happiness principle

What is wrong with this situation is that it is unjust. Why should a minority suffer simply to make a majority better off? Bentham has made the common good the sole arbiter of right and wrong. He has gone on to identify the common good with a simple aggregate in the form of the sum of human happiness. The sacrifice of the rights and interests of individuals and minorities to the common good is therefore possible; even, as in the example, to the unjust extent that they are sacrificed simply to make others better off. To avoid this outcome several modifications to traditional Benthamite utilitarianism have been suggested. One is to assess utility by what generally follows from acts of a certain kind rather than, as it seems to be with Bentham, what is actually going to happen in any particular case. 'What moral rule will maximize human happiness if it were universally followed?' becomes the crucial question rather than the simple case by case question of 'What will happen if **this** is done?' The aim is to arrive at general rules of conduct rather than decisions about the rights and wrongs of particular acts. It is therefore called 'rule utilitarianism' to distinguish it from the 'act utilitarianism' of Bentham. According to proponents, it can deal with problems of justice. They argue that the test of 'Is this moral rule conducive to the greatest human happiness?' will result in the sort of situation described in the example being deemed morally wrong. We cannot be permitted to disadvantage others simply because it will benefit us. If everyone did so we would all suffer. Overall, and in the long term, the outcome would be disutility.

Another modification abandons Bentham's aggregate method of

calculating utility for some form of averaging. That is, instead of merely adding up the total sum of happiness, we look also at its distribution. The highest mean or median (opinions vary) share of happiness is sought. That way, it is hoped, the injustice of some people getting much less than a fair share of happiness is avoided.

A third modification picks up on a point which Bentham himself acknowledged but was little developed by him or anyone else. It is that unhappiness in general, and pain in particular, are usually more intensely felt than happiness and pleasure. The greatest feeling of happiness, the strongest sensation of pleasure, is a relatively mild affair compared with the depths to which unhappiness and pain can take people. (Compare torture and malnutrition to love and fine food.) Given this, it can be argued, utilitarianism rules out gross injustices. Intense suffering by a minority will always outweigh any happiness the majority might derive from being advantaged by the suffering. A grossly exploited underclass will therefore not be permitted. The balance of disutility over utility would make the situation wrong.

A fourth and final modification is more radical still. It would stop either happiness or unhappiness being the only objective. It advocates we adopt a more broadly consequentialist approach in which the maximization of benefits and the minimization of harm remain the aim, but there is no attempt at further specification. Rather a pluralist, non-hedonistic, approach is adopted in which happiness and unhappiness simply take their place in an indefinite list of harmful and beneficial things. (Whether this could still be called utilitarianism is a terminological issue.) On this account, such things as freedom, friendship, knowledge, love, honesty, and so on, are seen as good in their own right and not merely for the happiness they promote. Likewise, tyranny, enmity, ignorance, hate, deceit, and so on, are seen as bad in their own right. This goes for justice and injustice also. So when a minority is exploited simply for the enhanced benefit of a majority, the increased happiness of that majority is just part of the equation. It must be balanced not only against the unhappiness of the minority but also against the harm of injustice. In such an equation, it could be argued, mere enhanced happiness will not be sufficient to justify gross injustice.

The effectiveness of any and all of these modifications to traditional utilitarianism, either alone or in combination, is a moot point. They all go some way in eliminating the sort of gross injustice involved in permitting a mere increase in benefits to justify the infliction of harm. In some judicious combination they could perhaps eliminate it all together. For hostile critics though, even this success would not be enough to make utilitarianism acceptable. For them the whole consequentialist approach is misguided. Its intrinsic error is to think that only outcomes matter. People are then not valued as persons it is argued. What is of value is not the individual person but the harm or benefit which accrues to the person. Thus morality becomes a matter of calculation. Principle inevitably gives way to expediency. The rights of individuals are always capable of being overridden. For such critics, only a non-consequentialist theory will do.

KANTIANISM: AN ETHIC OF DUTY

Non-consequentialism in ethics is often identified with an approach labelled 'deontological' (from the Greek for duty). Its classic, indeed definitive formulation, is that provided by the German philosopher Immanuel Kant (1724–1804). Although in many ways the diametric opposite of Bentham's utilitarianism, Kant's theory also makes the monistic claim that one thing and one thing only is 'good in itself'. The difference is that while for Bentham that one thing is happiness, for Kant it is a 'good will'. An action is morally right, according to Kant, only if the person performing it is motivated by a good will; morally wrong if it is not. The possession of such a will alone makes the action right; its absence alone makes it wrong. Nothing else matters.

What does Kant mean by a 'good will'? Essentially, he means the action is done for reasons of principle; from a sense of duty and nothing else. Self-interest can certainly not be the motive; but neither can kindness, loyalty, sympathy, or any other laudable sentiment. These are admirable things, says Kant, but they do not constitute a specifically moral motivation for acting. A sense of duty can alone provide that (hence the title 'deontological' for his theory).

How can we know when an act is done from a sense of duty? When, says Kant, it is done in accordance with what he calls the 'categorical imperative'. Kant expresses the categorical imperative in several ways, all of which are, he says, equivalent. Attention has, however, traditionally centred on just two definitions; and though they are certainly complementary, Kant's claim that they are equivalent is unconvincing. They are perhaps best seen as two separate but mutually supportive formulations of what constitutes the categorical imperative.

The first says:

'I ought never to act except in such a way that I can also will that my maxim should become a universal law.'[2]

The 'maxim' which Kant mentions is the principle on which I act. It may be either a good principle or a bad principle. If the personnel officer decides to break an employee's confidentiality, he or she might be acting on a maxim like, 'Whenever it is convenient to break a promise in circumstances such as this, I shall do so.' A more responsible decision on confidentiality might be expressed by a maxim like, 'When I am asked to disclose personal information, I will only disclose what is non-confidential.' In practice maxims may be more complicated than this; a personnel officer may wish to qualify circumstances in which he or she might exceptionally reveal confidential information, for example if the police asked for disclosure. But for the convenience of discussing Kant's philosophy, these relatively simple ones will suffice.

'Universalizing' a maxim basically means that the principle upon which we act (the maxim) should be one which we can, with consistency, wish all other people to act upon. Now, some maxims can be universalized, while others cannot. For example, it is perfectly possible for all personnel officers to maintain confidentiality concerning employees; we can conceive of all of them conscientiously doing this. But if we make a promise we have no intention of keeping, then the maxim on which we have acted is something like; 'When I make a promise I may subsequently decide whether or not to keep it.' But then, of course, the whole business of making promises becomes pointless, even nonsensical. The whole point of promises is that they ought to be kept. If everyone were free to break their promises when it suited them to do so then the practice of promise making would lose all purpose. It would become impossible to sustain. Consequently, the practice of promise breaking too would become meaningless. There would be nothing to be gained by it because there would be no expectation that promises are going to be kept. Hence the principle that we should make promises which we have no intention of keeping cannot be universalized. We cannot, as a matter of logical consistency, require everyone to act in that way. So actions performed under that maxim are contrary to the categorical imperative and therefore morally wrong. In contrast, there is no logical inconsistency in requiring that promises be made with the intention of keeping them. This is a maxim which can be universalized. So actions performed under

[2] Immanuel Kant, *Groundwork of the Metaphysic of Morals*; transl H. J. Paton (London: Harper and Row, 1964) p. 70.

it are in accordance with the categorical imperative and are therefore morally right.

Kant's second formulation of the categorical imperative is based on an idea which is nowadays called 'respect for persons'. At its simplest it contrasts human beings with objects: vegetables and minerals, chairs and tables. Objects have a merely instrumental value. They are things; their worth lies simply in the use to which human beings can put them. Human beings, on the other hand are persons. They are feeling, purposeful, rational, capable of having aims of their own which they can care for deeply. This, so the argument goes, means their lives have an intrinsic and not merely instrumental value. To deny this altogether, to treat people as being of purely instrumental value, is to deny their 'personhood'. It is to treat them as mere objects having no other purpose beyond the use to which they can be put. To do this, the argument goes on, is to act immorally. To act morally we must respect the personhood of people and never treat them simply as a means to an end but always, and primarily, as an end in themselves. As Kant puts it:

> 'Act in such a way that you always treat humanity . . . never simply as a means, but always at the same time as an end.'[3]

On either formulation Kantianism is distinguished from utilitarianism by the absence of any explicit and direct appeal to consequences in determining right and wrong. What is of central and perhaps sole importance is the motive for the action. With utilitarianism, in contrast, motives are incidental. They matter only in so far as they are conducive to performing actions which maximize utility. They are not, as they are with Kant, a good in themselves; but only as a means to the end of maximizing utility.

The result is a contrast of consequentialist flexibility and non-consequentialist inflexibility. It means that Kantianism is strong just where utilitarianism is weak and vice versa. Unlike utilitarianism, Kantianism would not permit the sacrificing of individuals or minorities to collective self-interest. This is not how we would expect to be treated ourselves and so such actions could not be universalized. They would also be actions which very clearly treated people simply as means to an end. The other side of this coin, of course, is that Kantianism can be accused of making no allowance for those extreme circumstances when, very arguably, the common good must have priority over everything

---

[3] *Ibid.*, p. 96.

else. In one of his earlier writings, for example, Kant stated that he disallowed all lying; even if an intending murderer were to ask us the whereabouts of his or her intended victim we would be obliged to tell the truth. Surely it is not only permitted but morally obligatory that we should lie to evil-doers to prevent them doing wrong? Also, and more seriously, faced with a choice between saving many lives at the price of sacrificing a few, is it not obligatory that we permit the sacrifice of the few – however much we would not want it done to ourselves or however much this is treating people simply as a means to an end?

Philosophers who defend Kant will point out that his insistence on universal truth telling appears in a very minor work which does not reflect his more mature position expressed in the *Groundwork of the Metaphysic of Morals*, and that the problem of whether or not to disclose information to intending murders can be solved by making the maxims on which we act rather more sophisticated than the simple formulae of 'Always tell the truth,' or 'Always keep your promises'. For example, one's maxim might be, 'I propose to tell the truth to those who seek information for honest purposes.' However, it is difficult to rule out qualifications which make nonsense of the idea of universalization; for example, why could not it be the personnel officer's maxim to tell the truth only to people who live, say, in Plymouth or Wolverhampton?

Another suggestion which is very much a modification of Kantianism is to allow for a difference between 'prima facie' and 'actual' obligations. We have a prima facie ('at first appearance') obligation to fulfil any moral duty, but whether it is actually performed depends on whether or not it conflicts with other, and perhaps more important, duties. If there is no conflict, the duty can and should be acted on. If there is a conflict, the most important duty is the one acted on. It becomes our actual duty while any other is set aside as merely a prima facie obligation. So, for example, our duty not to tell lies can be overridden by our duty to thwart wrongdoing, while our duty to not to permit innocent lives to be lost can be overridden by a duty to preserve the greatest number of lives we can.

Both moves to qualify maxims and this division into prima facie and actual duties are made to avoid unacceptable consequences from acting on principle alone. Conversely, the switch from act to rule utilitarianism would seem to be a move to introduce principles into what would otherwise be a simple calculation of consequences. In both cases the strengths of one theory are apparently being used to offset the weaknesses of the other.

NATURAL LAW: AN ETHIC OF RIGHTS

There is third tradition in ethical thinking which can be seen as complementary to Kantian deontologism. This is natural law doctrine. It has an immensely long history going back to classical times, has been variously interpreted, and has no single definitive version. Its distinctive feature however, at least since the seventeenth century, has been a concentration on rights. This arose because natural law theory was traditionally about protecting people from unjust or tyrannical actions by governments.

The basic idea was that over and above mere human law was an objective moral order, the 'natural law', which sets limits to the power of rulers. Governments which behaved unjustly transgressed that moral order. Their laws could, and in extreme cases should, be disobeyed. Gradually this idea became entwined with that of a 'contract' between government and governed; with governments being obliged to act within the natural law, and the governed obliged to obey them, provided they did.

By the seventeenth century a crucial modification was established. This was that the contract became 'social'. It was no longer deemed to be a contract between governments and people, but rather between the people themselves to set up and empower a government. With this the fundamental democratic principle of government by consent was established. An agreement of the people gave governments their power; and an agreement of the people, through the process of holding an election, could take that power away.

By this stage also, the idea of natural law was inextricably bound up with that of rights. In requiring justice of governments, the natural law conferred rights on the governed. In saying that certain things could not be done to people, the natural law was declaring that there were things they had a right to. The generally agreed list was life, liberty and, it was sometimes said, property. These were proclaimed as 'natural rights'; that is, rights bestowed on people by the natural law. As such, they were rights which governments could neither give nor take away. People possessed them simply in virtue of being human. They were, as we would now say, 'human rights'. The job of governments with regard to such rights was simply to recognize and protect them.

Many thinkers contributed to the developments leading up to this conclusion, but the key figure was almost certainly the British philosopher John Locke (1632–1714). After him, and perhaps partly because of him, it was a view of the role of governments which was put into practice by the American Declaration of Independence (1776) and the French Declaration of the Rights of Man (1789). While in the twentieth century, a plethora of declarations and conventions have committed governments to the recognition and protection of an ever-expanding list of 'human rights'. It includes the traditional generalities of life, liberty, justice, and sometimes property; but also the specifics of freedom of expression, belief, and association, as well as rights to education, welfare, fair trials, fair wages, and even holidays with pay.

The connection of such an ethic of rights with Kantianism is very strong. Firstly, the doctrine of respect for persons has an obvious affinity with that of human rights. In both there is a status common to all human beings which affords them protection from abuse by others. To infringe people's human rights is very much to fail to treat them as ends in themselves.

A second connection is perhaps less obvious. It lies in a certain logical correlativity between moral duty and human rights. Where there is a human right to be respected there is generally a moral duty to respect that right. The converse is perhaps less common in that it arguably admits of a frequent exception in the case of duties of benevolence: being kind, generous, charitable, and so on. We ought to be kind, generous and charitable, but arguably people have no right to demand this of us; there is no moral claim on us to behave towards them in this way. Following Kant, such merely optional duties of benevolence have come to be called 'imperfect'. The contrast is with 'perfect' duties which have to be fulfilled. These include all really important duties and with them there generally is a corresponding right. A duty not to murder, for example, is matched by a corresponding right to life. In such primary cases, duties and rights are but opposite sides of the same coin. Duties concern morality from the point of view of people performing an action; while rights concern morality from the point of view of people on the receiving end of the action. Kant's emphasis on duty can therefore be seen as complementary to the emphasis on rights provided by natural law doctrine.

This interpretation is supported by the third and perhaps most important point of contact between the two theories; which is that both are broadly non-consequentialist. Kantian duty imposes, we saw, a constraint on any unqualified adherence to the utilitarian goal of optimizing collective welfare. The same is no less true of the doctrine of human rights. We cannot sacrifice individuals and minorities to the common good when to do so would be to abuse their human rights – their right to life, liberty, justice, or whatever. Traditionally, the doctrine of human rights has been a bulwark not just against tyranny, but against any such single-minded pursuit of collective self-interest.

It follows from this third point that any uncompromising commitment to rights has the same problem of inflexibility as uncompromising Kantianism. It also is faced with the fact that in very extreme cases we do seem to be morally required to sacrifice individuals and minorities in order to preserve the common good. Most starkly, people do have a right to life but most would think it proper, if tragically regrettable, that a few lives should be sacrificed to save many.

The traditional natural law response to this dilemma parallels the deontologist's admission that duties can be merely prima facie. It is to allow that human rights are not absolute. They can be overridden. Some rights are more important than others. Faced with a clash, the more important right must prevail. A right to life, for example, will obviously override any right to property. Also, rights can be lost; we lose them when we fail to respect the rights of others. For example, we can lose our right to liberty (be imprisoned) when we fail to respect the rights of others to their property by stealing it from them. Perhaps most significantly, declarations of human rights will invariably accept that under extreme circumstances any and all rights can be set aside when the collective interest demands. This way, it is hoped, a commitment to human rights can be made compatible with the common good.

APPLYING ETHICAL THEORIES

None of the three theories seems adequate on its own; certainly not in any unqualified version. The aim of serving the common good has to be tempered by the admission of rights and duties. Rights and duties cannot generally be examined separately; and neither can be pursued regardless of any consideration of collective welfare. This would seem to point a tripartite approach to the resolution of moral problems where the general aim of optimizing collective welfare is pursued but with due allowance given to duties on the one hand, and rights on the other.

With regard to welfare, the first and most basic question to be asked is how will the action at issue affect the common good? What is its likely degree of utility or disutility? In making this calculation we can set aside the issue of whether, as hedonistic utilitarianism claims, it is all comes down to happiness and unhappiness. Whether it does or not, many things must still be recognized as good or bad for human beings, even if, in the last analysis, they all reduce to happiness or unhappiness. What we must also do in making this calculation is to look at those general rules which have, over time, been found to promote and protect collective welfare. We must not easily set them aside because of the contingencies of a particular situation. We must bear in mind that a general adherence to such rules is itself an important contributor to collective welfare; perhaps the most important contributor. Any exception to that general adherence will therefore require a powerful justification. In addition, the distribution of the resulting welfare must be considered. Who gets what kind of benefit or harm and to what extent? Have people received what is just? Finally, the relative distribution of benefits as opposed to harm must be considered. We must allow that the two are not equal; disutility carries greater moral weight than utility. The pain and deprivation of even a few, when it is severe enough, can count for more than the pleasure and privilege of the many. The relief of suffering and the avoidance of harm must therefore have a degree of priority over any maintenance or addition of benefits in calculations of collective welfare.

With duties the issue of motive is brought to the fore. When we act from duty we not only aim to do the right thing but to do it for the right reason. Acting from duty means that we deserve moral credit for our actions – and the benefits which might follow. In examining our motives, the test of universalizability is a useful guide. It will help determine whether we act from duty or purely self-interest. In the event of a conflict of duties, we can use the test of relative importance to separate the actual from the merely prima facie. While to separate the perfect from the merely imperfect, we can appeal to the presence or absence (respectively) of a corresponding right.

With regard to rights, the test of respect for persons will provide a guide to determine when rights exist and when they might be abused. Although there can be profound arguments about the specifics, it can be accepted that certain fundamental conditions must be met for persons' lives to flourish and be fulfilled. These fundamental conditions constitute the things to which all human beings have a right. They are their human rights. There is an abuse of human rights when these fundamental conditions are denied: when liberty, justice, security, and even life itself, are taken away. Then, as Kant puts it, people are treated as means rather than ends. Because different rights serve different ends, they can be in conflict. When they do then, as with duties, the most fundamental must be given priority.

With regard to both duties and rights, there is a broad distinction to be made between a very general kind which usually hold good for all human beings, and those which are specific to a particular social role. For example, and most pertinently for our purposes, there are duties or rights specific to roles as manager, director, partner, shareholder, employer, employee, customer, supplier and so on.

The point, of course, about these 'role-specific' duties or rights is that not everyone has them. They come, as it were, with the job. They are commitments and claims over and above those we all generally have. They do not, contrary to a frequently given excuse, replace or override our general moral duties and rights. Rather, they add to or supplement them. They are essentially an extension of our general moral duties and rights, imposing an additional responsibility here, awarding an extra privilege there, but always requiring to be broadly consistent with more fundamental principles.

Indeed, they derive their legitimacy from that consistency. We are morally bound by them because they are an extension of more fundamental duties and rights. The duty of a manager to ensure safe working conditions, for example, is largely an extension of the general moral duty to preserve and protect the lives of our fellow human beings. Consequently, such role-specific moral rules are binding only insofar as they are broadly consistent with the more fundamental kind from which they derive their legitimacy. To choose an admittedly extreme example, it did no good for defendants at the post-war Nuremberg trials to say their duties as officials of the Third Reich exempted them from responsibility for Nazi atrocities, or that their rights as citizens of a sovereign nation denied the court authority over them.

Given the restricted nature of role-specific duties and rights, the tests of universalizability and respect for persons (respectively) are not generally applicable. They are tests designed to reveal moral rules which will hold good for all human beings. By definition, role-specific duties and rights do not. All the other considerations mentioned do, however, apply to them. Role-specific duties can conflict and must therefore be divided into 'actual' and 'prima facie'; and they can also divide into 'perfect' and 'imperfect'. Likewise, role-specific rights are as capable of conflict as any other and so might need to be ranked in order of importance. For example, in the event of a conflict between responsibilities towards workers and an obligation to advance the interests of shareholders, a manager must determine an actual duty; and while responsibility for safe working conditions are likely to constitute a perfect duty (assuming a corresponding right), there is perhaps only an imperfect duty to make generous welfare provision for workers (assuming there is no corresponding right). Likewise, given the right of workers to safe working conditions and also right of shareholders to profits on their investment, these are rights which could be in conflict and the manager might well be in the position of deciding which one should prevail.

Taking all the above points together, the following checklist for moral evaluation emerges.

For welfare
1. Calculate the utility and disutility of actions;
2. try to maintain socially beneficial rules;
3. try to achieve a just distribution of benefits and harm;
4. give more weight to harm than benefits.

For duties
1. Examine motives (to determine the moral credit deserved);
2. apply the test of universalizability to motives (to help determine general moral duties);
3. distinguish actual from prima facie duties via the test of relative importance;
4. distinguish perfect from imperfect duties via the test of correlative rights;
5. recognize role-specific duties.

For rights
1. Apply the test of respect for persons (to help determine fundamental moral rights);
2. when rights conflict, use the test of relative importance;
3. recognize role-specific rights.

INTRODUCING THE READINGS

The much anthologized reading from Albert Z. Carr supports a kind of moral relativism by arguing that the moral rules governing business are different from, and less restrictrive than, those governing society at large. This point of view is strongly opposed in the second reading by Norman E. Bowie, who argues that, whether judged from a Kantian or utilitarian perspective, Carr's defence of deception in business is morally unacceptable. The third reading is a detailed defence of rule utilitarianism by John C. Harsanyi. He argues, in particular, that the rule version of utilitarianism can satisfactorily account for moral duties and rights. The final reading introduces a different ethical perspective to those dealt with in chapter 3. In it, Joseph R. DesJardins argues for the applicability of a virtue based ethic for business. Here the emphasis is not on the nature or results of actions (as determined by considerations of duty and rights or utility), but on the moral character of the person performing the action (an approach associated with the great Greek philosopher Aristotle, 384–322 BC). DesJardins makes the interesting connection between such a virtue based ethics and the idea of 'business excellence' (as advocated by Peters and Waterman in their best-selling book, *In Search of Excellence*). This, he says, entails businesses adopting what he calls the 'professional' view of people's roles within the organization, whereby their work is seen as fulfilling the purpose intrinsic to the business function (providing goods and services for the public good) rather than as a merely 'instrumental' means to some extrinsic end such as the securing of profits or even wages.

Is business bluffing ethical?

ALBERT CARR

A respected businessman with whom I discussed the theme of this article remarked with some heat, 'You mean to say you're going to encourage men to bluff? Why, bluffing is nothing more than a form of lying! You're advising them to lie!'

I agreed that the basis of private morality is a respect for truth and that the closer a businessman comes to truth, the more he deserves respect. At the same time, I suggested that most bluffing in business might be regarded simply as game strategy – much like bluffing in poker which does not reflect on the morality of the bluffer.

I quoted Henry Taylor, the British statesman who pointed out that 'falsehood ceases to be falsehood when it is understood on all sides that the truth is not expected to be spoken' – an exact description of bluffing in poker, diplomacy, and business. I cited the analogy of the criminal court, where the criminal is not expected to tell the truth when he pleads 'not guilty.' Everyone from the judge down takes it for granted that the job of the defendant's attorney is to get his client off, not to reveal the truth; and this is considered ethical practice. I mentioned Representative Omar Burleson, the Democrat from Texas, who was quoted as saying, in regard to the ethics of Congress, 'Ethics is a barrel of worms' – a pungent summing-up of the problem of deciding who is ethical in politics. I reminded my friend that millions of businessmen feel constrained every day to say *yes* to their bosses when they secretly believe *no* and that this is generally accepted as permissible strategy when the alternative might be the loss of a job. The essential point, I said, is that the ethics of business are game ethics, different from the ethics of religion.

He remained unconvinced. Referring to the company of which he is president, he declared: 'Maybe that's good enough for some businessmen, but I can tell you that we pride ourselves on our ethics. In 30 years not one customer has ever questioned my word or asked to check our figures. We're loyal to our customers and fair to our suppliers. I regard my handshake on a deal as a contract. I've never entered into price-fixing schemes with my competitors. I've never allowed my salesmen to spread injurious rumors about other companies. Our union contract is the best in our industry. And, if I do say so myself, our ethical standards are of the highest!'

He really was saying, without saying it, that he was living up to the ethical standards of the business game – which are a far cry from those of private life. Like a gentlemanly poker player, he did not play in cahoots with others at the table, try to smear their reputations, or hold back chips he owed them.

But this same fine man, at the very time, was allowing one of his products to be advertised in a way that made it sound a great deal better than it actually was. Another item in his product line was notorious among dealers for its 'built-in

Reading taken from *Harvard Business Review*, Jan.–Feb. 1968. Copyright © 1968 Harvard Business Review.

obsolescence.' He was holding back from the market a much-improved product because he did not want it to interfere with sales of the inferior item it would have replaced. He had joined with certain of his competitors in hiring a lobbyist to push a state legislature, by methods that he preferred not to know too much about, into amending a bill then being enacted.

In his view these things had nothing to do with ethics; they were merely normal business practice. He himself undoubtedly avoided out-right falsehood – never lied in so many words. But the entire organization that he ruled was deeply involved in numerous strategies of deception.

PRESSURE TO DECEIVE

Most executives from time to time are almost compelled, in the interests of their companies or themselves, to practice some form of deception when negotiating with customers, dealers, labor unions, government officials, or even other departments of their companies. By conscious misstatements, concealment of pertinent facts, or exaggeration – in short, by bluffing – they seek to persuade others to agree with them. I think it is fair to say that if the individual executive refuses to bluff from time to time – if he feels obligated to tell the truth, the whole truth, and nothing but the truth – he is ignoring opportunities permitted under the rules and is at a heavy disadvantage in his business dealings.

But here and there a businessman is unable to reconcile himself to the bluff in which he plays a part. His conscience, perhaps spurred by religious idealism, troubles him. He feels guilty; he may develop an ulcer or a nervous tic. Before any executive can make profitable use of the strategy of the bluff, he needs to make sure that in bluffing he will not lose self-respect or become emotionally disturbed. If he is to reconcile personal integrity and high standards of honesty with the practical requirements of business, he must feel that his bluffs are ethically justified. The justification rests on the fact that business, as practiced by individuals as well as by corporations, has the impersonal character of a game – a game that demands both special strategy and an understanding of its special ethics.

The game is played at all levels of corporate life, from the highest to the lowest. At the very instant that a man decides to enter business, he may be forced into a game situation, as is shown by the recent experience of a Cornell honor graduate who applied for a job with a large company.

This applicant was given a psychological test which included the statement, 'Of the following magazines, check any that you have read either regularly or from time to time, and double-check those which interest you most. *Reader's Digest, Time, Fortune, Saturday Evening Post, The New Republic, Life, Look, Ramparts, Newsweek, Business Week, U.S. News & World Report, The Nation, Playboy, Esquire, Harper's, Sports Illustrated.*'

His tastes in reading were broad, and at one time or another he had read almost all of these magazines. He was a subscriber to *The New Republic*, an enthusiast for *Ramparts*, and an avid student of the pictures in *Playboy*. He was not sure whether his interest in *Playboy* would be held against him, but he had a shrewd suspicion that if he confessed to an interest in *Ramparts* and *The New Republic*, he would be thought a liberal, a radical, or at least an intellectual, and his chances of getting the job, which he needed, would greatly diminish. He therefore checked five of the more conservative magazines. Apparently it was a sound decision, for he got the job.

He had made a game player's decision, consistent with business ethics.

A similar case is that of a magazine space salesman who, owing to a merger, suddenly found himself out of a job.

This man was 58, and, in spite of a good record, his chance of getting a job elsewhere in a business where youth is favored in hiring practice was not good. He was a vigorous, healthy man, and only a considerable amount of gray in his hair suggested his age. Before beginning his job search he touched up his hair with a black dye to confine the gray to his temples. He knew that the truth about his age might well come out in time, but he calculated that he could deal with that situation when it arose. He and his wife decided that he could easily pass for 45, and he so stated his age on his resume.

This was a lie; yet within the accepted rules of the business game, no moral culpability attaches to it.

THE POKER ANALOGY

We can learn a good deal about the nature of business by comparing it with poker. While both have a large element of chance, in the long run the winner is the man who plays with steady skill. In both games ultimate victory requires intimate knowledge of the rules, insights into the psychology of the other players, a bold front, a considerable amount of self-discipline, and the ability to respond swiftly and effectively to opportunities provided by chance.

No one expects poker to be played on the ethical principles preached in churches. In poker it is right and proper to bluff a friend out of the rewards of being dealt a good hand. A player feels no more than a slight twinge of sympathy, if that, when – with nothing better than a single ace in his hand – he strips a heavy loser, who holds a pair, of the rest of his chips. It was up to the other fellow to protect himself. In the words of an excellent poker player, former President Harry Truman, 'If you can't stand the heat, get out of the kitchen.' If one shows mercy to a loser in poker, it is a personal gesture, divorced from the rules of the game.

Poker has its special ethics, and here I am not referring to rules against cheating. The man who keeps an ace up his sleeve or who marks the cards is more than unethical; he is a crook, and can be punished as such – kicked out of the game or, in the Old West, shot.

In contrast to the cheat, the unethical poker player is one who, while abiding by the letter of the rules, finds ways to put the other players at an unfair disadvantage. Perhaps he unnerves them with loud talk. Or he tries to get them drunk. Or he plays in cahoots with someone else at the table. Ethical poker players frown on such tactics.

Poker's own brand of ethics is different from the ethical ideals of civilized human relationships. The game calls for distrust of the other fellow. It ignores the claim of friendship. Cunning deception and concealment of one's strength and intentions, not kindness and openheartedness, are vital in poker. No one thinks any worse of poker on that account. And no one should think any worse of the game of business because its standards of right and wrong differ from the prevailing traditions of morality in our society.

DISCARD THE GOLDEN RULE

This view of business is especially worrisome to people without much business experience. A minister of my acquaintance once protested that business cannot possibly function in our society unless it is based on the Judeo-Christian system of ethics. He told me:

> I know some businessmen have supplied call girls to customers, but there are always a few rotten apples in every barrel. That doesn't mean the rest of the fruit isn't sound. Surely the vast majority of businessmen are ethical. I myself am acquainted with many who adhere to strict codes of ethics based fundamentally on religious teachings. They contribute to good causes. They participate in community activities. They cooperate with other companies to improve working conditions in their industries. Certainly they are not indifferent to ethics.

That most businessmen are not indifferent to ethics in their private lives, everyone will agree. My point is that in their office lives they cease to be private citizens; they become game players who must be guided by a somewhat different set of ethical standards.

The point was forcefully made to me by a Midwestern executive who has given a good deal of thought to the question:

> So long as a businessman complies with the laws of the land and avoids telling malicious lies, he's ethical. If the law as written gives a man a wide-open chance to make a killing, he'd be a fool not to take advantage of it. If he doesn't, somebody else will. There's no obligation on him to stop and consider who is going to get hurt. If the law says he can do it, that's all the justification he needs. There's nothing unethical about that. It's just plain business sense.

This executive (call him Robbins) took the stand that even industrial espionage, which is frowned on by some businessmen, ought not to be considered unethical. He recalled a recent meeting of the National Industrial Conference Board where an authority on marketing made a speech in which he deplored the employment of spies by business organizations. More and more companies, he pointed out, find it cheaper to penetrate the secrets of competitors with concealed cameras and microphones or by bribing employees than to set up costly research and design departments of their own. A whole branch of the electronics industry has grown up with this trend, he continued, providing equipment to make industrial espionage easier.

Disturbing? The marketing expert found it so. But when it came to a remedy, he could only appeal to 'respect for the golden rule.' Robbins thought this a confession of defeat, believing that the golden rule, for all its value as an ideal for society, is simply not feasible as a guide for business. A good part of the time the businessman is trying to do unto others as he hopes others will *not* do unto him. Robbins continued:

> Espionage of one kind or another has become so common in business that it's like taking a drink during Prohibition – it's not considered sinful. And we don't even have Prohibition where espionage is concerned; the law is very tolerant in this area. There's no more shame for a business that uses secret agents than there is for a nation. Bear in mind that there already is at least one large corporation – you can buy its stock over the counter – that makes millions by providing counterespionage service to industrial firms. Espionage in business is not an ethical problem; it's an established technique of business competition.

'WE DON'T MAKE THE LAWS'

Wherever we turn in business, we can perceive the sharp distinction between its ethical standards and those of the churches. Newspapers abound with sensational stories growing out of this distinction:

> We read one day that Senator Philip A. Hart of Michigan has attacked food processors for deceptive packaging of numerous products.
> The next day there is a Congressional to-do over Ralph Nader's book, *Unsafe at Any Speed*, which demonstrates that automobile companies for years have neglected the safety of car-owning families.
> Then another Senator, Lee Metcalf of Montana, and journalist Vic Reinemer show in their book, *Overcharge*, the methods by which utility companies elude regulating government bodies to extract unduly large payments from users of electricity.

These are merely dramatic instances of a prevailing condition; there is hardly a major industry at which a similar attack could not be aimed. Critics of business regard such behavior as unethical, but the companies concerned know that they are merely playing the business game.

Among the most respected of our business institutions are the insurance companies. A group of insurance executives meeting recently in New England was startled when their guest speaker, social critic Daniel Patrick Moynihan, roundly berated them for 'unethical' practices. They had been guilty, Moynihan alleged, of using outdated actuarial tables to obtain unfairly high premiums. They habitually delayed the hearings of lawsuits against them in order to tire out the plaintiffs and win cheap settlements. In their employment policies they used ingenious devices to discriminate against certain minority groups.

It was difficult for the audience to deny the validity of these charges. But these men were business game players. Their reaction to Moynihan's attack was much the same as that of the automobile manufacturers to Nader, of the utilities to Senator Metcalf, and of the food processors to Senator Hart. If the laws governing their businesses change, or if public opinion becomes clamorous, they will make the necessary adjustments. But morally they have in their view done nothing wrong. As long as they comply with the letter of the law, they are within their rights to operate their businesses as they see fit.

The small business is in the same position as the great corporation in this respect. For example:

> In 1967 a key manufacturer was accused of providing master keys for auto-mobiles to mail-order customers, although it was obvious that some of the purchasers might be automobile thieves. His defense was plain and straightfor-ward. If there was nothing in the law to prevent him from selling his keys to anyone who ordered them, it was not up to him to inquire as to his customers' motives. Why was it any worse, he insisted, for him to sell car keys by mail, than for mailorder houses to sell guns that might be used for murder? Until the law was changed, the key manufacturer could regard himself as being just as ethical as any other businessman by the rules of the business game.

Violations of the ethical ideals of society are common in business, but they are not necessarily violations of business principles. Each year the Federal Trade Com-mission orders hundreds of companies, many of them of the first magnitude, to 'cease and desist' from practices which, judged by ordinary standards, are of ques-tionable morality but which are stoutly defended by the companies concerned.

In one case, a firm manufacturing a wellknown mouthwash was accused of using a cheap form of alcohol possibly deleterious to health. The company's chief executive, after testifying in Washington, made this comment privately:

> We broke no law. We're in a highly competitive industry. If we're going to stay in business, we have to look for profit wherever the law permits. We don't make the laws. We obey them. Then why do we have to put up with this 'holier than thou' talk about ethics? It's sheer hypocrisy. We're not in business to promote ethics. Look at the cigarette companies, for God's sake! If the ethics aren't embodied in the laws by the men who made them, you can't expect businessmen to fill the lack. Why, a sudden submission to Christian ethics by businessmen would bring about the greatest economic upheaval in history!

It may be noted that the government failed to prove its case against him.

CAST ILLUSIONS ASIDE

Talking about ethics by businessmen is often a thin decorative coating over the hard realities of the game:

> Once I listened to a speech by a young executive who pointed to a new industry code as proof that his company and its competitors were deeply aware of their responsibilities to society. It was a code of ethics, he said. The industry was going to police itself, to dissuade constituent companies from wrongdoing. His eyes shone with conviction and enthusiasm.
>
> The same day there was a meeting in a hotel room where the industry's top executives met with the 'czar' who was to administer the new code, a man of high repute. No one who was present could doubt their common attitude. In their eyes the code was designed primarily to forestall a move by the federal government to impose stern restrictions on the industry. They felt that the code would hamper them a good deal less than new federal laws would. It was, in other words, conceived as a protection for the industry, not for the public.
>
> The young executive accepted the surface explanation of the code; these leaders, all experienced game players, did not deceive themselves for a moment about its purpose.

The illusion that business can afford to be guided by ethics as conceived in private life is often fostered by speeches and articles containing such phrases as, 'It pays to be ethical,' or, 'Sound ethics is good business.' Actually this is not an ethical position at all; it is a self-serving calculation in disguise. The speaker is really saying that in the long run a company can make more money if it does not antagonize competitors, suppliers, employees, and customers by squeezing them too hard. He is saying that oversharp policies reduce ultimate gains. That is true, but it has nothing to do with ethics. The underlying attitude is much like that in the familiar story of the shop-keeper who finds an extra $20 bill in the cash register, debates with himself the ethical problem – should he tell his partner? – and finally decides to share the money because the gesture will give him an edge over the s.o.b. the next time they quarrel.

I think it is fair to sum up the prevailing attitude of businessmen on ethics as follows:

We live in what is probably the most competitive of the world's civilized societies. Our customs encourage a high degree of aggression in the individuals' striving for success. Business is our main area of competition, and it has been ritualized into a game of strategy. The basic rules of the game have been set by the government, which attempts to detect and punish business frauds. But as long as a company does not transgress the rules of the game set by law, it has the legal right to shape its strategy without reference to anything but its profits. If it takes a long-term view of its profits, it will preserve amicable relations, so far as possible, with those with whom it deals. A wise businessman will not seek advantage to the point where he generates dangerous hostility among employees, competitors, customers, government, or the public at large. But decisions in this area are, in the final test, decisions of strategy, not of ethics.

THE INDIVIDUAL AND THE GAME

An individual within a company often finds it difficult to adjust to the requirements of the business game. He tries to preserve his private ethical standards in situations that call for game strategy. When he is obliged to carry out the company policies that challenge his conception of himself as an ethical man, he suffers.

It disturbs him when he is ordered, for instance, to deny a raise to a man who deserves it, to fire an employee of long standing, to prepare advertising that he believes to be misleading, to conceal facts that he feels customers are entitled to know, to cheapen the quality of materials used in the manufacture of an established product, to sell as a new product that he knows to be rebuilt, to exaggerate the curative powers of a medicinal preparation, or to coerce dealers.

There are some fortunate executives, who, by the nature of their work and circumstances, never have to face problems of this kind. But in one form or another the ethical dilemma is felt sooner or later by most businessmen. Possibly the dilemma is most painful not when the company forces the action on the executive but when he originates it himself – that is, when he has taken or is contemplating a step which is in his own interest but which runs counter to his early moral conditioning. To illustrate:

> The manager of an export department, eager to show rising sales, is pressed by a big customer to provide invoices, which, while containing no overt falsehood that would violate a U.S. law, are so worded that the customer may be able to evade certain taxes in his homeland.
>
> A company president finds that an aging executive, within a few years of retirement and his pension, is not as productive as formerly. Should he be kept on?
>
> The produce manager of a supermarket debates with himself whether to get rid of a lot of half-rotten tomatoes by including one, with its good side exposed, in every tomato sixpack.
>
> An accountant discovers that he has taken an improper deduction on his company's tax return and fears the consequences if he calls the matter to the president's attention, though he himself has done nothing illegal. Perhaps if he says nothing, no one will notice the error.
>
> A chief executive officer is asked by his directors to comment on a rumor that he owns stock in another company with which he has placed large orders. He could deny it, for the stock is in the name of his son-in-law and he has earlier formally instructed his son-in-law to sell the holding.

Temptations of this kind constantly arise in business. If an executive allows himself to be torn between a decision based on business considerations and one based on his private ethical code, he exposes himself to a grave psychological strain.

This is not to say that sound business strategy necessarily runs counter to ethical ideals. They may frequently coincide; and when they do, everyone is gratified. But the major tests of every move in business, as in all games of strategy, are legality and profit. A man who intends to be a winner in the business game must have a game player's attitude.

The business strategist's decisions must be as impersonal as those of a surgeon performing an operation – concentrating on objective and technique, and subordinating personal feelings. If the chief executive admits that his son-in-law owns the stock, it is because he stands to lose more if the fact comes out later than if he states it boldly and at once. If the supermarket manager orders the rotten tomatoes to be discarded, he does so to avoid an increase in consumer complaints and a loss of good will. The company president decides not to fire the elderly executive in the belief that the negative reaction of other employees would in the long run cost the company more than it would lose in keeping him and paying his pension.

All sensible businessmen prefer to be truthful, but they seldom feel inclined to tell the *whole* truth. In the business game truth-telling usually has to be kept within narrow limits if trouble is to be avoided. The point was neatly made a long time ago (in 1888) by one of John D. Rockefeller's associates, Paul Babcock, to Standard Oil Company executives who were about to testify before a government investigating committee: 'Parry every question with answers which, while perfectly truthful, are evasive of *bottom* facts.' This was, is, and probably always will be regarded as wise and permissible business strategy.

FOR OFFICE USE ONLY

An executive's family life can easily be dislocated if he fails to make a sharp distinction between the ethical systems of the home and the office – or if his wife does not grasp that distinction. Many a businessman who has remarked to his wife 'I had to let Jones go today' or 'I had to admit to the boss that Jim has been goofing off lately,' has been met with an indignant protest. 'How could you do a thing like that? You know Jones is over 50 and will have a lot of trouble getting another job.' Or, 'You did that to Jim? With his wife ill and all the worry she's having with the kids?'

If the executive insists that he had no choice because the profits of the company and his own security were involved, he may see a certain cool and ominous reappraisal in his wife's eyes. Many wives are not prepared to accept the fact that business operates with a special code of ethics. An illuminating illustration of this comes from a Southern sales executive who related a conversation he had had with his wife at a time when a hotly contested political campaign was being waged in their state:

> I made the mistake of telling her that I had had lunch with Colby, who gives me about half my business. Colby mentioned that his company had a stake in the election. Then he said, 'By the way, I'm treasurer of the citizens' committee for Lang. I'm collecting contributions. Can I count on you for a hundred dollars?'

Well, there I was. I was opposed to Lang, but I knew Colby. If he withdrew his business I could be in a bad spot. So I just smiled and wrote out a check then and there. He thanked me, and we started to talk about his next order. Maybe he thought I shared his political views. I wasn't going to lose any sleep over it.

I should have had sense enough not to tell Mary about it. She hit the ceiling. She said she was disappointed in me. She said I hadn't acted like a man, that I should have stood up to Colby.

I said, 'Look, it was an either/or situation. I had to do it or risk losing the business.'

She came back at me with: 'I don't believe it. You could have been honest with him. You could have said that you didn't feel you ought to contribute to a campaign for a man you weren't going to vote for. I'm sure he would have understood.'

I said, 'Mary, you're a wonderful woman, but you're way off the track. Do you know what would have happened if I had said that? Colby would have smiled and said, "Oh, I didn't realize. Forget it." But in his eyes from that moment I would be an oddball, maybe a bit of a radical. He would have listened to me talk about his order and would have promised to give it consideration. After that I wouldn't hear from him for a week. Then I would telephone and learn from his secretary that he wasn't yet ready to place the order. And in about a month I would hear through the grapevine that he was giving his business to another company. A month after that I'd be out of a job.'

She was silent for a while. Then she said, 'Tom, something is wrong with business when a man is forced to choose between his family's security and his moral obligation to himself. It's easy for me to say you should have stood up to him – but if you had, you might have felt you were betraying me and the kids. I'm sorry that you did it, Tom, but I can't blame you. Something is wrong with business!'

This wife saw the problem in terms of moral obligation as conceived in private life: her husband saw it as a matter of game strategy. As a player in a weak position, he felt that he could not afford to indulge an ethical sentiment that might have cost him his seat at the table.

PLAYING TO WIN

Some men might challenge the Colbys of business – might accept serious setbacks to their business careers rather than risk a feeling of moral cowardice. They merit out respect – but as private individuals, not businessmen. When the skillful player of the business game is compelled to submit to unfair pressure, he does not castigate himself for moral weakness. Instead, he strives to put himself into a strong position where he can defend himself against such pressures in the future without loss.

If a man plans to take a seat in the business game, he owes it to himself to master the principles by which the game is played, including its special ethical outlook. He can then hardly fail to recognize that an occasional bluff may well be justified in terms of the game's ethics and warranted in terms of economic necessity. Once he clears his mind on this point, he is in a good position to match his strategy against that of the other players. He can then determine objectively whether a bluff in a given situation has a good chance of succeeding and can decide when and how to bluff, without a feeling of ethical transgression.

To be a winner, a man must play to win. This does not mean that he must be ruthless, cruel, harsh, or treacherous. On the contrary, the better his reputation for integrity, honesty, and decency, the better his chances of victory will be in the long run. But from time to time every businessman, like every poker player, is offered a choice between certain loss or bluffing within the legal rules of the game. If he is not resigned to losing, if he wants to rise in his company and industry, then in such a crisis he will bluff – and bluff hard.

Every now and then one meets a successful businessman who has conveniently forgotten the small or large deceptions that he practiced on his way to fortune. 'God gave me my money,' old John D. Rockefeller once piously told a Sunday school class. It would be a rare tycoon in our time who would risk the horse laugh with which such a remark would be greeted.

In the last third of the twentieth century even children are aware that if a man has become prosperous in business, he has sometimes departed from the strict truth in order to overcome obstacles or has practiced the more subtle deceptions of the half-truth or the misleading omission. Whatever the form of the bluff, it is an integral part of the game, and the executive who does not master its techniques is not likely to accumulate much money or power.

Does it pay to bluff in business?

NORMAN E. BOWIE

I

Albert Carr has argued in an influential article[1] that the ethics of business is best understood on the model of the ethics of poker.

> Poker's own brand of ethics is different from the ethical ideals of civilized human relationships. The game calls for distrust of the other fellow. It ignores the claim of friendship. Cunning deception and concealment of one's strength and intentions, not kindness and openheartedness, are vital in poker.
>
> Most executives from time to time are almost compelled in the interests

of their companies or themselves to practice some form of deception when negotiating with customers, dealers, labor unions, government officials, or even the departments of their companies. By conscious misstatements, concealment of pertinent facts, or exaggeration – in short, by bluffing – they seek to persuade others to agree with them. . . . A good part of the time the businessman is trying to do unto others as he hopes others will not do unto him. . . . A man who intends to be a winner in the business game must have a game player's attitude.

Although Carr's attitude is widely held, I think Carr's argument can be refuted. I begin with an appeal to Kant's ethics in order to show that unless business adheres to a minimum standard of justice, business practice would be impossible. In particular I will show that such practices as lying, cheating, and bribery are immoral and that business practice presupposes that such practices are immoral. I then consider a Carr-like two pronged rebuttal of the Kantian analysis – specifically that as a matter of fact business practice succeeds quite well with a certain amount of lying and cheating and that whatever the case against outright lying and cheating, in some institutions a certain amount of deception and nondisclosure of information might be morally permissible. In responding to this rebuttal, I appeal to utilitarian considerations to show that when Carr's poker model is adopted, bad consequences result. Deception and the nondisclosure of information are usually counterproductive in terms of long-term profit.

The first step of my argument is based on the moral philosophy of Immanuel Kant, particularly on Kant's first formulation of the categorical imperative.[2] Kant argues that a requirement of morality is consistency in action. Suppose that someone were to advocate discriminatory policies against Jews. To be consistent, that person would have to advocate discrimination even if he himself should turn out to be a Jew. Presumably, he would not be willing to be treated discriminatorily, and hence consistency in action requires that he not treat Jews in a discriminatory way. Morality is not simply a matter of treating others as you would like them to treat you. It is also a matter of not treating others in ways that you would not accept if you were they. Kant's point is that morality requires consistency of action and judgment when you are on both the receiving and the giving ends. Morality requires that you not make an exception of yourself, that you not engage in practices or follow rules that you could not recommend to everyone.

But suppose one were to reply to Kant as follows: 'I don't care if other people try to take advantage of the rules by making exceptions of themselves. If they can get away with it, more power to them.' In the business context, such a person would be willing to participate in a business environment in which deception is expected. This is precisely the position of Carr. In situations like this, the Golden Rule fails us. The answer it gives depends on how the person contemplating a given action wants to be treated himself or herself. Suppose the way in which one wants to be treated is immoral in itself – suppose one doesn't care if others try to deceive him or her. Such a business person could be consistent in action and still behave unjustly. How could Kant reply?

Kant has a ready answer. Some contemplated actions would be self-defeating if they were universalized. Kant's categorical imperative strengthens the Golden Rule so that the person who is willing to allow others to behave unjustly is defeated. Kant's categorical imperative says, 'I ought never to act except in such a way that I can also will that my maxim should become a universal law.' To use one of Kant's examples, consider whether or not a businessperson should tell a lie. If the business-person were to make the principle of her action a universal law, namely 'lying is permissible,' the act of lying would be self-defeating. For if lying were universally permitted, people would never know whether an assertion was true or false, and hence both the purpose of telling the truth and of lying would be defeated. Lying is possible only when it is not made universal.

Kant's point can apply specifically to business. There are many ways of making a promise. One of the more formal ways is by a contract. A contract is an agreement between two or more parties, usually enforceable by law, for the doing or not doing of some definite thing. The contract device is extremely useful in business. The hiring of employees, the use of credit, the ordering and supplying of goods, and the notion of warranty, to name but a few, all make use of the contract device. Indeed, the contract is such an important part of business operation that it is often overlooked. This is a serious blunder. I maintain that, if contract breaking were universalized, then business practice would be impossible. If a participant in business were to universally advocate violating contracts, such advocacy would be self-defeating, just as the universal advocacy of lying and cheating were seen to be self-defeating.

But Carr could correctly point out that he never advocated the breaking of contracts. He simply advocates the nondisclosure of information, bluffing, and the calculated use of exaggeration. Does this narrow interpretation of Carr's thesis enable him to escape Kant's trap? Perhaps not.

Let us take a simple business transaction and move on to more complicated ones. In almost every case of a cash-for-product transaction, either the purchaser receives the good before paying or the purchaser pays before receiving the good. Seldom is the transfer simultaneous. What would happen to business if, in an attempt to receive something for nothing, it was common practice for the purchaser to claim that he or she had paid when he or she had not, in other words, to bluff. Or suppose the salesperson bluffed by claiming that the customer had not paid when he or she had paid. If such behavior were universalized, ordinary commerce would become self-defeating. The modern grocery or department store could not exist if such bluffing were universalized, and hence the bluffers have nothing to gain if bluffing is universally advocated.

Kant's argument is meant to show that rational agents cannot will that certain maxims be universally acted upon. If the principles were universally adopted, the behavior described by the principles would be self-defeating. The maxim, 'It's morally permissible to lie' is a perfect example of just such a principle.

But does Kant's argument really apply in the bluffing example? There is nothing self-defeating about a world with no grocery stores or supermarkets. However, the observation misses Kant's larger point. A Kantian could argue that the acceptance of any practice requires acceptance of the rules that constitute the practice. To accept the practice without accepting the rules that underlie it is self-defeating. If you break the rules, consistency requires that you permit others to break the rules, and such universal rule breaking would undermine the practice. One purpose of the preceding discussion was to show how lying and bluffing undercut business practice. Since such actions cannot be universalized from the Kantian perspective, lying and bluffing by business persons is immoral.

II

Does this Kantian argument refute Carr's analysis? Many philosophers would think not. First, one does not need extensive experience in business to know that there are many types of deception, like bluffing, that are both widely practiced and widely accepted. A few examples suffice. It is common knowledge that automobile dealers do not expect people to pay the sticker price for automobiles. A certain amount of bargaining is taken for granted. The same is true for real estate prices. Unless a seller's market is in effect, the asking price for a house is seldom the selling price. At the initial bargaining session, labor leaders overstate wage demands, and management also understates the wage increases it is willing to grant. In all these instances, the final price or wage contract is arrived at through a process that does resemble the poker game Carr uses as an analogy. The price or wage contract does depend in part on the strength of one's hand and on one's bluffing ability. In the late 1970s, one did need to pay the sticker price for small foreign cars with good gas mileage.

Surely automobile dealers and sellers of homes cannot be accused of immoral behavior when they post prices above those that they are willing to accept. Surely the labor leader is not behaving immorally when he overstates the wage increases his union expects to receive.

The point that Carr and his defenders is making is simply this: In the real world of everyday business practice, there is a great amount of bluffing, exaggeration and manipulation. Since everyone knows that such bluffing, and the like take place, business does quite well – the logic of Kant not withstanding. There is no danger of a collapse – either of credit or of capitalism as a whole. Practical experience confounds the philosopher's theory. The ethics of poker is still the appropriate model for business ethics.

Second, so long as Carr's argument is limited to the nondisclosure of information, bluffing, and the calculated use of exaggeration, Carr can escape the Kantian trap after all. Carr might concede that once one has agreed not to bluff, then it would be wrong to do so. However, Carr could maintain that his recommendations apply to the practice itself. In other words, he is making a recommendation regarding business practices. If bluffing and the like are accepted as a part of business practice, then there is nothing wrong with bluffing in business situations. Indeed it is because bluffing and exaggeration are accepted as part of the game that the examples Carr cites are not viewed as threatening to business practice.

III

What response can be made to Carr and his defenders? First Kant has set some limits. If lying or cheating were universalized, they surely would be self-defeating. The fact that some lying and cheating occur is quite beside the point. Kant is not claiming that people never lie; rather he is providing reasons why they shouldn't. Indeed nothing Carr has said counts against either Kant's point or Kant's argument. After all, even Carr admits that cheating in poker is not permitted. Where Carr disagrees with a Kantian is that if bluffing and the like were universally practiced in business, it would be self-defeating.

Perhaps utilitarianism can be of some assistance here. The task is to compare Carr's recommendation that business practice permit widespread bluffing, exaggeration, and the nondisclosure of information with an alternative conception of business that seeks to eliminate or sharply circumscribe such activities. Which conception of business practice would produce the greatest good for society? For business itself? Perhaps a more utilitarian perspective might break the impasse.

Wouldn't it be in the best interest of business to adopt the poker model of business ethics? I think not. Let us consider labor relations, where Carr's poker model is implicitly if not explicitly adopted. In collective bargaining the relationship between the employer and the employee is adversarial. Collective bargaining is competitive through and through. The task of the union is to secure as much in pay and benefits as possible. The task of the employer's negotiators is to keep the pay and benefits as low as possible.

In the resulting give-and-take, bluffing and deception are the rule. Management expects the union to demand a percentage pay increase it knows it won't get. The union expects the company to say that such a pay increase will force it to shut down the plant and move to another state. Such demands are never taken at face value although they are taken more seriously on the ninetieth day of negotiations than they are on the first day.

Recently the conventional view of collective bargaining practice has been under attack. One of the most prominent criticisms of current practice is its economic inefficiency. The adversarial relationship at the bargaining table carries over to the workplace. As a result of the hostility between employee and employer, productivity suffers and many American products are at a competitive disadvantage with respect to foreign products. Japanese labor-management relations are not so adversarial and this fact accounts for part of their success. This particular criticism of collective bargaining has received much attention in the press and in popular business magazines. The most recent manifestation of the recognition of the force of this criticism is the host of decisions General Motors has made to ensure that labor relations are different at its new assembly plant for the Saturn.

Second, the practice of bluffing and deception tends to undermine trust. As some American firms lost ground to foreign competition, the management of many of the firms asked for pay reductions, commonly called 'give backs.' Other managers in firms not threatened by foreign competition cited the 'dangers' of foreign competition to request pay cuts for their employees – even though they were not needed. Use of this tactic will only cause future problems when and if the competitive threat really develops. This utilitarian point was not lost on participants in a labor-management relations seminar I attended.

Participant I: In the past, there was a relationship of mutual distrust.

Participant II: These are the dangers in crying 'wolf.' When the company is really in trouble, no one will believe them.

Participant III: To make labor/management participation teams work, you need to generate mutual trust. It only takes one bad deal to undermine trust.

These individuals are indicating that the practices of bluffing and deception have bad consequences in employer/employee relationships. These unfortunate consequences have been well documented by philosophers – most recently by Sissela Bok. Bok's critique of 'white lies' and the use of placebos applies equally well to deception in the collective bargaining process.

> Triviality surely does set limits to when moral inquiry is reasonable. But when we look more closely at practices such as placebo-giving, it becomes clear that. all lies defended as 'white' cannot be so easily dismissed. In the first place, the harmlessness of lies is notoriously disputable. What the liar perceives as harmless or even beneficial may not be so in the eyes of the deceived. Second, the failure to look at an entire practice rather than at their own isolated case often blinds liars to cumulative harm and expanding deceptive activities. Those who begin with white lies can come to resort to more frequent and more serious ones. Where some tell a few white lies, others may tell more. Because lines are so hard to draw, the indiscriminate use of such lies can lead to other deceptive practices. The aggregate harm from a large number of marginally harmful instances may, therefore, be highly undesirable in the end – for liars, those deceived, and honesty and trust more generally.[3]

However, there is more at stake here than the bad consequences of lying. Bluffing, exaggeration, and the nondisclosure of information also undermine a spirit of cooperation that is essential to business success. The poker model, with its permitted bluffing and the like, is a competitive model. What the model overlooks is the fact that the production of a good or service in any given plant or office is a cooperative enterprise. Chrysler competes with General Motors and Toyota but the production of Chrysler K cars in that assembly plant in Newark, Delaware, is a cooperative enterprise. Lack of cooperation results in poor quality vehicles.

Hence the competitive model of collective bargaining sets wages and working conditions for what at the local level is a cooperative enterprise. Labor-management negotiators forget the obvious truth that the production of goods and services cannot succeed on a purely competitive basis. There have to be some elements of cooperation somewhere in the system. Why shouldn't the collective bargaining process use cooperative rather than competitive techniques? When bargaining is conducted industry-wide, as it is with automobiles, the competitive mode seems natural. Auto production is a competitive industry. But just because Chrysler is competitive with General Motors, why must Chrysler management be in a competitive relationship with its own employees? Indeed, couldn't it be argued that the fact that Chrysler's management does see itself in competition with its unionized employees undercuts its competitive position vis-à-vis other automobile producers. To use the language of competition, if Chrysler is at war with itself, how can it win the war against others?

As long as collective bargaining is essentially adversarial and characterized by bluffing and exaggeration on both sides, the cooperative aspect of business will be underemphasized. The costs of ignoring the cooperative aspect are great – both for society and for business itself.

Hence this distrust that so concerned the participants in the seminar is only in part a function of the deceit and bluffing that go on in collective bargaining. It is in large part a function of using the wrong model. We shouldn't look at collective bargaining as a game of poker.

With this discussion of collective bargaining as instance, let us evaluate Carr's proposal on utilitarian grounds. Should the stockholders applaud a chief executive officer whose operating procedure is analogous to the operating procedure of a poker player? In Carr's view, 'A good part of the time the businessman is trying to do unto others as he hopes others will not do unto him.' But surely such a practice is very risky. The danger of discovery is great, and our experience of the past several years indicates that many corporations that have played the game of business like the game of poker have suffered badly. Moreover, if business practice consisted essentially of these conscious misstatements, exaggerations, and the concealment of pertinent facts, it seems clear that business practice would be inherently unstable. Contemporary business practice presupposes such stability, and business can only be stable if the chief executive officer has a set of moral standards higher than those that govern the game of poker. The growth of the large firm, the complexity of business decisions, the need for planning and stability, and the undesirable effects of puffery, exaggeration, and deception all count against Carr's view that the ethics of business should be the ethics of a poker game.

NOTES

1. Albert Z. Carr, 'Is Business Bluffing Ethical?' *Harvard Business Review*, 46 (January–February 1968): 143–153.
2. For a review of the essentials of Kant's moral philosophy see this chapter.
3. Sissela Bok, *Lying: Moral Choice in Public and Private Life* (New York: Pantheon Books, 1978), pp. 19, 31.

Rule utilitarianism, equality, and justice

JOHN C. HARSANYI

Utilitarianism and the Concept of Social Utility

In this paper I propose to discuss the concepts of *equality* and *justice* from a rule utilitarian point of view, after some comments on the rule utilitarian point of view itself.[1]

Let me start with the standard definitions. *Act utilitarianism* is the theory that a morally right action is one that in the existing situation will produce the highest expected social utility. (I am using the adjective 'expected' in the sense of mathematical expectation.) In contrast, *rule utilitarianism* is the theory that a morally right action is simply an action conforming to the correct moral rule applicable to the existing situation. The correct moral rule itself is that particular behavioral rule that would yield the highest expected social utility if it were followed by all morally motivated people in all similar situations.

It is clear from these definitions that utilitarianism, in either version of it, is a very simple theory because it tries to derive all moral values from one basic principle, that of social utility. Yet, the history of utilitarian theory shows that interpretation of this principle gives rise to some far-from-simple conceptual problems – and also to many disagreements among utilitarians. But this is really not surprising. Moral problems are notoriously complex and difficult; and any philosophic theory that makes a serious attempt to come to grips with them cannot fail to reflect these complexities.

More specifically, interpretation of the principle of social utility poses problems of three different sorts. First, it poses some technical problems about how to define social utility and, more fundamentally, how to define individual utilities. Second, it poses some specifically moral problems about the definition of social utility. Finally, it poses the problem of how to apply the principle of social utility and, in particular, whether its application should follow the act utilitarian or the rule utilitarian approach.[2]

Under the first heading, we have to decide whether individual utilities are cardinal and interpersonally comparable quantities so as to make their sum and/or their arithmetic mean mathematically well-defined. We have also to decide whether to define a person's utility function in terms of his preferences, or of his feelings of pleasure and pain, or of his mental states of 'intrinsic worth,'[3] or any other criteria. All of these are technical problems which raise no difficult moral issues.[4]

More difficult are the specifically moral problems posed by the concept of social utility. For example, how much weight should we give to people's patently irrational and/or antisocial preferences? Indeed, how much weight should we give to their socially very desirable altruistic preferences? (If we assign positive weight to people's preferences for *other* people's welfare, then we give unfair advantage to individuals

Reading taken from *Ethics and Economics* (ed.) by E. F. Paul *et al.* Copyright © 1985 Social Philosophy and Policy.

with many friends and relatives, who wish them well, over individuals who lack such support.) How much weight should we give to the preferences of people unable to find out whether their preferences have been met or not – such as dead people or, in general, people who cannot monitor the situation, for whatever reason? Is it ever morally permissible to do what we like to do, even if our action does not yield the highest possible social utility?

Notice that these moral problems are important, not only for utilitarian theory, but also for any other moral theory – even though utilitarian theory does bring them more clearly out into the open, simply because it operates at a higher level of analytical precision than most nonutilitarian theories do. Of course, it is all to the good that utilitarianism forces us to face up to these problems: we learn a lot about the nature of morality by trying to answer them.

Rule Utilitarianism vs Act Utilitarianism
Even though all of these are important problems, in my opinion the most important internal problem for utilitarian theory is the choice between act utilitarianism and rule utilitarianism. No doubt, act utilitarianism is the simpler one of the two versions of utilitarianism. But rule utilitarianism seems to be closer to common sense morality and to our basic moral intuitions. Moreover, much more importantly, I will try to show that by following the rule utilitarian moral code, society will achieve a much higher level of social utility than it could achieve by following the act utilitarian approach.

To be sure, act utilitarianism has no difficulty in dealing with the moral problem of benevolence. Surely, it is obvious enough that we can increase social utility by helping other people or at least by not causing them needless harm. Yet, it seems to me that act utilitarianism cannot deal adequately with the moral problem of *justice* and with many related issues because it cannot deal adequately with the problems of moral *rights* and of moral *obligations*. For instance, suppose the government wants to take away my home in order to build a freeway through my property. Is this a morally justified action? (Note that I am not asking here about the constitutionality or the legality of such an action. I am asking about its *morality*.)

According to act utilitarianism, it is morally justified if it creates more utility than disutility. The government's action will create positive utility for the prospective users of the freeway, and for the workers and their employers who will build it. It will create a negative utility for me and my family, who will lose our home, and for the taxpayers who will have to pay for the new freeway, etc. According to act utilitarian theory, taking away my home is justified if the benefits accruing to the first group will exceed, *however slightly*, the sacrifices imposed on the second group.

Yet, this conclusion is clearly inconsistent with common sense morality, according to which the government's action violates my individual rights, and more specifically, violates my property rights to my home. (It also violates my personal freedom to live my private life without government interference.) Therefore, even if the government offered me reasonable compensation, expropriation of my home could be justified only if the balance of the resulting total utility over the resulting total disutility were quite substantial. If the government were unable to pay proper compensation, then only extreme social emergencies could possibly justify expropriation.

What position should a utilitarian take on this? Obviously, any moral code protecting individual rights will generate both social benefits and social costs. Therefore, a utilitarian must try to compare the benefits people will obtain on occasions when this moral code protects their individual rights, with the inconvenience they will suffer on occasions when this moral code restricts their freedom of action by protecting other people's rights against them.

I think it is very clear that, by any reasonable standard, the social benefits of such a moral code will greatly outweigh the undeniable social costs. That is to say, most of us will strongly *prefer* to live in a society whose moral code gives clear protection to individual rights, and does not permit violation of these rights, except possibly in some rare and rather special cases. In my opinion, this fact is the basic argument for rule utilitarianism.

The situation is much the same with respect to our moral obligations. According to common sense morality, we have some special obligations resulting from our family roles, our occupations, our friendships, and our other special social relationships. These special obligations will, most of the time, take precedence over other moral obligations. But a consistent act utilitarian must deny this.

For example, suppose I have to decide whether to spend a given amount of money on my own children's education or on supporting some other children in urgent need of financial help. According to common sense morality, I must spend this money on my own children's education – unless denying the money to the second group of children would create very extreme hardship. In contrast, an act utilitarian would have to say that I should give the money to the second group of children if their need for the money were slightly greater, *however slightly greater*, than my own children's needs were – that is, I should give it to this group of children if they could be expected to derive slightly more utility, *however slightly* more utility, than my own children would derive from it.

Once more, a rule utilitarian must, by and large, side with traditional morality. In all known societies, there is a division of labor among adults in looking after the children of the community. This division of labor has considerable social utility because, if all adults had to look after all children, it would be virtually impossible for them to find out the various children's individual needs, and it would be virtually impossible for them to develop close emotional ties with individual children.[5]

The specifics of this division of labor are different in different societies. For example, in some societies, the mother's oldest brother is the principal person in charge of the children. Of course, in our own society looking after children is normally a responsibility of the two parents. But, in any case, the special relationship between a group of children and the relevant adults can be preserved only if this relationship normally takes precedence over most other social obligations. In contrast, if we followed the act utilitarian approach and permitted other – in some sense, perhaps momentarily more urgent – moral obligations to take precedence, this special relationship could not survive.

To put it differently, we must distinguish between local optimality, in the sense of maximizing social utility by each individual action we may take, and global optimality, in the sense of maximizing social utility by the moral code we adopt and by the entire system of moral rights and moral obligations this moral code brings into existence. Act utilitarianism focuses on local optimality, whereas rule utilitarianism focuses on global optimality. In some situations, local and global optimality pull in the same direction. But in all situations where they pull in different directions, we have to give preference to global optimality, which means adopting the rule utilitarian approach.

To put it still another way, the main difference between rule utilitarianism and act utilitarianism lies in the fact that the former recognizes, while the latter denies, the logical dependence of justice on the existence of suitable moral rules that define people's moral rights and moral obligations. Unlike some contemporary act utilitarians, John Stuart Mill clearly understood this relationship. After arguing that justice first meant conformity to positive legal rules, he wrote that later

> . . . the sentiment of justice became attached, not to all violations of law, but only to violations of such laws as *ought* to exist, including such as ought to exist, but do not.[6]

Mill here obviously refers to moral laws.

Let me illustrate the actual working of the rule utilitarian approach in more specific terms, using the example of promise-keeping. Suppose that A promises B to do X for him but does not deliver on his promise. According to act utilitarianism, this breach of promise will be morally wrong only if it creates more total disutility than total utility. Of course, the main utility created by the broken promise is the utility A derives from not implementing a presumably burdensome obligation. In contrast, the main disutilities created by A's action are:

(1) The disutility to B of losing the promised physical benefit, and the extra disutility to him of having his expectations of obtaining this benefit utterly disappointed.

(2) The disutility to society as a result of decreased public confidence in future promises when people learn about this breach of promise by A.

Note that normally disutility (2) will be negligibly small because one act of promise-breaking is unlikely to have any noticeable effect on public confidence in promises.

Consequently, for an act utilitarian, the basic question is whether A's utility gain by breaking his promise exceeds B's utility loss. If it does, however slightly, then A's breach of promise is morally justified. In contrast, a rule utilitarian must ask the question, 'Which particular moral rule about promise-keeping would yield the highest social utility?' Note that a rule utilitarian must judge the social-utility implications of any proposed moral rule on the assumption that, if this moral rule were adopted, this would automatically become public knowledge.[7] Therefore, in judging any proposed moral rule, he must always ask the question, 'What would be the effects on people's expectations, incentives, and behavior, if they knew that this was the moral rule adopted for a given class of situations?'

Consequently, under rule utilitarianism, the moral rule about promise-keeping must be chosen in such a way that it will maximize social utility by striking the right balance between two classes of social interests. On the one hand, there is the interest of the *promisee* in obtaining the promised performance and in avoiding disappointment of his expectations by nonperformance. There is also the interest of *society* in maintaining public confidence in promises. If the proposed moral rule permitted too many easy exceptions from promise-keeping, the promisee's interests would receive insufficient protection. Moreover, public confidence in promises would be significantly impaired (because people would know how lax this moral rule about promise-keeping actually was). This would be very undesirable because a good deal of social cooperation crucially depends on the credibility of promises – in fields ranging from commercial credit transactions to private agreements about where and when to meet, etc.

On the other hand, consideration must be given also to the promisor's interest in being morally released from his promise, when fulfilling it would cause him undue hardship. If the moral rule about promise-keeping permitted too few exceptions, the promisor would too often be saddled with excessively burdensome obligations.

Presumably, there will be a moral rule maximizing social utility by permitting just the right set of exceptions from promise-keeping. To be sure, it will often be a matter of difficult personal judgment whether a given situation does or does not represent a permissible exception under the rule utilitarian criterion. As I have argued elsewhere,[8] in practice it is often quite difficult to decide what specific moral rule, with what particular list of exceptive cases would in fact maximize social utility. Hence, the best course of action for a rule utilitarian moral decision maker will often be to defer to the social customs existing in his social environment (for example, as to permissible exceptions from promise-keeping) – unless he has strong reasons to believe that such conformity to these social customs would be definitely contrary to social utility.

Yet, even though there may often be practical difficulties in deciding what specific list of permissible exceptions to a given moral rule would in fact maximize social utility, I think it is very important from a philosophic standpoint that rule utilitarianism does provide at least a conceptually clear theoretical criterion for the set of morally permissible exceptions.

Let me draw three general philosophic conclusions from this discussion. First, in many cases rule utilitarianism and act utilitarianism will yield very different practical moral implications. In particular, as we have seen, rule utilitarianism will protect people's moral rights and their special moral obligations in a much wider range of cases, and will permit their infringement in many fewer exceptional situations, than act utilitarianism will. By the same token, rule utilitarianism will permit many fewer exceptions to the moral obligation of keeping our promises – or to that of gratitude to a benefactor, or to that of telling the truth, etc. – than act utilitarianism will. This should finally put to rest the surprising claim, sometimes made even by very distinguished moral philosophers,[9] that rule utilitarianism and act utilitarianism are equivalent as to their practical moral implications.

Second, it is *not* true, as some act utilitarian philosophers have claimed,[10] that rule utilitarianism amounts to 'rule worship,' in the sense of irrationally requiring observance of a moral rule even in cases where deviating from this rule would yield higher social utility. (At least, this is certainly not true about the version of rule utilitarianism that I am defending.) To the contrary, as we have seen, rule utilitarianism requires us to choose that particular set of permissible exceptions to any given moral rule that will maximize social utility. The only important moral philosopher who can be justly accused of 'rule worship' is Kant, who denied that there were *any* morally justified exceptions to our basic moral rules.

Finally, society will reach a much higher level of social utility by following the rule utilitarian moral code than it would reach by following the act utilitarian approach. As we have seen, this is so because it will be much better to live in a society in which all people, or at least all morally motivated members of society, respect other people's individual rights and their own institutional obligations, keep their promises, tell the truth on important matters, etc. (unless they have exceptionally important reasons not to do so). Such a society would be preferable to an act utilitarian society where people will disregard other people's rights and their own moral obligations whenever this is likely to yield slightly greater total utility than total disutility.

To put it differently, rule utilitarianism places itself on the high middle ground between act utilitarianism and various deontological theories. Like the latter, it takes the view that we cannot define a morally right action merely in terms of social expediency, which, by itself, would necessarily lead to a super-Machiavellian morality. Rather, the pursuit of social expediency must always be constrained by the deontological requirements of morality, such as observance of rationally chosen moral rules, and respect for a rational system of moral rights and moral obligations. On the other hand, rule utilitarianism agrees with act utilitarianism, that ultimately the rational justification of these moral rules, moral rights, and moral obligations must lie in their undeniable social utility.

In fact, rule utilitarianism is the *only* moral theory that can provide a rational explanation and justification for these deontological components of morality. Act utilitarianism cannot do so because the limitations of its conceptual framework prevent it from recognizing these deontological concepts as relatively autonomous elements of morality. On the other hand, deontological theories, of course, fully recognize their importance, but cannot provide any rational justification for them. For example, Prichard and Ross based their theories on the concept of moral duty but they could not explain where these moral duties are supposed to come from and why a rational person should care to discharge them. Likewise, Nozick built his theory on the concept of 'entitlements,' but never explained their logical basis and their morally binding force.[11]

Finally, contractarians like Locke, Rousseau, and Rawls tried to explain our moral and legal rules in terms of a hypothetical prehistoric social contract. But this social contract is obviously pure fiction and, therefore, cannot possibly explain real-life moral obligations. Indeed, even if this social contract had been a real contract concluded by our very remote ancestors many thousand years ago, it could hardly be morally binding, now, on the present members of our society.

But the decisive objection to this social-contract theory is that it is irredeemably circular. The hypothetical social contract, like *any* contract, would derive all of its moral binding force from the moral rule that contracts should be kept. Therefore, we cannot without circularity claim that this moral rule itself, and all other moral rules, owe their moral justification to this social contract in the first place.

Moral Values vs Other Human Values

Kant took the view that morality is the highest value of human life. A consistent utilitarian cannot share this view.[12]

The basic task of morality is to induce people to help other people in achieving their own objectives, which are in most cases *nonmoral* objectives, such as economic well-being, a good social position, health, friendship, love, knowledge, artistic experiences, etc.

Thus, in an important sense, morality is primarily a servant of many other human values, rather than itself the highest value. Moreover, even though no person can have a rich and well-balanced life without strong moral commitments, these moral commitments are less likely to occupy the center of the stage for him than are his work, his family and friends, and his intellectual, cultural, social, and political interests.

Of course, our moral duties must always take precedence over any other considerations. But this is true only in the trivial sense that we would not call anything our moral duty simpliciter had we not already decided that it has an overriding moral claim upon us. In contrast, our prima facie moral duties do not always take precedence over our nonmoral interests.

For example, if I make a promise, I will obviously have a prima facie moral duty to keep it. Yet, if breaking my promise would not cause any serious harm to the promisee, but keeping my promise would cause me a very substantial financial loss that I could not have foreseen when I made the promise, then it might be morally permissible for me to break my promise. This means that I might be morally free to give precedence to my financial interests over a prima facie moral obligation.

Likewise, a utilitarian cannot regard very high degrees of moral devotion always as unmixed blessings. Even less can he so regard high degrees of morally motivated devotion to idealistic political objectives.

Great devotion to one's moral values requires a willingness to make great sacrifices for them. Yet, as experience shows, people who are willing to make great sacrifices for their moral values are often equally willing to sacrifice other people to them. The unfortunate fact is that great devotion to high moral and political ideals may not be very far away from socially disastrous moral and political fanaticism. Robespierre was no doubt a man devoted to the highest moral principles.

Utilitarianism and Equality

As has often been pointed out, there are many different types of equality and of inequality. I will discuss only two: *equal consideration* for the interests of different individuals, and equality of social benefits for different individuals in terms of income, wealth, status, power, etc., which can also be described as *economic and social equality*.

The principle of equal consideration is a rather undemanding principle. All it requires is that, in dealing with different people, we should not provide rationally unjustifiable favorable treatment or unfavorable treatment for any one of them. This principle has a fundamental role in any version of utilitarian theory because it enters into the very definition of social utility: whether we define social utility as the *sum* or as the *arithmetic mean* of individual utilities, we must give equal weight to all individuals' utilities.

The principle of equal consideration is a direct corollary of one of the most basic general principles of rationality, viz., the principle of sufficient reason. Therefore, we may be tempted to conclude that the principle of equal consideration is morally binding on all human action. I do not think this is the case. For in some decisions we may have virtually unlimited moral discretion, and may be under no moral obligation to follow any objective criteria at all.

For example, it seems to me that if I pay my secretary out of my own private funds, and need a new secretary, I will be morally free to follow my own preferences in choosing among alternative candidates for the job. I will have no real moral obligation to give all candidates 'equal consideration,' or to use any specific criteria in order to select the 'most deserving' candidate – though, of course, it will be morally praiseworthy if I do so.

In contrast, if I am acting as a public official, or even as an official of a large, or at least a moderately large, social organization, I will be morally obliged to make any major decision on general and rationally defensible criteria (even if I am under no *legal* obligation to do so). This is so because such officials are, in an important sense, agents of society as a whole and ought to follow the standards of fairness and of rationality of society in all major decisions, even in situations where a private citizen would not be positively required to do so.

I now propose to discuss *economic and social equality*. It seems to me that, for a consistent utilitarian, economic and social equality is *not* an intrinsic moral value. To be sure, other things being equal, a more equal distribution of economic and noneconomic benefits is always preferable to a less equal distribution. But the main reason for this lies in the law of diminishing marginal utility of money and of most other good things in life. Thus, greater economic equality is morally desirable mainly because a poor man, who is likely to spend any extra money on important necessities, is also likely to derive a much higher utility from an extra $100 than will a rich man, who is likely to spend any extra money on relatively unimportant luxuries.

For this reason, a utilitarian will favor government policies for a moderate redistribution of income and wealth. But he will have to counsel moderation, because society has a vital interest in maintaining people's incentives for hard work, for enterprise, and for developing their talents. Some redistributive policies may increase poor people's incomes by a few percentage points but may decrease the rate of growth in national income, possibly making these poor people actually much worse off a few years later than they would have been in the absence of these policies.

On the other hand, there are strong utilitarian reasons for opposing both extreme poverty and extreme wealth, especially extreme levels of inherited wealth. Extreme poverty not only causes physical hardships, but also tends to paralyze the intellectual and cultural life of its victims, and tends to poison their moral attitudes. Surprisingly enough, the intellectual, cultural, and moral effects of extreme wealth, especially of very great inherited wealth, are often much the same. In many societies, children of very rich families are seldom conspicuous by their intellectual, cultural, and moral accomplishments, nor by their ability to lead a happy and well-balanced life. Moreover, extremes of poverty and of wealth also tend to hinder proper operation of our democratic political institutions.

No doubt, many moral philosophers take issue with the utilitarian view that economic and social equality is not an intrinsic moral value. But if these philosophers were right, this would mean that, in a distribution of social benefits, a poor person (or an otherwise disadvantaged person) should be given priority over a rich person (or an otherwise more fortunate person) even if, for a given benefit, the former is not expected to derive a higher utility than the latter is. For easier reference, I will describe the moral value judgment contained in this last sentence as *statement A*.

I now propose to show in two examples that statement A would be an utterly unacceptable moral value judgment. I will need examples involving noneconomic benefits because, in a distribution of economic benefits, owing to the law of diminishing marginal utility, a poor person will almost always derive a higher utility from any given benefit.

Consider a distribution of a scarce lifesaving drug, or a distribution of scarce university admissions, when the available supply of either falls very much short of existing demand. Suppose that, in the case of the drug, we have to choose between a rich patient and a poor patient, both of whom badly need this drug. Suppose, also, that the rich patient is definitely expected to benefit more from the drug. Or suppose that, in the university admissions example, we have to choose between a rich candidate and a poor candidate, both of whom have the qualifications required for admission. Suppose, also, that the rich candidate is clearly better qualified and can derive a greater benefit from university education.

Then, statement A would imply that we should give the lifesaving drug or the university admission to the poorer person, even though the richer person would derive a greater benefit from it – except, perhaps, if this richer person would derive a *very much* greater benefit from the lifesaving drug or from the university admission. Yet, even if the richer person is expected to derive only a moderately greater benefit from the drug or from the university admission, he will have a stronger moral claim to it. It would be morally unjustifiable discrimination against him if he were denied the drug or the university admission merely because he happens to be rich.

Thus, I conclude that statement A is a completely unacceptable moral value judgment. Utilitarian theory is right to take the view that economic and social inequality is not an intrinsic moral value, and that it is morally wrong to discriminate against a rich or an otherwise fortunate person in order to reduce the difference between him and the poorer or otherwise less fortunate members of society.[13]

Utilitarianism and Justice

As I have argued earlier, society has a very important interest in having its members respect each other's basic rights and institutional obligations – in other words, in having its members observe the basic standards of justice.

Yet, this coin also has another side. Preoccupation with minor violations of our rights, real or apparent, and the widespread passion for litigation so prevalent now in the United States, are highly counterproductive social practices. Indeed, not only is it often socially preferable if people put up with minor injustices, instead of engaging in endless litigation, it is often socially *desirable* to have social institutions whose very success depends on having some 'unfair' practices built into them.

For instance, the effectiveness of the free enterprise system (and even that of a socialist system) crucially depends on the fact that a successful business executive will be promoted and an unsuccessful one demoted. Yet, this is often 'unfair,' because this success or failure may be unrelated to the business executive's own effort and ability, and may be a matter of sheer luck. Likewise, in many parliamentary systems, a cabinet minister must take political responsibility for his subordinates' mistakes, regardless of whether he is really responsible for them by common sense criteria or not.

In both cases, of course, it would be possible to promote or to demote the individual in question only after an inquiry determined how much responsibility he really had for the outcome. But such inquiries are costly, time consuming, and often quite inconclusive. Thus, there are good arguments for acting without any such prior inquiry.

More fundamentally, it is possible to argue that it is 'unfair' to reward a person's superior performance by higher pay, higher prestige, and higher social status, if this performance is largely a result of his outstanding ability, rather than of his greater effort, or of his higher moral standards. But a utilitarian must fully support rewards based on performance because the alternative would destroy the incentives for gifted people to fully develop and use their talents to the benefit of society, and would encourage philistinism and hostility to excellence.

Again, it is hard to deny that proportional representation is the 'fairest' electoral system, and the only one really 'fair' to small parties. But this is not necessarily a convincing argument for proportional representation. From a utilitarian point of view, a question much more important than such 'fairness' considerations is, 'which particular electoral system is more likely to yield a stable and effective government, one able to take unpopular measures when they are called for on economic issues, on minority rights, on foreign policy and defense, etc.?' On this score, it seems to me that two-party systems, with the two parties from time to time alternating in government, have been in most cases far superior.

Conclusion

I have discussed the nature, and some of the internal problems, of the utilitarian point of view. In comparing act utilitarianism with rule utilitarianism, I have come down in favor of the latter, primarily on the ground that rule utilitarianism will yield a higher level of social utility because it requires wider respect for other people's rights and for our own special obligations. I have argued that, for a utilitarian, moral values will not be always the highest values of human life, and sometimes will have to yield precedence to other social values. I have also argued that, even though equality and justice (including fairness) are of fundamental importance from a utilitarian point of view, they cannot always be the decisive considerations for framing social policies.

NOTES

1. The author wants to thank the National Science Foundation for supporting this research through grant SES77-06394-A02, administered by the Center for Research in Management, University of California, Berkeley.
2. Any moral decision, under either version of utilitarianianism, is a *constrained maximization* problem, with social utility as the maximizand. But the actual constraints of maximization are different under the two versions of utilitarianism. An act utilitarian must try to maximize social utility under the assumption that the strategies of all *other* utilitarians are simply *given*, independent of his own strategy. In contrast, a rule utilitarian must try to maximize social utility under the assumption that *all* utilitarians will always use the *same* strategy. See J. C. Harsanyi, 'Rule Utilitarianism and Decision Theories,' *Erkenntnis* 11 (1977), pp. 44-48. As a result, the alternatives will also be different under the two utilitarian theories. Under act utilitarianism, they will be alternative individual acts. Under rule utilitarianism, they will be alternative moral rules; in fact, as closer analysis would show, they are alternaitve comprehensive moral codes.
3. G. E. Moore, *Principia Ethica* (London: Cambridge University Press, 1903), p. 17.
4. For a discussion of these problems, see my *Rational Behavior and Bargaining Equilibrium in Games and Social Situations* (Cambridge: Cambridge University Press, 1977), Chapter 4; and 'Rule Utilitarianism and Decision Theory,' pp. 27-30.
5. Harsanyi, 'Rule Utilitarianism, Rights, Obligations, and the Theory of Rational Behavior,' *Theory and Decision* 12 (1980), p. 128.
6. John Stuart Mill, 'Utilitarianism,' *Utilitarianism, Liberty, and Representative Government*, ed. Ernest Rhys (New York: Everyman's Library, E. P. Dutton and Co., 1926), pp. 43-44, quoted in J. Narveson, *Morality and Utility* (Baltimore: Johns Hopkins University Press, 1967), p. 148.
7. Presumably, under *any* moral theory, we would have to assume that moral rules will be made publicly known to enable people to comply with them. But under rule utilitarian theory there is an additional reason for assuming that moral rules will be publicly known. For, in principle, every individual can compute what set of moral rules will yield the highest social utility.
8. J. C. Harsanyi, 'Some Epistemological Advantages of the Rule Utilitarian Position in Ethics.' *Midwest Studies in Philosophy* 7 (1982), pp. 395-396.
9. See Richard B. Brandt, 'Toward a Credible Form of Utilitarianism,' *Morality and the Language of Conduct*, H. N. Castañeda and G. Nakhnikian, eds. (Detroit: Wayne University Press, 1963), pp. 120-123; D. Lyons, *The Forms and Limits of Utilitarianism* (London: Oxford University Press, 1965), *passim*; R. M. Hare, *Freedom and Reason* (Oxford: Oxford University Press, 1963), pp. 130-136.

10. J. J. C. Smart, 'An Outline of Utilitarian Ethics,' *Utilitarianism, For and Against* (London: Cambridge University Press, 1973), p. 10.
11. H. A. Prichard, *Moral Obligation* (Oxford: Oxford University Press, 1968); W. D. Ross, *Foundations of Ethics* (Oxford: Clarendon Press, 1939); R. Nozick, *Anarchy, State, and Utopia* (New York: Basic Books, 1974).
12. My argument in this section has greatly benefited from Professor Narveson's discussion of these topics (J. Narveson, *Morality and Utility*, pp. 34–37). But he may not agree with all that I will say.
13. Of course, there is a very strong case for remedial actions in favor of social groups unjustly treated in the past. But it is a more difficult question how far we may go in discriminating against people not belonging to these social groups, if these people have no personal responsibility for the unjust policies of the past.

Virtues and business ethics

JOSEPH R. DESJARDINS

Much of the work done by philosophers in business ethics has been structured by an overly narrow understanding of ethical theory. This understanding is characterized by an almost total reliance upon moral rules and principles and an almost total disregard of virtues and the ethics of character. As understood by many philosophers working in business ethics, the goal of ethical theory is to identify and defend some fundamental principle that can serve as the foundation for all morality. Such a principle will provide this foundation if it can, first, be defended as categorically binding on all rational agents and, second, be capable of moving such agents to specific acts that are required by the principle. Generally, this second goal is achieved if the principle can function as a major premise from which specific practical conclusions can be deduced.

Much of the first-order writing done by philosophers in business ethics has involved the second goal: applying general ethical principles to specific situations in business and from these principles deriving what one ought to do in that situation. Moral philosophers less interested in 'applied ethics' have been content in pursuing the first goal. Thus, moral philosophy today is often divided into two areas: Those working in ethical theory are charged with justifying certain principles (for example, utility, the categorical imperative) as binding on all persons, while those working in applied ethics attempt to show how these principles commit one to accepting certain specific conclusions about whistleblowing, employee rights, and so on. Thus applied ethics stands in the same relationship to ethical theory as engineering stands to physics. The theorist defends the general principle while the practitioner applies that principle to solve particular practical problems.

Given this principle-based understanding of ethical theory, the means for institutionalizing ethical responsibility within corporations is clear. The task is to get the corporation to accept some ethical principle as the guide for the activities of its members. A number of different strategies have been proposed to meet this goal. Milton Friedman, for example, suggests that corporations ought to adopt the principle of profit maximization as their guide. This principle, through the functioning of a free and competitive market, will lead the corporation to fulfill its social responsibility. Others have argued for a utilitarian principle broader than profit maximization, claiming that corporations ought to be guided by a more general understanding of social goods and by the recognition of a responsibility to bring about such goods.

Still others argue for non-utilitarian principles. Tom Donaldson, for example, defends a version of social contract theory of corporate social responsibility.[1] In this view, a corporation institutionalizes its ethical responsibility by obeying the implicit contract that exists between it and society.

These and many other similar strategies share a belief that the road to ethical responsibility lies with the internalization of some independently justified principle. In what follows, I suggest that there are good reasons for thinking that any such approach will fail. I then go on to consider an alternative strategy for institutionalizing ethical behavior.

THE FLAW IN PRINCIPLE-BASED ETHICS

What, then, is wrong with principle-based ethics? Why do I suppose that attempts to institutionalize ethical responsibility within corporations that rely upon principles will fail? There are both practical and theoretical reasons for this skepticism.

First, we should take seriously the fact that in practice, ethical principles seldom give any unambiguous practical advice. Adopting a principle-based approach in business ethics leads to numerous practical difficulties. A seemingly endless series of problems arises when one attempts to derive from such principles as the categorical imperative or the principle of utility, solutions to ethical problems faced by businesspeople. Hopeless ambiguity in application, apparent counterexamples, ad hoc rebuttals, counterintuitive conclusions, and apparently contradictory prescriptions create an overwhelming morass in the discussion of particular moral situations. The confusion is compounded even further when recommendations from competing principles are added to the discussion. Those of us who have tried to teach business ethics in this way can attest that ethics is not engineering: unambiguously correct or even generally accepted answers occur very seldom. This radical inconclusiveness of ethical debates should at least suggest that something is wrong with our approaches to moral problems.

Beyond these practical problems, and partly explaining them, lie additional conceptual difficulties. By far the most significant is the fact that no ethical principle has yet been established in any plausible fashion as categorically binding upon all people. Philosophers have simply failed to justify the principles they apply in business ethics. Principle-based ethical theories are committed to the view that without the prior independent justification of the principle, attempts to institutionalize ethical responsibility by appeal to a principle will fail. Since we must admit the outright failure of the project of justifying moral principles, we should be skeptical of attempts to ground business responsibility upon moral principles.

Two further problems with the emphasis upon principles can lead us into a discussion of the alternative approach. First, principle-based ethics tends to identify particular actions as the core of morality and tends to ignore the character of the person who performs those acts. Ethical principles, whether they be called rules, maxims, laws, or action guides, inevitably conceive of moral judgments in terms of the question What should I do? and disregard the equally practical question of What [kind of person] should I be? Consequently, business ethics often labors under the inadequate assumption that every particular act can, once and for all, be determined as obligatory, prohibited, or permissible. Borrowing a phrase from Robert Nozick, principle-based ethical theories are 'end-state' theories. They share a conviction that there is one unequivocable arrangement of this world (that is, arrangement that is in accord with the favored principle) which would be morally preferable.

Of course, this conviction can be seriously questioned. Why should we assume that the moral world is unambiguous? In light of the vast number of experiences that have given rise to the rapid recent growth of applied ethics, should we not assume just the opposite? I suggest that we recognize the moral life to be often fundamentally ambiguous. Ethics is not like problem solving in science or technology: There just may not *be* clear moral answers 'out there' waiting to be discovered if only we use the right method. Principle-based ethics encourages us to think that there are such answers. If only we apply the right principle carefully enough, we can determine the moral status of each individual action.

A second, not unrelated, problem concerns the impersonal nature of principles. Principles are distinct from the people who are to use them: They are external rules to be internalized, adopted, accepted as one's own, and applied. This creates a gap between person and principle, a gap that underlies some of the most serious problems in ethics. Even if moral principles were plausibly justified as binding on all rational agents (a goal that, I suggested above, has yet to be approached), the motivation question remains. Why should I do what is required by this principle? As a motivational question, this remains open. Even if the principle could give us unambiguous advice, we can (and do) sensibly ask Why should *I* do this? Principle-based ethics leaves us with an unbridgable motivational gap between the applied principle and the action. (On the face of it, it seems that the closer a principle comes to the goal of being rationally justified – for example, the categorical imperative – the more formal it is and the more empty it is of motivational content. On the other hand, the closer a principle is to providing a motive to act – for example, the utilitarian happiness principles – the farther it is from being rationally binding on all rational agents.)

AN ALTERNATIVE APPROACH

Let us suppose that, unlike technical or scientific problems, moral problems have no answers or solutions just waiting to be discovered. What if there were no single right answer to many of the moral problems confronting us? Besides despair, is any alternative open to us? I would like to suggest that there is, and that we can be guided to this alternative by Aristotle.

The Aristotelian Good

Aristotle characterizes good acts as those acts performed by the good man. Although this often is thought to be circular, it seems to me to contain a wealth of truth. Imagine that you are lost deep in a jungle. There is no *one* way out of this predicament and indeed you may never get out. What would you hope for? I would want neither a map nor a survival handbook. Since I don't know where I am to begin with, a map will be of little help. Since the handbook cannot hope to cover every situation that might be encountered, it can be only marginally helpful. Rather, I would like a person who is experienced in the ways of the jungle to act as my guide. I think that Aristotle saw moral problems in much the same way. Deciding how we should live our lives is like deciding what to do in the jungle. Principles and rules will be of little help since, like maps, they can be helpful only when you already know where you are (have already established that the rule is morally justified) and, like handbooks, they cannot hope to cover all situations. What we need is a person experienced in the ways of life.

Accordingly, the Aristotelian good world is not one that conforms to some pre-established principle. Rather, it is a world populated by good people. I suggest that the good business also is not one that conforms to some preestablished principle, but one that is populated by good people. A morally responsible business is not one that measures its actions against some external principle, but is one in which good people are making the decisions.

Such a good person would be a person of character, disciplined to avoid the temptations of immediate, short-term pleasures. She would recognize that much of what is worthwhile in life is not easily and immediately achievable. This person would not be overcommitted to rules and regulations; she would have the courage to be creative, to enocurage and entertain new ideas, to sometimes go on intuition. (The good person certainly would not be a bureaucrat!) The good person would also enjoy others, recognizing that solitude in a social world will result in the loss of great good. This might imply that the good person have a sense of humor. The good person would also foster her intellectual abilities. Reason and intelligence can contribute much (but not all) to the good life. Above all else, the good person possesses *phronesis*, or practical wisdom. Following Aristotle, since ethics is not a demonstrative science and since there are no unambiguous answers in ethics, a type of reasoning different from scientific reasoning will be required of the good person. The ability to make reasonable decisions in situations in which there is no right answer is the mark of phronesis: It is to possess practical wisdom.

It is the nature of phronesis that one cannot specify, a priori, what it will amount to in practice. In general, it is the ability to apply lessons learned in the past to new situations in the present. It is to be able to make appropriate adjustments so that general lessons fit the specific situation. Phronesis requires us to fit our reasoning to the situation and to avoid forcing present situations into preconceived categories. In this sense, phronesis is the antithesis of bureaucratic reasoning. It is the ability to adapt to changing situations without losing sight of one's ultimate goal. A business seeking to foster the development of good persons will be well advised to encourage the development of phronesis.[2]

The Nature of Virtues

I would now like to pursue some suggestions about the nature of the virtues that are found in Alasdair MacIntyre's book *After Virtue.*

Traditionally, the virtues have been conceptually tied to some *telos*, or some 'good life' for man. The virtues were those character traits that promoted the attainment of the good life. The good man, in turn, was that person who possessed these virtues. The history of moral philosophy from at least the seventeenth century essentially ignores the role of the virtues in ethical theory. At best, the virtues were given a position alongside sentiments and feelings as being part of the noncognitive, and therefore arbitrary and subjective, side of morality. The most compelling explanation for this view centers on the fact that modern philosophy has, by and large, rejected the notion that there is any single, nonarbitrary *telos* for man. Some writers would trace this to the individualism of post-Hobbesian liberalism. The focus of that liberalism is upon man as atomistic individual and away from man as social. Since individual men have different ends, it becomes folly to try to identify some one end for all men. Other writers of a Marxist bent trace this loss of a human *telos* to the alienation that results from the modern industrial-capitalist society. Still other commentators trace the rejection of a human telos to the rejection of teleology in general during the scientific revolution that took place during the sixteenth and seventeenth centuries. Whatever the cause, the lack of some one telos for all people prevented the development of anything but a subjective, variable account of the virtues.

I am not prepared to defend some conception of the good life for man. Nevertheless, some suggestions we find in MacIntyre might start us in the right direction. In regard to the good life, MacIntyre says:

> To ask 'What is the good for me?' is to ask how best I might live out that unity [of an individual life] and bring it to completion. To ask 'What is the good life

for man?' is to ask what all answers to the former question have in common. (p. 203.)

What all answers to the first question have in common involves what is necessary to live a unified, whole life. The unity of a life can emerge only when that life is situated in a social and historical context, a 'narrative' in MacIntyre's phrase, that gives meaning to that life. Individuals do not exist as solipsists, our every action – indeed, our every thought – can be meaningful only within a complex social, historical, and linguistic context. Thus, to try and live our life in isolation from others will undermine the very context that gives meaning to and ultimately unifies our lives. It will effectively prevent us from attaining our own good, the fulfillment of our life story or narrative.

What does this have to do with business ethics? It seems to me that there are two ways in which the roles people play in business can be understood. Only one of these will contribute to that unity of the human life by situating the person within a social and historical context.

In what I call *instrumental view*, individuals fill roles that are simply means to some other end (profit for the employer, wages for the employee). In this view, an individual fills a position in much the same way that components are plugged into a stereo system. Individuals are interchangeable parts, and as such they are denied any intrinsic value or meaning of their own. This essentially is the bureaucratic view of business in which an organizational chart gives meaning to each position. The position itself and the individual who fills it have value only so long as they are efficient means to some external end. In this view, individuals are encouraged to think of themselves as role-players. Like the manager in Albert Carr's 'Business Bluffing' article (see p. 108), individuals play a variety of roles: managers, spouses, parents, religious believers, political constituents. When stripped of these roles, however, the individual means little or nothing. As a result, individuals are denied the unity of life that is essential to the pursuit of their good life.

On the other hand, there is what I call the *professional view* in which the positions individuals occupy are valuable in themselves and not just as means to some other end. Like the medical or teaching profession, these positions derive their value from those goods (what MacIntyre calls 'internal goods') that can be achieved only through the practice of that activity. Individuals occupying these positions derive meaning and value from the pursuit and attainment of goods that are internal to those positions. These goods are essentially social, having developed during a long social history and, in turn, contributing to the future good of that society. As such, these positions are more likely to foster the unity (or integrity) that is necessary to live out one's life and bring it to completion. Unlike jobs, professions do not ask the individual participant to suspend the pursuit of the good life while at work.

In the instrumental view, work is what one does to earn the money needed to pursue what is valuable. Since value is therefore determined by money, the individual is left to assign her own value to anything at all. In the professional view, one pursues what has been established as valuable in itself by the social history of that profession. This pursuit of the objective social good is an intrinsic part of the profession. I would suggest that we develop the professional conception of business management by recognizing the intrinsic value of business as the supplier of goods and services. In this view the function of business (indeed, its social responsibility) is to produce goods and services that contribute to the good of society. Moral philosophers are encouraged to examine the character traits necessary to attain these goods in the attempt to describe the virtues of business management.

Tying some of these suggestions together, let us say that the 'good life' for man lies in the pursuit of excellence. Let us say that excellence for business is the pursuit of goods and services that contribute to and advance the social good. This social good, ultimately, is a decision that should be made in the political arena. (This calls for an approach to business ethics in terms of social and political philosophy rather than in terms of ethical theory.) Nevertheless, we can say that a business can institutionalize ethics by fostering the development of good people within its ranks. Ways of doing this include closely identifying employee positions with the pursuit of business excellence. In part, this requires avoiding the instrumental view of employee roles. It would also include the encouragement of phronesis as its decision procedure and the avoidance of bureaucratic formalism.

NOTES

1. See his *Corporations and Morality* (Englewood Cliffs, NJ: Prentice-Hall, 1981).
2. For an interesting parallel to this account of phronesis in business, see *In Search of Excellence* by Thomas Peters and Robert Waterman (New York: Harper & Row, 1982).

CASE STUDY

Assessing the ethics of businesses: the New Consumer survey

Assessing the economic performance of businesses is far from easy but it at least has the advantage of well established procedures for measuring profits growth, market share, turnover, and the like. Assessing 'social' performance is certainly no less difficult and has the added disadvantage of requiring the development of a wholly new set of indicators. In the UK, this has been done by New Consumer (NC), a not-for-profit public interest research organization based in Newcastle upon Tyne. Over a two-year period from late 1988 to 1990, it investigated 128 major companies based or operating in the UK, concentrating mostly on those involved in mass consumer markets for food and household goods. There were 79 British companies and 49 were foreign owned. Small though the sample was, a significant feature was the greater openness of the foreign owned firms, and in particular the American, compared to the British. In all, 32 of the 128 (25%) co-operated fully with the survey, 64 (50%) to some extent, and 32 (25%) to little or no extent; with nearly a third of the American companies in the fully co-operating category compared to barely a fifth of the British. The most frequently given reason for not co-operating was an inability to collect the data because of a lack of resources or of any central collation. However, the authors of the survey also noted a distinction between firms which see this kind of research as an opportunity to clarify their approach to social issues and those which see it as a threat – an attempt, presumably, to pillory them for their shortcomings. This is despite the fact that NC is concerned only to provide consumers with the information that will enable them to make informed choices and explicitly rejects a campaigning or pressure group role.

NC began by identifying more than 70 areas of business activity which raised ethical concerns. To make the survey manageable, this was reduced to 13 general areas. These covered:

1. disclosure of information
2. pay, benefits and conditions
3. industrial democracy
4. equal opportunities
5. community involvement
6. environment
7. other countries
8. respect for life
9. political involvement
10. respect for people
11. links with oppressive regimes
12. military sales
13. marketing policy.

The first general area concerned the degree of secrecy sorrounding corporate activity. Areas 2–4 were lumped together as 'employment issues'. They included such things as training, pensions, directors' pay, trade union recognition, profit sharing and policies towards women and ethnic minorities. Area 5 concerned charitable giving and involvement in community aid programmes. Area 6 covered a wide range of environmental issues from pollution control to conserving the rainforests. Area 7 was about involvement with developing countries. Area 8 was about concern for animal life and, in particular, the use of animals in scientific experiments. Area 9 was concerned with donations to political parties and any resulting conflicts of interest; also donations to politically aligned bodies and payments to the Economic League (an organization which blacklists potential employees on political grounds). Area 10 concerned involvement with alcohol, tobacco, and gambling. Area 11 was reduced to links with South Africa. Area 12 concerned involvement with the arms trade and defence contracts in general. Area 13 was an occasional category to cover cases where companies had adopted a morally controversial approach in advertising and marketing their products.

In addition to a descriptive evaluation of their performance in some or all of these 13 areas, companies were given given quick comparative ratings in 12 areas. These were basically the original 13 excluding 2, 3 and 13, with 4 split into separate ratings of equal opportunities for women and ethnic minorities, and 6 sub-divided into a rating for the environmental impact of a company's activities and another for activity aiming at environmental improvement. The ratings themselves were a mixture of comparisons with other companies, straight yes/no answers, and attempts to broadly quantify the degree of involvement in particular areas. For example, companies were compared to each other with regard to their disclosure of information, had yes/no ratings for political involvement, and a quantitative rating for military sales.

What emerged from the survey was a wide variation in company attitudes to ethical issues. Some companies, particularly the American, had well developed policies in the relevant areas and were obviously keen to be seen in a good ethical light, while others had neither the policies nor any very discernible concern about ethical matters. For example, it was concluded about the Kellogg Company that it 'clearly takes seriously the maintenance of its role as a good corporate citizen, and a high level of disclosure aids evaluation of its policies'. However for the House of Fraser it was concluded that 'this major retailing company presents an extremely negative record in both the social responsibility and business ethics fields'. The general lesson of the survey, however, is not just the range of company responses to these issues but the range of those issues themselves; involving just about every aspect of busiess activity be it organizational, financial, technological, political or environmental.

Source: R Adams, *et al.* (eds), *Changing Corporate Values* (London: Kogan Page, 1991).

DISCUSSION TOPICS

1. Are there some things that are wrong irrespective of the consequences? Give examples and reasons.
2. Consider the following ethical issues in business. How would they be viewed by
   (a) a utilitarian
   (b) a Kantian
   (c) a 'natural law' theorist
   (d) a non-cognitivist?
      (i)   factory farming
      (ii) 'whistle blowing'
      (iii) attitudes to 'shrinkage' of stock
      (iv) bribery
      (v)   an 'equal opportunities' employment policy.

3. Using the checklist for moral evaluation on p. 106, consider to what
   extent the following types of business practice are ethically acceptable:
   (a) offering someone a job because his or her father is a friend of
       yours;
   (b) declaring your work place a 'no smoking' zone;
   (c) declaring several redundancies in the interests of profitability;
   (d) starting a price war to put competitors out of business;
   (e) burning crops to boost market prices.

Not all of the points are necessarily applicable to each example, so
consider the ones which seem the most relevant. You may feel that these
brief descriptions provide insufficient detail to enable you to reach an
ethical judgment. If so, feel free to invent additional details as needed.
Devise examples of your own and test them in a similar way.

Capitalism, markets and justice

4

What is capitalism?
Markets, social markets and market socialism
Is capitalism just?

Introducing the readings

From unjust markets to just distribution   Saul Estrin
Can socialism change its spots?   Chris R. Tame
The capitalist system and the worker: Analysis and summary of the
  encyclicals   Phillip Hughes
Anarchy, state and utopia   R. Nozick
A theory of justice   John Rawls

Case study
Employee capitalism: the story of NFC

Discussion topics

WHAT IS CAPITALISM?

Although the term 'capitalism' is widely taken for granted amongst economists and students of business studies, relatively little attention has been given to offering any systematic analysis of what the term means. Although on the surface it may seem fairly obvious what a capitalist system is, there is scope for divergent views on the subject. We therefore intend to examine a number of possible defining characteristics of capitalism, and to suggest our own preferred definition.

The following may seem to be an acceptable way of defining capitalism: 'an economic system combining the private ownership of productive enterprises with competition between them in the pursuit of profit'.

The advantage of this formulation is that it picks out the three aspects which are generally accepted as defining features of the system. These are:

- private ownership
- competition
- the profit motive.

The adjective 'private' means that ownership is not vested in the state; 'competition' is essentially for sales to customers; and 'profit' is to be understood in the everyday business sense of a surplus of income from sales over costs incurred. It might be suggested that these three defining characteristics are insufficient, and that some additional ones are needed. For example, it might be suggested that with capitalism there is also minimal government intervention in the running of the economy. However, as a statement about what presently goes on in capitalist countries this would have to be rejected as false. In practice there is often a great deal of government intervention in the running of capitalist economies and it is certainly always more than any possible minimum. Most importantly, there is macro-economic management through government manipulation of interest rates, tax rates, public expenditure, and public borrowing. In addition, there is frequently a more direct kind of government economic intervention through the offering of tax incentives, subsidies, state aid for ailing industries, government rescue packages for bankrupt businesses and, in many cases, a degree of state ownership of businesses. There has undoubtedly been a general decline in this kind of direct intervention in recent years, with a strong trend towards policies of deregulation and privatization in many capitalist countries – most notably the UK. None the less, direct intervention by governments still remains a considerable feature of capitalist economies. In any case, the kind of indirect intervention represented by government macro-economic management remains essentially intact and seems to be a permanent part of any modern capitalist economy.

It follows that talk of minimal government intervention would seem to be less a description of capitalism as it is than a plea for it to take a particular form; specifically, the *laissez-faire* form. (*'Laissez-faire'* literally means 'leave to do', and hence a *laissez-faire* economy is one which is left free to operate without government intervention.) Its advocates argue that capitalism is that much more efficient if the economic role of the state is kept to some absolute minimum. The more extreme among them would restrict the economic activity of governments to the protection of property, the enforcement of contracts, the upholding of rules of fair competition, and not much else. Few might go that far, but the decline in direct economic intervention by governments in recent years is a testimony to the resurgence of this general approach. It remains, however, deeply controversial. But even supposing that it were not and that the *laissez-faire* view of the workings of capitalism was indubitably correct, this would still not require us to add the words 'minimal government intervention' to our list of core characteristics. All it would add is the qualification that capitalism works best when the economic role of the state is kept to some absolute minimum. In other words, 'minimal government intervention' becomes part of a definition of a better form of capitalism rather than capitalism as such.

It is open for advocates of *laissez-faire* to insist that we have 'capitalism proper' – capitalism in some pure and undiluted sense – where the role of the state is kept to some absolute minimum. This may well be correct. From a historical point of view it probably is. Large scale and widespread government intervention in the running of capitalist economies is very much a twentieth-century phenomenon. Moreover, the rise of capitalism in the eighteenth and nineteenth centuries was strongly associated with the spread of *laissez-faire* ideas. Even so, minimal government intervention need not be added to our list of defining features. The consequence of any reduced role for the state is an enhanced role for private ownership, competition, and the profit motive. It is precisely because proponents of *laissez-faire* believe that these three factors are more effective than the actions of government that they want state intervention kept to a minimum. It follows, therefore, that even in terms of a purist conception of capitalism we need not add minimal government intervention to our list. All we need do is add that for the capitalism under consideration to be pure and undiluted, the private ownership must be maximized, the competition unfettered, and the profit motive be given full rein. In short, all that is needed is our three defining features – with somewhat more emphasis.

It could of course be that something more modest than advocacy of *laissez-faire* is meant by talk of minimal government intervention. It could simply be the obviously correct claim that capitalism involves less intervention than in the almost totally state controlled economies of countries that are or were under communist control. Yet even when interpreted as making this obviously true claim, we still need not add minimal government intervention to the list of defining features. Given the requirements of private property, competition, and profit, there is no way the role of governments could be anything but significantly less than in an almost totally state controlled economy. As before, the addition would be superfluous.

There is a similar tale to tell with some of the more psychological characteristics which might be attributed to capitalism; such traits as 'individualism', 'independence', 'enterprise', and the like. Again, the extent to which they hold are open to doubt and they can, in any case, be accounted for by our core characteristics.

What is really being talked about when these traits are attributed to capitalism are entrepreneurs. These are people who both own and run businesses. They are presumably enterprising by definition. They are also independent in the sense that they are their own bosses; in their working lives at least, no one tells them what to do. For this reason, if no other, we can also presume that they are in some sense 'individualistic'. But however generous we are in attributing these traits to entrepreneurs, this does little to identify them with capitalist society in general. Entrepreneurs are a relatively small minority within a capitalist society. Most of the working population, including those that are managers, are employees. So as far as the traits under discussion are specific to entrepreneurs, they are not generally found in a capitalist society. One might even argue that as they are the traits of a boss, they require the prevalence of precisely contrary traits in that very much larger number of people who are bossed, namely conformity, dependence, and obedience.

In principle, it is open to anyone in a capitalist society to become an entrepreneur. In practice however, not everyone wants to be an entrepreneur, and not everyone can be. This is not just because many people lack the necessary qualities or resources – the commitment, capital, experience, expertise, or whatever. There are structural limits too. A modern economy involves centralized services and the mass production of goods. It requires large organizations, which require a large work force. Given capitalistic forms of ownership, the great mass of the working population have to be employees for such an economy to function. Moreover, entrepreneurship is only a worthwhile option if not too many people engage in it. The more that do, the more both chances of success and opportunities for growth are diminished. Thus, entrepreneurship and its attendant traits not only happen to have, but necessarily must have, a relatively restricted distribution if a modern capitalist society is to function effectively.

To make this point is not to lose sight of the vital role of entrepreneurship within capitalism. It may be in limited supply, but the supply is essential; 'the "life-blood" of the system', those unafraid of uttering clichés might say. Without it new businesses would not start up and the old ones would soon ossify. This is undeniably true; but it does not mean that those bundles of qualities we identify with entrepreneurship are to be added to the list of core features. Again, they can be explained as consequences of the three so far given. Entrepreneurial individualism, independence, enterprise, and even the very function of entrepreneurship itself, are understandable as responses to a situation in which there is private ownership, competition, and the possibility of personal gain through profits.

Individualism can of course be understood in some larger sense of a general social diversity and non-conformity rather than anything specifically entrepreneurial. This is, however, a kind of individualism to which capitalism seems positively antithetical. It is certainly not welcomed in large corporations or amongst business people in general. Here social conformity of behaviour, appearance, and even belief, is very much the order of the day. While with global production and marketing, modern capitalism is very arguably imposing a world-wide uniformity in consumer products, outlets, and even in the consumers themselves. (Witness McDonald's in Moscow.) It is perhaps unsurprising then that if we compare, for example, Britain with Germany, the USA with Japan, or western economies in general with those of the Far East, we could well be justified in concluding that the greater the social conformity the better a capitalist economy works.[1] This might be true of any kind of modern

[1] See W. G. Ouchi, *Theory Z* (Reading, Mass.: Addison-Wesley, 1981), p 51, on the idea that the collectivism of Japanese society is better suited to an industrial economy than the individualism of Western countries.

industrial economy of course; but it seems no less true of the capitalist kind.

Finally, it is possible to be just as brief with any idea that the presence of political democracy and material prosperity are defining features. The fact there have been and are capitalist societies without one or both of these things puts paid to this suggestion. This is so even given the highly significant fact that **only** predominantly capitalist societies have managed to successfully attain either. What this points to is the possibility that while capitalism is no guarantee of either democracy or prosperity, it is at least a prerequisite for them.

We can have capitalism without prosperity or democracy but not, it might be suggested, either of them without capitalism.[2] Given the undoubted desirability of democracy and prosperity, the very obvious point of this argument is to deny the possibility of any acceptable alternative to capitalism as an economic system. It is therefore very controversial. But even within the terms set by this controversial argument the characteristics of democracy and prosperity still do not become definitive of the system. Rather, they are seen as a consequence of it. Given profit-orientated competition, so the argument goes, we have the economic efficiency which makes material prosperity possible; and given the dispersal of power which comes with private ownership, we have a necessary precondition for political democracy. Yet again we have features which, if they hold at all, can be accounted for by our three core characteristics.

Capital employing labour – a fourth condition

There is, though, at least one critical aspect of the system for which our trio does not adequately account. This is the functional division between capital and labour within capitalist enterprises; the fact that capital employs labour. It means that the providers of labour are, within the terms of their employment, accountable to the providers of capital for what they do, either directly or through management appointees. It also means the providers of capital have sole right to the products of labour and to any profits derived from their sale. It is a relationship which holds because the enterprises concerned are both owned and ultimately controlled by the providers of capital as distinct from the providers of labour. In short, capital employs labour because the enterprises which

---

[2] See, for example, Milton Friedman, *Free to Choose* (Harmondsworth: Penguin, 1980), p 21.

do the employing are owned and ultimately controlled by capital rather than labour. (This is why the system is called 'capitalism'.) We can therefore sum up this fourth characteristic as:

- Ownership and ultimate control are vested in capital as distinct from labour.

To see that this fourth condition cannot be accounted for by any of the other three we need only look to that supposedly prime example of a non-capitalist enterprise, the worker co-operative. Like the capitalist enterprise, the worker co-operative is privately owned, has to compete with other businesses, and seeks to make a profit. The difference is that in a traditional worker co-operative, the work-force will collectively own and control the enterprise. They effectively employ themselves. They therefore own the product of their labour and with this any profit from its sale. Here then is an arrangement which combines private ownership, competition, and the profit motive, yet is regarded as manifestly non-capitalist; indeed, is very often set up as an alternative to capitalism. What this argument seems to demonstrate is that this condition is necessary to capitalism. Unless it holds, a business enterprise does not count as 'capitalist'. What then of our other three core characteristics? Are they also necessary to a capitalistic arrangement for business enterprises? Two at least seem to be.

Without the first – that of private ownership – we could not distinguish between capitalist businesses and commercially structured state owned companies; for example, the French car maker Renault. From a legal point of view such companies can be indistinguishable from capitalist firms. (The government can simply be the sole or major shareholder.) They can be required to compete with other businesses. They can make and distribute profits in exactly the same way as any capitalist firm and, like a capitalist firm, both ownership and ultimate control will be vested in suppliers of capital rather than labour. The only difference is that the capital which does the owning and controlling is public rather than private.

A similar argument applies to the third condition, that of profit. We need this to distinguish between capitalist businesses and mutual corporations. These include building societies, consumer co-operatives, and many large insurance companies. They have to compete with other businesses. They are also privately owned, but not by shareholders or entrepreneurs. Rather, they are run for the benefit of their customers: their members, depositors, policy holders, and so on. In that sense it can perhaps be said that their ownership and control is vested in capital rather than labour. Certainly, those who work for them are employees in exactly the same way as in a capitalist enterprise. Where they differ from capitalist enterprises is that in being run for the benefit of customers they are not being run for profit. They can show a surplus on their trading, but as this surplus belongs to the customers from whom it was derived and not a separate group of shareholders or entrepreneur owners, it cannot be counted as 'profit' in any properly capitalistic sense. (If worker co-operatives can be said to dissolve the distinction between capital and labour, the mutual corporation can be said to dissolve the distinction between capital and customer.)

The only one of our four central features which does not seem essential to distinguishing a peculiarly capitalistic form of business enterprise is competition. To demonstrate this we need look no further than the recently privatized gas, water, electricity, and telecommunications utilities in the UK. These companies face little or no competition; they are monopolies, or at least virtual monopolies. Yet they are manifestly capitalist, replete with shareholders, dividends, and the employment of labour by capital. They exemplify, in other words, private ownership and profit combined with ownership and ultimate control by capital. With the absence of just one of those features their status as capitalist organizations would presumably be lost; with the absence of competition it is not. They are necessary conditions while competition is not.

This is not a conclusion about either the prevalence or importance of competition. There is no denial of the fact that most capitalist enterprises are not monopolies or of the idea that competition between them will contribute to their efficiency. It is purely a conclusion about what it means for an enterprise to be capitalist. In the last analysis, it is an analysis of how to use the word 'capitalism'.

Those anxious to pursue a purist conception of capitalism might go for the option of giving equal status to competition and making all four conditions necessary. This would deny any monopoly the title 'capitalist' no matter how much it might otherwise fit the bill. (From a *laissez-faire* point of view this might be no more than they deserve.)

Those anxious to adopt a more flexible approach, while concerned for political reasons to retain the title 'capitalist' wherever possible, might go for the option of not making any of the four conditions necessary. This would make for a range of different kinds of capitalism. There would be what might, in deference to the purists, be called 'capitalism proper', when all four conditions held. But there could also be variation on this basic theme. (In practice, any three from four will do.) The absence of ownership and control by capital would not deny worker co-operatives the title 'capitalist'. They would merely become instances of what might be called 'worker capitalism'. Likewise, the absence of private ownership would simply make state firms instances of 'state capitalism'. While the absence of the profit motive in mutual corporations would distinguish a variant describable as 'consumer capitalism'. Finally, privately owned, profit making, capital based businesses without competition could be qualified as 'monopoly capitalism'.

None of this matters, provided we are clear about what is meant in each case. What is important is not the word 'capitalism' but what it is used to refer to. The problem is that faced with such a complex and politically fraught concept as capitalism, it is very difficult to be clear about what is being referred to without some agreed account of its central features.

We would recommend the account which keeps the combination of private ownership and profit along with ownership and ultimate control by capital as necessary features while allowing that competition, though usual and vital, is not a necessary condition. This puts the emphasis in defining capitalist on the internal structure of enterprises rather than the context within which they operate; on the kind of organization they are rather than the way they function in relation to other enterprises. This is, we would suggest, an account of what it is to be capitalist which not only best agrees with ordinary usage, but is the one which can be most usefully applied in dealing with debates about alternatives to capitalism (in the next section). The option of having no necessary conditions at all admits too much. Enterprises such as worker co-operatives, state owned companies, and mutual corporations which a few might be inclined to see as capitalist, are accorded the title. However, the option of insisting on competition as a necessary condition excludes too much. It refuses to admit enterprises such the privatized UK utilities which seem undeniably capitalist.

One final point to be noted is that this rejection of competition as a necessary condition is also supported by the blindingly obvious fact that, far from being integral to the existence of capitalist businesses, competition is very much something to be avoided. It is worth engaging in only when, paradoxically enough, it leads to the elimination of competitors. Otherwise it is simply a painful necessity which not only threatens the survival of a business but will, if pushed too far, lead to a reduced level of profit for all those competing businesses which do manage to survive. A tacit agreement to keep competition which limits can be an all too frequent outcome.[3] Left to themselves, businesses can even attempt to reduce or eliminate competition by tacit devices such as mergers, take-overs, and price fixing cartels. Consequently, governments seek to overcome this anti-competitive tendency in capitalism by passing anti-monopoly legislation and setting up agencies to oversee it. Were competition to be definitive of the system then presumably such outside interference would not be needed?

This is not to deny a spontaneous tendency to competition within capitalism. Firms need to make profits in order to survive and prosper, and this drive for profit is almost certainly a greater incentive to competition than the promptings of governments. The obvious paradox is that this same drive for profit is also, as we have just seen, the incentive for moves by businesses to restrict or suppress competition. In terms of our four core features, profit is the objective, private ownership and the employment of labour by capital are the means, while competition is merely an obstacle. Unsurprisingly, it is sometimes more advantageous to avoid the obstacle than overcome it.

MARKETS, SOCIAL MARKETS AND MARKET SOCIALISM

There is a tendency to use the words 'capitalism' and 'market economy' interchangeably. (One might even say the latter has become a euphemism for the former.) In the sense that, in practice at least, a capitalist economy is always a market economy this identification is not problematic. What is problematic is any assumption that the identification is somehow exclusive: that **only** capitalist economies can be market economies. Capitalism is certainly the usual way of organizing market economies but not, it can be argued, the only possible way. There are alternatives; some apparently very different from traditional capitalism, others less so. The least different allow that there is scope within a market economy for what can be seen as crucial modifications to traditional capitalist structures. The most different claim that these struc-

---

[3] An article in the *Sunday Times* of 18th August 1991 revealed that while the average mark up in British supermarket chains was 60%, in Germany it was only half that amount. It also revealed that at 8% the profit margins of British supermarket companies are four times the West European average. The article quotes an MP as saying: 'I don't believe the supermarkets are competitive on price. They know what each other is going to charge, they don't have to sit round a table and agree it among themselves.' (See Adam Smith's warning: reading 3, chapter 3.)

tures can be partially or totally replaced by distinctly non-capitalist alternatives while still preserving a market economy. The modificatory approach can take a variety of forms of which arguably the most significant is that of the 'social market'. The second approach – total or partial replacement – is 'market socialism'. To see just what they modify or replace we need only refer back to the account of capitalism already given. To see how, despite these departures, they might still be market economies we need to add an account of just what it is to be an economy of that sort.

The most general characteristic of a market economy is 'voluntary exchange'. What is exchanged are goods and services. What they are exchanged for are either other goods and services or, more usually, money. What makes the transaction 'voluntary' is a lot more complicated. It varies with three different but overlapping senses of that word.

The first is fairly obvious. It is 'freedom from coercion' in the sense that neither of the partners in the exchange is forcing the other to make the exchange through threats of violence, blackmail, and the like. This then, is an obvious and unconditional requirement of market transactions.

The second meaning raises many more questions. It is 'freedom from external control' in the sense that the partners are left alone to decide the terms of their exchange. What, in practice, they would have to be left alone from is state regulation. The rejection of state regulation by advocates of *laissez-faire* is an appeal for voluntariness in this second sense. It is also the very particular sense in which their approach to economic management is an appeal for markets. This follows because any kind and degree of government regulation of exchanges will, as a simple matter of definition, make them less voluntary and therefore less of a market transaction.

This does not mean that state regulation has to be completely absent from markets. Only regulation which totally controlled exchanges in every respect, would eliminate all voluntariness and with it all traces of market status. Regulation which is limited in the degree of control it enforces or in the areas it exercises control over, is perfectly possible. To the extent state regulation is limited in either or both of these ways, exchanges would be voluntary and so would, to that same extent, have a market status.

Nor does it even follow that every kind of state regulation of exchanges will, on balance, reduce their market status. Some positively promote it.

Most fundamentally, there have to be laws which establish property rights: laws which define who owns what. Without them people would not even know what was theirs to exchange. In addition, there have to be laws to protect those rights: laws against theft, fraud, and extortion. Without them exchange would probably be too hazardous to be worth engaging in. Such laws will certainly reduce voluntariness in the sense of freedom from external control, but would seem essential to voluntariness in the first and perhaps more fundamental sense of freedom from coercion. Finally, it is at least desirable that market economies have laws against cartels, monopolies, and against restrictive trade practices in general. Without them a market economy would be that much less efficient because it would be that much less competitive.

The place of competition within a market economy is not, however, merely that of an aid to efficient functioning. It is a definitive feature. Market exchanges are not just voluntary, they are competitive. This follows from the fact that anything worth exchanging, be it goods and services or money, will have to be something for which there is a demand but not also an unlimited supply. (Why else exchange?) It is a combination which means that, **unless** intervening action is taken, then there is almost inevitably going to be competition of some sort. It will be between buyers to acquire the things in limited supply, and between sellers to meet the demand. Supply will therefore have to be balanced against demand. To the extent that the supply of any particular item of exchange is low and demand high, buyers will have to compete with each other to purchase. To the extent that supply is high and demand low, sellers will have to compete with each other for sales.

Intervening action to prevent competition can be the formation of monopolies and cartels. It can also be the use of coercion by one of the partners in the exchange. (Someone imposing an exchange in this way clearly has no need to compete.) Likewise, particular kinds of state control can wholly or partly eliminate competition: actions such as rationing, price fixing, production quotas, and the like. In certain very important respects, therefore, voluntariness is a pre–condition for competition. This is, however, absolutely so only for freedom from coercion. For freedom from external control it will depend on the kind of controlling action the state takes. As we have seen, some kinds of state control work to make competitive exchanges possible. Some even work to make them more competitive than they would otherwise have been. There is, in short, no necessary correlation between voluntariness in the second sense of freedom from external (state) control and competition.

Voluntariness in our third and final sense is 'freedom of choice'. This is not, as with the other two senses, merely the absence of some kind of constraint. It is something positive; a freedom to choose between alternative options. With it there is a necessary correlation with competition. That correlation is, however, asymmetrical; the more it is granted to one side in an exchange, the more it is taken away from the other. Competition is, so to speak, a two-edged sword. It widens the freedom of choice of those whose goods and services are competed for, precisely because it restricts that of those who have to do the competing. The more buyers have to compete in purchasing products in short supply but great demand, the less freedom of choice they have with regard to price, quality, variety, and so on. In such a situation sellers can dictate the terms. Conversely, the more sellers have to compete in selling products in great supply but low demand, the less freedom of choice they have in these same areas. Here it is the buyers who can dictate terms. Given fierce enough competition, one side may have little choice but to accept what the other side offers. The only option might be to take it or leave it.

Since competition is something in which **both** buyer and seller engage, it is not a provider of freedom of choice but rather the determinant of how it is distributed between the two partners in the exchange. This is the approach adopted by economists when they talk about markets in terms of 'perfect competition'. What they mean, very roughly, is that a situation in which competition between buyers and sellers is so perfectly balanced that supply and demand exactly match each other and the price arrived at is the maximum buyers are prepared to pay and the minimum sellers are prepared to accept.[4] It is accepted that this is an idealization. In practice few if any markets will come near to meeting the conditions that are needed for perfect competition. The few that might include stock exchanges and perhaps some agricultural commodity markets – wheat, for example. These are all what might be called 'trading markets'; that is to say, markets in which professional traders, some in the business of buying and others in the business of selling, engage in one-to-one bargaining. Markets of this kind have an obviously large and important role within a modern market economy; but they are clearly not what such an economy is mostly about. What it is mostly about is consumption. It is a 'consumer market'. It is a society of material abundance; at

---

[4] For a non-technical exposition of perfect competition in a business ethical context see M. Velasquez, *Business Ethics* (Englewood Cliffs: Prentice-Hall, 1992), section 4.1.

least by the standards of the past. By and large, the availability of goods and services is restricted only by the willingness and ability of consumers to pay for them. There is general competition between consumers only in the rather narrowly technical sense that their collective demand for any particular item of consumption helps determine its average price and with that how much of it they can afford to consume. Consumers do not normally have to compete with each other in anything like the more everyday sense of having to win out against specifiable opponents in order to complete a transaction. Such active and individualized competition is, in a modern market economy, largely restricted to producers. What they compete for are consumer preferences. To win those preferences they must satisfy them with what they produce, which means that production must be geared to consumption. Thus there cannot be parity of either freedom of choice or of competition between consumer and producer in a modern market economy. Put crudely but effectively, consumers have the choice, producers do the competing. To the extent those roles are reversed, either through shortages or restrictive practices, we do not have a market economy of the modern consumer kind. In its broadest outline, therefore, a modern market economy is nothing more than a system of voluntary exchange in which there is a general subordination of production to consumption brought about through competition between producers.

In principle, there could be a subordination of production to consumption without competition. Producers could collectively attempt to give consumers what they require. This was attempted in communist 'command' economies. There was to be a rational organization of production to meet social needs. It was to be a 'production for use' which would avoid the misdirection of resources and wasteful duplication of products and services which were presumed to result from the competitively based 'production for profit' of capitalism. This rational organization was to be effected by central planning agencies setting production targets for individual enterprises. The function of the individual enterprises was simply to meet those targets. The price at which they could sell their products was generally fixed for them by the planners and was often heavily subsidized. There was an element of voluntary exchange only in the sense that consumers were free to decide what to spend their money on. There was though no direct consumer determination of what was produced. That was, at least in principle, left to central planning, though the reality seems to have been a good deal more chaotic.

This arrangement was not without its early successes when there was some very specific objective demanding the mass mobilization of labour: the establishment of heavy industry, the building up of an infrastructure, the exploitation of a natural resource, the achievement of some large scale technological breakthrough, and so on. (It is not for nothing that there is resort to command structures in market economies during war time.) But overall, there can be little doubt that central planning has proved greatly inferior to the decentralized competition of a market based capitalism in meeting consumer needs.

This has, moreover, proved to be a curious inversion of what was supposed to happen. The Marxist theory was that capitalism would collapse through its inability to manage its own productiveness. Those periods of economic recession endemic to capitalism when supply out-stripped demand, would culminate in a final and fatal 'crisis of over-production'. The great paradox of history is that the system which communism established to overcome that problem collapsed because of its inability to meet even the most basic needs of people; a crisis of **under-production**. The lesson of history, therefore, is that in so far as the choice lies between a centrally planned command economy and a market economy and the issue is one of relative efficiency, it is the latter which must be chosen. The only question is, what kind of market economy?

The social market

The answer which says a 'social market' is difficult to pin down. The phrase is German in origin and has a precise meaning only in so far as one can point to the way in which that country runs a market economy. This approach emerged in what was then West Germany during the aftermath of the Second World War. It started as the economic pro-gramme of the newly-formed Christian Democratic party but was eventually accepted, and even extended, by their Social Democratic opponents. Today it is a consensus view, enjoying broad support across the main political parties in Germany.

Despite now being part of a consensus, and despite also the fact the German Christian Democrats are not an exclusively Roman Catholic party, this view of how a market should be run has a distinctly Catholic intellectual origin. It stems from an approach to economic and political questions called 'Catholic social thought'. This began in the late nine-teenth century as the Catholic Church's response to liberalism and socialism. Both these two very different political movements were opposed for their generally secular and sometimes strongly anti-clerical policies. Both were also castigated as being, in their own very different ways, socially divisive. Liberalism by its adherence to a *laissez-faire* form of capitalism which had little regard for the rights or interests of workers, and socialism by its exploitation of the legitimate grievances of workers in the name of a class struggle aimed at toppling the capitalist order.

In their stead, Catholic social thought proposed co-operation between classes; in particular, between capitalists and workers. Capitalistic forms of ownership were defended as embodying a 'right to private property', while the force of socialist attacks on capitalism were to be blunted by recognizing a parallel right to just treatment for workers. For political parties operating within this tradition, putting these aims into practice produced a distinctive mix of policies. Adherence to capitalism and a general conservatism on social issues has been combined with support for state welfare provision and a willing acceptance of a role for trade unions within industry – even to the extent of supporting specifically Catholic or Christian trade unions.

In Germany this kind of politics has produced the idea of management and labour as 'social partners' needing to work together in the best interest of the company and of society. It is an idea which has taken concrete form in a series of laws requiring worker–management 'co-determination' in the running of commercial businesses.[5] This is imposed at two levels: that of the individual plant and of the company as a whole.

In all plants with five or more permanent employees, staff have the right to elect a 'work's council' which, depending on the numbers employed, will have anything from 3 to 31 members. (Below 20 employees they elect a single 'work's representative'). These staff representatives have equal power of decision making ('co-decision') with the plant management on a whole range of local issues ranging from health and safety matters to the fixing of break times and bonus rates. Here proposals can come from either side and have to be jointly agreed. On other issues the right of decision making belongs to management alone but they must either seek the consent of the work's council with what they propose or at least consult it before they take action. Matters requiring consent include grading, regrading, transfers of personnel, and vocational training. Those requiring consultation include any planned contraction or expansion in the work-force, alterations in production methods which affect staff requirements, as well as dismissal cases. In

---

[5] There are separate and weaker structures of participation for state employees. Also, family owned companies and media companies, as well as religious and political organizations, are exempt from many of the provisions of the co-determination legislation.

firms with more than 100 regular employees, the work's council has a right, through a system of 'economic committees', to information on the firm's financial situation and long term plans which is not commercially sensitive. The law also makes any agreements between management and the work's council legally binding on both parties, and charges both to act in the best interests of employees and the plant.

At the level of the company as a whole, co-determination is achieved through employee representation on 'supervisory boards'. Under German company law, every joint stock company (those owned through share-holdings) must have such a board. It is the ultimate governing body of the company. It appoints, and has power of dismissal over, a separate 'management board' that has charge of the day-to-day running of the company. The executives sitting on the management board are not only answerable to the supervisory board for their conduct of company affairs, they may (if the company charter says so) require its consent for major decisions on such matters as investment, borrowing, and the appointment and dismissal of senior staff.

In companies employing 500 people or less, only shareholders elect the supervisory board and employees have no representation. Where more than 500 people are employed, employees elect one third of the board and shareholders the other two thirds. Where more than 2000 people are employed the two have, in principle, equal representation. In practice, shareholders will usually have majority control. This happens for two reasons. Firstly, because at least one representative of senior management must be included among employee members and such representatives are likely to be sympathetic to shareholder interests. Secondly, and more crucially, because the chairperson can exercise a double vote in the event of a tie and this is an office which is normally held by a shareholder representative. Legally, this need not be so. The office can be held by a board member from either side. In practice, as the election of the chair requires a two thirds majority and after two ballots the shareholder representatives must decide alone, they have a virtual monopoly of the post and with it effective majority control. The exception to this shareholder dominance is in the mining and steel industries (in companies with more than 1000 employees) where there is fully equal worker–shareholder representation through the requirement of a neutral chairperson jointly agreed on by both sides.

Without co-determination, particularly at the supervisory board level, Germany's social market economy would amount to no more than a rather strong version of the 'welfare capitalism' generally practised in all advanced Western economies since the end of the second world war and, until the recent revival of *laissez-faire* ideas, generally accepted by mainstream parties in those countries. It is a form of capitalism involving comprehensive state welfare provision and extensive state economic intervention, very often coupled with attempts at nationally negotiated agreements between governments, employees and trade unions on economic matters.

With co-determination the social market is more than welfare capitalism. It represents an important modification in traditional capitalist structures. Though it leaves ownership of business to the providers of capital, it cedes partial control to the providers of labour. As such, it is a modification of the fourth of the defining features of capitalism; the one which makes both ownership and (ultimate) control the exclusive preserve of capital rather than labour.

The socialist market economy

Proponents of a social market can point to the concrete, and successful, example of Germany to back up their arguments. Proponents of market socialism have no such advantage. There are no examples of a fully functioning socialist market economy.[6] What they propose is therefore a largely theoretical construct.

Its starting point is the contention that markets can be socialist as well as capitalist. The aim is to uncouple markets as a system in which producers compete for consumer preferences from capitalism as a system involving a particular form of ownership and control for the productive enterprises doing the competing (hence the need to make this distinction in the previous section). The competitive system is endorsed, the peculiarly capitalist form of competing enterprise is rejected.

The grounds for that rejection are often twofold. There is always the broad objection that ownership and control are both too narrowly based in capitalist enterprises: vested in rich proprietors, wealthy private shareholders, anonymous fund managers, elite executives, and the like. As the work-force in general is far more numerous than any of these groups, it follows that if ownership and control of enterprises can be transferred

---

[6] It can be suggested that communist Yugoslavia was an actual (and unsuccessful) example of a socialist market economy. But whether, when, and to what extent Yugoslavia had such an economy is hotly debated. (See J. Buck, *Comparative Industrial Systems* (London: Macmillan, 1982), pp. 113–119). Whether, in any case, a one party dictactorship represents a fair example is another problem.

from capital to labour then this will achieve that dispersal of wealth and power which market socialists want. Secondly, there is often also the more specific objection that what is wrong with capitalist enterprises is that their ownership and control is vested in capital rather than labour. When combined these two criticisms lead to the contention that markets are capitalist to the degree that ownership and control of enterprises are narrowly based and vested in capital, socialist to the degree that they are broadly based and vested in labour.

On this criterion, the paradigm of a market socialist enterprise is the traditional worker co-operative. There both ownership and control are wholly vested in labour. If such enterprises could be made the norm throughout the economy then market socialism would achieve its inter-related aims of a dispersal of wealth and power and their transfer from capital to labour through a single mechanism. There is, though, some scepticism among many market socialists as to whether the worker co-operative is a suitable model for the economy as a whole. It is suitable, they say, for the smaller business but not the larger kind. The problem, very roughly, is that taking on extra workers can tend, at least in the short term, to reduce the per capita profit enjoyed by each member of the co-operative. The volume of profit may grow, but it will need to be shared among more people. In contrast, as long as the volume of profit is increased, however marginally, it will still pay a capitalist enterprise to take on more people. Consequently, so the argument goes, the capitalist firm will generally have a greater tendency to growth than the co-operative.[7]

If this argument is correct, then that distinction between capital and labour which the traditional worker co-operative dissolves will need to be preserved in the case of larger businesses. However, to meet market socialist objectives the relationship between the two will need, as far as possible, to be the reverse of that which holds with capitalism. Instead of capital employing labour, labour should employ capital. This can be attempted in a variety of ways.

With worker co-operative, there can be a combination of some degree of differential share holdings among members, the employment of a limited percentage of non-members, and the investing of non-voting share capital by non-members. Through such measures co-operative will

---

[7] See J. Legrand and S. Estrin (eds.), *Market Socialism* (Oxford: Oxford Univerity Press, 1989), for the source of most of this account of market socialism; and in particular, chapter 7, where Estrin discusses worker co-operatives.

hopefully have the tendency to growth of capitalist businesses while preserving their labour based character. (All these measures are, in fact, presently practised variants on the traditional model of equal and exclusive shareholding among all workers in enterprise.)

Another broader strategy is simply to expand employee share ownership in ordinary businesses through governments encouraging and requiring measures such as tax concessions, share options, loan facilities, and the like. In this market socialism would seem, rather surprisingly perhaps, to be at one with those advocating 'wider share ownership' as the means of establishing 'popular capitalism'. There is though, the crucial distinction that with market socialism the wider share ownership is a strategic move to alter the present balance of wealth and power in capitalist society rather than, as it often seems with advocates of popular capitalism, simply a tactical move to increase support for capitalism. The aim for market socialism is that to some significant extent workers will own and control the businesses they work for, rather simply holding a modest and perhaps merely nominal stake in it.

An alternative proposal would achieve some of the same objectives without requiring employees to have to buy shares. It would turn large firms into 'labour–capital partnerships'. This would be a radical extension of the social market idea. It would recognize that businesses require the coming together of labour and capital by giving each side an equal share not only in the control of the business but in its profits also (though with ownership of its assets remaining in the hands of shareholders).

More complicated proposals involve large firms being turned into worker-managed units at a plant level, while at a head office level the firm as a whole is turned into a financial holding company which would oversee and co-ordinate the operations of the local units. The holding companies themselves could have several different forms of ownership, no one form of which need be dominant. They could be collectively owned by the local worker-managed units. They could be wholly owned by shareholders with employees enjoying only a share in control. They could be organized as labour–capital partnerships in the way described above. They could have some kind of public ownership; either through direct state ownership, or through a state-sponsored investment fund set up to achieve the widest possible spread of ownership.

The sorts of proposal presented above represent a particular strand in socialist thinking. It is one which, although it has a long history and is now once again coming to the fore, has never been dominant in the socialist tradition. The dominant tendency has supposed incompatibility between markets and socialism. The basis of this supposition is that while markets are about competition, socialism is about co-operation. In reply, market socialists recognize this is so but deny the implication that socialism and markets are incompatible. They point out that markets also require co-operation between people, that they connect producers with consumers and that this connection can work to their mutual benefit. Nor, they insist, is competition necessarily the destructive force which socialists have generally supposed it to be. It depends on how the competing is organized. Provided there is equal opportunity to compete, and provided people are shielded from the harsher effects of competition by state action, then the benefits will outweigh the disadvantages.

The belief that markets and socialism are incompatible led socialists to espouse alternatives to market mechanisms in the form of central planning and the setting up of state-owned monopolies. This was always a means to an end. The end, very roughly, was the elimination of poverty and social disadvantage, along with the attainment of the widest possible spread of wealth and power in society. The hope was that central planning and the setting up of state monopolies would help attain these objectives. But if, as market socialists believe, socialism and markets can be compatible, then socialism does not necessarily have to resort to such non-market solutions. It has a choice between market and non-market mechanisms. The only question is which, on balance, and in any particular instance, will provide the best means for attaining socialist ends?

What defines market socialists is that, on balance, they favour market solutions as the means to socialist ends. They do so primarily on the grounds of superior efficiency. Only with the productive efficiency of markets can the socialist objectives of eliminating poverty and social disadvantage be attained. In addition, they compare the decentralization of markets to the centralization of planned economies and judge that, provided suitable mechanisms for ownership and control are implemented, markets are a superior vehicle for attaining the dispersal of wealth and power which all socialists seek.

IS CAPITALISM JUST?

Justice is a particular but pervasive and crucial aspect of morality. That aspect is the morally proper treatment of people. Justice is about ensuring that what is done to people is what ought to be done to them. It is about assessing actions affecting people in terms of the treatment those affected people are morally required to receive. It deals with these moral requirements as both constraints on action and also as imperatives to action. In everyday language, justice is about giving people what is 'fair', what they have a 'right' to and whatever it is that, to their advantage or disadvantage, they 'deserve'.

It follows that there can be different forms of justice depending on exactly what it is that people are morally entitled to. There is 'procedural' justice concerned with the fair and impartial administering of rules of procedure in trials and the like, 'corrective' justice concerned with giving proper recompense for wrongs suffered, 'retributive' justice concerned with dealing out morally appropriate punishments for wrongs committed, and so on. When questions about the justice of capitalism are raised, the form at issue is 'distributive' justice. This deals with fairness in the sharing out of benefits and burdens among people. The people concerned can be members of a particular group, society at large, or even humanity in general. When it is society at large, we can speak of 'social' justice and this is often the term used when the justice of capitalism is discussed.

The central point at issue in such discussions is the unequal distribution of wealth and income in capitalist societies. It is true that no one pattern of distribution precisely fits every capitalist society (a point to which we shall return), and that calculations are fraught with technical difficulties concerning the collection and assessment of data; nonetheless, the general form of the inequality is clear enough.

A substantial minority will receive incomes which fall significantly below the mean average for the population as a whole. Most will be around the average. A small minority will have anything up to several times average income. A tiny minority, decreasing in number as the size of their income increases, will exceed the average by much more: by tens or even hundreds, and in rare cases by thousands. Because distribution is so weighted towards the top, a majority will receive less than the mean average.

The distribution of wealth will broadly follow that for income. Anyone who is not reasonably close to an average income will probably have very little wealth. Those on around average income and few times above will probably have a fair degree of wealth. In total it will be a majority of the total wealth of society, though with much of it in the form of housing and pensions. Those on many times more than average income will have not only very much greater per capita wealth, but will tend to hold it in the 'marketable' forms of businesses, land, stocks, shares, and the like.

Those with the very largest incomes will probably derive most of it from their possession of wealth; that is, from the resulting profits, rents, dividends, and so on. Their wealth, like their income, can also exceed the average by tens, hundreds, and even thousands. (As income and wealth usually go together, we will generally use 'wealth' for both unless the difference needs to be made explicit.)

What is significant about this inequality is how very much more it relates to the top than the bottom. People can perhaps start to count as poor when they drop below half the average income. This means the average are usually only a couple or so times better off than the poor. The rich, on the other hand, can be almost any number of times better off than the average. There is a considerable gap between poor and average; one which can, moreover, make the difference between comfort and hardship. But in strictly quantitative terms, the really significant inequality is between the rich and the rest. This is shown in the fact that while it is possible to doubt that in advanced economies people are poor in any but strictly 'relative' sense, no one could say the same about being rich. The only question is at what stage, in the ever-increasing multiples of average wealth, it becomes impossible not to call a person 'rich'.

Wealth is not the only inequality at issue. There is an obvious correlation between different degrees of wealth and different degrees of power, with the richest having most power and the poorest having least. In a society where the rich are so much richer than the rest this correlation can lead to enormous concentrations of power; with again the really significant inequality being between the rich and the rest. On top of this, there is also the specifically capitalist arrangement of vesting control of enterprises in suppliers of capital. This provides a peculiarly direct correlation between wealth and power. It grants to the rich influence over people's working lives, over their economic fortunes and even, through purchase or ownership of the media of mass communication, their opinions. Thus, in terms of both a general correlation between wealth and power and a peculiarly capitalist way of controlling businesses, an unequal distribution of power is also at issue.

Those who find these inequalities questionable do not usually do so on the grounds that there ought to be a totally equal distribution of wealth and power. Their concern is invariably limited to the extremes; a sizeable minority being poor and mostly powerless, and a small minority being very rich and powerful. Nor are they even all concerned to redress every extreme, of riches as well as poverty, of power as well as wealth. For welfare capitalism, it is only inequality of wealth at the bottom end which is a problem. Tackling that problem could involve reducing the inequality of wealth at the top end through the use of progressive taxation to fund welfare programmes, but this need be nothing more than a means to an end of reducing poverty rather than a deliberate policy. For the social market economy a concern with inequalities of wealth is also limited to those at the bottom. What is added, through co-determination, is the aim of reducing those inequalities of work-place power that are specific to capitalism. For market socialism there is not only a concern with power as well as wealth, but with extremes of wealth at the top as well as the bottom. It seeks to transfer ownership as well as control from capital to labour as part of a general policy of aiming at the widest possible dispersal of both wealth and power.

Equality

Attitudes to distributive justice are largely distinguished by the extent to which it is identified with equality. Those who see a more or less close connection are 'egalitarians', while those who see little or no connection are 'anti-egalitarians'. But this measure, market socialism is egalitarian but in a qualified way which stops well short of demanding total equality. Welfare capitalism and a social market economy are a little more difficult to generalize about. They are, we can say, qualified anti-egalitarians with regard to wealth in that while they are not prepared to see people drop below an acceptable minimum, they see little or nothing wrong with extremes of wealth at the top. With regard to power, welfare capitalism is effectively anti-egalitarian, while the social market supports a very qualified egalitarianism in the area of people's working lives.

Though on balance both welfare capitalism and the social market economy could be said to fall within the anti-egalitarian half of the spectrum, they both represent forms of capitalism that are prepared to make considerable concessions to egalitarianism; in the case of the social market, very considerable concessions. Both can therefore be contrasted with an extreme *laissez-faire* capitalism which would accept no connection at all between distributive justice and equality. For advocates of extreme *laissez-faire*, their policy of non-interference in the operations of capitalist markets means accepting whatever distribution of wealth and power those markets produce. A distribution is just if it is the product of the free operation of capitalist markets unhindered by force, fraud, or government interference. How equal or unequal it is has no bearing on the matter.

This is a very radical position which would seem to run counter to our normal presuppositions. In our everyday thinking we seem to start from an initial assumption of equality. The paradigm of fair shares appears to be perfectly equal shares. Given a situation where things have to be divided among members of a group, the usual assumption seems to be that those things should be divided up equally unless there is some countervailing reason why not. Without such a reason, anything less than equal shares will almost certainly seem unfair – particularly to those whose share is less than equal.

On the other hand, there is no shortage of such countervailing reasons. There is a presumption in favour of perfectly equal shares only if it is accepted that the people concerned are not appreciably different from each other in any relevant respect. If this underlying assumption is not accepted, then the presumption in favour of equal shares becomes lost. It is, in short, equal shares for equal people only.

Need and merit

Here the radical position is the uncompromisingly egalitarian line that there are no relevant differences. It says that there is nothing about people which can distinguish them from each other in ways which warrant unequal shares. This is far from being our normal assumption. In everyday life we accept that there are ways in which unequal share can become not merely allowable but even obligatory. These ways divide, very roughly, into those which appeal to what people deserve and those which do not. Within the latter category, the principal criterion is probably need. Within the former it is usually merit. In fact, talk of 'desert' and 'merit' are often synonymous.

As a criterion of distributive justice, need is normally about remedying deficiencies. It is about helping the poor, the sick, and the generally underprivileged. It is about not permitting the quality of people's lives to fall below some acceptable and achievable minimum. Need is therefore an egalitarian principle, if only to the limited extent that it does not permit too much inequality at the bottom end of the social scale. It is the principle usually appealed to by those such as supporters of welfare capitalism, of social markets, and of market socialism who see poverty as unjust; but it has to be totally rejected by those who take the radical *laissez-faire* view that distributive justice and equality are wholly unconnected.

As a criterion of distributive justice, merit is very much the opposite of need in at least two ways. The first is that it is normally about matching distribution to contribution rather than to deficiency. It is about what is put in rather than taken out; with such things as differing degrees of effort, skill, ingenuity, and the like counting as relevant considerations. The second way merit is the opposite of need is that it has nothing to do with equality. The distribution is required to be proportional to merit, but this is not at all the same thing as equality. It means that as the merit of a contribution varies from individual to individual (as it most certainly will), so must the resultant distribution. For all to receive equal shares regardless of the value of their contributions would be deemed unjust. The just distribution is the one which matches distribution to contribution regardless of how equal or unequal this makes the resulting share-out.

Merit is therefore an anti-egalitarian principle and as such supports the *laissez-faire* view that a distribution does not need to be equal to be just. This is all it does, however. It does not demonstrate that capitalist distribution, particularly when based on unrestricted *laissez-faire*, is **in fact** just. For this to follow it would have to be that capitalist distribution actually is proportional to individual merit. This is arguably so to some extent, but it is clearly far from generally true. Capitalism does often reward merit, but not always or everywhere; nor does it reward every kind of merit. People can fail in business through no fault of their own. They can be rich because of inherited wealth, or because they were peculiarly unscrupulous, or just plain lucky. They can be poor through illness or misfortune. People can put tremendous effort and skill into poorly paid jobs. They can make an outstanding contribution as a scientist, scholar, social reformer, or whatever, and yet have very scant financial reward. Others of very much lesser talents can none the less make vast fortunes.

Utility

Given that they must reject appeals to need and that appeals to merit are difficult to sustain, defenders of *laissez-faire* will often attempt a utilitarian justification of inequality. It assumes a distribution is just if it maximizes aggregate utility. This may mean some people getting more or less than they need or merit; but if in terms of total utility people are better off, then this makes the distribution just. Granted that assumption, it is then pointed out that efficiency requires providing people with incentives in the form of unequal rewards, that efficiency makes society as a whole better off, and so in terms of maximizing total utility these unequal rewards are just.

As far as it goes, this is probably a sound enough argument. Efficiency does seem to require the incentives provided by unequal rewards, greater efficiency is generally conducive to greater all round utility, and there is a case for a utilitarian conception of justice.[8] The argument does not however necessarily support the *laissez-faire* view that there can be unlimited inequality. All that has been shown is that some unspecified degree of inequality is required if efficiency and utility are to be maximized. The degree required may in fact be rather limited; and as it turns out, there are good reasons for supposing that it is.

With regard to efficiency, international comparisons might on balance indicate that a market economy works best when there is a relatively modest degree of inequality; they certainly indicate that efficiency is not necessarily harmed by the inequality being modest. Taking the usual economist's measure of comparing the average bottom fifth of incomes with the average top fifth, we find some interesting variations. In highly successful Japan the top fifth have only 4.3 times the income of the bottom fifth. (This is slightly less than an estimated 4.4 gap in the former Soviet Union, and not much more than the 3 to 4 times ratio in the former communist countries of Eastern Europe.) In notably successful Germany the ratio is 5.7. In the less successful UK and USA the ratio is 6.8 and 8.9 respectively. In the less developed capitalist economies the gap is often wider. In Brazil, to choose a notoriously extreme example, there is 26.1 ratio. (It has been estimated that if this ratio could be reduced to 5, then the bottom fifth of the Brazilian population would enjoy a tenfold increase in income.)[9] The top fifth of incomes will range from a great majority who will earn around the average for the quintile to a small minority who will have incomes which are many times larger than that average; everyone, that is, from the merely well off to the super-rich. This is an enormously wide range of incomes. It can involve ratios measured in tens and even hundreds as compared to the merely single or (low) double digit ratios usual in comparing the average top and bottom fifths of the society at large. Thus, if there is a question about how wide the spread needs to be to provide incentives for society

[8] J. S. Mill attempts to give a utilitarian account of justice in his classic text *Utilitarianism* (1861).
[9] The figures are those of the 1991 'Human Development Report' of the United Nations Development Programme, and are quoted in M. Kidron and R. Segal, *The New State of the World Atlas* (London: Simon & Schuster, 1991), pp. 36–7. A Przeworski, *Democracy and the Market* (Cambridge University Press, 1991), p. 145, quotes older but very similar figures and gives the estimate on income inequality in the Soviet Union as well as the estimate of the effects of Brazilian re-destribution (p. 12).

at large, how much greater must it be for this very much more unequal top quintile? For example, on the basis of international comparisons, it seems reasonable to suppose that a shop floor worker might need around a fivefold increase in salary to be motivated to become a fairly senior executive in a medium sized company. But does that executive need a ten, twenty, or even a hundredfold increase to be motivated to become the executive in charge of a very large corporation? Would not a less accelerated increase motivate just as well?

Reason for thinking it might was provided during the 1992 visit to Japan of the US president, George Bush – the famous vomiting banquet tour. He took with him the chief executives of the three largest American motor companies. These executives came to plead for restrictions on the export of Japanese cars to the US. The force of their plea was somewhat blunted when it was pointed out that their opposite numbers in charge of Japan's very much more successful car companies were paid only around a tenth of their salaries. For example, the chairman of Chrysler, Mr Lee Iaccoca, received 4.5 million dollars a year, while the head of Honda was reputed to receive less than 400 000 dollars.

With regard to utility, constraints on inequality would seem to be imposed by what economists call 'diminishing marginal utility'. This is simply the point that the more of anything which anyone has, the less utility they are likely to derive from it. For example, the delight of a previously homeless person on moving into a new home will probably exceed that of the multi-millionaire buying his ninth or tenth mansion. On this basis, the aim of achieving a distribution which maximizes utility is likely to have a generally egalitarian emphasis. It will try to direct benefits to disadvantaged people who will derive the most utility from them, and away from advantaged people who will derive least, aiming for maximum average utility rather the potentially more unequal maximum total utility. (See chapter 3, Utilitarianism: an ethic of welfare.)

The disutilities stemming from unrestrained inequality are also relevant. These include the likely resentment of the poor at their position – a resentment which may spill over into crime and civil unrest. There is also the frustration which ambitious people from the lower and middle strata will probably feel when their route to the top is blocked by privileged access to positions of power and influence which the rich are likely to enjoy. There is the inefficiency which is likely to result from those positions being filled by people who obtain them through privileged access rather than ability. There is the inefficiency which comes from the fact that much of the wealth of society is going to be transmitted as inheritance rather than earned as incentives to work hard and progress.

Perhaps most of all, there is the threat to general social cohesion posed by widespread inequality – a cohesion which may well explain the success of such relatively egalitarian countries as Germany and Japan.

Nozick

All in all then, utilitarianism will probably not permit unrestricted inequalities. Neither, we have seen, will appeals to merit or to need. An alternative is to look at what people have a right to as a criterion of distributive justice and see if this can produce the desired outcome. It is the approach which has its best known contemporary representative in the work of the American philosopher Robert Nozick. In his book *Anarchy, State and Utopia*, Nozick offers what he calls an 'entitlement' theory of distributive justice. He does so as a contribution to a school of political thought known as 'libertarianism' which supports *laissez-faire* capitalism to the extent of advocating a 'minimal state' where the function of government is reduced to national defence, law enforcement, and not much else. His entitlement theory is integral to that programme because it makes the possession and enjoyment of private property an inviolable human right. Any attempt by governments or anyone else to interfere with that right, in the name of equality or anything else, will therefore be a violation of human rights and consequently unjust. The only requirement Nozick lays down for this inviolability is that the property be 'justly' possessed; both on first becoming private property and on any subsequent transfer to a new owner.

What will make the original acquisition justly possessed, according to Nozick, is that in gaining possession of it the person becoming the owner does not violate anyone else's human rights. He calls this 'the principle of justice in acquisition'. With regard to what would constitute a violation of human rights, Nozick takes a very restricted view. He favours the traditional assumption that these rights are strictly limited in scope and essentially negative in character. They are rights to life, liberty, and (of course) property; and their possession is all about other people having an obligation **not** to interfere in your enjoyment of them. Consequently, when Nozick says an original acquisition of property is just if it does not involve the violation of anyone's rights, he basically means no more than that force and fraud were not used: no one had the thing taken from them against their will, nor was anyone cheated out of it. Nozick then simply assumes without much question that once something has been justly acquired, the owner has now an inviolable right to dispose of it in any way desired and so only a voluntary transfer can make it the property of anyone else. It must, in other words, be freely sold, bartered, or given away in order to become the property of someone else. He calls this 'the principle of justice in transfer'. Once there has been such a transfer, the same inviolable rights of possession and disposal which belonged to the original owner will belong to the new owner and to any subsequent owner acquiring the property through just transfer. Using the term 'holding' to describe a person's property, Nozick defines the required sequence of events in the following way:

1. a person who acquires a holding in accordance with the principle of justice in acquisition is entitled to that holding;
2. a person who acquires a holding in accordance with the principle of justice in transfer, from someone else entitled to the holding, is entitled to the holding;
3. no one is entitled to a holding except by (repeated) applications of 1 and 2.

Nozick points out that this is a set of purely 'historical' criteria. All they attend to is the question of how someone came by a holding. **Any** spread of holdings is just provided it is produced by the required sequence of events. Only the process matters.

Nozick's view contrasts with what are called 'patterned' theories. They are concerned only with outcomes. With them a distribution is just only if it spreads out holdings in a particular way. For example, distribution based on need or merit is patterned. It requires that certain agreed holdings be given to the needy or the meritorious. So also is a distribution based on utility. Here the required spread of holdings is one which maximizes utility in some way. So also is any distribution which requires some degree of equality. Here it is only if the distribution meets that degree of equality that it is just.

In being dismissed along with all other pattered outcomes, considerations of equality now play no part in determining whether a distribution is just. The two issues become wholly separate. Provided it has been brought about in the required way, great poverty can exist alongside great riches without this situation being in any way unjust. What would be unjust, according to Nozick, would to remedy this situation by the forcible redistribution of property. That would violate the inviolable right of the rich to their property. The property of the rich can be given to the poor, but only if the rich agree to it. Helping the poor is, at best, what is described in chapter 3 as an 'imperfect duty'.

The definition of distributive justice which has produced this radical consequence has been designed to serve two principal objectives. The first is to make it true by definition that a capitalist distribution is just. He does this by laying down strictly historical criteria that are, and are meant to be, fully compatible with a capitalist way of distributing property. Given the process of acquisition and transfer he lays down, it will automatically follow that a capitalist distribution is just. The second objective is to make it true by definition that any attempt to alter a capitalist distribution will be unjust. He does this by adding to his historical criteria the proviso that only by that process can property be justly owned. From this it follows that to redistribute what capitalism has already distributed would be unjust.

Both consequences are only as good as the definition of distributive justive they derive from. Why should we accept that definition? Nozick offers no very conclusive arguments. In particular, he has great difficulty explaining how previously unowned assets can become owned. What, for example, is the moral justification for land which no one previously owned becoming the exclusive possession of a particular person to the exclusion of all others? Nozick talks of no one being made 'worse off' by such transitions to private ownership. The assets were, after all, previously unused and so unproductive. Also, Nozick claims, the transfer of assets to individuals (rather than to society at large) will optimize their efficient use and so compensate those excluded from possession through a general increase in productivity. This may be so. But what justifies particular individuals gaining possession of previously unowned assets? Why should it be person X rather than person Y that enjoys the extra advantage of exclusive ownership? Nozick relies on a simple 'first come first served' allocation, with those who got to the previously unowned assets first gaining exclusive possession. But is this fair? Does it even ensure that the most enterprising gain possession? And are those excluded adequately compensated? Why are they not required to give their consent to the transfer to private ownership? In any case, and though Nozick hotly denies it, is not all this talk of the collective benefits of private ownership a utilitarian appeal to the common good and just the sort of patterned account of distributive justice which Nozick categorically rejects?

It cannot be said that Nozick satisfactorily answers such questions about the justifiability and coherence of his theory. He seems, in fact, short of positive reasons for accepting it. His chief line of defence is to attack the alternatives, which he does mainly through the claim that any attempt to impose patterned theories of distributive justice will interfere with liberty.

In its basics, this is a very familiar argument. It repeats the traditional *laissez-faire* view that liberty and equality are incompatible, that the more there is of one the less there has to be of the other, and as liberty is assumed to have priority, then equality must be rejected. Nozick simply generalizes this reasoning to apply to patterned theories in general and not just egalitarianism in particular. He argues that, left to themselves, people will engage in voluntary exchanges which will produce a particular distribution. For those who favour patterned theories, the resulting distribution will be acceptable only if it matches the agreed pattern. As it is the result of masses of unplanned individual transactions, no such pattern will be very closely matched; in particular, it will certainly not produce anything like an equal distribution. Consequently, the implementation of patterned theories, and in particular egalitarian theories, will necessarily involve interference in voluntary transactions. To ensure the desired pattern, those transactions will have to be regulated, restricted, or even forbidden. In short, patterned theories require constant interference in liberty. Nozick's historical account of distributive justice, on the other hand, involves no such constant interference. It accepts whatever pattern the historical process throws up. It is therefore fully compatible with liberty, and so also is the *laissez-faire* capitalism which it endorses.

It is in virtue of giving this overriding priority to liberty that Nozick is called a 'libertarian'. This is, however, only part of a general appeal to rights as overriding all other moral considerations. Nozick starts from the (undefended) assumption that human rights are absolute. His very first words are, 'Individuals have rights, and there are things no person or group may do to them (without violating their rights)'.

There are obvious objections to such a position. As we saw in chapter 3, claims for an inviolable right to anything are highly questionable. Can rights not always be overridden by considerations of the common good when the situation is serious enough? And would not extremes of wealth and poverty be just such a situation? In adding an inviolable right to liberty to an inviolable right to property, Nozick is open to the charge that he is simply adding one questionable assumption to another. In any case (as we also saw in chapter 3), rights have to be balanced against each other. Arguably, and contrary to another initial presumption of Nozick's, do not rights include more than the bare life, liberty and property he allows? Are there not rights to security and welfare which, if they are pressing enough, can override a right to liberty?

Even if there are more rights than Nozick allows and rights in general are not inviolable, it is still true that liberty is a very basic right. So even with those two qualifications, the charge that equality is incompatible with liberty still constitutes an important challenge to egalitarianism. If egalitarianism is to avoid appearing to offer a stark choice between equality or liberty then it must show that, at least to some acceptable degree, the two are capable of being reconciled. This can be attempted in a variety of ways.

Equality and liberty

It can be argued that liberty is not the merely negative 'freedom from interference' which Nozick and other advocates of *laissez-faire* claim. It is also something positive; a power to act. We are not necessarily free to do something merely because there is nobody stopping us. More often than not we also need access to resources – in particular, financial resources. We can exercise a freedom to travel, to buy, to invest, or whatever, only if there is the money to do these things. From this it is said to follow that equality aids rather than threatens liberty. By providing the widest possible spread of resources, it helps ensure that a maximum number of people can exercise the freedoms given to them.

Another egalitarian argument is to point out that there is no general right to liberty, only to specific liberties. We are not, for example, free to rape and pillage. From the fact that something is a freedom it does not necessarily follow that we have a right to it. When we talk of 'liberty' we usually have in mind such political rights as freedom of speech, freedom of assembly, of association, and so on. These, it is said, are genuine rights. They are not to be confused with that liberty to engage in market activities which advocates of *laissez-faire* are so keen to defend. There is, it is claimed, no comparable right to these merely 'economic freedoms'.

In reply, defenders of *laissez-faire* will say that the political freedoms depend upon the economic. They claim that only with the decentralization which comes with private property and competition can political freedoms be maintained. (We encountered this argument at the beginning the chapter.) The usual egalitarian retort is to dismiss this claim. Any state interference in economic activity will certainly restrict the freedom of some people to some extent but there is, they will contend, no necessary spillover into restrictions on political freedoms. In fact, they add, what threatens those rights is inequality. They repeat the argument about the enjoyment of rights being dependent on the possession of resources. The right to free speech, for example, is hugely more effective in the hands of a millionaire newspaper proprietor than an ordinary citizen. Such inequality affronts, they may go on to suggest, because the whole point about political freedoms is that citizens are meant to enjoy equal rights. Every citizen should have them, and no citizen should have them to a greater extent than any other. They are about commonly held rights to freedom of speech, assembly, and association. They are about equal voting rights, equality before the law, equal employment opportunity, and so on. They are, in fact, nothing more than a political expression of those fundamental rights which everyone has simply in virtue of being human.

Rawls

The usual response then among egalitarians is to dismiss or at least play down any possible conflict between liberty and equality. An egalitarian thinker who is unusual in not adopting this course is the American philosopher John Rawls. In his now classic book *A Theory of Justice*, he takes the potential conflict seriously enough to require that political freedoms be given priority over economic equality in his theory. He also takes seriously the very much parallel *laissez-faire* charge (touched on earlier) that equality and efficiency are incompatible. He does this by permitting increases in efficiency to justify departures from equality. In short, he tries to produce an egalitarian theory of distributive justice which will reconcile equality with both liberty and efficiency.

In contrast to Nozick's, it is a theory which attempts a systematic defence of its criteria for distributive justice. This is not, despite its egalitarianism, through an appeal to selflessness or the common good. On the contrary, Rawls starts from the assumption that people are 'rational' in the utility maximizing sense beloved of economists. From this he seeks to arrive at a set of principles which all such rationally self-interested people would accept as fair. He asks what principles for organizing society they would accept if they were starting from scratch – from what he calls 'the original position'. (In this he consciously evokes the social contract theory touched on in chapter 3.)

It would not do, of course, to give basically self-interested people an absolutely free choice of distributive principles. They would then tend to choose criteria seen as favouring themselves. Labourers might choose the amount of physical effort expended, capitalists the amount of capital invested, intellectuals the amount of IQ possessed, and so on. Under such conditions there could be no chance of arriving at criteria which everyone could accept as fair. For this, the decision making needs to take place under conditions which will impose impartiality on the participants. It needs to be a choice which will serve everyone's interest in general but no one's interest in particular. In choosing for themselves the participants will need, in a sense, to choose for everyone. (This, as we saw in chapter 3, is a very Kantian notion; and Rawls speaks of his theory as 'highly Kantian in nature'.)

To impose the necessary impartiality, Rawls requires that the choice be made under what he calls a 'veil of ignorance'. By this he means that the people doing the choosing are presumed to know nothing about themselves which will distinguish them from other people: they are totally ignorant about their own talents, skills, family connections, physical qualities, tastes, predilections, or whatever. Consequently, they will have no means of knowing what distributive principles will be of particular benefit or disadvantage to themselves. They cannot opt for principles designed to serve their individual self-interest because they have no way of distinguishing themselves as individuals. They are forced to be impartial.

Under such conditions they will, according to Rawls, choose the following distributive principles as being in their own self-interest:

1. Each person is, to have an equal right to the most extensive total system of equal basic liberties compatible with a similar system of liberty for all.
2. Social and economic inequalities are to be arranged so that they are both:
   (a) to the greatest benefit of the least advantaged . . . , and
   (b) attached to positions open to all under conditions of fair equality of opportunity.

What Rawls is saying here is that faced with a situation in which they have no way of knowing how any **particular** benefit will accure to them, people will opt for an arrangement in which the very worst position in which they might find themselves will be as favourable as possible. They will choose a safety first option which guarantees that the worst possible outcome will be as good as it possibly can be. This, using a term derived from economics, Rawls describes as the 'maximin' strategy. That is, a situation in which the minimum is maximized.

With principle 1, this strategy is served by the fact that, no matter where in society individuals end up, they will not lose out in the distribution of political freedoms. They will have as much as they possibly can have because everyone will have as much as they possibly can have. Rawls calls this the 'principle of greatest equal liberty'. With principle 2, it is less obvious that a maximin strategy is being served. It begins by allowing that there can be 'social and economic inequalities' – that is, inequalities in wealth, income, power, status, and so on. But why allow this? Why not again simply opt for total equality? Will this not guarantee that no matter where people end up their position will be as good as it possibly can be?

Rawls says it will not for reasons of efficiency. He agrees with supporters of *laissez-faire* that efficiency demands incentives and the incentives require differential rewards. Consequently, he says, those self-interested individuals in the original position would not choose total equality in social and economic matters. It would not be in their interest because it would mean a less efficient and therefore less productive society than one based on unequal rewards. Given the greater productivity of a society providing unequal rewards, even its least advantaged members could still be better off than anyone in a society where the distribution of social and economic benefits is absolutely equal. Provided the worst off position is still better than the position everyone would be in under conditions of total equality, then the rational thing to do in terms of a maximin strategy is to prefer the unequal but more productive society to the equal but less productive one.

The optimum situation is one which productivity is as high as possible and inequality as low as possible. Gains in productivity have to be traded against degrees of inequality to arrive at an optimum correlation between the two. Then the worst position is indeed as good as it possibly can be. Given, for example, a situation in which wealth has to be distributed among ten people, it is better in maximin terms to have a twentieth share of £300 than a perfectly equal one tenth share of £100; better still to have a one twelfth share of £200; better than that to have even a thirtieth share of £600; worst off all to have a one hundredth share of £800; and so on.

What part (a) of principle 2 does is guarantee that this required correlation between gains in productivity and degrees of inequality will always hold. Rawls calls it the 'difference principle'. What it says is that inequalities are permitted only if they maximize benefits to the worst off in society. Consequently, it makes inequalities dependent on providing benefits for the least advantaged. The inequalities have not only to result in productive gains but as much as possible of those productive gains have to be passed on to the least advantaged. There is a trade-off between equality and efficiency but with only as much inequality permitted as will make the position of the worst off in society as good as it possibly can be. That way a maximin outcome is guaranteed.

Part 2(b) is called the 'principle of fair equality of opportunity' by Rawls. Here, as with 1, the connection with a maximin strategy is relatively straightforward. Given that under the veil of ignorance people do not know their eventual position in society and that according to the difference principle the rewards for different positions can be unequal, it follows that if the worst position is to be as good as it possibly can be then there has to be an equal opportunity to compete for those unequal rewards. This does not merely exclude discrimination on the grounds of race, sex, class, and the like. That would simply provide what Rawls describes as 'careers open to talents'. 'Fair' equality of opportunity, he insists, also requires positive action by the state to ensure that disadvantaged groups are able to compete effectively. Anything less would make the worst position less good than it possibly could be.

Rawls attempts the reconciliation of equality with liberty by giving priority to maximum equal liberty over the other two principles. In this way the requirement to better the lot of the worst-off and provide full equality of opportunity will not be at the expense of political freedoms. 'Liberty', he contends, 'can be restricted only for the sake of liberty'. In other words, the only ground for restricting anyone's liberty is to ensure that it is not at the expense of someone else's.

He attempts the reconciliation of equality with efficiency by the 'difference principle', only allowing departures from equality which benefit the worst-off. Hence, gains in efficiency can justify departures from equality. Thus Rawls offers a flexible egalitarianism, which does not insist on equality at any price but still gives equality priority over efficiency. What it excludes is the kind of utilitarian calculation which, as we saw in Chapter 3 would allow a majority to benefit at the expense of a minority. For example, and to revert back to our earlier illustration, given a distribution among ten people, the difference principle would prefer the worst-off receiving a twentieth share of £300 to a perfectly equal division of £100, but would prefer either of these distributions to a situation in which even a single person enjoyed only a hundredth share of £800. Though everyone else could be very much better off with this third arrangement, it would be rejected as unjust according to Rawls' difference principle. 'Injustice', he says, 'is simply inequalities that are not to the benefit of all'. He allows that in a large and complex society it will not be possible to ensure that every single person benefits from efficiency-promoting inequalities. But he insists that only if, as a general rule, everyone is better off as a consequence can inequalities be justified. In that sense, and despite its undoubted flexibility, Rawls' theory of distributive justice is radically egalitarian.

This balancing of apparently conflicting demands stems from Rawls' aim of arriving at a set of distributive procedures on which all rationally self-interested people can agree. It is an attempt at consensus. He seeks to pursue egalitarian objectives while meeting what he regards as the legitimate criticisms made by advocates of *laissez-faire*. He also attempts to be neutral between capitalism and market socialism. He presumes that his principles of justice are best served by the freedom and efficiency which seem to come with a market economy, but leaves open the question of which form of ownership and control should be adopted.

On the other hand, this same consensual approach leaves him open to criticism from several different directions at once. He can be attacked by utilitarians for giving priority to liberty over considerations of welfare. Less flexible egalitarians can charge him with setting no bounds to the degree of inequality which is possible (provided the worst-off are catered for). Libertarians can argue that his radical form of equality of opportunity can only be at the expense of liberty, and therefore excluded by the priority he gives to liberty. The list goes on, but perhaps the two most telling criticisms concern his adoption of the maximin strategy and his claim that **only** improvements in the condition of the worst-off can justify economic inequalities.

With regard to the maximin strategy, it can be argued that, rather than choosing this safety-first option, some people in the original position might make a riskier choice. They might decide to take a chance on society in which the worst position was not as good as it could be but, as a consequence, some other positions were a lot better than they would be otherwise. They might even be prepared to gamble on a society in which just a few people had almost everything and most of the rest almost nothing. To argue, as Rawls does, that this would be an irrational choice is to make assumptions about rationality which these critics would not be prepared to concede – namely, that it is always and necessarily a safety-first procedure.

With regard to his claim that only improvements in the lot of the worst-off can justify inequalities, Rawls is open to attack from two quarters. The first asks: what about different degrees of merit? Is it not the case that, as we have seen, in virtue of different degrees of merit some people just deserve more or less than others? The issue, it can be insisted, is not whether anyone else benefits from the extra shares that some people might get, but whether that extra is deserved or not.

Rawls will have none of this. He arrived at the 'difference principle' by not only rejecting a utility-based distribution but a merit-based one as well. His position is that differential rewards can never be justified by appeals to merit. Whatever merits or demerits people have are simply the effects of their upbringing or genetic endowment. They are clever, stupid, diligent, lazy, or whatever, because that is the way they were born or brought up. Their merits and demerits are therefore simply a matter of luck and so nothing at all to do with being deserving or undeserving. As Rawls puts it, 'the initial endowment of (people's) natural assets and the contingencies of their growth and nurture in early life are arbitrary from a moral point of view.'

This claim of Rawls leads on to the second line of attack. This comes from Nozick, who also, as we saw, rejects distribution based on merit (though in his case because it would be a patterned criterion). He points out though, that one of the reasons which Rawls gives for rejecting utilitarianism is that it treats people as mere aggregates of utility rather than autonomous human beings. 'Utilitarianism', Rawls says, 'does not take seriously the distinction between persons.' It can mean, he goes on to claim, treating people as a means to someone else's welfare – something which, on the Kantian principle (noted in Chapter 3) that people might be treated as ends in themselves, Rawls categorically rejects. Nozick fully agrees with this rejection but accuses Rawls of contradicting himself. In rejecting any idea that superior rewards can be deserved and requiring them to be only justified by improvements for the worst-off, Rawls has to treat the abilities of the more talented in society as assets to be put at the disposal of the less talented. It means, as Rawls acknowledges, regarding 'the distribution of natural abilities as a collective asset so that the more fortunate are to benefit only in ways that benefit those who have lost out.' This, Nozick argues, denies that distinctness of persons which Rawls is so keen to uphold.

In our view, this criticism of Nozick gets to the heart of the dispute between Rawls and Nozick. It is a choice between a qualified egalitarianism and a totally unqualified anti-egalitarianism. In very crude terms, the dispute comes down to whether or not there is, as someone once famously said, 'no such thing as society, only individuals'.

INTRODUCING THE READINGS

The first reading is a defence of market socialism by Saul Estrin. In it he argues that while markets will inevitably produce some inequalities (and indeed have to in order to provide incentives), those inequalities need not be as great as those which exist under a capitalistic form of market economy.

In his rejection of a market socialism, Chris R. Tame concentrates on what he sees as its fatal weakness; namely, that in being concerned to ensure a degree of equality, it will inevitably involve the use of a state power to restrict individual freedom (essentially the classic claim of an inevitable conflict between equality and liberty).

The third reading consists of key excerpts from summaries of Roman Catholic social teaching, as enunciated in Papal encyclicals (letters on church doctrine sent out by popes). The selections demonstrate that intention to steer a middle course between socialist collectivism and *laissez-faire* individualism which seems to define Roman Catholic social thought. To what extent Christian Democratic parties achieve that balance is, of course, subject to debate.

The final two readings are key extracts from Nozick's and Rawls' contending accounts of distributive justice.

From unjust markets to just distribution

SAUL ESTRIN

For too long, socialists have allowed themselves to be tarred with the brush of central planning. The *a priori* arguments against the use of such an allocative mechanism, highlighting in particular the problems for labour incentives, motivation and in processing information, are well established (on both right and left, in the works of, for example, F. A. Hayek or Alec Nove). Moreover, the autocracy and inefficiencies of planned economies in practice, brought to public awareness by recent developments in, for example, Poland or the Soviet Union, confirm the unacceptability of such a mechanism for voters schooled in Western traditions and patterns of consumption. By tying their social objectives to an inherently inefficient and unattractive way to allocate resources, socialists have seriously blurred the distinction between means and ends.

The problem arises because the early socialists confused the operation of markets with the evils of capitalism. The rise of capitalism coincided with the spread of markets. Though there was always some trading, capitalism seemed to be inextricably linked to a vast increase in the areas of economic life in which market relations prevailed. This linkage seemed particularly true in the labour market, with very low wages and severe poverty for the many industrial workers contrasting with the accumulation of vast fortunes for the new entrepreneurs. Marx in particular wanted to look behind what he saw as the veil of free labour contacts, to the exploitation that he sensed at the heart of capitalist accumulation. He believed that although, unlike the slaves and serfs of feudal societies, workers under capitalism exchanged their labour voluntarily for a wage, they were nevertheless exploited. The key to this puzzle lay in the ownership of capital used in production, and the resulting relations of power within the enterprise. Private ownership allowed the capitalists to extract an income from the enterprise over and above the underlying scarcity value of capital they provided to the production process. If exploitation in this sense was to be abolished, ownership of capital would have to be vested in the hands of workers. Moreover, the new arrangements of ownership would have to be collective rather than individual, or the process of accumulation and exploitation would simply begin again.

This is a very particular view of socialism, and one to which I do not necessarily subscribe. But it contains the key point that socialism is ultimately about the distribution of income and wealth in society, and about the relationship between the factors of production at the work-place. And Marxist or not, many socialists continue to see changes in the way that property rights to streams of income are distributed as being the fundamental element of a socialist reform.

Reading taken from *Economic Affairs*, August/September 1987. Copyright © 1987 Economic Affairs.

The early socialists were therefore clear about the theoretical problems of capitalism. The current incoherence on the left in large part arises because they were less lucid about the solutions. These were perceived to lie in collective ownership, but the precise way in which an economy where the bulk of capital was nationalised would conduct its affairs was not spelt out, it was left to 20th-century practitioners to resolve the operational details. It so happened that the first of these, and the most influential – the Russian Bolsheviks – chose, after eleven years of experimentation which included markets, to adopt a system of central planning. Although their circumstances were highly particular and not of practical relevance today, the result has been that planning and socialism have become inextricably linked in the mythology of the left.

Needless to say, the blanket identification of socialism with planning has been a major source of comfort to the right. Planning is at minimum inefficient and perhaps even infeasible as a way to run an economy sensibly. If socialists retain a commitment to planning, their social objectives can be dismissed as impractical without their opponents being drawn into arguments as to their broader desirability. If socialists instead accept markets, and especially competitive markets, as the only way to allocate resources in a modern economy, the debate can move to the more substantive issues.

The main reason that markets need socialism is that, with current arrangements of ownership, the market mechanism permits, and possibly encourages, a highly inegalitarian distribution of income and wealth. Without specifying an exact distributive rule along the lines of, for example, John Rawls,[1] my value-judgement is that economies should be as egalitarian as is consistent with efficiency in the allocation of resources. Indeed, one might go further to suggest that, in developed economies, one might be willing to sacrifice some element of additional output to buy more equality.

Egalitarianism is a slippery concept, and it should be emphasised that, because of incentive problems, I mean equality neither in the current distribution of income nor in holdings of wealth across individuals at a particular moment. Forces in the labour market mean that rewards must differ according to productivities, skills, training, region and type of employment. And because people are at different points in the life-cycle, or choose different patterns of consumption over their life-times (for example, to consume more in youth than in old age), holdings of wealth must vary across individuals at any moment.

Market socialists object to high incomes which reflect monopoly 'rents' (earned by privileged position rather than effort) more than marginal products, and vast differences in the distribution of wealth, evaluated over an individual's lifetime, particularly if transmitted from generation to generation. Competitive forces in the labour market must therefore be encouraged to dissipate the accumulation of monopoly rents as income and wealth, and taxes may also be required to reduce income gains of this sort. Moreover, it is a basic tenet of market socialism that a redistributive system which largely abolishes previously inherited economic privileges will be established.

Egalitarianism of this sort may still have some negative incentive effects, but fewer, it is hoped, than with a static concept of equality. Even if we start our hypothetical new market socialist regime with perfect income and wealth equality, with markets, particularly for labour and capital, it is certain that a new group of relatively rich people will emerge, either as a result of their own abilities or because of luck. Because wealth is accumulated at a compounding rate, initially small differences in holdings become enormously magnified over time, particularly if the time-scale spans generations. This effect explains the crucial importance of breaking the inequality cycle by drastically hindering the capacity of the rich to pass their ever-accumulating fortunes from generation to generation.

The right claim that inequality is required in a market economy to ensure that the allocative process is efficient. There is something to this argument. In the labour market, the price mechanism, and the resulting differentials in wages, are required to allocate labour between uses and skills. If its operation is suppressed, the alternative is direct allocation of labour, which, moral questions apart will have deleterious effects on the motivation of employees. In the capital market, where returns are risky, a low probability of large rewards may be an important incentive to invest. But the efficiency argument is overstated and its corollaries for wealth distribution unconvincing. One may have to reward particular labour skills very highly 'pour encourager les autres'. There is no good incentive reason that short-term luck – being in the right place at the right time – should be converted into a permanent advantage on product markets, transmitted across generations.

Traditional socialists have further misgivings about markets. For example, it is often argued that if resources are allocated through the market-place, the frivolous tastes of the rich will take precedence over the basic necessities of the poor. This reservation falls under the slogan, 'production for people, not for profit'.

There are two related problems here: monopoly and distribution. The first requires a vigorous policy on competition. But in the absence of serious spill-over effects or monopoly power, production for profit is socially desirable. Socialists are probably more worried that the price mechanism encourages producers to make goods for which there is a demand, so that, since the better-off have more to spend, producers will devote more resources to them. Market socialism does not entirely resolve this problem. Even if inequalities can be prevented from persisting across generations , at any moment there will be some people who are (relatively) rich and others who are (relatively) poor. To prevent a market system from penalising the poor, a full structure of welfare services will be required.

Traditional socialists also suspect that there is some process whereby markets inherently engender inequalities. An interpretation of this argument is linked to overshooting by the price mechanism under certain conditions. In practice, prices may significantly overshoot their new long-run position after, say, a change in demand and only gradually come down again. Recent examples probably include changes in the sterling exchange rate since 1979 and, perhaps, salaries in the City, post Big Bang. Markets can thus create excessive volatility of prices, with all the associated problems of uncertainty and waste. The problem will be particularly serious if the good in question is a particular type of labour skill, or the entitlement to a flow of income. The overshooting, up or down, then has consequences for the distribution of income and wealth.

Prices can deviate for a long time from their long-run positions since the required adjustments of supply to changes in technology or demand are too slow, because, for example, of gestation lags in investment or the necessary retraining of labour is time-consuming. This phenomenon undermines the costless signalling function which is commonly viewed as one of the crucial advantages of the market. For example, an increase in demand can stimulate price overshooting and thereby cause sizable fortunes to be accumulated during a long period of insufficient supply. There is then an over-response by producers which leads the price to fall below its long-run position, and leads to some losses. The allocative point is that, while the market is excellent for fine-tuning, it may not be the best way to stimulate non-marginal responses in the structure of the economy. The key point is that the resulting monopoly rents, paid out as income or wealth entitlements, do not start a new cycle of privilege and inequality.

Socialists' concern with distribution is intimately bound up with their attitude towards ownership of capital in the workplace. Two guiding principles are relevant here, first that capital should not appropriate rewards over and above its scarcity price, and, second, that the ownership of capital should not necessarily confer managerial rights. The first is clearly associated with the issues of exploitation raised above. The second allows socialism to be taken into enterprise itself, in the knowledge that markets are mediating the relationship between firms.

In a perfectly competitive world, the problem of what to do with profits is less critical because in long-run equilibrium they will be zero. This assumption hinges on the static nature of the model and the assumed absence of uncertainty. In a dynamic and uncertain world, profits will at best be zero in an expected sense, and more probably positive, since changing conditions will always open up the opportunity profitably to exploit short-term advantages. The question is then how the rights to those expected streams of profit should be allocated.

The answer is not straightforward. It is often argued that the rights should be concentrated in a few hands, to allow the pooling of risks. In an uncertain environment, owners of small quantities of capital are particularly susceptible to the disadvantages of the concentration of uncertainty. Professor James Meade has argued[2] that the reason that capital hires labour, rather than the other way round, is because labour cannot spread itself across various activities in order to spread risks. Capital, on the other hand, can. A similar line of reasoning favours the emergence of large-scale capitalists and the concentration of ownership.

The second advantage of concentrating responsibilities in this way is that it gives one person an incentive to organise or allocate resources efficiently. The property-rights approach to these problems starts from the assumption that all firms have to undertake monitoring of their labour forces to curtail shirking. But monitoring itself is hard to observe and cannot therefore be purchased in a free market. The monitor therefore enters into an arrangement of residual claimancy[3] with the labour force, and is rewarded by the extra output he earns from the workers by eliminating shirking. It is therefore asserted that there has to be an individual residual claimant; making all the workers residual claimants will not help because their incentives are too diffuse.

These are serious issues, of fundamental importance to the understanding of the market mechanism. I cannot claim to have resolved them, and must therefore prepare to temper my value-judgement if these arguments prove to have substance. But it is my suspicion that they are seriously overstated. The pooling of risks is properly the function of an insurance market, and is not necessarily best served by the concentration of property rights in the hands of a few risk-loving individuals. And it is stretching credulity to see the necessity of giving residual rights to monitors of work-teams as a justification for the huge concentrations of ownership that characterise most capitalist economies.

A socialist perspective would, instead, concentrate on the wider distributional implications of attributing residual profits to a small group. Restricting rights over all expected streams of profit to a small group, and one with no special characteristics in the labour or product markets, is unjust. It also allows the owning group to accumulate resources quickly, and thereby to take advantage of risk-pooling to strengthen further its position in the market-place. It would be preferable to distribute the profits around the society at large. The emergence of a small group of wealthy capitalists also has ramifications for the political process. Wealth confers political as well as economic power which, it can be assumed, the wealthy will use in their own interest. Linking rights over the residual income with the provision of capital services is therefore at the heart of the inequalities of income, wealth and power to which socialists object.

Finally, socialism offers a market system the opportunity to change the way that enterprises are run. Conventional ownership arrangements confer on owners the right to manage, either directly or indirectly, by setting the terms of reference for management who act in their stead. The shift of emphasis from plan to market on the left has brought to the fore the issue of how best to organise the enterprise, and the realisation that fundamental changes in society may not be bound up with extensions in role of the state, but rather with changes in the way that work itself is organised.

Capitalist enterprises are traditionally organised in an hierarchical way. An alternative paradigm, particularly relevant for the market socialist, involves workers' self-management of industry. Relevant, if not ideal, models include the Israeli *kibbutzim*, the Basque co-operatives in Mondragon, Spain, and certain elements of the Yugoslav economy. The advantages from the socialist perspective are clear. Self-managed firms institutionalise the rule that labour hires capital, rather than the reverse. To the extent that the attribution of residual rights underlies worker exploitation, such arrangements eliminate it.

More importantly, self-management of industry begins to break down the sharp contrast between democracy in the political arena and autocracy in the workplace. If involvement in decisions which affect the lives of ordinary people is regarded as an important principle of a just society, democratic processes must be extended to the enterprise. Current arrangements in the firm tend to undermine political democracy, by devaluing the contribution of people at the bottom of the hierarchy and devaluing their skills. Worker's self-management should act in the reverse way.

One of the key problems stressed by observers of the capitalist enterprise is the dissatisfaction or alienation felt by a significant proportion of the work-force. Workers have no say in the production processes used, the pace of manufacture, manning strengths or the layout of the plant. Their dissatisfaction comes out in their attitude to work, their supervisors and the owners, and often leads to uncooperative attitudes, and inflexibility to new work practices. Once again, many of these problems can be resolved in a system of workers' self management, where individual employees are given an equal vote in determining all aspects of company policy. The consequence of the reduced alienation may well be substantial gains in the productive efficiency of the organisation.

There are, of course, serious problems with a self-managed economy, which remain to be resolved. A large literature points to slugishness of responses in the market-place and problems with investment relative to the capitalist firm. While these problems are real, they could be solved by the introduction of institutions formed to counter them; in particular, competing holding companies motivated to create new co-ops to fill the gaps in the market-left by the sluggishness of existing firms. The debate on how best to increase workers' participation in the work-place is only beginning. But development along these lines is a crucial element of what socialism might bring markets.

For market socialists, the differences with the new right are not about the role of competitive processes in the allocation of resources. It is recognised that markets are the only efficient way to run a modern economy. But that is not to accept as unalterable the current distribution of resources, endowments and power in society. If one accepts socialist value-judgements, it is still necessary to transform the distribution of income and wealth and the way that firms are owned and run.

NOTES

1. Rawls' arguments are criticised in Anthony Flew, 'Inequality is not Injustice', *Economic Affairs*, Vol. 7, No. 5, June–July. 1987.–ED.
2. The Theory of Labour-Managed Firms and of Profit-Sharing', *Economic Journal*, Vol. 82, 1972, pp. 402–428.
3. I.e., claims to the profit net of all costs.

Can socialism change its spots?

CHRIS R. TAME

It is a tribute to the revival of liberal and libertarian ideas that they had previously consigned to the 'dustbin of history' that many contemporary socialists are now rephrasing their arguments in libertarian terms, conceding certain criticisms or admitting a 'role' for the 'market mechanism'.

In truth, the libertarian rhetoric of the 'New Socialists' is not new. It sounds rather like the justifications for statism made by the neo-liberals. (T. H. Green, Bernard Bosanquet, Thomas Whittaker, L. T. Hobhouse, *et al.*) of the late 19th and early 20th century. But there has always been a libertarian strand within socialism, as well as the collectivist, authoritarian or statist ones. And Marx himself characterised his ultimate communist society as one where 'the free development of each is the condition for the free development of all'.[1]

Simply to crow over the new socialists' abandonment of the goal of central planning and to see it as a decisive victory over socialist ideology is therefore profoundly mistaken. Many socialists never advocated central planning as the core of their position in the first place. Moreover, the new socialists are still socialists and still offer an erroneous critique of the market that must be vigorously refuted.

The most profound error of the new socialists is their very concept, a 'positive' one, of freedom.[2] By defining freedom as a positive capability or option, as 'an equal right to those positive resources which are necessary to action and agency' (Raymond Plant's words), and proclaiming certain positive freedoms as rights, they ignore the inescapable truth that these so-called rights can be maintained only by physically aggressing against others. In any real-world application of their ideas, one man's 'freedom' is always another man's slavery (i.e., loss of life, liberty and property).

So do libertarians have nothing to say about 'positive freedom' (as the new socialists frequently assert)? Our arguments is precisely that it is only ensuring negative liberty (freedom from invasive violence) that maximises positive liberty (choice, options in life, prosperity, and so on). The history of humanity, the rise of prosperity as the result of the freeing of the market, is eloquent evidence. The trouble with using the word 'freedom' to cover 'positive freedom' is that it obscures the unpleasant logic that the attempt to create positive freedom by state action by its very nature infringes freedom from coercion.

The new socialists frequently argue that libertarianism contains an inner contradiction. They assert that a free market requires a strong state to enforce market relationships.[3] It is, of course, true that all societies require some form of law enforcement and resolution of disputes. But the critics ignore many vital points. Firstly, free-market societies have depended more on the voluntary acceptance of a

Reading taken from *Economic Affairs* August/September 1987. Copyright © 1987 Economic Affairs.

just social order by its denizens than they do on the physical enforcement of law.[4] Market societies arose precisely because strong states were absent.[5] Moreover, the new socialists also ignore the extent that the law itself, in the relatively free-market societies of the West, has arisen as a result of decentralised, voluntaristic, market forces.[6]

It is a distortion to describe the classical liberal concept of a limited state as a strong state. For liberals the state should not be able to overwhelm civil society or interfere in voluntary, non-coercive relationships. Of course, whether the 'limited states' can be limited in practice is a readily admissible question, much discussed by liberals. But it is notable that the new socialists prefer not to mention the work of the 'anarcho-capitalist' libertarians, who argue that the state can and should be (in a phrase of Proudhon's) 'dissolved in the economic organism', that the services of defence, law enforcement can be better and more equitably supplied by market agencies.[7]

Another major argument of the new socialists is that the market cannot sustain itself, or maintain its own values, that a 'pure market' would be a 'war of all against all'. They possess a curiously Hobbesian view of humanity. If there is one lesson that every exponent of the market has proclaimed, it is that when individuals eschew violence and predation but pursue their self-interest in the market by creating and exchanging goods and services, the interest of all is served. A competitive market system is a harmonious one in which the self-interest of all is compatible. Free-market economics demonstrates the truth that 'selfishness' is mutually beneficial. The work of Robert Axelrod explains theoretically the rather obvious (except to socialists) reality of the way in which people recognise their mutuality of interest as market relationships evolve. And Ayn Rand's philosophy proclaims precisely that 'selfishness' is a virtue, that our nature as distinctive rational entities is served best by a rational egoism which manifests itself in those non-coercive, mutualistic relationships which are called 'capitalism'.[8]

It is especially ironic that the new socialists attack the market on the grounds that it generates 'unjust' privilege and that the state is required to prevent special privilege arising. Thus Andrew Gamble justifies state power in order to control those groups which seek to escape from market disciplines.[9] But the whole burden of the economic and class analysis of classical liberals, from Smith onward, is that powerful interests seek to exploit their fellows by coercive means. This is precisely *why* the liberals supported *laissez-faire*. 'Unjust' monopolies can arise *only* as a result of state interference in the market. An allegedly 'caring', interventionist state is the organ by which groups, classes and individuals exploit one another.

Ironically, socialism can be seen as a false consciousness that has repeatedly allowed special interests to gain exploitative power by masking their predations in the rhetoric of responsible state action for the common good.

When Gareth Stedman Jones speaks of 'society as a whole being in control of its productive resources' and 'control of economic destiny at a national democratic level' in 'new and democratic forms'[10] it must be remembered that 'society as a whole' is only a useful phrase for hiding the power of particular individuals who wield it.

'Society' as a conscious entity does not exist. There are only individuals. Either they dispose of their lives, liberty and property as they themselves see fit, or they are coercively prevented from so doing. 'Democratic participation' in a coercive political process is not much consolation to the losers. Moreover, the evidence of the real world does not give much credence to the idea that democracy will not prevent a powerful elite from manipulating such a system for its own power and privilege.

How genuine some of these new socialists are in their libertarianism is a moot point. Paul Hirst maintains as a central tenet in his definition of socialism the desirability of 'the greatest measure of equality of condition attainable between individuals'. But this desideratum is blatantly at variance with his support for a 'socialism which places freedom and autonomy first'.[11] If the differing aptitudes, skills, determination, interests, luck, and so on, result (as they do and will continue to do so) in differing economic success, will Hirst's proposed system interfere with their autonomy in the name of equality? Similarly, would his system interfere with the autonomy of millions of ordinary people's voluntary consumption choices that made, for example, Elvis Presley a very wealthy and decidedly unequal individual?

One suspects he would. For the new socialists frequently assert that individuals are influenced or moulded by others, with implication that freedom is therefore unreal.[12] The hidden (and sometimes not so hidden) agenda of this sort of assertion is that it is alright for (the presumably superior and autonomous) socialists to impose their values upon other individuals who suffer from alienation and false consciousness. The hegemony on the left of a reactionary, authoritarian and inhumane 'feminism' has reinforced this implicit statism. The *laissez-faire*/civil libertarian concept of 'freely contracting parties, in cultural and sexual as well as in purely economic matters' is thus rejected in favour of coercive intervention in 'the forms and content of culture' and in 'so-called "private life"'.[13]

But by far the most ominous characteristic of these writers is their repeated declaration that their socialism is a matter of 'commitment to the communal and the collective as a good in itself', as Stedman Jones has said.[14] Eric Hobsbawm is even more explicit: 'The good society', he writes, '[. . .] should certainly contain "the greatest sum of freedom", "the highest amount of choice" and "the most human happiness" achievable. But it cannot be *defined* by adding up individual freedoms, choices and happinesses.' It is 'more than the sum of its individual members'.[15] This is the perennial mystical rationale of totalitarianism, the essence of Hegel, Marx, Mussolini, and Hitler, the view that their society is somehow an entity independent of, and above, individuals, an entity which can have its own distinct interests, aims, and happiness. For if there is such an entity, what justication is there for not sacrificing individuals to it? And sacrificed they have been, in their millions, throughout history and still in the present day.

While not wishing to deny sincerity to all, one would certainly be more confident of the motivation of the new socialists if they behaved with more obvious intellectual honesty. The *New Statesman* symposium, 'Does Socialism Have a Future?', was replete with polemical tricks, abuse, and the attribution of foul motives to the proponents of the market. Its contributors constantly assert, but do not demonstrate, that their case is 'obvious' and 'self evident' (Peter Kellner). Libertarian scholars are characterised as 'idealogues' (Kellner) and 'gurus' (Roy Hattersley – who also suffers from a constitutional inability to spell Robert Nozick's name correctly), 'intellectually banal and their economic and social analyses sketchy' (Paul Hirst). Worse still, liberals are labelled 'hireling publicists and [. . .] client intellectuals' (Hirst).[16] It is striking that these 'new' socialists are apparently unwilling actually to read or admit of existence of the libertarian literature, let alone engage its arguments. This weakness reaches its apogee of absurdity in Sarah Benton's assertion that 'There are [. . .] an extraordinary number of issues about which the "new" right is silent [. . . :] culture, conservation and ecology, care of the sick, aged, children [. . . ,] the decline of manufacturing, especially research and development, defence, and all matters of political rights and civil liberties'.[17]

I have tried to focus on the core concerns of the new socialists. Insofar as they truly do have a libertarian motivation, their practical proposals cannot result in liberty. And what libertarian motivations do exist ride in tandem with authoritarian and coercive values. One must conclude with regret that the new socialists have no more to offer men and women of goodwill than the old socialists.

NOTES

1. Karl Marx and Friedrich Engels, *The Communist Manifesto*, Penguin, Harmondsworth, 1967, p. 105.
2. Roy Hattersley, 'A Party of Paradoxical Principle', *New Statesman*, 6 March 1987, p. 4, Raymond Plant, 'The Market: Needs, Rights and Morality', *ibid.*, p. 14.
3. Andrew Gamble, 'Smashing the State: Thatcher's Radical Crusade', *Marxism Today*, June 1985, pp. 21–22.
4. Indeed, the internalisation of social *mores* is a major factor in the preservation of orderly behaviour in all societies.
5. *Cf.* John A. Hall, *Powers and Liberties: The Causes and Consequences of the Rise of the West*, Penguin, Harmondsworth, 1986.
6. *Cf.* Murray N. Rothbard, *Power and Market*, Institute for Humane Studies, Menlo Park, California, 1970, p. 4, and Bruno Leoni, *Freedom and the Law*, Nash Publishing, Los Angeles, 1971.
7. The idea of an anarcho-capitalist society was originated by the great French classical economist Gustave de Molinari, and expounded by the largely American school of individualist anarchists like Benjamin Tucker. In recent years it has enjoyed a vigorous restatement by both free market economists and libertarian philosophers – *cf.*, for example, David Friedman, *The Machinery of Freedom*, Arlington House, New Rochelle, New York, 1978; M. and L. Tannehill and J. Wollstein, *Society Without Government*, Arno Press/New York Times, New York, 1972; Murray Rothbard, *For A New Liberty*, 2nd edn., Collier Macmillan, New York, 1973; John T. Sanders, *The Ethical Argument Against Government*, University Press of America, Washington DC: 1980; David Osterfeld, *Freedom, Society and the State*, University Press of America, Washington DC, 1983.
8. Robert Axelrod, *the Evolution of Cooperation*, Basic Books, New York, 1954; Ayn Rand, *The Virtue of Selfishness: A New Concept of Egoism*, New American Library, New York, 1963; *cf.* also D. J. Den Uyl and D. Rasmussen (eds.), *The Philosophic Thought of Ayn Rand*, University of Illinois Press, Urbana, 1984.
9. Andrew Gamble, *loc. cit.*, p. 22; Paul Hirst, 'Can Socialism Live?', *New Statesman*, 6 March 1987, pp. 6–10.

10. 'Paternalism Revisited,' *Marxism Today*, July 1983, pp. 26–28.
11. *Loc. cit.*, pp. 8, 9.
12. Ian Forbes (ed.), *Market Socialism: Whose Choice?*, Fabian Society, London, 1986.
13. Richard Sparks 'Special Discretion Required', *New Socialist*, April 1987, p. 23; Lucy Bland, 'Sex and Morals: Rearming the Left', *Marxism Today*, September 1985, p. 24. These two writers do not explicitly call for coercive action, but it is the only alternative to the liberal morality they reject.
14. *Loc. cit.*, p. 26.
15. 'Offering a Good Society', *New Statesman*, 6 March 1987, p. 13.
16. 6 March 1987, pp. 5, 4, 5, 6, 8.
17. 'The Hardening on the Right,' *ibid*, p. 20.

The capitalist system and the worker: analysis and summary of the encyclicals

PHILLIP HUGHES

RERUM NOVARUM OF LEO XIII (15 MAY 1891) AND

QUADRAGESIMO ANNO OF PIUS XI (15 MAY 1931)

THE ENCYCLICAL RERUM NOVARUM

I. THE SOCIAL CONFLICT: SOCIALISM NO SOLUTION

THE SOCIALIST THEORY OF OWNERSHIP. What is to be said of this, i.e. as a solution to the social problem? and, secondly, as to its intrinsic worth?

Socialists hold that individual possessions should become the common property of all, to be administered by the public authority. There are two objections to this theory; first, that the worker would be the first to suffer were it ever translated into fact; and, next, that it is contrary to justice.

As to the first objection, the pope notes how the impelling motive and reason of a man's work is to obtain property, i.e. something which, thereafter, he may hold as his very own. He intends not merely to acquire a full, real right to remuneration, but a right also to the disposal of such remuneration just as he pleases. It is in such power of disposal that ownership consists, whether the thing owned be land or some moveable object. Now the Socialist solution would deprive the worker of the liberty of disposing of his wages. For, given the Socialist system, he could not do anything with his wages except exchange them for things to consume. He could not, through his wages, increase his resources, exchanging the wages for things which might produce yet further wealth, and thus, in time, come to better his condition. Socialists, therefore, strike at the interests of the wage-earner himself.

Readings taken from *The Pope's New Order: A Systematic Summary of the Social Encyclicals and Addresses, from Leo XIII to Pius XI* (London: Burns Oates & Washbourne Ltd., 1943).

The second objection is that the Socialist solution is unjust. This criticism makes it necessary to set forth the Catholic teaching that private ownership is lawful, and to explain what lawful ownership really means. The Socialist solution, says the pope, is unjust, because 'every man has, by nature, the right to possess property as his own'; 'by nature,' i.e. because man is a *human* being and not a mere animal: because man is a being that directs its own activities by the use of its own reason. Now because man is a *rational* animal 'it must be within man's right to possess things, not merely for temporary and momentary use, as other living things do, but to hold them in stable and permanent possession'; to possess not only things that do not survive his use of them (food, for example) but things which, being used, still survive, and continue to exist for further use in a time to come. How does this follow?

Man, through his reason, can link the future with the present, and, master of his own acts, he can guide his life, under the protecting power of God. He can, therefore, make choices not only in regard to his present welfare, but also in regard to matters that will affect his welfare in the years ahead. Hence man needs to own not only the fruits of the earth, but also the earth itself, from which the provision for the future is to come. Man's needs recur for ever. 'Nature must, then, have given to man a source that is stable and remaining always with him, from which he might look to draw continued supplies. And this stable condition of things he finds only in the earth and its fruits.'

The Socialist says the State alone should own the land. But there is no place here for the State's intervention. For 'Man precedes the State. Prior to the formation of any state, man possesses the right to provide for the sustenance of his body.'

In support of the theory that the State alone should own the land, it is urged that 'God gave the earth for the use and the enjoyment of the whole human race.' This is true; but it does not mean that God so gave it that no individual can own a part of it. God gave it to all means that He did not assign particular parts to particular individuals, means that the whole race should profit from it; and what parts different individuals should own would be settled 'by man's own industry and the laws of individual races.' The whole race must profit from the earth, and in this sense necessarily have a use of it, for 'even though apportioned among private owners, the earth ceases not to minister to the needs of all, inasmuch as there is no one who does not sustain life from what the land produces.'

A further proof that private ownership is in accordance with the law of nature, lies in the relation of labour to the land and in the permanent effects of labour upon the land to which it is applied. 'When man turns his activity and strength to procure the fruits of nature, by such an act he makes his own that portion of nature's field which he cultivates – that portion on which he leaves the impress of his individuality. . . . It cannot but be just that he should possess this portion as his very own and have a right to hold it without anyone being justified in violating that right.'

Despite the strength of these arguments, however, obsolete opinions to the contrary are being revived, e.g., that while it is lawful for a man to own the fruits of the soil, or to have the right to use it, it is unjust that he should possess the soil outright, whether this be 'land on which he has built or land he has brought under cultivation.' But land tilled and cultivated is a different thing from that same land in its virgin state. The labour that has brought about the improvement becomes, in great measure, part of the land that has been improved, and 'indistinguishable and inseparable from it.' Who but the labourer should possess and enjoy this permanent fruit of his toil?

The common opinion of mankind is, then, right when it sees the origins of the system of private property in the nature of things. The practice of all the ages, the civil law and the divine law, all confirm and enforce this principle, that private ownership is a just institution. It is something pre-eminently in accord with the nature of man, and it undeniably makes for the peace of human existence. . . .

II. CATHOLIC TEACHING ALONE PROVIDES THE SOLUTION

THE GENERAL SOCIAL MESSAGE OF THE CHURCH. What is inherent in, and inseparable from, human nature must be borne with; for example the natural inequality which obtains between man and man. Men differ from one another in capacity, skill, health, strength; and from this inequality alone they differ inevitably in fortune. It is impossible to reduce society to one dead level. There is an inequality that is part of the nature of things, and all striving against the nature of things is in vain. Nor is this inequality an evil in itself. It is, of itself, far from being disadvantageous either to individuals or to the community. Again, pain and suffering cannot ever be wholly abolished. They are the consequences of sin and 'they must accompany man so long as life lasts.' To promise people a new age free from pain and trouble, where repose shall be undisturbed and enjoyment uninterrupted, is 'to delude and impose on them.' 'Nothing is more useful than to look on the world as it really is' – and at the same time to seek elsewhere for the solace to the world's troubles.

As regards the mutual relations of the employer and the workman, it is not true that these form classes which are by their nature, and inevitably, hostile each to the other. On the contrary, the nature of things calls for their constant cooperation. For each class needs the other, and one of the Church's most useful functions is to prevent the ever recurring strife, by reminding each class of its duties to the other, and especially of the obligations of justice.

What are these Obligations? For the Workers they are: 'to carry out honestly and fairly all equitable agreements freely entered into'; never to injure an employer's property or his person; never to resort to violence in defending their own cause, or to riots or disorder; to shun evil-principled agitators.

For the wealthy Owner and Employer, the obligations are: not to consider workmen as bondsmen; to respect the worker's dignity as a man and as a Christian; to remember that 'it is shameful and inhuman to treat men like chattels to make money by, or to look upon them merely as so much muscle and physical strength'; to remember the needs of the worker's soul, provide time and opportunity for his religious duties, and guard him from dangerous occasions of sin in his work; 'never to tax the workers beyond their strength, or to employ them in work unsuited to their sex or age.'

But above all else, the employer's 'great and principal duty is to give every one what is just'; in this matter of wages 'to exercise pressure upon the needy and the destitute for the sake of gain, to gather one's profit out of another's need is condemned by all laws, human and divine. To defraud anyone of his due wages is a sin that cries to Heaven for vengeance.' Hence the employer is bound 'to refrain, religiously, from cutting down wages whether by force, by fraud or by usurious dealing.' . . .

SPECIAL TEACHING ON THE STATE'S SOCIAL DUTIES. . . . The foremost duty of the State is to make sure that its laws and institutions are of a kind to bring about both public well-being and private prosperity.

This well-being and prosperity are dependent ultimately on a rule that is according to good morals, on well-regulated family life, respect for religion and justice, moderate and fair taxation, progress in the arts and in trade, an abundant yield of the soil.

It is by promoting these that the State benefits the citizens, and amongst these the poor especially. And 'the more that is done for the benefit of the working classes, by the general laws of the country, the less need will there be to seek for special means to relieve them.'

Moreover, the working classes, who are equally members of the State with the rich, are, in every State, very largely in the majority. 'The public administration must duly and solicitously provide for the welfare and the comfort of the working classes; otherwise that law of justice will be violated which ordains that each man shall have his due.' The chief duty of rulers is to act with strict justice – i.e., with *distributive*[1] justice – towards each and every class alike.

What exactly is meant by this due provision for the welfare and comfort of the working classes? In general, the purpose for which the State exists is 'to make men better.' More particularly, the distinctive purpose of the State is 'to see to the provision of those material and external helps, *the use of which is necessary to virtuous action.*'[2]

Now the labour of the working class is indispensable for the provision of such commodities. So much so that 'it may be truly said that it is only by the labour of working men that states grow rich.'

It is, therefore, Justice which demands that the interests of the working classes shall be protected carefully by the State – 'that being housed, clothed and bodily fit, they may find their life less hard and more endurable,' the commonwealth thus shielding from misery 'those on whom it so largely depends for the things that it needs.'

'The State must not,' of course, 'absorb the individual or the family.' Its intervention must be solely for the safeguarding of both the community and all its citizens. It is when there is no other way of meeting the general interest, or that of a particular class, no other way of preventing harm to it, that the public authority must step in and act. . . .

NOTES

1. The rule of distributive justice is that offices, honours, rewards, be distributed among the community by its ruler proportionately to the merits and capacity of the several members of the community.
2. St. Thomas Aquinas, *De Regimine Principum*, i. 15; the italics are the pope's.

III. THE LIVING WAGE

We come now to the most famous passage in the whole encyclical – the passage which is, perhaps, all that many people have in mind when they speak of 'the teaching of *Rerum Novarum*.'

The section opens with an explanation of what wages are, according to a well-known school of political economists. This is the theory, that just wages are the outcome purely of the free consent of master and workman. Whatever these agree to is, by the fact of the agreement, just. The master cannot owe more to the man than this, be the amount what it may. The only way in which a master can be guilty of injustice is by paying less than the agreement stipulates, and the State's only ground for interference, in matter of wages (according to this theory), is to enforce the contract made. The justice of the contract itself depends merely on the fact of its being an agreement.

The pope declines to accept this theory. There are important elements in the matter which this theory altogether ignores. A man's labour is a personal thing, it is true, that is to say it is something bound up with his personality, and it is therefore his own exclusive property. If this were all, doubtless it would be within the workman's right to accept any rate of wages whatsoever. But there is a further characteristic of human labour.

Man's labour is *necessary*, i.e., without its results man cannot live. Self-preservation is a law of nature, and it is wrong, is in fact a crime, to disobey this law. Our conclusion about wages must be very different from that of the economists the pope is criticising, once we recall that a man's work is the means by which he procures what is required to keep him alive.

We must, in fact, admit that, in agreements between employer and worker about wages, not only must there be freedom, but there must be regard for the underlying 'dictate of natural justice, more imperious and ancient than any bargain between man and man.' This dictate is that 'wages ought not to be insufficient to support a frugal and well-behaved wage-earner.'

Should it happen that either 'through necessity or through fear of a worse evil,' the worker consents to take less 'because the employer will afford him no better, "the worker" is made the victim of force and injustice.'

For the settlement of disputes in this matter – and indeed for the settlement of all the various matters connected with conditions of work, e.g., hours, health precautions, etc. – the pope recommends the institution of boards of arbitrators. This will prevent – what the pope never ceases to foresee and to warn against – 'undue interference on the part of the State.'

As to the amount which constitutes this wage sufficient 'to support a frugal and well-behaved wage-earner,' the pope, naturally, makes no attempt to define it in terms of money. What Leo XIII had in mind follows in the next paragraph. Here the pope declares that the worker should be encouraged to become himself an owner. 'Nature itself would urge him to this. . . . The law therefore should favour owner-ship . . . and induce as many as possible of the people to become owners.' The workman, if paid the kind of wage the pope has in view, 'wages sufficient to enable him comfortably to support himself, his wife, and his children . . . will find it easy, if he be a sensible man, to practise thrift . . . to put by some little savings and thus secure a modest source of income.'

If the workers, in their own small way, thus develop into owners, society will profit in many ways. 'Property will certainly become more equitably divided. The present evil state of things will tend to disappear, i.e., the division into two 'widely differing castes . . . the one holding power because it holds wealth; which has in its grasp the whole of labour and trade; . . . manipulating for its own benefit . . . all the sources of supply; . . . and the other, a needy and powerless multitude, sick and sore in spirit; ever ready for disturbance.' There will be, also, a greater abundance of the fruits of the earth; for 'men always work harder and more readily when they work on that which belongs to them.' Then, too, 'men would cling to the country in which they were born, for no one would exchange his fatherland for a foreign country, if his own afforded him the means of a decent and happy life.'

But one necessary condition, if these three important benefits are to be realised, is 'that a man's means be not drained and exhausted by excessive taxation.' The State, once again, has the right to a certain control over private property. But it has no right to absorb it altogether, and 'the State would therefore be unjust and cruel if, under the name of taxation, it were to deprive the private owner of more than is fair.'

IV. THE ROLE OF PRIVATE ASSOCIATIONS WITHIN THE STATE AND ESPECIALLY OF TRADE UNIONS

The pope has spoken of the role of the two public societies, i.e., the Church and the State. He now turns to what may be done by private societies, the last class of these agencies which are apt for the task of solving the great and urgent problem.

The most important of all these private organisations are the Trades Unions; and the pope explicitly prays that their number may increase.

He insists that such unions do not derive their right to exist from any permission given by the State. For 'to enter into a society of this kind is the natural right of man, and the State is bound to protect natural rights, not to destroy them.' So that 'if the

State forbids its citizens to form associations, it contradicts the very principle of its own existence.' . . .

THE ENCYCLICAL QUADRAGESIMO ANNO

I. THE FRUITS OF 'RERUM NOVARUM'

PIUS XI celebrates in this encyclical the fortieth anniversary of Leo XIII's letter *Rerum Novarum*.

The pope begins by recalling the times in which Leo XIII's letter appeared. It was the hey-day of almost uncontrolled capitalist development; the hey-day, too, of economic liberalism. Competition, it was almost everywhere believed, should be absolutely free, and the State should leave industrial problems to be solved by those directly concerned, the workmen and their employers. Mankind was increasingly dividing into two classes, those who enjoyed all the advantages supplied by the modern inventions, and the vast multitude of poverty-stricken workers who produced the profits on which the other class lived, 'and who struggled in vain to escape from the difficulties which encompassed them.' This state of things the wealthy found 'quite satisfactory,' though the workers were more and more restive under it.

Catholic opinion was divided. There were some 'who could in no way persuade themselves that so enormous and unjust a difference in the distribution of temporal goods' was what God intended, and who sought for a remedy: but such Catholics were often looked on with suspicion by their fellow-Catholics, and also they were by no means agreed among themselves as to remedies and policies. To all this Catholic questioning *Rerum Novarum* gave an authoritative answer.

Pius XI recalls the world-wide enthusiasm that greeted Leo's letter, and also the dismay in certain – even Catholic – quarters. It was 'so unexpectedly in advance of its time.' Hence the slow of heart scorned it, the timorous were afraid of it, and many who professed to admire it regarded it as no more than a utopian dream.

This fortieth anniversary is for Pius XI an opportunity to recall what benefits have resulted from Leo XIII's action, to defend Leo's teaching – his 'economic and social doctrine' – against certain doubts and to develop some of its details, and finally to pass a judgement on the economic regime of to-day and on modern Socialism, to explain wherein lies the root cause of the social disorder and to point out the only thing that will cure it. . . .

II. LEO XIII'S TEACHING DEFENDED AND DEVELOPED

This is the longest division of the encyclical (7000 words out of 18 000). In it the pope examines four points which concern directly the individual – namely, Ownership, Capital and Labour, the Emancipation of the Proletariat and the Just Wage – and then, in a long concluding section, he deals with the actual reconstruction of the social system.

This second main division of the encyclical opens with a boldly worded statement that the Church has the right, and the duty, 'to deal as an authority with social and economic problems': not, indeed, to decide the discussions of a technical kind that must arise once reform and reconstruction begin, but to decide the question whether the underlying principles of any particular reform are right or wrong. The reason is simple; 'the deposit of truth entrusted to Us by God, and Our weighty office of declaring, interpreting and urging, in season and out of season, the entire moral law, demand that both the social order and economic life be brought within Our supreme jurisdiction.'

Economic life, the pope continues, is something that is guided by its own principles in its own domain. The same is true of moral conduct. But these two spheres of activity are not so dissociated, so alien each from the other, that economic life is in no way dependent on morals. And to maintain the contrary is to maintain what is false. Economic laws determine what human effort can achieve, and by what means. These economic laws are the discovery of reason; but reason can also discover what, in the design of God, is the ultimate purpose of the whole system of things considered from the point of view of economics. The point of view of economics is, however, only one particular way of regarding the universe. Economic purposes and aims are only particular purposes and aims. And particular aims must be subordinated to the general, ultimate aim or purpose of things. It is the function of the moral law – in contradistinction with, say, the economic law – to direct our activities (in whatever sphere these may lie) towards those purposes or objects of that particular sphere of life which correspond with the general ultimate purpose of all. 'If this [moral] law be faithfully obeyed, the result will be that particular economic purposes . . . will fall into their due place in the general system of purposes,' and we shall be able, through the pursuit of economic purposes, to rise to the first purpose of all things, namely God.

OWNERSHIP OR THE RIGHT TO OWN. Leo XIII, and all Catholic theologians, have always taught that the right to own has a twofold character for it concerns the invididual, and it concerns the good of the community. They all, that is to say, assert that God gave man this right to possess things as his own first 'so that individuals might be able to provide for their own needs and the needs of their families' and then in order that, through the right of ownership, the goods provided by God 'for the whole human race may really serve this purpose.'

There is a twofold danger in discussions about ownership against which we must guard: if the second, i.e., the social or public, aspect of ownership is not sufficiently borne in mind, we risk falling into 'individualism'; on the other hand, if it is the first, i.e., the private and individual, characteristic of ownership that is minimised, we risk the error of 'collectivism.'

CAPITAL AND LABOUR. As to labour, there is one form of it – namely, the labour which a man employs as his own master – which gives him a claim to all its fruits. But there is another form also, the labour which a man hires out to another and which is applied to the capital of another. It is of this kind of labour that the pope is now going to speak. It is this of which Leo XIII spoke when he said: 'It is only by the labour of working men that States grow rich.' And, says Pius XI, it is self-evident that 'the huge possessions which constitute human wealth . . . flow from the hands of the working man.

On the other hand, it is no less evident that this toil would be ineffective had there not been already in existence the vast, God-created resources of natural wealth. And all this wealth is owned by someone; indeed, that everything should have somewhere its proper owner is a condition of order in life, and demanded therefore by the natural law. If, then, a man has not property of his own to which to apply his labour, 'an alliance must be formed between his labour and his neighbour's property.' That capital and labour form such an alliance is an obvious essential condition of social well-being.

There has not, however, always been, between these forces, that accord which the situation calls for. Capital, for instance, 'was able, for a long time, to appropriate too much to itself.' It 'left the worker with the barest minimum' sufficient to keep him alive and active. And this state of things was, as it were, consecrated by the political economists who agreed that this was an inevitable development due to 'inexorable economic law' and that things must always be like this. Certainly, for a long time, 'the steady pressure of economic and social tendencies was in this direction.'

The cause of the workers, exasperated as they were by such conditions – which the teachings of the so-called Manchester school would have riveted on them as an eternal yoke – was, however, not really helped when the 'intellectuals' who fought for them devised, in reply, a theory just as wrong, namely, that the worker had every right to 'all products and profits, excepting those required to repair and replace capital.'

The principle of just distribution of product and profit must, in fact, be sought elsewhere. To begin with, Leo XIII's telling words must be borne in mind: 'The earth, even though apportioned among private owners, does not thereby cease to serve the needs of all.' As to the distribution of wealth – which is another way of saying that the earth is meant to serve the needs of all – if this is to be just, the good of the whole community must be served by it, the needs of every member satisfied, i.e., 'No class must exclude any other class from a share in the benefits.' 'Each person must receive his due share, and the distribution of created goods must be brought into conformity with the demands of the general good or social justice.'

'The distribution of wealth to-day is gravely defective,' Pius XI remarks, 'as every sincere observer is aware, on account of the vast difference between the few who hold excessive wealth and the many who live in destitution.' . . .

THE JUST WAGE. But how can the worker save, except out of his wages? The question of wages still remains the important question that Leo XIII described. Pius XI now develops the teaching of *Rerum Novarum*. What he has to say can be summarised under six headings.

(1) It is not true to say that the wage contract is something always and everywhere unjust, and that a system of profit-sharing is the only system really fair to the worker.

But, all the same, given modern conditions, the pope thinks it advisable that the wage system should be supplemented by some kind of partnership. This has been tried with success in many cases, the wage-earners and the officers of the business sharing in some way in the ownership, in the managment or in the profits.

(2) This extremely serious business of the just wage cannot be solved, as some superficial people seem to think, by the simple application of some single principle. 'Many things have to be taken into account,' as Leo XIII has already said. It cannot, for example, be maintained that the just wage is a wage equal in value to the value of the work produced. The principle here is false.

(3) Labour – like property – has, besides its individual character, a social aspect also. Especially is this true of labour that is hired. In fact – and this is obvious – a man's labour cannot produce its fullness of fruit unless there be an organised social system, in which laws and customs protect the work; unless the different kinds of work cooperate; 'and – above all – unless intelligence, capital and labour combine in the common effort.' What the true value of human efficiency, what the adequate compensation it earns, can never be discovered if all this is left out of sight. Bearing in mind all that this twofold character of labour involves, certain extremely important consequences follow, which must be taken into account when wages are being fixed.

(4) Firstly, 'the wage paid to the working man must be sufficient for the support of himself and of his family.'[1] It is certainly right that other members of the family contribute, according to their means, towards the common maintenance. But 'to abuse the tender years of children, or the weakness of woman is an abomination.'[2] The true work for a mother is the work of her home. The state of things where a mother goes out to work because the father's pay is insufficient to keep the family is 'a most wicked abuse,'[3] a thing 'to be abolished at all costs.' The home in such cases is neglected and especially the mother's great function of training her little children. If present circumstances do not make it feasible to pay fathers of families 'such a wage that it meets, adequately, normal domestic needs . . . social justice demands that reforms be introduced without delay which will guarantee such a wage to every adult working man.'

(5) There needs also to be taken into account – in this matter of fixing wages – the business itself and those in charge of it. It would not, for example, be just to demand an exaggerated wage, which the business could not pay without ruin. Or again, the business it may be, is perhaps run at little profit because there is a want of energy or of enterprise in the management, or because new methods are neglected. The loss which is due to causes of this sort does not justify a reduction of the workers' wages. It may, however, happen that a business declines because it has no choice but 'to sell its products at an unjustly low price.' In such a case the real culprits – should wages be reduced – are those who have laid the unjust burdens, or who have unjustly brought about the unproductive sales.

These are cases to be met by concerted action between workmen and employers, and this joint action the State should assist.

(6) Finally, in fixing rates of wages the good of the country as a whole needs to be taken into account. 'Opportunities for work should be provided for every man able and willing to work. This depends in no small measure upon the level of wages. . . . All are aware that a rate of wages too low or too high causes unemployment. Unemployment . . . causes misery and temptation to the workers and endangers public order. . . . To lower or raise wages unduly, with a view to private advantage, and with no consideration for the common good, is therefore contrary to social justice, which demands that, so far as possible, by concerted plans and united wills, wages be so regulated as to offer to as many as possible opportunities of employment, and of securing for themselves suitable means of livelihood.'

Another point to which the pope draws attention is that there should be some kind of 'proportion between different wages' and also – what is closely connected with this – 'proportion between the prices charged for the products of the various economic groups, agricultural, industrial and so forth.' . . .

NOTES

1. The pope refers here to what he has said in the encyclical, *Casti Connubii*.
2. *Nefas est*, in the Latin text.
3. *Pessimus abusus* in the Latin; the English translation reads 'intolerable.'

III. THE ECONOMIC REGIME OF TO-DAY SURVEYED AND JUDGED

Since the date of Leo XIII's encyclical, the capitalist economic regime has spread everywhere. Its advantages, disadvantages, vices, now affect the whole human race.

And to-day, it is not only wealth that is accumulated but power to dominate the economic system despotically. It has now come to this that a few men – who are not the owners, but only the trustees and managers of the moneys invested – are thus masters of the whole economic world.

The source of their hold on that world is that, controlling money, they also control credit; it is this small group that decides who shall be given and who denied credit. They supply, 'so to speak, the life blood to the entire economic body.' They 'grasp in their hands the very soul of production, so that, against their will, no one can breathe.' 'This accumulation of power is the characteristic note of the modern economic order.' It is, also, 'a natural result of unrestricted competition.' For where this obtains, only the strongest survive; and the strongest, often enough, 'means those who fight most relentlessly, who pay least heed to the dictates of conscience.'

A threefold chronic struggle results from this accumulation of power by a few men. There is the endless struggle for supremacy in the economic field; there is the struggle to dominate the State and use it as a tool; there is the struggle between the different states.

The final results then, in economic life, of the once-vaunted spirit of individualism are lamentable. The pope describes the contemporary scene: 'Unbridled ambition to dominate has succeeded the lust for profit; the whole economic regime has become hard, cruel and relentless to a ghastly degree.' The confusion in the over-burdened, ill-organised State has added to the evils and the State, 'which should be the supreme arbiter, ruling in kingly fashion far above all party contentions ... has become instead a slave bound over to the service of human passion and greed.' In the relations of nation with nation, we can note two dangerous developments. On the one hand there is 'economic nationalism, or even economic imperialism; on the other hand, a no less noxious and detestable internationalism or international imperialism in financial affairs, which holds that where a man's fortune is, there is his country.'

IV. THE SOCIALISM OF TO-DAY SURVEYED AND JUDGED

Socialism, too, has undergone profound changes in the last forty years. It can no longer be termed a single system, defending 'certain definite and mutually coherent doctrines.' On the contrary, it has in the main split into two, often bitterly hostile, sections. But one thing both sections have in common, to wit, 'the anti-Christian basis which has always been characteristic of Socialism.'

One section has run headlong into Communism and openly, and by every means, it calls for the class war and the complete abolition of private property. Once the Communists succeed – and wherever they succeed – 'it is monstrous beyond belief how cruel and inhuman they show themselves to be.' It is likewise well known that they are militantly atheistic. The pope laments the heedlessness of so many before this terrible menace, and the apathy of states that do nothing to check that Communist propaganda which is always the beginning of the trouble. Still worse, and meriting still more severe judgement, is the sloth[1] 'of those who neglect to remove or modify those social conditions which drive people to exasperation,' and who are thus preparing the way for the overthrow and ruin of the social order.

The other section keeps the name of Socialism and is much less radical. It condemns the use of force, would mitigate the class war and not abolish private ownership entirely. In a sense this section might seem to be tending towards the Christian tradition, and 'it cannot be denied that its opinions sometimes closely approach the just demands of Christian social reformers.' If this development, in Socialists of this type, continues (and Pius XI explains with some detail in what such development would consist) 'it may well come about that gradually these tenets of mitigated Socialism will no longer be different from the programme of those who seek to reform human society according to Christian principles.' The pope gives an example, saying: 'It is rightly contended that certain forms of property must be reserved to the State, since they carry with them a power too great to be left to private individuals without injury to the community at large.' ...

NOTES

1. *Socordia* in the Latin text: 'foolhardiness' in the English translation (C. T. S., § 112).

Anarchy, state and utopia

ROBERT NOZICK

THE ENTITLEMENT THEORY

The subject of justice in holdings consists of three major topics. The first is the *original acquisition of holdings*, the appropriation of unheld things. This includes the issues of how unheld things may come to be held, the process, or processes, by which unheld things may come to be held, the things that may come to be held by these processes, the extent of what comes to be held by a particular process, and so on. We shall refer to the complicated truth about this topic, which we shall not formulate here, as the principle of justice in acquisition. The second topic concerns the *transfer of holdings* from one person to another. By what processes may a person transfer holdings to another? How may a person acquire a holding from another who holds it? Under this topic come general descriptions of voluntary exchange, and gift and (on the other hand) fraud, as well as reference to particular conventional details fixed upon in a given society. The complicated truth about this subject (with placeholders for conventional details) we shall call the principle of justice in transfer. (And we shall suppose it also includes principles governing how a person may divest himself of a holding, passing it into an unheld state.)

If the world were wholly just, the following inductive definition would exhaustively cover the subject of justice in holdings.

1. A person who acquires a holding in accordance with the principle of justice in acquisition is entitled to that holding.
2. A person who acquires a holding in accordance with the principle of justice in transfer, from someone else entitled to the holding, is entitled to the holding.
3. No one is entitled to a holding except by (repeated) applications of 1 and 2.

The complete principle of distributive justice would say simply that a distribution is just if everyone is entitled to the holdings they possess under the distribution.

A distribution is just if it arises from another just distribution by legitimate means. The legitimate means of moving from one distribution to another are specified by the principle of justice in transfer. The legitimate first "moves" are specified by the principle of justice in acquisition. Whatever arises from a just situation by just steps is itself just. The means of change specified by the principle of justice in transfer preserve justice. As correct rules of inference are truth-preserving, and any conclusion deduced via repeated application of such rules from only true premises is itself true, so the means of transition from one situation to another specified by the principle of justice in transfer are justice-preserving, and any situation actually arising from repeated transitions in accordance with the principle from a just situation is itself just. The parallel between justice-preserving transformations and truth-preserving transformations illuminates where it fails as well as where it holds. That a conclusion could have been deduced by truth-preserving means from premises that are true suffices to show its truth. That from a just situation a situation *could* have arisen via justice-preserving means does *not* suffice to show its justice. The fact that a thief's victims voluntarily *could* have presented him with gifts does not entitle the thief to his ill-gotten gains. Justice in holdings is historical; it depends upon what actually has happened. We shall return to this point later.

Not all actual situations are generated in accordance with the two principles of justice in holdings: the principle of justice in acquisition and the principle of justice in transfer. Some people steal from others, or defraud them, or enslave them, seizing their product and preventing them from living as they choose, or forcibly exclude others from competing in exchange. None of these are permissible modes of transition from one situation to another. And some persons acquire holdings by means not sanctioned by the principle of justice in acquisition. The existence of past injustice (previous violations of the first two principles of justice in holdings) raises the third major topic under justice in holdings: the rectification of injustice in holdings. If past injustice has shaped present holdings in various ways, some identifiable and some not, what now, if anything, ought to be done to rectify these injustices? What obligations do the performers of injustice have toward those whose position is worse than it would have been had the injustice not been done? Or, than it would have been had compensation been paid promptly? How, if at all, do things change if the beneficiaries and those made worse off are not the direct parties in the act of injustice, but, for example, their descendants? Is an injustice done to someone whose holding was itself based upon an unrectified injustice? How far back must one go in wiping clean the historical slate of injustices? What may victims of injustice permissibly do in order to rectify the injustices being done to them, including the many injustices done by persons acting through their government? I do not know of a thorough or theoretically sophisticated treatment of such issues. Idealizing greatly, let us suppose theoretical investigation will produce a principle of rectification. This principle uses historical information about previous situations and injustices done in them (as defined by the first two principles of justice and rights against interference), and information about the actual course of events that flowed from these injustices, until the present, and it yields a description (or descriptions) of holdings in the society. The principle of rectification presumably will make use of its best estimate of subjunctive information about what would have occurred (or a probability distribution over what might have occurred, using the expected value) if the injustice had not taken place. If the actual description of holdings turns out not to be one of the descriptions yielded by the principle, then one of the descriptions yielded must be realized. . . .

PATTERNING

The entitlement principles of justice in holdings that we have sketched are historical principles of justice. To better understand their precise character, we shall distinguish them from another subclass of the historical principles. Consider, as an example, the principle of distribution according to moral merit. This principle requires that total distributive shares vary directly with moral merit; no person should have a greater share than anyone whose moral merit is greater. (If moral merit could be not merely ordered but measured on an interval or ratio scale, stronger principles could be formulated.) Or consider the principle that results by substituting 'usefulness to society' for 'moral merit' in the previous principle. Or instead of 'distribute according to moral merit,' or 'distribute according to use-fulness to society,' we might consider 'distribute according to the weighted sum of moral merit, usefulness to society, and need,' with the weights of the different dimensions equal. Let us call a principle of distribution *patterned* if it specifies that a distribution is to vary along with some natural dimension, weighted sum of natural dimensions, or lexicographic ordering of natural dimensions. And let us say a distribution is patterned if it accords with some patterned principle. (I speak of natural dimensions, admittedly without a general criterion for them, because for any set of holdings some artificial dimensions can be gimmicked up to vary along with the distribution of the set.) The principle of distribution in accordance with moral merit is a patterned historical principle, which specifies a patterned distribution. 'Distribute according to I.Q.' is a patterned principle that looks to information not contained in distributional matrices. It is not historical, however, in that it does not look to any past actions creating differential entitlements to evaluate a distribution; it requires only distributional matrices whose columns are labeled by I.Q. scores. The distribution in a society, however, may be composed of such simple patterned distributions, without itself being simply patterned. Different sectors may operate different patterns, or some combination of patterns may operate in different proportions across a society. A distribution composed in this manner, from a small number of patterned distributions, we also shall term 'patterned.' And we extend the use of 'pattern' to include the overall designs put forth by combinations of end-state principles.

Almost every suggested principle of distributive justice is patterned: to each according to his moral merit, or needs, or marginal product, or how hard he tries, or the weighted sum of the foregoing, and so on. The principle of entitlement we have sketched is *not* patterned. . . .

HOW LIBERTY UPSETS PATTERNS

It is not clear how those holding alternative conceptions of distributive justice can reject the entitlement conception of justice in holdings. For suppose a distribution favored by one of these non-entitlement conceptions is realized. Let us suppose it is your favorite one and let us call this distribution D_1; perhaps everyone has an equal share, perhaps shares vary in accordance with some dimension you treasure. Now suppose that Wilt Chamberlain is greatly in demand by basketball teams, being a great gate attraction. (Also suppose contracts run only for a year, with players being free agents.) He signs the following sort of contract with a team: In each home game, twenty-five cents from the price of each ticket of admission goes to him. (We ignore the question of whether he is 'gouging' the owners, letting them look out for themselves.) The season starts, and people cheerfully attend his team's games; they buy their tickets, each time dropping a separate twenty-five cents of their admission price into a special box with Chamberlain's name on it. They are excited about seeing him play; it is worth the total admission price to them. Let us suppose that in one season one million persons attend his home games, and Wilt Chamberlain winds up with \$250 000, a much larger sum than the average income and larger even than anyone else has. Is he entitled to this income? Is this new distribution D_2, unjust? If so, why? There is *no* question about whether each of the people was entitled to the control over the resources they held in D_1; because that was the distribution (your favorite) that (for the purposes of argument) we assumed was acceptable. Each of these persons *chose* to give twenty-five cents of their money to Chamberlain. They could have spent it on going to the movies, or on candy bars, or on copies of *Dissent* magazine, or of *Montly Review*. But they all, at least one million of them, converged on giving it to Wilt Chamberlain in exchange for watching him play basketball. If D_1 was a just distribution, and people voluntarily moved from it to D_2, transferring parts of their shares they were given under D_1 (what was it for if not to do something with?), isn't D_2 also just? If the people were entitled to dispose of the resources to which they were entitled (under D_1), didn't this include their being entitled to give it to, or exchange it with, Wilt Chamberlain? Can anyone else complain on grounds of justice? Each other person already has his legitimate share under D_1. Under D_1, there is nothing that anyone has that anyone else has a claim of justice against. After someone transfers something to Wilt Chamberlain, third parties *still* have their legitimate shares; *their* shares are not changed. By what process could such a transfer among two persons give rise to a legitimate claim of distributive justice on a portion of what was transferred, by a third party who had no claim of justice on any holding of the others *before* the transfer? To cut off objections irrelevant here, we might imagine the exchanges occurring in a socialist society, after hours. After playing whatever basketball he does in his daily work, or doing whatever other daily work he does, Wilt Chamberlain decides to put in *overtime* to earn additional money. (First his work quota is set; he works time over that.) Or imagine it is a skilled juggler people like to see, who puts on shows after hours.

Why might someone work overtime in a society in which it is assumed their needs are satisfied? Perhaps because they care about things other than needs. I like to write in books that I read, and to have easy access to books for browsing at odd hours. It would be very pleasant and convenient to have the resources of Widener Library in my back yard. No society, I assume, will provide such resources close to each person who would like them as part of his regular allotment (under D_1). Thus, persons either must do without some extra things that they want, or be allowed to do something extra to get some of these things. On what basis could the inequalities that would eventuate be forbidden? Notice also that small factories would spring up in a socialist society, unless forbidden. I melt down some of my personal possessions (under D_1) and build a machine out of the material. I offer you, and others, a philosophy lecture once a week in exchange for your cranking the handle on my machine, whose products I exchange for yet other things, and so on. (The raw materials used by the machine are given to me by others who possess them under D_1, in exchange for hearing lectures.) Each person might participate to gain things over and above their allotment under D_1. Some persons even might want to leave their job in socialist industry and work full time in this private sector. I shall say something more about these issues in the next chapter. Here I wish merely to note how private property even in means of production would occur in a socialist society that did not fobid people to use as they wished some of the resources they are given under the socialist distribution D_1. The socialist society would have to forbid capitalist acts between consenting adults.

The general point illustrated by the Wilt Chamberlain example and the example of the entrepreneur in a socialist society is that no end-state principle or distributional patterned principle of justice can be continuously realized without continuous interference with people's lives. Any favored pattern would be transformed into one unfavored by the principle, by people choosing to act in various ways; for example, by people exchanging goods and services with other people, or giving things to other people, things the transferrers are entitled to under the favored distributional pattern. To maintain a pattern one must either continually interfere to stop people from transferring resources as they wish to, or continually (or periodically) interfere to take from some persons resources that others for some reason chose to transfer to them.

A theory of justice

JOHN RAWLS

THE MAIN IDEA OF THE THEORY OF JUSTICE

My aim is to present a conception of justice which generalizes and carries to a higher level of abstraction the familiar theory of the social contract as found, say, in Locke, Rousseau, and Kant.[1] In order to do this we are not to think of the original contract as one to enter a particular society or to set up a particular form of government. Rather, the guiding idea is that the principles of justice for the basic structure of society are the object of the original agreement. They are the principles that free and rational persons concerned to further their own interests would accept in an initial position of equality as defining the fundamental terms of their association. These principles are to regulate all further agreements; they specify the kinds of social cooperation that can be entered into and the forms of government that can be established. This way of regarding the principles of justice I shall call justice as fairness.

Thus we are to imagine that those who engage in social cooperation choose together, in one joint act, the principles which are to assign basic rights and duties and to determine the division of social benefits. Men are to decide in advance how they are to regulate their claims against one another and what is to be the foundation charter of their society. Just as each person must decide by rational reflection what constitutes his good, that is, the system of ends which it is rational for him to pursue, so a group of persons must decide once and for all what is to count among them as just and unjust. The choice which rational men would make in this hypothetical situation of equal liberty, assuming for the present that this choice problem has a solution, determines the principles of justice.

In justice as fairness the original position of equality corresponds to the state of nature in the traditional theory of the social contract. This original position is not, of course, thought of as an actual historical state of affairs, much less as a primitive condition of culture. It is understood as a purely hypothetical situation characterized so as to lead to a certain conception of justice.[2] Among the essential features of this situation is that no one knows his place in society, his class position or social status, nor does any one know his fortune in the distribution of natural assets and abilities, his intelligence, strength, and the like. I shall even assume that the parties do not know their conceptions of the good or their special psychological propensities. The principles of justice are chosen behind a veil of ignorance. This ensures that no one is advantaged or disadvantaged in the choice of principles by the outcome of natural chance or the contingency of social circumstances. Since all are similarly situated and no one is able to design principles to favor his particular condition, the principles of justice are the result of a fair agreement or bargain. For given the circumstances of the original position, the symmetry of everyone's relations to each other, this initial situation is fair between individuals as 'moral persons,' that is, as rational beings with their own ends and capable, I shall assume, of a sense of justice. The original position is, one might say, the appropriate initial status quo, and thus the fundamental agreements reached in it are fair. This explains the propriety of the name 'justice as fairness': it conveys the idea that the principles of justice are agreed to in an initial situation that is fair. The name does not mean that the concepts of justice and fairness are the same, any more than the phrase 'poetry as metaphor' means that the concepts of poetry and metaphor are the same.

Justice as fairness begins, as I have said, with one of the most general of all choices which persons might make together, namely, with the choice of the first principles of a conception of justice which is to regulate all subsequent criticism and reform of institutions. Then, having chosen a conception of justice, we can suppose that they are to choose a constitution and a legislature to enact laws, and so on, all in accordance with the principles of justice initially agreed upon. Our social situation is just if it is such that by this sequence of hypothetical agreements we would have contracted into the general system of rules which defines it. Moreover, assuming that the original position does determine a set of principles (that is, that a particular conception of justice would be chosen), it will then be true that whenever social institutions satisfy these principles those engaged in them can say to one another that they are cooperating on terms to which they would agree if they were free and equal persons whose relations with respect to one another were fair. They could all view their arrangements as meeting the stipulations which they would acknowledge in an initial situation that embodies widely accepted and reasonable constraints on the choice of principles. The general recognition of this fact would provide the basis for a public acceptance of the corresponding principles of justice. No society can, of course, be a scheme of cooperation which men enter voluntarily in a literal sense; each person finds himself placed at birth in some particular position in some particular society, and the nature of this position materially affects his life prospects. Yet a society satisfying the principles of justice as fairness comes as close as a society can to being a voluntary scheme, for it meets the principles which free and equal persons would assent to under circumstances that are fair. In this sense its members are autonomous and the obligations they recognize self-imposed.

One feature of justice as fairness is to think of the parties in the initial situation as rational and mutually disinterested. This does not mean that the parties are egoists, that is, individuals with only certain kinds of interests, say in wealth, prestige, and domination. But they are conceived as not taking an interest in one another's interests. They are to presume that even their spiritual aims may be opposed, in the way that the aims of those of different religions may be opposed. Moreover, the concept of rationality must be interpreted as far as possible in the narrow sense, standard in economic theory, of taking the most effective means to given ends. I shall modify this concept to some extent, as explained later, but one must try to avoid introducing into it any controversial ethical elements. The initial situation must be characterized by stipulations that are widely accepted.

In working out the conception of justice as fairness one main task clearly is to determine which principles of justice would be chosen in the original position. To do this we must describe this situation in some detail and formulate with care the problem of choice which it presents. These matters I shall take up in the immediately succeeding chapters. It may be observed, however, that once the principles of justice are thought of as arising from an original agreement in a situation of equality, it is an open question whether the principle of utility would be acknowledged. Offhand it hardly seems likely that persons who view themselves as equals, entitled to press their claims upon one another, would agree to a principle which may require lesser life prospects for some simply for the sake of a greater sum of advantages enjoyed by others. Since each desires to protect his interests, his capacity to advance his conception of the good, no one has a reason to acquiesce in an enduring loss for himself in order to bring about a greater net balance of satisfaction. In the absence of strong and lasting benevolent impulses, a rational man would not accept a basic structure merely because it maximized the algebraic sum of advantages irrespective of its permanent effects on his own basic rights and interests. Thus it seems that the principle of utility is incompatible with the conception of social cooperation among equals for mutual advantage. It appears to be inconsistent with the idea of reciprocity implicit in the notion of a well-ordered society. Or, at any rate, so I shall argue.

I shall maintain instead that the persons in the initial situation would choose two rather different principles: the first requires equality in the assignment of basic rights and duties, while the second holds that social and economic inequalities, for example inequalities of wealth and authority, are just only if they result in compensating benefits for everyone, and in particular for the least advantaged members of society. These principles rule out justifying institutions on the grounds that the hardships of some are offset by a greater good in the aggregate. It may be expedient but it is not just that some should have less in order that others may prosper. But there is no injustice in the greater benefits earned by a few provided that the situation of persons not so fortunate is thereby improved. The intuitive idea is that since everyone's well-being depends upon a scheme of cooperation without which no one could have a satisfactory life, the division of advantages should be such as to draw forth the willing cooperation of everyone taking part in it, including those less well situated. Yet this can be expected only if reasonable terms are proposed. The two principles mentioned seem to be a fair agreement on the basis of which those better endowed, or more fortunate in their social position, neither of which we can be said to deserve, could expect the willing cooperation of others when some workable scheme is a necessary condition of the welfare of all. Once we decide to look for a conception of justice that nullifies the accidents of natural endowment and the contingencies of social circumstance as counters in quest for political and economic advantage, we are led to these principles. They express the result of leaving aside those aspects of the social world that seem arbitrary from a moral point of view.

NOTES

1. As the text suggests, I shall regard Locke's *Second Treatise of Government*, Rousseau's *The Social Contract*, and Kant's ethical works beginning with *The Foundations of the Metaphysics of Morals* as definitive of the contract tradition. For all of its greatness, Hobbes's *Leviathan* raises special problems. A general historical survey is provided by J. W. Gough, *The Social Contract*, 2nd ed. (Oxford, The Clarendon Press, 1957), and Otto Gierke, *Natural Law and the Theory of Society*, trans. with an introduction by Ernest Barker (Cambridge, The University Press, 1934). A presentation of the contract view as primarily an ethical theory is to be found in G. R. Grice, *The Grounds of Moral Judgement* (Cambridge, The University Press, 1967). See also § 19, note 30.
2. Kant is clear that the original agreement is hypothetical. *See The Metaphysics of Morals*, pt.

I (*Rechtslehre*), especially §§ 47, 52; and pt. II of the essay 'Concerning the Common Saying: This May Be True in Theory but It Does Not Apply in Practice,' in *Kant's Political Writings*, ed. Hans Reiss and trans. by H. B. Nisbet (Cambridge, The University Press, 1970), pp. 73–87. See Georges Vlachos, *La Pensée politique de Kant* (Paris, Presses Universitaires de France, 1962), pp. 326–335; and J. G. Murphy, *Kant: The Philosophy of Right* (London, Macmillan, 1970), pp. 109–112, 133–136, for a further discussion.

TWO PRINCIPLES OF JUSTICE

I shall now state in a provisional form the two principles of justice that I believe would be chosen in the original position. In this section I wish to make only the most general comments, and therefore the first formulation of these principles is tentative. As we go on I shall run through several formulations and approximate step by step the final statement to be given much later. I believe that doing this allows the exposition to proceed in a natural way.

The first statement of the two principles reads as follows.

First: each person is to have an equal right to the most extensive basic liberty compatible with a similar liberty for others.

Second: social and economic inequalities are to be arranged so that they are both (a) reasonably expected to be to everyone's advantage, and (b) attached to positions and offices open to all. There are two ambiguous phrases in the second principle, namely 'everyone's advatage' and 'equally open to all.' . . .

By way of general comment, these principles primarily apply, as I have said, to the basic structure of society. They are to govern the assignment of rights and duties and to regulate the distribution of social and economic advantages. As their formulation suggests, these principles presuppose that the social structure can be divided into two more or less distinct parts, the first principle applying to the one, the second to the other. They distinguish between those aspects of the social system that define and secure the equal liberties of citizenship and those that specify and establish social and economic inequalities. The basic liberties of citizens are, roughly speaking, political liberty (the right to vote and to be eligible for public office) together with freedom of speech and assembly; liberty of conscience and freedom of thought; freedom of the person along with the right to hold (personal) property; and freedom from arbitrary arrest and seizure as defined by the concept of the rule of law. These liberties are all required to be equal by the first principle, since citizens of a just society are to have the same basic rights.

The second principle applies, in the first approximation, to the distribution of income and wealth and to the design of organizations that make use of differences in authority and responsibility, or chains of command. While the distribution of wealth and income need not be equal, it must be to everyone's advantage, and at the same time, positions of authority and offices of command must be accessible to all. One applies the second principle by holding positions open, and then, subject to this constraint, arranges social and economic inequalities so that everyone benefits.

These principles are to be arranged in a serial order with the first principle prior to the second. This ordering means that a departure from the institutions of equal liberty required by the first principle cannot be justified by, or compensated for, by greater social and economic advantages. The distribution of wealth and income, and the hierarchies of authority, must be consistent with both the liberties of equal citizenship and equality of opportunity.

It is clear that these principles are rather specific in their content, and their acceptance rests on certain assumptions that I must eventually try to explain and justify. A theory of justice depends upon a theory of society in ways that will become evident as we proceed. For the present, it should be observed that the two principles (and this holds for all formulations) are a special case of a more general conception of justice that can be expressed as follows.

> All social values – liberty and opportunity, income and wealth, and the bases of self-respect – are to be distributed equally unless an unequal distribution of any, or all, of these values is to everyone's advantage.

Injustice, then, is simply inequalities that are not to the benefit of all. . . .

THE MAIN GROUNDS FOR THE TWO PRINCIPLES OF JUSTICE

In this section my aim is to use the conditions of publicity and finality to give some of the main arguments for the two principles of justice. I shall rely upon the fact that for an agreement to be valid, the parties must be able to honor it under all relevant and foreseeable circumstances. There must be a rational assurance that one can carry through. The arguments I shall adduce fit under the heuristic schema suggested by the reasons for following the maximin rule. That is, they help to show that the two principles are an adequate minimum conception of justice in a situation of great uncertainty. Any further advantages that might be won by the principle of utility, or whatever, are highly problematical, whereas the hardship if things turn out badly are intolerable. It is at this point that the concept of a contract has a definite role: it suggests the condition of publicity and sets limits upon what can be agreed to. Thus justice as fairness uses the concept of contract to a greater extent than the discussion so far might suggest.

The first confirming ground for the two principles can be explained in terms of what I earlier referred to as the strains of commitment. I said that the parties have a capacity for justice in the sense that they can be assured that their undertaking is not in vain. Assuming that they have taken everything into account, including the general facts of moral psychology, they can rely on one another to adhere to the principles adopted. Thus they consider the strains of commitment. They cannot enter into agreements that may have consequences they cannot accept. They will avoid those that they can adhere to only with great difficulty. Since the original agreement is final and made in perpetuity, there is no second chance. In view of the serious nature of the possible consequences, the question of the burden of commitment is especially acute. A person is choosing once and for all the standards which are to govern his life prospects. Moreover, when we enter an agreement we must be able to honor it even should the worst possibilities prove to be the case. Otherwise we have not acted in good faith. Thus the parties must weigh with care whether they will be able to stick by their commitment in all circumstances. Of course, in answering this question they have only a general knowledge of human psychology to go on. But this information is enough to tell which conception of justice involves the greater stress.

In this respect the two principles of justice have a definite advantage. Not only do the parties protect their basic rights but they insure themselves against the worst eventualities. They run no chance of having to acquiesce in a loss of freedom over the course of their life for the sake of a greater good enjoyed by others, an undertaking that in actual circumstances they might not be able to keep. Indeed, we might wonder whether such an agreement can be made in good faith at all. Compacts of this sort exceed the capacity of human nature. How can the parties possibly know, or be sufficiently sure, that they can keep such an agreement? Certainly they cannot base their confidence on a general knowledge of moral psychology. To be sure, any principle chosen in the original position may require a large sacrifice for some. The beneficiaries of clearly unjust institutions (those founded on principles which have no claim to acceptance) may find it hard to reconcile themselves to the changes that will have to be made. But in this case they will know that they could not have maintained their position anyway. Yet should a person gamble with his liberties and substantive interests hoping that the application of the principle of utility might secure him a greater well-being, he may have difficulty abiding by his undertaking. He is bound to remind himself that he had the two principles of justice as an alternative. If the only possible candidates all involved similar risks, the problem of the strains of commitment would have to be waived. This is not the case, and judged in this light the two principles seem distinctly superior.

A second consideration invokes the condition of publicity as well as that of the constraints on agreements, I shall present the argument in terms of the question of psychological stability. Earlier I stated that a strong point in favor of a conception of justice is that it generates its own support. When the basic structure of society is publicly known to satisfy its principles for an extended period of time, those subject to these arrangements tend to develop a desire to act in accordance with these principles and to do their part in institutions which exemplify them. A conception of justice is stable when the public recognition of its realization by the social system tends to bring about the corresponding sense of justice. Now whether this happens depends, of course, on the laws of moral psychology and the availability of human motives. I shall discuss these matters later on. At the moment we may observe that the principle of utility seems to require a greater identification with the interests of others than the two principles of justice. Thus the latter will be a more stable conception to the extent that this identification is difficult to achieve. When the two principles are satisfied, each person's liberties are secured and there is a sense defined by the difference principle in which everyone is benefited by social cooperation. Therefore we can explain the acceptance of the social system and the principles it satisfies by the psychological law that persons tend to love, cherish, and support whatever affirms their own good. Since everyone's good is affirmed, all acquire inclinations to uphold the scheme. . . .

. . . I now wish to give the final statement of the two principles of justice for institutions. For the sake of completeness, I shall give a full statement including earlier formulations.

First Principle

Each person is to have an equal right to the most extensive total system of equal basic liberties compatible with a similar system of liberty for all.

Second Principle

Social and economic inequalities are to be arranged so . . . that they are both:
   (a) to the greatest benefit of the least advantaged, and
   (b) attached to offices and positions open to all under conditions of fair equality of opportunity.

First Priority Rule (The Priority of Liberty)

The principles of justice are to be ranked in lexical order and therefore liberty can be restricted only for the sake of liberty. There are two cases:
   (a) a less extensive liberty must strengthen the total system of liberty shared by all;
   (b) a less than equal liberty must be acceptable to those with the lesser liberty.

Second Priority Rule (The Priority of Justice over Efficiency and Welfare)

The second principle of justice is lexically prior to the principle of efficiency and to that of maximizing the sum of advantages; and fair opportunity is prior to the difference principle.

CASE STUDY

Employee Capitalism: the story of NFC

The National Freight Corporation (NFC) was set up by a Labour government in 1968 to bring the various state owned road transport businesses under a single organization. It was one of only three state owned businesses earmarked for privatization by the incoming Conservative government of 1979, and was eventually sold off in 1982 for £53.5 million. Though only a small part of what became a massive programme of privatization, what made the sale notable was that the buyers were the firm's employees.

The buy-out was organized by a team of senior managers led by the chief executive, Peter Thompson. Their motivation was, as he candidly puts it, a combination of 'fear, greed, and vision'. The fear was that if they did not buy the business someone else would and in an ensuing management restructuring they might lose their jobs. The greed motive was that at the price on offer they could make a lot of money from the deal. Their vision was that by making it an employee buy-out they could create a business based on participation and the sharing of wealth which would also, as a consequence, maximize commitment and therefore maximize efficiency; thus creating even more wealth to be shared out.

Thompson claims the vision motivation was dominant, and there is every reason to believe him. As he points out, his team could have gone for a straightforward management buy-out involving only senior executives. Instead they went for a scheme under which shares were on offer to any employee who wanted them, as well as to members of their immediate family and company pensioners. (Together they are known as 'family' to distinguish them from any shareholders with no employment connection with the company.) Moreover, each employee was offered an interest free loan·of £200 towards the cost of buying shares. Not only that, but when it turned out that the offer was over-subscribed, Thompson and his team decided that purchases up to £600 in value should be met in full while those above should be scaled down by 17%, ensuring a wider dispersal of shares.

In all, about 40% of the workforce bought shares amounting to 77.5% of the total equity. Another 17.5% were bought by the banks financing the deal. The team of 13 senior executives leading the buy out ended up with the remaining 5%. This worked out as far more than the average employee share allocation, but was still very much a minority holding and was, in part at least, a consequence of the banks insisting that they invest a minimum of £250 000 between them – a condition designed to ensure they had a substantial vested interest in the firm's future success.

Right from the start the new company was committed to preserving employee control. Dealing in 'family' shares was restricted to an internal market which only allowed sales to other 'family' members. A profit sharing scheme amounting to 15% of pre-tax profits encouraged employees who were not shareholders to buy shares. Assisted by this, the proportion of employees owning shares in the company grew to around 60% by 1986. When in 1989 the company was led by the need for new capital to have a stock exchange flotation, a preferential price for existing shareholders (one for every eight shares held) helped encourage 'family' members to buy 50% of the shares on offer. In addition, and despite some stock exchange doubts, employee shares were given double voting rights to help preserve employee control into the future.

NFC is undoubtedly a successful company, both financially and ethically. From an original equity of £7.5 million in 1982 it grew to stock exchange valuation of £900 million in 1989. It has a highly developed participatory system (which does not discriminate between employees who are shareholders and those who are not). As well as the 15% of pre-tax profit devoted to profit sharing, another 1% is given to charity. 1% of total shareholding belongs to a trust which devotes the profits to relieving hardship among former employees. Also, the company operates a Social Responsibility Council to oversee its charitable and community work. These are all very positive things. But they could be done by a conventional capitalist business. What is clearly special about NFC is its system of employee ownership and control within what is otherwise a conventional capitalist structure. This makes it difficult to categorize; to quote the *Guardian* (19th June 1981) after the proposed employee buy-out was announced: 'It is difficult to say whether the propsal is left wing (employee ownership of industry) or right wing in that the employees are being turned into mini capitalists.'

It is not a worker co-operative in that ownership and employment are clearly separate: in so far as employees do exercise control over the company they do so purely in their role as shareholders. Nor is NFC like employee owned companies such as the John Lewis Partnership and Scott-Bader where employee ownership is exercised through a trust which holds shares on behalf of employees: with NFC shares are held directly and individually. Nor is NFC an example of co-determination on the German model; employees are represented on the board of directors as shareholders and in no other capacity. None the less, NFC is still very different from an ordinary capitalist business. It is not simply a case of 'popular capitalism', with workers being encouraged to buy a few shares in order to have a stake in the company. It is, at least at the moment, something much more radical than this: an example of what Peter Thompson calls 'employee capitalism'.

Sources: Peter Thompson, *Sharing the Success*, Fontana, 1991; A. Nejad, *The Employee Buy-Out of the National Freight Consortium*, a report for Partnership Research Ltd, London, September 1986.

DISCUSSION TOPICS

1. Consider a company which has been under public ownership and which has recently been privatized. Which sectors of society have gained from privatization and which, if any, have lost? Explain why this is the case.
2. Consider the following extract from Cecil Northcote Parkinson's *The Short List* (pp. 31–2).

Only a little thought is needed to convince us that the perfect advertisement would attract only one reply and that from the right man. Let us begin with an extreme example:

Wanted: Acrobat capable of crossing a slack wire 200 feet above raging furnace. Twice nightly, three times on Saturday. Salary offered £25 per week. No pension and no compensation in the event of injury. Apply in person at Wildcat Circus between the hours of 9am and 10am.

The wording of this may not be perfect but the aim should be so to balance the inducement in salary against the possible risks involved that only a single applicant will appear. It is needless to ask for details of qualifications and experience. No one unskilled on the slack wire would find the offer attractive. It is needless to insist that candidates should be physically fit, sober, and free from fits of dizziness. They know that. It is just as needless to stipulate that those nervous of heights need not apply. They won't. The skill of the advertiser comes in adjusting the salary to the danger. An offer of £1000 per week might produce a dozen applicants. An offer of £15 might produce none. Somewhere between those two figures lies the exact sum to specify the minimum figure to attract anyone actually capable of doing the job. If there is more than one applicant, the figure has been placed a trifle too high.

What view of determining wages is this writer expressing? Consider arguments (a) in favour of this viewpoint; (b) against it.

Corporations and responsibility | 5

THE NATURE OF BUSINESS CORPORATIONS

The corporation is the dominant form of business enterprise in the modern world. Those that are not corporations will normally be small businesses involving a single working proprietor or a few people in partnership. The rest, including all very large businesses, will be corporations. It is not, however, the fact of being any particular size which makes a business a corporation. It is a question of how it is owned and legally identified. For an unincorporated business, ownership is nothing more than the ownership of its assets (if there are any). These are owned by individuals in exactly the same way as any other pieces of private property. It just happens that they involve, or can be put to, a business use. The business itself is legally identified with the people who, in their own person or as employees, carry out the work of the business. If they cease to operate, so does the business. Nothing so straightforward applies to corporate businesses. With them ownership takes the very much more indirect form of shareholdings and they are not legally identified with people at all.

It is this separateness from people which defines corporate status. A business is a corporation when it is regarded as a distinct entity in its own right, separate from all or any of the people associated with it, be they the work-force, managers, directors, or even shareholders. Having this status means that the courts will recognize the business as possessing legal rights and duties in much the same way as an individual human being. It is regarded as something which, of itself, can enter into contracts, own and dispose of property, incur and be owed debts, inflict and suffer damage, sue and be sued, be victim and perpetrator of crimes, and so on. In short, a business which has the status of a corporation is treated in law as if it were a person. It becomes what lawyers speak of as an 'artificial' or 'juristic' person as opposed to the 'natural' person which is an individual human being.

Corporate status is not confined to businesses, nor did it originate with them. In England, the idea of incorporation emerged during the Middle Ages and was probably first applied to religious and public bodies such as monasteries as self-governing towns ('boroughs'). To this day, these and many other such non-business institutions have corporate status, including, one example, universities. (The account given here follows L. C. B. Gower, *Gower's Principles of Modern Company Law* (London: Stevens & Sons, 1992), chapters 2 and 3. It is, in its details, specific to English law.)

The extension of this status to the business sphere begins with its granting to merchant guilds in the medieval period. These were bodies formed to represent (and tightly regulate) various crafts, trades, or professions such as butchers, bakers, and bankers. In modern terms, they would be trade associations representing businesses in particular industries. What was being incorporated were organizations to which businesses belonged. The businesses themselves remained unincorporated.

The first businesses to be incorporated were 'merchant adventurer companies' set up to trade with overseas countries. (Their establishment also marked the first general application of the word 'company' to a business.) These date from at least the fourteenth century, but did not become common until the expansion of overseas trade in the sixteenth century – the most famous example being the East India Company, formed in 1600.

At their inception they were not much like modern corporate businesses. In many important respects they were more like merchant guilds. Like the guilds, their incorporation was tied up with the granting of monopoly privileges – just as only guild members were allowed to carry on certain crafts, so only company members were allowed to trade with certain overseas areas. More importantly, the companies were like the guilds in that they did not trade as single unit. As with guild members, company members traded as individual businesses. The company, like the guild, was simply a organization to which, given its monopoly position, a merchant had to belong in order to carry out a particular kind of trading.

The transition to something like a modern structure began with the introduction of what was called 'joint stock trading' inside the merchant companies. This meant that instead of trading individually, some members would join together to purchase a stock of goods between them. The amount of money each member of the group subscribed to the purchase of that stock could vary, and any profit from trading in those goods would be proportional to that amount. At first this arrangement would only hold for a single voyage. Later, the practice became for it to continue for several years. Eventually, joint stock trading became not only permanent but universal, with individual trading being prohibited and the company operating as single unit which distributed profits on the basis of money invested in the company as a whole. At this stage we have not only a fully fledged business corporation, as opposed to a loose trading association, but also the establishment of shareholding as the means by which such businesses are set up and owned. (The use of the phrase 'joint stock company' for businesses based on shareholding stems from this historical development.)

These fully fledged corporate businesses emerged in the seventeenth century. Their practice of shareholding, along with their use of the title 'company', was widely adopted by other businesses. What they could not easily adopt, though, was the corporate status which went with these things. This could only be acquired through the granting of a royal charter or by act of parliament. Either way, it was a time consuming process requiring the winning of official approval – and still very much associated with the granting of monopoly rights. All that changed in 1844 with the passing of the first Joint Stocks Act. This created the modern situation in which incorporation is made available by a simple process of registration.

The passing of the act was probably more about regulation than anything else. An unincorporated business with freely transferable shares was a difficult entity to define legally and control. In the absence of incorporation it was assumed to be a partnership. As such it was identical with its presumed partners; in this case, its shareholders. These were though, not only potentially very numerous but could be constantly changing. It was therefore very difficult to know exactly to what or to whom legal rights and duties could be assigned. Even deciding the name or names under which actions could be brought presented something of a problem (Gower, p 32).

By making the company something separate from the people associated with it, incorporation resolved this problem of legal identification. It established what lawyers call 'perpetual succession'. This means that in being a separate legal entity from the people associated with it, a corporation is not dependent on the participation of any particular people for its existence. They can change completely, be they employees, directors, shareholders, or whatever. As the identifiable possessor of legal rights and duties, the corporation carries on.

Incorporation was not only about making regulation easier. It also provided advantages for the companies themselves. There were two principal benefits. The first was the very general one of continuity. The second was the very specific one of limited liability.

Continuity comes from perpetual succession. It means that one and the same company can legally carry on its activities regardless of changes in staffing, management, or even shareholding. The company persists through changes in the composition of these associated groupings. Moreover, because in a legal sense their association is with this enduring entity rather than to each other, this means their legal position is unaffected by changes in the composition of each group. People continue to have shares in the same company regardless of changes in the workforce or management. Conversely, because they are employed by the company rather than its shareholders, changes in shareholding do not, of themselves, affect the legal position of employees, be they managers or workers: they continue to be employed by the same company. In an important respect, changes in shareholding do not even affect ownership. It is the company as a corporate entity which owns the assets of the business. What the shareholders own is a right to a share of any distributable financial surplus. They in effect own the company rather than its assets. Consequently, the right of the company, acting through its employees, to utilize those assets is legally unaffected by changes in shareholding. Their utilization can continue regardless.

The benefit of limited liability as possible consequence of the general extension of corporate status to companies was not at first appreciated. It had long been recognized that in being a separate entity from the people associated with it, the debts of a corporation belonged to it and not those people. They were not, therefore, liable to have their assets seized to pay for their debts. This was admittedly a concession rather than a necessary consequence of corporate status,[1] but it obviously fitted in rather well with the idea of the corporation as a separate entity. None the less, limited liability was not at first given to companies incorporated by the new and simplified process of registration. It was only later, in 1856, that legislation was passed making shareholders in registered companies liable for company debts only up to the value of their unpaid shares. The argument was that because this greatly reduced the risk from shareholding, it would encourage people to invest and so aid economic development – still the chief reason offered. It was a reason which did not go unchallenged. *The Times* denounced the move as a 'rogues charter' because it would enable people to evade their moral responsibilities. As a warning to creditors the 1856 bill required that the word 'limited' be added to the title of companies – still a requirement for UK companies.

---

[1] It would be perfectly possible, for example, for the law to grant limited liability to unincorporated businesses such as partnerships. In the case of non-managerial 'sleeping partners' it does (Gower, p. 90).

SOCIAL RESPONSIBILITY

What are the social responsibilities of business corporations; that is to say, their moral responsibilities to the communities in which they operate and to society at large? One short, sharp, and endlessly discussed answer was provided by Nobel prize winning economist Milton Friedman, an uncompromising advocate of *laissez-faire* capitalism. In a famous article (see the first reading in this chapter) he claims that business corporations, along with businesses in general, have only one social responsibility and that is to increase their profits.

In saying this he denies, in effect, that businesses have social responsibilities. As the himself puts it, what is meant by talk of social responsibilities is that 'business is not concerned "merely" with profit'. Accordingly, and this will greatly simplify the discussion, we shall speak of Friedman as opposing the whole idea of social responsibility rather than proposing a particular conception of it when he says that businesses ought only to aim for profit maximization.

In proposing that single goal, he is presumed not to be arguing for a total disregard of morality. Though he does not say so directly (he couches it in terms of what shareholders want), Friedman does talk of the drive for profit being required to conform to law and 'ethical custom', and this is invariably interpreted as requiring that normally accepted moral standards should apply. Exactly what those standards demand of businesses he does not say; but as he combines acceptance of them with rejection of social responsibility, it follows that he has to be operating on the assumption that the moral demands of social responsibility are of a very much higher order to those of 'ethical custom'. In what way they are higher is also not made explicit; but he does speak of social responsibility as requiring businesses to be concerned with 'promoting desirable "social" ends': goals such as 'providing employment, eliminating discrimination, avoiding pollution'. From this we can infer that what Friedman sees as additional to 'ethical custom' in social responsibility is an active commitment to improving social conditions: a positive responsibility for doing good. In contrast, conformity to 'ethical custom' would have to be just a matter of businesses not doing things which society regards as wrong – a passive avoidance of evil.

In rejecting a morally active role in favour of the single goal of profit maximization, Friedman is not saying that businesses must never seek to do good. They may do so provided they do it in order to serve the goal of profit maximization. It is, for example, all right for a company to provide a local community with amenities if this is done to encourage recruitment, or for tax reasons, or to generate useful goodwill, and the like. When subordinate to profit in this way any such active do-gooding is, he supposes, 'hypocritical window-dressing'. None the less, it is acceptable because it is in accordance with his profit maximizing criterion. With the doctrine of social responsibility, this condition is reversed. Good must **not** be done for reasons of profit, otherwise (he seems to assume) it will be just another tactical application of the profit maximizing principle.

Thus, according to Friedman, the doctrine of social responsibility makes two distinguishing claims. They are that businesses must actively seek to do good, and that this good must not be done for profit. Before turning to Friedman's reasons for rejecting the doctrine, we must first see if he has correctly described it.

Broadly speaking we think he has. Take away the two factors he picks out and we would be left with something like the profit maximization within acceptable moral limits which he champions. Where he almost certainly goes wrong, however, is in adopting too narrow an interpretation of what its two distinguishing features mean for business social responsibility. To that extent, he fails to correctly describe it.

With regard to the first claim of actively doing good, he has assumed that this is readily distinguishable from a simple avoidance of evil. But it is not. If we take Friedman's own examples of what social responsibility demands of business by way of 'promoting desirable social ends', we see that they are as much about avoiding evil as doing good. To take action against unemployment, discrimination, and pollution is certainly to do good but is also, and very obviously, to get rid of social evils as well. What Friedman seems to be assuming is that social responsibility is confined to those optional acts of charitable benevolence which, as we saw in chapter 3, Kant labelled 'imperfect duties'. On his own examples, this is not the case. Those examples also illustrate the general point that very often the moral choice is between doing good or, by default, doing evil. In practice, the two can very often not be not separated. Consequently, Friedman's assumption of a neat division between 'ethical custom' and business social responsibility takes too narrow a view of both. The first cannot be confined to simply the passive avoidance of evil or the second to just the active pursuit of good because very often good and evil are simply two sides of the same moral coin. Friedman is therefore wrong to assume that acceptance of 'ethical custom' has no implication for the adoption of socially responsible policies by business. Clearly it has; if only because such is the power of business over people's lives that its failure to do good will very often result in great evils being permitted to flourish.

With regard to social responsibility requiring that good should not be done for profit, the way Friedman is too restrictive here is by denying all possibility of profit. He excludes it by definition when he declares that:

> 'to say a corporate executive has "social responsibility" . . . **must** [our emphasis] mean that he is to act in some way which is not in the interests of his employer'.

Acts of social responsibility, he goes on to make clear, can only involve the business in costs and never benefits. They are acts such as keeping sale prices down 'though a price increase would be in the best interests of the corporation', or an expenditure on pollution control which is 'beyond the amount that is in the best interests of the corporation', or providing employment 'at the expense of corporate profits'.

This total exclusion of financial benefit simply does not follow. From the fact that an activity has not been engaged in to serve the goal of profit, it does not follow that profit cannot **result**. It can happen as by-product. A company might, for example, decide to keep open an unprofitable plant for longer than is economically necessary in order not to inflict mass unemployment on a community and find that the workforce rewards this loyalty with productivity gains which make the plant profitable. What defines social responsibility is not the exclusion of profit as an outcome, but its exclusion as a motive: the fact that when an act is done simply as a means to the end of profit it is not then an act of business social responsibility. Friedman obviously fails to separate outcome and motive. Moreover, it seems plausible to suppose that he thinks profit should be totally excluded from the outcome because he starts from the assumption that it should be totally excluded from the motive. If so, he would be mistaken in his starting point as well as his reasoning from it. Social responsibility does not demand that all thought of profit should be absent. As we saw in chapter 3, being moral does not, and cannot, totally exclude self-interest. It is enough that it is neither the sole nor predominant motive. The same then is true of acting from reasons of business social responsibility. Such actions cannot be done solely or predominantly for profit, but thoughts of financial gain need not be totally absent. So if Friedman does suppose this then he takes too narrow a view of the possible motives for social responsibility as well as of its possible outcomes.

Turning now from Friedman's analysis of social responsibility to his case against it, we find he presents no less than five arguments. Two of them are central and argued for in some detail. The other three are mentioned only in passing and also raise issues which will be, or have been, looked at. They will, therefore, be only touched on here.

The first of these three subsidiary arguments is specific to the business corporation. It says that because a corporation is an 'artificial person', it cannot have moral responsibilities – at least not in the way that real people can. (This is a complex issue which we shall look at again later in this chapter.)

Both the other two subsidiary arguments depend on appeals to the kind of *laissez-faire* economics discussed in chapters 2 and 4. One states that because accepting social responsibilities means not having profit as the only goal of business activity, this 'involves accepting the socialist view that political mechanisms, not market mechanisms, are the appropriate way to allocate scarce resources'. As social responsibility is only meant to supplement profit as a goal and not totally replace it, this is clearly an exaggeration. Supply and demand will certainly not hold complete sway, but this is only a bad thing (whether it is called 'socialism' or not), given the controversial assumption that *laissez-faire* is a good thing.

The same goes for the other argument of the pair. It endorses Adam Smith's 'invisible hand' argument that the common good is best served by people pursuing their own self-interest rather than by the active do-gooding which social responsibility requires. It is also – literally – an argument which Friedman mentions only parenthetically. Yet it is crucial to his whole position. If self-interest is the best way to serve the common good, then the morally right thing for businesses to do is to confine themselves to pursuing profit. Friedman could even say, as at times he does, that profit maximization is the only 'socially responsible' course for business to follow. But again this is true only if the controversial claims of *laissez-faire* are true.

Friedman's two main arguments form the core of his case against business social responsibility. Both are specific to corporations.

One has been dubbed 'the agency argument'. It makes use of the legal concept of an 'agent' as someone appointed by another person (the 'principal') to act on his or her behalf. What Friedman contends is that managers are agents of shareholders in the businesses they work for. As such, they must only do what is in the interests of these shareholders, which, Friedman says, means making 'as much money as possible' for them. So as on his analysis, social responsibility can only be at the expense of financial gain for the business, it follows that a role as agents necessarily precludes managers setting social responsibility goals for the businesses they work for. They would not then be acting in the interest of their principal.

There are many counter-arguments to this. There is the point already made that Friedman is wrong to assume that social responsibility can only be at the expense of profit. He could also be said to be wrong about what shareholders want and is in their interest. He assumes that what they want is to make as much money as possible from their shares. But is this always and totally true? (Even Friedman allows that it is only 'generally' so.) Might they not also want to balance profit against 'desirable social ends'? In any case, what they want and what is in their interest might be two different things. Their interest could best be served by living in a society in which desirable social ends such as reductions in unemployment, discrimination, and pollution are promoted – even if this means their dividends are somewhat lower as a consequence.

These are all important points, but the really radical challenge to Friedman's position is to question his initial premise about managers simply being agents of shareholders. He presents this as a statement of fact about the legal position of managers but it is also, as part of his attack on business social responsibility, a situation he would want to obtain in any case.

As a statement of legal fact, the agency argument is questionable, but may well be essentially correct – at least as a statement of American and (as it happens) British law.[2] Friedman does not express the position correctly though. He says that this agency status follows because 'a corporate executive is an employee of the owners of the business'; but, as we saw in the previous section, this is not quite right. The shareholders are, in a roundabout way, the owners of the business; but neither the managers nor anyone else working in the business are employed by them. Their

[2] See D. Birsch, 'The Failure of Friedman's Agency Argument', in J. R. DesJardins and J. J. McCall, *Contemporary Issues in Business Ethics* (Belmont, California: Wadsworth, 1990), pp. 28–36, specifically pp. 33–4. For the British legal position, see Gower, *op cit*, pp. 554–5. The 1980 Companies Act permitted British company directors to have regard to the interest of employees, but as an option they are legally free to exercise rather than a duty which has to be fulfilled (see G. Morse, *Charlesworth & Morse: Company Law* (London: Sweet & Maxwell, 1991), pp. 398–9). For the difference between the Anglo-American and continental European view of companies see R. I. Tricker, *Corporate Governance* (Aldershot: Gower Publishing, 1984), pp. 120–1.

employer is the corporation. The corporation, however, is presumed in law to exist for the benefit of its 'members' – that is, the shareholders. It is their interest which the directors, and through them the managers, must ultimately serve. So though it does not happen in the direct way he describes, but rather through the intermediary of the corporation, Friedman seems broadly correct in his contention that managers are in fact agents of the shareholders.

With the deeper question of whether this ought to be the case, the key issue is whether the interests of the corporation ought to be exclusively identifed with its shareholders. Why not all the groups associated with it? Then managers would still be agents of the corporation but not just of the shareholders alone. Those who take this line reject what they call a 'stockholder model' of the corporation in favour of what, in contrast, is described as the 'stakeholder model'.[3] This has affinities with co-determination but has wider scope. According to the stakeholder model, the job of the manager is to strike an equitable balance between all the different groups of people who have a 'stake' in the company in the sense that their well-being is some way dependent on it. This will include shareholders and employees, but also customers, suppliers, the local community, and even society at large. In seeking to satisfy those various interest groups a company run on stakeholder lines will clearly have many goals other than profits for shareholders. On the stakeholder model, the interest of shareholders in profit will be only one of many interests which business executives must satisfy. It is therefore a model of how a corporation should be run which is compatible with the idea of business social responsibility, but clearly excludes Friedman's profit maximization criterion along with the agency argument which he uses to support it.

Friedman's second core argument is also based on the assumption that there can only be a financial loss in taking on social responsibilities. This means someone must pay: either shareholders in lower dividends, or alternatively customers in higher prices or workers in lower wages. From this Friedman reasons that managers are effectively 'taxing' one or more of these groups. They are making them pay for promoting social goals that are properly the preserve of government and would normally be paid for out of taxes. On top of this, as business people they are not competent to decide on social needs and priorities. Worst of all, when

---

[3] For the origins of the stakeholder concept in management theory, see R. E. Freeman, *Strategic Management: a Stakeholder Approach* (Marshfield, Mass.: Pitman, 1984), chapter 2.

they do decide they are imposing their political preferences on those they are compelling to pay – and all this without ever being elected.

The above is usually called the 'tax argument'; but this seems too limited a description. It might better be called the 'usurpation argument' in that the overall point being made is that business social responsibility entails managers usurping the role of democratically elected politicians. It could be said to be the more effective of Friedman's two core arguments in that one does not need to be in sympathy with his general political and economic position to find the thought of business executives taking on a quasi-political role worrying. There is the general objection that it is undemocratic. As Friedman points out, no one elected managers to the job. What right therefore have they to decide what is best for society? Even if the pragmatic line is taken that it does not matter who does these things as long as they get done, there is still the question of whether managers are the right people for that job. This is not simply Friedman's doubts about their expertise; there is the deeper issue that as a group they are unlikely to be representative of society at large in terms of their political and social values. By a process of self-selection, employers' preference, peer pressure, family connections, and so on, managers would seem to almost inevitably end up as more conservative than society at large. This is markedly so in terms of their political preferences; particularly it seems at entrepreneurial and higher executive levels.[4] To have them decide on social priorities is to invite a markedly unrepresentative group to do so. Moreover, it can be argued, this is an unelected and unrepresentative group which already exercises too much influence over society. In the name of democracy, this argument goes on, government should tightly control what businesses can do and confine them to a strictly economic role. This then, is radically different political position from Friedman; one deeply opposed to *laissez-faire*. It has, in contra-distinction to his 'invisible hand' approach, been called the 'hand of government' argument. None the less, it ends up agreeing with Friedman that business should confine itself to making a profit and keep out of tackling social issues.

How might these various worries about the apparently undemocratic nature of business social responsibility be resolved? It could be argued that the fears are unfounded because social responsibility only involves funding politically innocuous projects which everyone supports. That

---

[4] A poll taken by the *Financial Times* during the 1992 British general election campaign showed 94% support for the Conservatives among leading business people.

may be so in the majority of cases but it will clearly not be so in every one. An example is the setting up of city technology colleges by the UK government in a move designed to establish a school system outside local government control. By helping in their funding, an apparently charitable move by businesses was also very much a political gesture.

These problems could perhaps be avoided by setting limits to what businesses could or could not do by way of social responsibility. Only activities representative of a broad political and social consensus could be legally permitted. But even supposing such a consensus could be agreed on (a large supposition), it could have the result of severely limiting what business can do; perhaps at the expense of deserving causes. The consensus might not, for example, run to a role for business in funding the arts because of the objection, frequently voiced, that business funding inevitably constrains artistic freedom. In any case there could still be controversy in deciding priorities among the things that can be done. For instance are the arts to have priority over helping the inner cities?

We can perhaps cut through all these difficulties by saying that if not being democratically accountable and representative is the problem, then we should add these features to business corporations. We can give teeth to the stakeholder model by giving stakeholders a say in the running of the corporation. That way corporations will have the democratic credentials to take on social responsibilities. (This option will be looked at in the section on corporate governance at the end of the chapter.)

IDENTITY AND ACCOUNTABILITY

The issue of the previous section was what moral responsibilities corporations should have. The issue of this one is whether they can have any at all. It was a question raised by Friedman when he said that as 'artificial persons' corporations could not have responsibilities, that they could be had only by people. This repeats a familiar argument. What it entails is that talk of corporate responsibility is simply a shorthand way of talking about people within corporations having responsibilities. If true, this would not of itself rule out corporations taking on social responsibilities. All it would mean is that in practice it would be those in charge of corporations who took on the responsibility – a point Friedman needed to establish for his agency and usurpation arguments. None the less, as an issue in its own right, the question of whether corporations as such can have moral responsibilities has become a subject of debate in business ethics.

The basic premise of the case against is that we cannot attribute responsibilities to corporations because we cannot attribute intentions to them; at least not as anything separate from those of the people involved in them. Without that ability any attribution of moral responsibility is nonsense. It makes no sense, for example, to talk about machines being morally responsible for anything. They do not act on the basis of intentions. People do. They can decide to do something, deliberate on how to do it, and have reasons for doing it. That is why we can speak of them doing things deliberately or accidentally, carefully or carelessly, selflessly or selfishly, malevolently or benevolently, and so on. In brief, it is why moral judgements about their actions are possible and why, in particular, praise and blame are possible. So unless it can be shown that there are specifically corporate intentions at work in the activities of business corporations, there is no question of the corporation itself having moral responsibilities.

The contrary view tries to show just this: that there is a specifically corporate intention which is more than merely the sum of what is intended by the individual people who work within the corporation. The point is made that a business corporation, particularly a large one, is not a mere collection of individuals but a highly organized hierarchical structure. Use is made of organizational charts. These show how different parts of the operation are divided between different sections and how an often complex chain of command co-ordinates all their different functions. What emerges from this hierarchical structure is the systematic direction of individual activity towards a common end. This, it is claimed, establishes the existence of an over-arching level of corporate intentions which cannot be reduced to those of the individuals involved. It will embody the complex inter-relationships of a mass of individual intentions, giving them meaning and direction. It will have a life of its own, capable of continuing to direct individual intentions when the individuals themselves change. So while corporate intentions are certainly formulated and effected by individuals, the whole can be said to be greater than the sum of its parts. This greater part is held to constitute peculiarly corporate intentions to which attach peculiarly corporate moral responsibilities.

The reply to this counter-argument contends that the fact of indivduals working to a common end does not of itself demonstrate the existence of specifically corporate intentions. All it need show is that only particular individuals provide corporations with their intentions; namely those who dictate corporate policy. Their decisions set the common end to which those within the corporation work. The possibility that what results from all these interactions might indeed be greater than the sum of its parts does not make the directing policies any less individual in origin. At the end of the day, the unarguable fact that a corporation has to act through individuals means that only intentions formed by individuals can lie behind corporate activity. There is, in the last analysis, nothing else to account for what is done and therefore nothing else to which moral responsibility can be attached.

What this reply challenges is a rather sophisticated attempt to create a moral identity for corporation. An altogether simpler but perhaps more conclusive objection is to ask why the attempt is being made. What is the point of determining a peculiarly corporate level of moral responsibility?

Moral responsibility is mostly about accountability: it is about holding someone responsible **for** something. The purpose of this is partly to reward virtue but more particularly (probably because protection is our first concern) to punish vice. How, it can be asked, is this primary purpose of punishment served by giving moral responsibilities to corporations? Corporations are simply not capable of being punished. To be punished is to suffer harm and, as entities distinct from the people associated with them, corporations are incapable of suffering harm. They certainly cannot suffer physical harm: they cannot be flogged, imprisoned, executed, or whatever. It might seem they can suffer financial harm on the grounds that they can be fined, expropriated, boycotted, and so on. But it is obviously people in the shape of shareholders, employees, customers, and the like who will suffer any resulting harm. Their dividends will be reduced, their employment prospects damaged, their prices increased. There is then simply no way of punishing corporations; or at least no way of punishing them which is not in reality the punishment of people. This impossibility means that the primary point of assigning moral responsibilities has no application to corporations.

Not only is this so, critics go on to argue, but attempts at assigning moral responsibilities to corporations can even result in the innocent suffering and the guilty evading punishment. The first can happen because although shareholders, employees, and customers can suffer from financial punishments aimed at the corporation, they have, for the most part, little or no responsibility for what the corporation does. They simply have no control of it. Power, as the next section will detail, lies mostly in the hands of senior executives. For the most part, the responsibility for what the corporation does belongs to them. If, however, there is an area of overall moral responsibility which belongs to corporations as such, then it is not an area which belongs to executives. Despite their control of the corporation, executives are being excused any overall moral responsibility for what it does. Thus, critics conclude, the idea of a specifically corporate moral responsibility is not only pointless but pernicious; and doubly pernicious at that: it exposes the innocent to harm and offers a way for the guilty to evade punishment.

These are not merely theoretical problems. They become of great practical significance in law. The law perhaps copes well enough with them in the civil area where only the payment of demages is at stake. There is no real difficulty in suing a corporate entity, albeit that in holding the company responsible for damages the law is ignoring the fact that some particular individuals were responsible. The company simply pays up and individual accountability is left as an internal corporate matter.

Where, however, the law does run into great difficulties with corporate entities is in the area of criminal law. Here the point is not mere compensation for damage suffered but the infliction of punishment for wrongdoing. For this the law will usually require proof of some kind of intention behind the act; it needs to have been done deliberately, or at least carelessly or recklessly. The law calls this intentional element *mens rea* (Latin for 'guilty mind'). It is required because, as we have seen, without it there can be no responsibility. It is waived only for what are usually not very serious offences where a need to deter is thought to be more important than a need for rigorous proof of guilt. These are crimes of 'strict liability'. For businesses these are offences such as selling adulterated food or giving short measure, and can be dealt with by fining the company and so exposing it to harmful publicity. The sticking point comes with the more serious crimes where proof of *mens rea* is required.

The problem then, as we have seen, that it is very difficult to ascribe intentions to corporations. In any case, the punishment for these more serious crimes is often imprisonment; something which clearly cannot be done to corporations. The law can keep up the pretence of punishing corporate entities when it comes to strictly financial punishments, but the pretence breaks down when the prescribed punishment is a physical one such as imprisonment. Then the law has to get to the individuals responsible for what happened. It has to tear away what has been called the 'corporate veil'.

But here the very complex hierarchical structures which give corporations at least the appearance of intention become a formidable barrier. Take, for example, a case where someone is killed through company negligence – a case of what has become known as 'corporate manslaughter'. For example, an inexperienced construction worker is killed when an inadequately supported trench collapses. Was it the fault of the supervisor who knowingly permitted such a trench to be dug, or of the site manager who failed to insist on safe working practices, or of the chief executive who was pressing for the project to be finished on time regardless of safety considerations, or of the board of directors who appointed that chief executive precisely because of his capacity to exert that kind of ruthless pressure? To deal with these sorts of questions the law has had recourse to an 'organic' theory of the company, whereby its directors and senior executives are identified as the source of the intentions which give meaning and direction to a corporation. They are considered to be the 'brains' of the corporate organism, controlling its bodily movements and therefore ultimately responsible for its activities. Paradoxically then, the law makes use of the same idea of central control that is used to argue for a specifically corporate responsibility in order to establish a level of **individual** responsibility. Even so, as our case study will illustrate, in practice the complexity of corporate command structures will often defeat any attempt to fix blame on particular people; though, as the next section will suggest, reform of the way corporations are controlled could perhaps be of some help here.

CORPORATE GOVERNANCE

The issue of corporate governance, as the title suggests, is that of how companies should be governed. It is about mechanisms for allocating powers and responsibilities within companies. As with political government, the central question is how those who exercise power are to be accountable to those for whose benefit they exercise that power. It is a question of particular concern to public companies – that is, companies whose shares are on sale to the public, usually through a stock exchange listing. This is because with them a separation between ownership and control is particularly marked. There is a distinction between a small group of senior managers exercising controlling power and what can be a vast number of shareholder owners for whose benefit those managers are legally supposed to exercise that power. In private companies, this division between ownership and control will either not exist or, if it does, be very much less marked. Private companies are those whose shares are not on sale to the public and so do not have a stock exchange listing. They form the overwhelming majority of registered companies but are, with a few notable exceptions, almost always very small in comparison to public companies. With them, owners are usually also controllers; at least as directors and usually as executives also. Even when they are not, the fact of just a single or relatively few shareholders will greatly facilitate management accountability. This does not mean that questions of corporate governance are confined to public companies. (It depends, as we shall see, on what view is taken of the nature of companies.) But it does mean that those questions are seen as more immediate and acute there. Accordingly, we initially focus on public companies in what follows.

As far as the law is concerned a UK public company should work rather like a parliamentary democracy. The electors (the shareholders) vote in a government (the directors) who use a staff of senior civil servants (senior executives) to run the country (the company). The reality, as everyone knows, is somewhat different. In practice, shareholders do not exercise much of a controlling function over directors, nor directors over executives. The only opportunity shareholders have of exercising control over directors is by voting on proposals at company meetings; usually a strictly annual event. Any voting has to be by attendance; postal ballots are only permitted if allowed for in company articles, and this is very unusual (Gower, pp 524–5). In very large companies only a tiny fraction of shareholders ever attend meetings. They can nominate a proxy to vote for them but only a small minority do so.[5] In any case, the process of proxy voting is organized by the directors of the company and they will usually not only make a strong recommendation on how a vote should go but will also offer themselves to shareholders as proxy voters. On any issue to put before shareholders the directors are therefore very much in charge of events. The initiative belongs to them and they can utilize all the resources of the company to promote their views. Shareholders opposing those views are not only forced to be merely reactive, but have to organize independently of

[5] A survey of UK companies by K. Midgley gives figures of less than 16% for shareholder participation in proxy voting and 0.25% for shareholder attendance at annual general meeting. (See K. Midgley, ed., *Management Accountability and Corporate Governance* (London: Macmillan, 1982), p. 64.)

company resources and at their own expense. Thus, through a combination of shareholder apathy and the tactical advantages which accrue to directors, company meetings are almost always a rubber stamp for directoral decisions. As a general rule, the only shareholder opposition which directors of large public companies need to take seriously is that which might be provided by institutional investors; notably pension funds and insurance companies. They do have the voting strength and organizational resources to challenge executives effectively.

The single most significant reason why directors, in their turn, do not exercise much control over senior executives is that they are usually one and the same people. Most directors in the majority of large UK public companies are also executives in those companies. The chief executive not only sits on the board of directors but is very often also its chairman. On average, 'executive directors' have something near a three to two majority over 'non-executive directors' on the boards of these companies.[6] The fact of this preponderance would alone mean that executives effectively control these companies. They can outvote the non-executives on any issue and given they are in a majority it would be difficult for any non-executive to stay in office without their support. If that were not enough, the apparently rather informal way in which British company directors are recruited also seems to give the executive majority a predominant say in the appointment of the non-executive minority. It has been estimated that no less that 70% of non-executive directors in the 100 largest British companies were personally known to the chairman or another board member before appointment. Of the rest, half are recruited independently of such contacts, while half are there on the recommendation of shareholders and other investors.[7] In other words, only around 15% are nominees of the supposed owners of the company. This leaves the other 85% to be nominated by an executive-dominated body; mostly by way of personal recommendations. On top of all this, the fact that executive directors also have full-time jobs within the company means that they will nearly always know more about its affairs than non-executives. A non-executive director would need to be not just very independently minded but also very well informed in order to challenge an executive line.

The reality then is that public companies are controlled by their senior executives rather than their supposed owners or even, as something

[6] *Independent on Sunday*, 26 July 1992, quoting figures supplied by PRO-NED, an organization devoted to furthering the role of non-executive directors.
[7] 'Pay and the Old Boy Network', *Independent on Sunday*, 24 November 1991.

distinct from executives, their directors. This itself is not a problem if all it means is that strategic and administrative control of those companies is in the hands of their senior management. Who, after all, should exercise such essentially managerial power except managers? The worry is not so much that executives control companies as that no one seems to be controlling them.

Here the curiously hybrid nature of the executive director is a factor. As executives they are employees of the company, as directors they are not. In law, a director is a kind of representative who acts on behalf of shareholders in the periods between company meetings. This requires that they be distinguished from mere employees of the company and so any payment has to be by way of fees and expenses rather than a salary.[8]

When, as it is in large public companies, responsibility for the strategic and day to day operations belongs to a separate executive branch of the company, then the primary and perhaps even sole task of the director as a representative of shareholders will be supervision of that executive branch. This would be a tricky enough job at any time. It requires the confidence to challenge full-time professionals over things about which they have detailed knowledge. When the people supposedly doing the supervising are those same full-time professionals, then it cannot be done at all.

For some this loss of a supervisory role is not a problem. Everything comes down, they say, to personal integrity. Provided executive directors do not exploit their position nothing amiss will occur. There is no need to alter the structure of corporate governance. No amount of tinkering with mechanisms will prevent the person that lacks personal integrity from abusing power. They might add that to make a problem of executive accountability is to introduce an unnecessarily confrontational element into corporate affairs, with non-executives cast in the role of corporate policemen. They might even take the line that questions of corporate governance are strictly a matter for board room decisions and not shareholders – a position interestingly parallel to the political doctrine which says that those elected to govern must vote as their conscience decides and not as their electors instruct them.[9]

Others are both less sanguine and less trusting. They point to a trend to greatly increased executive earnings which, they would say, are not

---

[8] Morse, *op. cit.*, p. 381.
[9] This is the line taken by the Institute of Directors (*Guardian*, 30 July 1992) in response to the Cadbury proposals. The political position it emulates is that of the conservative thinker, Edmund Burke (1729–97).

only excessive but largely unrelated to company performance.[10] They point to the interlocking nature of directorships in the very largest corporations with senior executives in one company very often being non-executive directors in another and, in particular, sitting on each other's remuneration committees to decide on executive pay.[11] Most dramatically, they point to corporate scandals such as the Maxwell affair as demonstrating the lack of effective procedures for executive accountability. To leave it to directors themselves to introduce the necessary changes is, they would say, to expect an unrealistic degree of self-assessment and even self-denial; particularly so, they might add, when it is required of people who have grown accustomed to virtually untrammelled power.

These critics can take a broadly reformist view which simply proposes adjustments in the mechanisms of corporate governance, or they can take a radical line which argues for a basic restructuring. They can also argue their case from very different bases depending on whether they approach the problem from a stockholder or stakeholder view of companies.

Reformists will probably concentrate on strengthening the position of non-executive directors. They might want them to control remuneration committees and the financial auditing of companies. They might also want the roles of board chairman and chief executive kept separate.[12] Reform could even go as far as requiring a majority of non-executives on boards of directors. Radical restructuring would be the total exclusion of executives from boards. This might even go as far as adoption of a German two tier system, with a non-executive supervisory board appointing and controlling a separate executive board. As well as arguably increasing executive accountability for their stewardship of the company, this separation hopefully would clarify lines of responsibility within the company. The supervisory board would only be accountable for the quality of its appointment of executives and the degree to which it has exercised control over them, while the executive board could bear a direct and generally collective responsibility for what the company does. When something like corporate manslaughter occurs there would then be a legally distinct body of full-time professionals to which immediate responsibility could be attached. Any specifically corporate responsibility

[10] 'Greed Still the Boardroom Creed', *Guardian*, 2 July 1992.
[11] 'Pay and the Old Boy Network', *loc. cit.*
[12] These are the two main proposals of the Committee on Financial Aspects of Corporate Governance, chaired by Sir Adrian Cadbury, which delivered its draft report in May 1992.

would belong to them as people rather than some merely abstract and consequently unpunishable legal entity. They would have to prove they had done everything they reasonably should have. Only then would questions of individual blame arise. That way the 'corporate veil' would perhaps not be quite so obscuring.

In terms of the stockholder model the problem is exclusively one of making executives accountable to shareholders. At its root is the separation of ownership and control. The general objective is to achieve for public companies the kind of identity of ownership and control which is broadly true of private companies. This can be done directly by increasing the power of shareholders, or more circuitously by converting executives into owners. Perhaps unsurprisingly, the latter is the route preferred by executives. Short of a management buy out, it usually involves issuing them with shares on favourable terms. That way, it is argued, executives will not see their interests as essentially different from that of shareholders. With the more direct route of increasing shareholder power, measures could range from providing more and better information for shareholders, to insisting that only shareholders could nominate and stand for election to boards of directors. In between, there could be encouragement of a more active role for institutional investors and perhaps the use of postal ballots to supplement attendance and proxy voting.

From the stakeholder perspective the separation of ownership and control is at best only part of the problem. In fact, were the only alternative a switch to a strictly shareholder control, then proponents of this view would probably prefer to stay with the separation. In that way managers would at least have a chance of considering the interests of groups other than shareholders. Sticking with executive control is not the only option though. There is the alternative of electing stakeholder representatives to company boards. Exactly which ones, and how many of each there would be, is subject to debate. Obviously shareholders and employees would be represented, probably also consumers in the case of utility companies, and perhaps a public interest director to look after the interests of society at large in the case of the very largest companies. Accordingly, from this perspective a difference between public and private companies is not of prime importance. It is important only in so far as it takes care of the question of executive accountability to shareholders. This still does not cater for accountability to other stakeholder groups. To do so changes in corporate governance are required for private as well as public companies.

How far any changes go will depend on how radical or reformist a line is taken. Most basically, should the balancing of stakeholder interests be left to executives or must there be stakeholder representation on company boards? If the latter, is it to be by expending existing boards or through a German-style supervisory board? Similar choices face advocates of the stockholder approach. Is there simply to be increased shareholder participation at company meeting or also more non-executive directors? More shareholder nominees on the board or **only** share-holder nominees on the board? A single or two-tier board? From either stakeholder or stockholder perspectives there are very similar decisions to be made about how far to go. The difference is that with the latter executives will be ceding power only to shareholders, whereas with the latter it will be to other groups as well.

Whether constituted by a supervisory board or not, a by-product of the wider board membership envisioned by the stakeholder approach is that it could perhaps deal with the criticism (raised in the previous section) that for companies to take on social responsibilities is a usurp-ation of democratic procedures. Given that what executives do by way of social responsibility would be sanctioned by a board of directors representing a wide range of social groups, then, arguably, executives would have the democratic mandate they need to justify such actions. They would no longer also be open to the charge that they were using corporate resources to promote a narrow sectional viewpoint.

INTRODUCING THE READINGS

The first reading is Friedman's classic account of business social responsibility. The second is an outline of the radically different stakeholder model by Evan and Freeman. In it they offer a Kantian defence of the model, arguing that the right not to be treated merely as a means to some end entails consideration be given to groups other than shareholders in determining corporate policy – even to the extent of having those other groups participate in determining company policy.

The third reading by Goodpaster and Matthews tackles the difficult conceptual question of whether a corporation is the kind of entity to which moral responsibility can be attributed. They argue that it can. They reject the 'invisible hand' argument that market forces ensure that a concentration on profit maximizing will serve the common good as well as the opposing view that only a strong 'hand of government' regulation will ensure that outcome. They do this because both would, for very different reasons, confine businesses to a purely economic function and deny them any moral purpose.

This idea that corporations as such can be assigned moral responsibility is firmly denied by John R. Danley. He argues that attempts to assign specifically corporate intentions over and above those of people within the corporation, have failed. To this he adds the contention (outlined in this chapter) that it is pointless to attribute responsibility to corporations because they are not the kind of thing which can suffer punishment.

The social responsibility of business is to increase its profits

MILTON FRIEDMAN

When I hear businessmen speak eloquently about the 'social responsibilities of business in a free-enterprise system,' I am reminded of the wonderful line about the Frenchman who discovered at the age of 70 that he had been speaking prose all his life. The businessmen believe that they are defending free enterprise when they declaim that business is not concerned 'merely' with profit but also with promoting desirable 'social' ends; that business has a 'social conscience' and takes seriously its responsibilities for providing employment, eliminating discrimination, avoiding pollution and whatever else may be the catchwords of the contemporary crop of reformers. In fact they are – or would be if they or anyone else took them seriously – preaching pure and unadulterated socialism. Businessmen who talk this way are unwitting puppets of the intellectual forces that have been undermining the basis of a free society these past decades.

The discussions of the 'social responsibilities of business' are notable for their analytical looseness and lack of rigor. What does it mean to say that 'business' has responsibilities? Only people can have responsibilities. A corporation is an artificial person and in this sense may have artificial responsibilities, but 'business' as a whole cannot be said to have responsibilities, even in this vague sense. The first step toward clarity in examining the doctrine of the social responsibility of business is to ask precisely what it implies for whom.

Presumably, the individuals who are to be responsible are businessmen, which means individual proprietors or corporate executives. Most of the discussion of social responsibility is directed at corporations, so in what follows I shall mostly neglect the individual proprietors and speak of corporate executives.

In a free-enterprise, private-property system, a corporate executive is an employee of the owners of the business. He has direct responsibility to his employers. That responsibility is to conduct the business in accordance with their desires, which generally will be to make as much money as possible while conforming to the basic rules of the society, both those embodied in law and those embodied in ethical custom. Of course, in some cases his employers may have a different objective. A group of persons might establish a corporation for an eleemosynary purpose – for example, a hospital or a school. The manager of such a corporation will not have money profit as his objectives but the rendering of certain services.

In either case, the key point is that, in his capacity as a corporate executive, the

Reading taken from *The New York Times Magazine*, September 13, 1970. Copyright © 1970 the New York Times Company.

manager is the agent of the individuals who own the corporation or establish the eleemosynary institution, and his primary responsibility is to them.

Needless to say, this does not mean that it is easy to judge how well he is performing his task. But at least the criterion of performance is straightforward, and the persons among whom a voluntary contractual arrangement exists are clearly defined.

Of course, the corporate executive is also a person in his own right. As a person, he may have many other responsibilities that he recognizes or assumes voluntarily – to his family, his conscience, his feelings of charity, his church, his clubs, his city, his country. He may feel impelled by these responsibilities to devote part of his income to causes he regards as worthy, to refuse to work for particular corporations, even to leave his job, for example, to join his country's armed forces. If we wish, we may refer to some of these responsibilities as 'social responsibilities.' But in these respects he is acting as a principal, not an agent; he is spending his own money or time or energy, not the money of his employers or the time or energy he has contracted to devote to their purposes. If these are 'social responsibilities,' they are the social responsibilities of individuals, not of business.

What does it mean to say that the corporate executive has a 'social responsibility' in his capacity as businessman? If this statement is not pure rhetoric, it must mean that he is to act in some way that is not in the interest of his employers. For example, that he is to refrain from increasing the price of the product in order to contribute to the social objective of preventing inflation, even though a price increase would be in the best interests of the corporation. Or that he is to make expenditures on reducing pollution beyond the amount that is in the best interests of the corporation or that is required by law in order to contribute to the social objective of improving the environment. Or that, at the expense of corporate profits, he is to hire 'hardcore' unemployed instead of better qualified available workmen to contribute to the social objective of reducing poverty.

In each of these cases, the corporate executive would be spending someone else's money for a general social interest. Insofar as his actions in accord with his 'social responsibility' reduce returns to stockholders, he is spending their money. Insofar as his actions raise the price to customers, he is spending the customers' money. Insofar as his actions lower the wages of some employees, he is spending their money.

The stockholders or the customers or the employees could separately spend their own money on the particular action if they wished to do so. The executive is exercising a distinct 'social responsibility,' rather than serving as an agent of the stockholders or the customers or the employees, only if he spends the money in a different way than they would have spent it.

But if he does this, he is in effect imposing taxes, on the one hand, and deciding how the tax proceeds shall be spent, on the other.

This process raises political questions on two levels: principle and consequences. On the level of political principle, the imposition of taxes and the expenditure of tax proceeds are governmental functions. We have established elaborate constitutional, parliamentary and judicial provisions to control these functions, to assure that taxes are imposed so far as possible in accordance with the preferences and desires of the public – after all, 'taxation without representation' was one of the battle cries of the American Revolution. We have a system of checks and balances to separate the legislative function of imposing taxes and enacting expenditures from the executive function of collecting taxes and administering expenditure programs and from the judicial function of mediating disputes and interpreting the law.

Here the businessman – self-selected or appointed directly or indirectly by stockholders – is to be simultaneously legislator, executive and jurist. He is to decide whom to tax by how much and for what purpose, and he is to spend the proceeds – all this guided only by general exhortations from on high to restrain inflation, improve the environment, fight poverty and so on and on.

The whole justification for permitting the corporate executive to be selected by the stockholders is that the executive is an agent serving the interests of his principal. This justification disappears when the corporate executive imposes taxes and spends the proceeds for 'social' purposes. He becomes in effect a public employee, a civil servant, even though he remains in name an employee of a private enterprise. On grounds of political principle, it is intolerable that such civil servants – insofar as their actions in the name of social responsibility are real and not just window-dressing – should be selected as they are now. If they are to be civil servants, then they must be elected through a political process. If they are to impose taxes and make expenditures to foster 'social' objectives, then political machinery must be set up to make the assessment of taxes and to determine through a political process the objectives to be served.

This is the basic reason why the doctrine of 'social responsibility' involves the acceptance of the socialist view that political mechanisms, not market mechanisms, are the appropriate way to determine the allocation of scarce resources to alternative uses.

On the grounds of consequences, can the corporate executive in fact discharge his alleged 'social responsibilities'? On the other hand, suppose he could get away with spending the stockholders' or customers' or employees' money. How is he to know how to spend it? He is told that he must contribute to fighting inflation. How is he to know what action of his will contribute to that end? He is presumably an expert in running his company – in producing a product or selling it or financing it. But nothing about his selection makes him an expert on inflation. Will his holding down the price of his product reduce inflationary pressure? Or, by leaving more spending power in the hands of his customers, simply divert it elsewhere? Or, by forcing him to produce less because of the lower price, will it simply contribute to shortages? Even if he could answer these questions, how much cost is he justified in imposing on his stockholders, customers and employees for this social purpose? What is his appropriate share and what is the appropriate share of others?

And, whether he wants to or not, can he get away with spending his stockholders', customers' or employees' money? Will not the stockholders fire him? (Either the present ones or those who take over when his actions in the name of social responsibility have reduced the corporation's profits and the price of its stock.) His customers and his employees can desert him for other producers and employers less scrupulous in exercising their social responsibilities.

This facet of 'social responsibility' doctrine is brought into sharp relief when the doctrine is used to justify wage restraint by trade unions. The conflict of interest is naked and clear when union officials are asked to subordinate the interest of their members to some more general purpose. If the union officials try to enforce wage restraint, the consequence is likely to be wildcat strikes, rank-and-file revolts and the emergence of strong competitors for their jobs. We thus have the ironic phenomenon that union leaders – at least in the U.S. – have objected to Government interference with the market far more consistently and courageously than have business leaders.

The difficulty of exercising 'social responsibility' illustrates, of course, the great virtue of private competitive enterprise – it forces people to be responsible for their own actions and makes it difficult for them to 'exploit' other people for either selfish or unselfish purposes. They can do good – but only at their own expense.

Many a reader who has followed the argument this far may be tempted to remonstrate that it is all well and good to speak of Government's having the responsibility to impose taxes and determine expenditures for such 'social' purposes as controlling pollution or training the hard-core unemployed, but that the problems are too urgent to wait on the slow course of political processes, that the exercise of social responsibility by businessmen is a quicker and surer way to solve pressing current problems.

Aside from the question of fact – I share Adam Smith's skepticism about the benefits that can be expected from 'those who affected to trade for the public good' – this argument must be rejected on grounds of principle. What it amounts to is an assertion that those who favor the taxes and expenditures in question have failed to persuade a majority of their fellow citizens to be of like mind and that they are seeking to attain by undemocratic procedures what they cannot attain by democratic procedures. In a free society, it is hard for 'evil' people to do 'evil,' especially since one man's good is another's evil.

I have, for simplicity, concentrated on the special case of the corporate executive, except only for the brief digression on trade unions. But precisely the same argument applies to the newer phenomenon of calling upon stockholders to require corporations to exercise social responsibility (the recent G.M. crusade for example). In most of these cases, what is in effect involved is some stockholders trying to get other stockholders (or customers or employees) to contribute against their will to 'social' causes favored by the activists. Insofar as they succeed, they are again imposing taxes and spending the proceeds.

The situation of the individual proprietor is somewhat different. If he acts to reduce the returns of his enterprise in order to exercise his 'social responsibility,' he is spending his own money, not someone else's. If he wishes to spend his money on such purposes, that is his right, and I cannot see that there is any objection to his doing so. In the process, he, too, may impose costs on employees and customers. However, because he is far less likely than a large corporation or union to have monopolistic power, any such side effects will tend to be minor.

Of course, in practice the doctrine of social responsibility is frequently a cloak for actions that are justified on other grounds rather than a reason for those actions.

To illustrate, it may well be in the long-run interest of a corporation that is a major employer in a small community to devote resources to providing amenities to that community or to improving its government. That may make it easier to attract desirable employees, it may reduce the wage bill or lessen losses from pilferage and sabotage or have other worthwhile effects. Or it may be that, given the laws about the deductibility of corporate charitable contributions, the stockholders can contribute more to charities they favor by having the corporation make the gift than by doing it themselves, since they can in that way contribute an amount that would otherwise have been paid as corporate taxes.

In each of these – and many similar – cases, there is a strong temptation to rationalize these actions as an exercise of 'social responsibility.' In the present climate of opinion, with its widespread aversion to 'capitalism', 'profits', the 'soulless corporation' and so on, this is one way for a corporation to generate goodwill as a byproduct of expenditures that are entirely justified in its own self-interest.

It would be inconsistent of me to call on corporate executives to refrain from this hypocritical window-dressing because it harms the foundations of a free society. That would be to call on them to exercise a 'social responsibility'! If our institutions, and the attitudes of the public make it in their self-interest to cloak their actions in this way, I cannot summon much indignation to denounce them. At the same time, I can express admiration for those individual proprietors or owners of closely held corporations or stockholders of more broadly held corporations who disdain such tactics as approaching fraud.

Whether blameworthy or not, the use of the cloak of social responsibility, and the nonsense spoken in its name by influential and prestigious businessmen, does clearly harm the foundations of a free society. I have been impressed time and again by the schizophrenic character of many businessmen. They are capable of being extremely far-sighted and clear-headed in matters that are internal to their businesses. They are incredibly short-sighted and muddle-headed in matters that are outside their businesses but affect the possible survival of business in general. This short-sightedness is strikingly exemplified in the calls from many businessmen for wage and price guidelines or controls or income policies. There is nothing that could do more in a brief period to destroy a market system and replace it by a centrally controlled system than effective governmental control of prices and wages.

The short-sightedness is also exemplified in speeches by businessmen on social responsibility. This may gain them kudos in the short run. But it helps to strengthen the already too prevalent view that the pursuit of profits is wicked and immoral and must be curbed and controlled by external forces. Once this view is adopted, the external forces that curb the market will not be the social consciences, however highly developed, of the pontificating executives; it will be the iron first of Government bureaucrats. Here, as with price and wage controls, businessmen seem to me to reveal a suicidal impulse.

The political principle that underlies the market mechanism is unanimity. In an ideal free market resting on private property, no individual can coerce any other, all cooperation is voluntary, all parties to such cooperation benefit or they need not participate. There are no values, no 'social' responsibilities in any sense other than the shared values and responsibilities of individuals. Society is a collection of individuals and of the various groups they voluntarily form.

The political principle that underlies the political mechanism is conformity. The individual must serve a more general social interest – whether that be determined by a church or a dictator or a majority. The individual may have a vote and say in what is to be done, but if he is overruled, he must conform. It is appropriate for some to require others to contribute to a general social purpose whether they wish to or not.

Unfortunately, unanimity is not always feasible. There are some respects in which conformity appears unavoidable, so I do not see how one can avoid the use of the political mechanism altogether.

But the doctrine of 'social responsibility' taken seriously would extend the scope of the political mechanism to every human activity. It does not differ in philosophy from the most explicitly collectivist doctrine. It differs only by professing to believe that collectivist ends can be attained without collectivist means. That is why, in my book 'Capitalism and Freedom,' I have called it a 'fundamentally subversive doctrine' in a free society, and have said that in such a society, 'there is one and only one social responsibility of business – to use its resources and engage in activities designed to increase its profits so long as it stays within the rules of the game, which is to say, engages in open and free competition without deception or fraud.'

A stakeholder theory of the modern corporation: Kantian capitalism

WILLIAM M. EVAN AND R. EDWARD FREEMAN

I. INTRODUCTION

Corporations have ceased to be merely legal devices through which the private business transactions of individuals may be carried on. Though still much used for this purpose, the corporate form has acquired a larger significance. The corporation has, in fact, become both a method of property tenure and a means of organizing economic life. Grown to tremendous proportions, there may be said to have evolved a 'corporate system' – which has attracted to itself a

Reading taken from *Ethical Theory and Business* by T. L. Beauchamp and N. E. Bowie. Reproduced by permission of the authors.

combination of attributes and powers, and has attained a degree of prominence entitling it to be dealt with as a major social institutions.[1]

Despite these prophetic words of Berle and Means (1932), scholars and managers alike continue to hold sacred the view that managers bear a special relationship to the stockholders in the firm. Since stockholders own shares in the firm, they have certain rights and privileges, which must be granted to them by management, as well as others. Since the greatest good of all results from the self-interested pursuit of business, managers must be free to respond quickly to market forces. Sanctions, in the form of 'the law of corporations,' and other protective mechanisms in the form of social custom, accepted management practice, myth, and ritual, serve to reinforce the assumption of the primacy of the stockholder.

The purpose of this paper is to pose several challenges to this assumption, from within the framework of managerial capitalism, and to suggest the bare bones of an alternative theory, *a stakeholder theory of the modern corporation*. We do not seek the demise of the modern corporation, either intellectually or in fact. Rather, we seek its transformation. In the words of Neurath, we shall attempt to 'rebuild the ship, plank by plank, while it remains afloat.'[2]

Our thesis is that we can revitalize the concept of managerial capitalism by replacing the notion that managers have a duty to stockholders with the concept that managers bear a fiduciary relationship to stakeholders. Stakeholders are those groups who have a stake in or claim on the firm. Specifically we include suppliers, customers, employees, stockholders, and the local community, as well as management in its role as agent for these groups. We argue that the legal, economic, political, and moral challenges to the currently received theory of the firm, as a nexus of contracts among the owners of the factors of production and customers, require us to revise this concept along essentially Kantian lines. That is, each of these stakeholder groups has a right not to be treated as a means to some end, and therefore must participate in determining the future direction of the firm in which they have a stake.[3] . . .

The crux of our argument is that we must reconceptualize the firm around the following question: For whose benefit and at whose expense should the firm be managed? We shall set forth such a reconceptualization in the form of a *stakeholder theory of the firm*. Finally, we shall critically examine the stakeholder view and its implication for the future of the capitalist system.

II. THE ATTACK ON MANAGERIAL CAPITALISM

The Legal Argument

The law of corporations gives a relatively clear-cut answer to the question: In whose interest and for whose benefit should the modern corporation be governed? It says that the corporation should be run in the interests of the stockholders in the firm. Directors and other officers of the firm have a fiduciary obligation to stockholders in the sense that the 'affairs of the corporation' must be conducted in the interests of the stockholders. And stockholders can theoretically bring suit against those directors and managers for doing otherwise. It says further that the corporation exists 'in contemplation of the law,' has personality as a 'legal person,' limited liability for its actions, and immortality, as its existence transcends that of its members.[4]

The basic idea of managerial capitalism is that in return for controlling the firm, management vigorously pursues the interests of stockholders. Since the corporation is a legal person, existing in contemplation of the law, managers of the corporation are constrained by law. Until recently there was no constraint at all. In this century, . . . the law has evolved to effectively constrain the pursuit of stockholder interests at the expense of other claimants on the firm. It has, in effect, guaranteed that the claims of customers, suppliers, local communities, and employees are in general subordinated to the claims of stockholders. . . .

Central to the managerial view of the firm is that management can pursue market transactions with suppliers and customers in an unconstrained manner.[5] The existence of marketplace forces will insure that fair prices for goods will be taken. This supplier-firm-customer chain has been constrained by a number of legislative and judicial acts. The doctrine of 'privity of contract,' as articulated in *Winterbottom* v. *Wright* in 1842, has been eroded by the developments in products liability law. Indeed, *Greenman* v. *Yuba Power* gives the manufacturer strict liability for damage caused by its products, even though the seller has exercised all possible care in the preparation and sale of the product and the consumer has not bought the product from nor entered into any contractual arrangement with the seller. Caveat emptor has been replaced, in large part, with caveat venditor.[6] The Consumer Product Safety Commission has the power to enact product recalls, and in 1980 one U.S. automobile company recalled more cars than it built. . . . Some industries are required to provide information to customers about a product's ingredients, whether or not the customers want and are willing to pay for this information.[7]

The supplier-firm-customer chain is far from that visualized by managerial capitalism. Firms, in their roles as customers and suppliers of other firms, have benefited from these constraints, and they have been harmed to the degree to which the constraints have meant loss of profit. However, we can say that management is not allowed to pursue the interests of stockholders at the expense of customers and suppliers.

The same argument is applicable to management's dealings with employees. The National Labor Relations Act gave employees the right to unionize and to bargain in good faith. It set up the National Labor Relations Board to enforce these rights with management. The Equal Pay Act of 1963 and Title VII of the Civil Rights Act of 1964 constrain management from discrimination in hiring practices; these have been followed with the Age Discrimination in Employment Act of 1967.[8] The emergence of a body of administrative case law arising from labor-management disputes and the historic settling of discrimination claims with large employers such as AT&T have caused the emergence of a body of practice in the corporation that it consistent with the legal guarantee of the rights of the employees. . . . The law has protected the due process rights of those employees who enter into collective bargaining agreements with management. As of the present, however, only 30 percent of the labor force are participating in such agreements; this has prompted one labor law scholar to propose a statutory law prohibiting dismissals of the 70 percent of the work force not protected.[9] . . .

The law has also protected the interests of local communities. The Clean Air Act and Clean Water Act have constrained management from 'spoiling the commons.' In an historic case, *Marsh* v. *Alabama*, the Supreme Court ruled that a company-owned town was subject to the provisions of the U.S. Constitution, thereby guaranteeing the rights of local citizens and negating the 'property rights' of the firm. Some states and municipalities have gone further and passed laws preventing firms from moving plants or constraining when and how plants can be closed, and there is much current legal activity in this area to constrain management's pursuit of stockholders' interests at the expense of the local communities in which the firm operates. . . .

We have argued that the result of such changes in the legal system can be viewed as giving some rights to those groups that have a claim on the firm, for example, customers, suppliers, employees, local communities, stockholders, and management. It raises the question, at the core of a theory of the firm: In whose interest and for whose benefit should the firm be managed? The answer proposed by managerial capitalism is clearly 'the stockholders,' and we have argued that the law has been progressively circumscribing this answer.

The Economic Argument

In its pure ideological form managerial capitalism seeks to maximize the interests of stockholders. In its perennial criticism of government regulation, management espouses the 'invisible hand' doctrine. It contends that it creates the greatest good for the greatest number, and therefore government need not intervene. However, we know that externalities, moral hazards, and monopoly power exist in fact, whether or not they exist in theory. Further, some of the legal apparatus mentioned above has evolved to deal with just these issues.

The problem of the 'tragedy of the commons' or the free-rider problem pervades the concept of public goods such as water and air. No one has an incentive to incur the cost of clean-up or the cost of nonpollution, since the marginal gain of one firm's action is small. Every firm reasons this way, and the result is pollution of water and air. Since the industrial revolution, firms have sought to internalize the benefits and externalize the costs of their actions. The cost must be borne by all, through taxation and regulation; hence we have the emergence of the environmental regulations of the 1970s.

Similarly, moral hazards arise when the purchaser of a good or service can pass along the cost of that good. There is no incentive to economize, on the part of either the producer or the consumer, and there is excessive use of the resources involved. The institutionalized practice of third-party payment in health care is a prime example.

Finally, we see the avoidance of competitive behavior on the part of firms, each seeking to monopolize a small portion of the market and not compete with one another. In a number of industries, oligopolies have emerged, and while there is questionable evidence that oligopolies are not the most efficient corporate form in some industries, suffice it to say that the potential for abuse of market power has again led to regulation of managerial activity. In the classic case, AT&T, arguably one of the great technological and managerial achievements of the century, was broken up into eight separate companies to prevent its abuse of monopoly power.

Externalities, moral hazards, and monopoly power have led to more external control on managerial capitalism. There are de facto constraints, due to these economic facts of life, on the ability of management to act in the interests of stockholders. . . .

III. A STAKEHOLDER THEORY OF THE FIRM

Foundations of a Theory

. . . Arguments that question the legitimacy of the modern corporation based on excessive corporate power usually hold that the corporation has no right to rule for its constituents. Each person has the right to be treated, not as a means to some corporate end, but as an end in itself. If the modern corporation insists on treating others as means to an end, then at minimum they must agree to and hence participate (or choose not to participate) in the decisions to be used as such. If our theory does not require an understanding of the rights of those parties affected by the corporation, then it will run afoul of our judgments about rights. Thus, property rights are not absolute, especially when they conflict with important rights of others. The right to property does not yield the right to treat others as means to an end. Property rights are not a license to ignore Kant's principle of respect for persons. Any theory of the modern corporation that is consistent with our considered moral judgments must recognize that property rights are not absolute.

Arguments that question the legitimacy of the modern corporation based on externalities or harm usually hold that the corporation is accountable for the consequences of its actions. Persons are responsible for the consequences of their actions through the corporation, even if those actions are mediated. Any theory that seeks to justify the corporate form must be based partially on the idea that the corporation and its managers as moral agents can be the cause of and be held accountable for the consequences of their actions.

In line with these two themes of rights and effects, . . . we suggest two principles that will serve as working rules, not absolutes, to guide us in addressing some of the foundational issues. We will not settle the thorny issues that these principles raise, but merely argue that any theory, including the stakeholder theory, must be consistent with these principles.

Principle of Corporate Rights (PCR): The corporation and its managers may not violate the legitimate rights of others to determine their own future.

Principle of Corporate Effects (PCE): the corporation and its managers are responsible for the effects of their actions on others.

The Stakeholder Concept

Corporations have stakeholders, that is, groups and individuals who benefit from or are harmed by, and whose rights are violated or respected by, corporate actions. The notion of stakeholder is built around the Principle of Corporate Rights (PCR) and the Principle of Corporate Effect (PCE). . . . The concept of stakeholders is a generalization of the notion of stockholders, who themselves have some special claim on the firm. Just as stockholders have a right to certain actions by management, so do other stakeholders have a right to their claim. The exact nature of these claims is a difficult question that we shall address, but the logic is identical to that of the stockholder theory. Stakes require action of a certain sort, and conflicting stakes require methods of resolution. . . .

Freeman and Reed (1983)[10] distinguish two senses of *stakeholder.* The 'narrow definition' includes those groups who are vital to the survival and success of the corporation. The 'wide definition' includes any group or individual who can affect or is affected by the corporation. While the wide definition is more in keeping with (PCE) and (PCR), it raises too many difficult issues. We shall begin with a more modest aim: to articulate a stakeholder theory using the narrow definition.

Stakeholders in the Modern Corporation

Figure 1 depicts the stakeholders in a typical large corporation. The stakes of each are reciprocal, since each can affect the other in terms of harms and benefits as well as rights and duties. The stakes of each are not univocal and would vary by particular

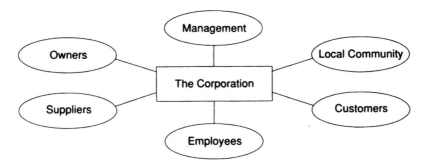

Figure 1 A stakeholder model of the corporation.

corporation. We merely set forth some general notions that seem to be common to many large firms.

Owners have some financial stake in the form of stocks, bonds, and so on, and expect some kind of financial return. Either they have given money directly to the firm, or they have some historical claim made through a series of morally justified exchanges. The firm affects their livelihood or, if a substantial portion of their retirement income is in stocks or bonds, their ability to care for themselves when they can no longer work. Of course, the stakes of owners will differ by type of owner, preferences for money, moral preferences, and so on, as well as by type of firm. The owners of AT&T are quite different from the owners of Ford Motor Company, with stock of the former company being widely dispersed among 3 million stockholders and that of the latter being held by a small family group, as well as a large group of public stockholders.

Employees have their jobs and usually their livelihood at stake; they often have specialized skills for which there is usually no perfectly elastic market. In return for their labor, they expect some security, wages, and benefits, and meaningful work. Where they are used as means to an end, they must participate in decisions affecting such use. In return for their loyalty, the corporation is expected to provide for them and carry them through difficult times. Employees are expected to follow the instructions of management most of the time, to speak favorably about the company, and to be responsible citizens in the local communities in which the company operates. The evidence that such policies and values as described here lead to productive company-employee relationships is compelling. It is equally compelling to realize that the opportunities for 'bad faith' on the part of both management and employees are enormous. 'Mock participation' in quality circles, singing the company song, and wearing the company uniform solely to please management, as well as management by authoritarian supervisors, all lead to distrust and unproductive work.

Suppliers, interpreted in a stakeholder sense, are vital to the success of the firm, for raw materials will determine the final product quality and price. In turn the firm is a customer of the supplier and is therefore vital to the success and survival of the supplier. When the firm treats the supplier as a valued member of the stakeholder network, rather than simply as a source of materials, the supplier will respond when the firm is in need. Chrysler traditionally had very close ties to its suppliers, even to the extent that led some to suspect the transfer of illegal payments. And when Chrysler was on the brink of disaster, the suppliers responded with price cuts, accepting late payments, financing, and so on. Supplier and company can rise and fall together. Of course, again, the particular supplier relationships will depend on a number of variables such as the number of suppliers and whether the supplies are finished goods or raw materials.

Customers exchange resources for the products of the firm and in return receive the benefits of the products. Customers provide the lifeblood of the firm in the form of revenue. Given the level of reinvestment of earnings in large corporations, customers indirectly pay for the development of new products and services. Peters and Waterman (1982)[11] have argued that being close to the customer leads to success with other stakeholders and that a distinguishing characteristic of some companies that have performed well is their emphasis on the customer. By paying attention to customers' needs, management automatically addresses the needs of suppliers and owners. Moreover, it seems that the ethic of customer service carries over to the community. Almost without fail the 'excellent companies' in Peters and Waterman's study have good reputations in the community. We would argue that Peters and Waterman have found multiple applications of Kant's dictum, 'Treat persons as ends unto themselves,' and it should come as no surprise that persons respond to such respectful treatment, be they customers, suppliers, owners, employees, or members of the local community. The real surprise is the novelty of the application of Kant's rule in a theory of good management practice.

The local community grants the firm the right to build facilities and benefits from the tax base and economic and social contributions of the firm. In return for the provision of local services, the firm is expected to be a good citizen, as is any person, either 'natural or artificial.' The firm cannot expose the community to unreasonable hazards in the form of pollution, toxic waste, and so on. If for some reason the firm must leave a community, it is expected to work with local leaders to make the transition as smooth as possible. Of course, the firm does not have perfect knowledge, but when it discovers some danger or runs afoul of new competition, it is expected to inform the local community and to work with the community to overcome any problem. When the firm mismanages its relationship with the local community, it is in the same position as a citizen who commits a crime. It has violated the implicit social contract with the community and should expect to be distrusted and ostracized. It should not be surprised when punitive measures are invoked.

We have not included 'competitors' as stakeholders in the narrow sense, since strictly speaking they are not necessary for the survival and success of the firm; the stakeholder theory works equally well in monopoly contexts. However, competitors and government would be the first to be included in an extension of this basic theory. It is simply not true that the interests of competitors in an industry are always in conflict. There is no reason why trade associations and other multi-organizational groups cannot band together to solve common problems that have little to do with how to restrain trade. Implementation of stakeholder management principles, in the long run, mitigates the need for industrial policy and an increasing role for government intervention and regulation.

The Role of Management

Management plays a special role, for it too has a stake in the fiction that is the modern corporation. On the one hand, management's stake is like that of employees, with some kind of explicit or implicit employment contract. But, on the other hand, management has a duty of safeguarding the welfare of the abstract entity that is the corporation, which can override a stake as employee. In short, management, especially top management, must look after the health of the corporation, and this involves balancing the multiple claims of conflicting stakeholders. Owners want more financial returns, while customers want more money spent on research and development. Employees want higher wages and better benefits, while the local community wants better parks and daycare facilities.

The task of management in today's corporation is akin to that of King Solomon. The stakeholder theory does not give primacy to one stakeholder group over another, though there will surely be times when one group will benefit at the expense of others. In general, however, management must keep the relationships among stakeholders in balance. When these relationships become unbalanced, the survival of the firm is in jeopardy.

When wages are too high and product quality is too low, customers leave, suppliers suffer, and owners sell their stocks and bonds, depressing the stock price and making it difficult to raise new capital at favorable rates. Note, however, that the reason for paying returns to owners is not that they 'own' the firm, but that their support is necessary for the survival of the firm, and that they have a legitimate claim on the firm. Similar reasoning applies in turn to each stakeholder group.

A stakeholder theory of the firm must redefine the purpose of the firm. The stockholder theory claims that the purpose of the firm is to maximize the welfare of the stockholders, perhaps subject to some moral or social constraints, either because such maximization leads to the greatest good or because of property rights. The purpose of the firm is quite different in our view. If a stakeholder theory is to be consistent with the principles of corporate effects and rights, then its purpose must take into account Kant's dictum of respect for persons. The very purpose of the firm is, in our view, to serve as a vehicle for coordinating stakeholder interests. It is through the firm that each stakeholder group makes itself better off through voluntary exchanges. The corporation serves at the pleasure of its stakeholders, and none may be used as a means to the ends of another without full rights of participation in that decision. We can crystallize the particular applications of PCR and PCE to the stakeholder theory in two further principles. These stakeholder management principles will serve as a foundation for articulating the theory. They are guiding ideals for the immortal corporation as it endures through generations of particular mortal stakeholders.

Stakeholder Management Principles

P1: The corporation should be managed for the benefit of its stakeholders: its customers, suppliers, owners, employees, and local communities. The rights of these groups must be ensured, and, further, the groups must participate, in some sense, in decisions that substantially affect their welfare.

P2: Management bears a fiduciary relationship to stakeholders and to the corporation as an abstract entity. It must act in the interests of the stakeholders as their agent, and it must act in the interests of the corporation to ensure the survival of the firm, safeguarding the long-term stakes of each group.

P1, which we might call The Principle of Corporate Legitimacy, redefines the purpose of the firm to be in line with the principles of corporate effects and rights. It implies the legitimacy of stakeholder claims on the firm. Any social contract that justifies the existence of the corporate form includes the notion that stakeholders are a party to that contract. Further, stakeholders have some inalienable rights to participate in decisions that substantially affect their welfare or involve their being used as a means to another's ends. We bring to bear our arguments for the incoherence of the stockholder view as justification for P1. If in fact there is no good reason for the stockholder theory, and if in fact there are harms, benefits, and rights of stakeholders involved in running the modern corporation, then we know of no other starting point for a theory of the corporation than P1.

P2, which we might call The Stakeholder Fiduciary Principle, explicitly defines the duty of management to recognize these claims. It will not always be possible to meet all claims of all stakeholders all the time, since some of these claims will conflict. Here P2 recognizes the duty of management to act in the long-term best interests of the corporation, conceived as a forum of stakeholder interaction, when the interests of the group outweigh the interests of the individual parties to the collective contract. The duty described in P2 is a fiduciary duty, yet it does not suffer from the difficulties surrounding the fiduciary duty to stockholders, for the conflicts involved there are precisely those that P2 makes it mandatory for management to resolve. Of course, P2 gives no instructions for a magical resolution of the conflicts that arise from prima facie obligations to multiple parties. An analysis of such rules for decision making is a subject to be addressed on another occasion, but P2 does give these conflicts a legitimacy that they do not enjoy in the stockholder theory. It gives management a clear and distinct directive to pay attention to stakeholder claims.

P1 and P2 recognize the eventual need for changes in the law of corporations and other governance mechanisms if the stakeholder theory is to be put into practice. P1 and P2, if implemented as a major innovation in the structure of the corporation, will make manifest the eventual legal institutionalization of sanctions. . . .

Structural Mechanisms

We propose several structural mechanisms to make a stakeholder management conception practicable. We shall offer a sketch of these here and say little by way of argument for them.

1. *The Stakeholder Board of Directors.* We propose that every corporation of a certain size yet to be determined, but surely all those that are publicly traded or are of the size of those publicly traded, form a Board of Directors comprised of representatives of five stakeholder groups, including employees, customers, suppliers, stockholders, and members of the local community, as well as a representative of the corporation, whom we might call a 'metaphysical director' since he or she would be responsible for the metaphysical entity that is 'the corporation.' Whether or not each representative has an equal voting right is a matter that can be decided

by experimentation; issues of governance lend themselves naturally to both laboratory and organizational experiments.

These directors will be vested with the duty of care to manage the affairs of the corporation in concert with the interests of its stakeholders. Such a Board would ensure that the rights of each group would have a forum, and by involving a director for the corporation, would ensure that the corporation itself would not be unduly harmed for the benefit of a particular group. In addition, by vesting each director with the duty of care for all stakeholders, we ensure that positive resolutions of conflicts would occur. While options such as 'stakeholder derivative suits' would naturally evolve under the law of corporations as revised, we are not sanguine about their effectiveness and prefer the workings of the political process, as inefficient as it may be. Therefore, representatives of each stakeholder group would be elected from a 'stakeholder assembly' who would initially meet to adopt working rules, charters, and so on, and whose sole purpose would be to elect and recall representatives to corporate boards. The task of the metaphysical director, to be elected unanimously by the stakeholder representatives, is especially important. The fact that the director has no direct constituency would appear to enhance management control. However, nothing could be further from the truth. To represent the abstract entity that is the corporation would be a most demanding job. Our metaphysical director would be responsible for convincing both stakeholders and management that a certain course of action was in the interests of the long-term health of the corporation, especially when that action implies the sacrifice of the interests of all. The metaphysical director would be a key link between the stakeholder representatives and management, and would spearhead the drive to protect the norms of the interests of all stakeholders.

2. *The Stakeholder Bill of Rights*. Each stakeholder group would have the right to elect representatives and to recall representatives to boards. Whether this is done on a corporation-by-corporation, an industry-by-industry, or a country-by-country basis is a matter for further discussion. Each stakeholder group would have the right to free speech, the right to grievance procedures inside the corporation and if necessary in the courts, the right to civil disobedience, and other basic political rights.

3. *The Management Bill of Rights*. Management would have the right to act on its fiduciary duty, as interpreted and constrained by the Board and the courts, the right to safeguard innovation and research and development, the right to free speech, grievance procedures, civil disobedience, and so on.

Both Bills of Rights merely recognize the fact that organizational life is pervasive in our society. If we are not to become what Orwell envisioned, then our organizations must guarantee those basic political freedoms, even at the cost of economic efficiency. If organizational members are to find meaningful work by participating actively in the modern corporation, then we must ensure that the principles of Jeffersonian democracy are safeguarded.

4. *Corporate Law*. The law of corporations needs to be redefined to recognize the legitimate purpose of the corporation as stated in P1. This has in fact developed in

some areas of the law, such as products liability, where the claims of customers to safe products has emerged, and labor law, where the claims of employees have been safeguarded. Indeed, in such pioneering cases as *Marsh* v. *Alabama* the courts have come close to a stakeholder perspective. We envision that a body of case law will emerge to give meaning to 'the proper claims of stakeholders,' and in effect that the 'wisdom of Solomon' necessary to make the stakeholder theory work will emerge naturally through the joint action of the courts, stakeholders, and management.

While much of the above may seem utopian, there are some very practical transitional steps that could occur. Each large corporation could form a stakeholder advisory board, which would prepare a charter detailing how the organization is to treat the claims of each stakeholder. Initially this stakeholder advisory board would serve as an advisor to the current board of directors, and eventually it would replace that board. Simultaneously, a group of legal scholars and practitioners, such as the American Law Institute, could initiate discussion of the legal proposals and methods to change corporate charters, while business groups such as the Business Roundtable could examine the practical consequences of our proposals. Given the emergence of some consensus, we believe that a workable transition can be found. . . .

NOTES

1. Cf. A. Berle and G. Means, *The Modern Corporation and Private Property* (New York: Commerce Clearing House, 1932), 1. For a reassessment of Berle and Means' argument after 50 years, see *Journal of Law and Economics* 26 (June 1983), especially G. Stigler and C. Friedland, 'The Literature of Economics: The Case of Berle and Means,' 237–68; D. North, 'Comment on Stigler and Friedland,' 269–72; and G. Means, 'Corporate Power in the Marketplace,' 467–85.
2. The metaphor of rebuilding the ship while afloat is attributed to Neurath by W. Quine, *Word and Object* (Cambridge: Harvard University Press, 1960), and W. Quine and J. Ullian, *The Web of Belief* (New York: Random House, 1978). The point is that to keep the ship afloat during repairs we must replace a plank with one that will do a better job. Our argument is that Kantian capitalism can so replace the current version of managerial capitalism.
3. Kant's notion of respect for persons (i.e., that each person has a right not to be treated as a means to an end) can be found in I. Kant, *Critique of Practical Reason* (1838 edition). See J. Rawls, *A Theory of Justice* (Cambridge: Harvard University Press, 1971) for an eloquent modern interpretation.
4. For an introduction to the law of corporations see A. Conard, *Corporations in Perspective* (Mineola, NY: The Foundation Press, 1976), especially section 19; and R. Hamilton, *Corporations* (St. Paul: West Publishing, 1981), Chapter eight.
5. For a modern statement of managerial capitalism, see the literature in managerial economics, for example R. Coase, 'The Nature of the Firm,' *Economica* 4 (1937): 386–405; M. Jensen and W. Meckling, 'Theory of the Firm: Managerial Behavior, Agency Costs and Ownership Structure,' *Journal of Financial Economics* 3 (1976): 305–60; and O. Williamson, *The Economics of Discretionary Behavior* (London: Kershaw Publishing, 1965).
6. See R. Charan and E. Freeman, 'Planning for the Business Environment of the 1980s,' *The Journal of Business Strategy* 1 (1980): 9–19, especially p. 15 for a brief account of the major developments in products liability law.

7. See S. Breyer, *Regulation and its Reform* (Cambridge: Harvard University Press, 1983), 133 for an analysis of food additives.
8. See I. Millstein and S. Katsh, *The Limits of Corporate Power* (New York: Macmillan, 1981), Chapter four.
9. Cf. C. Summers, 'Protecting All Employees Against Unjust Dismissal,' *Harvard Business Review* 58 (1980): 136 for a careful statement of the argument.
10. See E. Freeman and D. Reed, 'Stockholders and Stakeholders: A New Perspective on Corporate Governance,' in C. Huizinga, ed., *Corporate Governance: A Definitive Exploration of the Issues* (Los Angeles: UCLA Extension Press, 1983).
11. See T. Peters and R. Waterman, *In Search of Excellence* (New York: Harper and Row, 1982).

Can a corporation have a conscience?

KENNETH E. GOODPASTER AND

JOHN B. MATTHEWS, JR

During the severe racial tensions of the 1960s, Southern Steel Company (actual case, disguised name) faced considerable pressure from government and the press to explain and modify its policies regarding discrimination both within its plants and in the major city where it was located. SSC was the largest employer in the area (it had nearly 15 000 workers, one-third of whom were black) and had made great strides toward removing barriers to equal job opportunity in its several plants. In addition, its top executives (especially its chief executive officer, James Weston) had distinguished themselves as private citizens for years in community programs for black housing, education, and small business as well as in attempts at desegregating all-white police and local government organizations.

SSC drew the line, however, at using its substantial economic influence in the local area to advance the cause of the civil rights movement by pressuring banks, suppliers, and the local government:

> 'As individuals we can exercise what influence we may have as citizens,' James Weston said, 'but for a corporation to attempt to exert any kind of economic compulsion to achieve a particular end in a social area seems to me to be quite beyond what a corporation should do and quite beyond what a corporation can do. I believe that while government may seek to compel social reforms, any attempt by a private organization like SSC to impose its views, its beliefs, and its will upon the community would be repugnant to our American constitutional concepts and that appropriate steps to correct this abuse of corporate power would be universally demanded by public opinion.'

Reading taken from *Harvard Business Review*, January–February 1982. Copyright © 1982 *Harvard Business Review*.

Weston could have been speaking in the early 1980s on any issue that corporations around the United States now face. Instead of social justice, his theme might be environmental protection, product safety, marketing practice, or international bribery. His statement for SSC raises the important issue of corporate responsibility. Can a corporation have a conscience?

Weston apparently felt comfortable saying it need not. The responsibilities of ordinary persons and of 'artificial persons' like corporations are, in his view, separate. Persons' responsibilities go beyond those of corporations. Persons, he seems to have believed, ought to care not only about themselves but also about the dignity and well-being of those around them – ought not only to care but also to act. Organizations, he evidently thought, are creatures of, and to a degree prisoners of, the systems of economic incentive and political sanction that give them reality and therefore should not be expected to display the same moral attributes that we expect of persons.

Others inside business as well as outside share Weston's perception. One influential philosopher – John Ladd – carries Weston's view a step further:

'It is improper to expect organizational conduct to conform to the ordinary principles of morality,' he says. 'We cannot and must not expect formal organizations, or their representatives acting in their official capacities, to be honest, courageous, considerate, sympathetic, or to have any kind of moral integrity. Such concepts are not in the vocabulary, so to speak, of the organizational language game.'[1]

In our opinion, this line of thought represents a tremendous barrier to the development of business ethics both as a field of inquiry and as a practical force in managerial decision making. This is a matter about which executives must be philosophical and philosophers must be practical. A corporation can and should have a conscience. The language of ethics does have a place in the vocabulary of an organization. There need not be and there should not be a disjunction of the sort attributed to SSC's James Weston. Organizational agents such as corporations should be no more and no less morally responsible (rational, self-interested, altruistic) than ordinary persons.

We take this position because we think an analogy holds between the individual and the corporation. If we analyze the concept of moral responsibility as it applies to persons, we find that projecting it to corporations as agents in society is possible.

DEFINING THE RESPONSIBILITY OF PERSONS

When we speak of the responsibility of individuals, philosophers say that we mean three things: someone is to blame, something has to be done, or some kind of trustworthiness can be expected.

We apply the first meaning, what we shall call the *causal* sense, primarily to legal and moral contexts where what is at issue is praise or blame for a past action. We say of a person that he or she was responsible for what happened, is to blame for it, should be held accountable. In this sense of the word, *responsibility* has to do with tracing the causes of actions and events, of finding out who is answerable in a given situation. Our aim is to determine someone's intention, free will, degree of participation, and appropriate reward or punishment.

We apply the second meaning of *responsibility* to rule following, to contexts where individuals are subject to externally imposed norms often associated with some social role that people play. We speak of the responsibilities of parents to children, of doctors to patients, of lawyers to clients, of citizens to the law. What is socially expected and what the party involved is to answer for are at issue here.

We use the third meaning of *responsibility* for decision making. With this meaning of the term, we say that individuals are responsible if they are trustworthy and reliable, if they allow appropriate factors to affect their judgment; we refer primarily to a person's independent thought processes and decision making, processes that justify an attitude of trust from those who interact with him or her as a responsible individual.

The distinguishing characteristic of moral responsibility, it seems to us, lies in this third sense of the term. Here the focus is on the intellectual and emotional processes in the individual's moral reasoning. Philosophers call this 'taking a moral point of view' and contrast it with such other processes as being financially prudent and attending to legal obligations.

To be sure, characterizing a person as 'morally responsible' may seem rather vague. But vagueness is a contextual notion. Everything depends on how we fill in the blank in 'vague for ——— purposes.'

In some contexts the term 'six o'clockish' is vague, while in others it is useful and informative. As a response to a space-shuttle pilot who wants to know when to fire the reentry rockets, it will not do, but it might do in response to a spouse who wants to know when one will arrive home at the end of the workday.

We maintain that the processes underlying moral responsibility can be defined and are not themselves vague, even though gaining consensus on specific moral norms and decisions is not always easy.

What, then, characterizes the processes underlying the judgment of a person we call morally responsible? Philosopher William K. Frankena offers the following answer:

A morality is a normative system in which judgments are made, more or less consciously, [out of a] consideration of the effects of actions . . . on the lives of persons . . . including the lives of others besides the person acting. . . . David Hume took a similar position when he argued that what speaks in a moral judgment is a kind of sympathy. . . . A little later, . . . Kant put the matter somewhat better by characterizing morality as the business of respecting persons as ends and not as means or as things. . . .'[2]

Frankena is pointing to two traits, both rooted in a long and diverse philosophical tradition:

1. *Rationality*. Taking a moral point of view includes the features we usually attribute to rational decision making, that is, lack of impulsiveness, care in mapping out alternatives and consequences, clarity about goals and purposes, attention to details of implementation.

2. *Respect.* The moral point of view also includes a special awareness of and concern for the effects of one's decisions and policies on others, special in the sense that it goes beyond the kind of awareness and concern that would ordinarily be part of rationality, that is, beyond seeing others merely as instrumental to accomplishing one's own purposes. This is respect for the lives of others and involves taking their needs and interests seriously, not simply as resources in one's own decision making but as limiting conditions which change the very definition of one's habitat from a self-centered to a shared environment. It is what philosopher Immanuel Kant meant by the 'categorical imperative' to treat others as valuable in and for themselves.

It is this feature that permits us to trust the morally responsible person. We know that such a person takes our point of view into account not merely as a useful precaution (as in 'honesty is the best policy') but as important in its own right.

These components of moral responsibility are not too vague to be useful. Rationality and respect affect the manner in which a person approaches practical decision making: they affect the way in which the individual processes information and makes choices. A rational but not respectful Bill Jones will not lie to his friends *unless* he is reasonably sure he will not be found out. A rational but not respectful Mary Smith will defend an unjustly treated party *unless* she thinks it may be too costly to herself. A rational *and* respectful decision maker, however, notices – and cares – whether the consequences of his or her conduct lead to injuries or indignities to others.

Two individuals who take 'the moral point of view' will not of course always agree on ethical matters, but they do at least have a basis for dialogue.

PROJECTING RESPONSIBILITY TO CORPORATIONS

Now that we have removed some of the vagueness from the notion of moral responsibility as it applies to persons, we can search for a frame of reference in which, by analogy with Bill Jones and Mary Smith, we can meaningfully and appropriately say that corporations are morally responsible. This is the issue reflected in the SSC case.

To deal with it, we must ask two questions: Is it meaningful to apply moral concepts to actors who are not persons but who are instead made up of persons? And even if meaningful, is it advisable to do so?

If a group can act like a person in some ways, then we can expect it to behave like a person in other ways. For one thing, we know that people organized into a group can act as a unit. As business people well know, legally a corporation is considered a unit. To approach unity, a group usually has some sort of internal decision structure, a system of rules that spell out authority relationships and specify the conditions under which certain individuals' actions become official actions of the group.[3]

If we can say that persons act responsibly only if they gather information about the impact of their actions on others and use it in making decisions, we can reasonably do the same for organizations. Our proposed frame of reference for thinking about and implementing corporate responsibility aims at spelling out the processes associated with the moral responsibility of individuals and projecting them to the level of organizations. This is similar to, though an inversion of, Plato's famous method in the *Republic*, in which justice in the community is used as a model for justice in the individual.

Hence, corporations that monitor their employment practices and the effects of their production processes and products on the environment and human health show the same kind of rationality and respect that morally responsible individuals do. Thus, attributing actions, strategies, decisions, and moral responsibilities to corporations as entities distinguishable from those who hold offices in them poses no problem.

And when we look about us, we can readily see differences in moral responsibility among corporations in much the same way that we see differences among persons. Some corporations have built features into their management incentive systems, board structures, internal control systems, and research agendas that in a person we would call self-control, integrity, and conscientiousness. Some have institutionalized awareness and concern for consumers, employees, and the rest of the public in ways that others clearly have not.

As a matter of course, some corporations attend to the human impact of their operations and policies and reject operations and policies that are questionable. Whether the issue be the health effects of sugared cereal or cigarettes, the safety of tires or tampons, civil liberties in the corporation or the community, an organization reveals its character as surely as a person does.

Indeed, the parallel may be even more dramatic. For just as the moral responsibility displayed by an individual develops over time from infancy to adulthood,[4] so too we may expect to find stages of development in organizational character that show significant patterns.

EVALUATING THE IDEA OF MORAL PROJECTION

Concepts like moral responsibility not only make sense when applied to organizations but also provide touchstones for designing more effective models than we have for guiding corporate policy.

Now we can understand what it means to invite SSC as a corporation to be morally responsible both in-house and in its community, but *should* we issue the invitation? Here we turn to the question of advisability. Should we require the organizational agents in our society to have the same moral attributes we require of ourselves?

Our proposal to spell out the processes associated with moral responsibility for individuals and then to project them to their organizational counterparts takes on added meaning when we examine alternative frames of reference for corporate responsibility.

Two frames of reference that compete for the allegiance of people who ponder the question of corporate responsibility are emphatically opposed to this principle of moral projection – what we might refer to as the 'invisible hand' view and the 'hand of government' view.

The Invisible Hand

The most eloquent spokesman of the first view is Milton Friedman (echoing many philosophers and economists since Adam Smith). According to this pattern of thought, the true and only social responsibilities of business organizations are to make profits and obey the laws. The workings of the free and competitive market-place will 'moralize' corporate behavior quite independently of any attempts to expand or transform decision making via moral projection.

A deliberate amorality in the executive suite is encouraged in the name of systemic morality: the common good is best served when each of us and our economic institutions pursue not the common good or moral purpose, advocates say, but competitive advantage. Morality, responsibility, and conscience reside in the invisible hand of the free market system, not in the hands of the organizations within the system, much less the managers within the organizations.

To be sure, people of this opinion admit, there is a sense in which social or ethical issues can and should enter the corporate mind, but the filtering of such issues is thorough: they go through the screens of custom, public opinion, public relations, and the law. And, in any case, self-interest maintains primacy as an objective and a guiding star.

The reaction from this frame of reference to the suggestion that moral judgment be integrated with corporate strategy is clearly negative. Such an integration is seen as inefficient and arrogant, and in the end both an illegitimate use of corporate power and an abuse of the manager's fiduciary role. With respect to our SSC case, advocates of the invisible hand model would vigorously resist efforts, beyond legal requirements, to make SSC right the wrongs of racial injustice. SSC's responsibility would be to make steel of high quality at least cost, to deliver it on time, and to satisfy its customers and stockholders. Justice would not be part of SSC's corporate mandate.

The Hand of Government

Advocates of the second dissenting frame of reference abound, but John Kenneth Galbraith's work has counterpointed Milton Friedman's with insight and style. Under this view of corporate responsibility, corporations are to pursue objectives that are rational and purely economic. The regulatory hands of the law and the political process rather than the invisible hand of the marketplace turns these objectives to the common good.

Again, in this view, it is a system that provides the moral direction for corporate decision making – a system, though, that is guided by political managers, the custodians of the public purpose. In the case of SSC, proponents of this view would look to the state for moral direction and responsible management, both within SSC and in the community. The corporation would have no moral responsibility beyond political and legal obedience.

What is striking is not so much the radical difference between the economic and social philosophies that underlie these two views of the source of corporate responsibility but the conceptual similarities. Both views locate morality, ethics, responsibility, and conscience in the systems of rules and incentives in which the modern corporation finds itself embedded. Both views reject the exercise of independent moral judgment by corporations as actors in society.

Neither view trusts corporate leaders with stewardship over what are often called noneconomic values. Both require corporate responsibility to march to the beat of drums outside. In the jargon of moral philosophy, both views press for a rule-centered or a system-centered ethics instead of an agent-centered ethics. These frames of reference countenance corporate rule-following responsibility for corporations but not corporate decision-making responsibility.

The Hand of Management

To be sure, the two views under discussion differ in that one looks to an invisible moral force in the market while the other looks to a visible moral force in government. But both would advise against a principle of moral projection that permits or encourages corporations to exercise independent, noneconomic judgment over matters that face them in their short- and long-term plans and operations.

Accordingly, both would reject a third view of corporate responsibility that seeks to affect the thought processes of the organization itself – a sort of 'hand of management' view – since neither seems willing or able to see the engines of profit regulate themselves to the degree that would be implied by taking the principle of moral projection seriously. Cries of inefficiency and moral imperialism from the right would be matched by cries of insensitivity and illegitimacy from the left, all in the name of preserving us from corporations and managers run morally amok.

Better, critics would say, that moral philosophy be left to philosophers, philanthropists, and politicians than to business leaders. Better that corporate morality be kept to glossy annual reports, where it is safely insulated from policy and performance.

The two conventional frames of reference locate moral restraint in forces external to the person and the corporation. They deny moral reasoning and intent to the corporation in the name of either market competition or society's system of explicit legal constraints and presume that these have a better moral effect than that of rationality and respect.

Although the principle of moral projection, which underwrites the idea of a corporate conscience and patterns it on the thought and feeling processes of the person, is in our view compelling, we must acknowledge that it is neither part of the received wisdom, nor is its advisability beyond question or objection. Indeed, attributing the role of conscience to the corporation seems to carry with it new and disturbing implications for our usual ways of thinking about ethics and business.

Perhaps the best way to clarify and defend this frame of reference is to address the objections to the principle found in the last pages of this article. There we see a summary of the criticisms and counterarguments we have heard during hours of discussion with business executives and business school students. We believe that the replies to the objections about a corporation having a conscience are convincing.

LEAVING THE DOUBLE STANDARD BEHIND

We have come some distance from our opening reflection on Southern Steel Company and its role in its community. Our proposal – clarified, we hope, through these objections and replies – suggests that it is not sufficient to draw a sharp line between individuals' private ideas and efforts and a corporation's institutional efforts but that the latter can and should be built upon the former.

Does this frame of reference give us an unequivocal prescription for the behavior of SSC in its circumstances? No, it does not. Persuasive arguments might be made now and might have been made then that SSC should not have used its considerable economic clout to threaten the community into desegregation. A careful analysis of the realities of the environment might have disclosed that such a course would have been counterproductive, leading to more injustice than it would have alleviated.

The point is that some of the arguments and some of the analyses are or would have been moral arguments, and thereby the ultimate decision that of an ethically responsible organization. The significance of this point can hardly be overstated, for it represents the adoption of a new perspective on corporate policy and a new way of thinking about business ethics. We agree with one authority, who writes that 'the business firm, as an organic entity intricately affected by and affecting its environment, is as appropriately adaptive . . . to demands for responsible behavior as for economic service.'[5]

The frame of reference here developed does not offer a decision procedure for corporate managers. That has not been our purpose. It does, however, shed light on the conceptual foundations of business ethics by training attention on the corporation as a moral agent in society. Legal systems of rules and incentives are insufficient, even though they may be necessary, as frameworks for corporate responsibility. Taking conceptual cues from the features of moral responsibility normally expected of the person in our opinion deserves practicing managers' serious consideration.

The lack of congruence that James Weston saw between individual and corporate moral responsibility can be, and we think should be, overcome. In the process, what a number of writers have characterized as a double standard – a discrepancy between our personal lives and our lives in organizational settings – might be dampened. The principle of moral projection not only helps us to conceptualize the kinds of demands that we might make of corporations and other organizations but also offers the prospect of harmonizing those demands with the demands that we make of ourselves.

IS A CORPORATION A MORALLY RESPONSIBLE 'PERSON'?

Objection 1 to the Analogy

Corporations are not persons. They are artificial legal constructions, machines for mobilizing economic investments toward the efficient production of goods and services. We cannot hold a corporation responsible. We can only hold individuals responsible.

Reply

Our frame of reference does not imply that corporations are persons in a literal sense. It simply means that in certain respects concepts and functions normally attributed to persons can also be attributed to organizations made up of persons. Goals, economic values, strategies, and other such personal attributes are often usefully projected to the corporate level by managers and researchers. Why should we not project the functions of conscience in the same way? As for holding corporations responsible, recent criminal prosecutions such as the case of Ford Motor Company and its Pinto gas tanks suggest that society finds the idea both intelligible and useful.

Objection 2

A corporation cannot be held responsible at the sacrifice of profit. Profitability and financial health have always been and should continue to be the 'categorical imperatives' of a business operation.

Reply

We must of course acknowledge the imperatives of survival, stability, and growth when we discuss corporations, as indeed we must acknowledge them when we discuss the life of an individual. Self-sacrifice has been identified with moral responsibility in only the most extreme cases. The pursuit of profit and self-interest need not be pitted against the demands of moral responsibility. Moral demands are best viewed as containments – not replacements – for self-interest.

This is not to say that profit maximization never conflicts with morality. But profit maximization conflicts with other managerial values as well. The point is to coordinate imperatives, not deny their validity.

Objection 3

Corporate executives are not elected representatives of the people, nor are they anointed or appointed as social guardians. They therefore lack the social mandate that a democratic society rightly demands of those who would pursue ethically or socially motivated policies. By keeping corporate policies confined to economic motivations, we keep the power of corporate executives in its proper place.

Reply

The objection betrays an oversimplified view of the relationship between the public and the private sector. Neither private individuals nor private corporations that guide their conduct by ethical or social values beyond the demands of law should be constrained merely because they are not elected to do so. The demands of moral responsibility are independent of the demands of political legitimacy and are in fact presupposed by them.

To be sure, the state and the political process will and must remain the primary mechanisms for protecting the public interest, but one might be forgiven the hope that the political process will not substitute for the moral judgment of the citizenry or other components of society such as corporations.

Objection 4

Our system of law carefully defines the role of agent or fiduciary and makes corporate managers accountable to shareholders and investors for the use of their assets. Management cannot, in the name of corporate moral responsibility, arrogate to itself the right to manage those assets by partially noneconomic criteria.

Reply

First, it is not so clear that investors insist on purely economic criteria in the management of their assets, especially if some of the shareholders' resolutions and board reforms of the last decade are any indication. For instance, companies doing business in South Africa have had stockholders question their activities, other companies have instituted audit committees for their boards before such auditing was mandated, and mutual funds for which 'socially responsible behavior' is a major investment criterion now exist.

Second, the categories of 'shareholder' and 'investor' connote wider time spans than do immediate or short-term returns. As a practical matter, considerations of stability and long-term return on investment enlarge the class of principals to which managers bear a fiduciary relationship.

Third, the trust that managers hold does not and never has extended to 'any means available' to advance the interests of the principals. Both legal and moral constraints must be understood to qualify that trust – even, perhaps, in the name of a larger trust and a more basic fiduciary relationship to the members of society at large.

Objection 5

The power, size, and scale of the modern corporation – domestic as well as international – are awesome. To unleash, even partially, such power from the discipline of the marketplace and the narrow or possibly nonexistent moral purpose implicit in that discipline would be socially dangerous. Had SSC acted in the community to further racial justice, its purposes might have been admirable, but those purposes could have led to a kind of moral imperialism or worse. Suppose SSC had thrown its power behind the Ku Klux Klan.

Reply

This is a very real and important objection. What seems not to be appreciated is the fact that power affects when it is used as well as when it is not used. A decision by SSC not to exercise its economic influence according to 'noneconomic' criteria is inevitably a moral decision and just as inevitably affects the community. The issue in the end is not whether corporations (and other organizations) should be 'unleashed' to exert moral force in our society but rather how critically and self-consciously they should choose to do so.

The degree of influence enjoyed by an agent, whether a person or an organization, is not so much a factor recommending moral disengagement as a factor demanding a high level of moral awareness. Imperialism is more to be feared when moral reasoning is absent than when it is present. Nor do we suggest that the 'discipline of the marketplace' be diluted; rather, we call for it to be supplemented with the discipline of moral reflection.

Objection 6

The idea of moral projection is a useful device for structuring corporate responsibility only if our understanding of moral responsibility at the level of the person is in some sense richer than our understanding of moral responsibility on the level of the organization as a whole. If we are not clear about individual responsibility, the projection is fruitless.

Reply

The objection is well taken. The challenge offered by the idea of moral projection lies in our capacity to articulate criteria or frameworks of reasoning for the morally responsible person. And though such a challenge is formidable, it is not clear that it cannot be met, at least with sufficient consensus to be useful.

For centuries, the study and criticism of frameworks have gone on, carried forward by many disciplines, including psychology, the social sciences, and philosophy. And though it would be a mistake to suggest that any single framework (much less a decision mechanism) has emerged as the right one, it is true that recurrent patterns are discernible and well enough defined to structure moral discussion.

In the body of the article, we spoke of rationality and respect as components of individual responsibility. Further analysis of these components would translate them into social costs and benefits, justice in the distribution of goods and services, basic rights and duties, and fidelity to contracts. The view that pluralism in our society has undercut all possibility of moral agreement is anything but self-evident. Sincere moral disagreement is, of course, inevitable and not clearly lamentable. But a process and a vocabulary for articulating such values as we share is no small step forward when compared with the alternatives. Perhaps in our exploration of the moral projection we might make some surprising and even reassuring discoveries about ourselves.

Objection 7

Why is it necessary to project moral responsibility to the level of the organization? Isn't the task of defining corporate responsibility and business ethics sufficiently discharged if we clarify the responsibilities of men and women in business as individuals? Doesn't ethics finally rest on the honesty and integrity of the individual in the business world?

Reply

Yes and no. Yes, in the sense that the control of large organizations does finally rest in the hands of managers, of men and women. No, in the sense that what is being controlled is a cooperative system for a cooperative purpose. The projection of responsibility to the organization is simply an acknowledgment of the fact that the whole is more than the sum of its parts. Many intelligent people do not an intelligent organization make. Intelligence needs to be structured, organized, divided, and recombined in complex processes for complex purposes.

Studies of management have long shown that the attributes, successes, and failures of organizations are phenomena that emerge from the coordination of persons' attributes and that explanations of such phenomena require categories of analysis and description beyond the level of the individual. Moral responsibility is an attribute that can manifest itself in organizations as surely as competence or efficiency.

Objection 8

Is the frame of reference here proposed intended to replace or undercut the relevance of the 'invisible hand' and the 'government hand' views, which depend on external controls?

Reply

No. Just as regulation and economic competition are not substitutes for corporate responsibility, so corporate responsibility is not a substitute for law and the market. The imperatives of ethics cannot be relied on – nor have they ever been relied on – without a context of external sanctions. And this is true as much for individuals as for organizations.

This frame of reference takes us beneath, but not beyond, the realm of external systems of rules and incentives and into the thought processes that interpret and respond to the corporation's environment. Morality is more than merely part of that environment. It aims at the projection of conscience, not the enthronement of it in either the state or the competitive process.

The rise of the modern large corporation and the concomitant rise of the professional manager demand a conceptual framework in which these phenomena can be accommodated to moral thought. The principal of moral projection furthers such accommodation by recognizing a new level of agency in society and thus a new level of responsibility.

Objection 9

Corporations have always taken the interests of those outside the corporation into account in the sense that customer relations and public relations generally are an integral part of rational economic decision making. Market signals and social signals that filter through the market mechanism inevitably represent the interests of parties affected by the behavior of the company. What, then, is the point of adding respect to rationality?

Reply

Representing the affected parties solely as economic variables in the environment of the company is treating them as means or resources and not as ends in themselves. It implies that the only voice which affected parties should have in organizational decision making is that of potential buyers, sellers, regulators, or boycotters. Besides, many affected parties may not occupy such roles, and those who do may not be able to signal the organization with messages that effectively represent their stakes in its actions.

To be sure, classical economic theory would have us believe that perfect competition in free markets (with modest adjustments from the state) will result in all relevant signals being 'heard,' but the abstractions from reality implicit in such theory make it insufficient as a frame of reference for moral responsibility. In a world in which strict self-interest was congruent with the common good, moral responsibility might be unnecessary. We do not, alas, live in such a world.

The element of respect in our analysis of responsibility plays an essential role in ensuring the recognition of unrepresented or underrepresented voices in the decision making of organizations as agents. Showing respect for persons as ends and not mere means to organizational purposes is central to the concept of corporate moral responsibility.

NOTES

1. See John Ladd, 'Morality and the Ideal of Rationality in Formal Organizations,' *The Monist*, October 1970, p. 499.
2. See William K. Frankena, *Thinking About Morality* (Ann Arbor: University of Michigan Press, 1980), p. 26.
3. See Peter French, 'The Corporation as a Moral Person,' *American Philosophical Quarterly*, July 1979, p. 207.

4. A process that psychological researchers from Jean Piaget to Lawrence Kohlberg have examined carefully; see Jean Piaget, *The Moral Judgement of the Child* (New York: Free Press, 1965) and Lawrence Kohlberg, *The Philosophy of Moral Development* (New York: Harper & Row, 1981).
5. See Kenneth R. Andrews, *The Concept of Corporate Strategy*, revised edition (Homewood, Ill.: Dow Jones-Irwin, 1980), p. 99.

Corporate moral agency: the case for anthropological bigotry

JOHN R. DANLEY

In 'Corporate Moral Agency,'[1] Peter A. French argues for a position, increasingly popular, which would accept 'corporations as members of the moral community, of equal standing with the tranditionally acknowledged residents – biological human beings.' This is but one implication of accepting the claim that one can legitimately ascribe moral responsibility to corporations. To put the matter somewhat differently, again in French's words, 'corporations should be treated as full-fledged moral persons and hence . . . have whatever privileges, rights, and duties as are, in the normal course of affairs, accorded to moral persons.'

Unwilling to rest content with the usual assaults on prejudices against real persons based on race, creed, sex, religion, or national origin, French is among those[2] seeking to open yet another new front. The struggle is now being extended beyond real persons to eliminate discrimination against a particular class of *personae fictae*, fictitious persons, namely the corporation. Before too hastily endorsing this new 'corporate' liberation movement let us pause for reflection. If after serious consideration we do vote to admit these peculiar entities into our rather exclusivist and elitist community of moral beings, we should insist on their having equal standing with the rest of us run-of-the-mill featherless bipeds. After all, what moral neighborhood worthy of the name would allow second-class citizens? After examining the case for admission, however, I find myself driven to the uncomfortable position of defending apartheid, biological apartheid that is, of defending anthropological bigotry. I contend that corporations should not be included in the moral community; they should not be granted full-fledged moral status. Within this emotionally charged atmosphere

Reading taken from *Action and Responsibility, Bowling Green Studies in Applied Philosophy*, **II**, 1980. Copyright © 1980 Bowling Green Studies. Reproduced by permission of the author.

it is tempting to employ the standard *ad hominems* of bigotry ('Think of the value of your property'; or, 'Before you know it your daughter will bring a corporation home to dinner'; 'What about the children?'; and so forth), but I will attempt to ward off these temptations. My claim is that the corporatist programs of the kind represented by French would seriously disturb the logic of our moral discourse. Indeed, the corporatist position, while offering no substantial advantages, would entail the reduction of biological persons to the status of second-class citizens. Let us turn now to the dispute.

I

There is little doubt that we often speak of corporations as being responsible for this or that sin or charitable act, whether of microscopic or cosmic proportions. The question is what we mean when we speak in that way. Sometimes all we mean is that the corporation is the cause of such and such. In these instances we are isolating a cause for an event or state of affairs, an exercise not much more (or less) troublesome than saying 'The icy pavement caused the accident.' The debate revolves around a fuller sense of 'responsibility,' a sense which includes more than the idea of 'causing to happen.' In this richer sense, we ascribe responsibility only if the event or state of affairs caused was also intended by the agent.

When the concept of responsibility is unpacked in this fashion, the traditionalists appear to have victory already in hand. Whatever else we may say of them, collective entities are surely not the kinds of things capable of intending. Individuals within the corporation can intend, lust, have malice aforethought, and so forth, but the corporation cannot. Traditionalists, like myself, maintain that only persons, i.e., entities with particular physical and mental properties, can be morally responsible. Corporations lack these. For the traditionalists, to speak of corporations being responsible is simply elliptical for speaking of certain individuals within the corporation being responsible. On this point, and perhaps this one alone, I do not believe Milton Friedman[3] to be in error.

Undaunted by this venerable line of reasoning, the corporatists proceed to press their case. Although it is French's view that I am treating, I am concerned not so much with the details of his argument as with the general outlines of the corporatist position. Using French's theory as representative, however, provides us with one of the most forceful, sophisticated theories developed. French has worked for years in the area of collective responsibility.[4] His strategy is to accept the traditionalists' analysis of 'responsibility,' and then to attempt to show that some sense can be made of ascribing 'intentions' to a corporation.

The key to making some sense of corporate 'intentions' is what French calls the Corporate Internal Decision Structure, the CID. The CID is that which allows one, 'licenses' one, to redescribe the actions of certain individuals within a corporation as actions of the corporation. Although the notion is complicated, a CID contains two elements which are particularly relevant:

1. an organization or responsibility flow chart delineating stations and levels within the corporate power structure and
2. corporate decision recognition rules.

As French puts it, the organizational chart provides the grammar for corporate decision making; the recognition rules provide the logic. The purpose of the organizational chart is to locate which procedures will count as decisions for the corporation, and who may or must participate in those procedures. The recognition rules, we are informed, are of two sorts. The first sort are procedural recognitors, 'partially embedded in the organizational chart.' What these amount to, it seems, are directives more explicit than those contained in the chart, expanding upon it. The second sort of recognition rules are expressed primarily in corporate policy.

Employing the cumbersome apparatus of the CID, some acts may now be described in two non-identical ways, or so it is claimed.

> One of these . . . is 'Executive X's doing y' and one is 'Corporation C's doing z.' The corporate act, and the individual act may have different properties; indeed, they have different causal ancestors though they are causally inseparable.

The effect of this, of course, is that when certain individuals as specified by the organizational chart, engage in certain procedures as specified by the organizational chart and some recognition rules, and act in accordance with other recognition rules (corporate policy), then French claims we can redescribe the action as a corporate act, an intentional corporate act. It is critical to the corporatist position that the two descriptions are non-identical. Saying that 'Corporation C did z' is not reducible to the statement that 'Executives X, Y, and Z, voted to do y,' even though y and z are the same. Since they are non-identical the traditionalist is supposedly prevented from ascribing responsibility only to these individuals. The acts of the individuals are necessary for a corporate act but not identical with it.

Like a child with a new toy, one is strongly inclined by the glitter of this technical hardware to dismantle it, to try to find out how it all works, to see whether it really fits together, to see how and whether it can handle hard cases. To be sure, there are some problems which one can detect immediately. Let me mention two. First of all, it is unclear what French means by an organizational chart. Since his examples are those of nice neat black lines and boxes on a page, like the ones found in business textbooks and corporate policy manuals, one is left with the impression that this is what he has in mind. If so, there are severe difficulties. Most everyone is aware of the extent to which corporate reality departs from the ethereal world of black lines and boxes. Will French maintain that any decisions made by the managers of corporations which do not conform to the organizational chart are not decisions of the corporation? Biting the bullet here may be the best course but it is probable that most decisions are not strictly corporate decisions then. Few corporations act at all, if this criterion is used. French needs a more positivistic interpretation[5] of the organizational chart, one which would insure that the flow chart realistically captured the actual procedures and personages holding the powers. The difficulty with this modification, however, is that the CID begins to lose its function as a normative criterion by which to determine which acts are corporate acts and which are not. The positivistic interpretation would mean that a corporate act is whatever some powerful person within the corporation manages to get others in the corporation to perform, or gets others outside to accept as a corporate act. That will not work at all. The CID appears nestled upon the familiar horns of a dilemma. At least more work is necessary here.

There is a second difficulty. A basic component of the CID must be the corporate charter. Recently the general incorporation charters have become little more than blank tablets for the corporation to engage in business for 'any lawful purpose,' although some aspects of the organizational chart and a few recognition rules are delineated. Even these permissive rules of recognition have pertinence for French. Suppose every aspect of the CID was followed except that the board of directors voted unanimously to engage the corporation in some unlawful activity. According to the charter, a part of the CID, this is not possible. One could not redescribe such an act as a corporate act. This result of this is that corporations can never act illegally. Unlike the Augustinian doctrine that for fallen man it is not possible not to sin, the French doctrine appears to be that for the corporation it is not possible to sin at all.

These are but two of many queries which might be addressed to French's proposal. However, it is not my concern to dwell on such technical points here, lest we be distracted from the larger issue. Suppose, for the sake of argument, that we accept some mode of redescribing individual acts such that one could identify these acts as constituting a corporate intentional act. Accept French's. Would that establish the corporatist case? I think not. French tips his hand, for instance, when he writes that what 'needs to be shown is that there is sense in saying that corporations, and not just the people who work in them, have reasons for doing what they do.' But, obviously, French needs to show much more. All that is established by a device which redescribes, is that there is *a sense* in saying that corporations have intentions. The significant question is whether that sense of 'intend' is the one used by the traditionalists when explicating 'responsibility,' and when denying that corporations can have intentions. The traditionalists can easily, and quite plausibly, claim that the corporatist is equivocating on 'intend.' The sense in which a corporation intends is much different from that in which a biological person intends. The corporatist has further laid the foundation for this charge by finding it necessary to construct the apparatus so that the sense of 'intend' involved can be made clear. The more clearly this sense of 'intend' is articulated, the more clearly it diverges from what we usually mean by 'intend.' The arbitrariness of constructing a sense of 'intend' should be evident when we consider the possibility of ascribing intentions to numerous other entities, such as plants, animals, or machines. One could go to extraordinary lengths to provide a sense for attributing intentionally to many of these. Yet, few would contend that it was very similar to what we mean in attributing 'intention' to humans.

Consider a computer programmed to play chess which learns from previous mistakes. There is a sense in which the computer intends to respond P-K4 to my king pawn opening, but is this the same sense of 'intend' as when I intended P-K4? Furthermore, even ascribing an intention to the computer by no means entails that we would be ready to ascribe responsibility to it. The point is that it remains for the corporatist to demonstrate the relationship between the sense of 'intend' and the sense involved in ascriptions of responsibility to humans. Hence, a rather difficult task remains for the corporatist before the case is made.

II

Thus far I have established only that the corporatist has failed to establish the position. I must admit that I am not entirely enamored of the preceding line of argument. The dispute smacks of the theological controversies concerning whether 'wisdom' or 'goodness' when attributed to God have the same sense as when predicated of humans. Nonetheless, the corporatist has moved the debate in that direction by attempting to equate two markedly different senses. There are, fortunately, other factors to be considered in evaluating the corporatist position. These factors appear when one expands the focus of attention beyond the narrow conditions for ascribing 'responsibility,' and begins to examine the concept as it functions in the broader context of moral discourse.

Much hangs in the balance when ascribing 'responsibility.' Affixing responsibility is a prelude to expressing approbation or disapprobation – praise or blame. When the agent responsible is praised, that is the final move in the moral game. (Morality never pays very well.) But, when the responsibility is affixed and the agent in question is blame worthy, that is far from the end of the matter. In this case, affixing responsibility and expressing disfavor is itself a prelude to many further permissible or obligatory moves. Minimally, the blameworthy party is expected to express regret or remorse. More importantly, the agent may be required to pay compensation or be subject to punishment. Ascribing responsibility opens the door for these major moral moves. (There are other door openers as well, for example, the notion of cause in strict liability.) Any understanding of the concept of responsibility is incomplete without incorporting the role it plays in relation to these other moral moves. It is this which is lacking from the previous discussion of 'intend.' Such an analysis cannot be provided here. What can be done, however, is to sketch briefly how ascribing responsibility to corporations effectively blocks these moves, sundering many of the threads which tie 'responsibility' so intimately with concepts like remorse, regret, compensation, or punishment. Let me elaborate.

An indication of the consequences of admitting the corporation into the moral community have been foreshadowed by admission into the legal corpus as a person. That legacy is an odious one, marred by an environment within which the corporation has enjoyed nearly all of the benefits associated with personhood while shouldering but few of the burdens or risks. Much the same would result from admission into the moral world. That legacy is not solely to be explained by jaundiced justices or bad judicial judgments, but is a natural consequence of attempting to pretend that the corporation is just another pretty face. While the law early began holding the corporation liable (read: responsible) for certain specified acts, and the scope of things for which it was liable has dramatically increased over the years, there has been a hesitancy to judge that corporations could be subject to most criminal statutes. One of the major stumbling blocks was just the one which is the subject of this paper. It was clear that many of the criminal statutes required criminal intent, or a criminal state of mind, and unable to locate the corporate mind, it was judged that the corporation was not subject to these. The relevance of proposals such as French's is that the justices would now have a method for determining when the corporation acts with intent, with malice aforethought, with premeditation or out of passion. What I am anxious to bring to light, however, is that these proposals offer no advantage over the traditionalist view and in fact create further problems. Consider now the moral moves involved in extracting compensation from, or punishing, a guilty person. How is one to make these moral moves against a corporate person? One cannot. An English jurist put the point well in an often quoted quip to the effect that corporations have no pants to kick, no soul to damn. We may concur with the sentiment of that jurist who concluded that 'by God they ought to have both,' but they have neither, although French has given them a surrogate soul, the CID.

The corporation cannot be kicked, whipped, imprisoned, or hanged by the neck until dead. Only individuals of the corporation can be punished. What of punishment through the pocketbook, or extracting compensation for a corporate act? Here too, the corporation is not punished, and does not pay the compensation. Usually one punishes the stockholders who in the present corporate climate have virtually no control over corporate actions. Or, if the corporation can pass on the cost of a fiscal punishment or compensation, it is in the end the consumer who pays for the punishment or compensation. If severe enough, hitting the pocketbook may result in the reduction of workforce, again resting the burden on those least deserving, more precisely, on those not responsible at all. Sooner or later, usually sooner, someone hits upon the solution of punishing those individuals of the corporation most directly responsible for the corporate act. There are also moral difficulties associated with this alternative. For example, many top executives are protected through insurance policies, part of the perks of the job. That would be satisfactory if the intent is simply to compensate, but it neutralizes any deterrent or retributive effect. But let us pass over these considerations and examine more closely these recommendations to 'go inside' the corporation to punish an individual, whether stockholder, employee, agent, manager, or director of the corporation.

For the traditionalist there is little difficulty. The traditionalist recognizes the corporation as a legal fiction which for better or worse may have equal protection under the law of other persons, but the traditionalist many accept those legal trappings as at best a useful way of treating the corporation for legal purposes. For the traditionalist it makes moral sense for the law to go inside the corporation. After all, morally the corporation is not responsible; only individuals are. As long as those within the corporation pay for the deed, there is no theoretical difficulty.

What of the corporatist's position? The single advantage is that the adoption of that position would mean that some sense could be made of pointing an accusing finger or raising a fist in moral outrage at a fictitious person, a behavior which might otherwise appear not only futile but ridiculous. In the new corporatist scheme the behavior would no longer be ridiculous, only futile. The disadvantages, on the other hand, are apparent when one attempts to follow the responsibility assignment with the normally attendant moral moves as I have just shown. Either those moves are blocked entirely, since one may find no method by which to punish, or the moves are diverted away from the genuine culprit (the fictitious moral agent) and directed toward someone inside the corporation (non-fictitious moral agent). Either alternative is unacceptable. The former would entail that some citizens of the moral community, namely corporate persons, were not subject to the full obligations of membership. That reduces biological members to the status of second-class citizens, shouldering as they do all the burdens. The later alternative, 'going inside,' is equally offensive. This alternative means that biological agents are sacrificed vicariously for the sins of the corporation. This solution not only reduces the biological agents to second-class citizens, but would make scapegoats or worse, sacrificial lambs, of them. Thus would the admission of the corporation into the moral community threaten to disturb the logic associated with the ascription of responsibility.

In addition to these problems, the corporatists face other theoretical obstacles. It is not clear that 'going inside' a corporation is often, if ever, intelligible, given the analysis of a corporate act. To counter the traditionalist's claim that only individuals are responsible, French claims that the corporate act is not identical with the acts of individuals in the corporation. Given this, how is it possible now to reverse that claim and hold individuals responsible for something which they did not do? All they did at most was to vote for the corporation to do something, or to pay for something to be done on behalf of the corporation. The claim that individual acts and corporate acts are not identical opens the door to criminalless crime, a possibility admitted openly by French in another earlier paper. French there notes that a collective entity may be responsible yet no individual in that collectivity be responsible. Far from being an extreme case, that outcome may include all corporate acts. As mentioned above, such an alternative is unacceptable. But, again, can one make intelligible going inside to make one or more individuals responsible? In order to do so the corporatist must shift ground and concede that the individual acts and the corporate acts are identical, or perhaps that the individuals, by voting on a course of illegal or immoral action, coerced the hapless corporation to go along with the deed.

III

Although I have offered what I take to be a satisfactory defense of the traditionalist position, I would like to close by suggesting an alternative model for viewing the corporation. An alternative is needed because the corporatist's model has largely succeeded in warping many of our intuitions and is reinforced not only by legal idioms, but by managerial vocabulary. In many a corporatist's eye the corporation is an organism, and perhaps even much like a biological person. It has a brain, nerve receptors, muscle, it moves, reproduces, expands, develops, grows, in some periods the 'fat is cut off,' processes information, makes decisions, and so on. It adjusts to the environment. Such a metaphor may be useful but we have now begun to be victimized by the metaphorical model. Unfortunately, reformers have found it useful to accept that language and that model. It is useful to personify and then to vilify. The model, I fear, stands behind many attempts to endow the corporation with moral agency and personhood.

A more adequate model, especially for those who are reform minded, I would maintain provides a different perspective from which to view contemporary trends. The corporation is more like a machine than an organism.[6] Like machines they are human inventions, designed by humans, modified by humans, operated by humans. Like many machines they are controlled by the few for the benefit of the few. They are no longer simple, easily understandable, organizations, but as complicated as the latest piece of electronic hardware. It takes years of training to learn how to operate and direct one. Like machines they are created, yet they create and shape humans.

If a complicated machine got out of hand and ravaged a community, there seems something perverse about expressing our moral outrage and indignation to the machine. More appropriately, our fervor should be addressed to the operators and to the designers of the machine. They, not the machines, are morally responsible. To ascribe responsibility to such machines, no matter how complicated, is tantamount to mistaking the created for the creator. This mystification is a contemporary form of animism. Such is the case for anthropological bigotry.

NOTES

1. The basic argument of the article appears in a more detailed version in French's forthcoming book *Foundations of Corporate Responsibility*. I have not had the opportunity to consult that book. See also his article in the *American Philosophical Quarterly*, Vol. 13, No. 3, 1976.
2. Of those who apparently espouse this view to some degree are Norman Bowie and Tom L. Beauchamp in *Ethical Theory and Business* (Englewood Cliffs, N.J., Prentice-Hall, Inc., 1979) e.g. Chapter 1 and comments on page 128 and Christopher Stone in *Where The Law Ends* (Harper Colophon, New York, 1975).
3. See *Capitalism and Freedom*, (Chicago, IL, University of Chicago Press, 1962), pp. 133–136.
4. One of French's earliest works is 'Morally Blaming Whole Populations,' which appears in *Philosophy, Morality, and International Affairs* (New York, Oxford University Press, 1974) edited by Virginia Held et al., pp. 266–285.
5. The positive interpretation is suggested by, among other things, French's references to Austin and H. L. A. Hart. The distinction between organizational chart and recognition rules also resembles the positivistic distinction between secondary and primary rules.
6. Although I do not follow Ladd's argument, one good example of taking this alternative model seriously is demonstrated in his 'Morality and the Ideal of Rationality in Formal Organizations,' in *The Monist*, Vol. 54 (October 1970), pp. 488–516.

CASE STUDY

Making the punishment fit the crime:
the Zeebrugge disaster

On the evening of 6 March 1987, shortly after leaving the Belgian port of Zeebrugge, the cross-channel ferry *Herald of Free Enterprise* capsized with a loss of 150 passengers and 38 crew. The ship was owned by European Ferries Limited (trading under the name 'Townsend Thoreson'), a company that had just been taken over by the Peninsular and Oriental Steamship Company (P&O). It was a roll on-roll off (Ro-Ro) ferry, equipped with doors through which vehicles could be driven on and off. The astonishing reason for the capsize was that the bow doors had been left open on departure from Zeebrugge. A combination of increased speed and a sharp turn produced a bow wave that flooded through the open doorway. Within four minutes the ship ended up on its side half submerged in water. Only the good fortune of turning into relatively shallow waters prevented total submersion and an even greater loss of life.

The Department of Transport set up a Court of Formal Inquiry under Mr Justice Sheen. It sat from 27 April to 12 June 1987. Instituted under merchant shipping law, such a court is primarily concerned with investigating the causes of marine accidents. Its punitive powers only extend to the removal of officer's 'certificates of competence' (the licences to be merchant navy officers) and making shipowners contribute to the cost of the inquiry.

The court found that the reason the bow doors had not been closed was that the assistant bosun, Mr Stanley, had slept through a public address call to 'harbour stations' which should have alerted him to go and close the doors. This was, however, no simple case of one person's error. What the court also found was that there was no effective system for ensuring that the ship's doors were closed. They could be, and often were, closed by crew members other than Mr Stanley. Responsibility for ensuring the doors were closed belonged to the chief officer, Mr Sabel. He, though, was also required to be on the bridge during 'harbour stations'. From the position neither he nor ship's master, Captain Lewry, could see whether or not the doors were closed.

The court discovered that this problem of ensuring the doors were closed had been previously recognized and brought to the attention of senior management. In 1983 another Townsend Thoreson ship, *the Pride of Free Enterprise*, had set sail with both stern and bow doors open. In 1985 the then master of the ship, Captain Blowers, had sent a memorandum to the company's chief superintendent, Mr Develin, pointing out the problem and suggesting that indicator lights be fitted to show those on the bridge whether or not the doors were closed. Mr Develin circulated the memo to other senior managers who rejected the suggestion as unnecessary and even subjected it to some ridicule. Two other ship's captains raised the issue again in 1986; one of them being the senior master of the *Herald*, Captain Kirby (leader of a rota of masters captaining the ship).

On top of this the directors had also been alerted to shortcomings in the arrangements for counting the number of passengers on board (the limit was frequently exceeded) and measuring the draught of ships (a low draught was a factor in the *Herald* capsize). Another issue raised at the inquiry was the wider question of the stability of Ro-Ro ferries in general. Given their open car decks, they lack the sealed bulkheads which will normally separate sections of deck into watertight compartments. Hence, any flooding of those open decks can so rapidly destabilize such as to make evacuation virtually impossible. The *Herald*, for example, was supposed to need 30 minutes to evacuate but capsized in 90 seconds and sank in another 150. This basic design question was not, however, something which the court was prepared to consider, though as an issue involving all vehicle ferries of this sort, it remains a matter of grave concern to many people – including the families of the *Herald* victims.

The decision of the court of Formal Inquiry was that blame rested not only on the three principal crew members involved – Assistant Bosun Stanley, Chief Officer Sabel, and Captain Lewry – but also the Townsend Thoreson company. Mr Sabel had his certificate suspended for two years, Captain Lewry for one. The company was ordered to pay £350 000 costs.

Following the Sheen inquiry, a Dover coroner's jury was called to determine the cause of death of the disaster victims. In October 1987, and against the advice of the coroner, it returned a verdict of 'unlawful killing'. This opened the way for the criminal charges to be brought against the company and its officers. So as well as the civil law liability to pay damages from corporate funds (something the company had never contested), both the company and also specific individuals within it now faced the prospect of judicial punishment for the most serious kind of criminal misdeed.

After a 15 month investigation, the Kent police brought a charge of manslaughter against the Townsend Thoreson company and seven named individuals. As well as the three crew members, Stanley, Sabel and Lewry, the individuals were the senior master, Captain Kirby and three senior managers. The senior managers were the Deputy Chief Superintendent, Mr Alcindor; his immediate superior, Mr Develin; and the Group Technical Director, Mr Ayers – the last two also being directors of the company.

On 19 October 1990, after only 27 days, the trial judge, Mr Justice Turner, directed the jury to 'withdraw from consideration' the charges against the company and five of the seven individuals. The two individuals most closely connected with the accident, Stanley and Sabel, were left out of the direction, but the prosecution decided it was not in the public interest to continue the case against them alone.

The reason given for dropping charges was that while there obviously had been negligence to some degree, it could not have been proven that there was the 'gross negligence' required for manslaughter. For gross negligence there has to be a 'serious and obvious risk'. That the *Herald* had sailed under its admittedly defective arrangements on so many previous occasions without mishap was held to show that the risk of an accident was not 'obvious'.

This outcome does not mean that the companies and these individuals were left unpunished. As well as paying costs and damages, the company suffered disastrous publicity. (The name 'Townsend Thoreson' was rapidly dropped and with it any inclusion of 'Free Enterprise' in ship's names – a penchant of the previous owners.) All the charged individuals left the company; as, eventually, did the entire board. What was evaded was punishment under criminal law. Thus, the case does vividly demonstrate the two difficulties dealt with in this chapter: those of (1) applying criminal charges to corporations and of (2) 'piercing the corporate veil' to hold specific individuals responsible for crimes. A suggestion made in the aftermath of the *Herald* case has been that the first problem could be eased by 'aggregating' the *mens rea* of all the individuals involved to reach a corporate *mens rea* sufficient to establish the guilt of companies for crimes. We have questioned the point of establishing such a corporate intention in this chapter. Better, we would suggest, to use this idea of an aggregate intention to apportion blame between the individuals concerned; punishing them to the extent they contributed to a collective responsibility for criminal misdeeds.

Sources: J Cook, *An Accident Waiting to Happen* (London: Unwin, 1989), Chapter 2. Issues of the *New Law Journal*; 25 September 1987; 16 October 1987; 26 October 1990; 3 May 1991.

DISCUSSION TOPICS

1. How useful do you find Friedman's agent/principal distinction for determining whether matters are ethically acceptable in business?
2. Which of the following views is most appropriate for the business executive, (a) in Friedman's view; (b) in yours?
    (i) 'business is business';
    (ii) 'maximize profits since shareholders expect the maximum return for their investments';
    (iii) 'if you act within the law you have fulfilled your ethical obligations';
    (iv) 'adhere to conventional standards of morality';
    (v) 'there should be no difference between your own personal ethical standards and those you adopt when doing business'.

Explain the reasons for your answer.

The work place: employment   **6**

EMPLOYMENT AND RIGHTS

In the previous chapter we considered the obligations of companies to various stakeholders. In this chapter we consider the rights of the employee and the corresponding obligations of the management.

Before we consider employee rights, it is necessary to recapitulate and develop some of the points about rights which emerged in chapter 3. In the course of outlining an 'ethic of rights' we distinguished between human rights and 'role specific' rights. It is now appropriate to introduce a third (and perfectly familiar) category of right, namely **legal rights**. Legal rights are importantly different from the previous two types of right, and relate to entitlements which are enshrined in the law of the land and which can – generally speaking – be readily determined by the relevant statute books and by decisions made in contemporary courts of law.

It is easy enough, at least in principle, to determine what legal rights a citizen or a business organization has; it is a matter largely of determining what statutes and case laws exist. Human rights, on the other hand, are perhaps somewhat more nebulous. These are rights which are held to exist irrespective of where we have been born, or of any legislation which has been enacted. If we state that we have a right of free speech, or a right not to be detained without being charged, we are (normally) speaking of things to which we are entitled, irrespective of legislation. If we live in a regime which restricts freedom of speech or which permits detention without trial, we could still claim that these were **moral** (although not legal) rights.

We stated that human rights generally imply corresponding obligations. If we have the right to health, then there are obligations on others to ensure that we remain as healthy as possible. To claim the moral right we do not need to specify precisely who these people or bodies are: we may mean that an employer has an obligation to ensure that the work place is as safe and unpolluted as possible; we may mean that our doctor has an obligation to give us a consultation when we ask; we may mean that a government ensures that there is an efficient health service. What does not make sense is for someone to claim to have such a right, but for no one to have any responsibility for ensuring that our right is acknowledged.

A further point must be made about rights at this juncture; for a right to exist, it must be a genuine live possibility. University lecturers cannot meaningfully claim a right to earn one million pounds per annum or more; it is not merely that such a claim would be untrue, but that it is difficult to understand what University lecturers would **mean** if they made such a claim. In the present economic climate it is simply not feasible to give them such large sums of money; hence if such aspirations of grandeur are expressed in the language of 'rights' such claims become meaningless. Of course, we may **want** to earn one million pounds per annum; wants can be unlimited, but rights must be within the bounds of possibility.

Further, a human right is something which is **universal**. The United Nations declaration on human rights declares that all men (and, one presumes, women too) are free and equal in rights. Clearly there are certain rights which one might wish to claim for all humanity: a right to the basics of food, shelter and clothing; a right to health; a right to safety and freedom of passage and so on.

Where a right does not appear to be universal, such as the oft-cited right of a senior executive to hold the key to the executive cloakroom, it is likely that we are speaking of a 'role-specific right' rather than a fundamental human right. Executives are entitled to that key (their right) by virtue of their position in the company. A right to a pay cheque of £1500 a month is again a role-specific right; it derives from belonging to a certain position (from having a certain role) within an institution, where some workers have a (role-specific) right to a larger pay cheque and others to a smaller one. Such role-specific rights, however, may incorporate basic human rights; for example, the role-specific rights of workers to their salaries should incorporate the presumed human right to a minimum wage. Equally, role-specific rights often have a quasi-legal status. Sometimes they may be matters of convention; when one of the authors started teaching, he was informed that he should not have a desk with drawers on both sides, since he was not yet of Senior Lecturer status. At other times they have quasi-legal status, for example, if it becomes part of a formal contract (for example, what a Senior Lecturer's salary will be).

When the United Nation's *Universal Declaration of Human Rights* (1948) was drafted, presumably its authors were not envisaging a totally egalitarian society when they declared that 'all human beings are born free and equal in dignity and rights.'[1] Herein lies the problem for those who wish to implement a fair, non-discriminatory policy within the work place; how does one reconcile the claim that everyone is an equal bearer

[1] *Universal Declaration of Human Rights*, Article 1.

of rights with the obvious distinctions which we make within the work place? Not everyone earns £1500 per month, not everyone has the key to the executive cloakroom, not everyone can give orders to other employees.

THE 'RIGHT TO WORK'?

Having undertaken this general account of what rights are, we are now in a position to consider more concrete issues of employee rights.

The *Universal Declaration of Human Rights* states that, 'Everyone has the right to work, to free choice of employment, to just and favourable conditions of work and to protection against unemployment.'[2]

The problem of implementing such a 'right to work' policy lies in the notion of the reciprocal duty which such a policy entails. Who would have the obligation of ensuring that everyone had a right to work? An obligation of such proportions could not be the responsibility of any individual employer, who would not be financially capable of offering work to all and sundry. Such a policy could only be implemented at a higher level – the level of government intervention. Without a very firm interventionist government policy it is difficult to see how a right to work could be assured.

The notion of the 'right to work' presumably entails something different from an assurance that a society or government undertakes to **find** work for any citizen. What a 'right to work' policy can at least entail is everyone's right to offer themselves for employment. A government who imposed an employment ban on married women, or who restricted the type of job for which (for example) Jews could apply, would be in violation of this Article. Similarly, in the USA the term 'right to work' is linked with a 'no closed shop' policy; trade unions must not place barriers to potential workers such as requiring them to belong to a union before they are entitled to earn.

EQUALITY OF OPPORTUNITY

The *Declaration* goes on to state that, 'Everyone, without any discrimination, has the right to equal pay for equal work.'[3] Differentials must be justified. This applies both to employment policy and to wage

[2] *Ibid*, Article 23, paragraph 1.
[3] *Ibid*, Article 23, paragraph 2.

differentials. If an appointing panel appoints A rather than B, one normally assumes that they have good reason for doing so. Sometimes these reasons might be hard to articulate, as anyone who has been on an appointing committee knows, but it does not make very good sense for a personnel manager to claim that A was appointed rather than B, although there were no differences between them. As a consequence of the Race Relations Act and the Sex Discrimination Act, personnel departments are obliged to have relevant reasons for refusing to appoint a black person or a woman, since explanations like 'because you were female' or 'because you were black' are normally just not relevant.

Although race and sex are now reckoned to be irrelevant factors in determining who has the right to work, there are other possible grounds of unfair discrimination which are now coming into the arena of public debate. At the time of writing it is still permissible to decline to appoint someone on the grounds of age, religion, class, political affiliation, disability or physical appearance. If it is accepted that the sole criterion for employing someone ought to be their ability to do a job, then it follows that one ought not to discriminate against applicants on the grounds, for example, that they are over 35, or that they are over-weight, or that they use a wheel-chair – unless of course these characteristics are directly relevant to the job itself. (Someone with a visual impairment would not be a suitable coastguard, and a wheel-chair user would probably not make a good steeplejack.) So far all this may sound very reasonable. However, in matters of ethics things are never quite as simple as may appear at first. Laudable though such ideals of equal opportunity may seem, they invariably meet with resistance in certain circles. It is important to recognize that, however much one may disagree with the stance taken by certain employers, their position is not necessarily the result of sheer prejudice, but that they can adduce serious reasons for their position.

One reason which is frequently put forward is that employers have rights as well as employees. Surely employers have the right to choose who works for them (this is part of a 'freedom of contract'), and if they do not feel that they can comfortably work beside homosexuals, National Front members, or black people, then they have the right to refuse them employment. After all, do not those who pay the piper call the tune? One important point about rights (which we noted in chapter 3) is that they can conflict, and when they do a choice based on relative importance has to be made.

This problem highlights the issue which was raised in chapter 3, namely the extent to which a presumed human right may set a limit on what may be achieved by way of optimizing human welfare. Is the welfare of minority groups of workers, some of whom find serious difficulties in obtaining employment, to be limited by this presumed right of employers to choose freely the staff who work for them? It may be replied, however, that not every presumed right is indeed a genuine human right, and indeed to endow employers with such a right would be to endow them with the right to be prejudiced and to discriminate. As has been pointed out (see chapter 4), there is not a right to liberty, only to specific liberties. One might also add that, if employers have problems about their feelings towards certain groups of workers, an alternative and preferable way of dealing with the problem would be to work on these feelings and endeavour to alter them. That way the welfare of employer and employee alike would be optimized, and also the most competent person to carry out the job would be appointed, thus ensuring the optimum benefit to the firm.

Another somewhat similar argument, which is sometimes used to justify a *laissez-faire* approach to employment policy, appeals to the reactions, not of employers themselves, but of fellow workers or customers. An employer might take the view that the work-force would not take kindly to receiving orders from a woman or from a black person, or that customers would be deterred if ·the receptionist had an unsightly birth mark.

This argument is difficult to assess. Its critics argue that the sort of prejudice to which it appeals (a white man's refusal to be line-managed by a black person or a woman) ought to be outlawed in the work place, and that one effective way of doing this is to enforce a policy where managers are appointed solely on the grounds of their ability. The traditionalist, on the other hand, can argue that those who are likely to experience difficulties in managing white male workers have a serious shortcoming, of which it is reasonable to take account when making the appointment. In response, one might argue that if white male workers became more accustomed to taking orders from non-white or non-male managers, women and minority groups would have less difficulty in securing a foothold on the management ladder.

'AFFIRMATIVE ACTION'

In order to achieve greater equality for disadvantaged workers, some philosophers and some employers advocate a policy of 'affirmative action'. Affirmative action involves the recognition that certain groups or individuals have been disadvantaged in the past, and seeks to implement deliberate measures by way of compensation. These may involve special schemes to assist disadvantaged groups; a company may, for example, launch a publicity drive to attract women, or send female employees on assertiveness courses. Alternatively it may involve policies of 'positive discrimination' (sometimes also referred to as 'reverse discrimination'). Positive discrimination may involve the setting of quotas for disadvantaged groups, or it may simply involve letting a potential or actual employee's gender, race or sexual orientation 'tip the scales' when an appointment or promotion cannot be decided solely on the grounds of merit. Since it is likely that a work-force will be under-represented by women, disabled people, and ethnic minorities, it can be argued that, if such measures are taken to give these and other similar groups a positive advantage, we are likely to achieve a more balanced work-force.

Affirmative action policies are at best controversial. Employers who discriminate actively in favour of (instead of against) certain groups, may be accused of perpetrating the very kind of discrimination to which they are supposedly opposed. If it is right that jobs should be offered on the grounds of merit alone, then surely it is just as reprehensible to appoint someone 'because she is a woman' as it is to do so 'because he is a man'. Further, it may be argued that affirmative action does not ultimately serve the cause of disadvantaged groups, who, if they are the objects of affirmative action, leave themselves open to the charge that they only obtained their jobs, not because they were the best candidates, but because they came from disadvantaged groups. It may even become apparent that they perform worse than those who would have been appointed by traditional methods, thus reinforcing the possible prejudice that women (or disabled people or ethnic minorities) are 'not as good'. Supporters of affirmative action will adduce several reasons in support of such a policy. For some it is a matter of retributive justice that men (or able-bodied people or white people) should reap the consequences for their historical unfair advantage which they have usurped over others; thus affirmative action is a kind of sanction imposed on those groups who have traditionally dominated the corridors of power. The argument from retributive justice, however, is suspect; the white able-bodied man who is seeking employment in an organization with discriminates positively in favour of female employees and minority groups is not necessarily someone who deserves 'punishment' for the unfairness of others. He may not necessarily have downgraded women or disadvantaged minorities, so why should he pay the penalty for the past actions of able-bodied white males? Someone can only justifiably be the recipient of a sanction if he or she had a hand in the relevant misdeed; the teacher who 'punishes' the whole class for the misbehaviour of a few is acting unjustly, since only a few deserve punishment.

More plausible defenses for affirmative action lie in arguments resting on distributive rather than retributive justice. For example, it could be argued that, since employers still discriminate against women (notwithstanding recent legislation), the prospects for women (and others) are unlikely to be as good as those for men. Positive discrimination by other employers therefore serves to ensure that the prospects for women are enhanced, thereby bringing them nearer to a situation of sexual equality. A case can also be made for affirmative action in those areas where women have still to find a niche, and where the problems lie in associating femininity with a particular occupation. For example, it is often noted that their are few female physics teachers; the relative absence of women, it is argued, reinforces attitudes of children and schools that physics is a 'male' subject. Measures which were designed somehow to attract more women into this domain could have the effect of working towards a greater balance of the sexes in this area, thus ensuring that future generations of women with appropriate capabilities did not exclude themselves from this field simply because of their sex.

If these arguments are deemed to justify affirmative action policies, it is worth noting that they justify such discrimination in order to achieve a specific goal, namely greater (or equal) female representation. Once that goal is achieved, there can no longer be arguments for continuing with such policies. As Janet Radcliff Richards points out in *The Sceptical Feminist*, affirmative action can therefore only be justified as a short term measure, for very specific purposes relating to the status of women.

Another way of attempting to avoid discrimination in the work place is to impose quotas on categories of worker. Rather than letting gender, race or disability 'tip the scales', firms can allocate pre-determined percentages of the total work force to certain categories of disadvantaged groups, and make appointments accordingly – or at least set targets to be reached within a certain period of time, as indeed some firms have in the Opportunity 2000 scheme.

Like many ideas for eliminating or reducing discrimination, quota schemes are not without their problems. They can bring about situations where appointments are made not on merit but on the basis of having to make up a quota, thus leaving the appointee from the disadvantaged sector open to the same criticisms as might be made of someone appointed as a result of an affirmative action policy. The quota can also discriminate against conventional applicants who do not fall into the protected categories, and also – perhaps more importantly – to those minority groups who are not subject to a quota. To cite one example, the recent policy of the Indian government to reserve quotas of places for 'scheduled castes' in certain categories of job and in the universities, has made life much more difficult for Indian minorities, such as the Jains and Parsees, who fall outside the caste system. Since their members do not belong to the 'scheduled castes', being non-Hindu, they now have to compete for a reduced number of jobs and Higher Education places, together with the 'non-scheduled caste' Hindus.

In a world free from prejudice and discrimination, of course, policies of affirmative action and imposing quotas would not be needed, since only relevant factors would be taken into account by employers. In the imperfect world of the work place, however, such policies may be needed as a stepping stone towards the elimination of the prejudice and the ensuring of greater equality for minority groups and women. But if equal status is ever achieved, then it would surely be desirable for these perhaps necessary but not ideal means of achieving non-discrimination to be removed.

THE FAIR WAGE

Once an applicant is appointed to a post, how does one determine what he or she should be paid? In somewhat similar style to the Roman Catholic doctrine of the Just Wage, the *UN Declaration* proposes 'Everyone who works has the right to just and favourable remuneration ensuring for himself and his family an existence worthy of human dignity, and supplemented, if necessary, by other means of social protection.'[4]

The most obvious form of differentiation amongst workers is in earnings. Of all the issues discussed by trade unions, wages feature the most prominently. Why is it that, say, the chairman of a large corporation can earn sums which run into six figures, while the person who cleans his (not usually her) office can earn as little as three pounds per hour?

One answer (which was considered in chapter 4) is that such issues are

---

[4] *Ibid*, Article 23, paragraph 3.

determined by economic forces. Good cleaners are easier to find than good company directors, hence the price mechanism, which operates through the laws of supply and demand, dictates that they are priced much lower. The recent Conservative governments have consistently put forward the view that high wage earners need incentives, otherwise they are likely to become part of the 'brain drain', offering their services to countries which provide higher salaries. With this fear in mind, the Conservative Government of 1979 drastically reduced the rate of tax for top earners from 85% to 60%, and further reduced it to 40%, thus ensuring that company executives and the like received greater remuneration in real terms for their labour.

Similarly it might be argued that where jobs have features which seem to merit compensation (such as dirty, unpleasant or dangerous work, work with particularly long or unsocial hours, or jobs which carry high responsibility), there is an economic argument for offering enhanced pay. Other things being equal, the potential supply of workers for jobs will be lower, and therefore some incentive must be provided in order to attract personnel into such areas. The most obvious inducement which can be offered is enhanced pay.

Whether market forces alone ought to determine one's level of pay has been seriously debated. S. I. Benn and R. S. Peters, in their *Social Principles and the Democratic State* point out, trade unions are obliged to make out a case for wage claims when they are engaged in collective bargaining, and they do not normally consider it sufficient or appropriate to state that members are in shorter supply or that demand for their services is increasing. One can also point to situations where pay is set by the levels of supply and demand but yet seems inappropriately low for the efforts of the work force; for example, South African mine workers have been paid very low wages (about two pounds per day in the 1970s), but the majority of citizens in Great Britain remained unconvinced by their employers' justification, namely that the workers kept returning, hence the pay must have been set an appropriate level (in other words, the laws of supply and demand were operating effectively).

If it is the case that there are moral criteria which ought to determine wage differentials, what are these criteria? A number have been suggested. One such criterion is **parity**. We have already expressed the principle that differences between individuals require justification, hence it is a reasonable principle that employees should receive equal pay for work of 'equal value'. It is now commonly accepted that it is unjustifiable for an organization to offer different rates for male and female workers, although this was once common practice in the United Kingdom. What counts as equally valuable work, however, is open to debate. As the law currently stands, any worker (male or female) can bring a law suit against an employer on the grounds of discrimination, claiming parity with any other worker whatsoever in the firm, claiming that he or she does work of 'equal value'. The plaintiff may cite any other worker or job whatsoever, although clearly if there are obvious points of comparison, the action will stand a much higher chance of being successful. In 1988 a female cook successfully claimed parity with three male employees who worked respectively as a painter, a joiner and an insulation engineer.[5]

Where wage claims are pursued, claiming parity between workers in one firm and workers in another, or between workers in one country and workers in another, the situation is more difficult. Here economics undoubtedly plays a role as well as ethics: a firm or a country may simply be unable to pay someone the same as another firm or country; as we have argued, a right must be something which is possible to grant.

Other criteria which are frequently mentioned in the context of the fair wage are skill, qualifications and experience. Students in full-time education sacrifice wages for several years in order to improve their qualifications, and it seems just that they should be paid at enhanced rates after graduation in order to compensate for their financially unproductive period.

Responsibility is also held to warrant compensation in the work place. Again, it seems a matter of justice that those whose performance can have serious repercussions should not receive the same rewards as those whose occupations are carefree. For example, a doctor can cause the loss of a life; a solicitor can lose a client's money or reputation; a careless safety officer can potentially cause greater damage than a negligent clerk. Where negligence may result in one's having to compensate a victim, it seems right that the worker in question should financially be in a position to do this.

One further type of criteria is the **traditional relativities**. Status maintenance was very much a criterion of the just wage in Roman Catholic teaching on the subject. Certain types of work attract greater expectations than others in terms of the associated standards of living; a High Court judge, for example, expects to earn more than a bricklayer, and a company director more than a cleaner. It has sometimes been argued

---

[5] *New Law Journal*, May 13, 1988.

that status maintenance is important in ensuring that certain professions continue to be treated with the respect which their status entails; it can be argued, the Royal Family could not entertain foreign dignitaries if they lived in a semi-detached bungalow in suburbia, a judge might not be accorded the same respect if the public were to see him washing the dishes behind the kitchen window.

Where the 'status maintenance' argument entails that someone needs the appropriate conditions in which to work, it is difficult to quarrel with it. It has always been an accepted criterion of the just wage that the worker must earn enough to meet his or her occupational needs. Where the 'status maintenance' argument is simply designed to reinforce the status quo, the argument is more dubious. Certainly, there is a case for ensuring that workers' expectations are realized in the short term; abrupt changes in living standards can create obvious problems. However, whether the abolition of such differentials is desirable in the longer term is a different matter. We have argued the case for having some differentials in pay, but how wide such differentials should be is a matter of assessing the moral case for compensatory criteria, as well as determine the level of supply and demand for top paid occupations.

TRADE UNIONS

Finally, Article 23 states that 'Everyone has the right to form and to join trade unions for the protection of his interests.'[6] This right stems from the 'right of peaceful assembly and association'.[7]

The *Declaration* further states that 'No one may be compelled to belong to an association.'[8] At first appearance this may seem to exclude the policy of the 'closed shop' which is practised in certain professions. However, supporters of a closed shop policy have argued that a worker in such a profession has the choice to remain in the post or to leave; unless there is enforced labour, there is no such thing as enforced union membership. (One might compare this situation with that of belonging to an authoritative religious group; if one feels constrained by the practices of, say, Roman Catholicism, one has the option of leaving its ranks.) Further, it can be argued that all members of a trade or profession gain the benefits of collective bargaining, not simply those

---

[6] *Declaration*, Article 23, paragraph 4.
[7] *Ibid*, Article 20, paragraph 1.
[8] *Ibid*, Article 20, paragraph 2.

who belong to the union; hence it can be seen as unfair that those who do not pay subscriptions should receive equal benefits to those who do.

Those who support opting out will appeal to individual freedom. Surely workers have the right to determine who shall represent their interests, or indeed whether they will forgo representation. The strength of a union, it can be contended, should depend on whether workers are prepared to vote with their feet – or rather with their subscriptions. Those who support a closed shop will appeal to principles such as justice or fairness, no doubt claiming that those employers who wish to abolish closed shop policies are guilty of 'union busting' and of attempting to place workers simply at the mercy of amoral market forces.

EMPLOYER RIGHTS AND EMPLOYEE LOYALTIES

We have mentioned several rights of employees in the workplace. However, do not employers have rights too? The fact that most workers have a contract of employment and many a definite job description indicates that employees have legal and contractual obligations, and hence that there are corresponding rights on the part of employers that these be carried out. Normally this causes few ethical problems. But what happens when there is a conflict between the contractual obligations of a worker and his or her moral conscience? Conflicts of this kind are not infrequent in the field of medical ethics, where a nurse may be asked to assist with abortions, when the killing of a foetus runs counter to his or her moral beliefs. A situation of this kind is normally fairly easily resolved; usually the nurse will be given other duties, and, since there are plenty of nurses who do not feel uncomfortable with assisting, both the patient's right to choose and the nurse's presumed right to act in accordance with conscience are observed. In reality such actions of opting out on the part of such nurses and doctors do not normally make any material difference to the outcome; their choice not to comply is therefore presumably made on grounds of principle rather than consequences, although it is possible that anti-abortionist nurses might take the view that if everyone acted like them then there would be a significant difference in the outcome – and a difference for the better, in their opinion.

A more thorough-going consequentialist might take the view that one should fulfil one's contractual obligations, since, if an employee were to refuse, another colleague would comply. One of the authors used to know a sign writer who was a staunch evangelical Christian, and who strongly disapproved of football pools. One of his tasks was to paint advertisements for pools companies on double-decker buses – a task which he did without hesitation, arguing that if he refused several of his colleagues would take the task over, and so the result would be exactly the same. Was it fair, he reasoned, to leave tasks to one's colleagues which he was not prepared to do himself?

It is possible to entertain this kind of dilemma when contemplating the non-performance of an act. But the situation is different where a worker is contemplating a positive action which, once done, cannot be undone by one's peers. One particular type of action which falls into this category, and which has aroused much discussion of late, is the phenomenon of 'whistle blowing' – the activity of 'going public' with pieces of information which are normally regarded as confidential within the firm, but the disclosure of which is deemed to be in the best public interest.

The whistle blower is faced with a very difficult moral decision. If, say, the issue is one of public safety (for example, from fall-out from a nuclear reactor), there seem compelling consequentialist reasons why it is justifiable for a worker to break confidentiality. But either this must be done without the employer discovering the source of the 'leak', or the whistle blower can expect to pay very heavy penalties. Almost certainly, he or she will be dismissed (with obvious harmful consequences to spouses and families), or even worse. Sarah Tisdall, the Foreign Office clerk who leaked a memo to the *Guardian* about the arrival of Cruise Missiles in Britain, was sentenced to a six month prison sentence.

It is possible to adopt a strictly deontological approach to the issue of whistle blowing. An employee might take the view that moral principles such as loyalty were paramount, and took precedence over other prima facie principles which arguably operate regarding such issues, such as public benefit, or the public's presumed 'right to know'. Additionally, an employee might argue that it is the responsibility of management rather than the work-force to take decisions about what should or should not be disclosed. After all, the management are paid more than the employees precisely because they must assume the responsibility for safety and security and for deciding what information should be accessible to the public. If there are legal repercussions it is they and not the potential whistle blower who will be the object of any legal proceedings. In short, the shop floor employee might argue, 'Am I my brother's keeper? Why should I assume other responsibility on behalf of those who are paid to make crucial decisions?' The deontologist, however, need not necessarily be committed to deciding against whistle blowing. Deontologists may emphasize differing moral principles. The imaginary employee of the previous paragraph stressed company loyalty, but, equally, an employee who is contemplating blowing the whistle could appeal to a possible obligation to speak out against wrong. Loyalty, he or she might agree, is important enough, but there are limits to loyalty, and if being loyal involves acquiescing to unethical behaviour on the part of management, then one's duty to speak out takes precedence. Whether or not to blow the whistle, then, would depend on how a deontologist prioritized the moral principles which apply in a situation where 'going public' is a serious issue.

If the deontologist does not have a clear unequivocal answer to the question of whistle blowing, neither does the consequentialist. According to the consequentialist, it is not a matter of a priori principles, but rather what consequences whistle blowing will achieve. Consequentialist justifications would probably rule out whistle blowing which was simply aimed at seeking revenge on one's employers, 'leaking' information for personal gain (for example, from payment by a newspaper editor), or to further the aims of a competing firm who offered a bribe. For the consequentialist too, whistle blowing is very likely to be a last resort, since 'going public' inevitably has its undesirable effects which are best avoided if at all possible. Finally, a consequentialist justification would only support whistle blowing which was likely to succeed in its aims; if the whistle blower finds that the company continues to use unsafe practice after the whistle is blown, then the bad consequences are likely to outweigh the good; the whistle blower is worse off, and the company no better as a consequence. One piece of advice is often given to employees who contemplate whistle blowing; seek the support of one's union first. This may not be a particularly philosophical or even ethical observation, but it is a counsel of prudence which should be well heeded in view of the risks which the whistle blower runs.

INTRODUCING THE READINGS

Michael Fogarty's classic book *The Just Wage* gives a detailed analysis of the criteria which have been applied to determine when a wage may be considered to be 'just'; we have selected a passage where the author has expounded scholastic theories of the just wage, and attempts to show how market forces can combine with ethical criteria. David Ewing and Donald Martin debate the wider question of employee rights; Ewing supports the idea of a 'bill of rights' for employees, while Martin is unconvinced. Richard T. De George, building on the Universal Declaration of Human Rights' statements about the right to work, raises the question of whether the concept of the right to work is compatible with the significant unemployment rate which is accepted in the USA. The final two readings bring us back to the UK. Most writings about women in industry tend to support the struggle of the career-minded women in have access to the top managerial positions which have been traditionally reserved for men, and it is unusual to find an article such as J. R. Lucas, *Because You Are a Woman*, which actually argues that it can reasonable to treat a woman differently from a man on the grounds of gender. Lucas's article may well set readers' teeth on edge, but feminists should be aware of the arguments used by their opponents, if only to rebut them. (Some readers may also take exception to terms such as 'negroes' and 'Mahometans'; we chose not to edit out such references, in the interests of enabling Lucas's position to be clearly seen.) Janet Radcliff Richards is a complete contrast to Lucas, and offers some very forceful arguments to suggest that gender is quite irrelevant in appointing staff. Richards also considers the question of affirmative action, which we discussed above. It should be noted that, in place of this term, the author uses as synonyms 'positive discrimination' and 'reverse discrimination'.

The just wage

MICHAEL FOGARTY

The feeling remains that in matters of wages one should not try to be too clever. It is better to avoid forms of payment where error is particularly easy or where even a correct decision may cause scandal and confusion among those who do not know all the circumstances. The truck system, say Antonino, *can* be operated in a way fair to workers; but it is a 'discreditable' method of payment. Even a technique such as the payment of wages by cheque gives rise to some doubt.[1] 'Hidden compensation' *can* be licit if a wage is clearly unfair; but the conditions under which a worker can properly regard his wage as so unfair as to justify what would otherwise be theft from his employer came by the seventeenth century to be tightened up to the point of almost ruling such transactions out.[2] Perquisites, though often permissible, ought to be scrutinised rather closely.[3] Most of these are cases where transactions carry an atmosphere of fiddling or chiselling and so of dishonesty. But it would seem reasonable to read out of them, together with some supporting evidence from other fields, a general conviction that clarity is better than casuistry even if it means no more than rough justice.

To achieve the maximum of clarity and of mutual consistency between rates – a rate structure that corresponds to the common good – the scholastics call for the use of problem-solving techniques of all types, whether competitive, consultative, or based on direction. Their discussions have focused around four points.

First, they have a deep distrust of purely individual judgment: 'for by common consent we should always assume that an individual is more likely to judge badly and be deceived when calculating a Just Price than all the people together.'[4] Wage-fixing must be in the fullest sense a social process, drawing on all sources of information and points of view.

Secondly, therefore, the final court of appeal over wages or prices is the 'common estimate', the general opinion formed out of discussion and consultation between those who, in the phrase quoted earlier, 'can communicate with one another in the same place, district, or town.'[5] If the general run of people in a given market are not well enough informed, for instance about a new product, appeal may be made to the judgment of experts. The common estimate can over-ride even a legally fixed price if this is not 'reasonable and equitable', or is inspired by 'bribery, ill-will towards sellers, or crass ignorance',[6] 'for a law is not binding in conscience, 'except perhaps in order to avoid scandal or disturbance', if it is imposed inequitably or with a view to other than the common good.[7]

Thirdly, the common estimate should rest immediately on the innumerable detailed adjustments of a free labour market, for the foundations of mutual consistency are most likely to be laid by free mutual adjustment. The older scholastics considered certain cases where the freedom of movement of employees is restricted: in extreme cases by slavery, or sometimes by long hirings and penalties against breach of contract.[8] But the scholastics' working assumption is normally that employees will be free to seek and employers to offer the jobs that suit them best, and that this detailed competitive process of adjustment will be the immediate means of bringing the Just Wage to light. Their ordinary working test for a fair wage is, as has been said, that at that wage employees should be freely and willingly available and the labour market should just be cleared. Messner says simply that:

> 'The correctly functioning price mechanism much more easily and precisely works out the wage . . . than could be done by an army of statisticians.'[9]

Fourthly, however, the operative word is the 'correct' functioning of the price mechanism. If the price mechanism is to function correctly it needs regulation. Some scholastics have gone further than others in their belief that the directed economy is best. So, notably, Langenstein:

> 'Away, then, with the excuses of bad magistrates who, whether for bribes or because they are fools, allow prices to rise and fall according to the whim or greed of buyers and sellers. . . . These iniquities [monopolistic practices] should be exterminated with the most severe punishments, because they damn sellers with mortal sin, cause loss to buyers, and make guilty men of the magistrates through whose negligence these iniquities flourish.'

Governments, he says, should use statistics of the population and its class distribution, and of family budgets, to estimate required levels of consumption. Trial balances should then be struck between requirements and prospective supplies, home or imported, of each class of goods. If discrepancies show themselves, possible remedies include the forced sale of excess stocks, purchasing missions to possible sources of supply, export controls, reduction of import controls, forced labour for the idle, and deportation for the incorrigibly work-shy. Price controls should be general.[10]

Others have been less enthusiastic for the directed economy. But not even in their moments of strongest reaction against direction have the scholastics given its principle up. De Lugo, in the seventeenth century, perceives clearly all the deficiencies of a controlled market. But he still insists that price control, in particular, is 'most necessary' where there are few sellers, or to stabilise the prices of daily necessities whose purchase cannot be put off, or to avoid disputes or fraud on simple-minded or occasional buyers. He approves particularly warmly the practice of fixing hotel prices and requiring hotel-keepers to post these prices up.[11] So also in the twentieth century Messner, having made his declaration in favour of competition and the price mechanism, insists that social controls must be used to make this mechanism work properly. Controls are not to replace the free labour market: they are to provide the framework within which it can operate so as to allow a fair 'common estimate' to emerge. Nor are controllers authorised to supersede the wages or other conditions that the common estimate agrees to be fair; their business is to secure what is objectively right, not what they choose to declare to be so. But their work does constitute, in the scholastics' view, an essential link between the processes of consultation, by which it is finally agreed what the 'commonly estimated' rate is, and of competition in the free labour market, by which the conditions underlying this estimate are clarified and, very often, the commonly agreed rate is enforced. Consultation, in the last resort, decides wages policy: competition clarifies and, in detail, enforces it: but controls are also needed to stabilize, consolidate, accelerate, and at times supplement or correct both.

To stabilise or consolidate wages or prices is not, of course, at all the same thing as to freeze them. The scholastics do not object to change in the economy: far from it. But they insist that it shall move in a stable path along its trend, and that day to day or cyclical fluctuations, as well as possible deviations – what might be called 'vicious spirals' – shall be prevented by controls. So for instance in Antonino's conception it is for the market to set the rate for the lawyer's fee: but, given the fair market rate, it is right to prevent the less long-sighted members of the profession from under-cutting it. Modern writers say the same of the right of trade unions to maintain a reserve price for labour.[12] To stick to standard rates, so long as they represent the full value of each class of labour, is to the advantage of the individual, who needs a steady living: of the community, since the efficient organisation of production is encouraged when employers are forbidden to make a profit by paying labour less than its full value: and of those who have to solve the problems of a changing economy, since where rates are steady there is time to form a considered opinion on them.

NOTES

1. Antonino 2.1.17.7–8.
2. Cf. De Lugo 1.16.4.2: Lessius 2.24.4: and sources (e.g. Innocent XI, or Viva (17th–18th century) quoted by Rocha, 169.
3. Antonino 3.8.4.4.
4. Reginaldus (17th century), quoted in Rocha, 142.
5. Langenstein 1.5.
6. Molina 364: Lessius 2.21.2.
7. Aquinas, *Summa Theologica*.
8. E.g. Molina, 505, De Lugo 2.29.3, and material quoted by Rocha, p. 148–9.
9. Messner 764.
10. Langenstein 1.7 and 10–12.
11. De Lugo 2.26.4.
12. So for instance Lehmkuhl condemns (1.714) firms which force others into wage-cutting: or see Cronin.

An employee bill of rights

DAVID EWING

For nearly two centuries Americans have enjoyed freedom of press, speech, and assembly, due process of law, privacy, freedom of conscience, and other important rights – in their homes, churches, political forums, and social and cultural life. But Americans have not enjoyed these civil liberties in most companies, government agencies, and other organizations where they work. Once a U.S. citizen steps through the plant or office door at 9 *a.m.*, he or she is nearly rightless until 5 *p.m.*, Monday through Friday. The employee continues to have political freedoms, of course, but these are not the significant ones now. While at work, the important relationships are with bosses, associates, and subordinates. Inequalities in dealing with these people are what really count for an employee.

To this generalization there are important exceptions. In some organizations, generous managements have seen fit to assure free speech, privacy, due process, and other concerns as privileges. But there is no guarantee the privileges will survive the next change of chief executive. As former Attorney General Ramsey Clark once said in a speech, 'A right is not what someone gives you; it's what no one can take from you.' Defined in this manner, rights are rare in business and public organizations.

In effect, U.S. society is a paradox. The Constitution and Bill of Rights light up the sky over political campaigners, legislators, civic leaders, families, church people, and artists. But not so over employees. The employee sector of our civil liberties universe is more like a black hole, with rights so compacted, so imploded by the gravitational forces of legal tradition, that, like the giant black stars in the physical universe, light can scarcely escape.

Perhaps the most ironic thing is that only in recent years have Americans made many noises about this paradox. It is as if we took it for granted and assumed there was no alternative. 'Organizations have always been this way and always have to be,' we seem to say. One is reminded of an observation attributed to Marshall McLuhan: 'Anybody's total surround, or environment, creates a condition of nonperception.'

To put the situation in focus, let us make a brief review of rights in the workplace.

SPEECH

In many private and public organizations there is a well-oiled machinery for providing relief to an employee who is discharged because of his or her race, religion, or sex. But we have no mechanisms for granting similar relief to an employee who is discharged for exercising the right of free speech. The law states that all employers 'may dismiss their employees at will . . . for good cause, for no cause, or even for cause morally wrong, without being thereby guilty of legal wrong.'[1]

Of course, discharge is only the extreme weapon; many steps short of discharge may work well enough – loss of a raise in pay, demotion, assignment to the boondocks, or perhaps simply a cutback of normal and expected benefits.

Consider the case of a thirty-five-year-old business executive whom I shall call 'Mike Z.'. He was a respected research manager in a large company. He believed that his company was making only superficial efforts to comply with newly enacted pollution laws. In a management meeting and later in social groups he spoke critically of top management's attitude. Soon strange things began to happen to him, different only in degree from what happens to a political dissenter in the Soviet Union. First, his place in the company parking lot was canceled. Then his name was 'accidentally' removed from the office building directory inside the main entrance. Soon routine requests he made to attend professional meetings began to get snarled up in red tape or were 'lost.' Next he found himself harassed by directives to rewrite routine reports. Then his budget for clerical service was cut, followed by a drastic slash in his research budget. When he tried to protest this treatment, he met a wall of top management silence. Rather than see his staff suffer further for his dissidence, he quit his job and moved his family to another city.

Mike Z. could be almost anyone in thousands of companies, government agencies, and other organizations. It should not be surprising, therefore, that when it comes to speaking out on issues of company policy or management practice, employees make about as much noise as fish swimming.

So well-established is the idea that any criticism of the company is 'ratting' or 'finking' that some companies hang out written prohibitions for all to see. For instance, a private bus company on the West Coast puts employees on notice with this rule:

> The company requires its employees to be loyal. It will not tolerate words or acts of hostility to the company, its officers, agents, or employees, its services, equipment or its condition, or . . . criticisms of the company to others than . . . superior officers.

CONSCIENTIOUS OBJECTION

There is very little protection in industry for employees who object to carrying out immoral, unethical, or illegal orders from their superiors. If the employee doesn't like what he or she is asked to do, the remedy is to pack up and leave. This remedy seems to presuppose an ideal economy, where there is another company down the street with openings for jobs just like the one the employee left. But what about the real world? Here resignation may mean having to uproot one's family and move to a strange city in another state. Or it may mean, for an employee in the semifinals of a career, or for an employee with a specialized competence, not being able to find another suitable job anywhere.

In 1970 Shirley Zinman served as a secretary in a Philadelphia employment agency called LIB Services. One day she was instructed by her bosses to record all telephone conversations she might have with prospective clients. This was to be done for 'training purposes,' she was told, although the callers were not to be told that their words were being taped. The office manager would monitor the conversations on an extension in her office. Ms. Zinman refused to play along with this game, not only because it was unethical, in her view, but illegal as well – the telephone company's regulations forbade such unannounced telephone recordings.

So Ms. Zinman had to resign. She sought unemployment compensation. The state unemployment pay board refused her application. It reasoned that her resignation was not 'compelling and necessitous.' With the help of attorneys from the American Civil Liberties Union, she appealed her case to the Pennsylvania Commonwealth Court. In a ruling hailed by civil rights leaders, the court in 1973 reversed the pay board and held that Ms. Zinman was entitled to unemployment compensation because her objection to the unethical directive was indeed a 'compelling' reason to quit her job.[2]

What this interesting case leaves unsaid is as important as what it does say: Resignation continues to be the accepted response for the objecting employee. The Pennsylvania court took a bold step in favor of employee rights, for prior to this decision there was little reason to think that the Shirley Zinmans of industry could expect any help at all from the outside world. But within the organization itself, an employee is expected to sit at the feet of the boss's conscience.

SECURITY AND PRIVACY

When employees are in their homes, before and after working hours, they enjoy well-established rights to privacy and to protection from arbitrary search and seizure of their papers and possessions. But no such rights protect them in the average company, government agency, or other organization; their superiors need only the flimsiest pretext to search their lockers, desks, and files. The boss can rummage through an employee's letters, memoranda, and tapes looking for evidence that (let us say) he or she is about to 'rat' on the company. 'Ratting' might include reporting a violation of safety standards to the Occupational Safety and Health Administration (which is provided for by law), or telling Ralph Nader about a product defect, or giving the mayor's office requested information about a violation of energy-use regulations.

CHOICE OF OUTSIDE ACTIVITIES AND ASSOCIATIONS

In practice, most business employees enjoy no right to work after hours for the political, social, and community organizations of their choice. To be sure, in many companies an enlightened management will encourage as much diversity of choice in outside activities as employees can make. As noted earlier, however, this is an indulgence which can disappear any time, for most states do not mandate such rights, and even in those that do, the rights are poorly protected. An employee who gets fired for his or her choice of outside activities can expect no damages for his loss even if he or she wins a suit against the employer. The employee may only 'secure the slight satisfaction of seeing his employer suffer the statutory penalties.'[3]

Ironically, however, a company cannot discriminate against people whose politics it dislikes when it *hires* them.[4] It has to wait a few days before it can exercise its prerogatives.

DUE PROCESS

'Accidents will occur in the best-regulated families,' said Mr. Micawber in *David Copperfield*. Similarly, accidents of administration occur even in the best-managed companies, with neurotic, inept, or distracted supervisors inflicting needless harm on subordinates. Many a subordinate who goes to such a boss to protest would be well-advised to keep one foot in the stirrups, for he is likely to be shown to the open country for his efforts.

This generalization does not hold for civil service employees in the federal government, who can resort to a grievance process. Nor does it hold for unionized companies, which also have grievance procedures. But it holds for *most* other organizations. A few organizations voluntarily have established a mechanism to ensure due process.

The absence of a right to due process is especially painful because it is the second element of constitutionalism in organizations. As we shall think of it in this book, employee constitutionalism consists of a set of clearly defined rights, and a means of protecting employees from discharge, demotion, or other penalties imposed when they assert their rights.

Why bother about rightlessness is corporations, government agencies, and other organizations? They are much smaller than state and federal governments, are they not? Must an organization that 'rules' an employee only for forty or so hours per week be treated as a government?

For one answer, let us turn to the Founding Fathers. Of course, they did not know or conceive of the modern corporation and public agency, so we cannot read what their thoughts about all this might have been. Perhaps we can make a reasonable guess, however, by comparing some numbers.

If the original thirteen colonies were large and powerful enough to concern the Founding Fathers, it seems likely that those men, if here today, would want to extend their philosophy to other assemblages of equivalent size and magnitude. In the writings of James Madison, Thomas Jefferson, George Mason, Jonas Phillips, Richard Henry Lee, Elbridge Gerry, Luther Martin, and others, there is no inference that human rights were seen as a good thing only some of the time or for some places. Instead, the Fathers saw rights as a universal need.[5]

In 1776, and in 1789, when the Bill of Rights (first ten amendments to the Constitution) was passed by Congress and sent to the states for ratification, trading companies and government agencies were tiny organizations incapable of harboring bureaucracy. Indeed, to use Mr. Micawber's phrase, there was hardly room in them to swing a cat, much less create layer on layer of hierarchy and wall after wall of departmental structure.

Today all that has changed. Some of our corporate and public organizations have larger 'populations' than did the thirteen colonies. And a truly vast number of organizations have large enough 'populations' to rank as real powers in people's everyday lives. For instance:

- AT&T has more than 939 000 employees, nearly twice the size of the largest colony, Virginia, which had about 493 000 inhabitants in 1776.
- General Motors, with 681 000 employees, is nearly two and one-half times the size of the second largest colony, Pennsylvania, which had a population of about 284 000 people in 1776.
- Westinghouse, the thirteenth largest corporate employer today with 166 000 employees, is four times the size of the thirteenth largest colony, Delaware, which had a population of 41 400. Westinghouse's 'population' is also larger than that in 1776 of South Carolina, New Jersey, New Hampshire, Rhode Island, and Georgia.

In fact, 125 corporations have larger 'populations' than did Delaware, the smallest colony, in 1776. But can employee workforces legitimately be compared with state populations? Of course, there are important differences – the twenty-four-hours-per-day jurisdiction of the state as opposed to only eight hours per day for an employer, the fact that the state has courts and military forces while the employer does not, and others. Yet it is not an apples-and-oranges comparison. Decades ago, and long before corporations and public agencies achieved anything like their current size, political scientists were noting many important similarities between the governments of organizations and political governments. In 1908, for example, Arthur Bentley wrote:

> A corporation is government through and through . . . Certain technical methods which political government uses, as, for instance, hanging, are not used by corporations, generally speaking, but that is a detail.[6]

In numerous ways, sizable corporations, public agencies, and university administrations qualify as 'minigovernments.' They pay salaries and costs. They have medical plans. They provide for retirement income. They offer recreational facilities. They maintain cafeterias. They may assist an employee with housing, educational loans, personal training, and vacation plans. They schedule numerous social functions. They have 'laws,' conduct codes, and other rules. Many have mechanisms for resolving disputes. A few even keep chaplains on the payroll or maintain facilities for religious worship.

Accordingly, it seems foolish to dismiss minigovernments as possible subjects of rights, or to exclude employees from discussions of civil liberties. We have assumed that rights are not as important for employees as for political citizens. Our assumption is in error.

The bill of rights that follows is one person's proposal, a 'working paper' for discussion, not a platform worked out in committee.

1. *No organization or manager shall discharge, demote, or in other ways discriminate against any employee who criticizes, in speech or press, the ethics, legality, or social responsibility of management actions.*

   Comment: What this right does not say is as important as what it does say. Protection does not extend to employees who make nuisances of themselves or who balk, argue, or contest managerial decisions on normal operating and planning matters, such as the choice of inventory accounting method, whether to diversify the product line or concentrate it, whether to rotate workers on a certain job or specialize them, and so forth. 'Committing the truth,' as Ernest Fitzgerald called it, is protected only for speaking out on issues where we consider an average citizen's judgment to be as valid as an expert's – truth in advertising, public safety standards, questions of fair disclosure, ethical practices, and so forth.

2. *No employee shall be penalized for engaging in outside activities of his or her choice after working hours, whether political, economic, civic, or cultural, nor for buying products and services of his or her choice for personal use, nor for expressing or encouraging views contrary to top management's on political, economic, and social issues.*

   Comment: Many companies encourage employees to participate in outside activities, and some states have committed this right to legislation. Freedom of choice of products and services for personal use is also authorized in various state statutes as well as in arbitrators' decisions. The third part of the statement extends the protection of the First Amendment to the employee whose ideas about government, economic policy, religion, and society do not conform with the boss's.

   Note that this provision does not authorize an employee to come to work 'beat' in the morning because he or she has been moon-lighting. Participation in outside activities should enrich employees' lives, not debilitate them; if on-the-job performance suffers, the usual penalties may have to be paid.

3. *No organization or manager shall penalize an employee for refusing to carry out a directive that violates common norms of morality.*

   Comment: The purpose of this right is to afford job security to subordinates who cannot perform an action because they consider it unethical or illegal. It is important that the conscientious objector in such a case hold to a view that has some public acceptance. Fad moralities – messages from flying saucers, mores of occult religious sects, and so on – do not justify refusal to carry out an order. Nor in any case is the employee entitled to interfere with the boss's finding another person to do the job requested.

4. *No organization shall allow audio or visual recordings of an employee's conversations or actions to be made without his or her prior knowledge and consent. Nor may an organization require an employee or applicant to take personality tests, polygraph examinations, or other tests that constitute, in his opinion, an invasion of privacy.*

   Comment: This right is based on policies that some leading organizations have already put into practice. If an employee doesn't want his working life monitored, that is his privilege so long as he demonstrates (or, if an applicant, is willing to demonstrate) competence to do a job well.

5. *No employee's desk, files, or locker may be examined in his or her absence by anyone but a senior manager who has sound reason to believe that the files contain information needed for a management decision that must be made in the employee's absence.*

   Comment: The intent of this right is to grant people a privacy right as employees similar to that which they enjoy as political and social citizens under the 'searches and seizures' guarantee of the Bill of Rights (Fourth Amendment to the Constitution). Many leading organizations in business and government have respected the principle of this rule for some time.

6. *No employer organization may collect and keep on file information about an employee that is not relevant and necessary for efficient management. Every employee shall have the right to inspect his or her personnel file and challenge the accuracy, relevance, or necessity of data in it, except for personal evaluations and comments by other employees which could not reasonably be obtained if confidentiality were not promised. Access to an employee's file by outside individuals and organizations shall be limited to inquiries about the essential facts of employment.*

   Comment: This right is important if employees are to be masters of their employment track records instead of possible victims of them. It will help to eliminate surprises, secrets, and skeletons in the clerical closet.

7. *No manager may communicate to prospective employers of an employee who is about to be or has been discharged gratuitous opinions that might hamper the individual in obtaining a new position.*

   Comment: The intent of this right is to stop blacklisting. The courts have already given some support for it.

8. *An employee who is discharged, demoted, or transferred to a less desirable job is entitled to a written statement from management of its reasons for the penalty.*

   Comment: The aim of this provision is to encourage a manager to give the same reasons in a hearing, arbitration, or court trial that he or she gives the employee when the cutdown happens. The written statement need not be given unless requested; often it is so clear to all parties why an action is being taken that no document is necessary.

9. *Every employee who feels that he or she has been penalized for asserting any right described in this bill shall be entitled to a fair hearing before an impartial official, board, or arbitrator. The findings and conclusions of the hearing shall be delivered in writing to the employee and management.*

   Comment: This very important right is the organizational equivalent of due process of law as we know it in political and community life. Without due process in a company or agency, the rights in this bill would all have to be enforced by outside courts and tribunals, which is expensive for society as well as time-consuming for the employees who are required to appear as complainants and witnesses. The nature of a 'fair hearing' is purposely left undefined here so that different approaches can be tried, expanded, and adapted to changing needs and conditions.

Note that the findings of the investigating official or group are not binding on top management. This would put an unfair burden on an ombudsperson or 'expedited arbitrator,' if one of them is the investigator. Yet the employee is protected. If management rejects a finding of unfair treatment and then the employee goes to court, the investigator's statement will weigh against management in the trial. As a practical matter, therefore, employers will not want to buck the investigator-referee unless they fervently disagree with the findings.

Every sizable organization, whether in business, government, health, or another field, should have a bill of rights for employees. Only small organizations need not have such a statement – personal contact and oral communications meet the need for them. However, companies and agencies need not have identical bills of rights. Industry custom, culture, past history with employee unions and associations, and other considerations can be taken into account in the wording and emphasis given to different provisions.

NOTES

1. See Lawrence E. Blades, 'Employment at Will vs. Individual Fredom: On Limiting the Abusive Exercise of Employer Power,' *Columbia Law Review* 67 (1967):1405.
2. 8 Pa. Comm. Ct. Reports 649,304 A. 2nd 380 (1973). Also see *New York Times*, August 26, 1973.
3. Blades, 1412.
4. See 299 F. Supp. 1100, cited in *Employee Relations in Actions*, August 1971 (New York, N.Y., Man & Manager), pp. 1–2.
5. See, for example, Bernard Schwartz, *The Bill of Rights: A Documentary History*. Vol. 1 (Toronto and New York: Chelsea House Publishers in association with McGraw-Hill Book Company, 1971), pp. 435 ff.
6. Arthur Bentley, *The Process of Government*, cited in Arthur Selwyn Miller, *The Modern Corporate State* (Westport, Conn.: Greenwood Press, 1976), p. 188.

Is an employee bill of rights needed?

DONALD L. MARTIN

The perception of the corporation as an industrial form of government in which management plays the role of the governor and labor the role of the governed has been particularly popular since the end of World War II. 'Industrial democracy' has been the slogan of the labor movement in the industrial relations community. This analogy has recently given rise to demands for an 'Employee Bill of Rights.'[1] Such a bill would guarantee the worker the same *due process* that the Constitution guarantees the citizen. It would protect the worker from the arbitrary and inequitable exercise of managerial discretion.

WHERE THE INDUSTRIAL DEMOCRACY ANALOGY FALTERS

But, the industrial democracy analogy surely must be false. Two important considerations obviate it. First, a crucial distinction between government at any level and private economic organization, corporate or otherwise, is the right entrusted to government to exercise legitimate and reasonable force in its relations with its citizens. Second, the cost to a citizen of switching affiliation between governments is far greater than the cost to an employee of switching affiliations between firms. Since governments will surely violate public trust through their police powers, and since the costs to citizens of changing leaders or residences are relatively high, citizens will seek institutions to insulate themselves from the arbitrary and exploitative use of such powers by their elected and appointed representatives. These institutions include the first ten amendments to the United States Constitution (the Bill of Rights) and the Fourteenth Amendment (guaranteeing due process).

THE PROBLEM OF THE MONOPSONISTIC LABOR MARKET

Something close to an analogous use of exploitative power in the private sector occurs in the world of monopsonistic labor markets. In those labor markets, would-be employees have few, if any, alternative job opportunities, either because of an absence of immediate competitive employers or because of the presence of relatively high costs of moving to available job alternatives in other markets. With few or no job alternatives, workers are more likely to be the unwilling subjects of employer prejudice, oppression, and personal discretion than if labor market competition prevails.

Reading from *The Attack on Corporate America* (ed.) by M. Bruce Johnson. Copyright © 1978 University of Miami Press. Reprinted with permission.

No one would claim that the American economy is completely free of monopsony power. There is not a shred of evidence, on the other hand, that such power exists in the large American corporation of today. Indeed, there is impressive evidence to suggest that monopsony is not likely to be found in large, private corporations. Robert Bunting's examination of labor market concentration throughout the United States among large firms, for example, finds that employment concentration (measured by the fraction of total employees in a geographic area who are employed by the largest reporting firm in that area) is related inversely to labor market size, while firm size is correlated positively with labor market size.[2]

It is well known that monopsonistic powers reside in the collusive owners of professional sports teams, precisely because these powers are exempt from antitrust laws in the United States.[3] Professional sports firms, however, do not number among the large corporations at which 'Employee Bill of Rights' proposals are directed.

Interestingly, monopsonistic power in the labor market may be a significant factor at the local government level. Evidence of monopsony exists in such fields as public education, fire and police protection, and nursing.[4]

THE NATURE OF EMPLOYER-EMPLOYEE AGREEMENTS

The Constitution of the United States does not extend the Bill of Rights and the due process clause of the Fourteenth Amendment to the private sector unless agents of the latter are performing public functions [*Marsh v. State of Alabama*, 66 S. Ct. 276 (1946)]. Instead of interpreting this limitations as an oversight of the founding fathers, the preceding discussion suggests that the distinctive treatment accorded governments reflects the conscious belief that market processes, more than political processes, yield a degree of protection of their participants that is closer to levels that those participants actually desire. It also suggests that this inherent difference justifies the institutionalization of civil liberties in one form of activity (political) and not in the other form (market).

This interpretation is consistent with the repeated refusal of the United States Supreme Court to interfere with the rights of employers and employees (corporate or otherwise) to make mutually agreeable arrangements concerning the exercise of civil liberties (otherwise protected under the Constitution) on the job or in connection with job-related activities. (The obvious legislative exceptions to this generalization are the Wagner Act of 1935 and the Taft-Hartley Act of 1947. These acts proscribe the free speech rights of employers with regard to their possible influence over union elections on their own property, while allowing labor to use that same property for similar purposes.)

In the absence of monopsonistic power, the substantive content of an employer-employee relationship is the result of explicit and implicit bargaining that leaves both parties better off than they would be if they had not entered into the relationship. That both are better off follows because each is free to end the employment relationship at will – unless, of course, contractual relationships specify otherwise.

Americans have demonstrated at an impressive rate a willingness to leave current employment for better pecuniary and nonpecuniary alternatives. During nonrecessionary periods, employee resignations contribute significantly to turnover statistics. In an uncertain world, the workers who resign generate valuable information about all terms and conditions under which firms and would-be employees can reach agreement.

THE COSTS OF WORKPLACE CIVIL LIBERTIES

If information about each party to employment and information about potential and actual performance are costly, both firms *and* employees seek ways to economize. Indeed, the functions of a firm, from the viewpoint of employees, are to screen job applicants and to monitor on-the-job activities. A firm's final output is often a result of the joint efforts of workers rather than a result of the sum of the workers' separate efforts. This jointness of production makes individual effort difficult to measure, and on-the-job shirking becomes relatively inexpensive for any given employee. The reason is precisely that all employees must share the cost of one employee's 'goldbricking.' As a consequence, shirking, if done excessively, threatens the earning opportunities of other workers. Other white collar crimes, such as pilfering finished products or raw materials, have similar consequences.

To protect themselves from these threats, workers use the firm as a monitoring agent, implicitly authorizing it to direct work, manage tools, observe work practices and other on-the-job employee activities, and discipline transgressors. If employers function efficiently, the earnings of workers will be higher than if the monitoring function were not provided.[5]

Efficient *employer* activities, however, may appear to others, including some employees, to be flagrant violations of personal privacy from the perspective of the First, Fourth, Fifth, and Ninth Amendments to the Constitution. These employer activities, on the contrary, are the result of implied agreements between employers and employees, consummated by demand and supply forces in the labor market. The reduction in personal liberty that workers sustain in a firm has a smaller value for them, at the margin, than the increase in earning power that results. Thus, limitations on personal liberty in a firm, unlike such limitations in governments, are not manifestations of tyranny; they are, instead, the product of a mutually preferred arrangement.

It should not be surprising that higher-paying firms and firms entrusting more valuable decision-making responsibility to some employees would invest relatively more resources than would other firms in gathering potentially revealing information about the qualifications of prospective employees and about the actions of existing employees. Since the larger a firm is, by asset size or by employee number, the more likely it is to be a corporation, it should also not be surprising that corporations are among the firms that devote relatively large amounts of resources to gathering information of a personal nature about employees.

Prohibiting the gathering of such information by superimposing an 'Employee Bill of Rights' on the employment relationship has the effect of penalizing a specific group of employees. This group is composed of those persons who cannot otherwise compete successfully for positions of responsibility, trust, or loyalty because the high cost of information makes it unprofitable for them to distinguish themselves from other workers without desirable job characteristics. Thus, federal protection of the civil liberties of employees in the marketplace may actually harm those who wish to waive such rights as a less expensive way of competing.

Under an 'Employee Bill of Rights,' the process of searching for new employees and the process of managing existing employees are relatively more costly for an employer. This greater cost will be reflected not only in personnel policy but also in the cost of producing final outputs and in the prices consumers pay for them. An effect of an 'Employee Bill of Rights' would be limited dimensions on which employees may compete with each other. Although there are precedents for such limitations (for example, federal minimum wage laws), it is important to recognize that this kind of protection may have unintended effects on the welfare of large numbers of employees. The anticompetitive effects of institutionalizing due process and civil liberties have long been recognized by trade unions. These effects constitute an important reason for the interest unions have in formalizing the procedures employers use in hiring, firing, promoting, demoting, rewarding, and penalizing union employees. It is false to argue, nevertheless, that an absence of formal procedures and rules in nonunionized firms is evidence that workers are at the mercy of unfettered employers, or that workers are more likely to be exploited if they are located in corporations rather than in noncorporate forms of organization.

Even the most powerful corporations must go to an effectively competitive labor market for their personnel. Prospective employees see arbitrary and oppressive personnel policies as relatively unattractive working conditions requiring compensation of pecuniary and nonpecuniary differentials over and above what they would receive from alternative employments. Those workers who want more certainty in the exercise of civil liberties pay for that certainty by forgoing these compensating differentials. This reasoning suggests that the degree of desired democracy in the labor market is amenable to the same forces that determine wages and working conditions. There is neither evidence nor persuasive arguments that suggest that workers in large corporations somehow have been excluded from the process that determines the degree of democracy they want.

NOTES

1. Ralph Nader, Mark Green and Joel Seligman, *Taming the Giant Corporation*. (New York: Norton, 1976), pp. 180–197.
2. Robert L. Bunting, *Employer Concentration in Local Labor Markets*. (Chapel Hill: The University of North Carolina Press, 1962). And 'A Note on Large Firms and Labor Market Concentration,' *Journal of Political Economy* 74 (August 1966), pp. 403–406.

3. James S. Mofsky, *Blue Sky Restrictions on New Business Promotions.* (New York: Matthew Bender, 1971).
4. Eugene J. Devine, *An Analysis of Manpower Shortages in Local Government.* (New York: Praeger, 1970).
5. Armen A. Alchian and Harold Demsetz, 'Production, Information Costs, and Economic Organization,' *American Economic Review* 62 (December 1972), pp. 777–795.

The right to work: law and ideology

RICHARD T. DE GEORGE

Many people in the United States feel strongly about human rights. They champion human rights, criticize the violation of human rights abroad, and both support the U.S. Government's complaints about human rights violations in other countries and encourage a stronger policy on human rights than the Reagan administration has adopted. Yet listed in the Universal Declaration of Human Rights is the right to work – a right neither recognized nor respected in the United States, where unemployment is both accepted and expected. How are we to explain this apparent contradiction in attitudes, and what importance does it have for law?

I. THE HUMAN RIGHT TO WORK

The Universal Declaration of Human Rights, Article 23, states:

1. Everyone has the right to work, to free choice of employment, to just and favourable conditions of work and to protection against unemployment.
2. Everyone, without any discrimination, has the right to equal pay for equal work.
3. Everyone who works has the right to just and favourable remuneration ensuring for himself and his family an existence worthy of human dignity, and supplemented, if necessary, by other means of social protection.
4. Everyone has the right to form and to join trade unions for the protection of his interests.[1]

The right, as stated, requires both interpretation and defense. As every human right, it applies to all human beings simply by virtue of their being human. The right is appropriately implemented differently both in different societies and for people of different ages and circumstances. Infants as well as all other human beings have the

Reading taken from Richard T. De George, 'The Right to Work: Law and Ideology,' *Valparaiso University Law Review*, 19, Fall 1984, pp. 15–35. Reprinted by permission.

right to work; but being physically and mentally incapable of working, they do not actively exercise the right. Adults in primitive societies exercise the right differently from those in advanced industrial societies. . . .

The derivation that hinges on the right of all human beings to respect provides the most solid basis for the right to work. To be a human being is a matter not only of being of a certain biological type but also of belonging to human society. A full, able-bodied, competent member of society has a role and plays a role in it. Each has a right to do so. No adult is 'excess' or 'expendable' and the recognition of this fact is part and parcel of what it means for people to have the right to respect. Work is the typical way by which human adults assert their independence and are able to assume their full share of responsibility in a community. Work involves the assumption of one's place in the community, whether it is work in the home, the fields, the factory, or the office. One's self respect as well as the respect of others is closely linked with what one does, how a person expresses himself through his actions, and the extent to which one assumes the full burden of and responsibility for one's life and one's part in the social whole. A person who is not allowed to work, is not allowed to take a rightful place in society as a contributing, mature, responsible adult. The right to work is in this way closely related to the right to respect and derived from it for every society. It is for this reason that in many societies to deprive a person of a productive role in society is a form of ostracism, tantamount to punishment, and justifiable only for a serious social offense or crime.

The right to work can be interpreted as both a negative and as a positive right. As a negative right, no one, including the government, many legitimately prohibit someone who wishes to work from doing so, within the normal restrictions for negative rights, such as not infringing the similar, equal, or more important rights of others. As a positive right it requires at least that one's society provide one with the opportunity for full membership including the opportunity for participation in the productive activity of that society. . . .

II. IDEOLOGY AND LABOUR LEGISLATION

How are we to understand the failure of the United States to recognize the right to work? It becomes intelligible when we understand the ideology behind U.S. labour legislation. The ideology has two main aspects. The first is linked historically with the conception of free enterprise that has grown up in the United States and can be understood in terms of both social conditions and ideas. The second is related to how labour legislation develops in the United States and is linked to the adversarial relation of labour and management and the power conflict that results from this. Ideology helps prevent recognition of the right to work; but the portion of the ideology in question is a carry-over from an earlier age, no longer reflects reality, and should properly be replaced.

The aspects of the free enterprise ideology that prevents recognition of the right to work in the United States has its roots in the nation's history. At the time the Constitution was adopted the country was young and growing. The Bill of Rights did not include the right to work, for that right had not emerged as a matter of concern, either in its negative or in its positive sense, except in the case of slavery. Slavery was a different and separate issue. The right to life, liberty, and the pursuit of happiness were paramount, although behind the scenes the right to property was strongly upheld. The main fear was of government intrusion, and the rights to be secured were primarily against the government. The right to life was not interpreted as the right to work. A number of factors make this intelligible and make it acceptable.

The availability of the frontier was both a safety valve and an opportunity for people who wished to strike out on their own. The population was relatively small, and the opportunities many. It was not true, as would later be the case, that the only way for most people to live was to sell their labour to entrepreneurs for wages. Together with the land and opportunities available went three other ideological components, the roots of which can be traced to the conditions of the times.

The first of these was the doctrine of self-reliance. It was a trait that was cherished, and had to be cherished if one were to survive in a new land, especially on its frontiers. Self-reliance, of course, did not preclude helping one's neighbour. Yet each person was expected to stand on his own feet, work, and fend for himself.

Joined to this was the doctrine of competitive individualism. The ideology of incipient capitalism, which developed in the eighteenth and nineteenth centuries, incorporated the notion of competition. In the competitive battle each person was ego-centered. The best succeeded. The experience of the immigrants to a new land, joined with the experience of the frontier, complemented the capitalistic emphasis on the individual and the concomitant notion of competition. Individualism was ideologically joined with competition to become 'rugged individualism," according to which one competed and managed on one's own, whatever the outcome.

The third component comes from the 'Protestant work ethic.' This complemented the other two components and fostered the developing capitalist ideology. Industriousness was a virtue. Each person was expected to do his fair share. The belief was that those who worked hard prospered. Prosperity was an indication of the virtue of industry. The lazy reaped their own reward in the way of poverty and difficulty. Each person, it was believed, had the opportunity to succeed, and success depended on individual initiative.

This ideology had its basis in reality. There was, of course, unemployment. But the general belief was that opportunities were available for the industrious, those willing to take a chance, seek their own fortune, and if necessary tame the wilderness. The right to work did not emerge as an issue. It became an issue only when the labour supply exceeded demand; and only with the development of large industry, which carried with it the growth of a working force dependent on others for jobs. But the frontier had disappeared; there are no longer abundant opportunities for the self-reliant; and although industriousness is still deserving of reward, the equation of poverty with laziness is clearly not justified. . . .

If ideology stands in the way of recognizing the right to work, the history of the development of labour legislation, resulting from this ideology, hinders its implementation. . . . Labour legislation in the United States has developed largely out of the relations between management and labor, especially in the collective bargaining process. As a consequence, unless an issue is in the interest of either labour (as represented by the unions) or management such that it arises in collective bargaining, it usually fails for lack of an advocate. If, moreover, an issue is opposed by either labour or management outside the collective bargaining situation and without the full support of the other side, it has formidable opposition to overcome and slight chance of either getting a full hearing or of finding its way into legislation. The issue of the right to work is such an issue. It is opposed to the interest of management, does not arise in collective bargaining, and is given less importance by unions than issues that more directly affect their members.

The right to work, even if understood, at full employment, is clearly not in the interest of management. Unemployment guarantees the availability of people for at least some – usually lower level – jobs. It help keep wages down and helps enforce labour discipline, since fear of loss of one's job is a real threat. Given a choice, it is in management's interest to have a pool of unemployed from which to choose. Management would, therefore, not be anxious to have legislation that would guarantee full employment or recognize a right to work. If, however, full employment included people in training programs and people who were employed by the government only as an employer of last resort, there would in fact be a pool of people from which to draw when the need presented itself in times of expansion; and the presence of training programs might also guarantee a larger pool of qualified people than would otherwise be the case. . . .

In general, organized labour supports full employment legislation. But . . . United States unions have not been as vocal as one would expect in support of the right to work specifically as a human right. In practice individual unions have often been more concerned with benefits for their members than with the rights of unemployed workers. Some have even fought for benefits resulting in the laying off of some of their own members.[2] Moreover, although full employment with no unemployed would put unions in better bargaining position than otherwise guaranteed full employment would also undercut to some extent the need for the protection of jobs by unions.

A good deal of labour legislation has to do with the relation of labour and management, the rights of organized labour, and the workers represented by the union. Many of the unemployed are nonunion, unorganized, and unrepresented. Clearly the hard-core unemployed are of less concern to the unions than are union members, and in collective bargaining neither the unions nor management are concerned with the rights of the unemployed. While the history of labour legislation has been generated by collective bargaining and by the interests of the union on the one hand and management on the other, less than 30 percent of the American labour force belongs to a union, and the number of unionized workers has been diminishing for several years.

The history of labour legislation in the United States shows that negotiations between unions and management have not led to any serious consideration of the human right to work. Discussion of this right has not surfaced because in the context of collective bargaining this right is in the interest of neither organized labour nor management. While this fact makes the failure to notice this right understandable, it does not justify the absence of any legislation implementing the right of all to work and of those who desire it and are qualified. Consequently, the ideology underlying labour legislation should be brought out in the open and reevaluated. Similarly, the presuppositions of much of labour law jurisprudence that picture legislation as a means of arbitrating between contending factions – organized labour and management – should also be reexamined. This view is reinforced by the respective ideologies of both labour and management, who see themselves as opponents in an adversarial system. This opposition is fostered by collective bargaining. But since the right to work can sometimes be best implemented by collaboration rather than antagonism between management and labour, the ideology helps suppress implementation of the right to work.

The reexamination shows that the traditional ideology is partially defective. It is presupposed that organized labour and management are the only two contending parties. Since those who are outside of the organized labour force have no organized representative, their rights are systematically ignored and violated. The right to work is compatible with the best in the United States' tradition of free enterprise and of peaceful and productive labour relations. . . .

NOTES

1. I. Brownlie, *Basic Documents on Human Rights* 25 (2d ed. 1981).
2. The U.A.W., for instance, in 1982 insisted on higher wages for auto workers – twice the average for manufacturing workers – even as layoffs by auto manufacturers mounted.

'Because you are a woman'

JOHN R. LUCAS

The feminist debate turns on the application of certain concepts of justice, equality and humanity. Should the fact – 'the mere fact' – of a person's being a woman disqualify her from being a member of the Stock Exchange, the Bench of Bishops or the House of Lords, or from obtaining a mortgage, owning property, having a vote

Reading taken from *Philosophy*, vol. 48, no. 184, 1973, pp. 161–71. © 1973 Cambridge University Press. Reprinted by permission.

or going to heaven? Is it not, say the feminists, just as irrational and inequitable as disqualifying a man on the grounds of the colour of his hair? Is it not, counter the anti-feminists, just as rational as drawing a distinction between men on the one hand and children, animals, lunatics, Martians and computers on the other? Whereupon we come to enunciate the formal platitude that women are the same as men in some respects, different from them in others, just as men are the same in some respects as children, animals, lunatics, Martians and computers, and different in others. And then we have to embark on more substantial questions of the respects in which men and women are the same, and those in which they are different; and of whether any such differences could be relevant to the activity or institution in question, or could be comparable to the differences, generally acknowledged to exist, between *homo sapiens* and the rest of creation. Even if women are different from men, a feminist might argue, why should this be enough to debar them from the floor of the Stock Exchange, when, apparently, there is no objection to the presence of computers?

We are faced with two questions. We need to know first what exactly are the ways in which women differ from men, and this in turn raises issues of the methods whereby such questions may be answered. Only when these methodological issues have been discussed can we turn to the more substantial ones of morals and politics concerned with whether it can ever be right to treat a woman differently from a man on account of her sex, or whether that is a factor which must always be regarded as in itself irrelevant.

The facts of femininity are much in dispute. The development of genetic theory is some help, but not a decisive one. We know that men differ from women in having one Y-chromosome and only one X-chromosome whereas women have two X-chromosomes. Apart from the X- and Y-chromosomes, exactly the same sort of chromosomes turn up in men and women indifferently. The genetic make-up of each human being is constituted by his chromosomes, which occur in pairs, one of each pair coming from the father, the other from the mother. Men and Women share the same gene pool. So far as chromosomes, other than the X- and Y- ones, are concerned, men and women of the same breeding community are far more alike than members of different species, or even men of different races. This constitutes a powerful argument against the doctrine, attributed by some to the Mahometans, that women have no souls; contrary to the view of many young males, they are not just birds; or, in more modern parlance, it gives empirical suport to arguments based on the principle of Universal Humanity. Women are worthy of respect, for the same reasons as men are. If it is wrong to hurt a man, to harm him, humiliate him or frustrate him, then it is wrong to hurt, harm, humiliate or frustrate a woman; for she is of the same stock as he, and they share the same inheritance and have almost all their chromosome types in common.

Early genetic theory assumed a one-one correlation between pairs of hereditary genetic factors and their manifested effects in the individual. Whether I had brown eyes or blue eyes depended on whether I had the pair of factors BB, Bb or bB, in all of which cases I should have brown eyes, or whether I had bb, in which case I should have blue eyes. No other genetic factor was supposed to be relevant to the colour of my eyes, nor was the possession of a B or a b gene relevant to anything else about me. If this theory represented the whole truth, the feminist case would be simple. Sex is irrelevant to everything except sex. The fact of a man's being male or a woman's being female would be a 'mere fact' with no bearing on anything except sexual intercourse and the procreation of children. It would be rational to hold that only a male could be guilty of rape, and it might be permissible to have marriage laws which countenanced only heterosexual unions, and to look for proofs of paternity as well as of maternity. Perhaps we might go a very little further, and on the same grounds as we admit that negroes are not really eligible for the part of Iago, admit that males could not really expect to be employed as models for female fashions, and *vice versa*. Beyond these few and essentially unimportant exceptions, it would be as wrong for the law to discriminate between the sexes as it would be if it were to prefer blondes.

Simple genetic theory is, however, too simple. It needs to be complicated in two ways. First, although chromosomes occur in pairs, each single one being inherited more or less independently of every other one, each chromosome contains not just one, but many, many genetic factors, and these are not all independently inherited, and some, indeed, like the one responsible for haemophilia, are sex-linked. There are, so far as we know, relatively few effects – and those mostly bad – which are caused by factors contained in the Y-chromosome, and there is a slight *a priori* argument against many features being thus transmitted (because the Y-chromosome is much smaller than the others, and so, presumably, carries less genetic information): but there could well be more complicated effects due to a relatively rare recessive gene not being marked in the male as it probably would have been in the female. Mathematical talent might be like haemophilia or colour-blindness: it is consonant with what we know of genetic theory that only one in a thousand inherit the genetic factor, which if it is inherited by a boy then becomes manifest, but which if it is inherited by a girl, still in 999 cases out of a thousand is marked by a dominant unmathematicality. The second complication is more fundamental than the first. Genetic factors not only are not inherited independently of the others, but do not operate independently of the others. What is important is not simply whether I have BB, Bb, or bb, but whether I have one of these pairs in conjunction with some set of other pairs of factors. In particular, whether a person is male or female may affect whether or not some other hereditary factor manifests itself or not. Only men go bald. There are many physical features and physiological processes which are affected by whether a person is male or female. So far as our bodies are concerned, the fact of a person's being a man or a woman is not 'a mere fact' but a fundamental one. Although there are many similarities between men and women, the differences are pervasive, systematic and of great biological significance. Almost the first question a hospital needs to ask is 'M or F?'.

Many feminists are dualists, and while conceding certain bodily differences between men and women, deny that there is any inheritance of intellectual ability or traits of character at all. Genetic theory, as far as it goes, is against them. There is reasonable evidence for the inheritance of skills and patterns of behaviour in other animals, and in particular of those patterns of behaviour we should normally ascribe to the maternal instinct. Human beings are far too complicated to manifest many abilities or traits of character that are simple enough to be susceptible of scientific test; and although we often detect family resemblances in ways of walking and talking, as well as in temperament and emotion, it is not clear how far these are due to inherited factors and how far they have been acquired by imitation or learning. It is, however, a common experience to note resemblances between different members of the same family who have never seen each other and have had no opportunity of imitating one another. Such instances, when cited, are often dismissed as mere anecdotes, belonging to mythology rather than science, and unworthy of the attention of modern-minded thinkers in this day and age. It is difficult to stand one's ground in the face of the charge of being unscientific, for the word 'scientific' has strong evaluative overtones, and to be 'unscientific' smacks of quackery and prejudice. But it remains the case that all discussions about political and social issues must be 'unscientific' in that they are not exclusively based on the measurable results of repeatable experiments. For what we are concerned with is what people feel, decide, and ought to do about these things, and people are different, and feel differently and decide to do different things. If we refuse to admit to the argument any evidence other than the measurable results of reputable experiments, we may still be able to discuss questions of public health, but cannot even entertain those of justice or the political good. And if the feminist rejects all anecdotal evidence on principle, then she is making good her dualism by stipulation, because she is not prepared to recognize intellectual abilities or traits of character in the way in which they normally are recognized. This, of course, is not to urge that every story a boozy buffer cares to tell should be accepted as true or relevant; but only that the word 'scientific' needs to be handled with caution, and not used to rule out of court whole ranges of evidence and whole realms of experience. The canons of scientific evidence are, very properly, strictly drawn; and scientists accept the corollary that the topics amenable to scientific research are correspondingly limited. There are many discussions which cannot be evaluated within the canon of scientific argument upon the basis of scientific observations alone, among them discussions about what is right and good for individuals and societies. But they need not be any the worse for that, although they will be if the participants do not show the same fairness and reasonableness in their discussions as scientists do in their researches.

Another methodological issue is raised by those who acknowledge that there have been and are differences in the intellectual achievements and the typical behaviour of women as compared with men, but attribute all of them exclusively to the social pressures brought to bear upon women which have prevented them from exercising their talents to the full or giving rein to their natural inclinations. When the advocate of male supremacy marshals his masses of major poets against a solitary Sappho, the feminist explains that women have been so confined by domestic pressures and so inhibited by convention that those few with real poetic talent have never had opportunity to bring it to flower. Poets might be poor, but at least they could listen to the Muse undistracted by baby's cries: whereas potential poetesses, unless their lot were cast in Lesbos, were married off and made to think of clothes and nappies to the exclusion of all higher thoughts.

It is difficult to find hard evidence either for or against this thesis. In this it is like many rival explanations or interpretations in history or literature. What moves us to adopt one rather than another is that is seeems to us more explanatory or more illuminating than the alternative; and what seems to us more explanatory or illuminating depends largely on our own experience and understanding – and our own prejudices. But although we are very liable to be swayed by prejudice, it does not follow that we inevitably are, and although we are often guided by subjective considerations in deciding between various hypotheses, it does not follow that there is nothing, really, to choose between them. We can envisage evidence, even if we cannot obtain it, which would decide between the two alternatives. The feminist claim would be established if totally unisex societies sprang up and flourished; or if there were as many societies in which the rôles of men and women were reversed as there were traditional ones. Indeed, the existence of any successful and stable society in which the rôles of the sexes are reversed is evidence in favour of the claim. Evidence against is more difficult to come by. Few people deny that social pressures have a very considerable bearing on our behaviour and capacities. Some people argue from the analogy with other animals, whose behaviour is indubitably determined genetically and differs according to their sex; or argue, as I have done, by extrapolation from purely physical features. Both arguments are respectable, neither conclusive. Man is an animal, but very unlike other animals, particularly in respect of the extreme plasticity of human behaviour, nearly all of which is learned. Very few of our responses are purely instinctive; and it is unsafe to claim confidently that maternal feelings must be. What would constitute evidence against the feminist claim would be some intellectual ability or character trait which seemed to be both relatively independent of social circumstance and distributed unevenly between the sexes. Mathematical talent might be a case in point. It seems to be much more randomly distributed in the population than other forms of intellectual ability. If Ramanujan could triumph over his circumstances, then surely numerate sisters to Sappho should abound. But this is far from being a conclusive argument.

There are no conclusive arguments about feminine abilities and attitudes. But the discoveries of the scientists, so far as they go, lend some support to traditional views. It could well be the case that intellectual and psychological characteristics are, like physical ones, influenced by genetic factors. If this is so, the way in which a particular pair of genes in an individual genotype will be manifested in the phenotype will depend on the other genes in the genotype, and may depend greatly on whether there are two X chromosomes or one X and one Y. It could be that the masculine mind is typically more vigorous and combative, and the feminine mind typically more intuitive and responsive, with correspondingly different ranges of interests and inclinations. It would make evolutionary sense if it were, and would fit in with what else we know about the nature of man: but it is still possible to maintain the contrary view; and even if there are in fact differences between men and women, it does not follow that their treatment should be different too.

If it could be established that there were no innate intellectual or emotional differences between men and women, the feminists' case would be pretty well made; but it does not follow that to admit that there are differences carries with it an adequate justification for every sort of discrimination, and it is useful to consider what sort of bearing various types of difference might have. Suppose, for example, that mathematical ability were distributed unevenly and according to the same pattern as haemophilia, so that only one in n males have it and only one in n^2 females. This would be a highly relevant factor in framing our educational policy. It would justify the provision of far more opportunities for boys to study higher mathematics than for girls. But it would not justify the total exclusion of girls. Most girls prefer nursing to numeracy, but those few who would rather solve differential equations ought not to be prevented from doing so on the grounds that they are female. Two principles underlie this judgment. First that the connexion between sex and mathematical ability is purely contingent; and secondly that we are in a position in which considerations of the individual's interests and deserts are paramount. Even if there are very few female mathematicians, there is no reason why any particular woman should not be a mathematician. And if any particular woman is, then her being a woman is irrelevant to her actual performance in mathematics. Her being a woman created a presumption, a purely contingent although usually reliable presumption, that she was no good at mathematics. It is like presumptive evidence in a court of law, which could be rebutted, and in this case was, and having been rebutted is of no more relevance in this individual situation, which is all we are concerned with.

Female mathematicians are rare. Few disciplines are so pure as mathematics. In most human activities – even in most academic pursuits – the whole personality is much more involved, and the irrelevance of a person's sex far more dubious. Differences between the sexes are likely to come into play most in ordinary human relations where one person tells another what to do, or persuades, or cajoles or encourages or warns or threatens or acquiesces. In so far as most positions in society are concerned with social relations, it cannot be argued that the differences between the sexes are, of necessity, irrelevant. Although it might be the case that working men would as readily take orders from a fore-woman as a foreman or that customers would be as pleased to find a handsome boy receptionist as a pretty girl, there is no reason to suppose that it must be so. Moreover, life is not normally either an examination or a trial. It is one of the disadvantages of our meritocratic age that we too readily assume that all social transactions are exclusively concerned with the individual, who needs to be given every opportunity and whose rights must be zealously safeguarded. But examinations and trials are artificial and cumbersome exceptions to the general rule, in which no one individual is the centre of concern.

To deny people the fruits of their examination success or to deprive them of their liberty on any grounds irrelevant to their own desert is wrong: but it is not so evidently wrong to frustrate Miss Amazon's hopes of a military career in the Grenadier Guards on the grounds not that she would make a bad soldier but that she would be a disturbing influence in the mess room. Laws and institutions are characteristically two-faced. They set norms for the behaviour or different parties, and need to take into consideration the interests and claims of more than one person. They also need to apply generally, and cannot be tailor-made to each particular situation: they define rôles rather than fit actual personalities, and rôles need to fit the typical rather than the special case. Even if Miss Amazon is sure not to attract sidelong glances from the licentious soldiery, her sisters may not be; and it may be easier to operate an absolute bar than leave it to the recruiting officer to decide whether a particular woman is sufficiently unattractive to be safe. This type of case turns up in many other laws and public regulations. We lay down rigid speed limits because they are easier to apply. There are many towns in which to drive at 30 mph would be dangerous, and many suburbs in which to drive at 45 mph would sometimes be safe. Some boys of ten are better informed about public affairs than other voters of thirty. But the advantage of having a fixed speed limit or a fixed voting age outweighs its admitted unfairness.

We can now see what sort of facts would bring what sort of principles to bear upon our individual decisions and the general structure of our laws and institutions. We need to know not only whether there are differences, but whether these differences are integrally or only contingently connected with a person's sex, and whether they apply in all cases or only as a rule. The more integrally and the more invariably a difference is connected with a person's sex, the more we are entitled to insist that the mere fact of being male or female can constitute a conclusive reason against being allowed to do something. The less integral a difference is, the more the arguments from Formal Equality (or Universalizability) and from Justice will come into play, requiring us to base our decisions only on the features relevant to the case in hand. The less invariable a difference is, the more the arguments from Humanity and again from Justice will come into play, requiring us to pay respect to the interests and inclinations of each individual person, and to weigh her actual interests, as against those of the community at large, on the basis of her actual situation and actual and reasonable desires.

However much I, a male, want to be a mother, a wife or a girlfriend, I am disqualified from those rôles on account of my sex, and I cannot reasonably complain. Not only can I not complain if individuals refuse to regard me as suitable in those rôles, but I have to acknowledge that it is reasonable for society generally to do so, and for the state to legislate accordingly. The state is justified in not countenancing homosexual 'marriages', because of our general understanding of what marriage really is, and the importance we attach to family life. For exactly the same reasons, women are debarred from being regarded in a fatherly or husbandly light; and hence also in those parts of the Christian Church that regard priests as being essentially fathers in God from being clergymen or bishops. How far rôles should be regarded as being integrally dependent on sex is a matter of dispute. In very intimate and personal relationships it is evident that the whole personality is involved, and that since a man – or at least many, non-Platonic men – responds to a woman in a different way from that in which he responds to a man or a woman to a woman, it is natural that these rôles should be essentially dependent on sex. But as the rôles become more limited, so the dependence becomes less. I could hardly complain if I was not given the part of Desdemona or a job as an *au pair* boy on account of my sex: but if I had very feminine features and had grown my hair long and golden, or if I were particularly deft at changing nappies, I might feel a little aggrieved, and certainly I could call in question any law that forbade a man to play the part of a woman or be a nursemaid. Some substantial public good would need to be shown to justify a legal decision enforceable by penal sanctions being uniformly based not on my actual inability to fill the rôle required by only my supposed unsuitability on account of my sex. We demand a higher standard of cogency in arguments justifying what laws there should be than in those concerned only with individual decisions; and although this standard can be satisfied, often by admitting considerations of the public good, yet the arguments need to be adduced, because, in framing laws, we need to be sensitive to individual rights and careful about our criteria of relevance. Although it may be the case that a nurse is a better nurse for having the feminine touch, we hesitate to deem it absolutely essential; and although many more women than men have been good nurses, we do not believe that it must invariably be so. There are male nurses. We reckon it reasonable to prefer a woman in individual case, but do not insist upon it in all cases by law. We are reluctant to impose severe legal disqualifications, but equally would hesitate to impose upon employers an obligation not to prefer women to play female parts or to be nurses or to join a family in an *au pair* capacity. For we recognize that a person's sex can reasonably be regarded as relevant to his or her suitability for particular posts, and that many institutions will operate on this basis, and are entitled to. I am justified in refusing to employ a male *au pair* girl or a female foreman, although if there are many males anxious to be looking after young children or many women anxious to supervise the work of others, it may be desirable on grounds of humanity to establish special institutions in which they can fulfil their vocations. If we will not let Miss Amazon join the Grenadier Guards, let there be an ATS or WRAC for her to join instead.

Although we are rightly reluctant to impose legal disqualifications on individuals on grounds extraneous to their individual circumstances, it is inherent in all political thinking that we may find considerations of the general case over-riding those of the individual one; and often we frame our laws with an eye to what men and women are generally like rather than what they invariably are. A man may not adopt an infant girl unless she is more than twenty-five years younger than he; for some men might otherwise use adoption to acquire not so much a daughter as a wife. In many societies women have less freedom in disposing of their property than men; for else, things being as they are, some women would be prevailed upon to divest themselves of it to their long-term disadvantage. Ardent feminists have chafed at the shackles of marriage, and demand freedom from this degrading institution or their sisters as well as themselves. But if this freedom were established it would be the libertine males who would enjoy the benefits of liberation, being then free to leave the women to bear the burdens of parenthood all on their own. If most mothers care more for their children and their homes than most fathers do, then in the absence of institutions that recognize the fact they will in fact be disadvantaged. Some discrimination is needed to redress the balance. But discrimination, even positive discrimination, can work to the disadvantage of individuals, however much it may benefit most people on the whole.

The would-be female Stakhanovite is penalized by the law forbidding firms to employ female labour for sixty hours a week, just as the youthful entrepreneur is handicapped by his legal incapacity, as a minor, to pledge his credit except for the necessities of life, and the skilled racing motorist by the law forbidding him to drive, however safely, at more than 70. miles per hour. In each case the justification is the same: the restriction imposed on the individual, although real and burdensome, is not so severe as to outweigh the benefits that are likely to accrue in the long run to women in general, or to minors, or to motorists. It is in the nature of political society that we forgo some freedoms in order that either we ourselves or other people can secure some good. All we can in general demand is that our sacrifices should not be fruitless, and that if we give up some liberty or immunity it is at least arguable that it will be on balance for the best.

Arguments in politics are nearly always mixed, and involve appeals to different principles, according to how the question is construed. We can elucidate some canons of relevance for some of the principles which may be invoked. Where the principle is that of Universal Humanity, the reason 'Because you are a woman' is always irrelevant to its general applicability, though it may affect the way it is specified: perhaps women feel more strongly about their homes than men do, so that although we ought not, on grounds of humanity, to hurt either men or women, deprivation of her home would constitute a greater hurt to a woman than to a man. The principle of Universal Humanity is pervasive in its applications, but is conclusive only over a much more limited range. It is always wrong to torture; but often we cannot help hurting people's feelings or harming their interests if other values – justice, liberty, the public good – are to be preserved. And therefore arguments based on the principle of universal humanity may be over-ridden by ones based on other principles, also valuable. When the principle invoked is that of Formal Equality (or Universalizability) the reason 'Because you are a woman' cannot be dismissed out of hand as necessarily irrelevant. A person's sex is not a 'mere fact', evidently and necessarily separate from all other facts, and such that it is immediately obvious that no serious argument can be founded upon it. Particularly with those rôles that involve relationships with other people, and especially where those relationships are fairly personal ones, it is likely to matter whether it is a man or a woman that is chosen. When some principle of Justice is at stake, the criteria of relevance become fairly stringent. We are concerned only with the individual's actions, attitudes and abilities, and the reason 'Because you are a woman' must either be integrally connected with matter in issue (as in 'Why cannot I marry the girl I love?') or be reliably, although only contingently, connected with it (as in 'Why cannot I get myself employed for 60 hours a week?'); and in the latter case we feel that Justice has been compromised, although perhaps acceptably so, if there is no way whereby an individual can prove she is an exception to the rule and be treated as such. As the interests of the individual become more peripheral, or can be satisfied in alternative ways that are available, the principle of justice recedes, and we are more ready to accept rules and institutions based on general principles of social utility or tradition, and designed only to fit the general case. It is legitimate to base public feeling on such differences as seem to be relevant, but the more a law or an institution is based on merely a contingent, and not an integral, concomitance, the more ready we should be to cater for exceptions.

With sufficient care we may be able to disentangle what is true in the feminists' contention from what is false. At lease we should be able to avoid the dilemma, which seems to be taken for granted by most participants in the debate, that we must say that women either are in all respects exactly the same as men or else are in all respects different from, and inferior to, them, and not members of the same universe of discourse at all. I do not share Plato's feelings about sex. I think the sexes are different, and incomparable. No doubt, women are not quite as good as men, *in some respects*: but since men are not nearly as good as women in others, this carries with it no derogatory implication of uniform inferiority. Exactly what these differences are, and, indeed, what sort of differences they are, is a matter for further research; and exactly what bearing they should have in the application of the various principles we value in making up our mind about social matters is a matter for further philosophical thought. But without any further thought we can align our emotions with the proponents of Women's Lib on the most important issue of all. What angers them most is the depersonalization of women in the Admass society: and one cannot but sympathize with their protest against women being treated as mere objects of sexual gratification by men; but cannot avoid the conclusion that their arguments and activities in fact lead towards just that result which they deplore. If we are insensitive to the essential femininity of the female sex, we shall adopt an easy egalitarianism which, while denying that there are any genetic difference, allows us to conclude in most individual cases that women, judged by male standards of excellence, are less good than their male rivals. Egalitarianism ends by depersonalizing women and men alike.

The sceptical feminist

JANET RADCLIFF RICHARDS

SELECTION DISCRIMINATION

The question to be settled is this. Can we prove quite generally that it is always unfair to choose a man rather than a woman for something they would both like to do, when the woman could do it better than the man?

It is very important to get this question properly focused. We are considering at the moment only the rejection of women who are *actually* more suitable for the position in question than the competing men. If women are rejected because of poor education, that may show discrimination against them at an earlier point, but not at this one. If they are unsuitable because they will work badly with a prejudiced work force, or because someone is wanted who will not be away to have children, that may show unfairness in the structure of society, but does not involve the rejection of *actually suitable women* at this point. The selectors cannot be accused of selection discrimination as long as they choose the best candidate for the purpose in question. *Discrimination on grounds of sex is counting sex as relevant in contexts where it is not,* and leads to the rejection of *suitable* women. It is not discrimination on grounds of sex to reject women who are not suitable, even if their unsuitability is *caused* by their being women. When that happens it is their unsuitability, and not their sex, which has caused their rejection. The question at issue now is specifically whether discrimination against women who really are suitable for a position could ever be defended according to the principles of social justice which have been outlined here.

There is, of course, one perfectly obvious selection rule, applicable in any situation where people are competing for something they want. It is 'choose the candidate most suited to the position'. The question we are dealing with, therefore, is that of what possible reason there could be for adding to this eminently sensible rule, either openly or surreptitiously, the proviso 'but no women', or 'but make it harder for women'. There are various justifications around.

One which can be dismissed straight away is the suggestion which appears from time to time that the whole situation stems from kindness on the part of men, who want to protect women from all the hard things of life. It has already been argued that paternalism is not to be tolerated. Even if men did really think they were doing what was good for women in spite of themselves (which puts rather a strain on one's credulity) it would still not be justified. And while many women may still be perfectly willing to be grateful for any male chivalry which offers to take from them any chore they find burdensome, they can hardly be expected to respond with the same appreciation when men use their stranglehold on the running of everything to prevent women's doing the things they *want* to do. Feminists will believe men's good intentions when they make offers, not rules which they assure everyone are purely in women's interest.

However, although the kindness-to-women argument does appear, it is not the usual justification for discriminatory practices. By far the commonest argument takes the line that women are to be excluded because they are not equal to the task in question. They cannot be dockers or bus drivers because they are not strong enough, they cannot go into the professions or business because they are not clever enough, or can't concentrate, or are prone to hysteria, or will leave to have children or follow their husbands. The usual feminist response to this line is an indignant denial of the whole thing: either the accusations are false, or if women are in some ways inferior to men it is because men have deprived women of proper education. There is of course much truth in this. However, this is one clear case in which feminists would do better to forget about factual arguments for a while and concentrate on the logic. This reasoning is absolutely absurd for two reasons (both, incidentally, clearly pointed out by Mill).

In the first place, nearly all the differences claimed to exist between men and women are differences of *average*. No one with the slightest claim to sense could argue that *all* men were stronger or more intellectual or more forceful than *all* women. But the fact (when it is one) that the average woman cannot do something or other which the average man can do provides not a shred of justification for a rule or practice which also excludes all the exceptional ones who can do it, or demands that the women should perform better than the men to be admitted. You might as well try to argue that if black men were stronger on average than white ones, white men should not be allowed to lift heavy loads, or if Yorkshire people were cleverer than Lancashire ones, no one from Lancashire should be allowed to go to university. Average differences between men and women would account for different success rates in various activities, but they could not possibly account for selection policies which differentiated between them.

Second, even if there were cases where it looked as though all women actually might be worse at something than all men, that *still* would not account for a rule specifically excluding them or saying they should do better than men to be admitted, because, as Mill said, 'What women by nature cannot do, it is quite superfluous to forbid them from doing. What they can do, but not so well as the men who are their competitors, competition suffices to exclude them from . . .'. If men really think, for instance, that a certain level of strength is needed for driving buses, why not just say what that level is and test all applicants for strength? If they really think that all women will fail, why *add* 'but no women'? If the presumption were true no women would get in anyway. It is ridiculous to say that a rule specifically excluding women is needed *because* the work calls for a certain level of strength which women are presumed never to reach. If this is an example of the wonders of male logic, perhaps it is hardly surprising if women feel that they cannot aspire to it.

Some people try to escape this conclusion by saying that if women are inferior to men on average in certain respects it is a waste of time to look at women applicants, because there is so little likelihood of their succeeding. Certainly if such average differences did exist it would account for advising people who were making selections not to spend too much time interviewing women: it is not possible to interview everyone, and some principles of simplification have to be followed. But still, that would not in the least account for general rules excluding all women, which would apply even to the ones who happened to be so strikingly good at their work that they could not be overlooked, and the ones who produced good evidence that they did not suffer from the usual defects of their sex. Maxims for the guidance of selectors, giving some indication of where to look for what is wanted, are quite different from the lists of characteristics needed for the job. If most women are unsuitable for something, it is understandable that a selector should miss by accident some of the ones who are suitable. It is quite different, and not acceptable, to refuse to consider any women, even the ones whose excellence cannot be missed.

In fact there is no escape from the obvious conclusion, which is this. If a general rule is made saying what characteristics are needed for a certain position, and to the list of these characteristics is added the proviso 'but exclude women' or 'make it harder for women', it is *not* added because it is thought that all or most women do not reach the required standards. You do not make additional rules to prevent what would not happen anyway under the existing ones. *The only conceivable reason for a rule or practice excluding women is its perpetrators' thinking that without such a rule women would have to be let in*: that on grounds of strict suitability women, or more women, would have to be admitted. And since the rule against women cannot be justified by saying that women are not generally suitable, it must follow that they are being kept out on other grounds, unspecified.

Since they are unspecified, and since it appears to be necessary to hide them under specious arguments about women's unsuitability, it must be presumed that the real reasons are not of a sort people want exposed to the light of day. It is not, however, difficult to work out what they must be. What, for instance, must be happening if an employer passes over a competent woman in favour of a less competent man? It means that the job will be less well done, and therefore (to put it schematically) that he will be losing money by appointing the man. Why should he do that? He is actually willing to *pay* for something or other, and it is hard to see what it could possibly be other than the simple cause of male supremacy. In other words, individual women are apparently *suffering in the cause of male supremacy*, and individual men are gaining in the same cause. What could possibly be more unfair than that?

THE PROBLEM OF REVERSE DISCRIMINATION

We have, then, established that discrimination against women, treating their sex as a reason for putting them at a disadvantage in competitions where sex is not relevant, is always substantially unfair.

Clear and neat as that conclusion is, however, and useful in allowing us to pin down demonstrable injustice and charge individual culprits instead of having to rail in general about the unfair structures of society (for which it is hard to blame anyone in particular), it does raise problems for feminists in the context of the issue of reverse discrimination. The usual form recommended for reverse discrimination is that women of a lower calibre than men should be chosen for certain work in preference to them. It is a thing which many feminists think ought to happen, but the last section seemed to show that this would be absolutely unfair; that reverse discrimination would be open to exactly the same conclusive objections as ordinary discrimination.

More specifically, the argument seems to show that several explicit provisions of the Sex Discrimination Act must be unfair. For instance, the Act states that when appointments are made to various positions there are certain things which are not to be allowed to count against women applicants, the most striking of which, perhaps, is that they are not to be rejected on the grounds that they will meet prejudiced public and work force. There is no doubt that when people are prejudiced against women a man would often do the required work better; if the public have no confidence in a female door-to-door seller of insurance or encyclopaedias a man will sell more. To insist that this sort of thing should not be allowed to count against women is actually to say that women should be appointed even when they are less good than men. In other words, it provides for a certain amount of positive discrimination.

It will not do to say in a vague way that sometimes it must be all right to discriminate in favour of women. The argument of the last section showed that *whenever* considerations of sex entered into selections for whose purpose sex was not relevant that was unfair, and the whole point is to try to achieve fairness. We cannot simply assert that unfairness sometimes has to be tolerated. Of course it has already been argued that sometimes *formal* unfairness has to be tolerated in the interests of substantial fairness, but since the necessity of selecting the best candidate is *part of the account of what it is to be substantially fair* there is nothing higher which can override it. You cannot say that some substantial unfairness must be tolerated in the interests of greater substantial fairness, in the way that some bad must be tolerated to achieve a great deal of good, because fairness is not a thing to be shared out; it is a principle according to which other things are shared out. Anyone who is treated with substantial unfairness gets the wrong amount of good and bad.

If positive discrimination is to be justified, something much stronger is needed. Some of the usual defences of it which appear should be assessed.

Probably the commonest defence is the argument that since women have been badly treated in the past, what they should now be given is *compensation* for what they have missed. Compensation is a method of making up for past privation. It is not (to avoid confusion later on) a way of putting things right for the future, or improving matters generally; it is a means to give women the level of satisfaction they ought to have had anyway, by giving them enough now to fill the gap left by their previous deprivation. It is the sort of thing which would happen if an employer were to make up for employees' having been underpaid in the past by giving them all their back pay, with an allowance for interest and inflation, and perhaps damages.

If women have indeed been treated unfairly in the past, it does seem proper that they should be given compensation now. If men have had more than their fair share, they should have some of their ill-gotten gains to women, since they got them at women's expense in the first place. However, the question now is not of whether women should be compensated, but of whether the way to go about that is by means of positive discrimination. And there seems little doubt that it is not a proper means of compensation, for several reasons.

In the first place, you cannot actually compensate women in general for their past suffering by changing the rules now and allowing some women to achieve advantages for which they are not really qualified. Even if that would do as a compensation for the women chosen, it would be no compensation whatever for the others. It might perhaps improve things for the future, but that is not compensation. It would do nothing for the women who had been passed over earlier, and their unhappiness might even be increased by seeing other women being given advantages far beyond anything they had ever had. Reverse discrimination fails as a means of compensating women for their sufferings, both because you cannot compensate a group by giving benefits to some of its members (people need compensating individually or collectively, not by some method of representation), and anyway, the women who are individually compensated by discrimination are usually already the most privileged among women. Reverse discrimination is no compensation for women in general.

Perhaps then the idea is to compensate some individuals rather than the whole group, for their past injustice. That looks more promising. However it still does not work as justification of a general policy of reverse discrimination in favour of women. If the concern is really with underprivilege and its redress, why should it matter whether the person being helped is a woman rather than a man? Why should one discriminate generally in favour of women, when it might involve benefiting an already well off woman at the expense of a badly off man? If compensation is all that is at issue, why not have the rule that the worst off (of either sex) are to be compensated? To say that women's grievances should be redressed in preference to men's is to be unfair to men: it gives women the privilege of having their lack of privilege take precedence over men's lack of privilege, and when this is looked at from the point of view of deprived individuals there seems to be nothing to be said for it at all. Many men are less privileged than many women. The fact that women are on average less well off than men might justify someone's deciding to take particular care when assessing women candidates for anything, because there was a higher probability that they would need compensating than men would, but it would not justify a general rule.

Suppose, then, we argued that reverse discrimination should not be specifically in favour of women, but in favour of any underprivileged person. (That would still in practice tend to favour women, but would escape the charge that the practice was systematically unfair to men.) Even then it would not be justified.

This can be illustrated rather schematically. Suppose a benevolent man who runs a business is sympathetic to the problems of women, and is willing to do without some of his profit to benefit them. He has two position to fill, one responsible and interesting, and one rather dull. In competition for them are a well qualified man and a less well qualified woman. He has two options: to give the better job to the woman or to give it to the man. Suppose first he gives it to the woman. She then has a high degree of satisfaction; we are to suppose that she is not so hopelessly incompetent as to be unhappy, only less good than the man would have been. Her inefficiency loses money for the firm, but the employer does not mind that because he is willing to make sacrifices to benefit women. The man, on the other hand, has a low degree of satisfaction in the lesser job. Suppose, however, that the employer takes the other option, and appoints the man to the better job. The man then has a high degree of satisfaction, and the firm makes the usual profit. The employer is willing to forgo this in the interests of the woman, as before, and so gives her a high salary for her work in the lesser job. She therefore has also a high degree of satisfaction, though of course of a different sort. There seems, therefore, to be no doubt about which arrangement the employer should make. He should not make an arrangement which would benefit the woman only, if he could make one which would benefit the man as well.

Of course that example is very artificial, and no doubt objections could be brought against it in its present form, put it does illustrate a general point. To have a general policy of appointing women to positions for which they are not well qualified is not the best way to compensate them for past injustice. We should do much better to allow the best qualified people to do the work, because if work is worth doing it is in the interests of all that it should be done well. If we make such arrangements it will mean that we have a greater social product with which to compensate women, and others, for their past injustices, and that is what we should do. Compensation should come not in the form of unmerited advancement, but in the form of other primary social goods (to use Rawls's term).

The general conclusion of all these arguments is that although no doubt some compensation is due to women for their unjust treatment, the idea of compensation does not justify reverse discrimination in their favour.

Still, the defenders of reverse discrimination have no reason to retreat yet. All this talk of compensation, they can argue, is beside the point. If we are going to be fussy about the precise meaning of 'compensation', then let us concede that compensation is not what justifies reverse discrimination. What we want to achieve is not compensation but *an improvement of the position of women until society is fair to them*, and as a matter of fact probably the best way to achieve this is to appoint to positions of importance women who are rather less good at the work than the men who are in competition with them. As long as they are not such hopeless failures as to confirm everyone's ideas that women are not capable of any serious work, their holding those positions will be enough to make other women set their sights higher, and make people in general more used to seeing women in former male preserves ad expecting more of them. High expectations make an important contribution to high performance. That is quite a different point from the compensation argument, though the two are very often confused. Furthermore it escapes all the objections to which the other is open, including, most importantly, the general argument that is always unfair to select people for work on the basis of anything other than their suitability for it.

The point is this. If our present society is unfair to women, it is obviously fair that it should be changed; it is fair that we should set in motion social programmes to turn society into one which is better for women. We also think that when things are fairer to women society as a whole will benefit, because it will no longer waste their skills. Admittedly women now may not have the skills they should have had, and since it is probably too late for the women of this generation to acquire them we should perhaps think of compensating them for their disadvantage by other means, rather than giving them positions of responsibility. But that would be to take a short term view. We have to plan not only for the people who are alive now, but for the world our great-granddaughters will have to contend with. It would be unfair to them to let things go on as they are now, and unfair to their contemporaries to have potential skill wasted. Our social aims, therefore, become more complicated. We have to maintain our concern with high standards in the various professions, but we have also to think of the need to advance women. We want good doctors, certainly, but at the same time we want to encourage people to think of women as doctors. *If, as a matter of fact,* we think that the best way to achieve this is to have a good many successful women doctors, we may consider making rules which allow a woman to become a doctor with slightly lower medical qualifications than a man. *But this does not offend against the principle that there should be no discrimination in selection procedures, because we are still concerned to choose the best people for the job which needs doing.* It is just that the nature of the work to be done has changed, so that different people become suitable for it. We now want, for example, good doctors who *also* advance the position of women. As long as lowering the medical qualifications for women was causally relevant to the end to be achieved, it would be justified.

This way of looking at the matter does seem to remove the *prima facie* objections to reverse discrimination. Or perhaps a better way of putting it would be to say that reverse discrimination is not well named, because discrimination on grounds of sex involves counting sex as relevant in contexts where it is not, and the argument being put forward now is that in some unexpected contexts it *may* be relevant. In these contexts what appears to be discrimination in favour of women is not discrimination at all.

CASE STUDY

Opportunity 2000

Before the Sex Discrimination Act was passed in 1976, it was common for 'situations vacant' columns to specify which jobs were 'male' and which were 'female', and for many employers and professions to have separate salary scales for men and women. Yet, despite the fact that the Sex Discrimination Act made these and other practices illegal, women in the UK still typically earn on average 77% of the incomes enjoyed by men, and only a very small handful of women obtain top managerial positions. In 1991, women accounted for 7 out of 108 government ministers, 2 High Court judges out of 82, 2 national newspaper editors out of 21, 4 assistant chief constables out of 127. They were represented markedly more in school teaching (25% women secondary teachers) and as National Health Service managers (35%). They had no representation whatsoever as Cabinet Ministers, Civil Service permanent secretaries, BP and Lloyds Bank directors.

In the past, the Labour Party has attracted the reputation for championing the cause of working women, and in 1992 the Conservative Party recognized that there was a problem in continuing to attract support from that sector. A 1991 Gallup poll indicated that 56% of women approved of John Major compared with 52% of men, but 1987 General Election voting patterns revealed a marked leftward swing amongst younger women.

Since government action is costly, however, the Conservatives took the view that it would be a much less expensive way of tackling the problem if industrialists themselves were to pay for a campaign and to become actively involved in securing better employment opportunities for women.

Accordingly, on 28 October 1991 Prime Minister John Major announced the Government's support for Opportunity 2000, launched by Business in the Community (BITC), and comprised a team of senior business leaders chaired by Lady Howe. A total of 61 companies expressed a commitment to improving the status of women within their organizations by the year 2000 and set themselves definite targets for doing so. By October 1992 that total had risen to 123.

There is no single formula to be applied by companies who opt for membership of Opportunity 2000. Each company aims to enhance the prospects for female workers by formulating its own goals, which vary according to its circumstances. Some organizations have set very specific targets: for example, British Airways has stated that it intends by the year 2000 to employ a proportion of women which will reflect the total UK work force (42%); Natwest intends to increase the proportion of women in its management team from a current 16.3% to 33.3%; the BBC has set target ratios for senior executive positions (30:70), senior management (40:60) and management (40:60), to be achieved by 1996.

Other companies are less precise. Texaco's aim is 'to have a positive business environment conductive to realising the full potential of women by 1995', while the British Railways Board intends introducing new 'Quality of Life' policies, which will encompass sexual harassment, amongst others. Other employers, such as the Cabinet Office, intend focussing on pay schemes and nurseries.

The Opportunities 2000 target team plans to expand the membership, particularly institutions which have a high public profile and are likely to be influential. Target areas include the country's leading 500 companies, Universities, Trade Unions and Local Government departments. Any organization can join Opportunity 2000. In order to join, an annual contribution is solicited, which is based on the number of employees – £1000 for organizations with 1000 employees or more, and negotiable reduced rates for smaller firms. Apart from the annual fee, all that is needed is a letter to the campaign director from 'your Chairman (*sic!*), Chief Executive or Director of Personnel'.

Most people would agree that women are under-represented in business and industry, particularly at the top. Yet Opportunity 2000 has nonetheless attracted criticism. There are those who claim that it is little more than a token gesture towards women. Although over 120 major companies are represented, it has been pointed out that these companies employ only 20% of the country's female work force, most of whom work for small and medium sized companies. Other critics have argued that the status of women cannot be equal until more radical changes in society are effected – for example, persuading employers and husbands to elect to take extended paternity leave instead of having the wife take the traditional maternity leave. Such options currently exist in Scandanavian countries. At present, only British Gas mentions paternity leave in its Opportunity 2000 statement, and the permitted period is only four days.

Other critics will of course see the whole venture as pointless. After all, it might be argued, is not Opportunity 2000 supporting examples of 'positive discrimination', thereby patronizing women and leaving them open to the possible criticism that they have 'only got where they are today' by artificial interventionist measures, rather than by demonstrating their ability to compete with men for the same jobs on equal terms.

Supporters of the scheme will point out that employers' current lack of provision for women's needs discriminates unfavourably against them. The most obvious problem for women is that they bear children: and, as the champions of Opportunity 2000 frequently point out, until something is done to ensure that women can continue to progress in their careers despite interruptions to have children, women will never enjoy strictly equal opportunities.

Discussion questions on the case study

Comment on the Opportunity 2000 scheme. How necessary is it? Is there a case for formulating a more uniform set of policies for firms to adopt before they can gain membership? Opportunity 2000 monitors its overall progress, as do some individual firms which participate in the scheme. However, not all firms are committed to monitoring their progress; do you think this should be a prior condition for joining? Does the scheme go far enough, or is there a need for stronger government action?

DISCUSSION TOPICS

1. Firms often provide their employees with symbols of their status. Company cars, for example, are often graded in accordance with the rank of the employee, and the key to the executive cloakroom is often a coveted prize. How can such distinctions stemming from rank be justified? Would firms operate more or less efficiently if they were abolished?
2. You are interviewing applicants for the post of receptionist. Which of the following would you refuse to consider?
   (a) belongs to a fringe religious group.
   (b) has an unappealing birth mark.
   (c) is male, age 55.
   (d) is overweight (remember that obesity can lead to medical problems such as a heart condition).
   (e) belongs to the Paedophile Information Exchange.

Does it make a difference that some of these applicants are in this situation of their own free will (eg one could leave a religious group, one could diet)?

3. Find out what is required in order to implement an 'equal opportunities policy'. If your organization already has one, what is involved? Do you feel that a quota system, or a policy of 'affirmative action' would be desirable? (If you do, which categories of individual would you wish to identify and given particular help to?)

4. Should there be a minimum and/or a maximum wage? Consider arguments for and against.

Accounting and investment $\boxed{7}$

Ethics and the world of finance
The ethics of investment
Privatization

Introducing the readings

Creative accounting   Ian Griffiths
ED42 – the end of creative accounting?   Michael J. Brooks
Accountability and acquistions   Mike Allen and Robert Hodgkinson
The relevance of ethics: a practical problem analysed   J. G. Williams
Ethics in auditing   André Zünd
Auditor independence: a real issue?   Arnold Schilder

Case study
Polly Peck

Discussion topics

ETHICS AND THE WORLD OF FINANCE

To many people the world of finance seems incomprehensible or down-right boring, as the Monty Python caricatures of accountants in the 1970s suggested. The image of the financial world is often that of a desk-based job (the accountant in an office) or of yuppies watching share prices on a television monitor. What possible moral decisions are involved in preparing cash flow forecasts for a firm, auditing a company's books or advising a business on how to cost its goods or services? The apparent mathematical precision of accountants might cause the public to believe that – at least in so far as they are engaged in accounting procedures – there is no scope for making any kind of ethical decisions.

Alas, these conceptions of the accountant are mere stereo-types, as we shall show. The figures which an accountant prepares or scrutinizes are descriptions of reality, just like words. Although they should present a 'true and fair view', the picture the accountant paints can be either enlightening or misleading, depending on how he or she chooses to depict it. It takes a mere recollection of the Guinness scandal or the Robert Maxwell affair to know that manipulating figures on paper or VDU can give rise to serious crimes which affect the fortunes of many.

Of course, the actions of Saunders and Maxwell were illegal as well as immoral. But even within the law, however, various manoeuvres can be carried out by accountants which are often regarded as being in ethically grey areas. The most common practice of this kind is known as 'creative accounting', a phrase which is popularly associated with 'cooking the books' in a way which is legal although morally dubious.

The practice of creative accounting, however, is not necessarily un-ethical. Those who express outrage at the apparent creativity of certain firms' book-keeping are often those whose limits of accountancy are confined to their own personal accounting and perhaps to organizing small scale events where monetary transactions are clear and unambiguous. If we organize the annual Sunday School outing, there is no stretch of the imagination by which the coach hire cost £350 when we only paid the coach company £250, or where the monies received were £40 when 50 children paid one pound per head.

In the average company, by contrast, things are seldom so clear. To take a very simple example; suppose in the course of our employment within a large firm we are asked to organize a meeting. How much does it cost to do so? (In some major companies, managers who wish to call meetings are obliged to cost them first, in order to ascertain whether or not they are justified.) At first sight it might seem that a meeting costs nothing at all. If attendees are paid no overtime, if there are no rooms to be hired, if there are no external consultants demanding fees, it could be argued that the cost is zero. It is likely, however, that at least there were printed agendas that the telephone costs of calling the meeting; we could therefore cost the meeting on the basis of the cost of materials and services which would not have been incurred if no meeting had been contemplated. Most firms, however, would consider that these methods of costing were naïve; meetings have to be attended by people, and since attendees are present as part of their paid employment, a suitable proportion of salaries should be attributed to the cost of holding the meeting. Once embarked on the task of calculating what is a suitable proportion of each attendee's salary, the methods of calculation are manifold. One could calculate the average number of hours worked in the course of each member's week and determine what proportion of one's time (and hence one's salary) was attributable. A more con-servative approach might be to consider the costs of hiring part-time staff at cheaper rates to eke out the heavy workload of attendees, while at the other end of the scale one might consider the 'opportunity costs' incurred by tying up employees' time; after all, in most firms employees are worth more to the firm than they are paid. ('Opportunity costs' are the costs of not doing alternative tasks; if a member of a sales depart-ment can sell goods at a profit of, say, £500 an hour, then the opportunity cost of attending an hour-long meeting is £500.) And what are we to say about the costs of accommodation? Do we consider the marginal costs to the firm of holding the meeting, or the proportion of total costs of rents, heating and lighting? The point is that there is no clear or 'right' answer to the question, and different answers may well suit the different pur-poses of different firms. If holding the meeting means a reduction in selling then the firm might be well advised to include opportunity costs; if the attenders at the meeting are happy to work unpaid overtime, then more conservative methods of costing might be appropriate.

Accounting, like a wide range of other activities, is a way of describing part of the world, and the same part of the world is capable of being described in a variety of different ways. Just as a poet and a civil engineer might describe the same landscape differently because they have different purposes, so two accountants could present the accounts of the same firm in two entirely different ways. This is not in itself unethical, any more than civil engineers are unethical for describing the physical environment in terms of its potential use rather than for its inherent beauty, like the poet. Nearly all accounting is to some extent creative accounting, because there is no clear unarguable answer as to whether we regard something as a cost, as a loss, as an expense, or whatever. Examples of 'creative accounting' are legion. A firm whose profits are modest in a given financial year may decide to sell off some of its capital and treat the proceeds as profits. This could prove reassuring to shareholders, although obviously a firm could not continue such a policy indefinitely. Another technique of enhancing profits is called 'equity accounting'; under UK law, if a firm owns more than 20% of another firm it may declare that proportion of the other firm's profits as its own. (The same applies to losses.)

Faced with a problem of dropping sales, a firm might enhance its sales figures by allowing the bank to 'buy' goods, when in reality the goods are being offered as security for a loan. The company would 'buy back' its stock at a later date and for a higher price – exactly the same monetary transaction as taking out a loan. Meanwhile, the goods themselves do not change position; they remain in the warehouse, without any necessity for the company to deliver them physically to the bank and back again!

Even with something as seemingly clear as a sale, there can actually be ambiguity about whether a sale represents a profit or a loss. If a firm has sold a consignment of products, one would imagine that such a sale would be reflected in the accounts. However, if the buyer has been given credit, not only is it possible for the vendor to omit the sale figure in accounts during the period of credit, but it is possible for the vendor to consider the sale as a (temporary) loss of goods without payment, and hence a debit.

Another form of creative accounting involves placing a hypothetical monetary value on 'intangibles'. Companies are often worth more than their physical assets. If a firm has built up enough 'good will' amongst customers and suppliers then its name is surely worth something. The very name 'Coca-Cola' would presumably, if sold to another firm be of substantial value, even perhaps if that firm consisted of funeral directors. But precisely how much would the name 'Coca-Cola' be worth to a hypothetical buyer? To the best of our knowledge, no one has ever tried to buy the name, and Coca-Cola have never tried to sell it. Any figure therefore that is placed on its value must be a 'guesstimate', or maybe even just a guess. Yet well-known firms quite typically include intangible assets in their annual accounts.

All this, of course, does not mean that 'anything goes' in the name of accountancy. Although the world can be described in a variety of ways, not all ways are correct. Some ways are certainly false (for example saying we see a hill when there is a valley) and some, although not false, can be downright misleading (like claiming to be a student when he or she attends the occasional evening class). The same is true of accounting. For example, legally one may not claim under the heading of 'expenses' the costs of entertaining one's colleagues to dinner (unless they are from abroad), or keep two sets of accounts books, one for personal use and the other for the auditors.

It is not our task to enumerate the various creative accounting procedures which are carried out within the accountancy profession. Suffice it to say that the various manoeuvres which exist are large enough in number for whole books to be devoted to the subject. Our interest, as the reader should expect, lies in the ethical issues which are raised by the phenomenon.

The case which is often made for creative accounting is one of freedom, which, as we noted in a previous chapter, is a fundamental human right. It can be argued that companies should enjoy the fundamental right of deciding how to organize their own affairs, including how they decide to present their accounts. Any state insistence on a standardized method of accounting could be perceived as an unwarranted intrusion on individual liberty. Further, one system of accounting may be particularly appropriate to one firm, but inappropriate to another. Indeed at the present time the law recognizes that small businesses are not necessarily run by those who excel in accounting, and consequently a sole trader or partnership which has no limited liability is not obliged to present accounts with the same degree of exactitude as a PLC. Within the limited-liability sector, too, the affairs of an educational establishment, a charity, a chain store and a multi-national company are all very different, and it is difficult to see how some standard accounting scheme could be devised.

It can be argued too, that a company, like an individual, has the right to enjoy the best possible advantage within the law. Just as private citizens, if they are astute, will present their income tax returns in such a way as to maximize expenses and take full advantage of available tax allowances, so a firm may attribute as much as is legally possible to expenses, offer tax-saving advantages to executives (such as a company car instead of enhanced monetary payments), or minimize VAT by minimizing the sales turnover. The last of these can be done quite legally; one obvious example is for a car sales firm to treat a part-exchange as a reduced-price single sale, rather than two separate transactions in which the new car is sold for the full price and the old car bought as a separate deal. Indeed, it can be argued that since business executives have the duty of securing for their shareholders the best possible return for their investment (within the law, of course) that they have a positive obligation to ensure that the firm's statement of accounts is presented in such a way as to provide the maximum possible advantage to them.

These, then, are the major arguments in favour of creative accounting. At first appearance, they seem convincing and, given the inevitability of a creative element in accounting procedures in any case, one might wonder why anyone should object to such practices. Yet there are several objections to the procedures of accountants which merit serious consideration.

Firstly, it can be argued that if a firm engages in sharp practice which enables it to avoid (but not evade) taxation,[1] then other members of the public have to be called upon to make up the shortfall. Most private citizens, as we have noted, can do little to embellish their own tax returns with significant tax-saving devices. Indeed, in recent years, the law has closed in on astute private citizens; no longer do they have tax immunity for trust funds held for their children, children's bank accounts or even TSB savings accounts. If large companies avoid taxation, then it becomes incumbent on the government to reduce public spending or else for private citizens and less astute or smaller firms to make up the shortfall through higher taxation.

Secondly, some creative account clearly conflicts with a firm's duty to its investors. On several occasions firms have been known to present accounts in such a way as to enable investors to believe that profits are soaring, when in fact the opposite is the case. In a year in which business is bad, it is not unknown for a firm to decide that its pension fund should have a 'holiday' (that is, a year in which no payments are made into it) and to declare as additional profits the monies which would normally have been paid into pensions. This may cause investors to believe that a firm's financial health is better than actually is the case, and may encourage them to stay with that company rather than find a better return for investment elsewhere.

It may be thought that the ethical issues involved might be resolved by the auditors, who are bound by professional codes of practice such as

---

[1] Tax avoidance is something which is within the law, whereas evasion means the illegal avoidance of tax, usually by fraud.

that of the Institute of Chartered Accountants. Alas, this is far from the case. There is no agreed definition of what is a 'true and fair view' in accountancy, and different auditors have been known to have widely differing opinions on the matter. But this does not mean that a company is at the mercy of its auditors when it comes to deciding what it can get away with; on the contrary, although an auditor is obliged to be 'independent', he or she is appointed by the firm itself, and the decision as to whether or not to appoint an auditor is often decided by sounding out a possible candidate for an opinion relating to a potentially controversial accounting procedure. Clearly, the prospect of being fired or re-hired is bound to be a significant factor affecting the decision of an auditor on how to view certain pieces of creative accounting. As things stand at the moment, there is no independent and objective referee to blow the whistle on unacceptable accounting practices and to maintain consistency amongst companies concerning the way in which accounts are kept and presented.

It would be unfair to the accountancy profession to imply that it is complacent about the current situation, and proposals for changing the system have been suggested. The recent Accounting Standards Committee's draft ED42 (*Accounting for Special Purpose Transactions*), puts forward some proposals for standardizing the presentation of accounting procedures, at least in certain areas. (The article by Michael J. Brooks in the Readings section discusses the proposals.)

THE ETHICS OF INVESTMENT

When we turn to the area of investment, it is obvious that the accountant's figures and the prices quoted on the Stock Exchange are not merely numbers on paper. They record human activities of buying and selling, hiring and firing, and generally choosing between live options in the real world. Because share prices affect investors' decisions about whether to pull out or buy in, decisions relating to investment are votes for or against the continuation of a firm's activities. For example, buying shares in the main clearing banks (or even having an account there) could be construed as a vote in favour of their refusal to write off Third World debt.

So important is the whole area of finance and investment that it is sometimes even alleged that it is not the voters who determine democratically what decisions are taken by politicians, but large companies such as multi-nationals who can threaten to pull out of a country, putting jobs and material prosperity at risk, if it does not get its way. Large companies may have a vested interest in the perpetuation of oppressive regimes, for example if they permit cheap labour or if they permit irresponsible marketing (such as the selling of powdered baby milk in places such as Africa and India).

Starved of finance, of course, such companies could not continue to operate, and hence a convincing case can be made out for raising our consciousness on the issue of ethical investments. Indeed, on the surface it seems undeniable that, if one disapproves of a product or a process, one ought not to support it financially. We have seen (chapter 2) how the New Consumer raises public consciousness about ethically dubious business practices in well-known firms, although in theory it seems an inescapable conclusion that one should avoid such companies, in practice things are much more difficult. Although a private citizen can avoid directly investing in, say, the tobacco or the armaments industries, it may be difficult to avoid indirect investments in such areas. High street banks do not keep our money inside their counters, and it is sound financial sense to invest in as wide a portfolio as possible. As a result, even the ordinary practice of banking one's money may not be ethically 'clean'. From the point of view of the bank, managers will take the view that their first obligation is to their shareholders, who, they may argue, want the best possible return from the monies they have invested. Additionally, it can be argued that there is no unarguably 'right' answer to the question of which investments are 'clean' and which are not. While some people might regard tobacco companies as unacceptable, others will champion a citizen's 'right to smoke'; while some might claim that armaments are evil, others will argue that any country has the fundamental right to defend itself. What right has the bank, it might be argued, to act as the conscience of society, when such issues are fraught with controversy? (The Co-operative Bank is one possible exception to all this; it insists that customers' money is not used for unethical investments, and it refuses to speculate against currencies.)

Furthermore, companies themselves diversify and invest in other firms, and it can be difficult for the average consumer to keep track of which monies end up where. Investors might therefore be forgiven for thinking it morally fastidious to keep too close a watch on their funds and for taking the view that, so long as there are not flagrant breaches of basic moral standards, all is well – or at least as well as can be expected. Indeed, if one takes *The Ethical Consumer's* list, one might well find it hard to discover an investment which did not fall short of these standards in several respects. In the end, we may all be faced with the choice of deciding, not between black and white, but between different shades of grey.

It has been suggested that there is some advantage to be gained positively by investing in firms whose consciousness needs to be awakened. Ownership of shares carries some influence, and an investor can attend a company's Annual General Meeting and raise issues of concern from the floor. There have been remarkable occasions where this type of protest has succeeded; indeed, the campaign against Barclay's began with protesters buying small numbers of shares and voicing their protests at Barclay's AGM. However, despite the occasional remarkable success story, few citizens buy shares with the purpose of initiating reforms, and only a small handful of private investors ever attend shareholders' meetings. In any case, only a very few shares are needed in order to qualify for admission; this argument could scarcely be used for larger investments.

PRIVATIZATION

Until recently there have been industries in which private investment has not been possible at all. The succession of Conservative governments has changed all that. When the British Telecom flotation took place in 1986, a new breed of shareholder was born. The Conservative government, in its commitment to private enterprise, was determined to demonstrate that certain designated public services could actually be profitable, and that dealing in shares was an activity which did not require ordinary people to become speculators or to use stockbrokers.

Until its defeat in the 1979 election, Labour governments had typically taken the view that there were certain services which should not be sold to private individuals, but should be owned publicly. Such industries were those which appeared to be incapable of making a profit, which, although unprofitable, nevertheless provided the public with a social benefit which was believed to outweigh the cost of subsidizing the losses incurred by these industries. Such benefits might include the provision of employment to those who might otherwise be without work, or the supplying of socially desirable services such as railways, thus improving communications and syphoning off travellers and freight away from increasingly congested roads. Labour further took the view that there were certain industries which formed the 'bottlenecks' of the economy (such as water, electricity, communications) and that it was therefore desirable that the government should retain control of these key industries, rather than leave their fate to market forces, which might not necessarily result in the best interests of the nation. In fact all the recently privatized industries have been monopolies (even the new communications company Mercury only competes with British Telecom in a limited way), with the obvious disadvantages to the consumer. One suspects that at least one reason for privatization has more than a little to do with the Conservative philosophy of letting market forces decide the fate of business enterprises, as well as a presumed inherent desirability of private ownership. Whatever the reasons, the amount of campaigning, and – more especially – the pricing of Telecom shares was clearly designed to demonstrate to the average citizen that buying shares was 'a good thing'. It seems highly unlikely that the government accidently allowed these shares to be so greatly undervalued to the extent that many individuals became several thousand pounds to the good as a result of no effort other than filling in a simple application form. At the launch of British Petroleum, which coincided with the notorious 'Black Monday' in 1986, the Government was obliging enough to bale out those would-be investors who had been imprudent enough to go ahead with the purchase of plummeting BP shares. The sale of public utilities was therefore simultaneously the sale of an ideology; clearly the Government was determined that there would be a new breed of investor, the 'first time owner'.

Apart from political dogma and short term gain, convincing reasons for privatization are difficult to discern. If the aim was to generate income as a means of reducing taxation, privatization could be no more than a short term measure, owing to its 'one off' nature. If it was in the belief that privatized industries are more efficient than publicly owned ones, it could be argued that such a view confuses cause and effect; industries are likely to be nationalized because they are unprofitable, they are not necessarily unprofitable as a result of being nationalized. When Margaret Thatcher stated that one aim of privatization was to enable the public to 'take an interest' in the privatized services, it was difficult to see what this meant; levels of attendance at shareholders' meetings seems unaffected by privatization, and in any case it is unclear what advantage there would be in enabling the average private citizen to express views about how such industries should be run.

The first of the privatization advertising slogans announced, 'British Telecom goes public'. The implication presumably was that any member of the public who wished to do so could now share in the wealth of this profit-making industry. In point of fact, this was far from the case. The minimum investment was £50, a sum which many citizens simply could not afford, while those who could invest sums of £5000 or thereabouts almost literally doubled their money overnight. Meanwhile, revenues from the privatized sector of Telecom (49% after the original flotation) were lost to the exchequer, and had to be compensated by reductions of public services or by taxation. (Although the Conservative Government kept its 1979 pledge to reduce income tax, it slapped on 7.5% in the form of VAT, which more than offset any direct tax savings to the average citizen.) The programme of privatization tended to redistribute wealth in favour of the rich, rather than the poor, a pattern which runs counter to the 'need' principle of distributive justice which we articulated in chapter 4.

There is a justifiable fear by those who oppose privatization that a privatized industry will cut those sectors which are not financially profitable. If British Telecom and British Rail have their eye on profits, is it likely that they will continue to maintain respectively the isolated telephone booth near John O'Groats or the scenic line which carries only a handful of commuters?

There is a further, and important, criticism which has been voiced by those who are environmentally conscious. An industry which aims to maximize profits is likely to encourage consumption rather than con-servations of resources. To privatize power and water is therefore likely to involve consumers being encouraged to increase levels of consump-tion at a time when the environment is becoming threatened by excess pollution, erosion of top soil, and a general dwindling of non-renewable resources.

Clearly the issue of privatization raises the question of whether market forces should determine which services are offered and which are with-drawn, which industries flourish and which go to the wall, or whether a government has a duty to consider the common weal, including presumed rights of minorities, such as those who live in isolated areas or those who might find themselves unemployed if market forces dictate that their jobs no longer exist.

Our discussion has covered a range of issues relating to accounting and investment. Whether or not readers agree with our particular stance on issues such as privatization, we have endeavoured to show that the ethical dimension of these areas is not confined to obvious malpractices such as fraud. The very activities of accounting and investing themselves generate important ethical issues, which cannot be ignored by those who work in these professions.

INTRODUCING THE READINGS

Ian Griffiths, in the first chapter of *Creative Accounting*, which we reproduce here, sets out a number of techniques which have been used by the accounting profession, and examines the problems which these pose for potential investors. Proposals for change were outlined in the European Directive ED42, which Michael J. Brooks discusses in 'ED42 – The end of creative accounting?' Brooks focuses on three issues; controlled non-subsidiaries, the definition of a 'transaction' and how assets and liabilities are defined. In 'Accountability and Acquisitions' Mike Allen and Robert Hodgkinson focus their attention particularly on the way in which creative accounting is used in the area of acquisition accounting. J. G. Williams outlines some of the ethical dilemmas which may confront the newly qualified accountant. Although he does not claim to have easy solutions, the author provides techniques of breaking down such problems which will help the accountant to reach his or her own decision. The final two selections deal with auditing. André Zünd tackles issues relating to the ethical behaviour of auditors and auditees, while Arnold Schilder raises the question of the independence of the auditor, and the differing arrangements which exist in several European countries to ensure auditor independence.

Creative accounting

IAN GRIFFITHS

Every company in the country is fiddling its profits. Every set of published accounts is based on books which have been gently cooked or completely roasted. The figures which are fed twice a year to the investing public have all been changed in order to protect the guilty. It is the biggest con trick since the Trojan horse.

Any accountant worth his salt will confirm that this is no wild assertion. There is no argument over the extent and existence of this corporate contortionism, the only dispute might be over the way in which it is described. Such phrases as 'cooking the books', 'fiddling the accounts' and 'corporate con trick' may raise eyebrows where they cause people to infer that there is something illegal about this pastime. In fact this deception is all in perfectly good taste. It is totally legitimate. It is creative accounting.

This above-the-board means of achieving underhand ends is rife in boardrooms throughout the country as companies contrive to translate their activities of the year into reported results which flatter the management and the share price. The methods which are used to manipulate the figures and the dramatic impact they have on a company's profits are described in detail in later chapters. They range from the very simple to the latest, highly sophisticated schemes which defy detection. Whatever the degree of complexity, the end result is always exactly the same. The company produces figures which are only loosely based on fact.

The legacy for these rather crude adaptations of the year's events comes from the flexibility and vagueness of the accounting rules and company law which governs how financial statements should be prepared and presented. There is no black and no white, only grey. This country is blessed with a system of low definity monochrome accounting.

Yet no finance director can afford to be left behind in the creative accounting stakes. The opportunities to manipulate the profit and loss account, and the balance sheet which these schemes present, can no longer be overlooked. Financial information has become a propaganda weapon to be swung into action whenever the need arises. The days when a company's accounts were simply a record of its trading performance are long dead.

Having identified the financial statements, though, as the murder victim, and creative accounting as the murder weapon, all that is missing is the motive. The flat-footed sergeant turns to his inspector and asks, 'The only thing that puzzles me, chief, is why a company like that would want to do such a thing?'

The answer provides the key to creative accounting's growing popularity. The pressure on companies to report flattering results is greater than ever before. This necessity mothers the innovations in accounting creativity, which makes it increasingly difficult for users of financial information to discern fact from fiction.

Ironically, it is those users who have perhaps contributed most, directly and indirectly, to this climate of distortion. A combination of the increasing power of the big institutional investors and, at the same time, a move to encourage wider share ownership by small individual investors, has forced companies to tailor their results to meet more closely the demands of the stock market. Those demands dictate that a company produces a steady growth in profits and earnings and that it consistently lives up to the expectations imposed on it by an army of City analysts and research teams.

There is no doubt that a company which in four successive years produces pre-tax profits of £1, £2, £4, and £8 million will be regarded in a better light than one which produces profits of £4 and £15 million in years one and three and pre-tax losses of £1 and £3 million in years two and four. The net profits for both companies in the period is exactly the same at £15 million. But the first company has a record which reveals profits doubling each year; while the second enterprise has a trading record which is erratic to say the least.

It may well be that the second company's results represent a more accurate reflection of the trading pattern of the business. Unfortunately, the stock market simply does not take kindly to such vagaries and much prefers the fantasy of smooth growth to the reality of fluctuating operational performance. It falls to the creative accountant to ensure that those fluctuations are removed by hoarding profits in the years of plenty for release in the years of famine.

But profits-smoothing is only one side-effect of this subtle influence imposed by the City. There is also the requirement for companies to live up to the market's expectations. These are generated by the analysts from the big stockbroking houses who forecast the profits from a particular company and then use these projections as the basis for persuading clients to buy or sell the shares. It is not hard to imagine that if these clients have bought shares on the grounds that a company will make pre-tax profits of £50 million and it turns in only £40 million then questions will be asked. The buck is quickly passed and tends to stop with the company. There are few things to match the fury of a stockbroker who got his forecasts wrong. It is the kind of fury which a company does well to avoid and once again it is the finance director's responsibility to make sure that the figures match those anticipated by the City.

This relationship between companies and the City puts an entirely different perspective on the purpose of financial statements. They were originally intended to reflect how the entrepreneurs of the industrial revolution had looked after the cash, which had been put up as risk capital by shareholders to finance specific ventures. Today, though, the risk element of an investment, particularly in well-established business, is not linked to the company's operations but to the company's ability to keep the stock market sweet. Financial results have become a relative measure, not an absolute measure of success. Switching and swapping are the order of the day and a long term investment is one which won't be sold until a week on Tuesday.

The successful company is one which can strike the balance between giving out optimistic noises when the analysts' forecasts are being made and matching these later with the actual reported results. If a company is too conservative at the outset there will be no incentive for analysts to advocate that the shares be bought. But if it is too enthusiastic and the results do not match expectations, then not only will gains in the share price be lost but a lot of bad will is created. The whole aim is to create an atmosphere of 'buy the shares now and buy even more shares later'. The accomplished creative accountant, using the tools of his trade, will allow the company every opportunity to strike that balance, linking the absolute reality of trading performance with the relative illusions of reported results.

There is a danger, though, that this desire to keep the City happy and reap the rewards on an ever rising share price could get out of hand. For although the City is used as a collective noun to suggest a faceless legion of stockbrokers, bankers and financial institutions, it is in reality much more limited in its application. The City is rapidly becoming a handful of key analysts and institutions who between them have enormous power, and whose influence can make or break a company. The 'Big Bang' has radically changed the way the City is structured and operates, and the mighty financial conglomerates threaten to make a mockery of the concept of perfect knowledge. The perfect knowledge will be there all right, but in the hands of a few select organisations. Companies run the risk of becoming locked into a handful of these giants to the exclusion of the rest of the investment community.

That is a factor to be wary of in the future and for the time being many companies are more concerned with puffing up their share price. The creative accountant is supported in this task by a battery of press relations people, corporate communications consultants and investor relations advisers. Their life's work is to boost the company's share price and stock market rating. This may appear to be a worthy objective. A high share price, after all, reduces the chances of somebody else taking over a company, while at the same time increasing the chances of it making an acquisition of its own. Yet blind pursuit of a higher share price has its pitfalls.

Creative accounting, for all its scope to manipulate figures, cannot support the results of a company which is facing genuine and continuing trading difficulties. All that it can do is to defer and mitigate the bad news until there is a revival in trading fortunes. It cannot make bad news look good in perpetuity without resorting to out-and-out fraud. Therefore, if a company's share price tries to cross a bridge too far and comes unstuck, then untold damage can be done as a result of that setback. The wisest companies are those which use creative accounting to keep control not just of their figures but also of the share price itself. There is one well-known British company, a constituent of the FT 30 index, which does just this. The finance director has what he calls his bottom drawer, in which he keeps the fruits of his creative accounting – be they profits or losses – which he feeds out in order to ensure that the share price is kept within closely defined bands which reflect the company's genuine worth at a given moment in time.

When the creative accounting is so carefully controlled it is a relatively harmless weapon. It is merely reflecting the underlying trends in the value of the business, which would not always be apparent if the accounts were prepared and presented in accordance with a strict interpretation of the appropriate accounting rules and regulations. However, in the hands of a less scrupulous management it can be a highly dangerous instrument of deception. The investing community at large can be misled into making decisions on information which is neither full nor fair. Banks and other financiers might extend credit which, if the figures had been prepared in a different way, would have been withdrawn. Suppliers and other creditors may enter into a business relationship which otherwise would have been considered too risky.

The fact is, creative accounting is not just the prerogative of the quoted companies. Private companies have as much, if not more, to gain from manipulation of their annual accounts. This is particularly true of those which are considering making the transition either to the full Stock Exchange list or to the junior Unlisted Securities Market (perhaps better known as the Unlimited Surprises Market).

In these cases it is important to have created the right kind of trading record which will ensure that the flotation is accomplished with minimum fuss. Not only does the flotation provide the company with access to the massive funds of the existing City institutions but also presents the chance to entice the private investor to part with his hard-earned cash on the back of a campaign to promote wider share ownership.

That campaign had a tremendous boost from the giveaway privatisation of British Telecom, which has perhaps created some illusions among the wider share owner. The double-your-money characteristic of the Telecom flotation was unique to that company. It was a never-to-be-repeated offer, well, not before the next big privatisation anyway. However, it has perhaps given the impression that playing the stock market is like stealing candy from a baby. Nothing could be further from the truth. Yet there are now large numbers of private investors eager to repeat their Telecom success, who have very little idea of the real rules of the stock market game they are playing. It is this ever growing group of shareholders who have the most to lose from irresponsible creative accounting.

There is no reason why they should be conversant with the techniques which are employed to massage the accounts. Indeed there is no reason why they should have any grounding in basic accountancy anyway. It is dividends and capital growth which are important. The annual report and accounts do not even merit a placing in many shareholders' list of priorities. Yet this is the best opportunity the investor has to assess how his money is being managed. Ironically, the attitude among companies tends to be that, rather than to provide fuller and clearer statutory accounts, they concentrate instead on glossy superficial reviews of the business. It is a dangerous trend which will lead to a complete devaluation of the statutory accounts. The less attention paid to them, the more chance the creative accountant has of taking another step closer to the thin borderline which separates creativity from fraud. Once that divide is broken, then inevitably it will be the private shareholders who lose out most. There seems to be an unwritten rule that the big institutions will always suffer less then the small investor, be it as a consequence of fraud or simply of poor trading. This was illustrated by the tyre giant Dunlop's recent demise, which led to it being taken over by BTR – the industrial holdings group. The downturn in trading fortunes which left Dunlop on the verge of collapse was shared mainly by private investors. Most of the big institutions had sold out months earlier, confirming the view that perfect market information is only available to certain sections of the investing community. It leaves the small shareholders cruelly exposed to the wiles of the unscrupulous creative accountant. Not only are they last in line for being given the crucial information which might allow them to cut their losses and run, but more importantly they are actively dissuaded from taking an interest in the all-important financial statements which might give them a faint chance of seeing which way the wind is blowing.

But the use of creative accounting is not restricted to luring new investors into the company or keeping existing shareholders happy. It has also become very popular as a means of fighting takeover battles. The merger mania which has swept the country recently has forced both predators and defenders to search for new weapons which can be brought to bear on the opposition. Hardly a contested bid goes by without either or both sides resorting to creative accounting to bolster their own position, while at the same time criticising their opponent's methods of preparing and presenting financial information.

Yet this open acknowledgement of the distortion which takes place in financial statements seems to encourage the habit rather than pose questions about its acceptability. It is perhaps one of the few occasions when two wrongs seem to make a right, but then that is the creative accountant's stock in trade. As long as there are contested bid battles to be fought then creative accounting will always have its part to play.

However, while large elements of the creative accountant's armoury are being openly put on display, it has to be said there has been a steady increase in the number of schemes which are not visible even to the most highly trained eye. This is the most sinister aspect of creative accountancy and stems from what has been called off balance sheet financing. This involves adapting schemes which, rather than manipulate existing figures, actually exclude them altogether from the financial statements. It is impossible to detect them even from a detailed analysis of the small print in the notes to the accounts. The reason for a company to take advantage of these schemes is normally to allow it to obtain funding which it would otherwise have been unable to secure. Debt levels may already be uncomfortably high, making it impossible for a company to secure the additional cash it needs to finance its capital investment programme. The answer to this rather embarrassing problem has come in the shape of a variety of off balance sheet financing schemes which have been devised and are now being actively marketed. These schemes threaten to undermine completely the dwindling credibility of the statutory accounts.

Whether the moves underway to try and improve the disclosure of such schemes will work remains to be seen. The problem for the accountancy profession is that it has condoned, and in some cases quite properly encouraged, an element of creative accounting, by its corporate clientèle. For it to turn round suddenly and say that off balance-sheet financing is the unacceptable face of creativity may leave it with some awkward questions to answer about the acceptibility of tactics and techniques which have been permitted in earlier accounting periods. The crucial question which has to be answered is, where should the line be drawn?

There is of course no answer. If there were, the line would have been drawn a long time ago and there would be no such thing as creative accounting. The reason why it has survived and thrived is that the system of accounting standards is itself designed to encourage an element of flexibility. The standards are not intended, despite their name, to lay down specific accounting treatments, but rather to narrow down the range of options which should be consistently applied in order to improve the comparability of accounts year on year and between one company and another. The system recognises that different businesses will find different methods of accounting more appropriate for reflecting their performance more fairly. But in trying to strike the balance between flexibility and fairness it has erred, and quite rightly according to most finance directors, on the side of flexibility. Unfortunately, this leaves a system which gives the impression of laying down uniform standards but in practice it merely endorses the differing accounting treatments which are available.

The upshot is that accounts can be prepared in accordance with accounting standards and still show entirely different results for the same set of transactions. There is no need for a company to resort to non-compliance with those standards in order to implement a particular creative accounting technique, in fact to do so would only attract unwanted attention. All that is required of company accounts is that they show a true and fair view, and nobody has ever managed to define quite what this means. With such vague terms of reference to which to work, the creative accountant's job is made that much easier and the auditor's job that much harder.

Although the auditor is employed in theory to protect and act on behalf of the shareholders, there is little effective opposition he can mount against the determined manipulator of figures. Many of the arguments for or against a particular accounting treatment are fought purely on subjective grounds. The questions are those of judgement not of fact: all the auditor has to rely on for his defence is the rather feeble support of the true and fair view. His job is made even harder by his own admission that the figures shown in the accounts could be wrong by between 5 and 10 per cent, perhaps even more, without any impairment of their truth and fairness. In the light of this it becomes very difficult to argue that a certain approach is definitely wrong, when no one has laid down what is definitely right. In the end the auditor has to settle for an element of bartering over specific treatments; he gets his way on some and allows the company to take a more liberal interpretation of the rules on others.

But it is not just the theoretical difficulties of technical interpretation which makes the auditor's job difficult. He also has to face some quite difficult practical and commercial pressures. These are imposed by the intense competition in a stagnant audit market place. The companies are well aware of this and it is easy to see how an unscrupulous management might take advantage of this by subtly suggesting that failure to come round to their way of thinking on a particular issue might result, not directly of course, in the audit assignment being put out to tender. No firm likes to lose a client and it is surprising the extremes to which auditors will go in order to maintain cordial relations. This is not to suggest that the auditing profession is failing in its duties, but merely pointing out that when the question in dispute is one of judgement and there is no clearly defined right or wrong way of answering it, then pragmatism might prove to be the deciding factor.

It is not a situation which is likely to get any better. The competition in the market place is becoming increasingly intense, and some firms almost regard audit assignments as loss leaders which will give them the platform from which to sell their more lucrative services such as tax and management consultancy. And as the accounting practices, particularly the large international firms, set their sights on the type of corporate finance work which has traditionally been carried out by merchant banks, then the pragmatism might even be replaced by active incitement to adopt creative accounting techniques. There are already signs that this is happening, and these may still prove to be just the tip of the iceberg.

It is not, however, in the private sector alone where creative accounting is encountered: the public sector too has its own methods of manipulation. In these situations it is not the shareholders who are at risk but the taxpayers. The problem, though, is accentuated by the fact that the taxpayer has even less interest in the finances of the public sector than the small shareholder does in the accounts of his own company. The public's interest in the nationalised industries runs to such things as why trains don't run on time, why letters get lost in the post and why it takes the gasman such a long time to come and look at the boiler. Such practical questions are important, but they become even more so if they are asked against the background of a fuller understanding of a particular state industry's finances. At the moment the public is, by and large, quite happy to sit back and accept as gospel the figures which are broadcast as profits and losses for the year. The taxpayer seems quite happy to accept that the steel and coal industries lose lots of money while the gas and electricity industries make lots of money. No questions are asked about the methods of accounting which have been used to arrive at these conclusions.

Take the electricity industry for example. In 1983/84 it reported profits before interest of £914.4 million. It is a lot of money but not so much that the public gets too upset about it. However, that figure which is relayed to the taxpayer is based on current cost accounting principles which make an allowance for the impact of inflation. Had the electricity industry used the historical cost principles which are used in the private sector, the story would have been completely different. On the historical cost basis the pre-interest profits would have been £1,852.8 million. That is more than double the figure which is reported as the actual result for 1983/84. Suddenly questions might be asked about the prices which this public service company is charging to its customers, the taxpayer. The difference in the two figures works out at around a £20 a year reduction per person in electricity bills. On that basis some households would have been entitled to rebates. Yet the difference in the figures is purely a function of accounting treatment. It is exactly the same power stations producing exactly the same electricity for exactly the same consumers but one basis produces profits half those produced by another basis. And 1983/84 is not an isolated example. In 1984/85, when the results were affected by the miners' strike, the Electricity Council reported losses of £1,277.1 million before interest, using its favoured current cost accounting. Had it applied historical cost principles those losses would have reduced to just £146.6 million.

Clearly the chosen method of accounting will influence the budgets and forecasts which are critical in determining the level of price increases to be introduced. While the electricity industry insists on using current cost accounting which produce lower reported profits it will be able to justify more easily its price rises. Whether it is right to rely on the expediency provided by a particular accounting concept, which ironically, has now been totally discredited by the private sector and the accountancy profession is another matter altogether, but one which is very rarely discussed in the tap room or snug bar.

The use of creative accounting in determining pricing policies cannot, therefore, be underestimated. The Thames Water Authority showed this quite lucidly when it was attempting to resist government pressure for it to increase water rates. The government assumptions were based on current cost principles and showed that a price increase was needed in order for Thames to meet its required return on capital. The Thames assumptions, using historical principles, demonstrated quite the opposite and showed that more than adequate returns could be achieved without a price rise. Somebody had to be wrong.

It is not just in the area of pricing, however, where the chosen accounting treatment can influence the decision-making process. This was made horrifically clear during the bitter days of the year-long coal dispute. It was a conflict over pit closures. The National Coal Board insisted that it had to close uneconomic pits, while the union argued that the jobs could and should be preserved. However, one of the least controversial aspects of that dispute was over the definition of uneconomic. It was at the heart of the conflict yet it attracted very little publicity, and there is still no certainty that a satisfactory answer has been provided. The issue was raised by a team of independent accountancy academics who challenged the viability of certain key NCB accounting documents as the basis for making pit closure decisions. They raised important questions about fixed cost and overhead allocations which, if treated in different ways, produced different conclusions. It is a sad fact that people's jobs, and this is not just in the coal industry, could be put at risk simply because the accountants decide to treat certain costs in a particular way. Such arbitrary judgements are all well and good when the question is one of whether interest payments should be capitalised or not, but when that question could lead to somebody being deprived of their livelihood then a lot more care and caution is required from the creative accountant.

As the chapters unfold it will become clear that there is a tremendous amount of scope for making such arbitrary judgements. Carefully used the techniques outlined can provide a useful bridge between the artificial constraints of an annual reporting cycle and the reality of a trading cycle which may be either longer or shorter. Similarly, creative accounting can be used to iron out short term difficulties which might otherwise attract undue concern. However, the key to effective use of the various schemes is moderation. In the long run creative accounting is no substitute for sound trading and business development. Any attempt to make that substitution over a sustained period of time will result ultimately in catastrophe. It is, therefore, up to the company's management to use creative accounting with the integrity and respect which it deserves and it is up to individual shareholders to study financial statements more closely, to ensure that these standards are being upheld and maintained.

ED42 – The end of creative accounting?

MICHAEL J. BROOKS

The publication of the Accounting Standards Committee's exposure draft ED42 *Accounting for Special Purpose Transactions* represents a significant landmark in the development of standards of financial reporting in the UK. Not only does the proposed standard demonstrate a clear intention on the part of the ASC to eliminate much of what has euphemistically come to be known as 'creative accounting' but it is attempting to do so by means of a conceptual framework.

Creative accounting is clearly neither creative nor is it accounting in the generally accepted sense. It does not attempt to portray commercial events and financial conditions as they really are but, instead, presents them as the management of the reporting enterprise wishes them to appear. It has been suggested that the practice of creative accounting in the UK has been aided, at least in part, by certain recent accounting standards that have been flawed in concept and inadequate in their drafting. Presumably, these comments refer particularly to the standards on goodwill and acquisitions and mergers.

The latest proposals from the ASC are obviously intended to reverse the trend of recent years and, as such, will generally be welcomed by those who regard fair and neutral financial reporting as necessary to the proper working of the capital markets.

Reading taken from *Management Accounting*, December 1988. Copyright © 1988 *CIMA*. Reprinted with permission.

The conceptual approach taken by ED42 is also a welcome departure from what has often been criticised in the past as an excessively ad hoc process of developing accounting standards. Many of the ASC's pronouncements bear the marks of compromise and are, in certain instances, insufficiently consistent one with another, whereas a clearly articulated conceptual basis is better able to provide a sound framework for consistent and robust standards.

The purpose of this article is to describe the proposals contained in ED42 and to comment on them and their implications.

Special-purpose transactions

Special-purpose transactions, as defined and described in ED42, are not quite as unusual or esoteric as they might at first seem. Many special-purpose transactions are intended to facilitate off-balance-sheet financing and are often structured so as to present a legal form that may be quite different from their economic or business substance. While ED42 is at pains to point out that it does not specifically address the question of substance over form, this disclaimer is clearly intended to defuse the argument between the accounting profession and the legal profession regarding the ability of the former to prescribe non-statutory standards that appear to override the provisions of company law.

One particular feature of special-purpose transactions is that they may be arranged as a series of individual transactions such that the effect of the whole series differs from the apparent effects of each component when considered separately. The approach taken in ED42 is to have regard to the economic and financial effect of the whole series rather than that of each component when determining the appropriate accounting treatment to be applied. Such an approach is, of course, adopted already by most companies and their auditors and is considered by many in the profession to follow from the true and fair requirement of company law. Nevertheless, it is quite proper for the ASC to incorporate this point explicitly in the body of accounting standards.

Controlled non-subsidiaries

A particular cause for concern in relation to off-balance-sheet finance has been the use of companies which are controlled by another company but which are not subsidiaries of it. These are known as controlled non-subsidiaries. A subsidiary is currently defined in company law either in terms of the ownership of equity capital or the ability to control the composition of its board of directors. Both of these definitions provide scope for a company to set up another company which it can effectively control but which is not a subsidiary of it under company law.

The control over the financial and operational policies of such a non-subsidiary may be effected in a number of way. For example, an agreement may be made between the controlling company and the other shareholders in the non-subsidiary that the latter, who might include a merchant bank or other financial adviser to the controlling company, would only exercise their votes in accordance with the wishes of the controlling company. Alternatively, the equity capital could be split into equal numbers of voting and non-voting shares and only the voting shares issued to the controlling company. Different categories of shares might have different levels of voting rights.

Effective control over the operating policies of the non-subsidiary might be obtained by a provision in the articles giving disproportionate voting rights to certain directors at board meetings or by an agreement with a block of shareholders that their nominee directors would abstain from voting. None of these arrangements would involve the controlled company becoming a subsidiary of the controlling company.

Controlled non-subsidiaries clearly need not be consolidated into the group accounts of the controlling company and are therefore ideal vehicles for raising finance the existence of which could remain unknown to the users of the controlling company's accounts.

ED42 sets out to eliminate this opportunity for off-balance-sheet finance by requiring that the accounts of controlled non-subsidiaries be treated in group accounts in the same way as those of legally defined subsidiaries. The Department of Trade and Industry, with whom the ASC working party has been liaising closely on this topic has indicated that it is sympathetic to the view that control rather than ownership should be the main criterion for consolidation. Moreover, the European Commission's Seventh Directive on consolidated accounts, which is due for implementation in the UK in the next few years, also stresses control as the dominant factor in the decision as to whether the accounts of the company should be consolidated or not.

The substance of a transaction

At the heart of ED42's proposals is the proposition that a transaction should be accounted for in accordance with its commerical effect. While straightforward transactions do not usually present significant accounting problems, special-purpose transactions can package rights and obligations in a manner that makes it difficult to discern the appropriate accounting treatment and the effect that they have on the enterprise's assets and liabilities. This may occur due to a severance of legal ownership of an item from the ability to enjoy its benefits or exposure to the risks inherent in it or it may result from a series of transactions which can only be properly understood when considered in its entirety.

ED42 notes that the most familiar example of this is a finance lease for which the principle of recognising commercial substance rather than legal form has already been established in SSAP21. Other, more novel special-purpose transactions may involve the separate sale and re-purchase of goods which span the end of an accounting period or contain an option whose terms ensure that it will always be exercised.

Determining the substance of a transaction will involve identifying the relevant aspects of it and the manner in which they interact. It may not always be possible to be certain as to the effect of some transactions, in which case the accounting method should be chosen on the basis of the likely commercial effect.

Assets and liabilities

A key step in determining the substance of a transaction is in identifying the effect that it has on the assets and liabilities of an enterprise which have been recognised previously in its accounts and determining whether it has given rise to an asset or a liability not previously recognised.

While most accountants would argue that they already know from their training and experience what constitutes an asset or a liability, neither is currently fully defined either in UK accounting standards or in UK company law. ED42 offers definitions of assets and liabilities and sets these definitions in a conceptual framework which is clearly intended to provide a basis for the development of further accounting standards.

Assets are defined as probable future economic benefits, controlled by or accruing to a particular enterprise as a result of past transactions or events. This definition, which is essentially the same as that used by the US Financial Accounting Standards Board in its Conceptual Framework statements, has three main elements:

(a) probable future benefit – essentially this means future cash inflows to the enterprise. These cash flows need not, of course, be certain nor would the adoption of this definition suggest the abandonment of historical-cost accounting in favour of a discounted, economic-value approach;

(b) control by or accruing to the enterprise – this means that, for recognition in accounts as an asset, the benefit should not be available to another enterprise or the world in general. Thus the undoubted benefits to an enterprise of unpolluted air or the absence of exchange controls would not constitute assets that could be recognised in its financial statements;

(c) result of past transactions or events – this element requires that the event giving rise to the benefit must already have occurred. Consequently, the benefit that would arise in the future from a transaction that has yet to be undertaken or an event that has yet to occur cannot be considered an asset before the transaction or the event has taken place.

Once an asset is recognised in the accounts of an enterprise, it follows that it should remain in the accounts until events or transactions releasing or destroying the benefit have occurred. This release or destruction could occur merely by the passing of time, by physical or economic deterioration or by loss or confiscation. A clear distinction should be drawn between changes in assets and changes in associated liabilities.

For example, a transaction that purports to be the sale of an asset but which, in reality, is a financing transaction should be accounted for as an increase in the liabilities of an enterprise and not as a reduction in its assets.

ED42 defines liabilities in an analogous manner to assets. They are present obligations entailing probable future economic sacrifices by transferring assets or providing services to other entities in the future. Considering each of these elements in turn:

(a) present obligations include legal liabilities but are wider in scope. They encompass commitments which may not be legally binding but which may be inferred from an enterprise's dealings or policies, such as the payment of a pension to a retired employee who is not a member of a pension scheme;
(b) probable future economic sacrifices, like probable future benefits, do not have to be certain to qualify for recognition in financial statements although, clearly, they do have to be measurable;
(c) transfer of assets or provision of services to another entity – this part of the definition allows for uncertainty as to the identity of the recipient. For example, it would require recognition of a liability in respect of probable payments under a product warranty even though the identity of the potential claimant may not be known at the balance sheet date.

ED42 provides a detailed discussion of the implications of these definitions for financial reporting. Much of this discussion is conducted in a more academic tone than has been usual in previous ASC documents and this has given rise to some adverse criticism in certain of the responses to the proposals.

Some of this criticism no doubt reflects the lack of familiarity of many UK accountants with an overtly theoretical approach to accounting standard-setting and the practical nature of much of accounting education in the UK. While the final standard might be expected to have a slightly more pragmatic and familiar flavour, it is unreasonable to expect a standard that is intended to provide a sound conceptual basis to be couched in other than conceptual terms.

The proposals have also been criticised as not being specific enough. This kind of criticism is, however, somewhat misguided and presupposes that it is possible and desirable to legislate for every possible eventuality. To attempt to provide accounting standards of this sort would be to invite the 'cookbook' approach which not only produces detailed standards of enormous complexity but also encourages a standards-avoidance mentality whereby the less scrupulous members of the profession might actively look for loopholes in the rules.

Neither of these outcomes is to be preferred to the current UK approach which this exposure draft proposes to reinforce with a properly articulated theoretical framework. It is to be hoped that the process of exposure and debate will enable the ASC to build on the start provided by ED42 and that the standard that emerges from that process will strengthen rather than diminish the 'true and fair' principle so as to reassure the financial community that accounts really do mean what they say and say what they mean.

Accountability and acquisitions

MIKE ALLEN AND ROBERT HODGKINSON

Buying a business makes sense when the benefit exceeds the cost. Unless you happen to find a seller who accepts too low a price, you can only secure a net benefit from an acquisition by improving the target's performance.

Buyers, of course, run into problems which competition law when their plans to improve a target's performance depend on the creation and use of monopoly power, they can actually be said to create wealth. Either they use the target's resources more efficiently than the seller or they exploit opportunities for synergy with their existing business.

The principal argument for a free acquisitions market is that it should allow businesses to gravitate towards the managers who can do the most with them. However, the argument does collapse if nobody can tell whether an acquisition has resulted in a real and not just an apparent improvement in performance. It is our contention that buyers' accounts often do not reflect real success and failure. There is therefore a danger that businesses will gravitate towards the most creative accountants rather than the best managers.

The prospect of creating value from an acquisition arises whenever a potential target is poorly managed. Two courses of action are open to a corporate buyer or a buy-out or buy-in team. First, if the target is well positioned in a market with a good future, then the buyer should aim to turn the business round. Second, if the target is poorly positioned, perhaps in a stagnant market and with poor products and people, then it usually makes more sense to strip the target. These alternatives are not mutually exclusive. An asset strip of part of a target can help fund a turnround of the remainder of the business.

Most buyers other than management buy-out or buy-in teams also have an existing business to which they can add an acquisition target. This existing business provides a further opportunity for a buyer to create value from an acquisition through synergy. The concept of synergy is grandly paraphrased as 'the whole is greater than the sum of the parts' and it is captured in the formula '2 + 2 = 5'. Although the term is often viewed with suspicion, there are genuine circumstances in which two businesses can together achieve what is beyond their individual capabilities.

If the target's management is poor, little is lost by taking over the running of the acquired business and forcing the pace on realising synergy gains. But where target management is good, such a 'takeover' is likely to be damaging. The acquisition needs to be viewed as a merger and the two businesses need to be fused more gently.

The task of managing an acquisition to create value is likely to be difficult whether the acquisition takes the form of a turn-round, an asset strip, a takeover or a merger. Moreover, negotiating a deal so that the extra value is not given away to the sellers also requires particular skill, especially where there are rival buyers. Defining a successful acquisition in accounting terms does, however, appear to be easy.

Defining success

The successful turn-round leads to bigger operating profits although turnover can go up or down. The asset strip means the end of operating profits and turnover as trading assets are realised and liabilities are settled to generate a one-off non-operating profit. In a takeover or merger, profit margins can be improved by greater bargaining power, rationalised overheads and better asset utilisation. Turnover can be increased when the buyer's products are sold to the target's customers and *vice versa* and when a broader range of complementary products is sold to new customers who prefer 'one-stop shopping'.

It should be straightforward to translate the reasoning behind an acquisition into projections of profits, margins and sales. In most organisations this will be part of the normal process of planning and budgeting and the reporting of achievements will form the basis for determining the success of each acquisition and the effectiveness of management.

Outsiders are less well informed about the success or otherwise of acquisitions. Even if a target business remains a separate limited company, it is unlikely that its statutory accounts will allow a reliable comparison to be made of performance before and after an acquisition. Intercompany charges and the effects of positive or negative synergy on other parts of the buyer's group will conceal the real results of an acquisition.

Investors must therefore rely on the consolidated accounts of the buyer to judge the success of an acquisition. These accounts show the combined results of the buying company and the businesses it has bought using one of the two methods set out in SSAP 23, namely acquisition accounting and merger accounting.

In the UK, acquisition accounting principles can be applied to any deal. Merger accounting, which is seen as rather mischievous, is only allowed when all or almost all of the share capital of a target is acquired and the consideration consists entirely or almost entirely of shares in the buyer.

Nevertheless, we shall argue that the wider application of merger accounting principles would make it much easier to assess the success of an acquisitive company from its published accounts. There are three main areas of weakness in acquisition accounting: presentation of trends; effects of fair values; calculation of goodwill.

Trends

Under acquisition accounting, the results of an acquired business are consolidated from the date of acquisition. This makes a nonsense of trying to assess whether buying management have achieved real improvements in profits and sales. Spectacular growth is reported in the year of acquisition and in the following year. Further acquisitions disguise any subsequent stagnation.

By contrast, merger accounting requires a buyer to consolidate the results of a target for the whole of the year of purchase and for any previous periods that are presented. Only an underlying improvement in performance will generate an improving trend in reported sales and profits.

One of the main concerns with merger accounting is that management seem to take credit for results which were achieved prior to their stewardship. Such accounting is therefore often only seen as appropriate when two businesses and their managements really do 'merge'. To meet the criticism, SSAP 23 requires disclosure of the pre-purchase profits of a target. As a result, merger accounting does indicate the extent of management's stewardship and it provides the basis for judging the effectiveness of that stewardship.

A feature of both acquisition and merger accounting is that all companies included in the consolidated accounts should apply consistent accounting policies. With merger accounting, some educated guesswork may be needed to restate on a consistent basis the pre-purchase results which are consolidated. However, as we shall see, this difficulty is minor compared to that which is involved in squaring the consistency principle with the use of fair values under acquisition accounting.

Fair value

Merger accounting calls for the assets and liabilities of a target business to be brought into the buyer's consolidated accounts at their previous book values, subject only to adjustments to achieve consistency with the buyer's accounting policies. Acquisition accounting is different and requires adjustments to ensure that the consolidated balance sheet at the date of acquisition reflects the fair values of the target's separable assets and liabilities. The concept of fair value can be illustrated by looking at fixed assets and provisions.

The fair value of a fixed asset is represented by the cost of replacing it with an asset which would give the same service. Because of inflation, an asset's fair value is usually greater than its net book value. Consequently, the depreciation charges after an acquisition, which are calculated by reference to fair values, are higher than the pre-acquisition charges. This inconsistency makes it harder to compare performance before and after a purchase.

Turning to provisions, acquisition accounting recognises that a buyer allows for costs of reorganisation when deciding how much to pay for the profit-earning potential of a business. Therefore a provision for such costs is recognised as part of the fair value exercise at the date of acquisition.

With merger accounting, reorganisation costs are reported on a consistent basis through the profit and loss account regardless of whether they are connected with the purchase of a business and regardless of whether they arise before a purchase, in its immediate wake or afterwards. Acquisition accounting lacks this consistency and flatters the achievements of a buyer. Only the benefits of a post-acquisition re-organisation are reported in the profit and loss account, while the costs disappear under the general heading of 'goodwill'.

Goodwill

Acquisition accounting requires that goodwill be calculated as the difference between the fair value of the consideration given to buy a business and the fair values of separable net assets of that business. So goodwill cannot remain forever an asset on the consolidated balance sheet. Until SSAP 22, it must be written off immediately to reserves or amortised through the profit and loss account over its 'useful life'.

A buyer with substantial reserves will favour an immediate write-off of goodwill. Indeed such a buyer may try to maximize the goodwill write-off when putting the values on assets and provisions. If post-acquisition costs are recorded through goodwill write-off and not through the post-acquisition profit and loss account the apparent success of an acquisition is enhanced. It remains to be seen whether tighter disclosure requirements will curtail this abuse.

For other buyers, an immediate goodwill write-off could decimate their net assets and cause their gearing to soar. The amortisation of goodwill may be the only answer although this makes it harder to compare performance before and after an acquisition. The other alternative is to minimise the goodwill to be amortised by ascribing the values to recently discovered assets called brands, which never have to be written off through the profit and loss account!

There are no such choices with merger accounting. The consolidated balance sheets records the book values of a target's new assets and does not recognise any difference between these values and fair value of the consideration. There is no goodwill and there is no amortisation to distort preacquisition performance.

Conclusion

We have argued that merger accounting is more useful than acquisition accounting for assessing the success of acquisitive companies. It generates profit and loss accounts which are comparable between years and which therefore reveal real improvement in performance. Merger accounting is much less susceptible to manipulation, even though the reform of acquisition accounting which is underway may limit some of the unsavoury appeal. But what about the abuses of merger accounting? Surely companies use vending placings and gradual acquisitions through intermediaries to allow merger accounting to be used in circumstances where there is no real share-for-share exchange? One response is that such ruses would neither be necessary nor sinister if merger accounting was used for all acquisitions and corresponding mirror image treatment disposals are surely worth exploring.

And what of the limitations of the target's historic cost accounts which are perpetuated in merger accounting? The answer here is simple. If historic ex-accounts need to be reformed, for example to reflect fair values, they need to be reformed for all companies. It is not for acquisitive companies to reform the accounts of their targets, mix them up with their own unreformed accounts and so make themselves accountable to nobody.

The relevance of ethics: a practical problem analysed

J. G. WILLIAMS

Students attempting to pass their various examinations naturally see this test of competence as the critical part of the process of becoming a qualified management accountant.

After passing the examinations, completing the log book reminds them of the need for a range of relevant experience.

Later, having gained Associate status and in the process of seeking promotion (or a new position), they might with advantage stop to consider what else an employer expects of a newly qualified accountant. They might well with greater advantage consider this during the process of studying and qualifying.

The potential employer of a newly qualified management accountant is not just seeking a technician, however expert at using a spreadsheet for preparing and consolidating budgets. Nor is he merely seeking someone with experience – having previously done a similar job and able to apply existing skills and knowledge to the problems.

Think of this not unusual response from a manager after being presented with the analysis of a problem:

'Well, you've presented the figures; I assume they are correct, I understand the problem – but what should we do?'

The required reply usually involves some if not all of the following often over-lapping categories of judgments:

- factors which cannot be quantified easily, if at all;
- differences between long- and short-term profit;
- risk and uncertainty;
- moral and ethical judgment.

These are best illustrated by a practical problem.

Reading taken from *CIMA Student, August 1992. Copyright* © *1992 CIMA*. Reprinted with permission.

The problem
You have been appointed divisional accountant of a division of a large group which undertakes research and prototype development of electronic components. The Ministry of Defence is a major customer. Some contracts with the Ministry are fixed-price contracts whilst others, where development costs are impossible to estimate, are for the reimbursement of costs according to complex rules and a profit margin calculated by these rules.

In calculating the final costs and price to the Ministry on a recently completed contract you discover that your predecessor had misunderstood or misinterpreted the rules by which the costs should be calculated, and significantly overcharged the Ministry. The costs had not been queried, the invoices had been paid, and the profits reported had included these overstatements.

What do you say to the managing director?

Analyse the factors involved
Factors which cannot be quantified easily:

- Group reactions to disclosure of past error and reduced profits, views of divisional managerial competence, views of the advisability of further investment in the division if profit margins are reduced.
- Ministry reactions to disclosure:
  - Will honesty improve future relationships?
  - Will lower costs and prices lead to an increased business volume?
  - Will those in the Ministry who deal directly with the company be embarrassed by the disclosure?
  - Will they even be blamed for past errors and removed from their current responsibilities? In which case, will new executives favour other contractors?
  - Will the Ministry suspect deliberate miscalculation in the past and seek to impose penalties?

Differences between long- and short-term profit

- Short-term profits will be reduced by changing to the correct method of calculating.
- Past profits will be reduced and an adjustment made in this period which will be significant and very noticeable.
- Post-disclosure long-term profits will be less at risk and may improve.

Risk and uncertainty

- The chance of the Ministry discovering the error on a routine visit.
- The chance of an employee informing the Ministry.
- The problems that could arise if the miscalculations were deliberate.

Moral and ethical judgment

- The system of 'cost plus' depends on being able to trust supplying companies.
- The Ministry trusts qualified accountants to calculate accurately and honestly.

The list of factors involved is long, and is probably incomplete; different people will look at these problems in a variety of ways and express their analysis accordingly.

The analysis made, a recommendation is required.

The use of normal decision-making techniques

Applying normal decision-making techniques and listing possible actions can be useful, if only to clarify which actions are obviously unacceptable.

However, these techniques concern themselves only with the economics and probabilities of consequences, not with whether the actions are in any sense right or wrong. They indicate simply the highest expected value.

But using these techniques, and presenting the results clearly, does enable management to take decisions in as full knowledge as possible of the likely consequences.

This approach also helps when the managers involved find dealing with ethical arguments unfamiliar and uncomfortable.

Possible actions

- Use the correct calculation for this contract and disclose the past errors; this involves all the factors previously analysed.
- Use the correct calculation for this contract, but do not disclose past errors; this course of action leads to complications if the Ministry queries a lower-than-expected price or the group queries a lower-than-expected profit.
- Use the incorrect calculation used by your predecessor for this contract, and by implication for all future contracts. This may involve the delusion that safety lies in consistency; it also clearly involves deliberate error. Your predecessor's error may or may not have been intentional.

This analysis is designed to explore the problem and its implications; qualified accountants would not be expected to need to do it to reach an appropriate recommendation, though they may need to go through these arguments to convince others.

Choice of action

The right answer can be reached in at least three ways:

- applying moral or ethical judgment;
- applying the rules or directives of the Group Corporate Code of Conduct, if such exists – many larger companies now have codes of conduct;
- applying the guidance given in the CIMA *Ethical Guidelines*. To quote:

'INTEGRITY'

A professional accountant should be straightforward and honest in performing professional services.

Professional accountants should not be party to the falsification of any record or knowingly or recklessly supply and information or make any statement which is misleading, false or deceptive in a material particular.

Fundamental Principles, page 5

The right action is clear; the unacceptability of the wrong actions even clearer.

Disagreement with manager on course of action

But what do you do if your immediate superior disagrees and instructs you to take what you see to be a morally wrong course of action?

This is not a normal situation but one so difficult that it needs considerable thought, and a careful study of the appropriate section of the *Ethical Guidelines* – Resolution of Ethical Conflicts (pages 8–10).

The right course of action is clear but difficult, and involves following at least in the first instance organisational procedures and practices.

The steps recommended assume procedures typical of large British companies:

- explain to your manager why you cannot accept his instruction, with full reasons including reference to any Corporate Code of Conduct, and to the CIMA Statement;
- consider clarifying the position by discussing it in confidence with an objective outsider;
- at all times follow established procedures;
- at all times make clear that this is an issue of principle, not a matter of differing managerial judgment on a purely commercial consideration, nor a matter of different personalities;
- be prepared to take the issue beyond him to his superior, or all the way to the board or any audit committee of the board. This procedure will become much clearer as more companies establish audit committees and procedures for handling problems of this nature in line with the recent Cadbury Committee recommendations.

The reasonable assumption is that in a responsible public company senior managers will not be prepared to take formal decisions that are in any way morally questionable. Establishing an audit committee, and establishing ways to bring matters to an audit committee, makes these matters formal and less susceptible to informal pressure from managers.

Failure to resolve disputes

And if this fails? If you are still instructed to do what is to you morally wrong?

Resign and make it clear why you are resigning?

The problems are obvious: stay and be compromised or go and have all the problems of finding another post – and the problem of how to explain your resignation to potential employers.

Disclose the situation to the Ministry?

Whistleblowing is a difficult issue for the Institute. There is a fundamental principle of confidentiality in the Ethical Guidelines:

'A professional accountant should respect the confidentiality of information acquired during the course of performing professional services and should not use or disclose any such information without proper and specific authority or unless there is a legal or professional right or duty to disclose.'

This is reinforced at the end of the section of the *Ethical Guidelines* dealing with the Resolution of Ethical Conflicts:

'Except when seeking advice from the Secretary of the Institute or when legally required to do so communication of information regarding the matter to persons outside the employing organisation is not considered appropriate.'

Attitudes to whistleblowing are ambiguous; organisation members regard it as disloyalty and the courts have taken a very restrictive view of any potential public interest defence.

There have been cases of whistleblowing in the UK, involving (as this example) overcharging the Ministry of Defence and such matters as corporation tax. These have involved significant personal costs to the whistleblower, and their careers were jeopardised.

It is obvious that the difficulties are considerable, that no-one goes to this point without strong moral standards, and that there is every reason to try and make the position as clear as possible as early as possible to avoid getting to a hopeless situation by default.

Choice of action
It is worth thinking what the whistleblower is trying to achieve

- A sense of moral rightness after sacrificing one's career in doing what is seen to be duty?
- A sense of achievement from persuading the organisation to take the ethically correct action?

The first approach represents a deontological approach to ethics. The term derives from the Greek 'deon', meaning duty. This states that an action is correct if rooted in a true moral principle, regardless of the consequences.

The second approach represents utilitarianism – looking at the balance of the consequences of actions, rather than looking at the actions themselves.

Thinking about the issues involved, and how they should be analysed and handled – before they arise – is also beneficial in that it enables them to be handled more successfully.

Other problems
There is a wide range of similar potential problems for the qualified management accountant. Examples can include such problems as:

- pressures to overstate profit forecasts – for the group, for investment justification, for the bank to support borrowings, for a rights issue;
- pressure to produce misleading information for negotiations with a customer or supplier or with trade unions or employee representatives;

- problems created when independence is compromised or seen to be compromised by:
  - personal relationships;
  - financial involvement of any sort, and especially any leading to a potential conflict of interest;
  - the acceptance of any gift, favour or hospitality.
    There are morally similar problems when other members of the management team are compromised;
- problems when senior managers in your organisation tolerate actions which you regard as morally unacceptable, such as bribing the employees of potential customers.

There is potentially a very long list of problems. There are no easy solutions to be found but consulting appropriate texts or guidelines may help to clarify the issues.

Ethics in auditing

ANDRÉ ZÜND

The ethical challenge of auditing

The goal of *auditing* is to deliver an independent, competent judgement passed with due care, called an 'opinion', on the compliance of facts with norms. In cases when such an opinion is given by a person outside the social system to be audited the auditor is called an 'independent auditor'. An 'internal auditor', on the other hand, is an employee whose duty is to audit the firm on the instructions of the management; although he is not independent of the management, he should be unrelated to the persons and objects he audits.

The primary function of the independent auditor is to verify the annual financial accounts of a firm. He gives the financial statements the credibility they need; without such an audit the firm's presentation of the accounts is mere conjecture. According to Mautz/Sharaf, the *basic assumptions* of auditing consist of the *premises* which form the framework of the auditing process and the *principles* which are deduced from the premises, such as independence, competence and due care. The premises are divided into premises of verifiability and premises of behaviour. Without the premise of verifiability an audit would be nonsense. Only the provable is verifiable. The premise of behaviour concerns the auditees and has two aspects: the continuity

Reading taken from *Business Ethics - A European Review, vol. 1, no. 4*, Copyright © 1992 Blackwell. Reprinted with permission.

of past behaviour, and the 'true hypothesis', i.e., the premise that honest behaviour of the auditee may be assumed in the absence of clear evidence to the contrary.

Independent, external auditing has to contend worldwide with the growing discrepancy between public expectation and the auditor's self-understanding, the so-called *expectation gap*. One of the requirements made by the public is of an ethical nature: the auditor should behave ethically while remaining alert to the possibilities of unethical or ethically questionable behaviour on the part of the auditee.

Current teaching and research in auditing in Europe is characterized by a lack of reflection upon the 'philosophy' of auditing. Auditing evidences a deficit in theory and a predominance of the legal aspects, and the ethical point of view is largely neglected. Owing to public expectation, ethics in auditing have become a challenge for the auditors. Two aspects must be distinguished: the behaviour of the auditor himself and the behaviour of the auditee – although there are interdependencies between the two.

Ethical behaviour of the auditor

Ever since auditing became a profession, ethical conduct in auditing has been a main topic of professional organisations. The obligations of an auditor as a professional person are stated in a series of specific rules of conduct which emanate from the principle of self-regulation, proper to professional organisations. The rules of professional conduct represent a step from individual to social ethics and thus to progress in the solution of value conflicts within an organisation. *Codes of conduct* call upon reasoning; they are self-imposed obligations and are thus appropriate to human beings.

The behaviour of the auditor in conformity with the professional Code of Ethics is primarily characterized by three *principles of auditing*: independence, competence and due care. The principle of due care is synonymous with 'ethical conduct'. Conscientious (or conscience-compatible) correct behaviour on the part of the auditor is called *fairness*. The auditor is fair if he creates an atmosphere of confidence and presents himself as a partner of the auditee whom he needs in order to accomplish his mandate. Without the cooperation of the auditee a successful audit is impossible. Fairness in auditing is chiefly apparent in the *audit approach*. The *traditional approach* is authoritative and violates fairness because the auditee is not permitted to speak. The so-called *current moderate approach*, on the other hand, gives the auditee the right to reply. However, it is only the *participative teamwork approach* that includes the auditee in the auditing process. Fairness in auditing means entering into the ethical dimension of the subject of the auditing.

Ethical behaviour of the auditee

Examples of unethical or ethically questionable behaviour of auditees are: charging of private expenses to the firm's account; private use of the firm's cars and machines; inclusion of business acquaintances and their families on holidays financed by the firm; bribery of purchasers; manipulation of accounts of capital investments to achieve accordance with budgets; incorrect reconciliation of accounts in order to create budget reserves; exaggeration of cost budgets by means of 'slacks' to show favourable cost deviations, etc. All these examples have the following characteristics in common: they evidence misbehaviour within the limits of the law or within a grey zone, acting in one's personal interest or in the interest of the firm, they have the certainty of secrecy, and the firm's protection in doubtful cases.

If *auditability* is lacking, the competence of the auditor is lacking as well. If ethical norms are fixed, i.e., in a code of conduct, external standards are thereby internalised: they become part of the firm's principles and verifiability is then ensured. If the firm has no code of conduct, the question arises as to whether there are any generally accepted ethical norms from which behavioural standards can be deduced. Such general codes are partly included in professional codes of behaviour. The problem is not the acceptance of abstract norms, but the concretisation of such norms and the equation of divergent standards in actual situations.

In case of *special audits* ethics are the exclusive object of the audit (moral or ethics audit). This is the primary role of internal auditing. Its goal is to verify compliance with the codes of conduct. The environmental audit is a special audit by an external as well as an internal auditor.

As far as the *audit of annual financial statements* is concerned, we take the not undisputed standpoint that unethical and ethically questionable behaviour must be interpreted as *shortcomings of management*. Contemporary understanding decrees that management has to behave ethically. Unethical behaviour is a risk factor for the firm. Professional codes of conduct demand implicitly from the auditor that he does not close his eyes to any unethical behaviour he may find during his annual audit. He must analyse such facts critically and report on them. Otherwise the sacred principles of integrity, objectivity, credibility, quality, due care and confidence are idle words. In essence, to ignore unethical behaviour is a violation of the principle of fairness.

The auditor has to encourage the auditee to enter into a *dialogue*. If he is not successful in persuading him, the auditor may not leave the auditee in any doubt about the form and content of the *auditor's report*. The auditee should have the opportunity to react. *Whistleblowing* is only justified if life and health appear at risk and the official channels of the firm have been exhausted without any change in the auditee's behaviour.

References

KREIKEBAUM, H. 'Interne Revision und Ethik', in: *Handbuch Revision, Controlling, Consulting*. Editors: G. Haberland/P. R. Preisser/C. W. Meyer, Munich 1988, Part 1.9.
MAUTZ, R. K. and SHARAF, H. A. *The Philosophy of Auditing*. USA 1961.
ZÜND, A. *Revisionslehre*. Zurich 1982.
ZÜND, A. 'Revisionsethik – Wirtschaftsethik als Prüferverhalten und Prüfungsobjekt.' *Festschrift Carl Helbling*. Zurich 1992.

Auditor independence: a real issue?

ARNOLD SCHILDER

The concept – and some complications

Why are there auditors? In essence, to add credibility to accounts. Auditors derive their function from a formal or informal relationship between 'principals' (shareholders, investors, employees, treasury etc.), and 'agents' (management, sellers of shares to buyers, taxpayers etc.). The agents have to present accounts to the principals. The principals need assurance that these accounts are reliable. Auditors provide this assurance, and in that way they reduce uncertainty, add credibility. These notions are by definition relative: 100% certainty would be nice, but has to be balanced against relevance, timeliness, efficiency and costs. Principals hope to have chosen the best alternative, compared to making their own or others' inquiries. They base this hope on auditors' expertise, integrity and impartiality. Important guarantees for that are reputation and independence.

How is that regulated in the European Community (EC)? The Eighth EC Directive, dealing with 'the approval of persons responsible for carrying out the statutory audits of accounting documents', explicitly states the two notions of professional integrity and independence. But there is an interesting difference. Article 23 states positively that auditors 'shall carry out such audits with professional integrity'. (It is beyond the scope of my article to question what that exactly should be.) But Article 24 has been formulated negatively: 'Member States shall prescribe that such persons shall not carry out statutory audits which they have required if such persons are not independent in accordance with the law of the Member State which requires the audit'. Further specification of (non) independence might develop, and has been discussed for years, but no official drafts have yet been published by the European Commission.

Are the laws of the Member States so uniform, then, that further direction is not necessary? Are the Codes of Conduct as issued by the respective Institutes of Auditors in the Member States already harmonised? Yes and no.

Yes, if one looks at the general principles on independence. The recently revised Guide to Professional Ethics (United Kingdom and Ireland) (*Accountancy*, March 1992) states in its 'Fundamental Principles': 'A member should behave with integrity in all professional and business relationships ... (and) ... should strive for objectivity', and it elaborates in Statement 1.201: 'Objectivity is a state of mind, but in certain roles the preservation of objectivity needs to be protected and demonstrated by the maintenance of a member's independence from influences which could affect his or her objectivity'. Subsequent Sections provide many detailed requirements and illustrations.

Reading taken from *Business Ethics – A European Review Vol. 1, no. 4.* Copyright © Blackwell, 1992. Reprinted with permission.

In Germany *Unabhängigkeit* (independence), *Unbefangenheit* (objectivity) and *Unparteilichkeit* (impartiality) are required (*Wirtschaftsprüferhandbuch* 1992, Band I, pp. 47/48). Also here we find independence as a necessary condition of objectivity: 'Infolgedessen begründet Abhängigkeit gleichzeitig auch Befangenheit, weil die . . . Bindungen eine unwiderlegbare Vermutung begründen, dass der Abhängige auch befangen ist' (so dependence creates also auditor's bias because one might well suspect that the auditor is not objective when he appears to be dependent). German law comprises detailed requirements as well.

In France also it has been made very clear that independence as perceived by observers is important to support confidence in integrity and objectivity. In the *Normes* (principles) we read in statement 11: 'La loi, les règlements et la déontologie, sont une obligation au commissaire au comptes d'être et de paraître indépendant (the law, rules, and code of conduct create an obligation for the auditor to be and to appear independent). Il doit non seulement conserver une attitude d'esprit indépendante lui permettant d'effectuer sa mission avec integrité et objectivité, mais aussi être libre de tout lien réel qui pourrait être interprété comme une entrave à cette intégrité et objectivité' (He should not only preserve independence of mind, enabling him to audit with integrity and objectivity, but also be free of any constraint that might be seen as a breach of this integrity and objectivity). Again, this is followed by detailed rules.

The International Federation of Accountants (IFAC) has issued Guidance Ethics with similar contents. So, is there uniformity everywhere? Here we come to the 'no' to this question. Because if we look at some more detailed rules, we find interesting differences. *Table 1* illustrates this.

Is it not interesting that in Italy auditors are appointed for 3 years, may be again for another 3 and 3 years, but then have to leave? Whereas in Belgium there is also a 3-year term, this can be repeated indefinitely. In the UK auditors may be (re)appointed any time, but in France it is once in 6 years. Which situation creates more independence? The French one, because the auditor knows for many years that he can not be removed? The UK one, because reappointment is usually an annual formality, and the Stock Exchange might react negatively, anyhow, on an unusual auditor change? Or should we prefer the Italian situation, because the incumbent auditor knows that he will have to leave this client and his successor will object to unprofessional compromises?

There is an ongoing debate on the rotation subject. In Member States that currently have rotation mandated, abolition or mitigation is being considered. Arguments for this are that changing auditors is costly – and risky, because it takes time before the successor auditors have a thorough understanding of the company's business and organization. On the other hand, it has to be recognized that some form of rotation might be perceived as improving independence.

Usually, due to a mix of factors (staff promotion and turnover, new clients, changing planning deadlines), audit staff rotates anyhow. For partners this applies to a lesser extent, although possibly more than the public knows. So would the

Table 7.1 Different independence regulations in Europe

Subject	Country	USA	UK	NL	GER	BEL	SP	IT	FR
– Audit engagement period in years		n/r	1	n/r	n/r	3	3	3**	6
– Audit firm rotation mandated after n years		n/r*	n/r	n/r	n/r	n/r	9	9**	n/r
– MAS allowed for statutory auditors		yes	yes	yes	yes	yes†	yes	no	no
– Advertising allowed		yes	yes	yes	no	no	no	no	no
– Contingent fees allowed for non-audit work		yes	yes	yes	no	no	no	no***	no

n/r = not regulated

* For partners in SEC Practice Section rotation mandatory after 7 years
** For quoted and some other companies
† Only to a limited extent
*** Scale fees for certain engagements

mandatory partner rotation after some 7 years be a solution? And where often a second concurring partner is involved, he or she might rotate at a different schedule, to preserve continuity in understanding the company.

Another interesting matter is the scope of services. In some Member States the statutory auditors are allowed to provide all advisory services that they agree with their clients. This has of course to be within the limits of expertise. Why do companies and other organizations ask for other services? And why don't their shareholders object, if the Board buys such services from their auditors? The most obvious reason is that the auditor knows the company. For example, for tax services to smaller companies the tax advisor needs financial information that the auditors have already audited. So it saves time and costs if the audit staff assists in preparing the returns, and the company does not need to explain everything twice.

Another example is internal controls and information systems. The auditor will during and after his audit notify management of shortcomings in these areas. A natural question from management then is: How should I improve matters? That is where the advisory work starts. Should the auditor then say, 'Sorry, but I am not allowed to help you with solutions?'

Some Member States have answered this question positively: yes, the auditor should not interfere with the company's need for advice, because next year he has to audit the results of his advisory work. Suppose the auditor recommended a certain computer system to improve information processing quality. But the advice was wrong, or the computer firm was wrong, or the software house, or the client's staff. Will the auditor then be strong enough next year to criticize the situation? And will he be believed to be that strong? Along this line of reasoning non-audit services have been prohibited or restricted to statutory auditors.

It will be no surprise that many audit firms in such countries have their consultancy department next door. Some will say that is because these firms want to sell as many services as possible. Others argue that, if your mission is to reduce uncertainty in information and to add credibility to the processing thereof, you have a professional duty to care and service as much as possible.

A last example is advertising. In the early days of the profession auditors advertised and solicited for work like many other entrepreneurs. However, here also there is a threat to independence. If the auditor is very eager to be hired, will he be able to resist his client if he feels the accounts are not fairly presented? Or will he be afraid of losing his assignment? The consequence of this argument is that auditors should not expose themselves to commercial promotions, in order to keep their hands free. But this prudential behaviour has also been criticised, by business people as well as politicians, on the ground that auditors restrict competition by not promoting themselves. They behave like members of a guild who stay outside of means of communication that nowadays are seen as quite normal. Such a way of acting would facilitate keeping prices high, and also encourage hypocritical acquisitional activities. So several institutes have decided to allow advertisements. Contingent fees and cold calling are discussed in a similar manner.

Does all the above imply that there exist only differences? Certainly not. If one looks at such issues as the identity and ownership of the auditor's business, his financial independence of audit clients, prohibitions of serving in any management capacity to audit clients, or the criteria to be registered as a qualified auditor, then one also finds many similarities throughout Europe. To summarise, the auditing profession in Europe is guided by similar general principles of independence as a condition of objectivity and impartiality. But in practice there are not only similarities, but also substantial differences in the rules.

Variations in perceptions and some research findings

Reading all this one might feel some sympathy for those civil servants in Brussels who had to draft the European Commission's regulations on independence. It becomes understandable that Article 24 of the Eighth Directive restricts itself to the legal requirements of the individual Member States. Indeed, behind each State's law one might presume a more or less coherent system of culture, economics, contracting, taxation and division of wealth and power.

Nevertheless, Europe is in a process of unification by removing barriers. Harmonisation may often be too far away, but at least one can start with allowing to members of one country what is already permitted in other countries. This process had a well known start in 1979 when the European Court of Justice decided that the

Federal Republic of Germany had no right to impose its standards on French imports. In that case the French were allowed to export 'Cassis' to Germany, although by German criteria this drink did not contain enough alcohol to be sold as a liqueur.

This process of mutual recognition has been since 1987 enforced by the Single European Act. As a consequence one might expect liberalisation, gradual removal of barriers, European adaptation to practices accepted in any Member State.

Will all this happen automatically? I don't think so. So many social forces will exert their influence. The auditing profession itself, in Europe and worldwide, is discussing independence and is looking for constructive responses to established needs. Critics of the profession are also trying to legislate what they perceive as in the best interest of the public. One well-known example is the so called 'Fabian Document', published in 1991 in London by Austin Mitchell, Labour MP, and others. This document pleads for broad reform of auditing practices and offers detailed proposals.

Although personally I would object to more than one of the Fabian assertions, because they generalise to conclusions instead of providing a balanced analysis, the auditing profession has to listen carefully to these and other critics. So will national and European regulators. Prominent representatives of the profession recognize that 'audit is overdue for renaissance'. We have to abstain here from so many interesting topics that are beyond our scope, and ask only, what is at stake with independence – in fact and/or in appearance – and how can improvements be realized, if necessary?

Research

In the USA, the American Institute of Certified Public Accountants circulated in June 1991 a draft discussion paper entitled, 'A New Approach to Auditor Independence'. The paper began by saying that independence 'is the hallmark of the profession. The concept presumes integrity and encompasses objectivity. Independence reinforces awareness of the public interest in the quality of the auditor's work'. The paper then developed suggestions to concentrate upon 'independence in fact', and stated that it is important to have basic principles rather than detailed rules. These basic principles were:

1. the audit firm and the auditor should be financially independent of the client;
2. an auditor should not audit the results of decisions that are those of the auditor or the audit firm and that were not reviewed, understood and accepted by management;
3. the audit firm and the audit client should not be adversaries in litigation that is significant to the audit firm.

Guidelines and examples were added.

The paper supported this preference for broad principles by arguing that there are now so many detailed rules and pronouncements that they focus on the form and *appearance* of independence to the detriment of substance. There is thus serious concern for real independence, not only as it appears from the outside.

Nevertheless, this approach was firmly criticised by Professor Stephen Zeff, who served on the Planning Committee of the Auditing Standards Board as a public member on behalf of the public interest. He wrote to the Board: 'I believe that no statement of principles on auditor independence can justifiably exclude "appearance of independence", as this discussion paper does . . .' Professor Zeff referred to 'a world where perceptions, images and appearances influence public opinion and legislation' and stated that the paper 'ignores political reality in the last decade of the 20th century. This is a time when it is *more*, not less, important to demonstrate to lay observers that auditors have preserved their independence'.

This is an interesting debate, because both parties seem to be right. All regulations are useless when they do not succeed in objective, impartial, independent-in-fact judgment. But the public can neither observe this judgment nor test its quality. The public is dependent on the appearance, on its perception of the auditor's independence.

Independence in appearance and perception

We have already seen from *Table 1* that there are some differences in regulation with respect to this independence in appearance. But there are more differences in perception. Some research has been carried out in the past 20 years as to what various parties perceived as independent or dependent settings. The research design is that respondents receive a questionnaire comprising small, hypothetical, case descriptions. They have to score according to whether they perceive the auditor in these cases as independent or not. The results can be compared with professional rules and within the various categories of participants. In *Table 2* I have combined the results of 5 surveys. They relate to independence perceptions are held by auditors from the Big-Eight firms and smaller firms, accountants in industry, financial analysts and bankers/loan officers, in the USA, Canada, the United Kingdom and Germany. (It should be kept in mind, as appears from *Table 2*, that part of this research is rather dated. Institutional positions and rules may have changed since.) The respective cases are as follows.

1. An accounting firm had its office in a building which was owned by a client. The accounting firm occupied approximately 25% of the available office space in the building, and the client occupied the remainder.
2. In addition to the audit, an accounting firm provided services for the client which included maintaining the journals and ledgers, making adjusting entries and preparing financial statements.
3. In order to keep certain information confidential, the client had the accounting firm perform the following services in addition to the audit:
   (a) Prepare the executive payroll;
   (b) Maintain selected general ledger accounts in a private ledger.

Table 7.2 Combined survey results on perceived auditor independence

Situation	Position			Country – 'Independence' responses											
				U.S.A.			Canada			U.K.					Germany
	SEC	AICPA	ICAEW	CPA	LO	RFA	AUD	ANAL	BANK	CA8	CAO	CAIC	FA	LO	WP
1	NI	NI	I†	68	61	60*	–	–	–	90	94	80	69	71	76
2	NI	I	I	36	55*	53*	92	69	77	41	88	36	15	23	42*
3	NI	I	I	59	67	57*	–	–	–	74	90	60	49	54	78
4	NI	NI	NI†	12	42	30	–	–	–	33	30	17	15	13	78
5	NI	I	I†	86	70	63	42	34	42*	92	88	82	79	84	94
6	NI	NI	I†	50*	37	25	74	80	80	53	57	28	6	14	54*
7	NI	I/NI	n/a	58	78	69	–	–	–	–	–	–	–	–	85
8	I	I	I	88	93	96	96	90	85	87	90	80	84	84	96
9	NI	I	I	88	85	87	–	–	–	86	90	64	59	61	90
10	NI	NI	NI†	25	32	20	70	53*	41*	36	43	32	28	26	55*
11	n/a	n/a	I	–	–	–				28	52	29	9	14	–
# of respondents				202	114	74	191	163	102	92	69	90	68	70	108
Response rate (%)				58	35	42	48	41	26	53	51	47	57	54	28

† Interpretation, as the specific example was not referred to in the ICAEW statements (1977).
* Not significant at a level of ≤.05.

SEC, AICPA positions: per Lavin (1976). NI = Not independent
ICAEW positions: per Firth (1980). I = Independent

U.S.A.: CPA = Member AICPA; LO = Loan Officer of bank; RFA = Research Financial Analyst of brokerage house (Lavin, 1976 and 1977).

Canada: Aud = Auditor (member Canadian Institute of Chartered Accountants); Anal = Analyst (member Financial Analysts Federation of Canada); Bank = Banker (member of Canadian Bankers Association) (Lindsay et al., 1987).

U.K.: CA8 = Chartered Accountant working for Big Eight firm; CAO = Chartered Accountant in other professional practice; CAIC = Chartered Accountant employed in commerce or industry; FA = Financial Analyst in City of London; LO = Loan officer of bank/financial institution (Firth, 1980).

Germany: WP = Wirtschaftsprüfer (German auditors) (Dykxhoorn & Sinning, 1981).

4. A partner in an accounting firm managed a building owned by an audit client.
5. From the books of original entry, client personnel prepared printed tapes that could be read on an optical scanner and sent the tapes to the accountants' office. The accountants forwarded the tapes to a service bureau. The accountants received the print-outs of the financial statements and general ledgers and sent them to the client. The accountants did not edit the input data prior to transmission to the service bureau. The accountants provided this service in addition to the audit.
6. Pursuant to a plan of recapitalization, the existing debt of the company was exchanged for five-year promissory notes. The accounting firm received the same kind of promissory notes in payment of its audit fee.
7. *A* was the controller of Company *Z*. He was not an elected officer nor did he have any stock holdings in Company *Z*. *A*'s brother, *B*, was a partner in the public accounting firm that audits Company *Z*'s books. However, *B* was not the partner in charge of the audit.
8. A partner in a public accounting firm had a brother-in-law who was sales vice-president for a recently acquired client. The brother-in-law was not directly involved in the financial affairs of the company and the partner was not connected with the audit in any way.
9. An accounting firm rented block time on its computer to a client when the client's computer became overburdened.
10. A client of an accounting firm was engaged in the business of selling franchises. Two partners of this accounting firm invested approximately five per cent of their personal fortunes to buy one half of the stock of a corporation which held a franchise granted by this client. Except for the payment of a percentage of sales to the franchiser client, the franchisee operated independently.
11. An accounting firm receives 15% of its gross fees from one client.

The question for each case is: do respondents perceive the auditor to be independent? *Table 2* summarises the results.

There are various interesting differences. (Two big differences may have been caused by a slightly modified case formulation (Canada, second case) or a translation problem (Germany, fourth question).) In case 2 the auditors from smaller firms in the UK have no problem with the accounting firm auditing the books of the client and also preparing them; but the financial analysts oppose strongly, as well as the bankers in the UK. Cases 6 and 9 provide striking differences within the UK, but also with other countries. Case 11 is really surprising. Canadian auditors believed an accounting firm to be independent when receiving 15% of its gross fees from one client, while in the UK Big Eight-auditors and particularly the financial analysts and bankers criticize this strongly. And some answers from German auditors are worthwhile as well, although unfortunately some are not statistically significant.

We may *conclude* that there is quite some variety in perceptions of independence, what is acceptable and what is not, and how the profession, regulators and business environment should react.

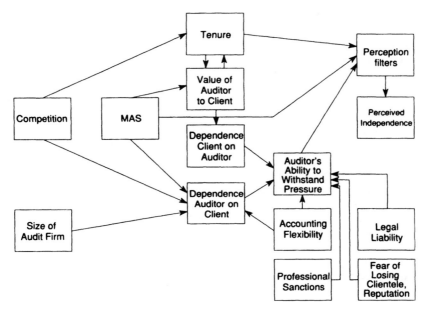

Figure 7.1 Conceptual model of perceived independence.

What factors influence perceptions of independence?

We can focus somewhat more deeply on the concept of independence. What factors are of influence on the perceptions that people develop and hold on auditors' independence? Here we find some help in the results of audit research. Let me introduce a model that was adapted from R. A. Shockley in 1982 (see *Figure 7.1*; from Shockley's model I have left out some details, and I have added the box with 'Perception filters').

The model shows how many factors influence 'Perceived Independence'. Let us review them briefly. I will add comments that are derived from research findings as described in some 60 articles; these have been summarized in the *Select Bibliography* elsewhere in this issue (pp. 251–263).

(a) *Size of audit firm.* Bigger firms may be perceived to be more independent than smaller firms because the fee of the individual client is relatively less important. Moreover, the combination of audit work and non-audit services in smaller firms is probably more in the hands of the same group of people, whereas bigger firms usually have them separately organized. It can be learned from *Table 2* (cases 2 and 11), that interesting differences in perception exist between users and investors compared with non Big-Eight auditors (cf. Shockley 1981; Amernic & Aranya; Knapp; Gul; and the references at *Table 2*).

(b) *Competition* is a complicated area. On the one hand it has been argued that the market for audit services will benefit from competition. Without competition clients might pay too high fees because their auditors would not pass on to them the benefits of 'knowledge spillovers' (the cost savings of possessing knowledge of the client's organization due to previous audit or advisory work) (Simunic). Here, of course, the smaller firms are competitive by number, whereas there is sometimes doubt expressed on the 'oligopoly' of the Big-Six firms – Arthur Andersen, Coopers & Lybrand, DRT/Touche Ross, KPMG, Price Waterhouse and Ernst & Young (as *Accountancy Age*, 23 April 1992, called it).

A Study of National Economic Research Associates (NERA), however, found no real threats to competition in the European market. 'Only further mergers between the Big Six are likely to pose any real threat to competition. Even if such mergers were to take place, they might also have pro-competitive features' (*Corporate Accounting International*, March/April 1992).

On the other hand, clients might be underserviced if intense competition would force the audit firms to decrease their fees far below a realistic cost level. The necessity of reducing cost would lead them to provide a lower service. Competition then might also threaten independence because incumbent auditors were eager to keep their clients and willing to compromise on critical issues (see further f, below). Shockley (1981) found that audit firms operating in highly competitive environments were perceived as having a higher risk of losing independence. So, it is not difficult to understand that debaters on competition identify both pro's and con's.

(c) *Tenure.* The tenure of a specific firm with one client is also debated. Countries that have mandated rotation believe that the auditor's objectivity will be impaired after many years of auditing the same client. Contrarily it appears that audit failures are more likely in the first or second year of a newly appointed auditor, because he/she has to acquire a thorough understanding of the auditee's business and organization. Audit committees therefore might decide to change auditors after a long tenure and accept the risks inherent in appointing new auditors (Knapp).

In this context it is understandable that the recent UK 'Cadbury Report' recommended, not to rotate firms as such, but their individual audit partners and staff.

(d) *Management Advisory Services (MAS).* This item has been much researched and debated. The range of these services is broad, and varies from traditional accounting and tax services (that are believed to belong to the accountant's core business) to very specialised advisory services like actuarial and appraisal work. Many studies concluded that non-audit services did not impair independence or objectivity (Scheiner; Glezen & Millar) or even made auditors more critical (Corless & Parker). Bankers and financial analysts had an equal (Pany &

Reckers), or high degree of confidence in CPA's independence while doing non-audit work along with the audit (Reckers & Stagliano), or even more than if only audit services were provided (Gul). Controls of professional ethics and liability reinforce this (Beck *et al.*). Disclosure of all types of services is recommended (Hillison & Kennelley, Pany & Reckers 1983).

The provision of some services (e.g., systems design) is more critical than others (e.g., tax) (Gul; Pany & Reckers 1983). Another quote from the NERA report seems to be in line with this: 'The close links that exist between the provision of audit and consultancy services do not pose a threat to competition, although they do have some implication for the regulation of professional independence'.

(e) *Regulation: professional sanctions and legal liability.* To preserve auditors' objectivity and impartiality they have to be made independent from their principals and the audited organizations as far as is sensible. This belief has led the profession's national and international representative bodies to provide for codes of conduct and professional sanctions. Apart from this self regulation national governments and the European Commission have also enacted laws and liability mechanisms.

It will not surprise readers that auditors appear to be sensitive to potential litigation (Farmer *et al.*) although only few law suits concern independence as such (St. Pierre). SEC disciplinary actions indeed caused loss of market share for the audit firms involved (Wilson *et al.*). Due to human nature a risk of moral hazard and loss of independence exists. Researchers suggest various approaches to reduce this risk, such as education, multi-period contracts, audit committees, penalties and lawsuits (Antle; Pearson; Yoon; Dopuch & King 1991; Van de Poel & Schilder). The peer review process in the USA seems to work satisfactorily (Wallace) and Big-Six firms assess risk significantly prior to acceptance of new clients (Huss & Jacobs); but on the other hand, mandated pre-acceptance inquiries with previous auditors were not made in a material number of cases (Lambert *et al.*).

Interestingly, Dopuch & King (1992) concluded from an experimental study that currently negligence by auditors is efficiently sanctioned by such market mechanisms as lawsuits and disciplinary courts; expansion of the scope of auditors' liabilities might be counterproductive.

(f) *Fear of losing clientele, reputation.* Auditors are sensitive to potential loss of client (Farmer *et al.*) and seem to accept compromises to a certain extent (although this may not be their firm's policy) (Van de Poel and Schilder). In this context it should be noted that different cultural backgrounds of auditors may cause different responses on (un)ethical cases (Park; Karnes *et al.*). What might be damaging to auditors' reputation in one culture or country, and therefore would prohibit unethical, dependent behaviour, may be acceptable practice elsewhere. This is important for Europe with its many cultures in particular, and may explain why the Eighth Directive so explicitly refers to national law.

However, why do auditor changes take place? If Big Eight auditor changes are mainly caused by factors like an audit firm's dominance in a particular industry, client financial health, size and growth, and not so much by qualified audit opinions (Haskins & Williams), then the auditor will not fear too much for negative consequences of his or her independent behaviour. According to Magee and Tseng an incumbent auditor's interest in an existing client presents a threat to independence only under limited circumstances. The fear of losing one's reputation is believed to have a major impact on maintaining and improving audit quality.

(g) *Accounting flexibility*. Various researchers point out that the flexibility of accounting principles causes threats to either perceived or in-fact independence. If auditors disagree among themselves as to the appropriateness of a reporting policy desired by the client, then a particular auditor may experience difficulties in taking a firm stance (Magee and Tseng; Grease; Shockley 1982). On the other hand this seems only a threat if it concerns issues that do not affect more than one reporting period, and that are not regarded by the client or the auditor as very important (Magee and Tseng).

Wolnizer argues that criticism of accountants results from widespread dissatisfaction with the product of their work. Independent verification is only achievable if financial disclosure consists of 'independent information'. By this he means information which can be tested inter-subjectively. As this is often possible only to a certain extent, independent professional judgment is also limited due to the absence of clear benchmarks. Especially here the important role of education and training in communication skills has to be emphasized (Pearson).

(h) *Value of auditor and dependence between client and auditor*. As *Figure 1* shows, there is dependence on both sides. So far as the auditor has more value to his or her client, the client is more dependent on the auditor. Such dependence increases the auditor's ability to withstand pressure. This explains why many audit firms' strategies aim to add value to their clients. From this it follows that serving clients in an optimal manner enhances independence: the client would not like to lose its auditor. The risk of qualifications to the auditor's opinion (especially on going concern and asset valuation, according to Firth) is important for clients (Gul). They may try to persuade the auditor not to issue a qualification (which then is a threat to independence) and the auditor may threaten to persist in doing so (which increases independence). This demonstrates their mutual dependence.

The auditor is dependent on the client for paying the audit fee. For that reason auditors often are prohibited from receiving more than a certain percentage (e.g., in the UK 15%) of practice income from any one client. Offering fees obviously below the cost of the related services (lowballing) exists (Turpen), but may not impair independence (DeAngelo). Contracts between client and auditor also influence their mutual dependence (Antle), as also do audit committees (Antle; Pearson).

(i) *Perception filters*. Shockley's model and the referenced research literature have made clear that many factors influence the perception of auditor's independence. Research findings also suggest that no easy conclusions can be drawn. The final picture is somewhat ambiguous. Certainly there are many potential threats. But it cannot be concluded that there is much more than potential. Indeed, many articles conclude that the issues studied did not impair independence, or at least would not necessarily do so. Despite the fact that not all articles or their methodology convince the reader to the same extent, the overall conclusions are quite interesting.

Nevertheless there is much public debate and criticism. So at least perceived independence is at stake, although independence-in-fact may pose no material problems. This raises the question whether perception as such needs more attention.

Various authors refer to matters of perception. New and higher expectations may arise (Causey; Berryman; Dykxhoorn and Sinning), leading to gaps with reality and misunderstanding of the auditor's role (Graese), or misunderstanding of the public's expectations (Mitchell et al.). Whereas dismissals of actions against auditors are less frequently reported publicly than resolution of actions by damage payments (Palmrose), there is some publicity bias. Perceivers of auditor behaviour who have a more field dependence cognitive style (being sensitive and responsive to social stimuli) (Gul), and therefore are more sensitive to public opinion than field independent persons, may be inclined to follow such publicity bias. On the contrary, field independent auditors perhaps lack understanding of public feelings. Could it be that training auditors in independency also makes them less sensitive to understanding public needs and expectations? To what extent are auditors educated in mass communication, sociology and political science, in matters of perception rather than facts, in TV-presentation rather than management letters?

We have already seen from Table 2 how many differences exist between auditors, providers and users of information regarding their perception of independence and ethics. To reflect what has just been noted I have therefore added the box 'Perception filters' to Shockley's model. All parties involved have their specific filters and these are nurtured day by day by different factors.

By way of summary, we have seen in this section how, on an overall basis, audit research findings on independence do not indicate much that is wrong with independence-in-fact. However, many factors influence the perception of such independence. The question arises whether a perceptional issue exists in the relationship between the audit profession and its perceivers. This would not necessarily surprise one, as the education of auditors pays little attention to mass communication and public affairs.

The ethical issue

Is auditor independence a real issue? So far, our conclusion is, not so much as far as independence-in-fact is concerned. There is a lot of regulation (some argue, too much), and more details might have an adverse effect. In cannot be proven from research that further rules would help – some authors state the opposite – and it has been demonstrated how natural and cultural influences require careful attention. So one might feel sympathy for the AICPA discussion paper, referred to in section 2?

Yes, certainly. But also for Stephen Zeff's criticism. We concluded in section 3 that the perceptional issue is the important one. Zeff pointed to today's world of 'perceptions, images and appearances and the political reality in the last decade of the 20th century'. And one would be ignoring this reality if one concluded that there is no issue at all.

Is it possible, then, to restate a concept of independence that can be observed (Bartlett)? Or heard? We may remember that 'auditor' is derived from Latin *audire*, to hear. In early Roman times the auditor heard public statements issued by accountable persons on their earnings and commented upon them also in public. And 'profession' is derived from Latin *profiteri*: to state openly, declare, avow. A profession has a duty to declare publicly (Sokolowski).

However, what is public in today's profession? Not very much, it seems. The audit profession started with individual auditors, professionals with a fiduciary relationship to their clients and other stakeholders. Today there are six big audit firms, each employing many tens of thousands of people in well established worldwide networks, and a lot of smaller but still quite substantial international firms. Referring to professional organizations of lawyers and physicians, Sass describes them as 'self-regulating guilds', that 'resemble "miniature governments" because they exercise all the types of power normally exercised by government', such as self-regulation, discipline and enforcement of behaviour, educational standards and influential publications.

One can look at the national institutes of auditors, and also at the big firms, to compare them with 'miniature governments'. From this comparison some lessons can be learned.

(a) The audit 'guilds' without doubt are perceived as exerting great influence on economic life. It should not surprise one that a general public then either expects more than is realistic, or just does not know what to expect, and becomes suspicious.

(b) Governments are controlled by democratic procedures, open information and public responsibility. Audit firms do not meet many of these criteria. They do not publish much information on the course of their business; there is no outside control, and they are not accountable on a regular basis to the public. Again, it should not surprise one that outsiders become mistrustful.

(c) If auditors' possibilities for providing reliable information on their audit clients are limited to a certain degree of reasonableness, then the standards that rule this degree have to be understood by users of financial statements. Here is needed what Sass calls 'cooperation-in-trust between client and provider and education-in-trust of the individual lay person and the public by professionals and professional organizations sharing technical knowledge in nontechnical language'.

Sass does not address the audit profession when he states, 'Of course there will be limits to the extent to which technical expertise can adequately be shared with lay persons, but professionals and their organizations have not yet tried hard enough, and the lay people have not yet requested it strongly enough'. Nevertheless this seems fully applicable to auditors as well.

- For the *individual auditor* this implies paying attention to all the parties involved. Not only management or supervisory board are important, but the implications for shareholders, creditors, employees and other stakeholders have also to be monitored. Evidence of such analysis should be reflected in the working papers.
- *Professional institutes* should try to work perception issues into the profession's education. Training in communication and networking deserves more attention.
- *Regulators* might shift their attention from all too detailed rules to addressing the more basic issues: how to guarantee that auditors are permanently improving the quality of their reporting to principals and agents.
- And the *audit firms* will perhaps concentrate more than ever upon such essential service qualities as reliability, responsiveness and empathy to the many stakeholders. This includes responses to broadly felt questions, as the Cadbury Report poses them: reporting on internal financial controls, going concern, interim accounts and best practice codes.

There is not so much an independence issue as such; there is primarily an issue of perception and communication. The perception of independence is relative to the perceived experience of service quality by a broad range of stakeholders. And the ethical issue is whether the audit profession will have the courage and the trust to take a proactive stance, to address issues of public relevance, to step out from behind its closed curtains, and to enter the 21st century as independent professionals – serving not only their direct clients but society as a whole.

CASE STUDY

Polly Peck

Polly Peck, who acquired ownership of Del Monte, the canned fruit firm, and Samsui, the electronics company showed an enormous profit for the year ended December 1989.

This remarkable profit, however, was a mirage, created by a practice known as 'currency mismatching'. What Polly Peck did was to make borrowing in hard currencies such as the Deutschmark and the Swiss franc, which enjoyed currency stability, but low rates of interest. These borrowings were matched by deposits in soft currencies, such as the Turkish lire, which attracted high interest rates, but which were unstable.

The foreign exchange losses incurred through the depreciation of the Turkish lire were not put through the profit and loss account, but declared in the balance sheet. As a result, Polly Peck was able to declare a £12.5 million interest income, after borrowing £530 million.

To account for the real loss the company made, the accountants made adjustments to the reserves of the consolidated accounts, amounting to £170.3 million for 1988, and £44.7 million for 1989, describing these amounts as 'exchange variances on net investment overseas'.

Although the 1989 profit and loss account made a provision of £10.5 million in unrealized losses, the Annual Report and Accounts camouflaged sizeable unrealized losses which never appeared on the profit and loss account, and hence did not affect the yield from the shares. Auditors, of course, approved these manoeuvres, but then the auditors (as in most firms) were not independent, but appointed by the company.

Because of the seemingly healthy accounts, Philips and Drew, a subsidiary of the Union Bank of Switzerland, were prepared to lend Polly Peck £7 million, which they subsequently were obliged to write off; they also lost a further £14 million by investing in Polly Peck, in what was effectively a gamble that the price of Polly Peck shares would not drop.

Polly Peck may have hoped that currency mismatching was a temporary cosmetic solution to a difficult financial period from which it would recover. Clearly in times of economic difficulty it is important not to cause shareholders to panic, with the inevitable consequence of a huge drop in share prices and in investment.

However, if this was intended as a short-term stopgap, it became apparent that such measures could not continue indefinitely. These measures did not allow the company a sufficient breathing space to get itself back on a sound financial footing, and Polly Peck collapsed in the summer 1991.

Critics of capitalism who are opposed to a system which encourages income which is effectively unearned may argue that those who were content to play the system of investing in shares and engaging in financial speculations deserve whatever consequences result. If one plays such a game, one might argue, it is incumbent on the speculator to take due steps to understand financial statements and to read the small print which explains how each figure is derived. This is, of course, not so easy as it sounds, and even professional accounts have gone on record as stating that they find many company's statements of accounts totally meaningless. But one might still argue that the burden of interpreting seemingly meaningless financial statements is part of the hazard of such financial speculation.

However, in reply it can be stated that investors are not necessarily speculators who chance their luck on the stock market. Ordinary people of modest means can often simply wish to make suitable provision for the future, and rely on financial advice given by professionals. If a company's Annual Report and Accounts misleads even the professionals in the field, then small private investors can lose hard-earned savings. Equally seriously, if a firm engages in financial transactions aimed at improving the cosmetics of its accounts, rather than directed at improving the overall health of the company, then jobs are at risk. A company which collapses means inevitable job losses, with all the resultant suffering which that causes.

Discussion questions on the case study

Should companies be allowed to 'dress up' accounts in such a way as to ensure that shareholders do not panic, and hence make a difficult situation even worse? Or should there be more consistent and standardized accounting procedures, with clear disclosure which enables investors to see properly what is happening?

Have investors a duty of care when it comes to investing, bearing the onus of making sense of firms' accounting procedures, or does a firm have the obligation to ensure that the implications of its Annual Report and Accounts are plain to all?

DISCUSSION TOPICS

1. You are a financial adviser in a finance company which arranges 'ethical investments' for members of the public. A member of the public has several thousand pounds to invest, and would like a portfolio of stocks and shares. Which of the following categories of activity would cause you to withhold recommendation?

   operation within oppressive regimes;
   poor trade union relations;
   low wage levels;
   pollution or damage of the environment;
   irresponsible marketing (for example, marketing powdered baby milk in the Third World);
   involvement in the production of nuclear energy;
   manufacture or supply of weapons;
   animal testing;
   factory farming;
   Sunday trading;
   political donations;
   subscribes to the Economic League (the right wing employee vetting agency).

   (All these are categories identified and used by ECRA – the Ethical Consumer Research Association).

   Having considered the general issues, you may care to research specific companies and determine how well they fare on these criteria.

   Finally, which do you feel is more important when offering advice on these matters to members of the public – your own personal values or those of your clients?

2. Mr Simon Cleverley of Manchester recently wrote to the *Guardian*, raising the intriguing question, 'Which offer the greater value to humankind – stockbrokers or wasps?' (*Guardian Supplement*, 16 November 1992, p. 14). Presumably this correspondent believed that certain members of the financial world do not obviously improve the country's standards of living, but make their wealth from the supposedly non-productive activity of speculating – an activity which has been accused of creating instability in the money markets, causing adverse effects to a country's balance of payments.

   Do you think those who deal in financial speculation can justify their activities – or are wasps really more useful to society?

Reaching the markets | 8

The ethics of persuasion
Persuasion and respect for persons
A consequentialist view
Advertising and ideology

Introducing the readings

The hidden persuaders   Vance Packard
Advertising in Britain   T. R. Nevett
The affluent society   J. K. Galbraith
The *non sequitur* of the 'dependence effect'   F. A. von Hayek
Advertising as communication   Gillian Dyer
Herself reappraised   Advertising Standards Authority
Speaking up for advertising   The Advertising Association

Case study
Cigarette advertising

Discussion topics

THE ETHICS OF PERSUASION

One of our colleagues recently received a letter informing him that he had won a major prize, which was specially reserved for his collection at an exhibition in Helston, some 60 miles from Plymouth. Attracted by the prospect of a weekend drive into deep Cornwall, he accepted the invitation, and on arrival learned that the prize consisted of a free ten-day holiday in the Mediterranean with his family. However, there were certain strings attached; the family had to attend a seminar on 'time-share' and would agree to participate in a promotional video on behalf of the firm which offered them the prize.

At this juncture our colleague declined to proceed any further, having heard (like most of us) the many atrocity tales relating to time-share agreements: high pressure sales tactics; agreements made under a foreign country's legislation to render legal redress difficult; lack of provision for a time-share company going out of business, leaving time-sharers without any means of booking, selling or liaising with each other; and so on.

Despite the cloud which overshadows the time-share industry, the product itself could actually be a good one, combining sensible financial investment with a useful facility. As things stand, however, time-share has attracted a poor reputation and many consumers are deeply suspicious, not only of the advertising of time-share, but of sales promotion more widely. It is very easy for a 'dark corner of the industry' (as time-share has recently been described by the Advertising Standards Authority[1]) to shape people's attitudes to advertising as a whole.

A market economy relies on the buoyancy of commercial transactions where sellers want to sell and buyers want to buy. It is only reasonable that sellers should be permitted to communicate with buyers, and that means of communication is, by definition, advertising; the process by which goods and services are brought to the consumer is, by definition, marketing. It is therefore difficult to see how anyone could justify the view that advertising or marketing 'ought to be banned' without radically calling into question the very basis of contemporary western economic systems. A more appropriate question therefore is not whether advertising or marketing should be abolished, but what constraints might reasonably exist to prevent the excesses of the more ruthless promoters in the advertising and marketing worlds.

We have entitled this chapter 'Reaching the Markets' and the authors

[1] The Advertising Standards Authority, Case Report 180, 11 April 1990, p. 1.

fully recognize that advertising and sales promotion are only part of the process which bridges the gap between production and consumption. Standard business textbooks identify four 'Ps' of marketing: Product, Price, Place and Promotion. All four, of course, raise substantial issues in business ethics. For example, what criteria might reasonably be used to ban goods and services from the market place completely (cannabis, prostitutes, faulty electrical goods) or restrict the way in which they are sold (cigarettes, alcohol, guns, prescription-only medicines)? Are suppliers morally entitled to charge whatever they want for their wares, leaving consumers to decide whether or not to accept an invitation to treat, or is there such a concept as a 'just price'?

It is not possible within the confines of a single volume to examine all the issues relating to the ethics of marketing. We touched briefly on the issue of the just price in chapter 1, and the ethics of 'dumping' inferior goods on Third World countries will be treated in the final chapter on the ethics of international business. Our passing treatment of these themes is not intended to downgrade their importance; it is simply that we have preferred to select one single area in the field of marketing – namely advertising – and to treat it in depth.

We have chosen advertising because there are few issues in business ethics which have polarized public opinion more. Opponents of advertising will claim that it is a 'con', that it puts consumers under undue psychological pressure to buy unnecessary items or strive for living standards beyond those they can afford. Critics will claim that advertising wastes money which would be better channelled into improving the product or reducing its price. Advertising, too, is allegedly a 'barrier to market entry'; we may be able to produce goods which are superior to those of the 'giant' companies, but, if we run only a small business, the chances are that we will be unable to advertise on the kind of scale which is necessary to break into the market.

Some critics will go so far as to claim that advertising is inherently a social evil, that it sets out to deceive, to encourage greed, and – particularly with the vast increase of credit facilities within the last 25 years – to persuade people to spend beyond their means. Furthermore, it is alleged, the persuasion industry sells more than the products it overtly promotes; advertising is, arguably, one means of propagating and perpetuating the capitalist value system, with its emphasis on consumer goods and material affluence. With only a few exceptions, advertising by its very nature must relate to goods and services on which money is spent; no one advertises a country walk or an evening by the fireside. As the economist Kenneth Galbraith argues, the advertising industry promotes consumables rather than public services such as education and health. It may be the case that expenditure on public services would bring greater benefits; if so, then advertising is helping to decrease the benefits we derive from our expenditure.

What limits, if any, should be required of the persuasion industry? If the advertising industry is justly the subject of criticism from time to time, that is of course no reason for objecting to advertising *per se*. After all, the occasional 'bent policeman' provides no good reason for abolishing the entire police force. Indeed it comes as no surprise that, in a recent survey carried out by the Advertising Association[2], no one was found who wanted to see the unqualified abolition of advertisements. If business is to take place at all, consumers must know of the existence of the goods and services which they are contemplating buying.

One possible view is that, because we live in a free society, freedom of speech is an important right, which applies equally to advertisers and private citizens alike. The etymological meaning of the word 'advertising' is 'to draw one's attention' (Latin: *advertere*). Just as the advertiser has the right to inform, so has the intending purchaser the right to be informed about the existence, availability and qualities of a product. Freedom of speech and freedom of information are thus the fundamental principles on which advertising should be conducted. If it is legal to sell a product or service, so some members of the marketing world have argued, then it ought to be legal to advertise it.

This view of advertising would of course be emphatically rejected by anyone who believes that morality has its basis in consequences rather than a priori principles. However, even the deontologist need not be committed to this *laissez-faire* view of the persuasion industry; there are other ethical principles which could equally be claimed to be a priori, and which have as much, if not more importance than the presumed right to free speech. For example, surely truth and honesty are moral principles which are relevant to the way in which an advertiser persuades the public to buy. Although the Advertising Standards Authority (ASA) has generally supported the principle that if it is legal to sell something it ought to be legal to advertise it, its British Code of Advertising Practice (BCAP) is based on the four fundamental principles, 'legal, decent, honest and truthful'[3]. The Trade Descriptions Act of 1968 re-

---

[2] *Speaking Up for Advertising* (London: The Advertising Association, 1983), p. 10.
[3] *The British Code of Advertising Practice* (London: Committee of Advertising Practice, 1988, 8th ed.), B.3.1, p. 24.

quires truthful presentation of all descriptions of goods and services, whether these descriptions are verbal or visual.

In terms of the ethical theories considered in chapter 3, it is unclear whether the ASA's position is based on a deontological view of business ethics or a consequentialist one; indeed it is more than likely that this question has not presented itself to the majority of the committee. The code itself is in fact compatible with either a Kantian 'respect for persons' or with a consequentialist view of ethics.

PERSUASION AND 'RESPECT FOR PERSONS'

The Kantian might contend that any form of persuasion which is dishonest, untruthful, or less than rational is an assault on the integrity of the individual, and can legitimately be the subject of moral censure. Kant's principle of 'respect for persons' may be construed as demanding that the rationality of the individual, which is his or her characteristic endowment, must be respected absolutely. This philosophical notion finds expression in certain public attitudes to advertising, for example, where consumers complain that advertising is insulting, and that the advertising industry 'treats us like morons'.

The view that human rationality is the touchstone by which modern advertising must be judged is, however, somewhat problematic. While we might all agree that our minimum expectation of the persuasion industry is that it propagates truthful information, in some cases it is what an advertisement withholds which is more objectionable than what it states. A washing powder might truly make one's clothes whiter than white, but yet have the unfortunate consequence of causing allergic reactions from the subsequent wearer. A advertisement which indicates a free offer, but which fails to disclose all the conditions which are required to obtain it, is justly subject to the ASA's sanctions.

It might be suggested that truthfulness is not quite sufficient to describe the specific virtue which should be required of the advertising industry. What we should demand, it has been suggested, is 'full disclosure'; advertisers should not simply to succumb to the 'puffery' which is so characteristic of the industry, but should provide full information about the product, warts and all. The problem about the demand for full disclosure is that it is simply not possible. There are almost endless numbers of statements about a product which can be made, and within the confines of an advertisement even the most conscientious and scrupulous advertiser must make judicious selection.

Even so, the view that the advertiser should inform rather than persuade (even if the information is of necessity incomplete) is questionable. It is often assumed that the distinction between informing and persuading is a clear one, indeed that the information and persuasion are two opposite poles, quite different ends of a spectrum. This is not so: to inform someone is often to persuade; if we are informed that there is a fire in the building, we are persuaded to leave; if we are informed that a substance is poisonous, we are persuaded not to eat it.

Further, it is not the case that we only approve forms of persuasion which are 'rational' and censure those which are not. We can persuade a friend to come to the cinema with us by informing him or her about what is showing, but we can also coax and tempt. ('Oh, come on then – you'll enjoy a night out!') Although there may occasionally be reasons why this is morally unacceptable (for example, if we know our friend should be studying for an examination) there is nothing necessarily wrong with this kind of non-rational persuasion, and indeed any censure is likely to relate either to the consequences of going to the cinema (a poor exam performance) or another moral principle which might be thought to come into play (decency, for example, if it is a 'blue movie'). So long as the persuasion is not downright deceptive, we do not normally censure that means of persuasion itself.

The same holds in the realm of advertising. If private citizens are allowed to coax and tempt, why, it may be asked, should not the advertiser? Indeed advertising would turn out to be very boring indeed if all it did was to bombard us with clinical facts about the products on offer. We do not believe, then, that the difference between acceptable and unacceptable advertising strategies can be based on a presumed distinction between information and persuasion.

A CONSEQUENTIALIST VIEW

If the information/persuasion distinction does not provide a means of distinguishing ethical from unethical sales promotion strategies, what alternative might be found? As we argued in chapter 3, the Kantian principles of rationality and respect for persons form only one possible answer to the question of what underlying basis there might be for ethical conduct, and at this point a consequentialist might suggest that the more appropriate ground for the distinction between ethically sound and ethically unsound advertising strategy lies in the **results** of persuasion, not in the **mode** of persuasion.

Advertising, the consequentialist would suggest, is acceptable if it brings good results, unacceptable if it brings bad ones. If advertising promotes human happiness by enabling higher standards of living to be achieved through consuming, and by encouraging consumers to buy products with which they are satisfied, then the persuasion industry has provided a useful service to society. Conversely, if certain forms of advertising increase human unhappiness by enabling the sale of shoddy goods or harmful products, or by encouraging consumers to incur serious debts, then such advertising is to be deplored.

The problem with a consequentialist view of advertising ethics is that it appears to make the end justify the means. (As we saw, this is an accusation frequently made against the utilitarian.) Recently, some manufacturers of burglar alarms were taken to task by the Advertising Standards Authority on the grounds that their advertising had aroused undue fear. One advertiser had distributed leaflets through people's letter-boxes stating that 'A burglar could enter your house as easily as this leaflet,' making certain people, particularly the elderly, unduly anxious about their safety. Even though this advertiser might have done home owners a good turn by inducing them to invest in home security, such benefits do not constitute a morally acceptable defence. Whatever the benefits, advertisers surely should not be – and indeed are not – permitted to appeal to fear, or to mislead the public. (Even when the cause is a charitable one, the same holds true. The Advertising Standards Authority has recently complained that charities often unduly play on people's good will, or resort to shock tactics.) Some time-share schemes may be thoroughly desirable (although the present authors do not know of any), but the fact that one was selling a thoroughly desirable time-share scheme does not justify failing to disclose information about a sales promotion or browbeating seminar attendees into submission.

ADVERTISING AND IDEOLOGY

There are more far-reaching criticisms of the advertising industry, however, than its methods of persuasion. Advertisers, it is often remarked, do not sell merely a product, but a whole way of life. It has been argued that the constant exposure to the concepts portrayed by the advertising industry conditions us to accept its fundamental presuppositions, that consumption and the acquisition of new goods is desirable. Affluence and high living are often upheld in advertisements as the ideals to strive for. It is argued that advertising reinforces the values of materialist ideology.

Advertising, it is argued, transmits other values too by means of ideological stereotyping. For example, family life is often portrayed as the norm, with the supposedly 'typical' family consisting of a father, mother, elder son and younger daughter, even though a mere 15% of the UK population live in families which correspond to this description. The father is generally white, the bread-winner, leaving the mother to act as the housewife who has little better to do than bake sponge cakes, wash floors and marvel at the results of the latest brand of detergent. Single parent families, elderly couples, black people, or people living alone are seldom portrayed as the heroes and heroines of television commercials. There are some notable exceptions, however. One national newspaper has focused its advertising on the up and coming career woman, and one washing machine firm, advertising in the Midlands, has shown a black man sounding its praises.

Defenders of the persuasion industry might well contend that stereotyping is an inevitable consequence of having to sell a product in limited space and time. The advertiser has to use some scenario in which to show the goods or services, and it is not feasible to show every possible lifestyle in the context of the product. Above all, the advertiser may argue, advertising requires 'targeting' and one has therefore to direct the advertisement to the particular group that one wishes most to reach. Since married men are generally the principal earners of income in a family, it may therefore seem reasonable that items of expenditure which involve fairly substantial outlays (such as motor cars, or expensive Christmas presents for children) should be aimed at the father. Further, the advertiser may point out, the aim of advertising is (generally speaking) to sell; an advertiser's task is to increase sales, and not to reform society, however much others may wish to question certain stereotypes.

There are problems, however, about stereotyping. First, there are some reasons to suppose that certain advertisers sell themselves short by introducing stereotypes. If an advertiser degrades women, it is very likely that he (not usually she) will lose women's custom. The traditional policy of the advertiser has been to enhance, indeed exaggerate the status of the people in advertisements with whom the public are supposed to identify. Indeed, psychological studies which have been carried out in the field indicate that a significant number of women are affected by negative portrayals of their gender and that this is reflected in their purchasing patterns.

Second, there are ethical objections to the negative portrayal of women. Stereotyping can be argued to be a subtle form of conditioning; subtle, because it is often unrecognized, or else, when it is noticed, it can be thought to be unimportant and not worthy of comment or complaint. To many women, however, the advertising industry forms part of the overall conditioning process within society which causes women to be downgraded, to be subservient to their husbands, and to settle for second-rate jobs or even for a life in front of the kitchen sink. The use of a nude or semi-nude female body, it is contended, reinforces the idea on the part of some men, that women are sex objects and can legitimate some of the sexual harassment and innuendo which is often rife in the work place.

Although it is no longer permissible to depict a naked or semi-nude woman to advertise some product unconnected with nudity, such as a car, the Advertising Standards Authority permits such portrayal where it is judged to be 'relevant' to the product – for example a shower, a perfume, or a set of bathroom scales. This ASA ruling, however, has by no means satisfied the feminist lobby, who argue that even this criterion of 'relevance' can justify sexism; after all, do **men** never take showers, put on after-shave or weigh themselves? Why do we so infrequently see a semi-nude man in magazine advertisements or TV commercials?

Faced with such complaints about advertising, the ASA's constant rule of thumb has always been whether the depiction of women in advertising causes 'grave or widespread offence', and two major studies have concluded that in general the public and women more particularly, are not offended by the way in which women are depicted by advertisers.

In this short chapter on advertising, it is not possible to provide a detailed critique of these two ASA reports. It is sufficient to say, however, that the scope of *Herself Appraised* (the first report, published in 1986) and *Herself Re-appraised* (1990), focus on the portrayal of the female body; they do not address wider questions of sex-role stereotyping, a matter on which the ASA has never, to the present authors' knowledge, upheld a complaint. When Hoover published a national advertisement for its Turbo vacuum cleaner, bearing the copy-line, 'Who's built a Turbo for women drivers?', the ASA refused to uphold the large numbers of nationwide complaints from women who believed that Hoover's style of advertising reinforced the traditional sexist value that the woman's place is in her home.[4]

The ASA hold the view that the advertiser is not a social reformer; if an advertisement depicts the status quo, then this is quite acceptable, however much some members of society may wish to change it. Critics of the advertising industry will point out that, in exaggerating people's standards of affluence, the industry is certainly not reflecting the status quo. If advertisers can portray living standards as they would like to see them, then why not women? We do not propose to resolve the issue in this chapter, but to leave the verdict to the reader. The fundamental issue, however, appears to relate to the role of the advertiser; how does the advertiser's 'role-specific duty' to sell relate to the wider issue of women's fundamental human right to be treated with equal dignity and respect to men? Does the advertiser simply have an obligation to **treat** women equally, or does that obligation also include helping to bring about a society in which all citizens are treated as having equal worth?

[4] The Advertising Standards Authority, Case Report 112, 15 August 1984, p. 15.

INTRODUCING THE READINGS

Should advertising simply inform, or is it acceptable for it to give consumers a psychological push and actually persuade? Vance Packard's classic *The Hidden Persuaders* was perhaps the first major popular work which articulated the criticisms of the 'persuasion industry' in the USA. The first reading is an extract which crystallizes many of Packard's misgivings about advertisers' methods. T. R. Nevett, the author of the second passage, cites some of the criticisms of advertising from a British point of view and outlines some of the more significant controls on advertising which have been introduced in recent times.

As the extracts from the debate between Galbraith and Hayek show, questions of the ethics of advertising spill over into questions of economics and politics. Theirs is a debate about what we should spend our money on and not (or not just) on what advertising tells us, Galbraith contends. In contrast, the criticisms made by feminists are not so much about whether and what things should be advertised, but rather **how** they are. Gilliam Dyer explores this dimension of advertising in her *Advertising as Communication*; we quote here an extract entitled 'What advertisements mean'. Dyer refers to 'images of women', taking up a common criticism of the ideology of advertising, namely that much advertising exploits, demeans or stereotypes women in society. While it is no doubt true that women have not yet achieved equal status with men, is it really the duty of the advertising industry to campaign for women's rights? The Advertising Standards Authority has commissioned two major surveys on the treatment of women in advertising – *Herself Appraised* (1982) and *Herself Reappraised* (1990) – which concluded that, by and large, the portrayal of women in advertisements did not 'cause grave or widespread offence' and that advertisers should reflect social conditions rather than feel any obligation to change them. We quote an extract from the more recent report.

Finally, the advertising industry answers its critics in the Advertising Association's publication, *Speaking Up for Advertising*. The AA takes the view that advertisers are sales people, not social reformers. It may have the last word in the present chapter, but readers will no doubt wish to add their own observations.

The hidden persuaders

VANCE PACKARD

The use of mass psychoanalysis to guide campaigns of persuasion has become the basis of a multimillion-dollar industry. Professional persuaders have seized upon it in their groping for more effective ways to sell us their wares – whether products, ideas, attitudes, candidates, goals, or states of mind.

This depth approach to influencing our behaviour is being used in many fields and is employing a variety of ingenious techniques. It is being used most extensively to affect our daily acts of consumption. The sale to us of billions of dollars' worth of United States products is being significantly affected, if not revolutionized, by this approach, which is still only barely out of its infancy. Two-thirds of America's hundred largest advertisers have geared campaigns to this depth approach by using strategies inspired by what marketers call 'motivation analysis'.

Meanwhile, many of the nation's leading public-relations experts have been indoctrinating themselves in the lore of psychiatry and the social sciences in order to increase their skill at 'engineering' our consent to their propositions. Fund raisers are turning to the depth approach to wring more money from us. A considerable and growing number of our industrial concerns (including some of the largest) are seeking to sift and mould the behaviour of their personnel – particularly their own executives – by using psychiatric and psychological techniques. Finally, this depth approach is showing up nationally in the professional politicians' intensive use of symbol manipulation and reiteration on the voter, who more and more is treated like Pavlov's conditioned dog.

The efforts of the persuaders to probe our everyday habits for hidden meanings are often interesting purely for the flashes of revelation they offer us of ourselves. We are frequently revealed, in their findings, as comical actors in a genial if twitchy Thurberian world. The findings of the depth probers provide startling explanations for many of our daily habits and perversities. It seems that our subconscious can be pretty wild and untuly.

What the probers are looking for, of course, are the *whys* of our behaviour, so that they can more effectively manipulate our habits and choices in their favour. This has led them to probe why we are afraid of banks; why we love those big fat cars; why we really buy homes; why men smoke cigars; why the kind of car we draw reveals the brand of gasoline we will buy; why housewives typically fall into a hypnoidal trance when they get into a supermarket; why men are drawn into auto showrooms by convertibles but end up buying sedans; why junior loves cereal that pops, snaps, and crackles.

We move from the genial world of James Thurber into the chilling world of

George Orwell and his Big Brother, however, as we explore some of the extreme attempts at probing and manipulation now going on.

Certain of the probers, for example, are systematically feeling out our hidden weaknesses and frailties in the hope that they can more efficiently influence our behaviour. At one of the largest advertising agencies in America psychologists on the staff are probing sample humans in an attempt to find how to identify, and beam messages to, people of high anxiety, body consciousness, hostility, passiveness, and so on. A Chicago advertising agency has been studying the housewife's menstrual cycle and its psychological concomitants in order to find the appeals that will be more effective in selling her certain food products.

Seemingly, in the probing and manipulating nothing is immune or sacred. The same Chicago ad agency has used psychiatric probing techniques on little girls. Public-relations experts are advising churchmen how they can become more effective manipulators of their congregations. In some cases these persuaders even choose our friends for us, as at a large 'community of tomorrow' in Florida. Friends are furnishing along with the linen by the management in offering the homes for sale. Everything comes in one big, glossy package.

Sombre examples of the new persuaders in action are appearing not only in merchandising but in politics and industrial relations. The national chairman of a political party indicated his merchandising approach to the election of 1956 by talking of his candidates as products to sell. In many industrial concerns now the administrative personnel are psychoanalysed, and their futures all charted, by trained outside experts. And then there is the trade school in California that boasts to employers that it socially engineers its graduates so that they are, to use the phrase of an admiring trade journal, 'custom-built men' guaranteed to have the right attitudes from the employer's standpoint.

What the persuaders are trying to do in many cases was well summed up by one of their leaders, the president of the Public Relations Society of America, when he said in an address to members: 'The stuff with which we work is the fabric of men's minds.' In many of their attempts to work over the fabric of our minds the professional persuaders are receiving direct help and guidance from respected social scientists. Several social-science professors at Columbia University, for example, took part in a seminar at the university attended by dozens of New York public-relations experts. In the seminar one professor, in a sort of chalk talk, showed these manipulators precisely the types of mental manipulation they could attempt with most likelihood of success.

All this probing and manipulation has its constructive and its amusing aspects; but also, I think it fair to say, it has seriously antihumanistic implications. Much of it seems to represent regress rather than progress for man in his long struggle to become a rational and self-guiding being. Something new, in fact, appears to be entering the pattern of American life with the growing power of our persuaders.

In the imagery of print, film, and air wave the typical American citizen is commonly depicted as an uncommonly shrewd person. He or she is dramatized as a thoughtful voter, rugged individualist, and, above all, as a careful, hardheaded consumer of the wondrous products of American enterprise. He is, in short, the flowering of twentieth-century progress and enlightenment.

Most of us like to fit ourselves into this picture, and some of us surely are justified in doing so. The men and women who hold up these glowing images, particularly the professional persuaders, typically do so, however, with tongue in cheek. The way these persuaders – who often refer to themselves good-naturedly as 'symbol manipulators' – see us in the quiet of their inter-office memos, trade journals, and shop talk is frequently far less flattering, if more interesting. Typically they see us as bundles of day-dreams, misty hidden yearnings, guilt complexes, irrational emotional blockages. We are image lovers given to impulsive and compulsive acts. We annoy them with our seemingly senseless quirks, but we please them with our growing docility in responding to their manipulation of symbols that stir us to action. They have found the supporting evidence for this view persuasive enough to encourage them to turn to depth channels on a large scale in their efforts to influence our behaviour.

The symbol manipulators and their research advisers have developed their depth views of us by sitting at the feet of psychiatrists and social scientists (particularly psychologists and sociologists) who have been hiring themselves out as 'practical' consultants or setting up their own research firms. Gone are the days when these scientists confined themselves to classifying manic depressives, fitting round pegs in round holes, or studying the artifacts and mating habits of Solomon Islanders. These new experts, with training of varying thoroughness, typically refer to themselves as 'motivation analysis' or 'motivation researchers'. The head of a Chicago research firm that conducts psychoanalytically oriented studies for merchandisers, Louis Cheskin, sums up what he is doing in these candid terms:

> Motivation research is the type of research that seeks to learn what motivates people in making choices. It employs techniques designed to reach the unconscious or subconscious mind because preferences generally are determined by factors of which the individual is not conscious . . . Actually in the buying situation the consumer generally acts emotionally and compulsively, unconsciously reacting to the images and designs which in the subconscious are associated with the product.

Mr Cheskin's clients include many of America's leading producers of consumer goods.

These motivational analysts, in working with the symbol manipulators, are adding depth to the selling of ideas and products. They are learning, for example, to offer us considerably more than the actual item involved. A Milwaukee advertising executive commented to colleagues in print on the fact that women will pay two dollars and a half for skin cream but no more than twenty-five cents for a cake of soap. Why? Soap, he explained, only promises to make them clean. The cream promises to make them beautiful. (Soaps have now started promising beauty as well as cleanness.) This executive added, 'The women are buying a promise.' Then he went on to say: 'The cosmetic manufacturers are not selling lanolin, they are selling hope. . . . We no longer buy oranges, we buy vitality. We do not buy just an auto, we buy prestige.'

The reason why I mention merchandisers more frequently than the other types of persuader in this exploration is that they have more billions of dollars immediately at stake and so have been pouring more effort into pioneering the depth approach. But the others – including publicists, fund raisers, politicians, and industrial personnel experts – are getting into the field rapidly, and others with anything to promote will presumably follow.

Advertising in Britain

T. R. NEVETT

Since World War II, advertising has probably been subjected to a greater volume of criticism than at any time in its history. This is not to say that it has become less truthful – standards in this respect are higher now than they have ever been. What has happened is that a change has taken place in the climate of public and political opinion which has brought advertisements under much closer scrutiny. Increased emphasis has been placed in general terms upon consumer protection. Consumers themselves have probably become more aware of advertising now that it is brought directly into their homes by the peculiarly intrusive medium of television. And a wide variety of writers have examined the ethics of 'persuasion', the possibilities of mass manipulation, and the economics of the advertising-inspired acquisitive society.

The Labour Party has tended to become particularly critical of the activities of advertisers. In 1959 a public meeting called by Francis Noel-Baker, M. P., set up the Advertising Inquiry Committee, an independent body which was to watch out for 'all kinds of socially harmful advertisement'. Two years later the party set up an independent commission under the chairmanship of Lord Reith, which recommended the establishment of a National Consumer Board financed by a levy on advertising. In 1972, a Green Paper on Advertising was published, in which advertising was condemned for creating an imbalance in the relationship between consumer and producer – a state of affairs which it was proposed to rectify by the creation of a National Consumers Authority:

> This Authority should be independent. It should have an income of millions rather than thousands, and thus be enabled to test claims on behalf of consumers,

to investigate complaints and to publish its work, (and that of others) effectively. The establishment of a statutory code to govern advertising practice is suggested. The Authority would advise on its provisions, enforcement and needed revisions.

The troubles besetting the newspaper industry were attributed to 'excessive reliance on advertising revenue', which it was felt might compromise the freedom of the press, together with 'the habit of advertisers of concentrating on papers already successful'. In addition, advertising was castigated for '. . . its tendency to over-encourage gross materialism and dissatisfaction and its tendency to irresponsibility'. Since many of the problems were seen as arising from 'an excess of advertising above a necessary and reasonable level', it was proposed to disallow 50 per cent of all advertising expenditure as a deductable expense for tax purposes. As well as financing the National Consumers Authority, it was felt that this would lead to competition in terms of price reductions on products rather than through advertising. The taxation of advertising was subsequently adopted as official party policy.

The teaching profession has at times been extremely critical of the influence of advertising on children. The Annual Conference of the National Association of Schoolmasters in 1962 heard Mr Terry Casey state their case in the following terms:

Perhaps the most pervasive anti-educational influence is that of modern advertising, for that *exists* to circumvent the reasoning faculty and weaken judgment. Some of it is puerile, but it can be subtle. Of the former kind are the many variants of the *ex parte* claim that 'Bloggs makes the best – whatever it is. This must be so because Bloggs says it is so'. Millions of young minds, which we seek to train to think, are constantly bombarded with this sort of nonsense. Not content with had logic, resort is had to bad manners. Children themselves are recruited as advertising agents, and are urged to make importunate demands upon their parents to buy this or that product. 'Don't forget my fruit gums, Mum!' is not even prefaced with the little word 'please'.

Under the rough treatment of the 'blurb' writers, adjectives have lost their vitality and almost their validity because of the excessive use of superlatives. In school we try to enrich vocabularies, but many children are reduced to the verbal poverty of using the prepositional prefix 'super' as an all-purpose adjective denoting approbation, thanks to the baleful influence of the 'Ads'. Psychology, the science which we thought was to be the handmaiden of education, has been prostituted to serve the ends of salesmanship, the panjandrum of the inflated economy. If advertising really is necessary to keep the wheels of industry and commerce turning, is it too much to ask that it be presented in ways which do not offend good taste nor affront good sense?

One result of the generally more critical attitude towards advertising has been an increase in the amount of legislation affecting the content of advertisements, both directly and indirectly. Apart from the widely known Trade Descriptions Act, there are over 60 statutes and statutory instruments currently in force which relate to advertising, the most important of them being listed in Appendix L of the British Code of Advertising Practice . . . for a detailed examination of their scope and significance the reader is referred to Dr Richard Lawson's definitive *Advertising Law*. Advertising on television is particularly tightly controlled, the Independent Broadcasting Authority having a statutory responsibility for programme content which includes advertising. This it discharged in respect of commercials by ensuring that they comply with its own Code of Practice, checking them before tranmission not only for points of presentation but also to make certain that all claims are capable of substantiation. Radio commercials, for which the I.B.A. is again responsible, are also subject to prior approval, but since the medium is used mainly for local campaigns, vetting in most instances is left to individual stations.

Mounting criticism has also forced the advertising business to tighten its own internal controls. Medical advertising in particular has come under increasingly close scrutiny, with the Proprietary Association of Great Britain revising its Code on a number of occasions, and the British Code of Standards in Relation to the Advertising of Medicines and Treatments, published under the auspices of the Advertising Association in 1948, subsequently being incorporated into the British Code of Advertising Practice. Voluntary action in this traditionally difficult area seems to have been successful. The Proprietary Association today works closely with the Department of Health, and regulations made under the Medicines Act of 1968 leave the detailed control of advertising very largely in the hands of the self-regulatory bodies. Even the Price Commission was impressed with the job which had been done:

> Self regulation of advertising by the industry has been initiated by the Proprietary Association of Great Britain (PAGB). This has been responsible for stopping the early advertising abuses which even now colour the image of the industry. The first Code of Practice was introduced in 1936 and this has been systematically updated since then to improve advertising standards and to take into account the development of new advertising media such as commercial television and radio. In addition to the controls imposed by the PAGB the advertising industry itself has imposed its own system of control through the Advertising Standards Authority.
>
> The number of complaints about proprietary medicines advertising is about 0.2 per cent of all complaints and the number upheld is less than 0.1 per cent. The conclusion is therefore that the system of control is effective.

The advertising business has also made considerable efforts to improve standards on a more general level, though in responding to public pressure it may have moved too little and too late. A notable step forward was taken in 1961 when the Advertising Association Conference saw the unveiling of the British Code of Advertising Practice, providing for the first time a set of formal standards to be observed and applied by all sides of the business. This was not enough to still the critical voices, objections being made to the framing of the Code on the grounds that it did not go far enough, and to the standing committee responsible for its enforcement because it represented advertising interests rather than those of the consumer. The following year therefore saw the setting up of a new body, the independent Advertising Standards Authority, which had as its object 'The promotion and enforcement throughout the United Kingdom of the highest standards of advertising in all media, so as to ensure in co-operation with all those concerned that no advertising contravenes or offends against these standards.' The chairman of the Authority was named as Professor Sir Arnold Plant of the London School of Economics, whose impartiality was beyond doubt; among its ten members was Vic Feather of the TUC. The sceptics still remained unconvinced, however, arguing that the Authority was not strong enough, was biased in favour of advertising, and that its working was comparable to that of the police investigating complaints against themselves.

By 1974 it was becoming abundantly clear that unless justice were seen to be effectively enforced, the Labour Government would introduce a statutory code of practice together with suitable machinery to ensure its observance. Faced with this threat, the industry made considerable revisions to its own system. The Advertising Standards Authority's permanent secretariat was strengthened. A revised edition of the Code of Practice was produced, with copies going to every Citizen's Advice Bureau in the country. Massive advertising campaigns were mounted, telling the public about the Authority and its work, and urging them to complain if they saw an advertisement that was not legal, decent, honest and truthful. Regular bulletins were introduced giving details of complaints received and the action taken. A monitoring system was begun to keep a check on particular categories of advertisement where problems were likely to occur. And the whole machinery of control was now financed by a levy on display advertising of 0.1 per cent to be collected by a new body known as the Advertising Standards Board of Finance (ASBOF). Meanwhile the Authority had also absorbed the work of the Advertisement Investigation Department of the Advertising Association, which had given so many years of faithful service.

The Council of the Advertising Standards Authority now consists of twelve members appointed by the Chairman, all of whom serve as individuals and not as representatives of any business or sectional interest. Eight are drawn from various areas of public life, and the others from the advertising industry to provide expert advice. The ASA is really the public face of advertising control. Another body, the Code of Advertising Practice Committee, co-ordinates activities within the advertising industry itself. Consisting of members of the twenty organisations subscribing to the Code, it is responsible for ensuring that people working in all branches of advertising are aware of and understand the provisions of the Code, and are prepared to enforce them. It can specify certain classes of advertisement for preclearance, currently vetting those for cigarettes, pregnancy testing and counselling, abortion, vasectomy, and sterilisation. It also deals with disputes on copy matters arising between advertisers, and if required will provide pre-publication advice on the admissibility of advertising claims.

The new method of working has undoubtedly been successful in ensuring stricter observance of the Code of Advertising Practice. The Authority's Annual Report for the year 1976–7 gives the following breakdown of complaints received during a sample period:

> The number of complaints which came within the ASA's remit over a nine week period were 1,592, against a background of something of the order of 4½ million advertisements published each week. Of that number, 183 were complaints not about advertisements but about a failure to deliver goods ordered by mail. (Because such goods are bought as a direct result of an advertisement, the ASA has a special responsibility for bringing such complaints to a satisfactory conclusion). Of the remaining complaints, 295 were found to be justified. This represents 18.5% of all complaints received in the period, but only 0.006% of the estimated total number of print advertisements published during the nine weeks concerned. The complaints which were upheld ranged from technical breaches of the Code and genuine over-sights to a very few intentionally misleading claims. A substantial proportion were concerned with questions of taste and decency: an area where self-regulation need fear no competition from the law.

In spite of this impressive record, there still remain some awkward loopholes. Enforcement of the Code is only effective if the media carrying the offending advertisement belong to one of the organisations which have agreed to uphold its provisions. In the case of an advertiser using 'rogue' media, or sending his material through the post, the Authority is powerless. In future it will surely be this area which will attract the attention of proponents of statutory control.

In addition to the part played by the Authority in advertising control, it should be remembered that considerable work is done behind the scenes by individual companies and organisations within the business. The Newspaper Society, by maintaining its own Advertisement Investigation Department, running training courses and seminars, and publishing essential information in handy reference form, keeps the regional press up to date and on its guard. Publishers' organisations operate guarantee schemes to protect readers against possible loss when sending off money in 'direct response' to mail order advertisements. The Incorporated Society of British Advertisers continues to supply its members with a confidential bulletin giving details of current sharp and illegal practices. Agency standards are upheld by the Institute of Practitioners in Advertising, which in 1957, for example, banned the use by its members of subliminal advertising – messages flashed at such speed that they are received by the brain without the recipient's conscious knowledge. Students taking the industry's professional examination – the Diploma of the Communication Advertising and Marketing Education Foundation – now also face compulsory questions on legal and voluntary controls. It remains to be seen whether all these efforts will be sufficient to head off the threat of tighter legal control, including compulsory prevetting of advertisements, as is the case on television. The British press has always been wary of any attempt to censor its columns, and there remains the fear that machinery established for the ostensible purpose of checking advertising could very easily be converted to control the editorial sections. Perhaps a few misleading advertisements are a small price to pay for democracy.

In addition to pressure for higher standards of advertising, the industry has also had to face calls for an end to the advertising of particular products. The case in which feelings have run highest has been that of cigarettes, following the publication of evidence linking smoking with lung cancer. At the outset the industry fiercely resisted any kind of curb. The public, it was argued, should be permitted to smoke themselves to death if they so desired. In any case, advertising did not encourage people to smoke but only to switch brands. A typical reaction was that of the poster industry's Joint Censorship Committee, which in 1962 banned a Ministry of Health poster with the wording 'Cigarettes cause lung cancer' on the grounds that this was not the same as saying 'Cigaratte smoking is a cause of lung cancer' – a decision described by Lord Hailsham as 'absolutely indefensible and indeed irresponsible, illogical quibbling'.

Gradually the industry was forced to give way. In 1962 the Independent Television Authority and the tobacco manufacturers agreed on a code of practice which put an end to the use of romantic situations, the over-emphasis on the pleasure to be derived from smoking, and the use of appealing personalities or settings. The screening of cigarette commercials was also limited to times when children were least likely to be watching. Three years later cigarettes disappeared completely from the commercial break, despite vehement protests from the Advertising Association, the Institute of Practitioners in Advertising, and the Incorporated Society of British Advertisers. Meanwhile, a number of newspapers and magazines was announcing that they would not accept any further cigarette advertising, among them the *Radio Times* and *Listener*, whose decision announced in 1969 was estimated to have cost them £500,000 in lost revenue within a year. The cigarette companies, for their part, actually increased their expenditure in the years after the television ban, and sought to circumvent it by such means as sponsorship.

At the time of writing, the appeals which can be made in cigarette advertising are set out in Appendix H of the *British Code of Advertising Practice*, which prohibits virtually every type of claim traditionally employed. Each advertisement also has to carry a warning that smoking can damage the health. Calls for a complete ban on cigarette advertising still persist, however, and there seems little doubt that this will eventually come, ending what must surely rank as one of the most contentious episodes in British advertising.

The affluent society

J. K. GALBRAITH

On Security and Survival

In our society, the increased production of goods – privately produced goods – is, as we have seen, a basic measure of social achievement. This is partly the result of the great continuity of ideas which links the present with a world in which production indeed meant life. Partly, it is a matter of vested interest. Partly, it is a product of the elaborate obscurantism of the modern theory of consumer need. And partly, we have seen, the preoccupation with production is forced quite genuinely upon us by the tight nexus between production and economic security. However, it is a reasonable assumption that most people pressed to explain our concern for production – a pressure that is not often exerted – would be content to suggest that it serves the happiness of most men and women. That is sufficient.

The pursuit of happiness is admirable as a social goal. But the notion of happiness lacks philosophical exactitude; there is agreement neither on its substance nor its source. We know that it is 'a profound instinctive union with the stream of life,'[1] but we do not know what is united. As just noted, precision in scholarly discourse not only serves as an aid in the communication of ideas, but it acts to eliminate unwelcome currents of thought, for these can almost invariably be dismissed as imprecise. To have argued simply that our present preoccupation with production of goods does not best aid the pursuit of happiness would have not nowhere. The concepts to which one would have been committed would have been far too vague.

Any direct onslaught on the identification of goods with happiness would have had another drawback. Scholarly discourse, like bullfighting and the classical ballet, has its deeper rules and they must be respected. In this arena, nothing counts so heavily against a man as to be found attacking the values of the public at large and seeking to substitute his own. Technically, his crime is arrogance. Actually, it is ignorance of the rules. In any case, he is automatically removed from the game. In the past, this has been a common error of those who have speculated on the sanctity of present economic goals – those who have sought to score against materialism and philistinism. They have advanced their own view of what adds to human happiness. For this, they could easily be accused of substituting for the crude economic goals of the people at large the more sensitive and refined but irrelevant goals of their own. The accusation is fatal.

The reader will now appreciate the care with which the defenses against such an attack have been prepared. The question of happiness and what adds to it has been evaded, for indeed only mathematicians and a few others are required to solve problems that can as sensibly be sidestepped. Instead, the present argument has been directed to seeing how extensively our present preoccupations, most of all that with the production of goods, are compelled by tradition and by myth. Released from these compulsions, we become free for the first time to survey our other opportunities. These at least have a plausible relation to happiness. But it will remain with the reader, and (since many of the opportunities can be served only by action of the state) one hopes with democratic process, to reconcile these opportunities with his own sense of what makes life better.

II

A society has one higher task than to consider its goals, to reflect on its pursuit of happiness and harmony and its success in expelling pain, tension, sorrow and the ubiquitous curse of ignorance. It must also, so far as this may be possible, ensure its own survival.

Once, in the not distant past, there was a simplistic association of security with an expanding economy – with a 'healthy' increase in the production of private consumer goods. This is no longer believed. As noted, ideas, along with the ability of the Soviet Union to extract awesome space accomplishments from a far less productive economy, joined to defeat this error and now it is hard to remember that we once believed such nonsense. But a dangerous, indeed an infinitely more dangerous, association of production with military policy still exists. The basic stabilization apparatus of the modern economy consists in a large public sector sustained by a large volume of taxation, which, being progressive, increases more than in proportion with increases in production and income, and releases income for private use when the rate of expansion is slower. Close to half of the expenditures which currently (in the mid-seventies) justify this taxation and thus justify this regulatory process are for military or related purposes. Economists have been quick to argue that other public expenditures would serve. But the fact cannot be eluded; as matters now stand, the stability of production depends on a large volume of military expenditures, quite a few of them for weapons thoughtfully designed to destroy all life.

Additionally, the weapons culture which underlies the macroeconomic stabilization of the economy also plays a deeply functional role in underwriting technology. If the notion that security depends on winning a race with the Soviet Union for increased production has been abandoned, the same cannot be said for the belief that it depends on winning a competition in technological innovation. Or rather, though the race is recognized as having no rational relation to the security of the participants, the commitment to it has been in nowise lessened. And one reason is that the race has, in fact, a deeply organic relation to economic performance. A consumer goods economy is limited in the resources it can allocate to research and development. The weapons competition sustains such effort on a vastly greater scale. This is interesting to the participant producers for its own sake. It also finances development with application to the consumer goods sector – the development of air transport and computer technology. And it is also a cover by which the cost of research and development for civilian purposes which is too expensive or too risky to be afforded by private firms can, on occasion, be conducted at public cost. Were we deeply concerned about survival, we would question the wisdom of these arrangements and we would work relentlessly to persuade the Soviet Union, as the principal focus of this competition, or their danger. But if economic performance is our primary concern – if production *qua* production is the thing that counts – then survival naturally takes second place. And so it does. Only as we get matters into better perspective will our priorities become more consistent with life itself.[2]

There are other if lesser problems which our present preoccupation with production leaves unsolved. Were the Russians to disappear from the world, or, even more remarkably, become overnight as tractable as church mice, there would remain vast millions of hungry and discontented people in the world. Without the promise of relief from that hunger and privation, disorder would still be inevitable. The promise of such relief requires that we have available or usable resources. If such is the nature of our system that we have production only because we first create the wants that require it, we will have few resources to spare. We will be rich but never quite rich enough to spare anything much for the poor – including our own. We shan't present a very enchanting picture to the world or even to ourselves. If we understand that our society creates the wants that it satisfies, we may do better.

Even when the arms race ends, as it must be made to end, the scientific frontier will remain. Either as an aspect of international competition, or in pursuit of the esteem and satisfaction which go with discovery, we shall want to seek to cross it and be in on the crossing. In the field of consumer satisfaction, as we should by now agree, there is little on which one can fault the American performance. But this is not all and, as we should now, hopefully, also agree, an economy that is preoccupied however brilliantly with the production of private consumer products is supremely ill fitted for many of these frontier tasks. Under the best of circumstances, its research will be related to these products rather than to knowledge. The conventional wisdom will provide impressive arguments to the contrary. No one should be fooled.

And not only does a great part of modern scientific work lie outside the scope of the market and private enterprise but so does a large area of application and development. Private enterprise did not get us atomic energy. It has shown relatively slight interest in its development for power for the reason that it could not clearly be fitted into commercial patterns of cost and profit. Though no one doubts the vigor with which it addresses itself to travel on highways within the United States, General Motors has little interest in travel through space.

As matters now stand, we have few civilian arrangements that are by central design and purpose directed to large-scale participation in modern scientific and technological progress and its large-scale application in advance of knowledge that these will be commercially feasible. Much has been accomplished by research and development not immediately subject to commercial criteria under the inspiration of military need. This has done more to save us from the partial techological stagnation that is inherent in a consumer goods economy than we imagine. But this is a hideously inefficient way of subsidizing general scientific and technical development, as nearly all scientists agree. And it has the further effect of associating great and exciting scientific advances with an atmosphere of fear and even terror.

III

Nor is this all. The day will not soon come when the problems of either the world or our own polity are solved. Since we do not know the shape of the problems, we do not know the requirements for solution. But one thing is tolerably certain. Whether the problem be that of a burgeoning population and of space in which to live with peace and grace, or whether it be the depletion of the materials which nature has stocked in the earth's crust and which have been drawn upon more heavily in this century than in all previous time together, or whether it be that of occupying minds no longer committed to the stockpiling of consumer goods, the basic demand on America will be on its resources of ability, intelligence and education. The test will be less the effectiveness of our material investment than the effectiveness of our investment in men. We live in a day of grandiose generalization. This one can be made with confidence.

Education, no less than national defense or foreign assistance, is in the public domain. It is subject to the impediments to resource allocation between private and public use. So, once again, our hope for survival, security and contentment returns us to the problem of guiding resources to the most urgent ends.

To furnish a barren room is one thing. To continue to crowd in furniture until the foundation buckles is quite another. To have failed to solve the problem of producing goods would have been to continue man in his oldest and most grievous misfortune. But to fail to see that we have solved it, and to fail to proceed thence to the next tasks would be fully as tragic.

NOTES

1. Bertrand Russell, *The Conquest of Happiness* (London: Allen & Unwin, 1930), p. 248.
2. These are matters which I discuss at great length, and I think with greater precision, in *The New Industrial State*, 2nd ed., rev. (Boston: Houghton Mifflin, 1971) and *Economics and the Public Purpose* (Boston: Houghton Mifflin, 1973). Indeed, the feeling that this somber and transcendent issue needed more attention was one of the inducements to these further books.

The Dependence Effect

The notion that wants do not become less urgent the more amply the individual is supplied is broadly repugnant to common sense. It is something to be believed only by those who wish to believe. Yet the conventional wisdom must be tackled on its own terrain. Intertemporal comparisons of an individual's state of mind do rest on technically vulnerable ground. Who can say for sure that the deprivation which afflicts him with hunger is more painful than the deprivation which afflicts him with envy of his neighbor's new car? In the time that has passed since he was poor, his soul may have become subject to a new and deeper searing. And where a society is concerned, comparisons between marginal satisfactions when it is poor and those when it is affluent will involve not only the same individual at different times but different individuals at different times. The scholar who wishes to believe that with increasing affluence there is no reduction in the urgency of desires and goods is not without points for debate. However plausible the case against him, it cannot be proven. In the defense of the conventional wisdom, this amounts almost to invulnerability.

However, there is a flaw in the case. If the individual's wants are to be urgent, they must be original with himself. They cannot be urgent if they must be contrived for him. And above all, they must not be contrived by the process of production by which they are satisfied. For this means that the whole case for the urgency of production, based on the urgency of wants, falls to the ground. One cannot defend production as satisfying wants if that production creates the wants.

Were it so that a man on arising each morning was assailed by demons which instilled in him a passion sometimes for silk shirts, sometimes for kitchenware, sometimes for chamber pots, and sometimes for orange squash, there would be every reason to applaud the effort to find the goods, however odd, that quenched this flame. But should it be that his passion was the result of his first having cultivated the demons, and should it also be that his effort to allay it stirred the demons to ever greater and greater effort, there would be question as to how rational was his solution. Unless restrained by conventional attitudes, he might wonder if the solution lay with more goods or fewer demons.

So it is that if production creates the wants it seeks to satisfy, or if the wants emerge *pari passu* with the production, then the urgency of the wants can no longer be used to defend the urgency of the production. Production only fills a void that it has itself created.

II

The point is so central that it must be pressed. Consumer wants can have bizarre, frivolous, or even immoral origins, and an admirable case can still be made for a society that seeks to satisfy them. But the case cannot stand if it is the process of satisfying wants that creates the wants. For then the individual who urges the importance of production to satisfy these wants is precisely in the position of the onlooker who applauds the efforts of the squirrel to keep abreast of the wheel that is propelled by his own efforts.

That wants are, in fact, the fruit of production will now be denied by few serious scholars. And a considerable number of economists, though not always in full knowledge of the implications, have conceded the point. . . . Keynes noted that needs of 'the second class,' i.e., those that are the result of efforts to keep abreast or ahead of one's fellow being, 'may indeed be insatiable; for the higher the general level, the higher still are they.'[1] And emulation has always played a considerable role in the views of other economists of want creation. One man's consumption becomes his neighbor's wish. This already means that the process by which wants are satisfied is also the process by which wants are created. The more wants that are satisfied, the more new ones are born.

However, the argument has been carried farther. A leading modern theorist of consumer behavior, Professor Duesenberry, has stated explicitly that 'ours is a society in which one of the principal social goals is a higher standard of living . . . [This] has great significance for the theory of consumption . . . the desire to get superior goods takes on a life of its own. It provides a drive to higher expenditure which may even be stronger than that arising out of the needs which are supposed to be satisfied by that expenditure.'[2] The implications of this view are impressive. The notion of independently established need now sinks into the background. Because the society sets great store by ability to produce a high living standard, it evaluates people by the products they possess. The urge to consume is fathered by the value system which emphasizes the ability of the society to produce. The more that is produced, the more that must be owned in order to maintain the appropriate prestige. The latter is an important point, for, without going as far as Duesenberry in reducing goods to the role of symbols of prestige in the affluent society, it is plain that his argument fully implies that the production of goods creates the wants that the goods are presumed to satisfy.[3]

III

The even more direct link between production and wants is provided by the institutions of modern advertising and salesmanship. These cannot be reconciled with the notion of independently determined desires, for their central function is to create desires – to bring into being wants that previously did not exist.[4] This is accomplished by the producer of the goods or at his behest. A broad empirical relationship exists between what is spent on production of consumer goods and what is spent in synthesizing the desires for that production. A new consumer product must be introduced with a suitable advertising campaign to arouse an interest in it. The path for an expansion of output must be paved by a suitable expansion in the advertising budget. Outlays for the manufacturing of a product are not more important in the strategy of modern business enterprise than outlays for the manufacturing of demand for the product. None of this is novel. All would be regarded as elementary by the most retarded student in the nation's most primitive school of business administration. The cost of this want formation is formidable. In 1974, total advertising expenditure – though, as noted, not all of it may be assigned to the synthesis of wants – amounted to approximately twenty-five billion dollars. The increase in previous years was by about a billion dollars a year. Obviously, such outlays must be integrated with the theory of consumer demand. They are too big to be ignored.

But such integration means recognizing that wants are dependent on production. It accords to the producer the function both of making the goods and of making the desires for them. It recognizes that production, not only passively through emulation, but actively through advertising and related activities, creates the wants it seeks to satisfy.

The businessman and the lay reader will be puzzled over the emphasis which I give to a seemingly obvious point. The point is indeed obvious. But it is one which, to a singular degree, economists have resisted. They have sensed, as the layman does not, the damage to established ideas which lurks in these relationships. As a result, incredibly, they have closed their eyes (and ears) to the most obtrusive of all economic phenomena, namely, modern want creation.

This is not to say that the evidence affirming the dependence of wants on advertising has been entirely ignored. It is one reason why advertising has so long been regarded with such uneasiness by economists. Here is something which cannot be accommodated easily to existing theory. More pervious scholars have speculated on the urgency of desires which are so obviously the fruit of such expensively contrived campaigns for popular attention. Is a new breakfast cereal or detergent so much wanted if so much must be spent to compel in the consumer the sense of want? But there has been little tendency to go on to examine the implications of this for the theory of consumer demand and even less for the importance of production and productive efficiency. These have remained sacrosanct. More often, the uneasiness has been manifested in a general disapproval of advertising and advertising men, leading to the occasional suggestion that they shouldn't exist. Such suggestions have usually been ill received in the advertising business.

And so the notion of independently determined wants still survives. In the face of all the forces of modern salesmanship, it still rules, almost undefiled, in the textbooks. And it still remains the economist's mission – and on few matters is the pedagogy so firm – to seek unquestioningly the means for filling these wants. This being so, production remains of prime urgency. We have here, perhaps, the ultimate triumph of the conventional wisdom in its resistance to the evidence of the eyes. To equal it, one must imagine a humanitarian who was long ago persuaded of the grievous shortage of hospital facilities in the town. He continues to importune the passersby for money for more beds and refuses to notice that the town doctor is deftly knocking over pedestrians with his car to keep up the occupancy.

And in unraveling the complex, we should always be careful not to overlook the obvious. The fact that wants can be synthesized by advertising, catalyzed by salesmanship, and shaped by the discreet manipulations of the persuaders shows that they are not very urgent. A man who is hungry need never be told of his need for food. If he is inspired by his appetite, he is immune to the influence of Messrs. Batten, Barton, Durstine & Osborn. The latter are effective only with those who are so far removed from physical want that they do not already know what they want. In this state alone, men are open to persuasion.

IV

The general conclusion of these pages is of such importance for this essay that it had perhaps best be put with some formality. As a society becomes increasingly affluent, wants are increasingly created by the process by which they are satisfied. This may operate passively. Increases in consumption, the counterpart of increases in production, act by suggestion or emulation to create wants. Expectation rises with attainment. Or producers may proceed actively to create wants through advertising and salesmanship. Wants thus come to depend on output. In technical terms, it can no longer be assumed that welfare is greater at an all-round higher level of production than at a lower one. It may be the same. The higher level of production has, merely, a higher level of want creation necessitating a higher level of want satisfaction. There will be frequent occasion to refer to the way wants depend on the process by which they are satisfied. It will be convenient to call it the Dependence Effect.

We may now contemplate briefly the conclusions to which this analysis has brought us.

Plainly, the theory of consumer demand is a peculiarly treacherous friend of the present goals of economics. At first glance, it seems to defend the continuing urgency of production and our preoccupation with it as a goal. The economist does not enter into the dubious moral arguments about the importance or virtue of the wants to be satisfied. He doesn't pretend to compare mental states of the same or different people at different times and to suggest that one is less urgent than another. The desire is there. That for him is sufficient. He sets about in a workmanlike way to satisfy desire, and accordingly, he sets the proper store by the production that does. Like woman's, his work is never done.

But this rationalization, handsomely though it seems to serve, turns destructively on those who advance it once it is conceded that wants are themselves both passively and deliberately the fruits of the process by which they are satisfied. Then the production of goods satisfies the wants that the consumption of these goods creates or that the producers of goods synthesize. Production induces more wants and the need for more production. So far, in a major tour de force, the implications have been ignored. But this obviously is a perilous solution. It cannot long survive discussion.

Among the many models of the good society, no one has urged the squirrel wheel. Moreover, as we shall see presently, the wheel is not one that revolves with perfect smoothness. Aside from its dubious cultural charm, there are serious structural weaknesses which may one day embarrass us. For the moment, however, it is sufficient to reflect on the difficult terrain which we are traversing. . . . We saw how deeply we were committed to production for reasons of economic security. Not the goods but the employment provided by their production was the thing by which we set ultimate store. Now we find our concern for goods further undermined. It does not arise in spontaneous consumer need. Rather, the dependence effect means that it grows out of the process of production itself. If production is to increase, the wants must be effectively contrived. In the absence of the contrivance, the increase would not occur. This is not true of all goods, but that it is true of a substantial part is sufficient. It means that since the demand for this part would not exist, were it not contrived, its utility or urgency, *ex* contrivance, is zero. If we regard this production as marginal, we may say that the marginal utility of present aggregate output, *ex* advertising and salesmanship, is zero. Clearly the attitudes and values which make production the central achievement of our society have some exceptionally twisted roots.

Perhaps the thing most evident of all is how new and varied become the problems we must ponder when we break the nexus with the work of Ricardo and face the economics of affluence of the world in which we live. It is easy to see why the conventional wisdom resists so stoutly such change. It is far, far better and much safer to have a firm anchor in nonsense than to put out on the troubled seas of thought.

NOTES

1. J. M. Keynes, *Essays in Persuasion*, 'Economic Possibilities for Our Grandchildren' (London: Macmillan, 1931), p. 365.
2. James S. Duesenberry, *Income, Saving and the Theory of Consumer Behavior* (Cambridge, Mass.: Harvard University Press, 1949), p. 28.
3. A more recent and definitive study of consumer demand has added even more support. Professors Houthakker and Taylor, in a statistical study of the determinants of demand, found that for most products price and income, the accepted determinants, were less important than past consumption of the product. This 'psychological stock,' as they called it, concedes the weakness of traditional theory; current demand cannot be explained without recourse to past consumption. Such demand nurtures the need for its own increase. H. S. Houthakker and L. D. Taylor, *Consumer Demand in the United States*, 2nd ed., enlarged (Cambridge, Mass.: Harvard University Press, 1970).
4. Advertising is not a simple phenomenon. It is also important in competitive strategy and want creation is, ordinarily, a complementary result of efforts to shift the demand curve of the individual firm at the expense of others of (less importantly, I think) to change its shape by increasing the degree of product differentiation. Some of the failure of economists to identify advertising with want creation may be attributed to the undue attention that its use in purely competitive strategy has attracted. It should be noted, however, that the competitive manipulation of consumer desire is only possible, at least on any appreciable scale, when such need is not strongly felt.

The non sequitur of the 'dependence effect'

F. A. VON HAYEK

For well over a hundred years the critics of the free enterprise system have resorted to the argument that if production were only organized rationally, there would be no economic problem. Rather than face the problem which scarcity creates, socialist reformers have tended to deny that scarcity existed. Ever since the Saint-Simonians their contention has been that the problem of production has been solved and only the problem of distribution remains. However absurd this contention must appear to us with respect to the time when it was first advanced, it still has some persuasive power when repeated with reference to the present.

The latest form of this old contention is expounded in *The Affluent Society* by Professor J. K. Galbraith. He attempts to demonstrate that in our affluent society the important private needs are already satisfied and the urgent need is therefore no longer a further expansion of the output of commodities but an increase of those services which are supplied (and presumably can be supplied only) by government. Though this book has been extensively discussed since its publication in 1958, its central thesis still requires some further examination.

I believe the author would agree that his argument turns upon the 'Dependence Effect' explained in Chapter XI of the book. The argument of this chapter starts from the assertion that a great part of the wants which are still unsatisfied in modern society are not wants which would be experienced spontaneously by the individual if left to himself, but are wants which are created by the process by which they are satisfied. It is then represented as self-evident that for this reason such wants cannot be urgent or important. This crucial conclusion appears to be a complete *non sequitur* and it would seem that with it the whole argument of the book collapses.

The first part of the argument is of course perfectly true: we would not desire any of the amenities of civilization – or even of the most primitive culture – if we did not live in a society in which others provide them. The innate wants are probably confined to food, shelter, and sex. All the rest we learn to desire because we see others enjoying various things. To say that a desire is not important because it is not innate is to say that the whole cultural achievement of man is not important.

This cultural origin of practically all the needs of civilized life must of course not be confused with the fact that there are some desires which aim, not as a satisfaction derived directly from the use of an object, but only from the status which its consumption is expected to confer. In a passage which Professor Galbraith quotes (p. 118), Lord Keynes seems to treat the latter sort of Veblenesque conspicuous consumption as the only alternative 'to those needs which are absolute in the sense

Reading taken from *Southern Economic Journal*, April 1961. Copyright © 1961 *Southern Economic Journal*. Reprinted with permission.

that we feel them whatever the situation of our fellow human beings may be.' If the latter phrase is interpreted to exclude all the needs for goods which are felt only because these goods are known to be produced, these two Keynesian classes describe of course only extreme types of wants, but disregard the overwhelming majority of goods on which civilized life rests. Very few needs indeed are 'absolute' in the sense that they are independent of social environment or of the example of others, and that their satisfaction is an indispensable condition for the preservation of the individual or of the species. Most needs which make us act are needs for things which only civilization teaches us to exist at all, and these things are wanted by us because they produce feelings or emotions which we would not know if it were not for our cultural inheritance. Are not in this sense probably all our esthetic feelings 'acquired tastes'?

How complete a *non sequitur* Professor Galbraith's conclusion represents is seen most clearly if we apply the argument to any product of the arts, be it music, painting, or literature. If the fact that people would not feel the need for something if it were not produced did prove that such products are of small value, all those highest products .of human endeavor would be of small value. Professor Galbraith's argument could be easily employed, without and [sic] change of the essential terms, to demonstrate the worthlessness of literature or any other form of art. Surely an individual's want for literature is not original with himself in the sense that he would experience it if literature were not produced. Does this then mean that the production of literature cannot be defended as satisfying a want because it is only the production which provokes the demand? In this, as in the case of all cultural needs, it is unquestionably, in Professor Galbraith's words, 'the process of satisfying the wants that creates the wants.' There have never been 'independently determined desires for' literature before literature has been produced and books certainly do not serve the 'simple mode of enjoyment which requires no previous conditioning of the consumer' (p. 217). Clearly my taste for the novels of Jane Austin [sic] or Anthony Trollope or C. P. Snow is not 'original with myself.' But is it not rather absurd to conclude from this that it is less important than, say, the need for education? Public education indeed seems to regard it as one of its tasks to instill a taste for literature in the young and even employs producers of literature for that purpose. Is this want creation by the producer reprehensible? Or does the fact that some of the pupils may possess a taste for poetry only because of the efforts of their teachers prove that since 'it does not arise in spontaneous consumer need and the demand would not exist were it not contrived, its utility or urgency, ex contrivance, is zero?'

The appearance that the conclusions follow from the admitted facts is made possible by an obscurity of the wording of the argument with respect to which it is difficult to know whether the author is himself the victim of a confusion or whether he skilfully uses ambiguous terms to make the conclusion appear plausible. The obscurity concerns the implied assertion that the wants of the consumers are determined by the producers. Professor Galbraith avoids in this connection any terms as crude and definite as 'determine.' The expressions he employs, such as that wants are 'dependent on' or the 'fruits of' production, or that 'production creates the wants' do, of course, suggest determination but avoid saying so in plain terms. After what has already been said it is of course obvious that the knowledge of what is being produced is one of the many factors on which it depends what people will want. It would scarcely be an exaggeration to say that contemporary man, in all fields where he has not yet formed firm habits, tends to find out what he wants by looking at what his neighbours do and at various displays of goods (physical or in catalogues or advertisements) and then choosing what he likes best.

In this sense the tastes of man, as is also true of his opinions and beliefs and indeed much of his personality, are shaped in a great measure by his cultural environment. But though in some contexts it would perhaps be legitimate to express this by a phrase like 'production creates the wants,' the circumstances mentioned would clearly not justify the contention that particular producers can deliberately determine the wants of particular consumers. The efforts of all producers will certainly be directed towards that end; but how far any individual producer will succeed will depend not only on what he does but also on what the others do and on a great many other influences operating upon the consumer. The joint but unco-ordinated efforts of the producers merely create one element of the environment by which the wants of the consumers are shaped. It is because each individual producer thinks that the consumers can be persuaded to like his products that he endeavours to influence them. But though this effort is part of the influences which shape consumers' tastes, no producer can in any real sense 'determine' them. This, however, is clearly implied in such statements as that wants are 'both passively and deliberately the fruits of the process by which they are satisfied' (p. 124). If the producer could in fact deliberately determine what the consumers will want, Professor Galbraith's conclusions would have some validity. But though this is skilfully suggested, it is nowhere made credible, and could hardly be made credible because it is not true. Though the range of choice open to the consumers is the joint result of, among other things, the efforts of all producers who vie with each other in making their respective products appear more attractive than those of their competitors, every particular consumer still has the choice between all those different offers.

A fuller examination of this process would, of course, have to consider how, after the efforts of some producers have actually swayed some consumers, it becomes the example of the various consumers thus persuaded which will influence the remaining consumers. This can be mentioned here only to emphasize that even if each consumer were exposed to pressure of only one producer, the harmful effects which are apprehended from this would soon be offset by the much more powerful example of his fellows. It is of course fashionable to treat this influence of the example of others (or, what comes to the same things, the learning from the experience made by others) as if it amounted all to an attempt of keeping up with the Joneses and for that reason was to be regarded as detrimental. It seems to me that not only the importance of this factor is usually greatly exaggerated but also that it is not really relevant to Professor Galbraith's main thesis. But it might be worthwhile briefly to ask what, assuming that some expenditure were actually determined solely by a desire of keeping up with the Joneses, that would really prove? At least in Europe we used to be familiar with a type of persons who often denied themselves even enough food in order to maintain an appearance of respectability or gentility in dress and style of life. We may regard this as a misguided effort, but surely it would not prove that the income of such persons was larger than they knew how to use wisely. That the appearance of success, or wealth, may to some people seem more important than many other needs, does in no way prove that the needs they sacrifice to the former are unimportant. In the same way, even though people are often persuaded to spend unwisely, this surely is no evidence that they do not still have important unsatisfied needs.

Professor Galbraith's attempt to give an apparent scientific proof for the contention that the need for the production of more commodities has greatly decreased seems to me to have broken down completely. With it goes the claim to have produced a valid argument which justifies the use of coercion to make people employ their income for those purposes of which he approves. It is not to be denied that there is some originality in this latest version of the old socialist argument. For over a hundred years we have been exhorted to embrace socialism because it would give us more goods. Since it has so lamentably failed to achieve this where it has been tried, we are now urged to adopt it because more goods after all are not important. The aim is still progressively to increase the share of the resources whose use is determined by political authority and the coercion of any dissenting minority. It is not surprising, therefore, that Professor Galbraith's thesis has been most enthusiastically received by the intellectuals of the British Labour Party where his influence bids fair to displace that of the late Lord Keynes. It is more curious that in this country it is not recognized as an outright socialist argument and often seems to appeal to people on the opposite end of the political spectrum. But this is probably only another instance of the familiar fact that on these matters the extremes frequently meet.

Advertising as communication

GILLIAN DYER

When we talk about advertisements or attempt to analyse them, most of us tend to assume that they are vehicles for the communication of usually somewhat distorted or exaggerated publicity; and that they are 'transparent' or invisible carriers at that.

We tend to take for granted that what is on the screen or page is what the ad means and we 'measure' ads against some assumed reality which could replace the 'unreal' images which constitute most ads. The images of men and women in ads, for example, are usually considered to be mythic rather than real, and also stereotyped. This kind of criticism usually gets bogged down in arguments about the extent to which such images are true or false and seeks to replace distorted images with representations of people and situations as they really are. It assumes that there is a simple and better reality with which to replace the stereotypes and myths and ignores the fact that ads are in themselves a kind of reality which have an effect. In this sense ads are not secondary to 'real life' nor copied or derived from it. Ads are what some critics call 'specific representational practices' and produce meanings which cannot be found in reality. There is no simple reality with which to replace the falseness of ads, and there are no simple alternatives to stereotypes. In order to gain better understanding of the role that advertising plays in our society, we need to ask how advertising organizes and constructs reality, how ideology and meanings are produced within the ad discourse and why some images are the way they are, or how they could have been constructed.

In order to approach these questions we need to consider a framework for analysis established by semiotics, described by its founder Ferdinand de Saussure as 'a science that studies the life of signs within society'. It is an approach which has adopted some concepts and tools of analysis from structural linguistics, which attempts to uncover the internal relationships which give different languages their form and function. Although language is a basic model, semiotics has cast its net wider, and looks at any *system of signs* whether the substance is verbal, visual or a complex mixture of both. Thus speech, myth, folktales, novels, drama, comedy, mime, paintings, cinema, comics, news items and advertisements can be analysed semiotically as systems of signification similar to languages.

This approach involves a critical shift from the simple interpretation of objects and forms of communication to investigations of the organization and structure of cultural artefacts and, in particular, to enquiry into how they produce meaning. It is argued that the meaning of an advertisement is not something there, statically inside an ad, waiting to be revealed by a 'correct' interpretation. What an ad means depends on how it operates, how signs and its 'ideological' effect are organized *internally* (within the text) and *externally* (in relation to its production, circulation and consumption and in relation to technological, economic, legal and social relations). Implicit in this approach is a rejection of much impressionistic criticism and 'scientific' content analysis which assumes that the meaning of an ad is evident in its overt, manifest content and ignores the form that the content takes. As I said at the beginning of this chapter, ads are not invisible conveyors of messages or transparent reflections of reality, they are specific discourses or structures of signs. As such we do not passively absorb them but actively participate in their production of signification, according to the way they 'speak' to or 'ensnare' us. We come to advertisements as social readers. According to Janice Winship 'We all, so to speak, bring our social positions with us to the reading of any discourse; and we are not automatically "interpellated" as the subject(s) which the discourse constructs' (1981, p. 28). She cites the example of a poster for a car which proclaimed: 'If it were a lady it would get its bottom pinched', and which was defaced with this rejoinder: 'If this lady were a car she'd run you down'. This challenge is effective because it uses the same means of representation as the ad. It also highlights the fact that the original ad was clearly addressed to a male and that the social reader objecting was a female. It matters, then, who an ad is implicitly addressed to, which may or may not include you.

Most semiotic/structural studies of advertising texts distinguish between their outward manifestation and inner mechanisms – the codes and conventions which organize and release the meanings of a text in the process of viewing or reading. Such codes are what makes meaning possible. Texts result from the dynamic interplay of various semiotic, aesthetic, social and ideological processes within them which also operate in the culture outside them. The audience member is involved in the work of the text and the production of its meaning; his or her own knowledge, social position and ideological perspective is brought to bear on the process of the construction of meaning. As Judith Williamson argues:

> Advertisements must take into account not only the inherent qualities and attributes of the products they are trying to sell, but also the way in which they can make those properties mean something to us . . . Advertisements are selling us something besides consumer goods; in providing us with a structure in which we, and those goods are interchangeable, they are selling us ourselves. (1978, p. 13)

Advertisements do not simply manipulate us, inoculate us or reduce us to the status of objects; they create structures of meaning which sell commodities not for themselves as useful objects but in terms of ourselves as social beings in our different social relationships. Products are given 'exchange-value': ads translate statements about objects into statements about types of consumer and human relationships. Williamson gives the example of the ad for diamonds ('A diamond is forever') in which they are likened to eternal love: the diamond means something not in its own terms as a rock or mineral but in human terms as a sign. A diamond cannot buy love, but in the ad it is the diamond which is made to generate love and comes to mean love. And once this initial connection has been made we almost automatically accept the object for the feeling. People and objects can become interchangeable as in, for example, the slogans 'The Pepsi generation', 'The Martini set'.

It is in this sense that advertisements should be seen as structures which function by transforming an object into something which is given meaning in terms of people. The meaning of one *thing* is transferred to or made interchangeable with another *quality*, whose value attaches itself to the *product*. In the simplest of cases, we can see how something (someone or some place) which we like or value transfers its qualities to the product. Two things are made interchangeable or equal in value – 'Happiness is a cigar called Hamlet'. Williamson calls this transfer of meaning between signs in an ad 'currency'. The cigar represents or replaces the feeling of happiness: 'Currency is something which represents a value and in its interchange-ability with other things gives them value too' (1978, p. 20).

Feminists have pointed out that ads addressed to women define women in terms of the commodity. Goods like convenience foods, domestic appliances, toilet products and fashions are sold not as commodities but in terms of what they can do for relationships (with men, with the family, with neighbours). Women are made to identify themselves with what they consume – 'You, Daz and your Hotpoint automatic', 'You and Heinz together make a perfect team'. Success with the family and friends can be purchased for the price of a packet of detergent, a bottle of cough syrup or a jar of moisturizing cream. Of course, it is women who usually do the washing and cook the meals, but they are made to feel inadequate without the commodities which help them perform the tasks which constitute their family and social relationships.

So in order to understand the image of a woman in an ad, it is important to identify how she is signified and positioned in the ad as a female person, and to remember that any representation is also partially defined in relation to the material position of women 'outside' the ad, within what feminists call 'patriarchal relations' – their economic, political and ideological position in society.

Herself reappraised

ADVERTISING STANDARDS AUTHORITY

Among critics it is commonplace that advertising degrades women and obstructs and delays the movement towards equality between women and men by 'stereotyping' women's lives as centring upon domesticities or being subordinated to men. In this way, it is said, advertising reinforces the barriers to women's achieving equality in the wider world. Some commentators also deplore what they describe as the use of women as 'sex objects' in advertisements. By this they mean that naked or partly covered women are pictured in some advertisements for no reason other than to attract the attention of the concupiscent generality of men. 'Stereotyping' and treating women as 'sex objects' are linked and often described as 'sexism' which some denounce as an attitude common to the advertising industry. These present day attitudes have been shaped by the experience of the pioneer feminists in Victorian days.

Apart from the vote, two of the main aims of movements for the emancipation of women before the First World War were to free women from their personal and legal subordination to men within the family and to secure the right to work for the high proportion of women, between one-quarter and one-third, for whom the large-scale emigration of men had denied husbands in a society which gave an assured status only to married women. The redundant women of the middle upper class who had neither father nor husband to support them sought freedom in their right to work and in opening the professions, monopolised by their brothers, to women. This explains why, into our own day, men and women often thought of the labour market as a place for single women who ought to vacate it upon marriage. Many upper class women thought abstention from marriage was an inevitable and proper cost of pursuing a career. They sometimes found themselves in conflict with working class women who sought freedom rather in regulating the conditions and restricting the hours of their over-abundant labour. Only in recent years have these clashes among the occupational interests of married and single women and of the working and upper class been resolved. But the emphasis which some still place on 'stereotyping' echoes the experience of women in the first half of our century when marriage and children meant the denial of a career. But the ways in which married women are now adapting to their dual roles as mothers and workers outside the home demonstrates that there is no longer an inevitable conflict between motherhood and career despite the difficulties and frustrations which affect many women.

The success of the Victorian and early-twentieth century movement for the emancipation of women in achieving formal institutional and legal equality in most spheres of life was, by all odds, one of the main social developments of the last hundred and fifty years. By the early 1960s it had brought one-half of humanity into the outward appearance of full citizenship. But that was the trouble. The promise was mocked by the daily realities of economic and occupational inequality and discrimination, and the result was a new phase in the women's movement which sought not the emancipation but the 'liberation' of women. The very titles of the period tell a part of the story. *The Second Sex*[1] felt compelled to exhibit the *Feminine Mystique*[2] by becoming the *Female Eunuch*[3] pursuing her *Sexual Politics*[4] through the *Dialectic of Sex*[5] with the aim of escaping from the *Patriarchal Attitudes*[6] of *The Naked Ape*[7] in the *Human Zoo*[8].

Stereotyping and Sexism

How then, we must ask, against the background sketched above, do the concepts of stereotyping and degradation by use as a 'sex object' help to an understanding of the treatment of women in advertisements in the present new phase of the one hundred and fifty year old women's movement. A recent Canadian study of *Sex Stereotyping in Advertising* thus summarises its findings about how women and men are portrayed in print advertising. 'The evidence . . . is overwhelming: in print advertising, woman's place is still in the home; women are still dependent on men; women still do not make independent and important decisions; women still view themselves and are viewed by others as sex objects.'[9] Some British critics of the treatment of women in advertising present similar conclusions. Nevertheless, it has often been pointed out that the indictment ignores the marked extent to which print, as distinct, perhaps, from some television advertising, has changed in this respect in the last ten years or so in these islands at least. But, even if it were accepted that the Canadian study presents a realistic picture, it has to be asked what is actually being argued by those who insist upon the stereotyping effect of advertising in the United Kingdom? It is difficult to support the view that social change has been obstructed for there have been striking transformations over the last generation in the direction of greater equality. The stereotypes and sexism of advertising has not hindered change in the central area of family law. In education, some of the oldest citadels are falling; there are now as many girls as boys being articled to solicitors and entering undergraduate medicine. Surely the generality of women are not so ignorant of the lives they lead that they are unaware of being workers as well as mothers in a society in which it is much more difficult to be a woman than a man? The fundamental inequalities of the labour market can neither be explained by the stereotypes of advertisers nor cured by tinkering with advertisements.

The very notion of stereotyping is over-simple and too narrow as a means of interpreting the rich variety of roles which women play in a single lifetime. Again, the argument from stereotyping assumes that advertising exercises great influence upon the way in which women think about their relationships with men, their attitudes to themselves and society, and of men and society to them. The evidence for this view is rarely examined. May it not be yet one more example of the present tendency to critics to regard the advertiser as a magician and of many to believe them?

The second limb of the argument is that women are stereotyped as sex objects by advertising and degraded in consequence. The present survey shows clearly that this view is not shared by the majority of people. Moreover, 'sex object' is itself an ambiguous term. There is no escaping that nature made women sex objects to men just as she made men sex objects to women, and most women and men have few complaints about nature's arrangement. It is the case, though, for many people brought up in our cultural and erotic heritage, that young women are nicer to look at than men, especially when they are naked, with obvious consequences on 'Page Three' and elsewhere. So it is natural and inevitable that permissiveness spreads to advertisements.

Some critics insist that what they object to is not naked women in advertisements but the portrayal of nakedness which is irrelevant to the product or service being advertised. The Authority's Council has concurred with this view and has adjudicated accordingly upon complaints. Council judges such advertisements from the point of view of accepting the erotic in art as in life, to the extent that it is contextually apt, and therefore to be treated as legitimate in advertising which is itself a major form of popular art.

Attitudes towards Advertising

The problem for the Authority is compounded by the undoubted fact that the clerisy has always disliked and condemned advertising. In the past, it fashioned a stereotype in which advertising confronted Puritan doctrine and challenged the Protestant ethic by urging people to consume and to enjoy, to spend and not to save. By promoting consumption, advertising was said by some to devalue in others the virtues of thrift and frugal living and to seduce young and old alike by the siren call that present joys are not hereafter. Many superior folk still feel that the good taste and sound culture of their fellow citizens are corrupted because advertising is mass persuasion in the interests of mass consumption and therefore encourages the proliferation of the meretricious.[10] Behind this catalogue of criticisms lies a vision of the advertiser as a thaumaturgist, manipulating flocks of docile consumers at will by inculcating wants which they did not previously possess leading to purchases of goods which they do not really need. Dr Richard Hoggart was stating a representative view when he argued twenty years ago[11] that the case against advertising is the same as that against political propaganda and 'any other form of emotional blackmail', it tries to achieve its ends by 'emotionally abusing its audiences'.

Similar assessments of the evils of advertising persist in some quarters. A distinguished physician recently responded to the Chairman of the ASA, who had rejected his complaint about an advertisement published by the British pharmaceutical industry, by observing that 'like most people, I have always supposed it to be the primary function of advertising to mislead . . .'.

But people at large by no means share his opinion that advertising is devious and dishonourable. Regular surveys of public attitudes to advertising have been conducted during the last twenty years, and they have shown that advertising is favourably regarded by at least two-thirds of the population though the degree of approval has fluctuated between high points in the early 1960s and early 1980s.[12] A limitation of those surveys is that respondents were faced with questions requiring undifferentiated answers of the order 'do you approve/disapprove of advertising a lot/little'. A survey commissioned by the Advertising Association in 1988 showed that 81% of a sample of the general population approved of advertising and only 3% disliked advertisements in newspapers and magazines. However, those who approved divided into 51% who approved 'a little' and 31% 'a lot'. When asked about print advertising, 31% of respondents said they 'liked' it, whilst 8% 'disliked' it and 59% were 'not bothered'. In the present survey the components of approval or disapproval have been broken down into a set of questions with the result that a more differentiated and, in consequence, at times a more critical, token of the public's attitudes to advertising emerges. Nevertheless, the upshot is that many of us rather like and approve in a discriminating way what some of our intellectual betters consider bad for us. The fact is, though, that the social and economic influence of advertising remains more talked about than studied.[13]

NOTES

1. Simone de Beauvoir (1949)
2. Betty Friedan (1963)
3. Germaine Greer (1970)
4. Kate Millett (1969)
5. Shulamith Firestone (1970)
6. Eva Figes (1970)
7. Desmond Morris (1967)
8. Desmond Morris (1970)
9. By Alice E. Courtney and Thomas W. Whipple, 1983, p. 14.
10. On this theme see D. G. MacRae, *Ideology and Society* (1968), pp. 77–86.
11. In Alexander Wilson (ed.), *Advertising and the Community* (1968), pp. 50–54.
12. Michael Barnes, 'Public Attitudes to Advertising', *International Journal of Advertising*, 1982, vol. 1, no. 2, pp. 119–128.
13. See the instructive analysis of M. J. Waterson of 'Some Popular Advertising Fallacies', *ibid.*, vol. 3, no. 3. 1984.

Speaking up for advertising

THE ADVERTISING ASSOCIATION

Is 'persuasion' desirable?

There is a view that giving people straightforward, uncluttered information is socially acceptable, but trying to persuade them to buy something, or to do something, is wrong. Persuasion can be made to have an almost Goebbels-like ring to it. A moment's reflection will show that what might be termed 'static information', which does not call for action of any kind, is most unlikely to exist in any form of communication. No one gives out information unless they want it to be used, whether it is simply the sign 'Exit' over a door or a listing in a telephone directory: these are the beginnings of persuasion.

The real question is not whether persuasion is desirable – it is virtually impossible to avoid it – but how far, in advertising, it should go, and whether it can get in the way of factual information. Firstly, the question of the level of persuasion. It is all too easy to overlook the fact that an advertisement is a partial statement: it has been described as 'truth in the most favourable light'. Provided that he stays within the limits of the law and the advertising codes, an advertiser can blow his own trumpet. The advertising industry in the UK has a well-deserved reputation for acting in a restrained, reasoned manner, without overwhelming consumers. So an acceptable level of persuasion is perfectly right and proper.

The second question is whether persuasion takes up valuable time and space in advertisements, which could better be used to give facts about products and services. This overlooks the first objective of an advertisement, which is to gain attention. If it can do this with facts, all well and good, but it may instead have to use fantasy or humour. Some critics would say that the fantasy or humour should be replaced by hard information. But for everyday products like tins of beans there is little that can be said that is not already known, so information on its own could be boring or even trivial. For more complex items, such as a washing machine, the reverse may be the case: an advertisement cannot encompass all that a consumer needs to know, so it is likely to encourage further action prior to purchase, such as sending off for a brochure or visiting a showroom. The chances of a consumer making an expensive purchase purely because of a persuasive message in an advertisement are pretty remote, instead he will read the manufacturer's leaflets, consult friends, study 'Which?', and so on.

Some critics maintain that persuasive advertising encourages excessive materialism – 'keeping up with the Joneses'. There is the added point that, at a time when millions are unemployed, it is socially divisive to show continuously on television commercials for the good life that many people cannot afford. But with or without advertising the differences in society would exist. 'The rich man in his castle, the poor man at his gate' was apparent long before the advent of a well-developed advertising industry. Indeed, it can be said that advertising, coupled with mass production, has helped the 'poor man' to narrow the gap between himself and the 'rich man' to achieve a better standard of living. Whether aspects of materialism are excessive is very much in the eye of the beholder, because one man's luxury can be another man's necessity. Certainly advertising as regulated in the UK encourages reasonable consumption rather than excessive binges.

As for those unfortunate enough to be unemployed, they do not need advertising to tell them that they are worse off – they are only too well aware of it – so curbs would achieve nothing except taking information away from the majority who do have spending power. It is all too glib and easy to blame advertising for creating social ills, instead of trying to find real cures.

Does advertising create 'false wants'?

Advertising, it is claimed, can persuade people to buy what they do not really require – the concept of 'false wants'. This is the strange suggestion that, by hammering home a message about a new product, an advertiser can induce consumers to purchase it, although deep down they do not want it – only through advertising can sales be initiated and maintained. Not only is this insulting to the public, it is simply not borne out by the facts.

Firstly, hundreds of new products – many of them widely advertised – fail each year because consumers do not want them. Secondly, there has to be a latent need or desire for a product before it can be successfully launched. A few years ago hardly anyone had heard of video recorders, now there is a well-established market, a clear example of latent need (to record programmes and watch films at home) that has been properly exploited. At a different level, advertising on its own could not sell instant potato or even chips if consumers did not already have a requirement for convenience foods of this kind. The requirement was already there, advertising merely exposed it with the offer of appropriate products.

Sometimes the 'false wants' criticism is made by those who believe, often with the best of intentions that they know best what the people ought and ought not to want. This 'nanny philosophy' is not limited to any one political creed and it is democratically dangerous.

Is product differentiation wasteful?

Some products use virtually identical ingredients – all that differs is the image and the packaging, including how they are advertised. This, the critics claim, is unnecessary and wasteful. But economists increasingly accept the concept of 'added value', which means, among other things, that a product can have non-physical differences from similar products and thus gain in value in the eyes of the consumer. Cosmetics are an obvious example, as are various brands of drinks. Different lipsticks, or a wide range of perfumes, would not exist if consumers did not perceive differences, similarly there would not be as many choices in the lager market. The differences may be in image (a perfume may be aimed at a particular age group) or in promotion (a lager may 'reach the parts other beers cannot reach'). All this means added value.

From time to time researchers and journalists publish 'exposés' showing how little difference there is between competing brands in particular product fields. Some consumers may find this information of value and will shop accordingly, but many others choose products on the basis of which best suit their life style, or the image with which they have most affinity.

Once there are perceived differences between brands there can be competition, with price and special offers, which clearly benefit consumers. The alternative is drab conformity, with people having reduced opportunities to express their personalities, and with the lack of competition encouraging inefficiency and high prices.

There are those who would say that because there is so much product differentiation, with new products (frequently with only minor changes to old ones) coming on to the market all the time, this encourages what has been termed the 'throw-away society' – people continuously buy new lines which are virtually identical to what they already have, then discard existing models that are in perfect working order. But who is to decide when a product improvement is not a product improvement? What one person perceives as a waste of money may be of positive benefit to another. If a new product actually offered nothing new to anyone then it would fail.

And let us not forget, in the context of product replacement, that advertising can help consumers dispose of unwanted items. Weekly newspapers in particular are full of small ads, for sales of individual products, car boot sales and so on. The so-called 'throw-away society' does not, in practice, throw away as much as some people imagine.

Are there too many advertisements?

Any speaker will occasionally have thrown at him the claim that there are 'too many advertisements'. A few people believe that advertising is too intrusive, and should be curbed for that reason. This is clearly a personal matter, so it is impossible to satisfy everyone, because tolerance of the volume of advertisements will differ. But what one can say is that it is comparatively easy to avoid advertisements that you do not wish to see or read. On ITV, for example, advertising has to be clearly indicated and must appear in 'natural breaks', and there are limits on the amount of advertising per hour. In the press, if an advertisement is designed in such a way that it might be mistaken for editorial matter, then the word 'advertisement' must appear above it.

Some people protest at the fact that the same commercial may appear several times during one evening's television viewing. But the advertiser wants to be sure that he reaches 'light' viewers as well as those who sit in front of the set for several hours. This seems a small price for the viewer to have to pay to ensure that there is revenue for two television channels.

Many people find nothing wrong with the volume of advertisements. To set against those who object, there are those who would say that on television the commercials are frequently more entertaining than the programmes, because creative standards in advertising are high in the UK. And classified advertisements in the press – for jobs, houses, entertainment – provide a real reader benefit.

Does advertising debase culture?

Arguments about cultural standards are rather complex, because this is obviously a subjective matter, centring on personal taste. The principal argument is that advertising is vulgar, and debases the English language. But advertisers have to use language that their customers will understand so they cannot be expected to use words that are only likely to be appreciated by graduates in literature. Advertisements, which frequently play on words, can use language in a vivid and entertaining manner.

The use of classical music in commercials comes in for some criticism. Purists protest that it is wrong to use, say, snatches of Beethoven to sell lager. In practice only a few bars of music are played, and it is hard to see how this detracts from the effect of the full piece when played in the surrounds of somewhere like the Royal Albert Hall. Indeed, it could well be that a snatch of music could encourage someone to wish to hear the whole piece, and so encourage a taste for classical music.

Does advertising exploit the vulnerable?

Advertising, say the critics, exploits the vulnerable. The honest answer to this is that there are small pockets of people who will always be misled by advertisements (or indeed by anything else!), no matter how strong the regulations. For example, some consumers go through life unable to cope with money management, and tend to overspend all too easily. Advertising may well guide such people towards purchases they cannot afford, but it is difficult to see how this can be avoided, because even if there were a totalitarian ban on advertising, it would easily be replaced by other forms of 'temptation'. And we should never lose sight of the fact that the vast majority of the public, who understand what advertisements are trying to do and know how to use them, have rights as well.

This does not, of course, mean that advertisers should be free to prey on the gullible or those who are socially insecure. Advertising regulations, for example, give detailed protection to children (see below), and also seek to prevent unfair exploitation of people who are excessively worried about their appearance or who have an obsessive fear of burglary, mugging and so on.

It is interesting to note one of the conclusions reached by the Office of Fair Trading in its report on advertising countrols in the print media published in November 1978:

'There is no evidence from the research which identifies any demographic or social group, for example the relatively poor, the young or the old . . . as particularly vulnerable to advertising in that the group could be shown to be less critical of advertising, or more disposed to like or accept it. The pattern of responses corresponded closely with the overall pattern'.

Does advertising reinforce stereotypes?

This is an argument that can never be concluded to the satisfaction of all. For example, an advertisement which shows modern mums going out to work could please progressive women, but upset those with a more traditional outlook who might be concerned at the supposed harmful effect on family life. What spokesmen for advertising can say is that it is first and foremost the job of most advertisements to sell products or services, not to make major changes in public attitudes, and it would be socially wrong if it was otherwise. To take an extreme example, imagine the reaction if a soap manufacturer were to campaign in his advertisement for Christianity as well as cleanliness.

But if most critics can be persuaded to take the point that product advertising should not initiate social engineering, there will still be those who will say that, like it or not, it may at least reinforce existing stereotypes: Dad as the sole bread-winner, children beautifully behaved, and so on. There is much truth in this, and rightly so, because in an advertisement an advertiser will use settings and language with which his potential customers readily associate, or to which they aspire. Stereotypes are understood as being a necessary form of shorthand demanded by the need to create a situation in a 30 second commercial, or in one illustration.

If advertising were to disappear overnight, it is hardly likely that there would be a rapid speeding-up of social change. The reinforcement of stereotypes through advertisements is only a very minor way in which society accepts that change should be gradual. Such factors as the way friends and relatives live their lives are much more important in this context.

Some would still claim that ultra-cautious advertisers keep behind social change rather than in step with it. The fact is that the articulate campaigner who believes passionately in a cause can be unwilling to accept that his view is held by a minority, and is not (yet) accepted by the world at large. By comparison advertisers do their research, and have evidence of what people are thinking in Halifax as well as in Hampstead. Nationwide campaigns have to reflect nationwide taste and lifestyles.

Does advertising exploit children?

There are basically three main areas of criticism regarding children's advertising: that it encourages materialism and artificial demands which parent cannot gratify; that it exploits children's natural credulity and sense of loyalty; and that it encourages bad eating habits and thus affects children's health.

With regard to the first criticism, children are, of course, dependent on their parents to supply their needs, and it is a fact of life that they will attempt to influence their parents and state their preferences for all kinds of things – not just products advertised on television, but what they do after school, the time they go to bed, the friends they choose, and the food they eat. This is a natural part of growing up and the forming of a relationship between parent and child, and will sometimes naturally cause friction. But how great a role does advertising play in causing a child to demand the unattainable and create dissatisfaction?

Research carried out by the Children's Research Unit in 1978 showed that children's demands were felt to be triggered off by many sources other than television, and were usually of a temporary nature. Peer groups in particular – what their friends had or wanted – were found to be of far more influence, as well as displays in shops, adults, parents and school.

Advertising is only one source of information, along with the others mentioned above, which enables a child to make a choice. If the parent feels that the choice is wrong – as they may with other choices such as general behaviour patterns – the decision is theirs.

The second criticism is that young children do not understand the purpose of advertising, and are therefore more vulnerable than adults. It is claimed that children cannot distinguish between fact and fantasy, and that advertising takes advantage of this natural credulity and lack of experience.

Advertisers fully recognise that the younger child needs protection on this point, and it is specifically covered in the codes of practice. But they do not accept this as an argument for a complete ban on children's advertising. Children are far more sophisticated then most people imagine, and all but the youngest are perfectly capable of evaluating advertising messages.

The ability to evaluate advertising messages increases with age, and by the age of seven the majority of children are competent in this respect. Indeed, advertising can be a valuable way of teaching consumer skills: it is far better for children to be exposed to advertising and to learn to distinguish advertising messages whilst they have little purchasing power and are under the control of their parents, than for them to be suddenly confronted with it at a later age.

Without anything to judge, it is difficult to see how judgment will develop. Children are subject to all kinds of influence every day – friends, comics, television programmes, shop displays – and advertising must be one of the very few which is rigidly controlled and restrained.

The third major criticism centres on the advertising of specific products: food such as sweets, sugared cereals, crisps and biscuits which, it is argued, are bad for childen because they cause tooth decay or obesity. This argument embraces more than advertising – for if such products are as harmful as critics say, they surely would seek to ban not just their promotion but their manufacture. Who, on that assumption, should decide that x is harmful but y is not, and on what grounds? The fact is that virtually any food taken to excess can be harmful, not just sugar or starch.

Even if the advertising of 'undesirable' foodstuffs to children were banned – and the codes have particular rules which govern such advertising – it is unlikely that this would have much effect. Although nearly half the sugar confectionery bought in 1978 was eaten by children, for example, only a fifth was actually bought by children; a third of all chocolate sold was eaten by children, but they only bought a tenth. So it is clear that adults, who play the most important part in deciding what is right or wrong for their children feel that sweets are right.

A ban on children's advertising would be ineffective without a corresponding change in adult behaviour, which influences children far more than television advertising in their attitude to categories of products. A child's interest in food is not created by advertising; nor will withdrawal of advertising destroy it. It is not what children eat that matters, but how much, at what time, whether they clean their teeth; in short, it depends on parental control. Advertising regulations can support parents, but can in no sense replace them.

Are women wrongly portrayed in advertisements?

In the context of stereotyping, it is the portrayal of women that is most often attacked. Critics argue, for example, that women are frequently shown as 'mere' housewives with little or no financial sense. It is indeed true that women are more often seen in advertisements for household products, than those for banks or building societies. This argument can be supported with facts. Although more and more women do a job outside the home, they are still responsible for the majority of household purchasing decisions. They are the ones who do a large amount of the family cooking and washing. It therefore makes sound commercial sense that advertisements for household products should be aimed at them.

Advertising messages must be brief, single-minded and to the point. They therefore need to use a form of shorthand in communicating with the public. This means that while it may be very true that the 'typical housewife' shown doing the washing, baking a cake, or cleaning the carpet, may also attend yoga classes two evenings a week, work as a part-time dental nurse 5 mornings a week, and enjoy visiting the theatre and walking in the country in her spare time, these facts are all irrelevant to the point the advertiser is trying to get across, and therefore sadly it is not practical to include them within the precious and expensive 30 seconds allowed for the selling message.

Some women feel that advertisements for household products do not portray sufficiently accurately the actual drudgery of housework, that advertisements glorify what can often be tedious chores. An argument that can be used in reply to this criticism is that an advertiser needs to portray the aspirational values of his potential customers in order to demonstrate his product most effectively.

In 1981 the Advertising Standards Authority undertook a survey of the attitudes of a representative national sample of women. The findings of this study were published under the title of 'Herself Appraised: The Treatment of Women in Advertisements' in the spring of 1982. This did not reveal widespread dissatisfaction about advertisements among the women interviewed. Where offence was caused, notably by nudity or by explicit references to sexuality and menstruation, it was not sufficiently widely shared for advertisements containing such material to be declared offensive in terms of the British Code of Advertising Practice. Neither was the reaction of respondents sufficient to suggest that there is, at present, any need for additional rules within the Code specifically related to the depiction of women in advertisements. However, a substantial minority of respondents were inclined to think that some women, not necessarily themselves, might feel degraded as a direct result of the manner in which their sex is depicted in advertisements.

The Authority noted in its 1982–83 Annual Report that an examination of the altered treatment of women and the family in advertisements over the last decade or so indicates that prudent advertisers have already made, and are acting upon, their own assessments of the directions of change. It trusts that the findings of its preliminary research will serve to persuade other advertisers to follow and thus to become more conscious of the sensitivities of one half of their audience.

CASE STUDY

Cigarette advertising

In 1954 the American Cancer Society and the British Medical Research Council independently published results of research which convincingly linked cigarette smoking with lung cancer. Tobacco tar contained carcinogenic substances, with the result that male smokers were six times as likely to contract lung cancer than their non-smoking peers.

At first the tobacco industry tried to promote smoking materials on the grounds of improved safety, such as filter tips and cigarette holders, but the evidence suggested that consumers did not want to be reminded of the health hazards at all, and that a better marketing strategy was to ignore the risks and promote the brand image.

Meanwhile the US and UK governments began to introduce measures designed to curb cigarette smoking. In both countries health warnings became obligatory on cigarette packets, and in 1965 a ban on all television advertising of cigarettes was imposed in the UK. The US government followed suit in 1971. The Advertising Standards Authority, founded in 1962, permitted the continuation of cigarette advertising, but drafted special regulations which controlled advertising copy produced by the cigarette companies. The ASA now insists that its permission must be sought for all cigarette advertising within the UK and that all advertisements are scrutinized to ensure their complicance with a fairly exacting code of practice.

Cigarette manufacturers have alleged that they are trapped in by a morass of legislation and advertising restrictions. Although there is nothing in law or in BCAP regulations to prevent cigarette manufacturers making truthful statements about their products (so long as these can be substantiated), there is little they would wish to tell which would attract the consumer. Benson and Hedges were the first cigarette company to circumvent the problem by resorting to 'abstract' advertising. Apart from the obligatory health warning, the advertisement said nothing about the cigarette at all, not even the name. The first in the series was the famous 'raining cigarettes' advertisement, which portrayed a 'pure gold' umbrella with diagonal cigarettes representing raindrops. ('Pure gold' was the Benson and Hedges slogan in their halcyon days of television advertising.)

This advertising strategy was pure inspiration. Surprisingly, it was pre-faced by no market research whatsoever, yet it proved to be amazingly successful. Benson and Hedges devised further abstract advertisements based on the theme of pure gold, while other companies followed suit with abstract advertising which related to their own brand image. Of all the competitors, probably Silk Cut is the best recognized, with its visual puns on purple silk being cut. Winston attempted a slightly different tactic by stating (not wholly accurately), 'We're not allowed to tell you anything about Winston, but here's a . . .', followed by something totally irrelevant, such as an aardvark or a 'tart leaning on a bar' (depicted by a crowbar and a jam tart!). Winston were not so successful on the sales front, although the entertainment value of their advertising was quite popular.

While the cigarette manufacturers complain about undue restrictions, anti-smoking campaigners do not believe that advertising controls have gone far enough. Action on Smoking and Health (ASH) would like to see a complete ban on cigarette advertising, and the Health Education Council has not the funds to produce anti-smoking publicity on the same scale as the multi-million pound advertising campaigns of the cigarette companies.

Pro-smoking organizations such as the Tobacco Advisory Council, FOREST (For the Right to Enjoy Smoking Tobacco) contend that a total advertising ban would be a violation of the principles of free speech and freedom of expression of the tobacco industry. Furthermore, they claim – and this is echoed by the Advertising Association – a complete ban would not be in the public interest. Cigarette advertising, they contend, does not increase the primary consumption of cigarettes; indeed this is not allowed by current advertising regulations which seek to ensure that advertisements are not directed at young people and do not encourage new smokers to take up smoking. Cigarette advertising, rather, is for companies to compete for their share of the market, encouraging those who have already taken up the habit to switch brands.

Not only is this the case, the pro-smoking lobby argues, a total ban would prevent the tobacco manufacturers disseminating information about their products. Smokers would be likely to continue with their existing loyalties if there were a total ban, and would not have the opportunity to be informed about safer forms of cigarette smoking, such as improved filter tips or lower tar brands. The Advertising Association supports this position by pointing to the evidence that countries with long-term advertising bans have a lower proportion of filter tip consumption, and that in countries such as Italy, Norway and Poland, cigarette smoking continued to climb during the years in which the respective bans were imposed.

Sources: Vance Packard, *The Hidden Persuaders* (Harmondsworth: Penguin, 1960); M. J. Waterson, *Advertising and Cigarette Consumption* (London: The Advertising Association, 1982); Tobacco Advisory Council, *The Case for Tobacco Advertising* (London, August 1988).

DISCUSSION TOPICS

1. 'Advertising degrades women'. In what ways do some contemporary feminists allege that advertising does this? Find examples, and justify your own conclusion on the subject.
2. Consider the ways in which advertising is said to support the dominant ideology. Do you think it is possible for advertising to be 'ideologically neutral'?
3. Ascertain which controls affect specific areas of the advertising industry (for example, television, journals, mail order). Do you think that advertising should be more closely controlled, and – if so – in what ways?

The 'greening' of business 9

WHAT IS A 'GREEN' BUSINESS?

The adjective 'green' covers a multitude of virtues. To be 'green' can mean responsible disposal of industrial waste, affirming animal rights and saving endangered species, saving trees and preserving the country-side, recycling, reducing or avoiding 'noise pollution', prohibiting CFCs, minimizing the 'greenhouse effect' and damage to the ozone layer, conserving energy (principally fossil fuels) and employing alternative sources of energy (such as solar, wind or wave power) and banning nuclear power. Some would contend that vegetarianism forms part of what it means to be 'green', while other protagonists wish to include employee health and safety as part of a 'green' programme.

Although the aim of 'being green' may seem a laudable one, the apparent comprehensiveness of 'green' issues has weaknesses as well as strengths. It is difficult to see what could **not** be included under this comprehensive umbrella. Literally everything is our environment, and therefore everything we do (whether as private individuals or as business men and women) affects it; we are always inside our environment and can never go outside it – whatever that would mean.

The fact that the term 'environmental' is so all-embracing means that it is often not clear what issues should be incorporated under that umbrella and what should not. For example, are health and safety issues green issues or not? Is a firm being 'green' if it obliges its workers to sit in front of VDU screens without offering eye strain checks or exploring the possibility of installing filters to reduce the risk of radiation? It might be argued that employee health and safety is an issue which has always been with us, and that it is a traditional and general responsibility of management to its employees, falling under the heading of employee rights and industrial law. On the other hand, it could be argued that, just as a (literally) green working environment with sunlight and views of landscapes and trees is conducive to the psychological well-being of workers, there is a similar obligation on the part of management to provide a working environment which is free of hazardous fumes, dangerous machinery and high levels of noise.

Does it really matter whether or not we define a particular issue in the business environment as 'green'? After all, it may be asked, 'What's in a name?', and it could be argued that so long as businesses treat the environment with due respect, then this is all that counts. Unfortunately the issue is not quite so simple. First, because the word 'green' is so versatile, it is possible for a firm to claim that a product is 'green' on account of one specific environmental feature when other qualities are potentially harmful environmentally. For example, one petrol company advertised lead free petrol as 'environmentally friendly', and added the claim that the fumes emitted from cars using it would not damage the ozone layer. The Advertising Standards Authority, with justification, took them to task for making an 'environmentally friendly' claim when lead free exhaust fumes, like any other exhaust fumes, contain carbon dioxide and therefore contribute to the 'greenhouse effect', unless a catalytic converter is fitted to the vehicle.[1] A product like recycled toilet paper may inherently be 'green' (in the sense of being composed of 100 per cent recycled materials), but it may have been manufactured by means of a process which used up large amounts of energy, or it may have had to be transported hundreds of miles by road in an articulated lorry before it secured its place on the supermarket shelf.

Further, a product can be 'green' in one respect but also very 'un-green' in another. The all-pervasiveness of the slogan 'green' often blurs together and disguises several different issues which may be at stake. Take for instance the issue of 'saving the whales'. One reason for attempting to preserve the life of whales is that it is an animal rights issue; whales are living beings which are capable of suffering, and (it may be argued) it is a form of 'speciesism' to suppose that the human manufacture and use of certain cosmetics may acceptably take precedence over the sparing of the whale. It is quite a different matter to object to whaling on the grounds that whales are at risk of dying out as a species because they are over-hunted. The 'anti-extinction' lobby typically uses a quite different set of arguments from the 'animal rights' campaigners; the problem for the anti-extinctionist is not animal suffering, but somewhat different considerations. It is not altogether clear what these are, but one consideration is the fact that the annihilation of a species is an irreversible environmental act (an argument encapsulated in the slogan 'Extinction is for ever'). Another type of argument is an ecological one, and it draws on utilitarian principles: nature has a fine balance which relies on a 'chain' of species which depend on one another; if one of these links is removed, then the balance can be seriously disturbed. A third type of argument might involve religious considerations; according to one Christian tradition, when God created the world he wanted as many species as possible to inhabit it and enjoy it. This principle has been labelled the 'principle of plenitude' and of course any

---

[1] The Advertising Standards Authority, *Case Report 171*, July 1989, p. 1.

human action which renders a species extinct would run counter to the divine purpose of 'plentitude' in creation.[2]

We do not propose to evaluate these different reasons for saving species; this would be too long an avenue to go down in a general discussion of 'greening' business. The important matter to notice is that there can be quite radically different reasons which the labels 'green' and 'environmental' blur together. The fact that there can be different reasons for preserving a species is not a mere academic matter; the underlying reasons behind conservationism determine what an acceptable alternative might be. For example, the cosmetics company Estée Lauder uses basking shark oil rather than whale oil – an acceptable alternative if a firm is simply 'anti-extinction', but an unacceptable alternative if one's hostility to whaling is based on a respect for animal and marine life.

To turn to another example, it is not particularly helpful for those who champion the greening of business to introduce 'no smoking' policies on the grounds that non-smoking is green. Opposition to tobacco can stem from a number of reasons. Smoking can be seen as a form of 'air pollution' (possibly an environmental issue). Smoking damages health (not so obviously 'environmental' although it is an important health and safety consideration). The purchasing of tobacco, arguably, exploits workers in the Third World, who are exposed to unfavourable trading conditions and who might fare better by growing edible crops for domestic consumption rather than non-essential plants like tobacco. Finally, in certain circles opposition to tobacco is opposed on religious grounds, either because it is seen as a prohibition (for example amongst Sikhs and Mormons) or because, being a stimulant, it alters one's state of consciousness and prevents the religious aspirant from seeing the world as it really is.

Are we able to impose any order on these diverse issues which are said to comprise the 'green' movement? Is there any common feature which they have, or is it the case that, as the philosopher Ludwig Wittgenstein might have said, we can find no more than some kind of 'family re-semblance'? In the *Philosophical Investigations*[3] Wittgenstein took the example of a 'game'. What do all games have in common? We might try suggesting that the common factor is winning and losing, but that would exclude games like patience or ring o' roses. We might try saying that

---

[2] Augustine, *De Civitate Dei*, XI, 22.
[3] Ludwig Wittgenstein, *Philosophical Investigations*, I.66 (Oxford: Blackwell, 1963).

they involve more than one participant – but what about solitaire? Or what about the suggestion that games are not 'serious'? Football and cricket are certainly taken extremely seriously by a large sector of the public, and Russian roulette can have some pretty serious consequences for the losers. According to Wittgenstein, there is no uniform set of factors which are common and peculiar to all games; all we can do is to identify a number of features which are typically found in games, and suggest that something is a game if it contains a significant number of these. Just as members of a family do not all have exactly the same common distinctive features, but a somewhat more nebulous set of overlapping points of resemblance, so it is with most, if not all, words we use, whether it is 'game' or whether it is 'green'.

Turning to the concept of 'green' we can identify a number of features which are commonly, but not necessarily always found in 'green' issues: responsible use of non-renewable resources, pursuit of sustainable growth and development, minimization of pollution, avoiding the irreversible destruction of aspects of the environment (ozone layer, greenhouse effect, extinction of species), conservation and preservation of beauty and the preservation of animal and plant life.

Having made some attempt at identifying the various strands which comprise 'green business', what should be the response of business companies to the 'green revolution'? It is possible for business men and women to conclude that green issues are irrelevant to business activity. As we have seen, Milton Friedman has argued that any firm's aim ought to be to maximize its profits on behalf of its shareholders.[4] If one accepts Friedman's view, then it is positively immoral to sacrifice profits in favour of the environment; rather, it is the government's role to intervene where environmental risks appear to take precedence over profit making. For Friedman, the central principle is **ownership**: the shareholders are the people to whom a business belongs, and business managers are wrongly appropriating the shareholders' money if they divert it to the purposes of conservation. For other commentators environmental matters will be resolved by purely economic considerations. Former US President Ronald Reagan is reported to have said about trees, 'When you've seen one, you've seen them all!' On such a view, trees are simply commodities which increase or decrease in economic value as numbers fall or rise. Controlling trees would therefore be accomplished automatic-

[4] Milton Friedman, 'The Social Responsibility of Business Is to Increase Its Profits'; *The New York Times Magazine*, 13 September 1970. Reprinted in chapter 5.

ally by the operation of market forces, Adam Smith's 'invisible hand'. When humankind is about to fell its last tree, that tree, being such a scarce commodity, would have become so expensive that it would have priced itself out of the market in favour of some substitute material, such as metal or plastic.

For the green campaigner, of course, our responsibilities cannot be shed so easily. Our obligations, they argue, must place respect for the environment above those of commercial gain. Even if economic considerations prevented us from killing the last whale or felling the last tree, it may be contended that we have duties to our environment and, especially, to subsequent generations who ought not be deprived of resources, scenery or species simply because the present generation has depleted the stocks.

GREEN BUSINESS OR CUSTOMER CHOICE?

Once we grant that 'green' issues are relevant in business transactions, who is ultimately responsible for ensuring that commodities are bought and sold with due regard for the environment? There are three possible views on the subject:

1. the 'greening' of businesses should be achieved by government legislation;
2. 'green' policies and products should be consumer-driven;
3. environmental protection should be company-led.

It is certainly the case that some areas of environmental protection are already covered by legislation. The Department of the Environment enforces compliance regarding levels of noise and disposal of at least some industrial waste. Propellants such as CFCs are now a thing of the past (even though their demise cannot reverse the ozone layer's recession). However, there are several difficulties in introducing legislation to cover a greater range of environmental issues. Some areas are controversial, such as animal testing, the abolition of which would be resisted by those who hold that it is better that animals should suffer in a laboratory than that humans should suffer by having adverse reactions to chemicals used in the manufacture of perfumes and other goods. In the meantime, legislation controls the **way** in which animal testing is carried out; for example, the experimenter must have a licence, and there are limits to the kinds of suffering which animals may endure. (They must be

destroyed immediately after the experiment, to prevent further unnecessary suffering). Whether such legislation goes far enough is debat-
able; at the time of writing the present Conservative government has set
its face against banning the hunting of animals for sport; hence it will
be a much greater step to control by law the treatment of animals for experimentation which, at least arguably, has a definite purpose. (Whether
it actually has a purpose or not has been questioned, of course; the
British Union for the Abolition of Vivisection has consistently argued
that animal experiments are useless as well as cruel.)

Further difficulties about introducing legislation lie in the sheer vagueness of 'green' concepts, to which we drew attention earlier. This makes
the area of 'eco-labelling' particularly problematic, for what does it mean
to declare a product to be 'environmentally safe', 'environmentally
friendly' or 'environmentally friendlier', as many packets declare? Are
such expressions synonymous, or do they reflect subtle distinctions which
the consumer is supposed to recognize? Proposals have been considered
within the EC to introduce some scheme of labelling, where products
could be scored against various 'green' criteria and be awarded symbols
to reflect how well they are faring. At present there exists the (currently
unresolved) problem of defining symbols and meanings, and also the
contentious issue of whether products should be obliged to carry symbols,
where this is appropriate, to connote that they are environmentally
harmful.

A further very practical problem lies in the vested interests of governments. Given that contributions to political parties come substantially
from business companies, unpopular legislation could mean withdrawal
of financial support. From the point of view of industry, legislation is
likely to be unwelcome: if 'going green' helps to increase a firm's sales,
then legislation should prove unnecessary; if, on the other hand, 'green'
entails 'costly' then firms are likely to be reluctant to see the introduction
of legal controls which would increase their production costs and hence,
arguably, reduce their profits.

If green consumerism is not to be government-driven, it may seem
that businesses themselves should be responsible for the environmental
implications of their activities. After all, is not the business company
who discharges effluent into rivers the moral equivalent of the vandal or
the litter lout who destroys and defaces in a private capacity? Surely, it
may be argued, the company which is harming the environment through
pollution or noise is cutting corners on production costs by not paying
for the 'externalities' – that is to say, the costs of production which

accrue outside the company itself. Surely those who pollute should pay the full costs of the pollution?

Although the 'polluter pays' principle may seem just, there are several problems about the notion. First, there are practical problems; it can be difficult to attribute the costs of cleaning up pollution or for compensating those who are affected by noise, smoke or inconvenience. In some cases it is not possible to put a price on environmental damage; since it is not possible to replace holes in the ozone layer, no amount of compensation seems great enough.

Although it may seem difficult to relate environmental damage to sums of money, this ought not to be beyond the wit of the accountant, who is quite familiar with cost benefit analysis and with placing valuations on 'intangible assets'. If it is possible for firms to assign values to intangible assets, then it ought to be possible to attribute notional figures to disbenefits which are caused by the activities of certain companies.

However, even though it may seem just that polluters should pay the costs of their production processes, companies who pollute may argue that they are competing with rivals and simply could not survive if they did not take full advantage of the maximum latitude allowed within the law. If greater care for the environment is necessary, then it is up to a government to introduce appropriate legislation, which would be binding on all competitors alike. A single company's unilateral concern for the environment could cause it to go out of business by becoming uncompetitive. Monies entrusted to executives are not to be squandered on good causes, however worthy they may seem. The aim of a firm, says Friedman, is to maximize profits, and if this is the case then firms should only 'go green' if this contributes to profit maximization.

If Friedman is right, then the greening of business should be consumer-driven rather than company led. If it becomes obvious that consumers prefer a 'green' to a 'non-green' product, then there are good grounds for supposing that 'greenness' will satisfy the demands of consumers, shareholders and campaigners all at once. It may be argued, what right have companies to insist that customers must buy environmentally friendly goods unless they want to? Surely customers should have choice, since the customer is king – or queen? One supermarket manager expressed the view to us that his role was to satisfy customer demand; to remove bleaches and dyes from his shelves, he maintained, would be a form of censorship, and although he expressed strong approval of environmentally friendly goods, he maintained that it was not his role to force consumers against their will to purchase in conformity with his own personal thinking.

The 'censorship' argument is an interesting one, but, whilst acknowledging the importance of individual choice in consumer affairs, we do not believe it to be as decisive an argument as this supermarket manager thought. Stores cannot stock everything, and hence are always having to 'censor' their shelves to exclude poor selling lines, items which do not accord with the firm's mission statement or indeed in some cases where the management has ethical objections to certain categories of goods. Some newsagents and book stores, for example, do not sell pornography, even though there may be a demand for it.

It is not by any means a widely accepted principle in business that firms begin from consumer demand and unequivocally provide it. It is commonly acknowledged that firms can create new wants and needs, particularly through their advertising strategy. Patterns of consumer behaviour can be changed, and indeed are changed. Although the Body Shop has a policy of not advertising, Anita Roddick's business policy is based on the assumption that the public are capable of being educated to think in an environmentally responsible way. As Roddick has shown, it is possible for a company to 'think green' and carry a significant proportion of the public along with it.[5]

In fact, consumers cannot become involved in the drive towards 'greenness' unless they are offered the choice by retailers and manufacturers. The 'freedom of choice' argument must at least entail that stores offer such choices to the consumers, who can find themselves shopping as would-be 'green' consumers, but unable to find products which are as friendly towards the environment as they would wish. There is a further problem in a firm having a consumer-driven environmental policy. If a firm is only 'green' to the extent of satisfying consumer demand that this is so, then its policies are likely to be less than consistent. Such a firm is likely to 'window dress' its policies so as to satisfy the consumer in the short term. By doing so, it may end up concealing other less obvious examples of environmentally irresponsible policies, leaving it open to critics such as environmental organizations to point out not only the shortcomings but the apparent lack of genuine commitment to the 'green' movement. British Rail, for example, recently tried to jump on the green bandwagon by labelling the buffet car paper bags 'recyclable'. If this was an attempt to win the green consumer, British Rail's efforts backfired, firstly because 'recyclable' is not synonymous with 'recycled' (after all, any paper product is 'recyclable', so it was difficult to see what special properties, if any, these bags were supposed

---

[5] Anita Roddick, *Body and Soul* (London: Vermillion, 1992).

to have). Secondly, the Friends of the Earth pointed out that no facilities were provided for actually recycling the bags which, by and large, simply went into the general litter bins in train compartments and stations, to be dumped like any other waste. By contrast, a firm who expresses its commitment to environmental awareness by commissioning a 'cradle to grave' environmental audit – a comprehensive examination of everything which occurs within every product's life-cycle from its production to its destruction – is much less likely to find itself the object of criticism for inconsistent, insincere or incomplete policies on 'green' issues.

We have considered arguments for and against the views which attribute environmental responsibility variously to government, manufacturer and consumer. In the end, it seems arbitrary to suggest that any one of these parties alone should be responsible for 'green' issues. If manufacturers attempt to devolve responsibility by appealing to the notion of consumer choice, then they are at least obliged to provide that choice. But their obligations are wider than that; manufacturers cannot provide every good and service and are therefore already 'censoring' their choices, and sometimes on ethical grounds. It is therefore difficult to see why such choices should not include choices made on the grounds of environmental awareness. As far as the consumer is concerned, if we acknowledge that the act of buying is not morally neutral, then it is difficult to deny that consumer responsibilities apply to environmental matters also. To buy a product simply on the grounds that it is the cheapest could mean that we have not paid the full costs of manufacture, and that we have encouraged a manufacturer to cut corners on price by leaving others the costs of cleaning up waste or by worsening the quality of the environment, for example by emitting excess noise or fumes. Finally, environmental matters cannot escape being the subject of legislation, which exists to ensure that gross malpractices are outlawed. Legislation also has the further advantage of ensuring that competing firms are on an equal footing with regard to environmental matters, and that less scrupulous competitors do not steal a march on those firms who are more responsible by cutting corners on 'green' issues.

INTRODUCING THE READINGS

In 1968 a group of prominent international scholars who were concerned about the future of the earth's environment formed the Club of Rome. Professor Jay W. Forrester of the Massachusetts Institute of Technology tried to create a computerized model of the earth's possible future states, given various choices which lay open concerning the use of the earth's resources. Jay Forrester, together with Donella Meadows, produced the famous study which appeared in 1971, *Limits to Growth*. Although the study has been much criticized, it raised public awareness of our planet's plight and the need for responsible use of the earth's resources. The 'green revolution' in the business world can be seen as a major outcome of the Club of Rome's study.

The address to the World Council of Churches by Jørgen Randers and Donella Meadows, *The Carrying Capacity of our Global Environment* gives a summary of the Club of Rome's analysis. In his celebrated book *Small is Beautiful*, E. F. Schumacher makes a similar plea for responsible stewardship of the earth's resources, but – unlike the Club of Rome – his arguments are based on Buddhist philosophy rather than on modern technology. (Perhaps Schumacher would have reconsidered his stance on working women if he were still alive today, but we reproduce his chapter on 'Buddhist Economics' with warts and all.)

In *A Bill Of Goods? Green Consuming In Perspective*, Debra Lynn Dadd and André Carothers consider the responses of the business world to our environmental predicament, and highlight some of the problems of 'green consumerism' and eco-labelling; the only solution, they argue, is to decrease consumption. R. M. Solow, by contrast, sees no reason why economic growth cannot continue, and believes that the price mechanism offers the key to humankind's predicament. Solow is highly critical of the Club of Rome model. Finally, the recent Government White Paper, *This Common Inheritance*, offers a similar solution to Solow's. If the price mechanism could be adjusted so that the polluter pays the full costs of pollution, then problems of supply and demand of non-renewable resources would be self-regulating.

The carrying capacity of our global environment – a look at the ethical alternatives

JØRGEN RANDERS AND DONELLA MEADOWS

For which of you, intending to build a tower, sitteth not down first, and counteth the cost, whether he have sufficient to finish it?

Luke 14:28

Introduction

The main thesis of my talk is very simple: because our environment – the earth – is finite, physical growth cannot continue indefinitely. In spite of its simplicity, the consequences of this fact pose an unprecedented challenge to mankind. The challenge lies in deciding on the ethical basis for making the trade-offs which will confront us in the near future – trade-offs which arise because our globe is finite.

The environment is finite

It should be quite unnecessary to point out that our environment is finite. However, most considerations of our future options lose sight of this fact. Thus, it will be worthwhile to spend some time discussing the physical limitations of the earth – especially because it is not generally recognized that we are already quite close to several of the physical limitations which define the carrying capacity of our globe.

Agricultural land

The quantity which most obviously is in finite, completely inelastic supply on our earth is land. There is about 3.2 billion hectares of land suitable for agriculture on the earth. Approximately half of that land is under cultivation today. The remaining half will require immense capital costs to settle, clear, irrigate, or fertilize before it can produce food. The costs will be so high that the United Nations' F.A.O., which is seeking desperately to stimulate greater food production, has decided that in order to expand food output it must rely on more intensive use of currently cultivated land, not on new land development.

If we do decide to incur the costs and to cultivate all possible arable land and to produce as much food as possible, how many people could we expect to feed? The lower curve in Figure 1 shows the amount of land *needed* to feed the growing world population, assuming that the present average of 0.4 hectares per person is sufficient.

Reading taken from an address before the Working Committee on Church and Society, World Council of Churches, Nomi, Italy, 1971. Copyright © 1971 World Council of Churches. Reprinted with permission of WCC Programme Unit III on Justice, Peace and Creation.

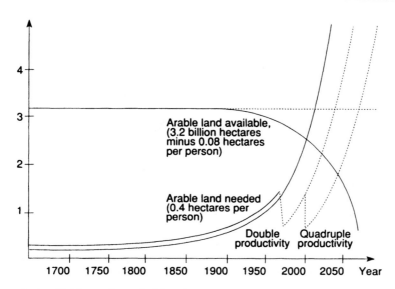

Figure 1 Available and needed land area.

(If we wanted to feed all of our 3.6 billion people at U.S.A. standards, we would require 0.9 hectares per person.) The actual growth in population from 1650 to 1970 is depicted with a heavy line; the projected growth at 2.1% per year after 1970 by a lighter line. The upper curve indicates the actual amount of arable land available. This line slopes downward because each additional person requires a certain amount of land (0.08 hectares assumed here) for housing, roads, waste disposal, power lines, and other uses which essentially 'pave' land and make it unusable for farming.

The graph in Figure 1 tells us that, even with the optimistic assumption that we will utilize all possible land, we will still face a desperate land shortage before the year 2000. The graph also illustrates some very important facts about exponential growth within a limited space. First, it shows how one can move within a few years from a situation of great abundance to one of great scarcity. The human race has had an overwhelming excess of arable land for all of our history, and now within 40 years, or one population doubling time, we will be forced to learn to deal with a sudden and serious shortage.

A second lesson to be learned from Figure 1 is that the exact numerical assumptions we make about the limits of the earth are essentially unimportant when we are faced with the inexorable progress of exponential growth. For example, we might assume that *no* arable land is taken for cities, roads, or other non-agricultural uses. In that case, the land available is constant, as shown by the horizontal dashed line, and the point at which the two curves cross is delayed by only about 10 years. Or we can suppose that we will double, or even quadruple the productivity of the land, through advances in agricultural technology. The effect of increasing productivity is shown by the dotted lines in Figure 1. Each doubling of productivity gains us just one population doubling time, or about 30 years.

Some people look to the sea to provide the extra requirements. But the total world fish catch in 1969 represented only a few percent of the world's protein, and the total catch in 1970 decreased from 1969. That was the first decrease since World War II. Most experts agree that the world's fish banks have been overfished and that prospects are for further decline, not advances, in protein output. The seas thus can not eliminate the constraints imposed on growth by limited land.

Heat release

We are faced with further obvious constraints in connection with natural resources like fresh water, metals, and fuels. Indications are that several of these will be in short supply even at higher prices within the next forty years, if present growth continues. However, it is argued that mining low grade ores and desalting the sea's water can alleviate these problems, and it may indeed be so, assuming that we can satisfy the concurrent enormous demands for energy.

A consideration of the energy that will be necessary to meet man's growing needs leads us to a more subtle and much more fundamental physical limitation imposed by our environment. Even if we assume that we find the means to *generate* the energy needed – for instance, controlled fusion – we are still faced with the fundamental thermodynamic fact that all energy generated finally ends up as heat. This is so, irrespective of whether the energy was generated by burning of coal or oil, or by nuclear reactions – and irrespective of what the energy is being used for. It is theoretically impossible to avoid this release if we want to consume energy.

The crucial point is that this heat will begin to have worldwide climatic effects when the released amount reaches some appreciable fraction of the energy normally absorbed from the sun. Thus, if we want to avoid major changes in the climate there is a fundamental limit to the amount of energy we can consume on the earth.

It may be of interest to you to know that if the energy consumption increases at 4% per year for another 130 years, we will at that point in time be releasing heat amounting to 1% of the incurring solar radiation – enough to increase the temperature of the atmosphere by $\frac{3}{4}$°C. That may sound like an unimpressive figure, but on a worldwide basis it could amount to climatic upheavals like increased melting of the polar caps. Local perturbations may come much sooner. In just 30 years it is estimated that in the Los Angeles basin heat released through energy consumption will be 18% of the normal incident solar energy of that area.

Pollution absorption

The third limitation I would like to mention is our globe's finite absorptive capacity for pollution. Until quite recently our environment was considered finite. It seemed incredible that the use of soap for one's laundry and pesticides for one's roses should possibly be able to affect the workings of the world ecosystem. But after the death of Lake Erie, the global increase in atmospheric CO_2, and the prohibition in the U.S.

of swordfish due to its content of mercury, it is abundantly clear that our environment is only able to absorb and degrade a limited amount of emissions and waste every year. When we exceed this absorptive capacity, we not only cause pollutants to accumulate in nature, but we also run the risk of completely destroying the natural degradation processes themselves, and thus decreasing the future absorptive capacity.

Thus we realize that absorptive capacity – far from being a good in unlimited supply – is an extremely valuable, scarce resource, which in fact limits the total possible emissions from human activity.

The present trend: growth

Growth in a finite world
Having established the existence of purely physical limitations of our earth, and I have described only a few of the many biological, physical, and social limits which exist, we may ask whether mankind's present behavior takes into account their existence.

On a global scale we are presently experiencing an exponential growth in population and in what I will call capital – houses, roads, cars, power plants, machinery, ships, etc. Some inevitable consequences of this growth are exponentially increasing demands for food and energy and also exponentially increasing emissions of pollution to the environment.

Since we know that there exist upper limits to the supply of food and energy and also to the amount of pollution which can be absorbed by the environment, it seems obvious that the growth we are presently experiencing cannot continue indefinitely. More important, as the last section indicated, we will surpass several constraints within the next couple of generations.

Hence, we are led to ask: are there mechanisms in the world system as it is currently organized which will cause a smooth shift from present growth trends to some other kind of acceptable behavior consistent with the world's finite capabilities? Or are we heading for some sort of disaster? These are the questions our group at M.I.T. set out to answer when we embarked last fall on an effort to make a mathematical simulation model of population and capital growth in the world system.

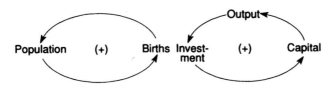

Figure 2 The positive feedback loops governing the growth in population and capital.

The WORLD model

Our model is a set of assumptions which relate world population, industry, pollution, agriculture and natural resources. The model explicitly represents the growth forces as a function of the biological, political, economic, physical, and social factors which influence them. Let me give you a brief description of main ideas underlying our model, and hence, the world system.

The exponential growth of population and capital is an important cause of all global problems – unemployment, starvation, disease, pollution, the threat of warfare, and resource shortages. All are influenced importantly by the interaction of population and capital. No attempt to understand our long-term options can succeed unless it is firmly based on an understanding of the relationships between these two forces and of the ultimate limits to their growth.

Population and birth constitute a positive feedback loop. More people produce more births and more births result in more people. Wherever there is a dominant positive feedback loop of this form, exponential growth will be observed. Capital produces industrial output. Greater output, all else equal, results in a larger investment and thus in more capital. Thus capital and investment constitute another positive feedback loop. The interactions among population and capital determine the rate at which each of them grows. The interaction takes many forms (Figure 3).

As a greater fraction of output is diverted from investment, the growth rate of capital decreases. Output may be diverted to consumption and services, to agriculture, and to military expenditures. As consumption and services increase, health and education improve, average lifetime becomes greater, deaths decrease, and population grows. Similarly, output may be diverted into agricultural capital which results ultimately in more food and a higher average lifetime. The primary determinant of the fraction of output reinvested is the output per capita. Where production per capita is low, most of the output must be diverted to consumption, services, and food. Those allocations reduce the rate of accumulation of the capital base and, at the same time, stimulate the growth of population. Population can increase much easier than capital in traditional societies. Hence, output per capita remains low in these countries and they find it very difficult to achieve economic growth.

Output diverted into military expenditures subtracts capital from the system and does not generate future growth directly. Industrial output also leads to the depletion of natural resources. As natural resources decline, the efficiency of capital decreases and the output-capital ratio goes down. Output per capita is the single positive force acting to slow the population explosion. As output per capita increases, the desired family size declines, the birth rate goes down, and population growth typically decreases. The influence of this is accelerated somewhat by the fact that as death rates decline there is a further decrease in desired family size. A large portion of the world's parents bear children primarily as a source of support in their old age. If there is a high mortality rate, one must bear three or four sons to insure that one will live. Thus, as the perceived death rate decreases, birth rates also decline. Output has one additional impact. Output leads to the generation of pollution. Pollution decreases food, and also decreases the average lifetime.

Most global problems have important roots in this simple set of interactions.[1] Formalizing these interactions into a simulation model is useful because it makes it possible to study the future implications of the world system's present organization. The model further permits analysis of the policy alternatives for natural resources,

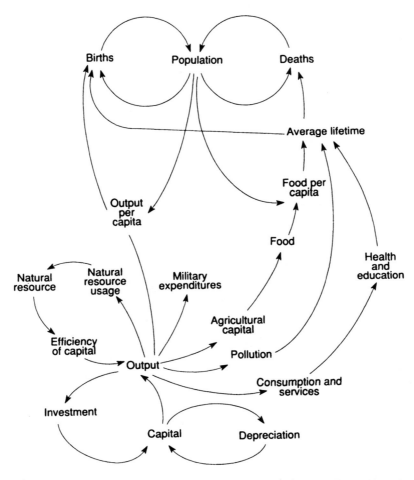

Figure 3 Basic interactions between population growth and capital accumulation.

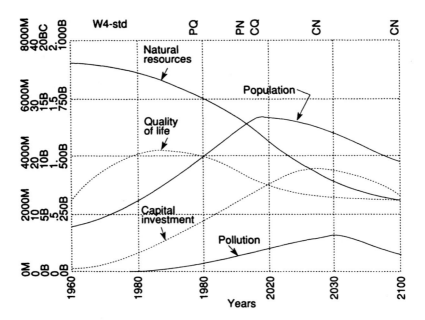

Figure 4 Basic world model behaviour showing the mode in which industrialization and population are suppressed by falling natural resource.

birth control, food production, economic development, etc. which we must now begin to evaluate. (See Figures 4, 5, 6.)

The inevitable collapse
Simulation runs like these, have led us to conclude that there are no mechanisms currently existent that will bring the present growth to a smooth stop when we reach the maximum level consistent with our finite environment.

Of course this does not mean that growth will not stop. It only means that, instead of an orderly transition to some feasible state, we will overshoot the physical limitations and then be forced into a traumatic decline back down to some level of population and industrialization which can be supported by our physical environment – which by then will be sorely depleted. For once we exceed a constraint, tremendous pressures will develop to halt the growth. If it so happens that we begin by exceeding the absorptive capacity for pollution, the pressures will take the form of radical increases in death rates due to impurities in food, water and air, decreases in crops and fish catches due to similar reductions in plant and animal life, and significant reduction in the effectiveness of investment due to high costs of controlling the high pollution in all *input*-factors. These pressures will mount until the population and

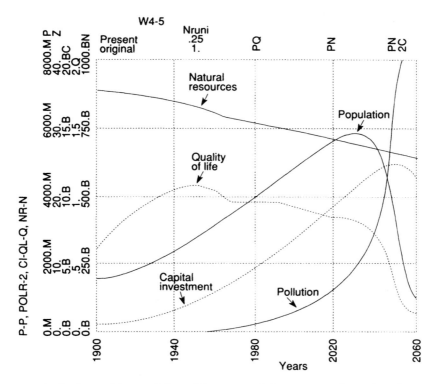

Figure 5 Pollution crisis precipitated by successful attempt at lowering the usage rate of natural resources. In 1971 natural resource usage is reduced 75% by more effective technology without affecting material standard of living.

industrialization finally involuntarily start to decline, and the pressures will only cease when levels are reached which are acceptable to the physical environment.

If we attempt to continue growth by removing one set of pressures – for instance, by introducing complete pollution control – we alleviate the situation only until we encounter the next constraint. And so on. Because the environment is finite, physical growth will always bring us into conflict.

The ethical basis for action

The short-term objective function
Thus we are faced with the fact that continuation of current growth practices will inevitably lead us to some sort of collapse, with a subsequent decrease in the cul-

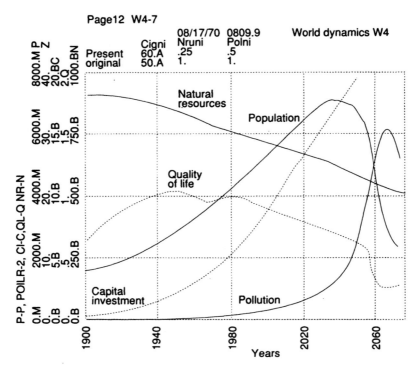

Figure 6 The capital investment rate is increased in order to arrest the beginning of the decline in the quality of life and the reduced natural resource usage from Figure 5 are retained. In addition in 1971 the normal rate of pollution generation is reduced 50%. The effect of pollution control is to allow population to grow 25% further and to delay the pollution crisis by 20 years.

tural and economic options of the human race. The natural question to ask is: what can we do?

It is important to realize that our answer to this question is completely dependent on our choice of criteria for what is 'good'. If we do not know what we want to obtain, if we don't know our 'objective function,' it is meaningless to try to decide what to do in a given situation. If our objective is to maximize the benefits of the people alive today, our course of action will be quite different from our actions if the goal is to maximize the benefits of all people which are going to live on our planet over the next 200 years.

At least in principle present human behavior is guided by the general idea that all people alive *today* are equally important and that the objective function is to maximize the total current benefits for all of these people. We have decided, at least in the Western democracies, that this objective is best served by letting each individual be free to pursue his own interest. It is assumed, very simply that if every citizen and institution in our society acts to maximize his own position in the short term, the society as a whole will benefit.

This acceptance of 'The Invisible Hand' has, however, introduced a strong emphasis on short-term benefits in our societies. When an action will bring both benefits and costs over time, individuals use the concept of net present value and discount the future implications so that they can determine whether an action should be taken now or ten years from now or never. The result of this procedure is that we assign essentially zero value to anything happening more than twenty years from now.

If we choose to adhere strictly to the objective of maximizing the short-term rewards of the present generation, there are in fact no environmental trade-offs to be made where we will have to weigh current benefits against future costs. In this case we would simply continue as before, maximizing the current benefits and neglecting any future costs which will result.

The question about use or non-use of DDT, for example, would be easily resolved. The fact that 1.3 billion people today can live safety from malaria due to DDT would grossly outweigh the costs inflicted upon future generations through our continued use of the chemical.

It is only this short-term objective function which can lead to the currently accepted conclusion that the value of an additional human being is infinite. The severe restrictions his existence will impose on the choices and perhaps even the lives of future generations – because of his consumption of non-renewable natural resources – is completely neglected. Thus we see that adherence to the short-term objective function resolves very simply all trade-offs between current benefits and future cost. Of course we will be left with the ordinary trade-offs among people alive today – for instance, the choice between denying the firm upstream freedom to dump waste in the river and denying those who live downstream pure drinking water. But these short-term conflicts are not relevant to our discussion, because we *do* have mechanisms in our society to resolve conflicts between two people alive today.

We do *not* have, however, mechanisms, or even moral guidelines, for resolving conflicts between the current population and the people of the future. And at the same time our simulation model demonstrates that the present preoccupation with what seems pleasant or profitable in the short-run fuels the growth which is finally going to make the world overshoot some physical constraint, forcing us into a period of abrupt and significant changes.

The long-term objective function
It is, however, possible to change the objective function – in the same way as Christianity changed the objective of man from selfish gratification to consideration for the welfare of all other people living at the same point in time.

Today we could change again, and for example adopt as our cardinal philosophy the rule that no man or institution in our society may take any action which decreases the economic and social options of those who will live on the planet 100 years from now. Probably only religion has the moral force to bring such a change.

We are basically facing only one ethical question in the impending global crisis. This is to decide on whether we want to continue to let our actions be guided by the short-term objective function, or whether we should adopt a longer-term perspective. In other words: the ethical question confronting global society today is to decide on the length of the time period used when comparing the costs and benefits of current actions.

Some of you might think that we should stay with the goal of maximizing the benefit of the present population, simply because we are still so *very* far from having attained this goal, as evidenced by the unequitable distribution of the world's wealth between the industrialized and the developing countries. However, before making this choice, one should remember our conclusion from the last section, indicating that a continued reliance on short-term objectives only makes it certain that there will be no acceptable future – for any country.

It is my feeling that the Church should adopt the goal of increasing the time-horizon implicit in mankind's activities – that is, introducing the longer-term objective function which maximizes the benefit of those living today, subject to the constraint that it does not decrease the economic and social options of those who will inherit this globe, our children and grand-children.

This goal is of course not completely foreign to contemporary society. It seems to be the value implicit in the actions of conservationists. However, ultimately it must be present in all of our activities.

Equilibrium – a desirable possibility

A lasting solution
Assuming that we accept the long-term objective function as the guide-line for our actions, what will we do about the approaching collision between our growing societies and the physical limits of the earth?

As soon as we are committed to the creation of a long-term, viable world system our most important task becomes to avoid the trauma connected with actually exceeding any environmental limitation. We must deliberately stop physical growth. We must engineer a smooth transition to a non-growth situation – an equilibrium, a steady state – which is in accordance with environmental limits. We must ourselves develop and employ legal, economic or religious pressures as substitutes for those pressures which would otherwise have been exerted by nature to halt physical growth.

By starting now we may still be able to *choose* the set of pressures we prefer to employ in stopping population and capital growth. We cannot avoid pressures. Counter forces *will* rise until growth stops. However, a deliberate choice is likely to leave intact many more of our fundamental, long-term objectives than is the blind and random action of natural forces such as starvation, social breakdown, etc. The

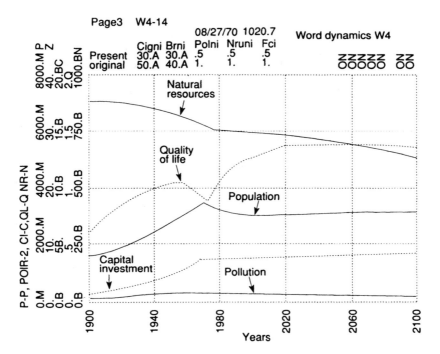

Figure 7 One set of conditions that establishes a world equilibrium. In 1971 capital investment rate is reduced 40% birth rate is reduced 50%, natural resource usage rate is reduced 75%, and food production is reduced 20%.

steady state is first of all defined by constant population and capital (see Figure 7). The second requirement is equally important. Since we want to create a system capable of existing for a long time, the state of equilibrium must be characterized by minimal consumption of non-renewable materials and by minimal emissions of non-degradable waste.

In this equilibrium mode of human civilization, science and technology will be busily developing ways of constructing products which last very long, do not emit pollution, and can be easily recycled. Competition among individual firms will continue, but the total market for material goods will no longer expand.

Although equilibrium implies non-growth of all *physical* activities, this will not be the case for cultural activities. Freed from the preoccupation with material goods, people will throw their energy into development of the arts and sciences, into the enjoyment of unspoiled nature, and into meaningful interactions with their fellow man.

The golden age

Only an orderly transfer into an equilibrium state will save us from the tumult of an environmental crisis, and again put the human race into harmony with the world's ecosystem. The presence of equilibrium could permit the development of an unprecedented golden age for humanity. Freedom from ever-increasing numbers of people will make it possible to put substantial effort into the self-realization and development of the individual. Instead of struggling merely to keep people alive, we could employ our energy in developing the human culture – that is, in increasing the quality of life for the individual to a level high above the present subsistence. The few periods of equilibrium in the past – for example, the 300 years of Japan's classical period – often witnessed such profound flowering of the arts.

The freedom from ever-increasing capital – i.e., from more concrete, cars, dams and skyscrapers – would make it possible even for our great-grandchildren to enjoy solitude and silence.

But more importantly, equilibrium would ultimately lead to an equitable distribution of the wealth throughout the world – because one would no longer be able to accept inequalities in the present under the pretence that they would be removed through future growth. Or in the words of H. E. Daly,[2] the American economist:

> . . . the important issue of the stationary state will be distribution, not production. The problem of relative shares can no longer be avoided by appeals to growth. The argument that everyone should be happy as long as his absolute share of the wealth increases, regardless of his relative share, will no longer be available. Absolute and relative shares will move together and the division of physical wealth will be a zero sum game.

The desirable aspects of the steady state were realized long ago. John Stuart Mill[3] wrote in 1857:

> It is scarcely necessary to remark that a stationary condition of capital and population implies no stationary state of human improvement. There would be as much scope as ever for all kinds of mental culture, and moral and social progress; as much room for improving the Art of Living and much more likelihood of its being improved, when minds cease to be engrossed by the art of getting on. Even the industrial arts might be as earnestly and as successfully cultivated, with this sole difference, that instead of serving no purpose but the increase of wealth, industrial improvements would produce their legitimate effect, that of abridging labor.

This, then, is the state of equilibrium, which seems to be the logical consequence of the adoption of the long-term objective function.

The changes needed during the transition from growth to equilibrium are tremendous, and the time is very short. But the results seem worth striving for, and the first step – the acceptance of a long-term objective function – is one in which the churches have always been a leader.

NOTES

1. Further information about our modeling effort can be obtained from System Dynamics Program Office, A. P. Sloan School of Management, E40–214, Massachusetts Institute of Technology, Cambridge, Massachusetts 02139, U.S.A.
2. H. E. Daly, 'Towards a Stationary-State Economy,' forthcoming in *The Patient Earth*, John Hartre and Robert Sorolow, eds., Holt, Rinehart and Winston, 1971.
3. J. S. Mill, *Principles of Political Economy*, Vol. II, London: John W. Parker and Son, 1857.

Buddhist economics

E. F. SCHUMACHER

'Right Livelihood' is one of the requirements of the Buddha's Noble Eightfold Path. It is clear, therefore, that there must be such a thing as Buddhist economics.

Buddhist countries have often stated that they wish to remain faithful to their heritage. So Burma: 'The New Burma sees no conflict between religious values and economic progress. Spiritual health and material wellbeing are not enemies: they are natural allies.'[1] Or: 'We can blend successfully the religious and spiritual values of our heritage with the benefits of modern technology.'[2] Or: 'We Burmans have a sacred duty to conform both our dreams and our acts to our faith. This we shall ever do.'[3]

All the same, such countries invariably assume that they can model their economic development plans in accordance with modern economics, and they call upon modern economists from so-called advanced countries to advise them, to formulate the policies to be pursued, and to construct the grand design for development, the Five-Year Plan or whatever it may be called. No-one seems to think that a Buddhist way of life would call for Buddhist economics, just as the modern materialist way of life has brought forth modern economics.

Economists themselves, like most specialists, normally suffer from a kind of metaphysical blindness, assuming that theirs is a science of absolute and invariable truths, without any presuppositions. Some go as far as to claim that economic laws are as free from 'metaphysics' or 'values' as the law of gravitation. We need·not, however, get involved in arguments of methodology. Instead, let us take some fundamentals and see what they look like when viewed by a modern economist and a Buddhist economist.

There is universal agreement that a fundamental source of wealth is human labour.

Now, the modern economist has been brought up to consider 'labour' or work as little more than a necessary evil. From the point of view of the employer, it is in any case simply an item of cost, to be reduced to a minimum if it cannot be eliminated altogether, say, by automation. From the point of view of the workman, it is a 'disutility'; to work is to make a sacrifice of one's leisure and comfort, and wages are a kind of compensation for the sacrifice. Hence the ideal from the point of view of the employer is to have output without employees, and the ideal from the point of view of the employee is to have income without employment.

The consequences of these attitudes both in theory and in practice are, of course, extremely far-reaching. If the ideal with regard to work is to get rid of it, every method that 'reduces the work load' is a good thing. The most potent method, short of automation, is the so-called 'division of labour' and the classical example is the pin factory eulogised in Adam Smith's *Wealth of Nations*.[4] Here it is not a matter of ordinary specialisation, which mankind has practised from time immemorial, but of dividing up every complete process of production into minute parts, so that the final product can be produced at great speed without anyone having had to contribute more than a totally insignificant and, in most cases, unskilled movement of his limbs.

The Buddhist point of view takes the function of work to be at least threefold: to give a man a chance to utilise and develop his faculties; to enable him to overcome his egocentredness by joining with other people in a common task; and to bring forth the goods and services needed for a becoming existence. Again, the consequences that flow from this view are endless. To organise work in such a manner that it becomes meaningless, boring, stultifying, or nerve-racking for the worker would be little short of criminal; it would indicate a greater concern with goods than with people, an evil lack of compassion and a soul-destroying degree of attachment to the most primitive side of this worldly existence. Equally, to strive for leisure as an alternative to work would be considered a complete misunderstanding of one of the basic truths of human existence, namely that work and leisure are complementary parts of the same living process and cannot be separated without destroying the joy of work and the bliss of leisure.

From the Buddhist point of view, there are therefore two types of mechanisation which must be clearly distinguished: one that enhances a man's skill and power and one that turns the work of man over to a mechanical slave, leaving man in a position of having to serve the slave. How to tell the one from the other? 'The craftsman himself,' says Ananda Coomaraswamy, a man equally competent to talk about the modern west as the ancient east, 'can always, if allowed to, draw the delicate distinction between the machine and the tool. The carpet loom is a tool, a contrivance for holding warp threads at a stretch for the pile to be woven round them by the craftsmen's fingers; but the power loom is a machine, and its significance as a destroyer of culture lies in the fact that it does the essentially human part of the work.'[5] It is clear, therefore, that Buddhist economics must be very different from the economics of modern materialism, since the Buddhist sees the essence of civilisation not in a multiplication of wants but in the purification of human character.

Character, at the same time, is formed primarily by a man's work. And work, properly conducted in conditions of human dignity and freedom, blesses those who do it and equally their products. The Indian philosopher and economist J. C. Kumarappa sums the matter up as follows:

'If the nature of the work is properly appreciated and applied, it will stand in the same relation to the higher faculties as food is to the physical body. It nourishes and enlivens the higher man and urges him to produce the best he is capable of. It directs his free will along the proper course and disciplines the animal in him into progressive channels. It furnishes an excellent background for man to display his scale of values and develop his personality.'[6]

If a man has no chance of obtaining work he is in a desperate position, not simply because he lacks an income but because he lacks this nourishing and enlivening factor of disciplined work which nothing can replace. A modern economist may engage in highly sophisticated calculations on whether full employment 'pays' or whether it might be more 'economic' to run an economy at less than full employment so as to ensure a greater mobility of labour, a better stability of wages, and so forth. His fundamental criterion of success is simply the total quantity of goods produced during a given period of time. 'If the marginal urgency of goods is low,' says Professor Galbraith in *The Affluent Society*, 'then so is the urgency of employing the last man or the last million men in the labour force.'[7] And again: 'If . . . we can afford some unemployment in the interest of stability – a proposition, incidentally, of impeccably conservative antecedents – then we can afford to give those who are unemployed the goods that enable them to sustain their accustomed standard of living.'

From a Buddhist point of view, this is standing the truth on its head by considering goods as more important than people and consumption as more important than creative activity. It means shifting the emphasis from the worker to the product of work, that is, from the human to the sub-human, a surrender to the forces of evil. The very start of Buddhist economic planning would be a planning for full employment, and the primary purpose of this would in fact be employment for everyone who needs an 'outside' job: it would not be the maximisation of employment nor the maximisation of production. Women, on the whole, do not need an 'outside' job, and the large-scale employment of women in offices or factories would be considered a sign of serious economic failure. In particular, to let mothers of young children work in factories while the children run wild would be as uneconomic in the eyes of a Buddhist economist as the employment of a skilled worker as a soldier in the eyes of a modern economist.

While the materialist is mainly interested in goods, the Buddhist is mainly interested in liberation. But Buddhism is 'The Middle Way' and therefore in no way antagonistic to physical well-being. It is not wealth that stands in the way of liberation but the attachment to wealth; not the enjoyment of pleasurable things but the craving for them. The keynote of Buddhist economics, therefore, is simplicity and non-violence. From an economist's point of view, the marvel of the Buddhist way of life is the utter rationality of its pattern – amazingly small means leading to extraordinarily satisfactory results.

For the modern economist this is very difficult to understand. He is used to measuring the 'standard of living' by the amount of annual consumption, assuming all the time that a man who consumes more is 'better off' than a man who consumes less. A Buddhist economist would consider this approach excessively irrational: since consumption is merely a means to human well-being, the aim should be to obtain the maximum of well-being with the minimum of consumption. Thus, if the purpose of clothing is a certain amount of temperature comfort and an attractive appearance, the task is to attain this purpose with the smallest possible effort, that is, with the smallest annual destruction of cloth and with the help of designs that involve the smallest possible input of toil. The less toil there is, the more time and strength is left for artistic creativity. It would be highly uneconomic, for instance, to go in for complicated tailoring, like the modern west, when a much more beautiful effect can be achieved by the skilful draping of uncut material. It would be the height of folly to make material so that it should wear out quickly and the height of barbarity to make anything ugly, shabby or mean. What has just been said about clothing applies equally to all other human requirements. The ownership and the consumption of goods is a means to an end, and Buddhist economics is the systematic study of how to attain given ends with the minimum means.

Modern economics, on the other hand, considers consumption to be the sole end and purpose of all economic activity, taking the factors of production – land, labour, and capital – as the means. The former, in short, tries to maximise human satisfactions by the optimal pattern of consumption, while the latter tries to maximise consumption by the optimal pattern of productive effort. It is easy to see that the effort needed to sustain a way of life which seeks to attain the optimal pattern of consumption is likely to be much smaller than the effort needed to sustain a drive for maximum consumption. We need not be surprised, therefore, that the pressure and strain of living is very much less in, say, Burma than it is in the United States, in spite of the fact that the amount of laboursaving machinery used in the former country is only a minute fraction of the amount used in the latter.

Simplicity and non-violence are obviously closely related. The optimal pattern of consumption, producing a high degree of human satisfaction by means of a relatively low rate of consumption, allows people to live without great pressure and strain and to fulfil the primary injunction of Buddhist teaching: 'Cease to do evil; try to do good.' As physical resources are everywhere limited, people satisfying their needs by means of a modest use of resources are obviously less likely to be at each other's throats than people depending upon a high rate of use. Equally, people who live in highly self-sufficient local communities are less likely to get involved in large-scale violence than people whose existence depends on world-wide systems of trade.

From the point of view of Buddhist economics, therefore, production from local resources for local needs is the most rational way of economic life, while dependence on imports from afar and the consequent need to produce for export to unknown and distant peoples is highly uneconomic and justifiable only in exceptional cases and on a small scale. Just as the modern economist would admit that a high rate of consumption of transport services between a man's home and his place of work signifies a misfortune and not a high standard of life, so the Buddhist economist would hold that to satisfy human wants from faraway sources rather than from sources nearby signifies failure rather than success. The former tends to take statistics showing an increase in the number of ton/miles per head of the population carried by a country's transport system as proof of economic progress, while to the latter – the Buddhist economist – the same statistics would indicate a highly undesirable deterioration in the *pattern* of consumption.

Another striking difference between modern economics and Buddhist economics arises over the use of natural resources. Bertrand de Jouvenel, the eminent French political philosopher, has characterised 'western man' in words which may be taken as a fair description of the modern economist:

'He tends to count nothing as an expenditure, other than human effort; he does not seem to mind how much mineral matter he wastes and, far worse, how much living matter he destroys. He does not seem to realise at all that human life is a dependent part of an ecosystem of many different forms of life. As the world is ruled from towns where men are cut off from any form of life other than human, the feeling of belonging to an ecosystem is not revived. This results in a harsh and improvident treatment of things upon which we ultimately depend, such as water and trees.'[8]

The teaching of the Buddha, on the other hand, enjoins a reverent and non-violent attitude not only to all sentient beings but also, with great emphasis, to trees. Every follower of the Buddha ought to plant a tree every few years and look after it until it is safely established, and the Buddhist economist can demonstrate without difficulty that the universal observation of this rule would result in a high rate of genuine economic development independent of any foreign aid. Much of the economic decay of south-east Asia (as of many other parts of the world) is undoubtedly due to a heedless and shameful neglect of trees.

Modern economics does not distinguish between renewable and non-renewable materials, as its very method is to equalise and quantify everything by means of a money price. Thus, taking various alternative fuels, like coal, oil, wood, or water-power: the only difference between them recognised by modern economics is relative cost per equivalent unit. The cheapest is automatically the one to be preferred, as to do otherwise would be irrational and 'uneconomic'. From a Buddhist point of view, of course, this will not do; the essential difference between non-renewable fuels like coal and oil on the one hand and renewable fuels like wood and water-power on the other cannot be simply overlooked. Non-renewable goods must be used only if they are indispensable, and then only with the greatest care and the most meticulous concern for conservation. To use them heedlessly or extravagantly is an act of violence, and while complete non-violence may not be attainable on this earth, there is nonetheless an ineluctable duty on man to aim at the ideal of non-violence in all he does.

Just as a modern European economist would not consider it a great economic achievement if all European art treasures were sold to America at attractive prices, so the Buddhist economist would insist that a population basing its economic life on non-renewable fuels is living parasitically, on capital instead of income. Such a way of life could have no permanence and could therefore be justified only as a purely temporary expedient. As the world's resources of non-renewable fuels – coal, oil and natural gas – are exceedingly unevenly distributed over the globe and undoubtedly limited in quantity, it is clear that their exploitation at an ever-increasing rate is an act of violence against nature which must almost inevitably lead to violence between men.

This fact alone might give food for thought even to those people in Buddhist countries who care nothing for the religious and spiritual values of their heritage and ardently desire to embrace the materialism of modern economics at the fastest possible speed. Before they dismiss Buddhist economics as nothing better than a nostalgic dream, they might wish to consider whether the path of economic development outlined by modern economics is likely to lead them to places where they really want to be. Towards the end of his courageous book *The Challenge of Man's Future*, Professor Harrison Brown of the California Institute of Technology gives the following appraisal:

'Thus we see that, just as industrial society is fundamentally unstable and subject to reversion to agrarian existence, so within it the conditions which offer individual freedom are unstable in their ability to avoid the conditions which impose rigid organisation and totalitarian control. Indeed, when we examine all of the foreseeable difficulties which threaten the survival of industrial civilisation, it is difficult to see how the achievement of stability and the maintenance of individual liberty can be made compatible.'[9]

Even if this were dismissed as a long-term view there is the immediate question of whether 'modernisation', as currently practised without regard to religious and spiritual values, is actually producing agreeable results. As far as the masses are concerned, the results appear to be disastrous – a collapse of the rural economy, a rising tide of unemployment in town and country, and the growth of a city proletariat without nourishment for either body or soul.

It is in the light of both immediate experience and long-term prospects that the study of Buddhist economics could be recommended even to those who believe that economic growth is more important than any spiritual or religious values. For it is not a question of choosing between 'modern growth' and 'traditional stagnation'. It is a question of finding the right path of development, the Middle Way between materialist heedlessness and traditionalist immobility, in short, of finding 'Right Livelihood'.

NOTES

1. *The New Burma* (Economic and Social Board, Government of the Union of Burma, 1954).
2. *Ibid.*
3. *Ibid.*

4. *Wealth of Nations* by Adam Smith.
5. *Art and Swadeshi* by Ananda K. Coomaraswamy (Ganesh & Co, Madras).
6. *Economy of Permanence* by J. C. Kumarappa (Sarva-Seva Sangh Publication, Rajghat, Kashi, 4th edn, 1958).
7. *The Affluent Society* by John Kenneth Galbraith (Penguin Books Ltd, 1962).
8. *A Philosophy of Indian Economic Development* by Richard B. Gregg (Navajivan Publishing House, Ahmedabad, 1958).
9. *The Challenge of Man's Future* by Harrison Brown (The Viking Press, New York, 1954).

A bill of goods? Green consuming in perspective

DEBRA LYNN DADD AND ANDRÉ CAROTHERS

The phenomenon of 'green business' has made its most noticeable impact upon the ordinary consumer-in-the-street in the form of a new variety of 'green' products available on the supermarket (and other) shelves. As a response to people's widely-held and strongly-voiced belief that environmentally-friendly products should be available for the sake of the planet's future, this entry of new items into the consumer arena represents, on the one hand, a welcome breakthrough of ecological consciousness into the world of business.

On the other, less positive, hand, the willingness of business to exploit the green label also epitomizes the very worst and most deceitful characteristics of the so-called free market economy. All too often, instead of genuinely changing business practices, processes and products, the response of corporations has been to cash in on the green bandwagon in a cynical exploitation of the latest market fad.

The ad opens with a tableau of children laughing and skipping as they carry green garbage bags across a verdant meadow strewn with litter. As they stuff the trash in bags, a voice-over speaks of the virtues of a clean environment and biodegradable garbage bags. With the field nearly cleaned, a spectral Native American in ceremonial regalia appears, intoning to one awed youngster, 'Take what you need, but always leave the land as you found it.'

In another commercial, a butterfly flits across the screen, and a pleasant voice patiently details the magnanimity of Chevron, the multinational oil giant, which has set aside land near one of its refineries to ensure that the rapidly dwindling El Segundo Blue butterfly does not fade into extinction. Who performs such acts of selfless altruism, the viewer is asked? 'People Do,' responds the oil company.

Reading taken from *Green Business: Hope or Hoax?* (ed.) by C. Plant and J. Plant. Copyright © 1991 Green Books

This is the new environmental advertising, the big-business response to the ecological mood of the public. We'll be seeing a lot more of it in the '90s. The
environment, for better or worse (mostly better), is now an 'issue.' The Michael
Peters Group, a design and new products consulting firm, found in a 1989 market
research poll that 89 percent of Americans are concerned about the impact on the
environment of the products they purchase, more than half say they decline to buy
certain products out of concern for the environment, and 78 percent would pay more
for a product packaged with recyclable or biodegradable materials.

Environmental concern 'is a bigger market than some of the hottest markets of the
'80s,' says the journal *American Demographics*. 'This is not a small market niche of
people who believe in the *Greening of America*,' says Ray Goldberg of the Harvard
Business School. 'It is becoming a major segment of the consuming public.' Little
wonder, then, that Madison Avenue has turned caring for the environment into a
marketing strategy. 'The selling of the environment,' says Minnesota Attorney
General Hubert Humphrey III, 'may make the cholesterol craze look like a Sunday
school picnic.'

In the case of these two TV ads, the sell is all hype. The first, for Glad 'biodegradable' garbage bags, fails to mention that truly biodegradable plastic is as rare as
the El Segundo Blue. Even if it were available, the pollution released in plastic
production puts the Glad Bag's ecological balance sheet squarely in the red. And
Chevron is first and foremost an oil company, an industry that is directly and
indirectly responsible for much of the pollution on Earth. Back-of-the-envelope
calculations suggest that Chevron has probably spent five times as much to boast in
magazines and on television of its skimpy list of environmental initiatives than the
actions actually cost. (And many of them were required under the provisions of their
permits anyway.)

Navigating the misleading claims of opportunistic advertisers is just one of the difficulties facing the consumer intent on 'ecologically correct' shopping. So complicated
is the terrain, in fact, that what is becoming known as 'green consuming' may prove
to be nothing more than a costly diversion from the campaign to save the Earth.

Blue Angels and Green Seals

The rush to fill the stores of Europe and North America with consumer goods is just
one of several leading causes of environmental destruction. The influence of big
business has foiled the effort to rein in the consumer culture's worst side effects. One
method is to inform consumers of the implications of their purchases, a tradition that
inspires consumer rights groups all over the world. Informative labeling is now the
method of choice for environmentalists and manufacturers.

The first labeling scheme keyed for ecological concerns was West Germany's Blue
Angel program, begun in 1978. The Blue Angel symbol graces over 2000 products,
calling consumers' attention to benefits such as recycled paper and the absence of
toxic solvents. Similar schemes are being proposed in nearly every country in

Western Europe and now in the United States. They come in three versions: independent, non-governmental efforts, like the United States' new Green Seal program (managed by the Alliance for Social Responsibility in New York); quasi-governmental schemes like those being developed in the United Kingdom and Canada; and identification programs from the manufacturers themselves, like Wal-Mart's new line of 'green' products.

Industry's fear of the consumer has produced some notable successes. Before Friends of the Earth in the United Kingdom had launched a planned boycott of CFC-contaminating aerosols, the industry pledged to phase them out. The Blue Angel program can lay claim to preventing 40 000 tons of solvents from entering the waste stream through glossy paints. The concern over agrochemicals in food has given a much-needed boost to the organic food industry, and the boycott of tuna, in conjunction with a federal labeling requirement that may pass the U.S. Congress this year, will play a large role in saving dolphins from the fishing fleet's nets.

But green consuming has its limits. First, seals of approval may be awarded indiscriminately and for the wrong reasons. The Blue Angel, for example, is bestowed on one brand of gasoline-powered lawn mower because it is quieter than a rival. The push variety, soundless and emission-free, gets no award. Loblaws, a Canadian chain of grocery stores, has among its self-proclaimed 'green' products a brand of acid-free coffee, so labeled because it does not cause stomach upsets. 'Green' batteries are being marketed in the United Kingdom and Canada that contain mercury – considerably less than other brands, but enough to put the lie to claims of environmental friendliness.

Some claims are absurd. 'Biodegradable' diapers are filling the developed world's landfills, with no sign that they will ever disappear. West German manufacturer AEG launched a two million dollar ad campaign in England claiming that their dishwashers saved newts. The logic runs like this: since the AEG appliances are slightly more energy efficient, they use less electricity and are therefore responsible for less acid-rain-causing power plant emissions (which, we assume, kill newts). Arco has launched a 'clean' gasoline in California with the slogan, 'Let's drive away smog.' Both Volkswagen and Audi have touted their cars' low emissions, including 'harmless carbon dioxide.' If they had done a little homework, they would have discovered that carbon dioxide is a leading greenhouse gas.

The environmental advertising bandwagon offers companies an opportunity to spruce up their images at relatively low cost. Many of the recycled paper products now flooding the market are made by companies with otherwise reprehensible environmental records. In the United Kingdom, according to the company's slogan, 'Green means Heinz.' But in the Pacific, thanks to tuna fishing, it means dead dolphins. And the term 'biodegradable' has been attached to so many different brands of polluting petroleum-based plastics that it has become virtually meaningless, as well as highly misleading.

These companies rely on government regulations for some of their claims, leading to situations like McDonald's declaration that their styrofoam burger trays are CFC-free, when in fact they contain CFC-22, a less potent member of the same chemical family. The lie is based on a glaring example of regulatory sleight of hand: according to the U.S. Environmental Protection Agency, CFC-22 is 'technically not a CFC,' although for the ozone layer the distinction is far less clear. Under federal law, paper manufacturers can call paper 'recycled' when it includes 40 percent recycled content, and that portion consists mostly of paper left over from production processes, not paper that has already been through a consumer's hands and recycled. In Canada, where the Canadian Standards Association creates guidelines for green products, business does its best to ensure that standards are not too stringent. 'We make the draft of a guideline,' says one insider, 'and the industry fights to lower the standard.'

All this should raise doubts about industry's claims that they have seen the light, and that hiding behind the advertising pitch is a real concern for the environment that transcends the bottom line. In fact, the record shows that big business is not inclined toward public service. According to a study by Amitai Etzioni of the Harvard Business School, two-thirds of the Fortune 500 companies have been charged with serious crimes, from price-fixing to illegal dumping of hazardous wastes. And these are only the ones that have been caught.

But even if we could count on the good faith of all concerned, the role of green consuming in the fight to save the planet is destined to remain small and marginal. Consumption's role in destroying the environment is a complex and poorly understood phenomenon. A truly green economy, for example, would require that all products be audited for their effect. Such an audit would analyze the product from 'cradle to grave,' and include the amount of energy used to produce and transport the item, the pollution generated in its manufacture, the role of the commodity in the economic and social health of the country of origin, the investment plans of the company in question and all its subsidiaries, and the final disposal of the product.

The questions raised by this approach are endless. Does the use of rainforest nuts justify the energy expended transporting them here? Are the labor practices in processing these nuts fair? We all thought the right thing to do was to use paper bags, but if energy use is factored in, some studies show that plastic grocery bags are more environmentally benign (bringing a bag from home doesn't make money for anyone, so you won't see that solution advertised). Should we buy recycled paper from a company known to pollute rivers with pulp mill effluent? Should magazines be printed on chlorine-bleached paper contaminated with dioxin, even if it is recycled and recyclable? Or should they use dioxin-free paper from Europe, even though it is at the moment rarely recycled, and fossil fuels are used to transport it?

Moreover, much of the pollution generated by business is out of reach of the average consumer. For example, as Barry Commoner points out, one of the reasons we have air pollution is that much of the work done by railways has been taken over by trucks, which generate four times as much pollution for each ton hauled. How would the average store owner respond if we demanded only goods that had been delivered by train? And when the beer industry consolidated and discovered that it was cheaper to sell beer in throwaway bottles than in returnables, what possible role could the consumer have played? Between 1959 and 1970, the number of beer bottles produced increased five-fold, while consumption only went up by one-third. Detroit pushes big cars with high-compression, high-pollution engines on the American public not because 'that's what we demand,' but because that's where the biggest profits are. These decisions aren't illegal, they are simply part of 'doing business' in the usual way – a way that puts environmental considerations last.

Finally, individual action, when limited to the supermarket aisles, does little to forward the fundamental changes required to save the Earth. Not only is this collection of individual actions completely outdistanced by the pact of destruction throughout the world, but as Friends of the Earth in the United Kingdom points out, green consuming 'leaves totally unanswered the basic questions about global equality and the chronic poverty and suffering of the millions of people in the Third World. . . . There is a real danger that green consumerism will divert attention from the real need to change institutional structures.' Green consuming labeling schemes, they conclude, 'must complement, not become a substitute for, firm government action.'

To consume or not to consume: *that* is the question

Green consuming is still consuming, which is the fundamental paradox. The answer to the problem we face is not only to consume appropriately; it is primarily to consume less. Green labeling schemes are similar in philosophy to the end-of-pipeline pollution control strategies that have failed to stem pollution. They put a dent in the pollution problem, but they do not solve it. The key to protecting the planet is to prevent a problem at the source, rather than tinkering with it after it is already created. In the consumer society, this means intervening early in the game in the decisions about what is produced and how it is produced. A society in which consumption is conscious and restrained requires that new any different decisions be made in corporate boardrooms as well as in national capitals, decisions that put the needs of the planet ahead of the profits of the corporation.

Is the end of the world at hand?

ROBERT M. SOLOW

I was having a hard time figuring out how to begin when I came across an excerpt from an interview with my MIT colleague Professor Jay Forrester, who is either the

Reading taken from *The Economic Growth Controversy*. Copyright © Macmillan

Christopher Columbus or the Dr Strangelove of this business, depending on how you look at it. Forrester said he would like to see about a hundred people, the most gifted and best qualified in the world, brought together in a team to make a psychosocial analysis of the problem of world equilibrium. He thought it would take about ten years. When he was asked to define the composition of his problem-solving group, Forrester said: 'Above all it shouldn't be mostly made up of professors. One would include people who had been successful in their personal careers, whether in politics, business, or anywhere else. We should also need radical philosophers, but we should take care to keep out representatives of the social sciences. Such people always want to go to the bottom of a particular problem. What we want to look at are the problems caused by interactions.' I don't know what you call people who believe they can be wrong about everything in particular, but expect to be lucky enough somehow to get it right on the interactions. They may be descendants of the famous merchant Lapidus, who said he lost money on every item he sold, but made it up on the volume. Well, I suppose that as an economist I am a representative of the social sciences; and I'm prepared to play out the role by talking about first principles and trying to say what the Growth vs. No-Growth business is really all about. This is going to involve me in the old academic ploy of saying over and over again what I'm not talking about before I ever actually say what I think I am talking about. But I'm afraid that some of those boring distinctions are part of the price you have to pay for getting it right.

First of all, there are (at least) two separate questions you can ask about the prospects for economic growth. You can ask: Is growth desirable? Or you can ask: Is growth possible? I suppose that if continued economic growth is not possible, it hardly matters whether or not it's desirable. But if it is possible, it's presumably not inevitable, so we can discuss whether we should want it. But they are separate questions, and an answer to one of them is not necessarily an answer to the other. My main business is with the question about the possibility of continued growth; I want to discuss the validity of the negative answer given by the 'Doomsday Models' associated with the names of Forrester and Meadows (and MIT!), and to a lesser extent with the group of English scientists who published a manifesto called 'A Blueprint for Survival.' Dr Mishan's main concern, on the other hand, was with the desirability of continued economic growth (and, at least by implication, with the desirability of past economic growth). If I spend a few minutes poaching on his territory, it is mainly because that seems like a good way to get some concepts straight, but also just to keep a discussion going.

Sorting out the issues

Arguments about the desirability of economic growth often turn quickly into arguments about the 'quality' of modern life. One gets the notion that you favor growth if you are the sort of person whose idea of heaven is to drive 90 miles an hour down a six-lane highway reading billboards, in order to pollute the air over some crowded lake, itself polluted, with the exhaust from twin 100-horsepower outboards, and whose idea of food is Cocoa Krispies. On the other hand, to be against economic growth is to be a Granola-eating, back-packing, transcendental-meditating canoe freak. That may even be a true statistical association, but I will argue that there is no necessary or logical connection between your answer to the growth question and your answer to the quality-of-life question. Suppose there were no issue about economic growth; suppose it were impossible; suppose each man or each woman were equipped to have only two children (one bomb under each wing); suppose we were stuck with the technology we have now and had no concept of invention, or even of increased mechanization through capital investment. We could still argue about the relative merits of cutting timber for building houses or leaving it stand to be enjoyed as forest. Some people would still be willing to breathe carbon monoxide in big cities in return for the excitement of urban life, while others would prefer cleaner air and fewer TV channels. Macy's would still not tell Gimbel's. Admen would still try to tell you that all those beautiful women are actually just looking for somebody who smokes Winchesters, thus managing to insult both men and women at once. Some people would still bring transistor radios to the beach. All or nearly all of the arguments about the quality of life would be just as valid if the question of growth never arose.

I won't go so far as to say there is no connection. In particular, one can argue that if population density were low enough, people would interfere much less with each other, and everyone could find a part of the world and style of civilization that suited him. Then differences of opinion about the quality of life wouldn't matter so much. Even if I grant the truth of that observation, it is still the case that, from here on out, questions about the quality of life are separable from questions about the desirability of growth. If growth stopped, there would be just about as much to complain about; and, as I shall argue later on, one can imagine continued growth with reductions in pollution and congestion and less consumption of sliced white bread.

I suppose it is only fair to admit that if you get very enthusiastic about economic growth you are likely to be attracted to easily quantifiable and measurable things as objects of study, to point at with pride or to view with alarm. You are likely to pay less attention to important, intangible aspects of the standard of living. Although you can't know whether people are happier than they used to be, you can at least determine that they drink more orange juice or take more aspirin. But that's mere weakness of imagination and has nothing to do in principle with the desirability of economic growth, let alone with its possibility.

There is another practical argument that is often made, and although it is important, it sometimes serves as a way of avoiding coming to grips with the real issues. This argument says that economic growth, increasing output per person, is the only way we are likely to achieve a more equitable distribution of income in society. There is a lot of home truth in that. It is inevitably less likely that a middle-class electorate will vote to redistribute part of its own income to the poor than that it will be willing to allocate a slightly larger share of a growing total. Even more pessimistically, I might suggest that even a given relative distribution of income, supposing it cannot be made more equal for political or other reasons, is less unattractive if the absolute standard of living at the bottom is fairly high than it is if the absolute standard at the bottom is very low. From this point of view, even if economic growth doesn't lead to more equity in distribution, it makes the inequity we've got more tolerable. I think it is one of the lessons of history that this is a realistic statement of the prospects.

It is even clearer if one looks, not at the distribution of income within a rich country like the United States, but at the distribution of income between the developed countries of the world and the underdeveloped ones. The rich Western nations have never been able to agree on the principle of allocating as much as one percent of their GNP to aid underdeveloped countries. They are unlikely to be willing to share their wealth on any substantial scale with the poor countries. Even if they were, there are so many more poor people in the world that an equally shared income would be quite low. The *only* prospect of a decent life for Asia, Africa, and Latin America is in more total output.

But I point this out only to warn you that it is not the heart of the question. I think that those who oppose continued growth should in honesty face up to the implications of their position for distributional equity and the prospects of the world's poor. I think that those who favor continued growth on the grounds that only thus can we achieve some real equality ought to be serious about that. If economic growth with equality is a good thing, it doesn't follow that economic growth with a lot of pious talk about equality is a good thing. In principle, we can have growth with or without equity and we can have stagnation with or without equity. An argument about first principles should keep those things separate.

Well, then, what *is* the problem of economic growth all about? (I'm giving a definition now, not stating a fact, so all I can say is that I think this way of looking at it contributes to clarity of thought.) Whenever there is a question about what to *do*, the desirability of economic growth turns on the claims of the future against the claims of the present. The pro-growth man is someone who is prepared to sacrifice something useful and desirable right now so that people should be better off in the future; the anti-growth man is someone who thinks that is unnecessary or undesirable. The nature of the sacrifice of present enjoyment for future enjoyment can be almost anything. The classic example is investment: We can use our labor and our resources to build very durable things like roads or subways or factories or blast furnaces or dams that will be used for a long time by people who were not even born when those things were created, and so will certainly have contributed nothing to their construction. That labor and those resources can just as well be used to produce shorter-run pleasures for us now.

Such a sacrifice of current consumption on behalf of the future may not strike you as much of a sacrifice. But that's because you live in a country that is already rich; if you had lived in Stalin's Russia, that need to sacrifice would be one of the reasons you would have been given to explain why you had to live without comfort and pleasures while the Ministry of Heavy Industry got all the play. If you lived in an underdeveloped country now, you would face the same problem: What shall you do with the foreign currency earned by sales of cocoa or copper or crude oil – spend it on imports of consumer goods for those alive and working now, or spend it on imports of machinery to start building an industry that may help to raise the standard of living in thirty years' time?

There are other ways in which the same choice can be made, including, for instance, the direction of intellectual resources to the invention of things (like the generation of electricity from nuclear fusion) that will benefit future generations. Paradoxically, one of the ways in which the present can do something for the future is to conserve natural resources. If we get along with less lumber now so that there will be more forests standing for our grandchildren, or if we limit the present consumption of oil or zinc so that there will be some left for the twenty-first century, or if we worry about siltation behind dams that would otherwise be fun for fishermen and water-skiers, in all those cases we are promoting economic growth. I call that paradoxical because I think most people identify the conservation freak with the anti-growth party whereas, in this view of the matter, the conservationist is trading present satisfaction for future satisfaction, that is, he is promoting economic growth. I think the confusion comes from mixing up the quality-of-life problem with the growth problem. But it is nonetheless a confusion.

Why should we be concerned with the welfare of posterity, given the indubitable fact that posterity has never done a thing for us? I am not anthropologist enough to know how rare or common it is that our culture should teach us to care not only about our children but about their children, and *their* children. I suppose there are good Darwinian reasons why cultures without any future-orientation should fail to survive very long in the course of history. (But remember that they had a merry time of it while they lasted!) Moreover, we now enjoy the investments made by our ancestors, so there is a kind of equity in passing it on. Also, unless something terrible happens, there will be a lot more future than there has been past; and, for better or worse – probably worse – there will be more people at each future instant than there are now or have been. So all in all, the future will involve many more man-years of life than the present or the past, and a kind of intergenerational democracy suggests that all those man-years-to-be deserve some consideration out of sheer numbers.

On the other hand, *if* continued economic growth is possible – which is the question I'm coming to – then it is very likely that posterity will be richer than we are even if we make no special efforts on its behalf. If history offers any guide, then, in the developed part of the world at least, the accumulation of technological knowledge will probably make our greatgrandchildren better off than we are, even if we make no great effort in that direction. Leaving aside the possibility of greater equality – I have already discussed that – there is hardly a crying need for posterity to be on average very much richer than we are. Why should us poor folk make any sacrifices for those who will in any case live in luxury in the future? Of course, if the end of the world is at hand, if continued economic growth is *not* possible, then we ought to care more about posterity, because they won't be so well off. Paradoxically, if continued economic growth is not possible, or less possible, then we probably ought to do more to promote it. Actually, there's no paradox in that, as every student of economics will realize, because it is a way of saying that the marginal return on investment is high.

Overshoot and collapse

There is, as you know, a school of thought that claims that continued economic growth is in fact not possible any more, or at least not for very long. This judgment has been expressed more or less casually by several observers in recent years. What distinguishes the Doomsday Models from their predecessors is that they claim to much more than a casual judgment: they deduce their beliefs about future prospects from mathematical models or systems analysis. They don't merely say that the end of the world is at hand – they can show you computer output that says the same thing.

Characteristically, the Doomsday Models do more than just say that continued economic growth is impossible. They tell us why: in brief, because (a) the earth's natural resources will soon be used up; (b) increased industrial production will soon strangle us in pollution; and (c) increasing population will eventually outrun the world's capacity to grow food, so that famine must eventually result. And, finally, the models tell us one more thing: the world will end with a bang, not a whimper. The natural evolution of the world economy is not at all toward some kind of smooth approach to its natural limits, wherever they are. Instead, it is inevitable – unless we make drastic changes in the way we live and organize ourselves – that the world will overshoot any level of population and production it can possibly sustain and will then collapse, probably by the middle of the next century.

I would like to say why I think that the Doomsday Models are bad science and therefore bad guides to public policy. I hope nobody will conclude that I believe the problems of population control, environmental degradation, and resource exhaustion to be unimportant, or that I am one of those people who believe that an adequate response to such problems is a vague confidence that some technological solution will turn up. On the contrary, it is precisely because these are important problems that public policy had better be based on sound and careful analysis. I want to explain some of my reasons for believing that the global models don't provide even the beginnings of a foundation of that kind.

The first thing to realize is that the characteristic conclusion of the Doomsday Models is very near the surface. It is, in fact, more nearly an assumption than a conclusion, in the sense that the chain of logic from the assumptions to the conclusion is very short and rather obvious.

The basic assumption is that stocks of things like the world's natural resources and the waste-disposal capacity of the environment are finite, that the world economy tends to consume the stock at an increasing rate (through the mining of minerals and the production of goods), and that there are no built-in mechanisms by which approaching exhaustion tends to turn off consumption gradually and in advance. You hardly need a giant computer to tell you that a system with those behavior rules is going to bounce off its ceiling and collapse to a low level. Then, in case anyone is inclined to relax into the optimistic belief that maybe things aren't that bad, we are told: Imagine that the stock of natural resources were actually twice as big as the best current evidence suggests, or imagine that the annual amount of pollution could be halved all at once and then set to growing again. All that would happen is that the date of collapse would be postponed by T years, where T is not a large number. But once you grasp the quite simple essence of the models, this should come as no surprise. It is important to realize where these powerful conclusions come from, because, if you ask yourself 'Why didn't I realize earlier that the end of the world was at hand?' the answer is not that you weren't clever enough to figure it out for yourself. The answer is that the imminent end of the world is an immediate deduction from certain assumptions, and one must really ask if the assumptions are any good.

It is a commonplace that if you calculate the annual output of any production process, large or small, and divide it by the annual employment of labor, you get a ratio that is called the productivity of labor. At the most aggregative level, for example, we can say that the GNP in 1971 was $1050 billion and that about 82 million people were employed in producing it, so that GNP per worker or the productivity of a year of labor was about $12 800. Symmetrically, though the usage is less common, one could just as well calculate the GNP per unit of some particular natural resource and call that the productivity of coal, or GNP per pound of vanadium. We usually think of the productivity of labor as rising more or less exponentially, say at 2 or 3 percent a year, because that is the way it has in fact behaved over the past century or so since the statistics began to be collected. The rate of increase in the productivity of labor is not a constant of nature. Sometimes it is faster, sometimes slower. For example, we know that labor productivity must have increased more slowly a long time ago, because if we extrapolate backward at 2 percent a year, we come to a much lower labor productivity in 1492 than can possibly have been the case. And the productivity of labor has risen faster in the past twenty-five years than in the fifty years before that. It also varies from place to place, being faster in Japan and Germany and slower in Great Britain, for reasons that are not at all certain. But it rises, and we expect it to keep rising.

Now, how about the productivity of natural resources? All the Doomsday Models will allow is a one-time hypothetical increase in the world supply of natural resources, which is the equivalent of a one-time increase in the productivity of natural resources. Why shouldn't the productivity of most natural resources rise more or less steadily through time, like the productivity of labor?

And of course it does for some resources, but not for others. Real GNP roughly doubled between 1950 and 1970. But the consumption of primary and scrap iron increased by about 20 percent, so the productivity of iron, GNP per ton of iron, increased by about 2.5 percent a year on the average during those twenty years. The

U.S. consumption of manganese rose by 30 percent in the same period, so the productivity of manganese went up by some 70 percent in twenty years, a bit under 2.25 percent a year. Aggregate consumption of nickel just about doubled, like GNP, so the productivity of nickel didn't change. U.S. consumption of copper, both primary and secondary, went up by a third between 1951 and 1970, so GNP per pound of copper rose at 2 percent a year on the average. The story on lead and zinc is very similar, so their productivity increased at some 2 percent a year. The productivity of bituminous coal rose at 3 percent a year.

Naturally, there are important exceptions, and unimportant exceptions. GNP per barrel of oil was about the same in 1970 as in 1951: no productivity increase there. The consumption of natural gas tripled in the same period, so GNP per cubic foot of natural gas fell at about 2.5 percent a year. Our industrial demand for aluminum quadrupled in two decades, so that productivity of aluminum fell at a good 3.5 percent a year. And industrial demand for columbium was multiplied by a factor of 25: in 1951 we managed $2.25 million of GNP (in 1967 prices) per pound of columbium, whereas in 1970 we were down to $170 000 of GNP per pound of columbium. On the other hand, it is a little hard to imagine civilization toppling because of a shortage of columbium.

Obviously, many forces combine to govern the course of the productivity of any given mineral over time. When a rare natural resource is first available, it acquires new uses with a rush; and consumption goes up much faster than GNP. That's the columbium story, no doubt, and, to a lesser extent, the vanadium story. But once the novelty has worn off, the productivity of a resource tends to rise as better or worse substitutes for it appear, as new commodities replace old ones, and as manufacturing processes improve. One of the reasons the productivity of copper rises is because that of aluminum falls, as aluminum replaces copper in many uses. The same is true of coal and oil. A resource like petroleum, which is versatile because of its role as a source of energy, is an interesting special case. It is hardly any wonder that the productivity of petroleum has stagnated, since the consumption of energy – both as electricity for domestic and industrial use and in the automobile – has recently increased even faster than GNP. But no one can doubt that we will run out of oil, that coal and nuclear fission will replace oil as the major sources of energy. It is already becoming probable that the high-value use of oil will soon be as feed stock for the petrochemical industries, rather than as a source of energy. Sooner or later, the productivity of oil will rise out of sight, because the production and consumption of oil will eventually dwindle toward zero, but real GNP will not.

So there really is no reason why we should not think of the productivity of natural resources as increasing more or less exponentially over time. But then overshoot and collapse are no longer the inevitable trajectory of the world system, and the typical assumption-conclusion of the Doomsday Models falls by the wayside. We are in a different sort of ball game. The system might still burn itself out and collapse in finite time, but one cannot say with any honesty that it must. It all depends on the particular, detailed facts of modern economic life as well as on the economic policies that we and the rest of the world pursue. I don't want to argue for any particular counterstory; all I want to say now is that the overshoot-collapse pattern is built into the models very near the surface, by assumption, and by implausible assumption at that.

Scarcity and the price system

There is at least one reason for believing that the Doomsday story is almost certainly wrong. The most glaring defect of the Forrester–Meadows models is the absence of any sort of functioning price system. I am no believer that the market is always right, and I am certainly no advocate of *laissez-faire* where the environment is concerned. But the price system is, after all, the main social institution evolved by capitalist economies (and, to an increasing extent, socialist economies too) for registering and reacting to relative scarcity. There are several ways in which the working of the price system will push our society into faster and more systematic increases in the productivity of natural resources.

First of all, let me go back to the analogy between natural resources and labor. We are not surprised to learn that industry quite consciously tries to make inventions that save labor, i.e., permit the same product to be made with fewer man-hours of work. After all, on the average, labor costs amount to almost three-fourths of all costs in our economy. An invention that reduces labor requirements per unit of GNP by 1 percent reduces all costs by about 0.75 percent. Natural resource costs are a much smaller proportion of total GNP, something nearer 5 percent. So industry and engineering have a much stronger motive to reduce labor requirements by 1 percent than to reduce resource requirements by 1 percent, assuming – which may or may not be true – that it is about as hard to do one as to do the other. But then, as the earth's supply of particular natural resources nears exhaustion, and as natural resources become more and more valuable, the motive to economize those natural resources should become as strong as the motive to economize labor. The productivity of resources should rise faster than now – it is hard to imagine otherwise.

There are other ways in which the market mechanism can be expected to push us all to economize on natural resources as they become scarcer. Higher and rising prices of exhaustible resources lead competing producers to substitute other materials that are more plentiful and therefore cheaper. To the extent that it is impossible to design around or find substitutes for expensive natural resources, the prices of commodities that contain a lot of them will rise relative to the prices of other goods and services that don't use up a lot of resources. Consumers will be driven to buy fewer resource-intensive goods and more of other things. All these effects work automatically to increase the productivity of natural resources, i.e., to reduce resource requirements per unit of GNP.

As I mentioned a moment ago, this is not an argument for *laissez-faire*. We may feel that the private decisions of buyers and sellers give inadequate representation to future generations. Or we may feel that private interests are in conflict with a distinct public interest – strip-mining of coal is an obvious case in point, and there are many others as soon as we begin to think about environmental effects. Private market responses may be too uncoordinated, too slow, based on insufficient and faulty information. In every case there will be actions that public agencies can take and should take; and it will be a major political struggle to see that they are taken. But I don't see how one can have the slightest confidence in the predictions of models that seem to make no room for the operation of everyday market forces. If the forecasts are wrong, then so are the policy implications, to the extent that there are any realistic policy implications.

Every analysis of resource scarcity has to come to terms with the fact that the prices of natural resources and resource products have not shown any tendency to rise over the past half century, relative to the prices of other things. This must mean that there have so far been adequate offsets to any progressive impoverishment of deposits – like improvements in the technology of extraction, savings in end uses, or the availability of cheaper substitutes. The situation could of course, change; and very likely some day it will. If the experienced and expert participants in the market now believed that resource prices would be sharply higher at some foreseeable time, prices would *already* be rising, as I will try to explain in a moment. The historical steadiness of resource prices suggests that buyers and sellers in the market have not been acting as if they foresaw exhaustion in the absence of substitutes, and therefore sharply higher future prices. They may turn out to be wrong; but the Doomsday Models give us absolutely no reason to expect that – in fact, they claim to get whatever meager empirical basis they have from such experts.

Why is it true that if the market saw higher prices in the future, prices would already be rising? It is a rather technical point, but I want to explain it because, in a way, it summarizes the important thing about natural resources: conserving a mineral deposit is just as much of an investment as building a factory, and it has to be analyzed that way. Any owner of a mineral deposit owns a valuable asset, whether the owner is a private capitalist or the government of an under-developed country. The asset is worth keeping only if at the margin it earns a return equal to that earned on other kinds of assets. A factory produces things each year of its life, but a mineral deposit just lies there: its owner can realize a return only if he either mines the deposit or if it *increases in value*. So if you are sitting on your little pile of X and confidently expect to be able to sell it for a very high price in the year 2000 because it will be very scarce by then, you must be earning your 5 percent a year, or 10 percent a year, or whatever the going rate of return is, each year between now and 2000. The only way this can happen is for the value of X to go up by 5 percent a year or 10 percent a year. And that means that anyone who wants to use any X any time between now and 2000 will have to pay a price for it that is rising at that same 5 percent or 10 percent a year. Well, it's not happening. Of course we are exploiting our hoard of exhaustible resources; we have no choice about that. We are certainly exploiting it wastefully, in the sense that we allow each other to dump waste products into the environment without full accounting for costs. But there is very little evidence that we are exploiting it too fast.

Paying for pollution

I think that what one gets from the Doomsday literature is the notion that air and water and noise pollution are an inescapable accompaniment of economic growth, especially industrial growth. If that is true, then to be against pollution is to be against growth. I realize that in putting the matter so crudely I have been unjust; nevertheless, that is the message that comes across. I think that way of looking at the pollution problem is wrong.

A correct analysis goes something like this. Excessive pollution and degradation of the environment certainly accompany industrial growth and the increasing population density that goes with it. But they are by no means an inescapable by-product. Excessive pollution occurs because of an important flaw in the price system. Factories, power plants, municipal sewers, drivers of cars, strip-miners of coal and deep-miners of coal, and all sorts of generators of waste are allowed to dump that waste into the environment, into the atmosphere and into running water and the oceans, without paying the full cost of what they do. No wonder they do too much. So would you, and so would I. In fact, we actually do – directly as drivers of cars, indirectly as we buy some products at a price which is lower than it ought to be because the producer is not required to pay for using the environment to carry away his wastes, and even more indirectly as we buy things that are made with things that pollute the environment.

This flaw in the price system exists because a scarce resource (the waste-disposal capacity of the environment) goes unpriced; and that happens because it is owned by all of us, as it should be. The flaw can be corrected, either by the simple expedient of regulating the discharge of wastes to the environment by direct control or by the slightly more complicated device of charging special prices – user taxes – to those who dispose of wastes in air or water. These effluent charges do three things: they make pollution-intensive goods expensive, and so reduce the consumption of them; they make pollution-intensive methods of production costly, and so promote abatement of pollution by producers; they generate revenue that can, if desired, be used for the further purification of air or water or for other environmental improvements. Most economists prefer this device of effluent charges to regulation by direct order. This is more than an occupational peculiarity. Use of the price system has certain advantages in efficiency and decentralization. Imposing a physical limit on, say, sulfur dioxide emission is, after all, a little peculiar. It says that you may do so much of a bad thing and pay nothing for the privilege, but after that, the price is infinite. Not surprisingly, one can find a more efficient schedule of pollution abatement through a more sensitive tax schedule.

But this difference of opinion is minor compared with the larger point that needs to be made. The annual cost that would be necessary to meet decent pollution-abatement standards by the end of the century is large, but not staggering. One estimate says that in 1970 we spent about $8.5 billion (in 1967 prices), or 1 percent of GNP, for pollution abatement. An active pollution-abatement policy would cost perhaps $50 billion a year by 2000, which would be about 2 percent of GNP by then.

That is a small investment of resources: you can see how small it is when you consider that GNP grows by 4 percent or so every year, on the average. Cleaning up air and water would entail a cost that would be a bit like losing one-half of one year's growth between now and the year 2000. What stands between us and a decent environment is not the curse of industrialization, not an unbearable burden of cost, but just the need to organize ourselves consciously to do some simple and knowable things. Compared with the possibility of an active abatement policy, the policy of stopping economic growth in order to stop pollution would be incredibly inefficient. It would not actually accomplish much, because one really wants to reduce the amount of, say, hydrocarbon emission to a third or a half of *what it is now*. And what no-growth would accomplish, it would do by cutting off your face to spite your nose.

In the end, that is really my complaint about the Doomsday school. It diverts attention from the really important things that can actually be done, step by step, to make things better. The end of the world *is* at hand – the earth, if you take the long view, will fall into the sun in a few billion years anyway, unless some other disaster happens first. In the meantime, I think we'd be better off trying to pass a strong sulfur-emissions tax, or getting some Highway Trust Fund money allocated to mass transit, or building a humane and decent floor under family incomes, or overriding President Nixon's veto of a strong Water Quality Act, or reforming the tax system, or fending off starvation in Bengal – instead of worrying about the generalized 'predicament of mankind.'

Environmental problems in our daily lives

BRITISH GOVERNMENT WHITE PAPER

The environment does not raise a single issue. It lumps together a wide and diverse collection of problems. Inevitably, people notice most those that affect their daily lives. They dislike dirty streets and want them cleaned up. They object to what they regard as the onslaught of planners and developers on their towns and villages and fields, recoiling in particular from buildings that seem out of harmony with their familiar neighbourhood. They are worried about health risks and want reassurance that their environment is not becoming a health hazard. They ask for cleaner water in their rivers and taps, cleaner beaches and bathing waters when they go on holiday, and cleaner air to breathe. They want goods that can be produced and disposed of without harming the environment. They want more quiet and less hustle, and to be able to escape from their towns and cities to a countryside that can cater for their leisure without losing its beauty and its character. They want the benefits of prosperity to include the improvement of their surroundings and the safeguarding of the natural world. What can a Government best do to address these aims? There are no easy and instant solutions; much has already been done but there is still more to do.

The foundation of policy: stewardship

The starting point for this Government is the ethical imperative of stewardship which must underlie all environmental policies. Mankind has always been capable of great good and great evil. That is certainly true of our role as custodians of our planet. The Government's approach begins with the recognition that it is mankind's duty to look after our world prudently and conscientiously. It was the Prime Minister who reminded us that we do not hold a freehold on our world, but only a full repairing lease. We have a moral duty to look after our planet and to hand it on in good order to future generations. That is what experts mean when they talk of 'sustainable development': not sacrificing tomorrow's prospects for a largely illusory gain today. We must put a proper value on the natural world: it would be odd to cherish a Constable but not the landscape he depicted. The foundation stone of all the policies in this White Paper is our responsibility to future generations to preserve and enhance the environment of our country and our planet.

In order to fulfil this responsibility of stewardship, the Government has based the policies and proposals in this White Paper on a number of supporting principles. First, we must base our policies on fact not fantasy, and use the best evidence and analysis available. Second, given the environmental risks, we must act responsibly and be prepared to take precautionary action where it is justified. Third, we must inform public debate and public concern by ensuring publication of the facts. Fourth, we must work for progress just as hard in the international arena as we do at home. And fifth, we must take care to choose the best instruments to achieve our environmental goals.

The best instruments

Once it is clear which environmental problems need to be tackled and with what urgency, the next question is how best to tackle them. Safeguarding the environment can be very costly in the short term, whatever the longer term benefits. Control of pollution is estimated to cost 1–1.5% of Britain's gross national product – perhaps £7 billion in 1990. Action on the environment has to be proportionate to the costs involved and to the ability of those affected to pay them. So it is particularly important for Governments to adopt the most cost-effective instruments for controlling pollution and tackling environmental problems. And we need to ensure that we have a sensible order of priorities, acting first to tackle problems that could cause most damage to human life or health, and could do most damage to the environment now or in the future.

If Governments want to stop something happening, or make something happen in a different way, they have broadly two choices: they can by law lay down rules and regulations on standards to be met or equipment to be installed; or they can use the market to influence the behaviour of producers and their customers. Whichever course they choose, the objective is to make those who cause environmental damage face the costs of control in full, without subsidy. That is called the 'polluter pays' principle which the Government, in common with many other Governments, adopts. If we impose higher standards centrally, this puts extra costs on producers and on their customers in turn; if we use price signals, for example by imposing charges or taxes on certain activities, extra costs again fall on the manufacturers, and then on their customers. This 'polluter pays' principle is an important means of influencing potential polluters.

Regulation

In the past, governments in Britain and elsewhere have mostly used regulation to control pollution. 'Fog everywhere', wrote Dickens about Victorian London. Eventually, the British Government used the law to impose regulations to clean up London's air. And there are large numbers of laws and regulations to protect the quality of our water and air and to control disposal of wastes on land. This regulatory approach has served Britain and other countries well, and it will remain an important part of future environmental controls. For example, our new system of integrated pollution control will regulate industrial processes of all types to ensure the best outcome for the environment as a whole.

Regulation, however, does have limitations. It can be expensive to monitor and difficult to up-date quickly in response to scientific and technical advance. It cannot always pitch controls at the level which strikes the most cost-effective balance between environmental benefits and compliance costs. Compliance costs can fall widely – on business, on Government, and on consumers – and are easy to under-estimate in advance. And so long as it remains the responsibility of the regulator, usually central Government, to lay down the ways in which pollution targets should be met, there will always be the danger that insufficiently flexible systems will be created and some better options overlooked. In short, regulation has always been required and is still required, but it has its shortcomings.

Market forces

For these reasons the Government, along with other Governments throughout the world, has begun to look for ways to control pollution which avoid some of these problems by working with the grain of the market. The ideas include various forms of pollution charges, as well as taxes and other economic instruments, all designed to encourage consumers and producers to behave in ways which benefit the environment.

These new approaches have been described loosely as the market-based approach to the environment, since they involve integrating economic and environmental concerns and applying market economics more broadly. In the Government's view, market mechanisms offer the prospect of a more efficient and flexible response to environmental issues, both old and new. There is nothing new about markets being influenced by environmental factors: houses in the quieter parts of towns have generally commanded the best prices; and, recently in particular, people across the world have been voting with their purses and wallets by preferring merchandise which seems environmentally-friendly, and manufacturers and suppliers have responded. Many Governments are now considering going a stage further by deliberate Government intervention to establish a new set of price signals.

We know what happens when price levels send the wrong environmental signals: the Amazon rain forests have been devastated at least in part because state subsidies there distorted economic choices and artificially favoured forest clearance instead of more sensible policies. The new Brazilian Government is trying to put that right. Just as the wrong price signals can cause disasters like that, so the right price signals should be able to cause very significant environmental improvements. There is evidence of that nearer to home. We have known for some time that lead in petrol produces harmful emissions, but motorists were slow to respond by switching to unleaded petrol. It was only when the Government intervened through a differential tax to give motorists a price incentive to switch to unleaded petrol that things started to move quickly.

The price mechanism will be the key, too, to the environmental consequences of the consumption of energy, which will much preoccupy people all over the world over the next 50 years. It is the price of energy more than any Government regulations or controls which will drive us to be more efficient about its use and more resourceful about the means of producing it. This is regardless of the political complexion of governments. It is impossible to be precise about the level of energy prices year by year, as the events of Summer 1990 have demonstrated. Increases in energy taxation or other measures directly raising the relative price of energy, outside transport, will not be necessary in the next few years. But we do not seek to duck the fact that energy prices will inevitably rise eventually, and we propose measures for promoting energy efficiency and reducing greenhouse gas emissions against that background.

The market can also help pay for improvements to the environment. Investment in cleaning up our rivers and beaches was held back for years by constraints on public expenditure under successive Governments. It took the privatisation of the water industry to allow the market to help. The new water companies will raise private funding for an extensive overhaul of the industry's capital equipment and for significant improvements to environmental standards. This will be reflected in the level of charges, and consumers will see for themselves the true market cost of the services that they consume and the quality they rightly demand. Private investment reflected in consumer charges is securing a public good. The forthcoming privatisation of the electricity supply industry will bring similar benefits.

Implications for people

We are all used to the idea that developments which change our surroundings bring gains to some and losses to others. A new industrial process can provide more jobs and more national wealth, but at the expense of the quality of our landscape or the air we breathe. A new housing estate on a green field can provide better living standards for those who move into it, but at the expense of those who delighted in this previously unspoilt countryside. Environmental gains and losses like this are familiar, and we have found ways of trying to reconcile them through public consultation and participation, the planning system and compensation schemes. Not everyone can be satisfied, but we have established systems to achieve a fair balance between different interests.

We are not, though, as used to balancing shorter term economic losses against longer term environmental gains. Closing down polluting industries can lose jobs but help preserve our inheritance. Changes in the pattern of energy use can cause problems and expense for some individuals, some industries and some countries, but are necessary if global warming is to be avoided. We may find ourselves apparently both gaining and losing in different parts of our lives; different groups in every country and different countries in every region will face similar adjustments. There can also be conflicts between environmental objectives: a tidal barrage produces emission-free electricity but floods important wildlife habitats.

The fact that almost every environmental issue faces us with an arduous agenda of choices in which some may initially have to shoulder greater burdens than others is another strong argument for basing decision-making on the best available evidence, and on the fullest possible public debate. If we avoid these difficult decisions, we will be putting our short-term convenience ahead of the lasting needs of future genertions.

Attempting to bring together all the policies which affect the environment is not and cannot be an exact scientific process. There is no anatomical or mechanistic relationship between them all. We cannot calibrate with precision the effect of this or that policy switch or modification on all the other related parts of the whole. To try to reduce all these issues to a table of figures is neither helpful nor honest: these are three-dimensional problems in a fast-changing world. So we are not dealing with a science, but with an area where political judgement will properly have a central role, constrained by the impertinent but implacable realities of the world.

We are attempting to cope not only with immense and imprecise complication, but also with great diversity. We travel all the way from chalk-land to the heavens, from saving the wild orchids and sea cabbage on the cliffs above Dover to beginning the international environmental negotiations which will ensure that the atmosphere around our planet is no longer treated like a dustbin. In almost every area of work, there is already writing on the page; we do not begin with a blank sheet – we should be in deep trouble were it otherwise. So progress is not made from a standing start. We are already on the move but recognise that we have to go further and faster.

CASE STUDY

The Body Shop

Anita Roddick opened the first Body Shop in Brighton in 1976. She had no previous business knowledge and underwent no formal business training. Indeed she has stated that the Body Shop would not have been the resounding success that it is, if she had followed the advice given in today's business schools.

Roddick's motivating force was the lack of integrity which she believed was inherent in the 'beauty' business. Essentially controlled by men, they sold false dreams to women by offering expensively packaged products, principally for skin care, which do nothing more than moisturize the skin. Since there are no miraculous ways of reversing the ageing process, Roddick believes that it is immoral to sell such products to middle-aged women offering false promises about looking and feeling years younger and using younger models to delude older women that they too can regain a youthful appearance.

Ageing women, Roddick alleges, will pay astronomical sums in pursuit of these false dreams. The cosmetics industry can charge £100 a gram for something which cost a mere £1 to produce, with the customer's money helping to finance multi-million pound advertising budgets which enable top companies to achieve a 30% profit and £50 million per year sales turnover.

Repulsed by these practices, Anita Roddick started her own small shop. She decided that the word 'beauty' would never be used at all; instead she would provide honest information about her goods and their ingredients – what they might do and what they could not. Packaging would be simple, and opportunities would be afforded for recycling jars and bottles. Roddick could not support the cosmetic industry's policy of ensuring product safety by means of animal testing, and it has therefore always been the Body Shop's policy never to sell anything that has been tested on animals.

In its early stages the Body Shop could not possibly have afforded the enormous advertising budgets which were characteristic of the industry. But the shop's refusal to advertise reflects Anita Roddick's belief that manufacturers and retailers should not enagage in high-pressure persuasion to make customers buy goods they do not really want. Body

Shop staff are therefore briefed to talk to customers and inform them, but to be prepared to let them leave the shop empty-handed. The company has always relied on its reputation in order to attract and on free publicity from journalists and feature writers; in fact, the business was enormously helped at its inception by a funeral director who threatened to sue Anita Roddick on the grounds that clients would not wish to hire an undertaker whose premises were near a 'Body Shop'!

Campaigning against animal testing was the Body Shop's prelude to educating the public in other areas of environmental concern. In 1985 the Body Shop sponsored posters for Greenpeace, and used its shop floors as campaign platforms to raise public consciousness about endangered species, the burning of tropical rainforests, acid rain and the receding ozone layer, amongst others. The shop has an Environmental Projects Department which actively encourages trade with the Third World, and many of the products are derived from materials used by the indigenous people in Third World countries.

The Body Shop itself seeks to be socially responsible in the way it conducts its business. In 1989 the firm commissioned a 'cradle to grave' environmental audit of all its practices, but focusing especially on packing and waste. Customers are discouraged from taking carrier bags; 'refillable' cotton bags are on sale, and recycled (and recyclable) polyethylene is now used for free carriers; recycled paper is always used, whether it is toilet paper or headed stationery. In 1990 the Body Shop became the first company in the UK to recycle plastic waste after it had been used by consumers.

Roddick has never seen profit maximization as her main motivating force. Indeed, it was with a certain incredulity that she saw Body Shop shares rise from 95 pence to £1.65 on the day of its flotation on the Stock Exchange in April 1984, making her an instant millionaire. Roddick's philosophy has never been based on profits, but on people, whether they be customers, staff or suppliers, all of whom she wants to see happy and fulfilled. She endeavours to make work interesting by encouraging staff to interest themselves in the campaigning carried out within the shop and to engage customers in conversation both about products and campaigns. Customers are not pressurized, and Third World suppliers are not exploited by being paid ridiculously low sums for their goods and labours.

Anita Roddick believes that her business philosophy breaks most of the rules which are taught in modern business schools; lack of concern for profits, shop windows promoting campaigns rather than products, informing customers rather than persuading them to buy, and so on. But

Roddick believes that 'running in the opposite direction' (as she puts it) is the key to her success, and that several major companies are now taking the Body Shop's cue and allowing environmental issues to have a significant impact on how their business is conducted.

Source: Anita Roddick and Russell Miller, *Body and Soul* (London: Ebury Press, 1991)

Discussion questions on the case study

Does the Body Shop's success show that it is possible to combine profitability with ethical responsibility? Or has Anita Roddick simply captured a 'niche market' by appealing to a minority of ethical consumers?

Does Anita Roddick's disregard for conventional business school education demonstrate that business schools have an underlying ideology which can successfully be called into question? Or is Roddick really as unconventional as her autobiography suggests?

DISCUSSION TOPICS

1. The 'green lobby' has consistently urged that, if we are to conserve the earth's resources, it is not sufficient simply to avoid aerosols and buy detergents which do not contain phosphates. 'Sustainable growth' requires that the average consumer simply consumes less. However, it has equally been argued by some manufacturers that goods with 'planned obsolescence' are good for the economy, because more frequent repeat purchases ensure a buoyant employment market. Is it possible to have a society where due regard is paid to sustainable growth, and where consumption is restrained, without incurring problems of mass unemployment and economic stagnation? How would an economy which implemented 'sustainable growth' policies differ from the 'consumer society' which the West has enjoyed since the Second World War?

2. ECRA (The Ethical Consumer Research Association) regularly recommends boycotts of firms who, in its opinion, have acted reprehensibly in some way. In November 1992, ECRA's boycott list, surprisingly, included that paragon of virtue, the Body Shop, 'for the use of the "5 year rolling rule" rather than a "fixed cut-off date" for animal testing' (*The Ethical Consumer*, Issue 22, November/December 1992, p. 30). In other words, the Body Shop will trade with firms once they have completed a five-year period without animal testing, whereas ECRA

believes in defining a definite date for the cessation of animal testing, after which there is no scope for relenting on a decision not to trade with the animal tester.

Who is right, in your view? Consider the following possible comments on ECRA's decision.

(a) 'A "rolling rule" enables a firm who no longer **needs** to test on animals to get "off the hook". A firm may cease to test on animals, not out of moral conviction, but because it is no longer felt to be necessary.'

(b) 'There is no clear answer to the question of how long firms should have ceased animal testing to be judged to be ethically acceptable. The Body Shop should therefore make its own decision on such matters.'

(c) 'The Body Shop at least does more than most other companies to act ethically and show responsibility to the environment. It is unfair to boycott them, rather than competitors who are probably much worse.'

(d) 'There is nothing wrong with animal testing in the first place. It is surely better to test on animals than to discover that products are harmful to humans.'

Ethics and international business 10

When we examined the relationship between morality and religion, we saw that different religions seemed to generate different moral codes. A society in which there is a dominant religion or ideology can be expected to produce a reasonably uniform set of values. In contemporary Europe, capitalism flourishes with its emphasis on private ownership, competition and the profit motive. A nation's success is measured in terms of its GNP (gross national product), and consumption is encouraged by means of an advertising industry which attempts to stimulate wants and boost demand. The means of production results from a system in which the investment of money is rewarded by interest which the investor does not earn through his or her immediate labour.

A prevailing norm exists in which work is good, and ambition is encouraged; unemployment is undesirable (although often unavoidable by some). At the level of personal ethics, certain agreed ethical standards are normally taken for granted; reasonable standards of integrity are expected, even if there are those who do not aspire to the ideal. Sexual harassment, racial discrimination, bribery, embezzlement, insider dealing, industrial espionage and breaches of confidentiality are all types of action which fall short of ideals which are normally expected in the business world.

As business has become increasingly internationalized, there is an increasing likelihood of Europeans and Americans encountering business partners from very different cultures, who subscribe to radically different ethical systems. Indeed we do not need to go abroad to encounter internationalization in business: EC countries have many migrant workers from India, Africa, the Middle East or the Far East, and, as migrant workers settle, a cosmopolitan new generation of business people emerges. Japanese companies now have many subsidiaries within Europe, bringing staff and their distinctive methods with them.

It may be questioned whether different cultures really have different value systems. Might it not be the case, for example, that most, if not all cultures disapprove of bribery, but some are more inclined in practice to yield to the temptation to resort to it? Not all British or European managers necessarily subscribe to the same set of values; hence it might be questioned whether international variations amongst managers are any more diverse than the differences between managers in the same single country or the same continent. This view has sometimes been labelled 'universalism'; according to this school of thought there is only one fundamental 'world management culture', with minor variations in attitudes and values amongst different managers. An alternative view is that international differences in attitudes and values amongst managers can be attributed to the political and economic differences which exist between different countries. This view has been labelled the 'economic clusters' view.

Two highly important studies of international business culture lead us to believe that both these views do not adequately account for the variations in values which we find on an international level. The first is by Haire, Ghiselli and Porter,[1] who surveyed a total of 3641 managers, examining their concepts of leadership, decision making, participation, cheating, amongst others; significant differences emerged, indicating that there was no single uniform 'management culture' and that the differences which became apparent were not related to the economic and political systems of the countries in which they worked. Haire *et al.* concluded that, in general, world management styles could be classified into five broad cultural clusters:

1. Nordic-European (Denmark, Germany, Norway, Sweden);
2. Latin-European (Belgium, France, Italy, Spain);
3. Anglo-American;
4. developing countries (Argentina, Chile, India);
5. Japan.

The second important study of international managerial values is by George England, entitled *The Manager and his Values*.[2] England examined the personal values of over 2500 managers in five countries: the USA, Japan, Korea, India and Australia. England extracted a total of 66 concepts from literature dealing with organizations and with individual and group behaviour, and devised a questionnaire with two modes of evaluation. First, managers were asked to rate the level of importance of a concept; they could rate, say, 'patriotism' as being of high, average or low importance. Second, they were asked to define the category of reason which made them give the concept the level of importance. One might value patriotism for pragmatic reasons ('Being patriotic makes one successful'), for ethical/moral reasons or because of one's feelings or affections ('I like the Royal Family'). Again, England found significant differences between the five cultures, and perhaps with some surprises; for instance, Japan and Korea, despite their historical hostility and apparent culture clashes, came second closest, only surpassed by simi-

---

[1] Mason Haire, Edwin E. Ghiselli, Lyman W. Porter, *Managerial Thinking: An International Study* (New York: Wiley, 1966).
[2] George England, *The Manager and His Values* (Cambridge, Mass: Ballinger, 1975).

larities between the USA and Australia. There were very significant differences between India and Japan, but not as much as those between Australian managers and those from Japan and Korea.

Within the discussion of international cultural and moral diversity the role of religion should not be forgotten. British business managers often underrate or ignore it, probably because religious affiliation is weak in the UK, with only some 4% of the population attending church more often than once a month, and a significant proportion of the population declaring no religious affiliation at all. It would be parochial, however, to assume that what is true of the UK is true of most other countries: British irreligiosity is probably only exceeded by the Dutch, the Australians, the Swedes, and the former communist bloc (in ascending order). Although it can be tempting to believe that religion has a low key in one's business dealings, this view is certainly not shared by most other business partners on the international scene.

The fact that there are different management cultures with different value systems means that there are no easy solutions to ethical dilemmas in international business, or in dealing with ethnic minorities within a culture. What does a British supervisor do when a Sikh insists that he must wear his turban instead of a safety helmet? Should secular Europeans be obliged to go without alcohol in an Arab country, when it is not part of their personal agenda to submit to the prescriptions of the Qur'an? When seeking planning permission in India, should a westerner resort to giving bribes to officials, especially when most other business people do?

Of all the various theories of ethics which we have discussed, moral relativism may seem to offer the easiest solution. 'When in Rome do as the Romans do,' might well serve as the cultural relativist's motto. This would entail the western business executive being prepared to forgo alcohol in countries where it is shunned (notably Arab countries, but also in states like Utah in the USA, where the teetotal Mormons constitute the majority of the population). It would probably entail going along with the practice of bribery in countries where this is the norm; indeed it could even be argued that bribery is not so insidious in these countries as it is in the West, since – as we saw in chapter 3 – it is regarded as quite a normal way to supplement one's rather low wages.

We have already expressed our reservations about cultural relativism. However, there is one serious problem which it entails in the context of international business. If it is desirable for western executives abroad to conform to prevailing norms in the countries in which they do business, equally the same would have to apply in reverse. Immigrant workers in Europe and the USA ought, on this view, to be expected to conform to the norms of western society. This would have the consequence that the cultural relativist would probably make no concessions to the Sikh who insisted on the importance of the turban, the practising Jew who wished to observe the sabbath, the Muslim who wished to set aside time for prayer on Friday at noon, and so on. Such conclusions would certainly be unpalatable to most people; not only do they reflect an inherent intolerance to cultural diversity, but implementing them would be disastrous for industrial relations. More especially, they run counter to principles of religious freedom, which are inherently bound up with respecting the individual.

KANT'S 'KINGDOM OF ENDS'

Kant's principle of respect for persons seems to fit much better with more enlightened attitudes towards international business today. Respect for persons implies that each person is to be respected in terms of his or her own cultural identity, beliefs, values and goals; in his *Groundwork of the Metaphysic of Morals* Kant developed his principle of 'respect for persons' (see chapter 3) into a concept which he called the 'kingdom of ends'. What he meant was this. Each one of us has his or her own goals and ambitions ('ends'), but these have to be developed in a society which incorporates other individuals who are often striving for different and sometimes incompatible ends. Thus a company's shareholders may want profits, while some of the workers within a firm may be striving for higher wages, increased leisure, or perhaps the pursuit of a religious life. (Jews who observe the sabbath take the view that worship is to be preferred to profit making, at least for one day in the week.) How a company holds its own goals together with the sometimes different goals of workers is no easy matter; systems of systematic staff appraisal and development, if sensitively handled, provide one major opportunity for synthesizing an employee's objectives for personal development with the strategic plans of the company.

When we look outside a single company, we find that Kant's concept of the 'kingdom of ends' points to an even greater complexity. Employees whose 'ends' are not those of the firm have the choice between sacrificing their own personal goals in favour of the company's collective ones, or else leaving the firm. (The choice at least exists in theory; whether leaving is a practical option is a different matter, of course.) But if one's goals differ from those of society, one cannot opt out of society. If a distiller aims to maximize sales, he or she has to compromise this aim with the wider aim of society, namely that there should not be widespread drunkenness and disorderly behaviour on the streets or chronic alcoholism. In our society's 'kingdom of ends' there are laws and voluntary codes of practice regulating the sale and marketing of alcoholic beverages. Teetotallers, on the other hand, cannot expect to attain their possible goals of having everyone sign the pledge and having all wines and spirits thrown into the local river; if that is their 'end', then it must be compromised to take account of the will of the majority. So the distiller will not engage in high pressure sales of spirits, and will grant the anti-alcohol campaigner the right to persuade others with the freedom of speech to do so.

In many cases there can be little objection to conforming to the conventions of another culture; indeed it can only be advantageous to avoid the almost unlimited number of situations where one might cause amusement, embarrassment or even offence. Avoiding eating with the left hand in India and in Arab countries may require some conscious effort on the part of the westerner, but it can only serve to please easterners who regard the left hand as the 'toilet hand'.[3]

It is not merely matters of etiquette which are affected by international business culture. Moral dilemmas are more difficult to resolve. Consider the matter of 'dumping' goods on the Third World which are unsaleable in the West. Kant's concept of the 'kingdom of ends' might seem to provide a possible defence of such actions. It could be argued that if a Third World country does not want, say, medicines which are past their sell-by date to be marketed, it should define such an 'end' by passing relevant consumer laws which would outlaw such practices. (Six out of ten Third World countries have no consumer laws at all there; the principle of *caveat emptor* is alive and well.) Further, the exporter could argue (in utilitarian fashion) that it is better for poorer countries to have substandard medicinal supplies than none at all – as might well be the case if the sale of medicines was more closely regulated. Just as a country can define its ends by passing relevant pieces of legislation, so international business partners can define their ends and, on the basis of these decide whether they can conscientiously operate as immigrants with potentially different values and goals in a different culture.

[3] There is no justification, as far as the present writers can see, for the statement found in some business textbooks that the left hand is the hand the Devil uses.

For the private citizen pursuing his or her ends within society, opting out of that society is seldom a live option. But for business on the international scene, opting out and opting in are precisely the options of which astute companies take advantage, particularly the large multi-nationals. If a company's ends conflict significantly with those of a government (for example, if a firm wants to market its goods freely but is hampered by restricting legislation), then it can – and often does – find a country where its aims can be pursued more freely. Where the ends of different nations are in stark conflict, then a government will impose embargoes on trade, or pressure groups may attempt to introduce boycotts, as happened when many British citizens were enraged by the former apartheid system in South Africa.

The decision, then, often has to be whether to modify one's ends or not to engage in international business within a given country. Suppose a European firm wants to do business in Saudi Arabia and they need to send out a representative. The firm has an equal opportunities policy, but unfortunately the aim of securing equal opportunities regardless of sex cannot be realized in this context, for in Saudi Arabia a woman is not even permitted to drive a car, let alone engage in business negotiations with male counterparts. The firm therefore sends out a man. His first reaction on arriving after a long journey might understandably be to want a drink but alcohol is strictly prohibited, even for non-Muslims. If he were to protest that he did not subscribe to the Qur'an, he might well be informed that the Qur'an provides rules for all men and women, and not merely for those who call themselves Muslims. In any case, any infringement of the laws laid down in the Qur'an is *ipso facto* against the law of the land, and it is a normal presumption that we act within the law, unless the law itself is grossly immoral. Thus we have a clash of 'ends'; if business affairs are to take place successfully, accommodation of one culture to another, together with its aims and values, is essential.

OTHER POSSIBLE APPROACHES

There can be no easy solution about whether to co-operate as trade partners on the international scene or to sever relations because of differing ideologies. Should one boycott Saudi Arabia on account of their treatment of women, just as many British citizens boycotted South Africa? A deontologist might take the view that if a type of action is wrong (like treating one category of people unequally to others) then one should be seen actively to disapprove and to refuse to co-operate with such a system. A more utilitarian approach would suggest that co-operation and trade open the channels of communication, which mght serve in the longer term to help to persuade a country that a regime was oppressive and that it should be ended. But there is yet another way of looking at the situation along utilitarian lines; it could be argued that in Islamic countries men and women are happy with their respective roles, very few women are campaigning for 'women's rights', and the Qur'an prescribes that they should be well looked after by their husbands. Has not Saudi Arabia therefore already achieved the greatest happiness of the greatest number?

Indeed, it could further be argued that in terms of justice and equality, Islam officially teaches the equality of women. This is often a point which westerners find difficult to grasp; if one equates equality with what western feminists demand then Islam is at a very far remove from female equality and the emancipation of women. A man can divorce his wife, but a wife cannot divorce her husband; a man can (at least in theory) have four wives, but a wife may only have one husband; a woman can inherit, but only half the legacy of any brothers. (It should be borne in mind, however, that in his time Muhammad was a champion of women's rights; in pre-Islamic Mecca a woman had no inheritance rights what-soever, and, on being divorced, could simply be turned out of the husband's home without any financial provision at all.) However, Muslims typically contend that this is not inequality. When a women marries she benefits equally from the husband's double portion of his inheritance; although the husband is permitted to have four wives, there are stringent requirements to secure equality of treatment (they must not only have equal status in terms of wealth, but also of sexual attention), such that few contemporary Muslims in practice are polygamous. The claim is that Islamic women are 'equal but different'. It may with some justification also be argued: why does the Muslim definition of the equality of women have to correspond to that given by western feminists?

Business partners simply cannot afford to tread upon the sensitivities of their international trade partners. The task of business men and women is to sell goods and services, not to sell their ideologies. The fact that Saudi Arabia does not accept the ideals of western feminism may be a matter of regret to many Europeans, but the business executive is there to do business, not to serve as a social reformer or a missionary. This does not have to mean that the business executive must accept any prevailing standards abroad; a manager, faced with the alternatives of giving someone a bribe or else failing to obtain planning permission for erecting essential premises, can always pull out of the country which imposes such a dilemma.

We do not pretend to be able to offer an instant formula to enable those engaged in international business to resolve dilemmas about whether to accept prevailing norms in a foreign culture or whether one should pull out completely, or at least allow someone else to work in a culture with which one found ethical difficulties. In the long run, a company or a government might take the view that to refuse to trade would be economically disastrous and hence there was no choice. It might therefore be argued that co-operation with a morally reprehensible regime is the lesser of two evils.

To sum up this part of the discussion, we can suggest some questions which business men and women might ask themselves when faced with ethical dilemmas on the international front:-

1. How seriously do we disagree with the practices of the competing ideology?
2. To what extent does the competing ideology further the 'ends' of those who live within it? (For instance, Muslim women may be happy with their lot, whereas black South Africans have certainly not been, and have often urged westerners to apply sanctions.)
3. Where a culture has different practices, are these regarded as acceptable and justified accordingly? Or are they wide-spread moral lapses on the part of citizens? (Perhaps an Indian would regard bribery as a regrettable fact of life, while the Muslim would insist that the place assigned to women is prescribed by the Aur'an.)
4. What are the consequences of (a) co-operation and (b) no co-operation? What is the likelihood of success in changing attitudes, if the westerner firmly believes they are mistaken? (But it is worth remembering that those in a foreign culture may be asking similar questions in connection with the West.)
5. Is there some way in which the 'ends' of the immigrant business partner and those of the host country might be jointly attainable? Can one set of partners be true to their own consciences while acknowledging the fundamental freedoms of others?

Whatever policy one adopts on these ethical culture clashes, it is important to try to understand, as far as possible, the global system of thought on which specific practices are based (such as the Hindu caste system, the Islamic system of law, and so on). Chris Patten, the

Governor of Hong Kong, betrayed a woeful ignorance of Buddhist culture when he said, in connection with the presumed lack of co-operation by the Chinese, that there was a prevalent saying that 'it was difficult to clap with one hand'.[4] By misquoting the Zen *koan*, 'What is the sound of one hand clapping?', a problem posed by Zen masters to enable the aspirant to reflect on the enigmatic nature of life, Patten assumed, incorrectly, that it meant that it takes two to make a bargain. Not only do such *faux pas* send signals to the host culture that the immigrant westerner feels little need to take that culture seriously; but it also shows that small fragments of information and advice do not enable business executives, diplomats and negotiators to anticipate new problems which inevitably arise. It is not sufficient merely to take individual pieces of specific advice about protocol abroad. One may be told not to ask for alcohol in parts of the Middle East, but does that mean that alcohol-free lager is acceptable? A non-Jew might know that Jews avoid pork, but then wonder why they seemed unwilling to accept an invitation to a pork-free meal which the former had arranged,[5] not realizing that kitchen utensils and combinations of food are also covered by Jewish dietary laws.

It was Wittgenstein who stated that understanding an activity entailed the participant 'knowing how to go on'. We cannot understand, say, arithmetic if we know only a few piecemeal equations like $1 + 1 = 2$, $2 + 3 = 5$ and $3 + 5 = 8$. Unless we understand what the activity of adding means and how it is accomplished, we cannot begin to become mathematicians. Rote learning the answers to simple equations is only a small step towards understanding arithmetic, but once we know **how to add**, we need no longer rely on individual snippets of memory and we can cope with new problems which we have never encountered before. The reader may not have been told specifically that $135 + 293 = 428$, but because he or she knows the relevant rules of arithmetic, this new sum can be worked out.

Ethics is not dissimilar. It is easy enough to memorize and copy individual pieces of advice, such as those the travel guides mention, but what is to happen in those situations which are not covered by the particular and somewhat fragmented instructions? Knowing that Jews and Muslims do not eat pork only takes a small step of the way towards

---

[4] Reported on 24 October 1992.
[5] In order to understand the reason, one has to know rather more about Jewish dietary law, and the principles upon which it is based. Isolated rules cannot enable the business executive or the student to make further inferences.

understanding and co-operating, and it does not enable us to anticipate new situations which cannot be coped with by this simple piece of information. If, however, the business negotiator knows that such dietary restrictions are connected with a wider system of religious law (the Talmud-Torah and *shari'ah* law respectively), and understands something about what that means, then he or she can be alerted to the fact that there are likely to be further religious and ethical obligations, and perhaps can have some understanding of what these are likely to be. To understand a set of complicated ethical, religious and political ideals may seem a tall order for the western business partner, who is probably unqualified in religion and politics (and perhaps ethics), but unfortunately there are no short cuts to successful cross-cultural business negotiation.

SOME WORDS OF ADVICE

We have stated that there are no easy solutions to the problem of adjusting to cultures which have different values and ideologies, but can offer several pieces of advice, which, if implemented, will make for more harmonious business relationships and greater business success. These are not 'top tips' which can be instantly put into operation; putting them into practice will involve considerable supplementary study and development of personal attitudes and skills. They are certainly not the kinds of 'home truths' which can be read on a aircraft and put into immediate operation.

- **Do not assume that 'we' are normal and 'others' are not.** This is western arrogance, and ignores the obvious point that westerners are in a minority when they are in a different culture. Our own value systems will probably need to adjust.

- **Always respect the beliefs and values of others.** This means refusing to dismiss them as 'superstitious', 'illogical' or 'unscientific'.

- **Find out as much as possible about the culture with which you are working.** This involves studying its political system, its ideology, its religions, its 'management culture' – in fact everything one can reasonably find.

- **Do not judge a country by stereotypes.** Often the media portray Sikhs as terrorists or Muslims as belligerent fanatics. Nothing could be further from the truth. It is surprising that when we have asked students about how to prepare for international business negotiations, the consideration of how to avoid being taken as a hostage is often at the forefront of their minds! Needless to say, the vast majority of business men and women are not taken hostage, and there is a far greater risk of being injured in a traffic accident. No one in the business world refuses to carry out their duties because they might get run down by a car.

- **Do not expect others to act contrary to their consciences.** The chances are that they will not do so in any case. Equally it is important to be true to one's own conscience, and sometimes this may involve considering whether you are the right person to operate at international level.

- **Do not underestimate the role played by religion in shaping people's thought and method of doing business.** If religion is unimportant to the reader, it must not be assumed that the majority of business partners share this value; they do not.

- **Talk to people who have already visited the country in which you will be the guest.** Find out the ways in which they found their experience rewarding, and possible problems they encountered. If they were faced with ethical dilemmas, how did they resolve them?

- **Try to speak at least a few words in the language of the culture in which you work.** This may seem a minor point, but unfortunately the British have attracted the worst reputation of all countries in failing to accommodate and adapt. One Greek colleague remarked to one of the authors that the British seldom learn even basic greetings like 'kal'emera' (Good morning). It costs little to do this, and shows that one does not expect foreign trade partners to do all the running.

- **Are you the right person to engage in international business?** Not everyone has the sensitivity and patience which it demands, and many business executives' expertise is better channelled elsewhere.

- **Finally, do not rely on a few 'top tips' picked up on easy guides which are freely available at airports.** If this is the beginning of your preparation for conducting international business, then you should cancel your flight!

INTRODUCING THE READINGS

In the readings which follow, we have attempted to span a number of business cultures. First, Haire, Ghiselli and Porter argue that differences in 'management culture' cannot simply be equated with differences in political or economic systems. We follow this with an extract from George England's important research on international business culture. England addressed the question of precisely **how** different different business cultures really are, examining which values managers took seriously and for what reason. England's study has the interesting feature of being thoroughly empirical; it is often assumed that moral beliefs and value systems are matters of pure theory, found in key textbooks or discussed in the confines of an academic seminar. England has shown that it is possible, and indeed important, to study values empirically, and his work is the result of collecting a formidable amount of data. It is therefore perhaps unsurprising that England was forced to confine himself merely to five business cultures: the USA, Japan, Korea, India and Australia. The study is interesting because he does not necessarily confirm our intuitive preconceptions about congruence and divergence amongst these different cultures on matters of morals.

There follows a series of readings based on different business cultures. Waqar Masood Khan outlines the Islamic alternative to the western system of borrowing and investing. Western students often wonder how an interest-free economic system is possible, and Khan provides an explanation not only of how it works, but what its advantages are. We then include a Jewish perspective from Meir Tamari, Director of Jerusalem's Institute for Ethics in Economics, who shows how matters of market entry, competition and employment (which we have discussed in earlier chapters) are dealt with by interpreting the Talmud-Torah. An extract from H. N. S. Karunatilake's *This Confused Society* argues from a Buddhist standpoint that contemporary western culture is based on greed, or *tanha* (craving), and that a Buddhist alternative based on *dana* (giving) can be devised. Finally, we include a very brief extract from Richard Tanner Pascale and Anthony G. Athos, *The Art of Japanese Management*. In so short a space we cannot hope to give an adequate account of the basis and nature of values in Japanese business, but Matsushita's statement of his 'spiritual values', his 'basic business principles' and the 'employee's creed' give at least a flavour of how Japanese management perceives the relationship between the individual employee, the company, and society at large. All three readings highlight ways of ordering society which might serve as alternatives to the methods employed within western corporate capitalism.

Managerial thinking: an international study

MASON HAIRE, EDWIN E. GHISELLI AND LYMAN W. PORTER

The map in Figure 1 is only partly facetious. It shows which countries are close to one another in terms of the similarities of managerial attitudes. This is exactly what the book is about: managers' thinking in different countries. The text will provide the detail for the groupings and distances we have represented, but the map does reasonable justice to the diversity. Unfortunately, the map is limited to two dimensions, whereas managerial views distribute themselves along a number of dimensions. In any case, it will probably do us all good to remember that, in addition to the geography of longitude and latitude, there is also a geography of motivation and attitude. As spatial geography shrinks with transportation and communication, it becomes doubly important for us all to concern ourselves with the psychological geography of neighborhoods and clusters.

This is the report of a research study on the attitudes of managers in various countries. It asks the questions: When managers think about managing, are their ideas all pretty much the same, or does managerial thinking differ from country to country? And, if it does differ, how do the countries group themselves together? Is there a readily discernible pattern in managers' responses by clusters or groups of countries? To answer these questions simply for the moment, it seems clear from the data reported here that there is a very high degree of similarity among managers' attitudes in all the countries studied. On the other hand, of all the differences observed among managers, about 25 percent of the variations were associated with national differences, so that there is an identifiable determinant of attitudes within each country. Furthermore, these national differences do tend to group themselves into intelligible patterns. These two points – the similarity and difference of managerial attitudes, and the clustering by countries – will, of course, have to be developed in considerable detail as the report progresses.

This introductory chapter will touch briefly on:

1. the form of the research instrument;
2. the problem of translation;
3. the sample surveyed; and
4. findings.

The reader can, if he likes, skip over the first three topics, since they are designed only to provide enough information to make the subsequent chapters on detailed findings more easily understood. If one wishes to avoid preliminaries, it is possible to plunge right into findings, and come back later, if necessary, to see how they were

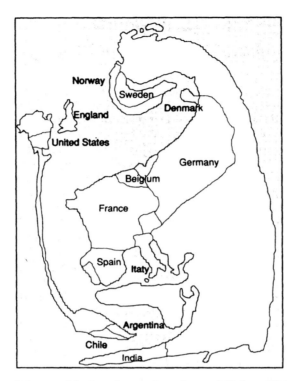

Figure 1 Map of the world after the explorations of Haire, Ghiselli and Porter.

obtained. A more orderly method, however, would be to carry forward at least a cursory view of the research procedures.

The form of the research instrument

To answer the research questions stated above, we prepared a questionnaire which each manager-respondent could complete for himself. . . . This form of tapping attitudes has real drawbacks – among them being that it makes it harder to go into great depth in the exploration of attitudes. Its virtue, however – and the consideration that seemed overriding in this case – is that it is possible to assure oneself that each respondent answered exactly the same questions, and that the results are strictly comparable from one group to another. Ths seemed an important exchange – giving up some depth for exactitude – in this case. As the problem of understanding managers' attitudes in other countries has grown, we have had a host of somewhat casual tourist-anecdotal reports on 'What managers are like in Transylvania or

Zenda.' The problem in reading these reports is to know just what it is that one learns from them. Did the studies raise the same issues fom country to country? With the same kinds of people? Can the studies be compared with one another?

An impressionistic study – or even an interview study with a small, casually selected sample – of the way an institution is imbedded in a culture encounters real pitfalls. It is easy to bring to the fore the problems of capital formation in one country, the loose labor market in a second, and family succession in management in a third. Unless variables are checked in each country, however, their relative weights remain a puzzle. In one country, friendly government officials may be easy sources of information; in another, it may be managers of manufacturing; in a third, bankers. Are the observed differences characteristic of the country, or are they the somewhat inadvertent results of the kind of people chosen? Finally, the culture itself is hard to separate from the impression of the institution. The *gemüilichkeit* of one country, the *bonhomie* of a second, or the studied casualness of a third, may provide unwitting distortion in one's view of the scene. For all these reasons, a very careful attempt was made in this study to ask identical questions of each manager, and to ask them of the same kinds of managers in each country so that the answers could be compared with as little error as possible.

The content of the questionnaire was limited to three main areas: Leadership; the role of the manager in his culture; and the motives managers want to satisfy on a job and the degree to which managers feel these motives are satisfied. (This is the sequence in which these topics are treated in the text, although they appeared in a somewhat altered order in the questionnaire itself.)

The first set of questions – on leadership – consisted of 8 items to which the manager responded by checking on a 5-point scale ranging from 'strongly agree' to 'strongly disagree.' The items were constructed logically to provide a series of steps from a somewhat unilateral, autocratic approach to management, to a more group-oriented team approach. They covered managers' beliefs in the capacity of subordinates, and their view of the efficacy of participation, of sharing information, and of providing opportunities for internal self-control on the job.

A second part of the questionnaire provided cognitive descriptions of the managerial role; they were obtained by use of a Semantic Differential format. . . .

Finally, a third part of the questionnaire, dealing with motivation, was made up of a series of 11 items designed to elicit responses geared to the Maslow hierarchy of needs for Security, Social needs, Esteem needs, and needs for Autonomy and Self-Actualization. . . . For each item, three questions were asked: How much is there now (of the opportunity to satisfy a given need)? How much should there be? And, how important is it? The respondent answered each question by checking a 7-point scale labeled from minimum to maximum. The difference between 'How much is there now?' and 'How much should there be?' provides a measure of the satisfaction of a need in question.

In addition to these three main parts of the questionnaire, a final page asked for demographic data relating to age of respondent, size of company, and the like.

The problem of translation

The research was faced immediately with the problem of translating the questions, since they were, in each case, presented in the managers' own native language. Translation presents two special difficulties in such a comparative study: First, the language of management today is largely English – and American English at that; second, a study of cultures that approaches the comparative problem through language is immediately trapped in the fact that the language itself is part of the culture. To whatever extent one disregards the differences in connotation in the interest of comparability, one may be spuriously removing true cultural differences which are germane and important to the study itself. Questions in this study had to be rephrased or eliminated to meet this difficulty; and special steps had to be taken to try to assess the cultural loading on terms related to management.

Americans speak frequently of 'leadership.' The term itself, in any simple sense, is probably translatable only into the Scandinavian languages. The Latin countries tend to use the English word. Even before *Il Duce* and *Der Führer* gave special historical connotations to the term, it was not the same in direct translation. We also speak blithely in the United States about 'the management team.' The French would use the same word for 'team' (*une équipe*) in sports that they would use for describing an hourly paid work group or gang; however, the word would sound distinctly odd if used to refer to the policy-making group. Is this a difference in language alone, or is it a cultural difference reflecting part of the very comparative difference in management philosophy under study? To keep the responses comparable, words like 'leader' and 'team' had to be eliminated, even though their elimination may have resulted in the loss of some of the substance of the differences under investigation. The very word 'manager' is almost impossible to translate simply. Its Latin root in *manus* makes it mean 'to handle,' but in the Latin languages the cognate word is used almost only to refer to the management of a horse by a rider. One 'manages' the horse by tugging at the reins – a more unilateral and directive sense of the term than would be perfectly comfortable for most American managers. Even the British use of the term 'managing director' implies partly a different corporate organization and partly a different view of the process of managing. The language of management is a problem for the research designer. For the person who wants some feeling for the meaning of the function of management in a culture, the variations in language provide a rich source of insights.

To deal with the problem of language, each questionnaire was translated from English into the language in question by a native of the country involved. The foreign-language version was then translated back into English, independently, by a second person to whom the language was native. This often led to a process of adjustment until a preliminary translation was obtained. This version was modified in the country of use (by conference with bilingual social scientists and managers) in order to get a formulation that was easy and idiomatic as well as linguistically correct. In the final stage of this process, the translated versions seemed reasonably satisfactory. . . .

The sample surveyed

The results of this study are based on a sample of 3641 managers from 14 countries. . . . In each country, the sample is drawn from many companies and from various ages, levels of management, and sizes of companies. In general, nationalized and quasi-nationalized industries were excluded from the sample, though in some countries the defining line was so fuzzy that it was difficult to apply this criterion rigidly. Managerial cooperation in the research came through the medium of employers' associations, universities, management training centers, foundations, and individual companies. It is perhaps worth noting that in all the countries, managers were most cooperative in the study. In only two cases – one in England and one in the United States – did groups explicitly refuse to take part in the research.

Is this a representative sample of management? It is a broad and varied sample by which we attempted to represent the dominant dimensions of management in each country. It is not, however, strictly a representative sample. To produce such a sample, one might do one of two things. First, armed with a complete list of all the companies in a country, one might draw a random sample of them. Several things argue against this method. One is that no such list is generally available. Another is that if such a sample were drawn, there is no guarantee that the companies would all cooperate; and bias would be introduced, just as it is in our sample, because those companies who are willing to take part in studies of management probably have managerial attitudes different from those of companies who are less approachable. Finally, such a random sample would draw less heavily on large and medium-sized firms. While this would represent the population, it seems likely that these larger firms are opinion leaders in a sense that gives their responses greater diagnostic and predictive power than the responses of the more numerous tiny companies.

The second course in drawing a representative sample of management would be to sample proportionately along various dimensions – age, education, company size, etc. – in such a way as to reproduce the makeup of a country's population of managers. Unfortunately, again, no such knowledge of the distribution of the population of managers exists; nor even of the relevant dimensions along which the distributions should be made. Even in Sweden and the United States – probably the two most researched-upon groups of managers – we are painfully lacking in such demographic detail. Consequently, in the sample represented here, an attempt was made to sample different industries and different companies within an industry; different parts of the country; sizes of companies; and levels of management. It is not possible, therefore, to say that if another sample were drawn with the same rules we would expect the same results plus or minus a determinable error term. The sample was drawn impressionistically and sometimes opportunistically, but it is a broad and diverse group in each case, and probably comes close to representing the country involved. Of even more importance, where other studies of management exist, our proportions agree reasonably well with those reported by other research workers. The tables of demographic data . . . show marked differences, in some cases, from one country to another. Are these to be interpreted as characteristic differences between countries, or as a failure of the sampling to draw upon a uniform population? Probably, to a large extent, they are characteristic differences. For example, in Spain, Italy, Belgium, and France, about 25 percent of the managers professed to have a major capital interest in the company they managed. In the other countries, this representation of equity was extremely rare. Clearly, to equate countries on this variable would vigorously distort the management community in many instances. Again, in most countries, the modal age of the managers surveyed was 35–45. In Germany, Italy, and India, it was 30–34; in Japan it was 50–54. It is not at all clear that the modal ages should be the same from country to country. In the exceptional cases noted here, major building or rebuilding of industry characterizes the postwar period, and one might expect these countries to differ from, for example, Chile, Argentina, and Spain. In a good many of the cases represented, the variation in demographic detail from country to country must probably be accepted as a characteristic of the country, and as one of the early steps toward a description of the population of managers.

A preliminary look at findings

As was suggested before, the two basic questions of our study are: Are the managers' attitudes the same or different? How do the countries cluster together? To these, a third can be added: Within the segments of the study – leadership, the concept of the manager's role, and motivation – how do countries and managers differ from one another? In this chapter, the briefest possible report of the highlights relevant to these questions will be indicated without any of the supporting evidence or detail. For these supporting points, the reader should follow each of the issues through the chapter devoted to it.

To answer the question 'Do managers from different countries differ from one another?' two figures were obtained. On any one of the scales in any of the three parts of the questionnaire, the total variation of the entire sample of 3641 managers was computed. This figure – the standard deviation of the scores of all managers – gives an estimate of the difference observed among managers. On the other hand, the standard deviation of the means of countries gives an estimate of the differences among countries in the sample. If the standard deviation of the means of countries were to be as large as the standard deviation of all managers – so that the ratio of the two is 1.00 – it would mean that all of the observed variation among managers was associated with national origin. In this case, the differences between managers could be completely accounted for by their country, with no room for individual differences of opinion of any other sort – a most unlikely situation. On the other hand, if all of the countries had the same average score, so that the standard deviation of their means was 0, it would signify that all of the observed variations in managers' attitudes were ascribable to individual differences, and none to country of origin. In this case, the ratio of the two standard deviations would be 0.

Among the three parts of the questionnaire the following ratios were obtained:

Attitudes and assumptions underlying management practices, .32; cognitive descriptions of the managerial role, .26; needs and need satisfaction, .27 – an average of .28. This means that of all the variation observed, about 28 percent was associated with national groupings; the differences among individuals are about 2½ times as great as the differences among countries. The three ratios reported here are remarkably similar, suggesting considerable stability in the pooled estimate. In each case, the ratio was made up of sub-parts: Four scores for attitudes and assumptions related to managerial practices, five factors in the descriptions of the managerial role, and three measures of motivation. These twelve measures also show rather close agreement, ranging from .17 to .48, with only three varying by more than .05 from the mean. The estimate seems reliable. If all differences arising from national origin were eliminated, the difference in managers' attitudes would be reduced by about 25 to 30 percent.

Is this difference arising from countries a big difference? It is, of course, impossible to answer this question in any absolute sense. The difference measured here is a relative one – the ratio of individual differences to national differences. However, two things can be said clearly: National differences make a consistent and substantial contribution to the differences in managers' attitudes. On the other hand, in terms of the possible differences in response to the items on the questionnaire, all of the responses tend to cluster fairly closely at one end of the scale. One might take the position that being a manager is a way of life and that, as such, a French manager might be expected to be more similar to an Indian manager, say, than to a French non-manager. The considerable similarity among managers' responses throughout the instrument lends some real support to this belief in the universality of managerial philosophy. On the other hand, one might believe that the fact of being a Frenchman, for instance, outweighs all else; so that a French manager is more like another non-managerial Frenchman in his attitudes about management than he is like an Indian manager. In support of this belief, there is the fact that 25 to 30 percent of the observed difference can be attributed to national origin. The cultural influence is present and substantial. It is not overwhelming.

This point about the simultaneous existence of similarity and diversity needs to be dealt with in a little more detail. It is an important point, and one that will come up again throughout the book. There is a very strong and consistent tendency for managers to express similar beliefs about management. In this sense, the values, perceptions, and attitudes of management can be said to be universal. To be a manager is to have a philosophy of management much like that of other managers everywhere. This similarity is so strong that the national groups, taken as units, tend to be remarkably similar. Popular stereotypes of the democratic Swedes, the Prussian mentality, and the tradition-ridden Japanese seem to demand widely and strikingly disparate scale positions on any measures of managerial strategy and tactics. These notions are not supported, insofar as they imply large and radical differences among the countries. Managers are so similar that countries find themselves, perforce, in the same region of the scale. However, in this considerable unanimity, a real diversity among countries exists. As has been mentioned, of all the differences among managers, 25 to 30 percent of the variation is associated with national origin. There are differences between countries, and the differences are real and substantial. Moreover, they cluster together in intelligible units which help to give us insight into the nature and origin of the observed differences.

In order to answer the second main research question – How do the countries group together? – each country's pattern of scores was compared with that of every other country. If, across a number of scales, country *B* is high when country *A* is high, and low when *A* is low, their scores are highly correlated and their patterns of response are similar. To the extent to which this tendency to vary together across a series of scales diminishes, the correlation and similarity diminish. In this manner, countries were compared each to each to see which ones are most similar to which other ones, and what clusters or groupings of countries come out of the data.... One further technical word: In obtaining these correlations, a total of 94 scales was used from the three parts of the questionnaire, weighted to give each part – leadership, role descriptions, and motivation – equal representation. The scores used were standard scores of the entire population; they weighted countries equally, regardless of sample size.

The first thing that is clear from these intercorrelations is that some countries are much more similar to one another than they are to other countries. The correlations run from .89 (Argentina and Chile) to −.76 (India and Norway, and India and Sweden). These figures indicate, on the one hand, a very close similarity; and on the other, a rather high degree of dissimilarity. Of the 91 comparisons – the fourteen countries with each other – about 20 percent showed no consistent relationship (correlations between .15 and −.15); about 20 percent were very dissimilar (more than −.40), and about 20 percent were fairly similar (more than .30). The countries are not all alike or uniformly scattered. Some of them are like others, and some are different from others. What patterns can we find in their relationships?

Major clusters of countries appear in a fairly simple way from these relationships: The Nordic-European countries (Norway, Denmark, Germany, and Sweden); the Latin-European countries (France, Spain, Italy, and Belgium); the Anglo-American pair; a group which might be called Developing countries (Argentina, Chile, and India); and, finally, Japan, which stands by itself and does not fit with any of the countries or clusters. These four clusters and one lone country have the following characteristic: Countries within a cluster are similar to one another and dissimilar to those in other clusters. Within a cluster, excluding Japan, the average correlation or similarity of one country to another is about .57. The average correlation with countries outside one's own cluster is −.38. In only two exceptional cases out of 37 possible comparisons is one country's correlation with another country outside its cluster higher than the average correlation within the country's own cluster. The conclusion is inescapable: There are groups of countries. The countries within each group are more like one another than they are like other countries. Moreover, it should be stressed that these clusterings are simple empirical facts which appear in the data when all the managers are asked the same questions. They are not *a priori* logical groupings forced on the data as a result of prejudged notions about relationships, but are the relationships which stand out from an analysis of the responses as they are.

The thing that emerges most clearly from the clusters is the strong pattern of cultural influence in these data. The first three clusters – Nordic, Latin, and Anglo-American – all include countries with strong bonds of similarity in language and religion; and with many common elements in their cultural background. Indeed, in one case, where a country was divided into two samples, the same trend was evident. In Belgium it was necessary to use a French-language questionnaire in the South and a Flemish one in the North. Even though the two parts of Belgium tended to go together, their differences tended to split along cultural lines. North Belgium, with its Protestant history, moved in the direction of the Nordic cluster, while predominantly Catholic South Belgium was more like the other Latin countries. The influence of cultural background and a broad sweep of values is unmistakable.

At first glance, the first three clusters seem to be language clusters, tempting one to ask: Is this merely an artifact of translation? Two responses seem clearly relevant here: First, one of the tightest clusters – Argentina, Chile, and India – is not a language cluster in that sense. Indeed, it cuts across two of the languages represented in earlier clusters. Clearly, the empirical findings do not support the explanation on the basis of language. Secondly, the close relation of language and culture, as was mentioned under the heading 'The Problem of Translation,' appears again here, as the two are, to some extent, inextricable.

At this point, let us consider another explanation that is often suggested in dealing with national differences in managerial styles. The bulk of comparative studies of management has been done by economists. As might be expected, they tend to find economic explanations for observed differences. As a result, there is a strong suggestion in these studies – though it is seldom stated or defended very explicitly – that differences in managerial style and strategy are primarily associated with differences in level of industrialization. The statement is usually made with a passing obeisance to the fact that cultural differences are present; but, after this brief mention, the cultural factor is ignored. The groupings of countries that emerge from these data fit remarkably poorly with any hypothesis flowing from the level of industrialization. The tight cluster of Spain, France, Belgium, and Italy, for example, or that of Norway, Sweden, Denmark, and Germany, provide a very mixed bag in terms of industrialization, but an understandable homogeneity in cultural strain. On any of the conventional measures of industrialization – percentage of non-farm workers, for instance, or production of fabricated goods – there is a wide gap between Spain, on the one hand, and France and Belgium, on the other; or between Norway and Denmark, and the more industrialized Sweden and Germany. Yet, in responding to questions about managing, these countries hang very closely together. In the Nordic cluster, for example, the average intercorrelation of each of the four countries with each other is about .40. Of the 40 correlations of these four countries with the ten others in the study, only 1 (Norway – England = .43) is of that order. Twenty-nine of the 40 correlations are negative. In the Latin cluster, similarly, the average intercorrelation is about .30. Of the 40 external comparisons only 3 are of that order; 29 are negative. The cultural groups are similar on these data, and different from the other countries.

This argument is not meant to suggest that the level of industrialization – or its history, pattern, and nature – are of no importance in determining managerial style and strategy. The data do not justify such a conclusion, and it does not seem useful to allow the explanation to degenerate into a simple *either-or* set of alternatives. Indeed, the Argentina-Chile-India cluster, cutting across language and cultural homogeneities as it does, is striking evidence of the effects of level of industrialization coming out in these data. What is clear, however, is the powerful strain of cultural differences in management thinking that appears repeatedly and consistently across these countries on these data.

Some areas of implications

The cultural patterns in managerial strategy that emerge here would seem to have immediate and practical implications for managers, particularly for those interested in international business, in establishing operations in other countries, or in developing foreign nationals within their own organizations. Three main issues stand out: (1) the opportunity to examine and understand managerial attitudes in one's own country; (2) the implication for firms sending managers to work in foreign climates; and (3) the problems of executive development across cultures. Let us take them up briefly, one at a time.

The responses of managers from any one of the countries provide a kind of profile of the country's managerial attitudes. What does the manager think is the way to lead? What does he see to be the role of the manager? What does he hope for from his job? What does he get? How dissatisfied is he? How do variables such as age, ownership, education, level in the firm, size of company, and the like, cut across these attitudes? It would seem to be a worthwhile exercise for groups of managers in any country to examine these profiles and ask themselves: Is this the way it is here? Is this the way it should be here? And if it is not: What can we do about it? The possibility of comparing one's own profile with those of other countries, similar and different, goes a long way toward heightening understanding of the meaning of a particular pattern, and sharpening the evaluation of the observed state of affairs. In these days of an intensified competitive climate among countries in international business, such an analysis and understanding of one's own strengths and weaknesses is of special importance.

The proper training program for managers in overseas operations is intimately bound up with these cultural clusters, too. Many companies in the flush of international expansion feel that they have only enough time to pick the man with the right functional specialty, check to see that he has been relatively adaptable on his last few local assignments, and ship him off. What more can be done? If there is time enough, something on local competitive history, anti-trust or cartel climates, and a word on politics about does it. Typically, almost nothing is said about the relation between the culture to which the man is going and the managerial attitudes he will meet. The strong groupings of countries along cultural lines here suggest that this variable should not be neglected. A well-equipped manager should go into a country with some knowledge of the cultural streams relevant to management's thinking there. At the very least, some knowledge of the country's religious values, political climate, and literary traditions seems essential. More than that, however, he should be at home with a series of questions like: What is the meaning of egalitarianism and what form does it take? Is there an elite? How is it recognized? What is honesty? How is it seen? What assumptions about the nature of human nature are implicit in, for instance, notions of original sin or of salvation – in a single-vote principle – in the role of caste or family? How are industriousness and self-actualization seen? How hard should one work? How much time should one invest in his family, his work, his friends? Questions like these are typically far removed from the portfolio of a manager going to a new country. Yet they are the clues to the cultural values which shape the managerial attitudes with which he will have to deal. The evidence of cultural clusters makes these questions imperative. So far, we have solved the problem by sending the best possible men and letting them learn the answers on the spot, or replacing them if they don't. The pressures of time and numbers mean that we can no longer afford this solution.

Finally, a consideration of the cultural influences on management's thinking leads us to the reverse process: training foreign nationals for leadership positions. In many cases, the tacit assumption seems to have been made that one can take a man from whatever pattern of life one finds him in and add a set of managerial and industrial skills, leaving the rest of the organization of his life unchanged. The close relation suggested by our data between general cultural patterns and managerial style and strategy seems to deny this. The problem is not just to inject our techniques of leadership and control into an otherwise unchanged man, but to help him to develop the whole view and practice of life that goes with certain kinds of managerial philosophy. In a sense, you can't make a manager without making a man. To try to abstract a potential manager's general values of life, and to manipulate in a training program only the on-the-job practices of leadership and management, is a form of latter-day sociological colonialism which will probably have results similar to those of the geographical expansionist colonialism of an earlier day, managerial strategy and practices are inextricably linked with general cultural values. To try to deal with one while keeping the other aloof and inviolate is, probably, eventually futile. It is necessary to go *all* the way in.

Subsequent chapters will cover more specifically – country by country and point by point – the manager's attitudes and assumptions underlying leadership techniques, his role, his motivations and satisfactions, the effects of his age and level, size of the firm, and the like. Through this wealth of detail, the reader is urged to keep in mind the central questions: How different are these managers' views from one another? What patterns are there to the differences? Where do the differences come from? In a sense, the respondents are all talking about the same thing – managing. Since we are all increasingly going to work together in these areas across countries, it becomes doubly important to recognize and understand the similarities and differences in managers' viewpoints.

Managers and their value systems

GEORGE W. ENGLAND

This article provides a summary and implications from the study of the personal value systems of over 2500 managers in five countries: Australia, Japan, Korea, India, and the United States of America. Its results and implications stem from a long-term research project aimed at the description, measurement and understanding of the personal value systems of managers and their impact on behavior.

A personal value system is considered to be a relatively permanent perceptual framework, likely to shape and influence the general nature of an individual's behavior. Values are similar to attitudes but are more deeply embedded in the personality and more permanent.

A personal value system, as used here, more closely resembles ideology or philosophy than any attitude. In some respects, an individual's personal value system at any given time can be thought of as that integrated group of attitudes and beliefs resulting from the interaction of his physical or biological self with his environment.

Basic rationale

A framework was developed to describe the relationship of values to behavior for managers. This framework was subsequently used to develop a measurement approach to personal value systems that

1. was representative of contemporary value theory[1]
2. was designed in light of the characteristics of the group being studied (managers), and

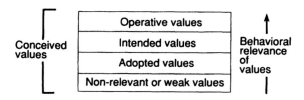

Figure 1 Value framework.

3. was clearly in accord with the primary role of values in influencing behavior (behavioral relevance of values).

Several major classes of overlapping values are shown in the framework in Figure 1. All possible values which might be held by an individual or by a specific group constitute the total value space and are known as *potential values*. The potential values are composed of two types: *nonrelevant* or *weak values* for a specific group or individual (those which would have little or no impact on behavior) and *conceived values* (those which may be translated from the intentional state into behavior). Conceived values are comprised of operative values (those which have a relatively high probability of being translated from the intentional state into actual behavior); *intended values* (those which are viewed as important, but may have only a moderate probability of being translated from the intentional state into behavior because of situational factors); and *adopted values* (those which are less a part of the personality structure of the individual and affect behavior largely because of situational factors).

Methodology

The development of a Personal Values Questionnaire (PVQ) was based on the rationale that the meanings attached by an individual to a carefully specified set of concepts will provide a useful description of his personal value system, which may in turn be related to his behavior in systematic ways. This approach to personal values measurement was influenced by the work of Charles Osgood[2] and his associates and represents an adaptation of their methodology.

To specify a set of concepts relevant to the personal value systems of managers, 200 concepts were selected from literature dealing with (a) organizations and (b) individual and group behavior. Ideological and philosophical concepts were also included to represent major belief systems. A panel of experts reduced the original 200 concepts to a set of 96 which was further trimmed to 66 based on pilot studies.

In the PVQ for managers, four scales are used to represent two modes of valuation. The primary power mode of valuation utilized is the *importance* scale. To the extent that it is possible to determine a consistent rationale as to why an individual or a specific group assigns importance to certain concepts, one has a reasonable basis for determining the behavioral significance of different classes of values. In this process, three secondary modes of valuation were developed from the literature.

The *pragmatic* mode of valuation suggests an individual's evaluative framework is primarily guided by success-failure considerations: e.g. will a certain course of action work or not; how successful or unsuccessful is it apt to be. The pragmatic mode of valuation runs throughout much of the literature dealing with managers.

The *ethical-moral* mode of valuation implies ethical considerations influence behavior toward actions and decisions which are judged to be 'right' and away from those judged to be 'wrong.'

The *affect or feeling* mode of valuation suggests a framework guided by *hedonism*; one behaves in ways that increase pleasure and decrease pain.

In the PVQ, the pragmatic mode of valuation is represented by a 'successful' scale; the ethical-moral mode of valuation is obtained through a 'right' scale; and the affect or feeling mode of valuation is measured through use of a 'pleasant' scale.

A combination of primary and secondary modes of valuation was thought to be a better behavioral predictor than either mode alone. For example, if Manager A is pragmatically oriented (i.e., concepts which were important to him were also seen as being successful as opposed to right or pleasant), his behavior would be predicted best by viewing it as a joint function of those concepts he thought were important and successful. In a more general sense, an individual's behavior (insofar as it is influenced by his personal values) is best explained by utilizing both those things he considers important and his primary personal orientation.

For a pragmatically oriented individual, behavior is best indicated by those concepts considered important and successful; for a morally-ethically oriented individual, behavior is best predicted by those concepts considered important and right; for an affect-oriented individual, behavior is best predicted by those concepts considered important and pleasant.

A theoretical framework of the relationship of values to behavior is presented in Figure 10.3. This framework[3] attempts to delineate the relationship of values to behavior for managers and is used in interpreting data about the personal value systems of managers.

The framework indicates two major ways in which values can influence behavior; *behavior channeling* and *perceptual screening*. Behavior channeling is illustrated by the behavior of an individual who places a high value on honesty and integrity when he is approached with a proposition which involves deception and questionable ethics. His behavior would be channeled away from the questionable proposition due to his operative values. Behavior channeling represents a rather direct influence on behavior in contrast to the more indirect influence of perceptual screening. Perceptual screening underlies the common expressions, 'he hears only what he agrees with', and 'you can't teach an old dog new tricks.' The power of personal values to select, filter, and influence what one 'sees' and 'hears' is well known in common experience as well as in the study of behavior.

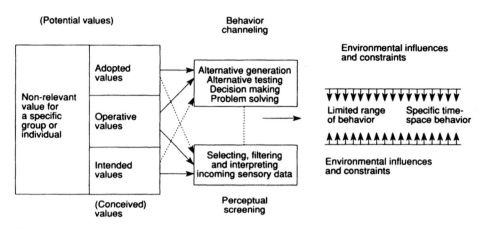

Figure 2 The relationship of values to behavior.

The impact of values on behavior must be considered in relation to environmental influences and constraints before specific statements can be made about an individual behaving in a certain way at a given time. Values are one part of the story, but certainly not the whole story. (See Figure 2.)

Our starting point is the individual manager in a work organization: our interest is in his personal values and what they tell us about his work behavior and outcomes of this behavior. We are not studying organizations, industries, nations or cultures, although each manager studied certainly can be placed within these broader frames of reference.

The managers studied[4]

National samples of managers in the U.S., Japan, Korea, India, and Australia were selected from major directories of corporation executives in each country. The national samples were developed to be roughly comparable in terms of three stratifying variables:

- size of organization in terms of number of employees,
- level of the manager within the organization, and
- organizational function of the manager.

The sample selection procedure was designed to obtain a diverse group of managers in each country in terms of organizational variables (type of company, size of firm, department or function, organizational level, salary level and line-staff position), and in terms of personal variables (years of managerial experience and age). The samples of managers come from private organizations, and represent a large number of firms. No more than four managers were selected from any one organization.

The number of managers in each country who provided complete information is as follows:

United States	997
Japan	374
Korea	211
Australia	351
India	623
Total	2556

In sum, we are dealing with over 2500 top and middle-management level managers from a variety of industries. The managers come from organizations of all sizes and represent the major functional areas of management. They are an experienced group; the average number of years spent in a management position is about 15, while the average age in our total sample is about 45.

Summary of study results

While space limitations make it impossible to present detailed results of all our work, we can indicate the general nature of our findings.

1. *There are large individual differences in personal values within each group we have studied.* Among managers in each country, some have a pragmatic orientation (they view ideas and concepts in terms of whether or not they work or are successful), some have an ethical-moral orientation (they view ideas in terms of being right or wrong), while a few have an affect or feeling orientation (they view ideas in terms of whether or not they are pleasant). Some managers have a very small set of values while others have a large set and seem to be influenced by many strongly-held values. The important values of some managers include concepts which are almost solely related to their organizational life, while other managers include a wide range of personal and philosophical concepts among their important values. Some managers have what might be termed individualistic values as opposed to group-oriented values. Some managers are highly achievement-oriented as opposed to others who value status and prestige more highly. Finally, it is clear that some managers have a personal value system that might be characterized as 'hard.' Their important values include concepts such as ambition, obedience, aggressiveness, achievement, success, competition, risk and force. Other managers have value systems that are often characterized as 'soft' and include such concepts as loyalty, trust, cooperation, compassion, tolerance, employee welfare, social welfare and religion. Personal value systems, then, are like most other human characteristics; individuals differ greatly with respect to them.

2. *Personal value systems of managers are relatively stable and do not change rapidly.* In 1966 we measured the personal value systems of a national sample of U.S. managers. In 1972. Professors Edward Lusk and Bruce Oliver of the University

of Pennsylvania's Wharton School repeated our earlier study on a comparable national sample of U.S. managers.[4] They reasoned that the widespread airing of environmental and social issues (e.g., pollution, the Vietnam war, lifestlye changes, changing expectations of the labor force, and minority and disadvantaged group employment problems) between 1966 and 1972 had probably been accompanied by changes in the value systems of managers. However, the differences between the value systems of the 1966 sample and the 1972 sample of managers were very small. Across all 66 concepts in the PVQ, the average difference in value importance was only 3.3 percentage points between the two time periods. A difference of 10 points or greater between the two samples was found on only four of the 66 concepts. (The 1972 sample placed greater value on the concepts dignity, trust, and change, and lower value on the concept 'my boss' as compared to the 1966 sample).

These results show quite clearly that the personal value systems of 1972 managers are very similar to those of 1966 managers, and thus do not appear to change rapidly even during periods of major environmental and social flux. Factors explaining this stability probably include the fact that personal values are a relatively stable human characteristic, the nature of the selection and development process managers go through, and the requirements and constraints that the job of managing places upon managers.

3. *Personal value systems of managers are related to and/or influence the way managers behave on the job.* While several of our analyses show this to be the case, the clearest evidence emerges in the study of Indian and Australian managers. Here we assessed the personal values of each manager and measured his behavior on five job incidents, each representing a typical problem which a manager might encounter in the performance of his job. Prior to analyzing the data, we made 25 predictions about how managers with certain values would be expected to behave. Examples of these predictions are:

(a) managers who have profit maximization as an important goal will be less willing to spend money on cafeteria and rest room facility improvements than will managers who do not have profit maximization as an important value;
(b) managers for whom compassion is an important value would be less willing to seek research and development funds by depriving employees of part of a potential wage increase than would managers for whom compassion is not an important value; and
(c) managers for whom cooperation is an important value would promote a more congenial department member as opposed to a highly creative but less appealing person.

Across all five incidents, 19 out of 25 predictions are supported by the data for Indian managers, and 18 of 25 predictions are supported for Australian managers. These results offer strong support for the contention that values are related to managerial behavior in meaningful ways.

4. *Personal value systems of managers are related to career success.* We defined career success in terms of managerial pay relative to the manager's age in our study

of American, Japanese, Indian and Australian managers. The heterogeneous nature of our samples seemed to dictate measuring success in terms of objective data that were relatively easy to collect. Relative salary level for one's age group provided such a measure.

We then developed and cross-validated a value profile pattern that was related to success in each of the four countries. The value patterns that were related to success were similar in the four countries and correlated with success as follows: USA (.32), Australia (.47), India (.35), and Japan (.26). These correlations are of similar magnitude to the validity coefficients generally reported for predicting managerial success by other types of predictors. We view these results as solid evidence that value patterns and success are meaningfully related in a similar fashion across the four countries.

The more successful managers favor an achievement orientation and prefer substantial interaction with other individuals. They value a dynamic environment and are willing to take risks to achieve organizationally-valued goals. Relatively less successful managers have values associated with a static, protected environment in which they take relatively passive roles and often enjoy extended seniority in their organizational positions.

Since the value systems of American managers seem relatively stable over time, and since values are related to success, we have explored the possibility of using values as a selection or promotion device in attempting to pick people who will turn out to be successful. Table 1 shows that value patterns are predictive of success and could be used in selection and placement decisions. We are hesitant, however, to recommend the use of personal values in selection because we do not know the full consequences of an individual organization having managers with similar value profiles. Persuasive arguments can be made that organizational vitality and adaptation to changing social and technological conditions may come about in part because of the value mix in an organization; we simply do not know what that optimal mix is for any given organization.

Table 1 Managerial success and managerial values

Value Score		Success Expectancy*
Very High	(top 20 percent)	72
High	(next 20 percent)	63
Medium	(next 20 percent)	47
Low	(next 20 percent)	41
Very Low	(bottom 20 percent)	34

* Chances in 100 of being among the top half of managers in terms of success.

5. Our results suggest that the value systems in the five countries contain elements of both similarity and difference. There is considerable variation in the primary orientations of managers in the five countries. The percentage of pragmatists is 67% in Japan, 57% in the U.S., 53% in Korea, 40% in Australia and 34% in India. The extent of moralistic orientation was 44% in India, 40% in Australia, 30% in the U.S., 10% in Japan and 9% in Korea. These differences, however, should be placed in the context of primary orientation similarity among countries. At least 34% of managers in each country were pragmatists, at least 9% in each country were moralists, at least 1% in each country were affect-oriented and at least 11% in each country had a mixed orientation. This suggest a similarity of primary orientation for about 55% of the managers across all five countries.

There are differences in the homogeneity of value systems within the five countries. Japanese managers are markedly most similar to each other in this respect, while Korean managers are most dissimilar to each other. The other three countries are in a middle position in terms of within country similarity of their value systems.

Viewing all our results, it seems that countries are contributing from 30–45% to the variability we find, while individuals are contributing from 55–70%. Thus we might say that individual differences account for about two-thirds of the variation in value systems of managers, while country differences account for about one-third of the variation in value systems of managers in the five countries studied.

There are certainly differences in the value patterns of the managers in the five countries. A thumbnail sketch of several observations about the values of managers in each country will highlight some of these differences.

U.S. Managers
- Large element of pragmatism.
- Have a high achievement and competence orientation.
- Emphasize traditional organizational goals such as Profit Maximization, Organizational Efficiency and High Productivity.
- Place high value on most employee groups as significant reference groups.

Japanese Managers
- Very high element of pragmatism.
- Value magnitude very highly (size and growth).
- Place high value on competence and achievement.
- Have the most homogeneous managerial value system of the countries studied.
- Indicate a high degree of value change occurring.

Korean Managers
- Large element of pragmatism.
- Place low value on most employee groups as significant reference groups.
- Display a self-oriented achievement and competence orientation.
- Moderate value placed on organizational goals.
- Show an intended egalitarian orientation.

Indian Managers
- High degree of moralistic orientation.
- Value stable organizations with minimal or steady change.
- Value personalistic goals and status orientation.
- Value a blend of organizational compliance and organizational competence.
- Place low value on most employee groups.

Australian Managers
- High degree of moralistic orientation.
- High level of humanistic orientation.
- Place low value on organizational growth and profit maximization.
- Place low value on such concepts as achievement, success, competition and risk.
- Major regional (geographical) differences in values of managers.

Implications and conclusions

Despite the value differences among managers in the five countries and the value diversity within each country, there is a common pattern of translation of values into behavior across the countries. Figure 3 shows the types of relationships among managerial values and various organizational, personal and behavioral variables. Organizational level, personal success, decision-making behavior and job satisfaction are related to value patterns in ways which permit generalization across countries. Organizational size and the individual manager's age are related to values of managers, but in a country-specific way. The type of industry in which a manager is employed is not related to values either across countries or within any given country. The important generalization that emerges is that values get translated from states of intention into behavior outcomes in a similar way across countries. Our results argue strongly for the possibility of generalization across countries and thus for the significance of further comparative studies.

Another major implication concerns distinctions among managers with different primary orientations, particularly the distinction between managers who have a pragmatic orientation and those having a moralistic orientation. This distinction is important in a number of ways. First, there is a major difference in the value patterns of the two types of managers. Pragmatists have an economic and organizational competence orientation as opposed to a humanistic and bureaucratic orientation for moralists. Pragmatists will be more responsive to the economic aspects of behavior and decisions, while moralists will be more responsive to the human and bureaucratic consequences of actions. Second, pragmatists are apt to be influenced more by training, persuasion and leadership approaches which focus on the notion of whether or not a particular act or decision will work or is likely to be successful. Moralists, on the other hand, would be more influenced by positions and approaches utilizing philosophical and moral justification. Even should the two types behave in a similar fashion, they would probably rationalize and/or explain the reasons for their

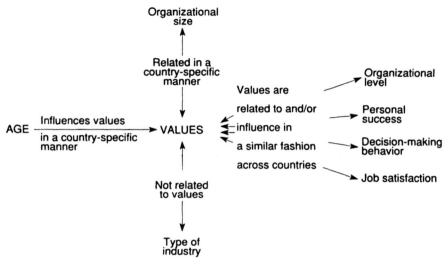

Figure 3 The type of relationships among managerial values and various organizational, personal and behavioral variables.

behavior in different terms. Third, pragmatists probably have more 'situational anchors' to guide their behavior, and seem to be more responsive to external rewards and controls while moralists are more responsive to internal rewards and controls. Moral and ethical norms, even though they are more subjective and more variable, are probably more firmly ingrained in the individual's personality than are success standards. Thus, it would be more difficult to change the behavior pattern of a moralist than a pragmatist. In short, we are arguing that the concept of a personal primary orientation for a manager is useful not only in determining internationality in value statements, but that the different orientations (particularly pragmatic and moralistic) have important implications for types of stimuli selected and the effectiveness of techniques of intervention and efforts to change behavior.

The fact that India and Australia have the largest proportion of moralistic managers suggests that change in managers is apt to be slower and/or more difficult in these two countries. This seems particularly true in India, where there are very few value differences between younger and older managers, thus providing very little internal management stimulus toward change.

The value system of Japanese managers was found to be the most homogeneous of all countries. (Whitehill and Takezawa likewise found more homogeneity in values and attitudes among Japanese production workers than among American production workers).[7] Japanese managers were also found to be the most pragmatic and to exhibit the greatest value differences between younger and older managers. These factors indicate a high degree of readiness for change by Japanese managers, when and if such change is necessary.

Affect-oriented managers (those viewing important concepts as pleasant) are relatively few in each of the five countries, and are the least successful and least satisfied of the orientation groups. Only 36 percent of the affect-oriented managers are in the top half of our success measures as compared to 52 percent of pragmatists and 49 percent of moralists in the international sample. Likewise, the average job satisfaction score for affect-oriented managers is 20.2 as compared to 21.4 for pragmatists and 21.5 for moralists. We are not certain if these lower success and satisfaction levels for affect-oriented managers are a function of their primary orientation per se, or if they come about because affect-oriented managers form such a small part of the total management group that their values find little support from the predominant orientation groups (pragmatists and moralists). Whatever the explanation, it is clear that the affect-oriented managers are at a disadvantage in terms of success and satisfaction.

About the future

A final set of observations deals with questions of future organization and management. Do our results suggest a movement towards such 'ideal' forms of organization design as Likert's Management System 4? As a guide to this analysis, we have assumed that tomorrow's cadre of important and influential managers will come primarily from the younger age group in our sample. They are already managers, and they have 25 to 35 years of their career ahead of them. With this assumption in mind, we have compared the value systems of younger managers in the international sample with those of older managers to search for clues about the future. While many of the age differences found are country-specific, there are a few trends at the international level which are relevant to this present concern:

- Younger managers place less relevance on organizational goals.
- Younger managers place less relevance on groups of people with whom they interact and greater relevance upon themselves (me).
- Younger managers place lower relevance on trust and honor.
- Younger managers place greater relevance on money, ambition and risk.
- Younger managers are slightly more pragmatic than are older managers.

None of these differences indicate any strong or likely movement toward Management System 4; in fact, most of the differences seem to work counter to such movement. Thus, in terms of the value systems of managers themselves, we would not forecast movement toward ideal types of organization and management, such as that proposed by Likert.

While one can doubt that there will be management initiative for change toward System 4, it is useful to remember that many managers are pragmatic and can adapt to whatever system seems most appropriate to their circumstances. The notion of situational organizational design thus seems most in accord with the value systems of managers in the future.

Finally our work leads us to the conclusion that the personal values of managers are both measurable and important to measure. Values are related to such practical and important concerns as decision making, managerial success, managerial satisfaction and organizational context differences. While we have learned a great deal about values and their role in organizational life. I am personally struck with how much there is to know. We know little, for example, about how value systems develop and how they are changed by organizational experiences; what are acceptable or optimal levels of value disparity within organizations or suborganizations to aid in the achievement of organizational success; what are the effects upon individuals of providing them with valid information about their own value systems; what values are most compatible with movement toward a post-industrial era or multinational corporate life; and finally how value measurement might aid in the strain toward consistency that all must make between what we believe and value and how we actually behave. In short, we view the study of value systems and their role in organizational life as an important and on-going venture. It is our sincere hope that the theory, the methodology, the result, and the ideas presented will lead to more effective and more enlightened management practices.

NOTES

1. McLaughlin, G. Values in Behavioral Science. *Journal of Religion and Health*, 1965.
2. Osgood, E.C., Suci, G.J. and Tannenbaum, P.H. *The Measurement of Meaning*. Urbana: University of Illinois Press, 1957.
3. England, G.W. 'Organizational Goals and Expected Behavior of American Managers.' *Academy of Management Journal*, Vol. 10, No. 2, 1967, pp. 107–117.
4. For more detailed information about the managers studied, see: England, G.W. *The Manager and His Values: An International Perspective*. Cambridge, Mass.: Ballinger Publishing Co., 1975.
5. For detailed data, analyses and procedures utilized, the reader is again referred to *The Manager and His Values: An International Perspective*.
6. Lusk, E.J. and Oliver, B.L. *The impact of organizational interactions on the American manager's personal value system*. Philadelphia: The Wharton School, University of Pennsylyania, 1972.
7. Whitehill, A.M. and Takezawa, S. *The Other Worker*. Honolulu: East–West Center Press, 1968.
8. Likert, R. *The human organization*. New York: McGraw-Hill Book Co., 1967.

In the market place

MEIR TAMARI

Competition among buyers and sellers in goods and services will serve to provide the quantity and quality the market desires, at prices it is prepared to pay. At the same time that competition provides economic benefits for society, it creates moral problems. Some people, sometimes a minority but always the weak and inefficient members of that society, lose their jobs or businesses. Society must balance the economic benefits·earned against the human loss caused by competition. Free market economists will argue that forces of supply and demand will ultimately restore equilibrium, so that the unemployed or the displaced entrepreneur will find alternative means of earning a livelihood.

Unfortunately, in real life there exist many obstacles to the interplay of free market forces, which often prevent the restoration of equilibrium. Furthermore, the time needed for this adjustment may be so long that the individuals or society can be destroyed. This has led to solutions such as the planned economy favored by socialist or communist societies. Experience, however, has shown that in these societies, the loss of the benefits of competition has led to poverty and economic deprivation, and, has created moral problems of its own.

The choice of the type of economy which lies between these two extremes, is not an economic judgment but an ethical one. It is a choice which will depend on the value structure of the particular society concerned.

Our mishnah and the one from *Baba Metzia* discussed in Chapter Four offer a framework for a market economy that balances the benefits and costs of competition, yet is neither socialist nor capitalist, but a specifically Jewish value structure. Each mishnah deals with a different type of competition; the above mishnah with the free entry of entrepreneurs, the one from *Baba Metzia*, with price and non-price competition.

The above mishnah discusses the rights of neighbors to protect themselves against the damage caused by the economic activities in their courtyard. This is extended, in the Talmudical discussion, to refer to the citizens of a city. Such damage can be ecological – noise and smell – or economic, e.g., the loss caused to existing businesses by the entry of new firms. The following discussion is restricted to the economic problems caused by competition.

The Talmudic sages queried whether the accepted protection afforded by the halakha against the noise, overcrowding, dirt, and the like resulting from business activities could be used to prevent the opening of new businesses that were owned by either local people or 'foreign' firms.[3] If such new·businesses are considered to be a

form of theft of the livelihood of existing businessmen, they woι
forbidden. If the 'veterans' do not have property rights, or the ι
of the general population overshadows these rights, the compet.
permitted.

Forestalling the competition need not take the form of new firms. ⅹ
created by the intervention of a new party into an ongoing negotiation to b᷒
estate, obtain a contract, or gain employment. A modern halakhic responsum ᷒
with such a case.

> You write to ask me concerning one of the teachers in your yeshivah who was
> approached by a parent to teach his son during the summer vacation. While the
> negotiations were being conducted, a fellow teacher accepted the position. Now,
> the first teacher claims redress according to 'ani mehapech' [the Talmudical
> dictum that when a poor man was examining a cake for sale, he who forestalls
> him is called an evildoer]. My answer is that the second teacher may not accept
> the position, even though he had no knowledge of the negotiations and even if he
> thought they had failed.
>
> We have to also consider the opinion of the Rama [Choshen Mishpat, Section
> 103] that the concept of forestalling does not apply in those cases where the seller
> asks for a higher price than the buyer is willing to offer. This has been modified
> by another authority to include only those cases where the buyer has shown that
> he is definitely rejecting the seller's offer. In other cases, like the present one,
> however, where negotiations are still continuing, the intervention of the third
> party causes the seller to refuse the buyer's offer, so it is a case of 'hasagat gevul'
> [the biblical injunction against removing a neighbor's landmark, understood by
> the rabbis to include depriving another of his livelihood], which is forbidden.[4]

There are other authorities who hold that the whole concept of forestalling is only
a moral injunction, not something enforceable in a court of law; a form of admirable
piety or righteousness, but not an economic right.[5]

Free entry

Regarding entry of new firms, the halakhic codes, within the limitations discussed
below, rule that existing merchants cannot prevent others from competing with
them.[6] The Middle Eastern bazaar, with its rows of similar businesses, is a present-
day example of the effect of this dictum. This is in contrast to those modern
shopping centers where only one of each type of business is allowed, thus restricting
competition.

There was a business concept limiting competition, however, which was accepted
by many authorities. This is called marufiyah, an Arabic term meaning, literally, a
friend, or, in Eastern Europe, arunda. Until modern times, most economic activity
was done under license, which conferred monopoly status. For example, people
bought the right to sell liquor, timber, or salt, or to lend money at interest or collect

axes. This was not merely a Jewish phenomenon, but part of the general economy in the world. The rabbis, generally speaking, did not allow one Jew to offer a higher price for such trading rights already enjoyed by another.[7] This would seem to be a contradiction of the free competition described above. The contradiction, however, is not a real one, since the *marufiyah* was the result of an investment which entitled the occupier to protection, the resultant monopoly.

The possessor of the '*marufiyah*' obtained it by literally cultivating the grantor of the license, usually the feudal lord. He invested time and money in winning his 'friendship' and the resultant monopoly. The idea of an investment that limits the free entry principle is also borne out by a Talmudical ruling, 'A fisherman must distance himself from his neighbor's nets.' This is explained by some authorities to refer to the special bait or hooks (the investment) used by the first fisherman.[8] Rabbenu Meir, the medieval Tosaphist, argued that 'monopoly' results from the fact that the fish are considered to already be in the possession of the fisherman. Customers, however, are free to enter and leave stores without being considered the owner's property.[9]

Non-citizens

The problem of free entry for non-citizens is more complicated than that of members of the same courtyard, town or state. In the latter case, all parties are 'citizens' of the same unit, liable to the same obligations and entitled to the same benefits. In the former case, the displacement of competitors and workers, or the decline of their profits, is aggravated by the fact that 'foreign' competitors are causing it.

The cry for protection of local labor and national interests is an ancient as well as modern one, so the halakhic treatment has important present day connotations. Such protection is usually in the form of higher prices and/or inferior goods and services. Once again, the welfare of the total population has to be considered in relation to the loss suffered by local merchants, industry, or labor. In the Talmudic discussion, the ruling was quite clearly that foreign and out-of-town merchants cannot be excluded, provided that they pay the local taxes. This ruling was incorporated in all of the halakhic codes – *Mishneh Torah*, *Arba'ah Turim*, and *Shulchan Arukh*.[10]

The insistence on payment of taxes is morally justified, since the 'foreigners' benefit from the local infrastructure; to rule otherwise would grant them an advantage that does not flow from their efficiency or productivity and cannot be matched by the local entrepreneurs. Clearly, the rabbis considered the benefit of the majority, the consumers, over the loss of the minority, and this is expressed in many responsa which limit free entry, not only by payment of taxes, but with the requirement that the imported goods be cheaper, better than the local products, or unavailable locally.[11]

The logic behind many of these responsa may be seen in a responsum by Rabbi Abraham ben Moses di Boton [16th-century Salonika], regarding a tailor who migrated to the city from an outlying village. The local craftsmen claimed that owing to his lower standard of living and his willingness to work longer hours, he was able to produce clothes at half the price, this constituting unfair competition. They argued, therefore, that he should be prevented from selling and producing in their town even if he paid taxes. Rabbi di Boton ruled, on the basis of the decision of Ibn Migash, that he could not prefer the few, the local manufacturers, over the interests of the majority, the consumers.[12] In those cases, however, where the consumer has no benefit either in price or quality, there is no logic, economic or moral, in causing loss to local entrepreneurs, and so foreign competition would be curbed.

There are other instances where competition is detrimental to the welfare of the community. This is shown by the ruling of the authorities in Franco-Germany that even where the foreigners are prepared to pay taxes, the local merchants have the right to protection. The best example of such rulings is the legal right which became known as *cherem hayishuv*. This sanctioned a public ban organized by a community against the free entry of foreign entrepreneurs. The *cherem hayishuv*, in effect, created a monopoly of residence, a legal asset which could be sold or bequeathed.[13] Jewish law has always recognized that the community has the right to protect itself against criminals, slanderers or other immoral people by the use of a ban on residence.[14] What is new in the *cherem hayishuv* is its use to provide economic protection. Many authorities objected to the *cherem*, especially those in the Sephardic world.[15] It would seem that the reason for this objection is to be found in the different social effects of competition in the two major blocs of medieval Jewish life. The Jewish economy in the pre-capitalist Moslem world of Spain, North Africa, and the Middle East was relatively free of restrictions, and as widely based as that of the general one. This made competition beneficial to the community as a whole. In medieval Christian Europe, however, the business base of the Jewish communities was so narrow that foreign competition, could involve not just a loss to some local merchants, but the economic destruction of the community. Thus, in this case, the halakhic authorities, whose interest has always been moral action, not economic policy, preferred the communal welfare over the short-term economic benefits of competition in those countries, and so supported the *cherem hayishuv*.[16]

At the same time, in view of the pre-eminence of learning in Judaism, Torah scholars were exempt from the *cherem* and encouraged to settle and operate businesses, even if this meant increased competition.[17] Sometimes they were granted monopoly rights or precedence in selling their goods – in effect, a public subsidy to Torah study. Refugees, too, were granted right of settlement as part of Jewish national obligations. Sometimes, however, the economic realities of life meant that their ability to do business, while permitted, was limited in order not to destroy the economic basis of the host community.[18]

Redundancy

It is not enough for a moral system to deal only with the economic effects of competition on the general public. The personal problems and social issues involved demand that the system also provide answers for the redundant worker and the displaced competitor.

Those authorities who would prohibit competition do so because it would destroy another's livelihood, with all the resultant problems. At the same time, they are proposing restrictions which would deny the consumer the benefits of technological and marketing progress. If the restriction is to be more than temporary, the community's or competitor's losses may be far too great. So it is not surprising to find many responsa which, indeed, limit the time a restricitive ruling may be in force. For example, an employee who left his former job and wished to open his own business was restricted by *Dayan* Weiss of Manchester from using the marketing knowledge he had gained from his former employer; understanding that this would prevent him from ever being able to operate his own business successfully, the *Dayan* limited the restriction to a reasonably short period.[19]

Naturally, such decisions at the individual level have only limited application and do not relate to the major social problem of unemployment. It is true that a competitor does not have any legal responsibility for the welfare of displaced workers or competitors in those cases where the competition is halakhically permitted. Nevertheless, there is a certain moral obligation which he is expected to assume, at least as an act of charity. Furthermore, he, together with all the other members of the community, is obligated to provide the unemployed workers or displaced entrepreneur with their basic needs, which would also include aid for any; psychological or moral damage suffered; this is not merely an act of sympathy, but a communal obligation which may even be financed by taxation.[20] Maimonides rules that the highest forms of charity in Judaism are those actions which prevent the descent into poverty – offering a job, giving advice, or providing a loan.[21] The successful competitor fulfills this act of personal charity through providing retraining, job information, and interest-free loans for the purpose of establishing the unemployed in their own businesses.

There is an additional Jewish way of handling unemployment, which could serve as a parallel solution, as may be seen in the following 20th-century responsum. The question deals with the problem of which employees should be dismissed when a factory finds that it does not have enough work for its workforce. Present-day practice in most firms is to apply the rule of 'last in, first out,' by which the last workers hired are the first to lose their jobs. This assumes, in effect, that the more senior workers have acquired a property right in their jobs.

Rabbi Moshe Feinstein's following answer has many parallels in modern labor negotiations, which reflect a mixture of mutual help and legal rights:

> If there is a contract stipulating the order of dismissal, or if there is a local custom [an important halakhic principle that offers protection in the absence of a specific contract], these have to be followed. Lacking such arrangements, the workers are in a situation similar to that of two partners who wish to divide up their common property; in our case, the work. The workers can each do half a day's work, thus dividing the wages between them [a practice often followed by workers when

they decide to accept a cut in wages in exchange for the retention of every worker's job.] Alternatively, one can say· to the other, 'Buy my share or sell me yours.' [In effect, this denies the veteran workers a property right in the place of employment.][22]

Such a policy would leave decisions of priorities in dismissal to the workers themselves rather than to management.

[3] *Talmud Bavli, Baba Batra* 21b.
[4] *Iggrot Moshe, Choshen Mishpat*, part 1, sec. 59.
[5] *Talmud Bavli, Kiddushin* 29a.
[6] *Mishneh Torah, Hilkhot Shecheinim*, ch. 6, halakha 8; *Tur* and *Shulchan Arukh, Choshen Mishpat*, sec. 156, subsec. 5.
[7] *T'shuvot Maharikh*, sec. 132.
[8] Tosafot, *Talmud Bavli, Kiddushin* 59a.
[9] Ibid.
[10] *Shulchan Arukh, Choshen Mishpat*, sec. 156, subsec. 5.
[11] Ibn Migas, *Chidushim, Baba Batra* 21b. Also see HaMeiri, *Baba Metzia* 40b; Rosh, *Baba Metzia*, sec. 16; *Tur, Choshen Mishpat*, sec. 231, subsec. 26; Rama, *Shulchan Arukh, Choshen Mishpat*, sec. 156, subsec. 4.
[12] *Lechem Rav*, sec. 216.
[13] *T'shuvot Chochmei Roma, Beit Ha'otzar*, vols. 57–58.
[14] *Ruach Chaim*, sec. 7, subsec. 4.
[15] *T'shuvot HaRashba*, sec. 132.
[16] Mordechai, *Baba Batra*, par. 517; *T'shuvot HaMaharam Mi Rothenburg*, sec. 883.
[17] Rama, *Shulchan Arukh, Yoreh De'ah*, sec. 145, subsec. 22; *T'shuvot Maharil Weil*, 106a; *T'shuvat Chatam Sofer, Orach Chayim*, sec. 130.
[18] Rama, *Shulchan Arukh, Choshen Mishpat*, sec. 156, subsec. 5.
[19] *Minchat Yitzchak*, part 2, sec. 94.
[20] *Shulchan Arukh, Yoreh De'ah*, sec. 248.
[21] *Mishneh Torah, Hilkhot Matnot Aniyim*, ch. 10, halakha 7.
[22] *Iggrot Moshe, Choshen Mishpat*, part 1, sec. 81.

Towards an interest-free Islamic economic system

WAQAR MASOOD KHAN

The Islamic Alternatives to Ribā*

There are two types of financial contracts which are presented in Islamic jurisprudence for replacing *Ribā*-oriented transactions. These are (i) *Shirkah* (partnership), and (ii) *Muḍārabah* (agency relationship).

* 'Ribā' means 'usury' or 'interest' (Editors' note).

There are differences among jurists regarding the conditions governing these contracts. We will note some important differences in the following discussion.

Although there are several kinds of partnership contracts the common feature in all these is that two or more people enter into a contract by providing capital in different amounts for running a business with the provision that they will share in the profit or loss in some pre-determined proportions (13).

Muḍārabah on the other hand is a contract in which one party, the owner (*Rabbul-Māl*) provides capital while the other party (*Ḍārib*) brings labour and effort with the provision of profit sharing in some pre-determined proportions.

We will confine ourselves to a discussion of *Muḍārabah*, since it is analytically more convenient to contrast this contract with a *Ribā* contract and also because it has the potential of replacing the so-called 'working capital' available only on the basis of a *Ribā* contract in the present banking system. This topic will be thoroughly discussed later.

In Islamic jurisprudence several terms are used to define this contract: *Qirāḍ*, *Muqāraḍah*, and *Muḍārabah* are used to identify the same contract. It has also been called Commenda. These terminologies reflect geographical identification of this contract rather than any other essential difference. The people of Arabia called it *Muqādarah* while in Iraq it was known as *Muḍārabah*. In the Western world it came to be known as Commenda (17).

It is unanimously agreed by jurists that the legal validity of this contract is basically traditional practice (*Sunnah*) and the consensus of the community (*Ijmā'*).

It has also been noted by the jurists that one of the major reasons for its acceptance is the resulting ease and efficiency achieved in the functioning of the economic system. This is reflected in the following paragraph from a leading jurist, Sarakhsī's discussion on *Muḍārabah* in his seminal work *Al-Mabsuṭ*:

> [This contract was allowed] because people have a need for this contract. For the owner of capital may not find his way to profitable trading activity, and the person who can find his way to such activity, may not have the capital. And profit cannot be attained except by means of both these, that is, capital and trading activity. By permitting this contract, the goal of both parties is attained (18).

Unlike the case of *Shirkah*, there is uniformity of treatment among jurists regarding the conditions governing the *Muḍārabah* contract. Before we discuss these conditions, let us list different kinds of *Muḍārabah* contracts. There are three kinds of contracts, viz (i) money *Muḍārabah*, (ii) commodity *Muḍārabah* and (iii) productive *Muḍārabah* (2).

The distinction reflects the form of initial investment and intermediary forms until the final stage of sharing. In money *Muḍārabah* and commodity *Muḍārabah* the form of initial investment provided by the principal is legally accepted money and goods, respectively. For the majority of jurists the latter form of capital is not acceptable, as a basis for *Muḍārabah*, unless the goods are first sold and the resulting revenue is considered as the base capital.

Islamic jurists have generally recommended *Muḍārabah* for exploiting the gains from price differentials that exist in different parts of the world. Thus many jurists have rejected the formation of a *Muḍārabah* contract that required manufacturing of goods and sharing the production, or what is called the productive *Muḍārabah*. But, as Udovitch points out (19), this can be avoided 'by the employment of a simple device involving sale of the goods in question', and sharing in the profits afterwards. This type of *Muḍārabah* is approved by the later jurists of the Ḥanafī school. Sarakhsī writes:

> For the work stipulated for the agent is the kind of work that the merchants practice in the pursuit of the attainment of profit. It is comparable to buying and selling. Similarly, if the investor instructs the agent to use capital to purchase leather and hide and then cut it into boots, buckets, and leather bags, this is all part of the practice of merchants in the pursuit of the attainment of profit, and its stipulation is permissible in a commenda (*Muḍārabah*) (20).

Mālikī and Shāfi'ī jurists, two other major schools of thought, have rejected any such kind of contract. They argue that, since the agent performs a productive act he should be compensated by a fixed wage rate and the profit/loss should go to the principal (3). Imām Mālik has rejected it on the ground that it was not the practice of Muslims of his time (14).

Islamic economists have differed from the Ḥanafī school on the legal validity of productive *Muḍārabah*. Indeed the Ḥanafī school, having the largest following in the Islamic world, appears to be more flexible and caters to current economic needs in its formation of Islamic laws.*

Conditions of *Muḍārabah*

(I) *Sharing of Profit/Loss:* There is no disagreement among Islamic jurists on the conditions governing the responsibilities of principal/agent in the case of profit or loss. The entire loss has to be borne by the principal while the profit has to be shared between them in some pre-specified proportions. This is so because in case of loss the agent has suffered a loss of his effort and labour so he cannot be asked to share any loss of capital. Since the principal, on the other hand, provides capital his loss is the capital lost in the business (15).

(II) *Agent's Reponsibilities:* Unless specifically restricted from engaging in certain activities, the agent is generally free to act 'as he sees fit' for the pursuit of profit. 'Hanafi law distinguishes', writes Udovitch, 'two types of contract: a limited mandate and an unlimited mandate commenda. A commenda with unlimited mandate is one in which the investor authorizes the agent to act completely at the latter's discretion in all business matters. Such authorization is conveyed by investor's statement to the agent: 'act with it (the investment) as you see fit'. In this case the agent may:

1. Buy and sell all types of merchandise as he sees fit.
2. Buy and sell for cash and credit.
3. Give goods as *Bid'ah*, leave them as a deposit or pledge.

4. Hire helpers as needed.
5. Travel with the capital.
6. Rent or buy animals and equipment.
7. Mingle it with his own resources.
8. Give it as a commenda to a third party.
9. Invest it in a partnership with a third party.'

Sarakhsī summarizes this as follows:

> If the investor says to the agent 'act with it as you see fit' then he may practice all of these except the loan. For the investor has consigned the control of this capital to the agent's descretion in a comprehensive wav; and we know that his intention is the inclusion of all that is customary to the practice of the merchants. The agent, thereby, has the right to engage in commenda, a partnership, and to mingle the capital with his own capital because this is of the practice of the merchants (21).

In case of limited mandate commenda the activities of the agent are restricted mainly in his relationship with the third party. In some cases there were geographical restrictions on the domain of the agent's operations.

(III) *Duration of Business:* There may or may not be a specified contractual period for the business, depending on the agreement between the principal and the agent. However there is little disagreement among jurists regarding cancellation of *Muḍārabah*. The dominant Ḥanafī school allows the cancellation by any party during its currency, provided that the other party is informed of the decision and it will not be harmful to the other party (16). It will be automatically cancelled in case of death, insanity, or apostasy from Islam of either party (22).

Some comments

As we noted earlier, Islamic economists have accepted that version of the *Muḍārabah* contract which has been approved and elaborated on by jurists of the Ḥanafī school. We shall have this contract in mind when talking of an Islamic financial contract in subsequent chapters.

It is important to emphasize at this point that a *Muḍārabah* contract has the potential of forming the basis of an Islamic financial system compatible with modern needs. The provision of forming a *Muḍārabah* or partnership with a third party or mingling one's own capital, as a part of the responsibilities of an agent, has far-reaching implications for devising an Islamic financial system. It seems clear that present banks under an Islamic system will play the rôle of agents. They can use the funds of depositors (principal) along with their own equity funds to form *Muḍārabah* or partnership with other investors.

NOTES

* The flexibility in accommodating various activities in the *Muḍārabah* contract, in the Ḥanafī school, is reflected in the following quotation of Imām Muḥammad, a legend in the Ḥanafī

school and a noble student of Imām Abū Ḥanīfah, the leader of the Ḥanafī school of thought:

'In *Muḍārabah* contract the limits on agent's activities will be determined by the practice of merchants. Imām Muḥammad has written that the agent has the right to rent a piece of land and from the *Muḍārabah* capital buy the wheat for cultivation on that land. He can also choose the plantation of dates or any other crop. These are legal acts and profit sharing will be according to agreed terms. These are among the practices of merchants and the agent has the right to adopt them.' (See Siddiqi, ibid, p. 153.)

Siddiqi has considered it as the basis for industrial *Muḍārabah*.

1. Haque, Z. (1979): 'The Theory of *Muḍārabah* (Profit Sharing) in Islamic Jurisprudence.' Paper presented at the International Seminar on Islamic Economics, Islamabad, pp. 12–13.
2. Haque: ibid., p. 7.
3. Haque: op. cit., p. 13.
4. Maududi, S. A. (1961): *Sūd* (Interest), (Islamic Publications, Lahore), (Urdu).
5. Maududi: ibid., pp. 150–1.
6. Maududi: op. cit., p. 165; and Shafī', Muftī M.: *Mas'ala-e-Sūd* (The Problem of Interest), (undated), (Idārat-ul-Ma'ārif, Karachi), p. 18.
7. Maududi: op. cit., Chapter 4.
8. Maududi: op. cit., Supplement 1; Shafī': Part II. See also Kahf, M. (1978): *The Islamic Economy*, (M.S.A. of U.S.A. and Canada).
9. Maududi: op. cit., Supplement 2.
10. Maududi: op. cit., p. 293.
11. Saud, M. A. (1979): 'Money, Interest and *Qirāḍ*' in *Studies in Islamic Economics*, ed. Khurshid Ahmad (Islamic Foundation, U.K.), pp. 59–84.
12. Shafī', op. cit.
13. Siddiqi, M. N. (1969): *Islamic Principles of Shirakat and Muḍārabat*, (Islamic Publications, Lahore), pp. 18–19.
14 Siddiqi: ibid., p. 154.
15 Siddiqi: op. cit., Chapter 2.
16 Siddiqi: op. cit., Chapter 5.
17 Udovitch, A. (1970): *Partnership and Profit in Medieval Islam*, (Princeton University Press), pp. 174–5. See also Haque, op. cit.
18 Udovitch: ibid., p. 175.
19 Udovitch: op. cit., pp. 183–6, and Haque, op. cit., p. 13.
20 Udovitch: op. cit., p. 186.
21 Udovitch: op. cit., pp. 204–5.
22 Udovitch: op. cit., p. 248.
23 Uzair, M. (1979): 'Some Conceptual and Practical Aspects of Interest-Free Banking', in *Studies in Islamic Economics*, op. cit., pp. 37–57.

This confused society

H. N. S. KARUNATILAKE

[I]n the past an incorrect interpretation has been given to Buddhism with the result that no one has explored the scope for Buddhist Economic planning. A large number of books on the subject has so far dealt only with its philosophy and so catered only to man's spiritual faculties. A broad based interpretation of Buddhism as a doctrine that relates to man as an earthly living being has received little consideration, with the result that people have tended to cast aside Buddhism on the grounds that it is other-worldy and it is primarily of interest to a select band of intellectuals. The logical outcome has been the conclusion that Buddhism cannot offer a plan for man's economic well-being and that it has no economic foundations. This is clearly a distorted and unwarranted interpretation of the doctrine. Since Buddhism is concerned with man, and as material things are essential for him, the doctrine specifically offers a program for his development, even though it may conflict with the fundamentals of orthodox Economics. To a large extent, his material welfare would be subservient to certain spiritual values and a code of conduct, because one must be able to determine those material things that are best for him.

The thesis has been maintained throughout in this book that Buddhist Economics is not neutral to ends and is positively concerned with the ends themselves, because value judgements are closely intertwined with man's spiritual and material improvement. Economics cannot be neutral to ends as long as man in modern society degenerates rapidly in an inhospitable environment by having access to unwholesome goods and services. The essence of Buddhist Economic planning is based on his being selective in the choice of what he needs. It makes serious value judgements on the objectives of planning, what activities must be promoted, those that must be discouraged and the kind of goods and services that must result from the process of economic development.

Specification of objectives

In a modern economic development plan one of the first objectives is to increase per capita income and human welfare. The performance of the plan is judged largely on how far and how quickly a country is able to increase its per capita income. Evaluation of progress is only made in terms of aggregates; the wealth and the economic progress of a country is appraised in terms of per capita income, even though very large numbers of poor people would be living in the so-called rich countries with very high per capita incomes. For instance, in the rich oil producing countries in the middle east, per capita income-wise some of them take precedence over all others, but the bulk of the ordinary people are poor because there are severe disparities in income distribution. A Buddhist Economic system would in practice not pay a great deal of attention to aggregates such as per capita income, because it is only a deceptive statistical figure derived by dividing the value of all goods and services produced in the country by the number of persons living there. All goods, irrespective of whether they are essential or non-essential, are taken into account in computing per capita income, and a large number of items which are harmful to man normally comes within its ambit. In a Buddhist Economy only goods that will enhance man's material and spiritual wellbeing would be produced. It would exclude harmful drugs, alcoholic liquors, narcotics, weapons, the slaughter of animals, chemicals which are dangerous to man and other goods and services which would ultimately result in his moral and material degeneration. In other words, per capita income would in this case become a more meaningful indicator of economic achievement to the extent that it includes only goods useful to man. Raising per capita income would then mean increasing the production of those goods and services which people need most.

Another objective of modern development planning is to make full use of the productive resources of a country. This is consistent with the basic tenets of Buddhist Economics. Buddhism advocates the prudent and economic use of resources in the interest of man, but it does not advocate the indiscriminate and irresponsible use of resources in the way it is done now. A Buddhist Economy would use resources rationally while promoting their conservation. Conservationists are often treated by economic planners as a group of fashionable enthusiasts whose main object is to obstruct progress. For instance, virgin forests are depleted creating erosion, changing valuable eco-systems, causing flash floods and the rapid silting up of reservoirs. By depleting forest resources man destroys at one stroke what nature has taken a millenium to build. Buddhism would automatically conserve a nation's wild life resources because it does not advocate the taking of any form of life. It would promote the establishment of sanctuaries for birds and animals. Man does not have to kill animals for his survival. Science has found many other avenues through which man could obtain the proteins and other nutriment that he needs.

Today, the bulk of the non-renewable resources like coal and oil, are being wastefully deployed in the production of large quantities of goods and services which are not really useful to man. With the result that these primary sources of energy are being fast depleted, whereas they should be conserved for the future use of generations to come. In the case of oil it would appear that one generation seems to have exploited the bulk of the known oil reserves. Oil causes less pollution than other forms of energy and its conservation is an important factor. In Buddhist Economic planning non-renewable and scarce resources would be automatically conserved because the priorities in production would be determined according to man's basic needs where the focus of attention would be on food, clothing, housing and other necessities. Within this compass, allowance could be made to accommodate needs which would tend to differ according to cultural patterns. Productive resources would be diverted to produce the most essential goods. For example, the resources used in the production of armaments, drugs, alcohol and harmful chemicals would be diverted to produce food, clothing and building materials.

The provision of full employment is an important objective in all development plans. But in practical terms, Buddhist Economics pays much greater attention to this because the achievement of the other objectives are dependent on this. The Buddha says in the 'Kutadanta Sutta' that poverty can be eliminated and the country made to prosper by providing employment. In this way, food, clothing, housing and medical attention can be provided. Then again the 'Vyagghapajja Sutta' refers to employment opportunities that will provide man with the scope for production through right knowledge and right effort. Buddhism places great value on the individual because the moral stature of the community could only be improved by developing the individual. The community is made up of individuals and it is not possible to think of the community outside the individual. For everyone employment is the source of income and income is the source of sustenance. Even if 5 per cent of the labour force is unemployed it means that society, in effect, has neglected a valuable group of people in the community. In this context, not only would a Buddhist Economy have a state of permanent full employment, but the organisation of production and the development and use of technology would be such that there could be no possibility of the economy veering away from it.

Modern economic theory says that more goods must be produced to provide more employment and that people are assured of jobs only if the demand for goods increases progressively. The irony, however, is that unemployment occurs at frequent intervals even in economies which are continually producing more goods. Why does this happen? It is mainly because modern planning ignores the composition of goods and how goods are produced. It has been maintained that the advanced economies of the west are able to keep their population at near full employment levels by producing armaments and other means of destruction. In a Buddhist Economy there is no need to do this. Since in the Buddhist system the attitude to man is different, his welfare would be safeguarded by a very pragmatic approach to development.

One way of providing more employment is to use more men than machines in production. Buddhist Economics does not say that machines should be dispensed with. Modern technology plays an important role in the process of development; but with a difference. It does not advocate the use of sophisticated technologies where it is really not necessary. Technology must be subservient to man, it is his servant and not master, it should not dominate him. In the production process man should be given pride of place and not technology. In a Buddhist Economic plan the traditional techniques of production would be judiciously combined with the modern methods. It will not take up uncritically the position that modern techniques of production are always superior. This implies that the scale of economic operations becomes an important factor. It is not necessary to have large scale industries; especially in developing societies they can be dispensed with without any resulting disadvantage. The thesis that more goods should be produced is valid, but the level of employment need not necessarily depend on this. Human labour must be deployed on production for the masses and not on the mass production of a selective range of goods.

Furthermore, production should not be looked upon as a national exercise confined to territorial limits. Nations should produce for each other. Man should be internationally oriented, and the common understanding to eliminate poverty within a Buddhist framework might be the unifying force. In this context, it would be more meaningful if the rich western countries would use their resources to produce food and clothing for the world's poorest nations, than to produce armaments in order to maintain full employment. In this sense Buddhist Economics transcends national frontiers. It is a prescription for a world economy where man, the individual, whether he is in a rich country or a poor country, becomes the focus of the development effort. There would be no room for selfishness on national lines, and healthy human international relationships should emerge. Economic development can flourish in a world community rooted in a healthy concept of group living. A spiritually enlightened man would think of the human race and not in terms of very parochial national or racial groups.

A few objectives of modern economic development have been used to show how the objectives in Buddhist plan would tend to differ from them. The most important objective in a Buddhist plan would be the development of the individual, materially and spiritually. It would be incorrect to use the word economic development in this context, a Buddhist Economy would be concerned with human development. Since economic planning is concerned with the material aspects of life how could it contribute to man's spiritual upliftment? In the modern world man himself has created conditions where materialism has restrained the development of spiritualism. A Buddhist development plan would tend to indicate the most important material needs of man and it would lay stress on the fruitlessness of certain economic activities of man. The programme of work outlined here shows that it is through man's self knowledge, self effort and self control that his true material welfare could be furthered. Planners must be conscious of the fact that it is not necessary to stimulate economic activity by artificially multiplying human wants. A place cannot be given to the dominance of economic motivating forces such as Tanhā or the excessive craving for wealth. Each person's motivation should rather be the desire to improve the material and spiritual wellbeing of all others.

Spirit of Dana

The spirit of Dana or giving would be the factor around which activity will be vitalised. This is not a new concept, it is found in most religions, but has a more important place in Buddhism. The narrower current interpretation and practice of Dana would be extended in terms of its true meaning. For the businessmen it would mean that he must realise that it is not necessary to make very large profits. Profits could be scaled down and economic expansion need not depend on large profits. The latter is not necessary to induce a large amount of savings because industries and enterprises would operate on a reduced scale. In place of monopolies there would be a large number of small enterprises which will correspondingly require less capital.

For the consumer it would mean sacrifices and it would also result in reducing his Tanhā or craving. Dana means giving and sharing. He will have to be ready to share his goods with others who have less. It would also mean that he must be prepared to sacrifice what he can do without. Earlier it has been pointed out that modern materialism is concerned with more goods, and as the range of goods and services increase, the new items that come within this range are less and less useful. This would be taken into consideration in the planning process. The main objective would be to produce a wide range of basic essential goods in adequate quantities so that everyone will have the right to enjoy an equal share. In order to ensure an equitable distribution of goods a great deal of emphasis would be given to the removal of income disparities. The plan would be positively concerned with how much and what is produced. The consumer himself should not need unnecessary goods because he could overcome his excessive craving through spiritual development.

Targets in a Buddhist development plan would be placed not in terms of a particular growth rate, but in terms of quantities of goods required in accordance with the needs of the population and the number of people having less than their minimum requirements being supplied with their needs during the plan period. The Buddhist planner should frequently carry out surveys on the social and economic conditions of the people. He will be primarily concerned with not those who have, but with those who have not. In the 'Kutadanta Sutta' the Buddha emphasised that the primary aim of social and economic policy was to eliminate poverty. The latter cannot be achieved unless attention is focussed squarely on those who are in greatest need.

Excluded activities

The exclusion of certain non-essential industries and activities would be the essence of Buddhist planning. In the 'Anguttara Nikaya' the Buddha has prohibited trade in weapons, trade in human beings, trade in the rearing of animals for slaughter, trade in liquor, trade in poisons, drugs and narcotics. On the other hand, materialistic planning works on a scheme of priorities, but does not exclude any activity. As the scope and capacity of production widens less important economic activities begin to figure in the plans. Whether these activities become the responsibility of the private or public sector is not material. In a Buddhist plan some economic activities would not find a place even if all production possibilities have been exhausted and resources are freely available, as they are fundamentally inconsistent with the development of man. In the first place, industrial planning would exclude the production of harmful goods, non-essential goods and others which are destructive to man. It has already been indicated that in some of the most advanced countries and others that have been built on ideological foundations, at least 25 to 35 per cent of the national product is diverted to the production of armaments and sophisticated weaponary, merely to outdo competitors and rival nations, or for the sake of propagating and sustaining an ideology. No estimates are available of the volume of narcotics, poisons and other harmful drugs which are produced, but judging from increasing drug addiction in the world today their production must be rising steadily. In the United Kingdom alone some 3,000 million anti-depressent tablets are sold every year to those who have become addicted to them. The production of alcoholic beverages would not find a place in a Buddhist Economy because liquor has a debilitating effect on man. Under the influence of liquor man loses his capacity for right thought and action. It is one of the trades that the Buddha has specifically prohibited. This is not difficult to achieve because in some Islamic countries there is total prohibition of liquor, and there is no reason why other countries could not act likewise.

Planners will have to be selective about the production of goods which cannot be classified as essential for a comfortable existence. Modern Economics maintains that as the standard of living improves goods, which are otherwise classified as luxury goods, come to be treated as essential goods by people who enjoy a higher standard of living. This thesis cannot be sustained, as long as such luxury or semi-essential goods are being produced at the expense of essential goods, which have been denied to the bulk of the world's population. Perhaps if the world's population is provided with an adequate amount of essential goods, resources would not be readily available to produce luxury goods and those which are harmful to man. Buddhist Economics does not advocate that production must be reduced to very utilitarian levels, rather it gives man the freedom to act in accordance with the broad perimeters it has laid down, and within this area the production possibilities are quite extensive.

Resources

After the specification of objectives and the exclusion of certain activities the next problem in planning is the question of resources. The latter is identified with how much people can save out of what they produce. Now Buddhist Economics pays a great deal of attention to saving because the Dhamma is founded on principles such as frugality, resourcefulness and control over excessive craving for material goods. The inculcation and the practice of these principles helps the savings process. The rational organisation of the economy also involves the proper deployment and generation of basic resources. The importance of saving has been emphasised by all religious philosophies without exception, but Buddhism has specifically laid down the quantum in view of the singular importance of saving as a social discipline.

No country which has fruitlessly wasted its resources and encouraged conspicuous consumption has been able to grow rapidly. The rich economies of today have advanced through the process of progressively increasing savings, either through compulsion or by voluntary means. Buddhism does not advocate compulsory or forced saving. Buddhist Economic planning creates an awareness among the public that this is the only process through which progress can be achieved. Since it promotes the elimination of waste, advocates a simple way of life and changes the current attitude towards materialism, it automatically creates conditions for more savings to take place. There would be no need to carry out savings drives, promotion campaigns or offer very high interest rates. Savings would come essentially out of the Buddhist way of living. The interest rate would only have a symbolic meaning, it would be only a reflection and a reward for wholesome living, right mindfulness and frugality. Such a society would save even without a rate of interest, because social values would not be conditioned by the rate of interest.

Public and private savings

The Buddha has advised laymen to save one fourth of what a person earns, but this may be difficult for a poor nation even though an individual might achieve this.

There are countries today that save as much as one-fourth of the gross income and this is achieved by a co-operative effort among individuals. If a nation could limit consumption to about three-fourths of the national product it would be saving one-fourth, and what it does not consume could be invested to develop the economy. This implies that at least one-fourth of the total production of the community should be set apart for the future, to strengthen the economy not only to ensure that basic needs are catered to, but also, to meet the needs arising out of unforeseen circumstances created by drought, floods, pestilence and disease; and also for reasons of precaution.

The Buddha has preached in the 'Dasaraja Dhamma Sutta' that a country that plans on this basis is bound to be a prosperous one. It would be free from the multifarious hardships which are experienced today by a great many nations. A common problem in most countries is the tendency towards excessive consumption and the failure to save for development purposes. The Buddha used the word 'Sammajivikata' to indicate that people must live within their means; in other words, spend only according to the capacity of their incomes. Economists in developed countries encourage people to spend, because they say that economic activity declines due to such factors as a fall in demand or underconsumption.

The 'Vyagghapajja Sutta' refers to savings as one of three cardinal requirements for economic development, and that such savings must arise out of a prudent pattern of expenditure. In many economies savings are low because consumption is high or incomes are too low. In such economies orthodox Economics advocates that incomes must be raised for savings to increase. This thesis could be sustained only in a social system which looks upon savings as a residue resulting from a very high level of consumption. This is where consumption is geared to the level of income, and where consumption in its totality is given a higher value than savings. Where consumption is artificially stimulated it is only a higher level of income that could generate savings; but on the contrary in a Buddhist Economy, where consumption has been maintained at modest levels, with human sustenance as the main objective, an increase in income must necessarily result in a higher level of savings because human values do not get distorted with higher income. In fact, the basic problem in modern living is the distortion in values that result from higher incomes, where people begin to look upon sophisticated and luxury goods as part and parcel of their standard of living. Buddhism advocates that the standard of living must be progressively raised, and this would be most important where significant differences in income levels occur in the community. But this must not be accompanied by the acceptance of false values, which in turn, tends to distort the way of life by a craving for goods and services that create conditions for social and moral degeneration.

Savings need not come from restraints on the level of consumption and this is what is commonly advocated today. It does not imply that one must subject oneself to heavy sacrifices and that consumption should be cut down to the detriment of the living standard already attained. In this context a distinction has to be made between the conventional high living standards and a high standard of living in Buddhist terms. According to the latter this is not determined by the diversity of material goods and services and the absolute freedom to enjoy them. Without the moral and spiritual development of man there cannot be a high standard of living. The latter in itself could cut down waste and people could save enough. The process of saving is the essence of building up a resource base for the development effort through a new way of life, whatever the economic philosophy.

In Buddhist Economics a high level of savings is desirable and to this extent it agrees with modern Economic theory. The main difference is that a Buddhist Economy would be able to get further afield with the same level of savings than the modern planner, because savings would not be used in the same way and would not flow into certain kinds of investments. It would be more rationally distributed among economic activities which are essential for man's development. More savings will be available for forms of investment which are neglected today, because they are not so profitable, although man needs them badly. Savings would not be used to produce armaments, harmful drugs, poisons, liquor, weapons, non-essential luxury goods and propagate a trade in pornography. To take an example in the context of non-essential goods, eight-cylinder luxury motor cars that waste non-replenishable energy resources and cause more pollution would not be produced. People can travel in equal comfort in a smaller and a more economical four-cylinder vehicle. Similarly there would be no need to produce supersonic aircraft with all the attendant unknown hazards attached to travel in them while he can get about just as quickly with the type of air transportation that is available today.

In Sri Lanka's own case the level of savings has barely exceeded 12 to 13 per cent at any time, while the desirable rate is in excess of 18 per cent. The question may be asked why the level of savings has been low in a poor country, where basic wants of the bulk of the population are not satisfied? To some extent, this is because even the poorer people do not always make it a point to spend their purchasing power on the most essential things due to a wrong sense of values. They do not save because limited money in their hands is often diverted to harmful, speculative or adventurous forms of expenditure. On the other hand, incomes have been low partly because savings have been low and the distribution of income has been so unequal that the amount of income in the hands of poor has not produced any savings.

Modern economic theory says that it is only through income disparities that savings could be maximised and that the bulk of the savings come mainly from those who have the highest incomes, thus belittling the contribution that the less affluent could make. In a Buddhist Economy, in the absence of very wealthy people, large corporations and monopolies, savings must necessarily come from the medium and small size economic units. Furthermore, savings will take place with positive objectives in view. There would be a clear cut idea of what goods are produced, the methods of production and how the product is being distributed. If the most essential goods are produced in very large quantities they should be freely available at relatively low prices which will always enable people to put by what they have not spent.

In such a society inflation cannot occur because there could not be a global shortage of goods. Changing prices would largely reflect changes in the priorities in production and distribution. It will be production for the people and there would be no erosion of purchasing power through inflation. Today people cannot save because of inflation. Prices increase sharply because not enough esssential goods are produced, or because goods are produced and distributed by monopolies, which either restrict supplies or artificially limit production with the objective of keeping very comfortable profit margins. For instance, the recent global price increases could be partly attributed to the cartel of petroleum producing countries raising the price of crude oil. In this process they have enhanced their own profits, while they have eroded the purchasing power of a very large number of poor nations, who are now unable to save.

Within a Buddhist Economic framework it is not only the individual that would save but this will be equally true of the government. The 'Kutadanta Sutta' emphasises government savings and by such means how the Treasury is frequently replenished with adequate funds. Government investment and expenditure would automatically receive a different orientation. The state would not have to spend considerable sums of money on an army or on the manufacture or procurement of armaments. This would help the state to increase its savings. Even its expenditure on the police force would be limited. There would be little crime, fewer violation of laws, addiction to drugs and other misdemeanours that would require police intervention. The function of the police force would be primarily to inform the public about the laws of the country and advise the community. Expenditure on health services would also be lower because the incidence of disease arising from the tensions of modern living, sexual promiscuity, through alcoholism and the use of narcotics would also be much less. The environment would be preserved; the land, sea and inland waterways would be largely free of all forms of pollution and this in itself will promote health and longevity.

International tension arising from ideological conflict would become less important because there will be no place for materialistic ideologies. The only ideology would have a spritual base and would be united through a common interest in the promotion of peaceful living and spiritual harmony. The latter will greatly ease all tensions. In such a society the role of administration would be considerably simplified, bureaucratic controls would be at a minimum and government expenditure would be mostly on its employees who would be entrusted with the maintenance of essential services. The greater savings resulting therefrom would be used in the further development of man, both on the economic and spiritual levels.

The art of Japanese management

RICHARD TANNER PASCALE AND ANTHONY G. ATHOS

'Spiritual' is an unlikely term in a narrative of corporate life. Yet nothing less suffices to capture the strong belief system that underlies Matsushita's philosophy. Some of the perplexing near contradictions of the Matsushita style become more understandable as we explicitly consider the values which underlie them. It is difficult, for example, to reconcile how senior management criticism can be perceived as 'training'; how the firm can transfer its poor performers and develop 'character' rather than demoralization. It is puzzling to witness a firm of such insistent efficiency, yet hear key executives speak of acceptance time and their desire to 'win people over.'

Any human organization must inevitably juggle internal contradictions – usually between the imperatives of efficiency and the countervailing human tradeoffs. Perhaps the phenomenon of 'spirituality' evolved as a means of making sense out of these inescapable dilemmas – between the individual and society, between man and efficiency. For Matsushita, the roots of his approach were specifically religious. In 1932, as the world recession deepened, Matsushita encountered a religious movement in Japan which had gained wide appeal and grown rapidly. The experience impressed Matsushita deeply. 'It comes clear to me,' he wrote, 'that people need a way of linking their productive lives to society.' Matsushita reconsidered his organization's purpose in this light. What emerged was a management philosophy tying business profitability to the social good in a kind of Darwinian paradigm. 'A business should quickly stand on its own,' said Matsushita, 'based on the service it provides the society. Profits should not be a reflection of corporate greed but a vote of confidence from society that what is offered by the firm is valued. When a business fails to make profits it should die – it is a waste of resources to society. A firm should not adopt a paternal attitude toward its failing divisions and subsidize them.'

At first encounter, we skeptical citizens in a time of government bailouts find such a rationale for profitability somewhat artificial and contrived. A Matsushita executive offers this explanation. 'When you think about it unideologically, societies give rise to organizations which serve their needs and societies reward them for this service. Many Westerners tend to smirk at the higher purposes to which Japanese organizations avowedly dedicate themselves and assume that these calls to higher values are just thinly disguised manipulation. But when one of your organizations – like IBM, for example – *really* gets its members to 'think,' or to believe, that 'IBM means service,' it is no longer an ad slogan. It becomes a belief system for thousands of people who work for that company – a human value beyond profit to which their productive lives are dedicated. No less is true for the business philosophy of Matsushita.'

The Matsushita philosophy provides a basis of meaning beyond the products it produces. Matsushita was the first company in Japan to have a song and a code of values. 'It seems silly to Westerners,' says one executive, 'but every morning at 8:00 A.M., all across Japan, there are 87 000 people reciting the code of values and singing together. It's like we are all a community.' Matsushita foresaw that a lifetime's organizational experience shapes one's character indelibly. It was unthinkable, in his view, that work, which occupies at least half of our waking hours, should be denied its powerful role. The firm, therefore, had an inescapable responsibility to help the employees' inner selves. This responsibility could best be realized by tying the corporation to society and the individual by insisting that management serve as trainers and developers of character, not just as exploiters of human resources. Some Western minds will find these ideas at best remote, at worst delusive. But such a connection between philosophy and hard-headed business objectives business objectives is one that the Japanese take as natural. One observer notes that Matsushita provides two distinct kinds of training. One is basic skills training, but the second and more fundamental one is training in the Matsushita values. These values are inculcated through a long apprenticeship across one's career. The newly hired are exposed to them continually. As a member of any working group, each person is asked at least once every other month to give a ten-minute talk to his group on the firm's values and its relationship to society. It is said that nothing is so powerful in persuading oneself as having to persuade others. Matsushita has long employed this technique of 'self-indoctrination.' Subordinates may be asked to consider a proposal they have set forth in light of the values of Matsushita. And everyone has heard and reheard the famous words of the founder: 'If you make an honest mistake, the company will be very forgiving. Treat it as a training expense and learn from it. You will be severely criticized (read: dismissed), however, if you deviate from the company's basic principles.' The basic principles, beliefs, and values of the firm are as follows:

BASIC BUSINESS PRINCIPLES
To recognize our responsibilities as industrialists, to foster progress, to promote the general welfare of society, and to devote ourselves to the further development of world culture.

EMPLOYEES CREED
Progress and development can be realized only through the combined efforts and cooperation of each member of our Company. Each of us, therefore, shall keep this idea constantly in mind as we devote ourselves to the continuous improvement of our Company.

THE SEVEN 'SPIRITUAL' VALUES
1. National Service Through Industry
2. Fairness

3. Harmony and Cooperation
4. Struggle for Betterment
5. Courtesy and Humility
6. Adjustment and Assimilation
7. Gratitude

These values, taken to heart, provide a spiritual fabric of great resilience. They foster consistent expectations among employees in a work force that reaches from continent to continent. They permit a highly complex and decentralized firm to evoke an enormous continuity that sustains it even when more operational guidance breaks down. And when we compare Matsushita with American firms of the same age – firms that were born in the 1920s such as General Motors, American Telephone and Telegraph, Westinghouse, and RCA – it is difficult to find many that have sustained their original vitality. Any inquiry into how Matsushita has sustained itself while so many others have fallen behind must surely turn to its value system as a central ingredient in its success.

The director of a major Matsushita subsidiary comments: 'Matsushita's management philosophy is very important to us. It enables us to match Western efficiency without being one bit less Japanese. Perhaps the ultimate triumph of Matsushita is the balancing of the rationalism of the West with the spiritualism of the East.'

CASE STUDY

City of Joy

One of the servants returned with a tray of cigars tied together in a bundle. The Mafia boss untied the cord and offered a cigar to the priest, who declined it. The godfather took his time lighting his own.

'You must be an altogether special person,' the godfather declared, exuding a puff of smoke, 'because it has been reported to me that you have made an application ... I can't actually believe it ... for Indian citizenship.'

'You are decidedly well informed,' Kovalski confirmed.

The godfather chuckled and settled himself comfortably in his chair.

'You must admit that it might seem somewhat surprising that someone should be tempted to exchange his affluent and privileged status of foreigner for that of a poor man in an Indian slum.'

'We probably don't have the same understanding of wealth, you and I.'

'At all events, I shall be proud to count someone like you among the ranks of my compatriots. And, if by any chance the response to your request is delayed, do let me know. I have connections. I shall try and intervene.'

'Thank you, but I put my trust in the Lord.'

The godfather made an effort to believe what he had just heard: was it possible that someone was refusing his support?

'Father,' he said after a growl, 'I have heard some strange rumours. It would seem that you intend to create a leper hospital in the slum. Is that right?'

'"Leper hospital" is a very grandiose expression. It's to be more a dispensary to treat the worst cases. I've asked Mother Teresa for the help of two or three of her Sisters.'

The godfather surveyed the priest sternly.

'You must know that no one can concern himself with the lepers in that slum without my authorization.'

'In that case, what's keeping you from helping them yourself? Your assistance would be most welcome.'

The godfather's eyebrows puckered above his thick glasses.

'The lepers in the City of Joy have been under my protection for twelve years, and that's probably the best thing that has ever happened to them. Without me the other inhabitants of this place would have thrown them out ages ago.' He leaned forward with a sudden air of complicity. 'My dear Father, have you asked yourself how the people next door to your "dispensary" will react when your lepers start to show up?'

'I have faith in the compassion of my brothers,' Kovalski said.

'Compassion? You holy men are always talking about compassion! All you'll get by way of compassion is a riot. They'll set fire to your dispensary and lynch your lepers!'

The priest gritted his teeth, preferring not to reply. 'This scoundrel is probably right', he thought.

The godfather relit his cigar and took a long draw on it, throwing his head back. 'I can see only one way for you to avoid all these trials and tribulations,' he said, throwing his head back again.

'Which is?'

'That you subscribe to a protection contract.'

'A protection contract?'

'It will cost you a mere three thousand rupees a month. Our rates are ordinarily much higher. But you are a man of God and, as I'm sure you realize, in India we are used to respecting what is sacred.'

Then, without waiting for any reply, he clapped his hands. His eldest son came hurrying in.

'The Father and I have come to an amicable agreement,' the godfather announced with evident satisfaction. 'The two of you can agree on the terms and conditions of the arrangement.'

The godfather was a nobleman. He did not concern himself with details.

That evening the founders of the Committee for Mutual Aid in the City of Joy assembled in Stephan Kovalski's room to discuss the godfather's ultimatum.

'The godfather's family is all-powerful,' declared Saladdin. 'Remember the last elections – the Molotov cocktails, the blows with iron bars . . . the people killed and all those injured! Is it really worth the risk of setting it all off again, for the sake of a few crippled carcasses? We'll just have to agree to pay.'

'All the same, three thousand rupees for the right to take in and nurse a few lepers is exorbitant.' Margareta was indignant.

'Is it the sum that bothers you,' asked Kovalski, 'or the principle?'
She seemed surprised at the question.

'Why, the sum of course!'

'A typical answer,' thought Kovalski. 'Even here in the depths of the slum, extortion and corruption sticks to their skin like flies.' All the others shared Saladdin's view, all, that was, except Bandona, the young woman from Assam.

'May God damn this demon!' Bandona exclaimed. 'To give him one single rupee would be to betray the cause of all the poor.'

Her words had the effect of an electric shock on Kovalski.

'Bandona is right! We must take up the challenge, resist it, fight it. It's now or never that we can show the people here that they are no longer alone.'

Early the next morning, the bulbous, backfiring motorcycle belonging to the son of Kartik Baba came to a halt outside Kovalski's room. As his father had ordered, Ashoka had come to discuss the payment terms for the 'contract'. The meeting, however, lasted only a few seconds, just long enough for the priest to intimate his refusal to the young ruffian. This was the first defiance ever laid before the authority of the all-powerful head of the Mafia in the City of Joy.

One week later the little dispensary was ready to receive the first lepers. Bandona and a number of volunteers set out to bring back the six extreme cases Kovalski wanted to hospitalize first. He himself went at dawn to Mother Teresa's house to collect the three Sisters who were to nurse the lepers. Hardly had they reached the square on which the mosque stood, however, when Bandona's group was intercepted by a commando of young thugs, armed with sticks and iron bars.

'No one's going any further!' shouted the leader, a pimply adolescent whose front teeth were missing.

The young Assamese girl tried to move forward but an avalanche of blows stopped her. At that same moment the priest arrived from the other end of the slum, accompanied by his three nuns. Seeing the commotion at the far end of the alley, he clenched his teeth. Then he heard a loud explosion and an outcry. A second gang had begun to use iron bars and pickaxes to ransack the old school that was to serve as the leper clinic. Terrified, the neighbourhood shopkeepers hastily barricaded their shop windows. On the Grand Trunk Road, the shrill grinding of dozens of metal shutters could be heard as traders rushed to lower them. When the destruction of the dispensary had been completed, a third gang appeared. They were carrying bottles and explosive devices in knapsacks strung over their shoulders. The street emptied in a flash. Even the dogs and the children, who were always swarming everywhere, took off. A series of detonations shook the entire neighbourhood, their echo resounding far beyond the boundaries of the City of Joy, as far as the railway station and beyond.

Taken from *City of Joy*, Dominique Lapierre (London: Arrow Books, 1986).

DISCUSSION TOPICS

1. You are arranging a two-day international business conference which will include representatives from Iran, India (Hindu and Sikh), Israel, Thailand, Japan and Europe. What information would you wish to obtain from them prior to this meeting? What situations might you be anxious to avoid? What kind of lunch menu would be suitably inclusive. (What might you avoid, and why?)

2. The extract from Dominique Lapierre, *City of Joy* is the true story of a Roman Catholic priest who plans to build a leper hospital in Calcutta. If you had been involved in the project, what would have been your reaction to the demand for protection money? Would the sheer amount involved have been the point at issue for you, or do you object on principle to paying money to a mafia? Kovalski's project was a 'good cause'; does this make a difference to you ? Does the end justify the means, or is encouraging extortion wrong irrespective of the end result?

FURTHER READING

Chapter 2

Relatively brief introductory surveys of business ethics are provided by the following:

J. Donaldson, *Key Issues in Business Ethics* (London: Academic Press, 1989)

W. H. Shaw, *Business Ethics* (Belmont, California: Wadsworth, 1991)

M. G. Velazquez, *Business Ethics: Concepts and Cases* (Englewood Cliffs: Prentice-Hall, 1992)

There are numerous American anthologies of introductory readings and commentaries. For example:

T. L. Beauchamp and N. E. Bowie, *Ethical Theory and Business* (Englewood Cliffs: Prentice-Hall, 1988)

J. R. DesJardins and J. J. McCall, *Contemporary Issues in Business Ethics* (Belmont, California: Wadsworth, 1990)

M. Hoffman and J. M. Moore, *Business Ethics: Readings and Cases in Corporate Morality* (New York: McGraw-Hill, 1990)

Chapter 3

Ethical theory, and ethics in general, is a vast field of study. Students of business ethics will probably find more than enough additional reading by consulting the theory sections of the introductory books listed for chapter 2. However, for those seeking a broader outline a relatively painless initiation is provided by:

L. J. Pojman, *Ethics: Discovering Right and Wrong* (Belmont, California: Wadsworth, 1990)

Those wanting to explore utilitarianism in more detail should consult:

J. J. C. Smart and B. Williams, *Utilitarianism: For and Against* (Cambridge: Cambridge University Press, 1973)

For a not-too-scholarly introduction to natural law and rights (a perspective not often dealt with in ethics text books), a useful starting point is chapter 4 of:

S. I. Benn and R. S. Peters, *Social Principles and the Democratic State* (London: Allen & Unwin, 1959)

Chapter 4

Issues of capitalism, markets and justice are approached from a broadly *laissez-faire* perspective in:

N. P. Barry, *The Invisible Hand in Economics and Politics* (London: Institute of Economic Affairs, 1988)

The best starting point for an investigation of market socialism is:

J. L. Le Brand and S. Estrin (eds.), *Market Socialism* (Oxford: Oxford University Press, 1989)

For a generally favourable view of Germany's system of co-determination, see:

V. R. Berghahn and D. Karsten, *Industrial Relations in West Germany* (Oxford: Berg Publishers, 1987)

For a generally hostile view (and a survey of co-determination in Western Europe in general) see:

A. L. Thimm, *The False Promise of Co-determination* (Lexington, Mass: D. C. Heath, 1980)

Chapter 5

An account of company law which deals with historical and political issues is provided by:

L. C. B. Gower, *Gower's Principles of Company Law* (London: Stevens & Sons, 1992)

A broad survey of ethical issues surrounding the corporation is provided by:

T. Donaldson, *Corporations and Morality* (Englewood Cliffs: Prentice-Hall, 1982)

The practicalities of corporate social responsibility are investigated in:

M. Jennings, *The Guide to Good Corporate Citizenship* (Cambridge: Director Books, 1990)

Issues of corporate governance are explored in:

L. R. Tricker, *Corporate Governance* (Aldershot: Gower Publishing, 1984)

Chapter 6

Discussion of the fair wage can be found in the following. Although both books are now quite old, they have become almost classics, and Fogarty provides very thorough analysis and detailed historical study of the area.

M. Fogarty, *The Fair Wage* (London: Chapman, 1961)
S. I. Benn and R. S. Peters, *Social Principles and the Democratic State* (London: Allen & Unwin, 1959)

For women's rights, a comprehensive and balanced analysis of the case for feminism can be found in:

J. Radcliff Richards, *The Sceptical Feminist* (Harmondsworth: Penguin, 1984)

Richards's book is primarily philosophical, but issues like workplace discrimination are discussed.

Chapter 7

There is relatively little by way of solid material on the ethics of accounting. The following gives an overview of some of the principal techniques which accountants use:

I. Griffiths, *Creative Accounting* (London: Routledge, 1992)

Griffiths' first chapter touches on some of the ethical implications of creative accounting.

A section on the significance of scandals in financial services can be found in:

J. Donaldson, *Business Ethics: A European Casebook* (London: Academic Press, 1992)

Statements of the ethical standards which accountants are expected to observe can be found in official handbooks of their professional bodies, such as: The Institute of Chartered Accountants in England and Wales, *Members Handbook 1992, Volume I: Constitutional, Ethical, Legal* (London: The Institute of Charted Accountants, 1992).

On ethical investments, information can be obtained from EIRIS (Ethical Investment Research and Information Service, 266 Pentonville Road, London N1 9JY). Various financial advisers have now set themselves up as ethical investment specialists and provide information on the track record of selected companies. Advertisements for such services can generally be found in journals such as *The Ethical Consumer*.

Chapter 8

The best-known work in the field is:

V. Packard, *The Hidden Persuaders* (Harmondsworth: Penguin, 1955)

Packard tends to focus on the techniques used by modern advertising, although in places he entertains the 'defence' of these practices. More recent landmarks are:

The Advertising Standards Authority, *Herself Appraised* (London: ASA, 1986), and
The Advertising Standards Authority, *Herself Reappraised* (London: ASA, 1990)

Both concern the treatment of women in advertising.
For a discussion of the relationship between advertising and ideology, see:

J. Williamson, *Decoding Advertisements* (London: Marion Boyars, 1978)

For a statement of the standards which are accepted within the advertising industry, see:

The Advertising Standards Authority, *The British Code of Advertising Practice* (London: ASA, 10th edn., 1991)

Chapter 9

Proably the best-known book to plead for responsible use of the environment in business is:

E. F. Schumacher, *Small is Beautiful* (London: Abacus, 1974)

Most of the literature in this field, like Schumacher, is 'pro-green', and the bulk of publications in the field are more concerned with **how** to be 'green' than with appraising arguments on each side. Examples of 'pro-green' literature include:

J. Elkington and T. Burke, *The Green Capitalists* (London: Gollancz, 1989)
C. Plant and J. Plant (eds.), *Green Business: Hope or Hoax?* (Bideford: Green Books, 1991)

Plant and Plant explore some of the ways in which businesses have jumped on the 'green' bandwagon and exploited consumers by feigning environmental friendliness.

For the government's vision of environmental preservation, see:

This Common Inheritance (London: HMSO, 1990)

For a defence of the view that the firm's prime obligation is profit maximization rather than environmental enhancement, we can do no better than refer the reader to Milton Friedman's classic essay, *The Social Responsibility of Business Is to Increase Its Profits*, which is reproduced earlier in this volume.

Chapter 10

The two classic empirical cross-cultural studies of managers and their values are:

M. Haire, E. E. Ghiselli, and L. W. Porter, *Managerial Thinking: An International Study* (New York, London, Sydney: John Wiley & Sons Inc., 1966)
G. W. England, *The Manager and His Values: An International Perspective from The United States, Japan, Korea, India and Australia* (Cambridge, Mass: Ballinger, 1975)

A useful 'how to do it' book is:

G. Kennedy, *Negotiate Anywhere!* (London: Business Books, 1985)

Kennedy produces fascinating examples for discussion, many of which have ethical dimensions, but there is no solid discussion of the ethical issues.

More solid treatment of alternative philosophies of business can be found in the works by Temari and Khan, from which we have reproduced extracts. There are many books on Islamic business and Islamic banking, which can be obtained most easily from specialist Islamic bookshops.

Index

Lightning Source UK Ltd.
Milton Keynes UK
UKOW021100270911

179347UK00001B/3/P